THE ARTHASAṀGRAHA OF LAUGĀKṢI BHĀSKARA

THE ARTHASAṀGRAHA OF LAUGĀKṢI BHĀSKARA

Edited with an Introduction, Translation into English and Notes (Explanatory and Critical) by

A.B. GAJENDRAGADKAR
R.D. KARMARKAR

With Introduction by

DR. SHIV KUMAR

MOTILAL BANARSIDASS PUBLISHERS PRIVATE LIMITED • DELHI

4th Reprint : Delhi, 2016
First Edition : Bombay, 1934

ISBN: 978-81-208-1442-4 (Cloth)
ISBN: 978-81-208-1443-1 (Paper)

MOTILAL BANARSIDASS
41 U.A., Bungalow Road, Jawahar Nagar, Delhi 110 007
8 Mahalaxmi Chamber, 22 Bhulabhai Desai Road, Mumbai 400 026
203 Royapettah High Road, Mylapore, Chennai 600 004
236, 9th Main III Block, Jayanagar, Bangalore 560 011
8 Camac Street, Kolkata 700 017
Ashok Rajpath, Patna 800 004
Chowk, Varanasi 221 001

Printed in India
by RP Jain at NAB Printing Unit,
A-44, Naraina Industrial Area, Phase I, New Delhi–110028
and published by JP Jain for Motilal Banarsidass Publishers (P) Ltd,
41 U.A. Bungalow Road, Jawahar Nagar, Delhi-110007

विषयानुक्रमणी

तृतीयो मन्त्रविभागः

चतुर्थो नामधेयविभागः

पञ्चमो निषेधविभागः

षष्ठोऽर्थवादविभागः

INTRODUCTION

By Dr. Shiv Kumar

The Mīmāṁsā School

The Mīmāṁsā school of Indian philosophy got the place of highest honour in the *āstika darśanas* or the Brāhmaṇical philosophies. It is the strongest propounder of the supersensuous matters like post-mortem existence, other worlds, acts and their results etc. which form the main basis of the ethical, religious and philosophical teachings of the Brāhmaṇical philosophies. Mīmāṁsā is closely related to the Vedas. It has provided the principles of Vedic interpretation which are held in high esteem even at present. Since it conducts discussion on *Vedavākyas*, it came to be termed *Vākyaśāstra* also. As an aid to achieve its main purpose of interpreting the Vedas and explaining the ritualistic acts it has developed its own philosophy, logic and psychology and, thus, has contributed a lot to the stock of Indian thought. It also offered some maxims which serve as rules of guidance in all walks of Indian life. Even today the Hindu literature on law does not violate the maxims fixed by Mīmāṁsā. Thus, Mīmāṁsā has greatly influenced Indian literature, culture and life.

The word *Mīmāṁsā* is derived from the root *man*, to know, with the desiderative suffix *san* and means a desire to know or an enquiry or investigation. Since the object of desire to know, enquiry or investigation here is *dharma* or religious duty, it is also called *dharmamimāṁsā* or *karmamimāṁsā*. It undertakes discussion about the problems relating to ritualistic acts. Jaimini gives this meaning to the *śāstra* in the opening *sūtra* of *Mimāṁsā* which marks the beginning of the enquiry into *dharma*.

The Mīmāṁsā system owes its origin to the practical needs arising in connection with the performance of ritualistic acts. The Ṛgvedic Aryas believed in the fulfilment of their desires through prayers to gods. In course of time the prayers were accompanied by offerings to the gods and the methods and manner of making the offerings most acceptable to the gods became rather complicated. The clarification is found in the Brāhmaṇa literature and it was further elaborated in the Sūtra literature.

The explanation, however, could not satisfy all the queries and reconcile all traditions of sacrificial performance. Hence, many preceptors laid down various rules for the clarification of various intricacies of the sacrificial rituals. The *Mīmāṁsāsūtra* of Jaimini compiled and systematized these principles of Vedic interpretation prevailing in different circles just as Bādarāyaṇa systematized the spiritual teachings of the Upaniṣads. In this way, the early Mīmāṁsakas aim at interpreting the sacred texts, and the science of interpretation and rituals reaches its peak at their hands. Besides, the Mīmāṁsā texts give a mystic meaning to the rituals with a philosophical justification and, thus, are not confined to the explanation of sacrificial performances.

The Mīmāṁsā Philosophy

The main purpose of Mīmāṁsā philosophy was a methodical interpretation of *dharma* or duty embodied in the ritualistic portion of the Veda. Its philosophical position aims to provide epistemological, metaphysical and ethical justification to the ritualistic doctrines. In view of the above purpose the Mīmāṁsakas have stressed Vedic testimony as the highest source of valid knowledge requiring no external test for its validity. They believe in the reality of the world, pluralism of souls, heaven, hell, impressions of acts lasting till the attainments of fruits, potency and acts as the regulating force of the world and methodical performance of sacrifices.

Knowledge

Knowledge, according to the Mīmāṁsakas, is the activity of the cogniser (*jñātṛvyāpāra*) which is inferred through the effect viz., cognisedness characterising the object cognised. It is of two types—valid and invalid. The latter involves some defect in the totality of causal conditions and is erroneous in nature. The former is, according to Kumārila, the knowledge which is in agreement with the real nature of an object, novel and not contradicted by a sublating knowledge, or, according to Prabhākara, the direct experience of an object as distinguished from remembrance.

The Pramāṇas

As the source of valid knowledge the Mīmāṁsakas of the Prābhākara school recognise five *pramāṇas*—perception, inference, verbal testimony, *upamāna* and presumption, while the followers of the Bhāṭṭa school recognise six with the addition of *anupalabdhi* to the above.

Perception is the immediate knowledge of an object arising through sense-object contact. A sense-organ comes in contact with its object and gets its impression. This knowledge is the indeterminate knowledge (*ālocana* or *nirvikalpa*). Then the mind interprets it by assimilating it to the past experience which determines the class, quality, activity and name of the object. It is called determinate (*savikalpa*) knowledge.

Inference is the knowledge of one of the relata after perceiving the other when the invariable association between the two is already known. It is of two kinds—for one's own self and for convincing others. The former is informal and does not require all the methodical steps while the latter consists of three statements—*pratijñā* (statement of the probandum), *hetu* (probans) and *dṛṣṭānta* (example). Kumārila further divides it into (i) *pratyakṣatodṛṣṭasambandha* (where the invariable concomitance between two objects has been directly perceived) and (ii) *Sāmānyatodṛṣṭasambandha* (where the invariable concomitance is seen in a general way).

Upamāna is the means of knowing the similarity of the object remembered at the sight of some resembling object. For example, a person having seen a cow in his house happens to come across a *gavaya* in the forest and then he comes to know that his cow is similar to the *gavaya*. Actually, Upamāna is postulated by the Mīmāṁsakas to get the knowledge of the sacrificial details of a rite from some other similar rite. Here, Prabhākara, unlike the Bhāṭṭa, considers similarity to be an independent entity.

Verbal testimony is the most important source of knowledge because it justifies the supreme authority of the Veda as the most authentic source of knowledge of *dharma* which is eternal, absolute and supreme. It is defined as the statement made by a reliable authority. Prabhākara restricts it to the scriptural statements only while Kumārila believes in the authority of worldly persons also. The Vedas are not composed by any person—human or divine. The Vedic statements give directions for sacrificial ritual or persuade persons for the performance of them. The Vedas are eternal and impersonal in origin and hence are free from all possible mistakes due to human weakness and are unchangeable and infallible in authority.

Postulation is the supposition of some unperceived fact to explain some otherwise inexplicable facts. For example, when a man, Devadatta, is observed to be fasting in the daytime but still growing fat, we have to presume his eating at night to explain the contradictory facts of fasting at daytime and growing fat.

The Bhāṭṭa school believes in non-perception (*anupalabdhi*) as a means of cognition of absence of something e.g. a jar on the ground. The Bhāṭṭas argue that absence cannot be perceived through senses because it cannot come in contact with the sense-organs. It cannot be an object of inference because there is no valid probans to lead to such a conclusion. Nor can it be a case of verbal testimony or presumption because the conditions necessary for them, viz., words and two seamingly contradictory facts are not present in this case. Prabhākara, on the contrary, holds that knowledge of absence arises through perception of the mere location devoid of the object to be negated.

In view of the fact that the sole purpose of Mīmāṁsā is to ascertain *dharma* it should be observed that the Veda, i.e. the verbal testimony is the only means of knowledge directly leading to the above. The other means of knowledge are accepted firstly to prove that *dharma* cannot be ascertained by them, secondly for refuting some antagonistic views questioning the authoritative character of the Veda, and thirdly to settle various questions regarding the details about *dharma*.

Self-Validity

As regards the genesis and ascertainment of validity of knowledge the Mīmāṁsakas hold that validity is intrinsic to knowledge, i.e., it arises and is ascertained by the totality of causal conditions giving rise to knowledge itself, while invalidity is extrinsic. Thus, regarding validity the view of the Mīmāṁsakas is opposed to that of the Naiyāyikas who maintain that validity is produced in knowledge by extrinsic conditions like the sharpness of the senses and it is also ascertained extrinsically just as that of perception by inference. The Nyāya view, however, would, according to the Mīmāṁsakas, involve the fault of infinite regress insofar as one knowledge will be ascertained through the other and so on. Moreover, it would defeat the very purpose of

Mīmāṁsā which believes in the infallibility of the Vedas without further questioning their validity.

The Mīmāṁsakas believe in the reality of the world vehemently setting aside nihilism and idealism. They accept the eternity of the world, and do not indulge in any controversy about the origin of the universe. Here they differ from the Nyāya-Vaiśeṣikas who believe in periodic creation and dissolution. The world is eternal and has ever been running the same without any creation or dissolution. Therefore, there is no need of any creator of the universe like God. Nor do the Mīmāṁsakas admit God for supervision over *dharma* and *adharma*. On the contrary, they think that acceptance of God will involve further absurdities. The Mīmāṁsakas firmly believe in the super-sensuous objects like heaven, hell and the deities on the strength of Vedic statements.

The Categories

As regards the analysis of the contents of the universe, the Mīmāṁsakas accept the Vaiśeṣika categories and their sub-categories with some notable deviations. Unlike the Vaiśeṣikas, the Mīmāṁsakas attach importance to *Śakti* as an independent category (or as a quality inherent in a cause). The efficiency of cause in giving rise to effect depends upon the presence of potency in it. The followers of Prabhākara, unlike the Vaiśeṣikas, do not accept *abhāva* as an independent category but take it as the form of the locus itself. Kumārila accepts the categories of substance, quality, action, generality and negation while Prabhākara believes in substance, quality, action, generality, inherence, potency, number and similarity. The Mīmāṁsakas add sound and darkness to the Vaiśeṣika list of nine substances. The *viśeṣa* of the Vaiśeṣikas is not accepted by the Mīmāṁsakas. Mind, according to the Vaiśeṣikas, is atomic, but according to the Mīmāṁsakas it is all-pervasive. Air is only to be inferred according to the Vaiśeṣikas but can be directly perceived according to the Mīmāṁsakas. Atoms are perceptible in the theory of the Mīmāṁsakas but can be inferred, or perceived by the *yogins* only, according to the Vaiśeṣikas. The Mīmāṁsakas, unlike the Vaiśeṣikas, do not accept God as the creator of the universe and the author of the Vedas. Ether, time and space are perceptible according to the Mīmāṁsakas but are the objects of inference only according to the Vaiśeṣikas.

The followers of Kumārila accept the classification of the qualities given by the Vaiśeṣikas but substitute tone for sound, accept manifestation as a quality rejecting merit and demerit. According to the Mīmāṁsakas, unlike the Vaiśeṣikas, one quality may exist in the other. The Mīmāṁsakas reject the Vaiśeṣika position that knowledge is perceptible through mental perception (*anuvyavasāya*). Sound is a substance according to the Mīmāṁsakas but a quality according to the Vaiśeṣikas. The Vaiśeṣikas hold that conjunction does not exist in all-pervasive substances and is produced and non-eternal, while Kumārila thinks that it is found in any two substances and is both eternal and non-eternal.

Soul is an indestructible eternal substance different from body, sense-organs and *Buddhi*. It is not destroyed at the time of death, but survives to reap the results of its actions. It is the agent of sacrificial rituals. Like the Nyāya-Vaiśeṣika the Mīmāṁsā also holds that knowledge etc. are adventitious qualities of soul and arise when it is conjoined with the mind-body complex. Souls are many in number each occupying one individual body. The Mīmāṁsaka's reply to the question as to how soul is known is notable. Kumārila holds that it is known through mental perception as the object of self-consciousness (*ahaṁpratyaya*) when one reflects on the soul, while Prabhākara is of the opinion that soul is manifested as the subject of knowledge—in all types of cognition the three things, the cogniser, the object of cognition and the cognition itself, are simultaneously revealed.

Mīmāṁsā attaches supreme importance to the performance of sacrifice. It is the best means to attain the highest end of life. The source of knowledge of such an end and the means thereof is the Veda. Sacrifice is to be performed because it is prescribed by the Veda, and as such forms the most sacred duty of a person. If they are performed with some purpose in mind, one gets his desires fulfilled and if performed disinterestedly, they lead to liberation. Such a stand led the Mīmāṁsakas to believe strongly in the law of Karma and to the further acceptance of latent impressions of acts done to explain the above phenomena. Acts do not vanish absolutely but leave their impressions on the agent, which when mature give appropriate results. One attains salvation by exhausting the fruits of acts through experiencing them and stopping their further accumulation. This situation is brought about through refraining from the performance of *kāmya karmas* and through avoiding the evil effects by performing the *nitya karmas* only.

Jaimini

The Mīmāṁsā sūtra of Jaimini is the earliest available text of the Mīmāṁsā school. However, the scattered references to the earlier *Ācāryas* and their views by Jaimini either for the support of his views or for refutation make it quite evident that many teachers of Mīmāṁsā in different circles held divergent views on several topics of Mīmāṁsā and several interpretations of Vedic sentences. Having summed up all efforts of his predecessors, Jaimini gave the final shape to the Mīmāṁsā doctrine with the contribution of his own.

We have no authentic source of information about Jaimini's personal history, date and place of birth. The *Pañcatantra* mentions that he was killed by an elephant. In an account of a semi-mythical nature Jaimini is mentioned as a disciple of Pārāśarya Vyāsa. In another account of the same type it is stated that Vyāsa, son of Parāśara, had four disciples, one of whom was Jaimini. He divided the Vedas into four and gave instructions in the Sāmaveda to Jaimini. As regards his date, we are still in a whirlpool of conflicting currents. Jacobi is of the opinion that he is not later than the 2nd century B.C. while Keith's opinion is opposite to it. S. N. Dasgupta assigns the probable period of 200 B.C. and Radhakrishnan thinks that Jaimini flourished in the fourth century B.C.

Śabarasvāmin

After Jaimini there is a literary gap of a few centuries till the commentary of Śabarasvāmin. The existence of some *Vṛttis* by Upavarṣa, Bodhāyana and Bhavadāsa on the *sūtras* of Jaimini is known from the scattered references to them. Śabara mentions the name of Upavarṣa with great reverence. The *Prapañcahṛdaya* mentions Bodhāyana and Upavarṣa as the authors of commentaries on the 20 chapters of the *Pūrva* and *Uttara Mīmāṁsā* (16 chapters in *Jaiminisūtras* including the four known as *Saṅkarṣakāṇḍa* and 4 of the *Uttaramīmāṁsā*). Kumārilabhaṭṭa refers to some *Vṛttis* which according to Pārthasārathi means the *Vṛttis* by Bhavadāsa etc. No details are available about these *Vṛttis* and their authors.

We meet with the explanation of the *sūtras* of Jaimini in the extensive commentary by Śabarasvāmin. This is the earliest extant commentary on the *Mīmāṁsāsūtra*. It is through this commentary that we come to know for the first time about the arrangement of the *sūtras* of Jaimini into prima facie topics or *adhikaraṇas* consisting of subject, doubt, prima facie view (*pūrvapakṣa*), reply (*uttarapakṣa*), and decision or *siddhānta*. Śabara introduced some metaphysical and epistemological theories like proofs for the distinction of soul from objective world, emancipation through *dharma*, reasons for the validity and invalidity of knowledge, etc. which were later on developed by Kumārila and Prabhākara. Nothing authentic is known about the date and personal life of Śabara. Ganganath Jha places him at about 57 B.C. on the authority of the tradition that king Vikramāditya was the son of Śabarasvāmin from a Kṣatriya wife. He had four wives of four castes and had six sons from them. Traditionally it is stated that his original name was Ādityanātha, but afterwards for the fear of Jaina persecution he changed his name to Śabara and disguised himself as a forester.

Kumārilabhaṭṭa

Again there is a gap of a few centuries till we come to Kumārilabhaṭṭa. During this gap some commentators of Śabarasvāmin might have existed as Pārthasārathi Miśra believes. He refers for example to Bhartṛmitra as having introduced several wrong theories (*apasiddhāntas*) in the system of Mīmāṁsā. Nothing more is known about Bhartṛmitra.

Now we come to the medieval period in which Kumārila figured as a great scholar of Mīmāṁsā. In this period different schools of Brāhmaṇical philosophy came in direct mutual contact and in conflict with the Buddhists. The conflict arose because the various theses about reality put forth by different systems, especially the Bauddhas, questioned the validity of self-complacent beliefs of the Mīmāṁsakas. Kumārilabhaṭṭa supplied broad basis of logical and epistemological theories to the Mīmāṁsā hypotheses and at the same time justified them through refutation of the opponents amongst whom the Bauddhas figured prominently. By means of his theory of the balanced combination of acts and knowledge and the concept of neutral and pure state of soul in the state of liberation Kumārilabhaṭṭa further gives a metaphysical basis to the discussions in the system. Thereby he certainly contributed immensely to the advancement of Mīmāṁsā thought and brought it into the arena of philosophy while earlier it was mainly a science of interpretation of the *śruti* texts.

Most probably Kumārilabhaṭṭa belonged to Mithilā in North Bihar and flourished in the middle of the seventh century. He wrote three reputed works—the *Ślokavārttika*, the *Tantravārttika* and the *Ṭupṭikā*. The first is a commentary in verse on the first *pāda* known as *Tarkapāda* of the first chapter of the *Śābarabhāṣya*. The second is a commentary mainly in prose on the *Śābarabhāṣya* and runs from *adhyāya* I, *pāda* II to the end of the third chapter. *Ṭupṭikā* is a brief commentary on the rest of the *Śābarabhāṣya*. Kumārila is also said to have written two more commentaries, namely *Bṛhaṭṭikā* and *Madhyamaṭikā*.

It is very difficult to say anything definitely about the personal life of Kumārilabhaṭṭa. There are many stories regarding the debates which were carried on between Kumārila and the Buddhist philosopher Dharmakīrti. According to a traditional account Kumārila in disguise learnt all the secrets of Buddhism from monks and then defeated them in open debate. Kumārilabhaṭṭa took it as a great sin against his teachers and for the expiation of such a sin he burnt himself alive on the banks of Triveṇī in Prayāga.

Prabhākaramiśra

Another important commentator of the *Śābarabhāṣya* is Prabhākaramiśra generally called Guru. According to tradition he was a pupil of Kumārilabhaṭṭa. There are many stories about the relation between the two. On the basis of the above tradition which makes him a junior contemporary of Kumārila he may be assigned to the later half of the seventh century. Ganganath Jha holds that Prabhākara flourished earlier than Kumārila, but this is not supported by tradition.

Scholars are of the opinion that he wrote two commentaries on *Śābarabhāṣya*—*Vivaraṇa* also called *Laghvī* and *Nibandhana* also called *Bṛhatī*. It is a point worth deep probing why Kumārila and Prabhākara wrote two commentaries each on the Bhāṣya of Śabara. C. Kunhan Raja has made a surmise that Kumārila may have first written the Ṭikās; then Prabhākara may have written *Laghvi* or *Vivaraṇa*; then Kumārila may have defended his position in the *Vārttikas* and Prabhākara may have re-asserted his position in *Bṛhati* or *Nibandhana*.

The Two Schools

Both Kumārila and Prabhākara claim to have faithfully explained the *Śābarabhāṣya*. Both of them try to prove the authority of Veda or āgama as the source of *dharma*, eternity of the world, and the supremacy of *dharma* determining the ethical conduct. Their commentaries mutually differ on many points and the differences became so famous and prominent that they came to be regarded as having founded two different schools antagonistic to each other and named after them as the Bhāṭṭa and the Prābhākara. Their differences relate to all the fields of epistemology, logic, metaphysics and ethics. It will be worthwhile to list some important points of difference.

Their Differences

Since Kumārilabhaṭṭa recognises *abhāva* as a separate category, he recognises *anupalabdhi* as a reparate means of knowledge for knowing *abhāva*, while Prabhākara considers *abhāva* as the *adhikaraṇasvarūpa* i.e. of the form of the location itself, and hence does not accept *anuplabdhi* as a separate means of knowledge. Thus Prabhākara recognises only five means of knowledge, viz. perception, inference, *Upamāna*, verbal testimony and presumption, while Kumārila admits *anupalabdhi* in addition to these. Kumārila thinks that knowledge is known through presumption which explains the manifested character of the object known, but according to Prabhākara it is directly perceived as knowledge is self-manifesting.

There is a difference between Kumārila and Prabhākara regarding the explanation of illusion e.g., when a conch-shell piece erroneously appears to be silver. Prabhākara believes in *akhyāti* theory while Kumārila holds the theory called *viparītakhyāti* or *anyathākhyāti*. According to the former in the above example the illusion is due to the fact that one does not note the peculiarity of the conch-shell as different from silver and remembers the silver seen at some other time, and so takes the conchshell to be silver, not cognising the difference between the remembered thing and the directly perceived one. Kumārila, however, goes a step further and says that the remembered silver is falsely identified with the conch-shell piece and thus one erroneously takes it to be silver. It further implies that according to Prabhākara no knowledge is false. The so-called wrong knowledge is partial knowledge. But Kumārila thinks that knowledge may be invalid also under certain circumstances.

Pervasion (*vyāpti*) for inference is ascertained by repeated observations according to Kumārila, but by observation of a single case according to Prabhākara.

The authoritative statement in verbal testimony is the scriptural statement only according to Prabhākara, but is both the scriptural and that uttered by human authority for Kumārila. In case an incomplete sentence is uttered, the words, are imported according to Kumārila, while according to Prabhākara what is imported is the sense of the words. As regards the rise of verbal cognition from a sentence Kumārila holds the theory of *abhihitānvayavāda* while Prabhākara believes in *anvitābhidhānavāda*. According to the former words convey their meanings and those meanings are capable of conveying their syntactical relation which is considered to be the *vākyārtha*, while according to the latter sentence is the unit of language and each word in a sentence conveys both the meaning and its *anvaya*.

Prabhākara considers *arthāpatti* through seen case only while Kumārila takes it as resulting from seen and heard.

Prabhākara admits eight categories—substance, quality, action, generality, inherence, potency, similarity and number, while Kumārila accepts five—substance, quality, action, generality and non-existence. Kumārila includes potency in qualities. Prabhākara like the Vaiśeṣikas accepts substantiality of nine—earth, water, air, fire, ether, soul, mind, time and space, while Kumārila adds darkness and sound to them.

Kumārila thinks that individuality applies to both the eternal things and to the products, while according to Prabhākara individuality applies to eternal things only.

The relation of generality to the individual is that of difference according to Prabhākara while that of difference and non-difference according to Kumārila.

Soul is cognised through mental perception according to Kumārila, but is perceptible as the experience of 'I' in all cognitions in the view of Prabhākara.

Kumārila thinks that in the state of release there is the mental experience of happiness but according to Prabhākara there is the destruction of all the specific qualities of soul.

Existence, etc. according to Kumārila are genera but not according to Prabhākara who holds that genus exists in perceptible things only.

Kumārila holds like the Vaiśeṣikas that action is perceptible while Prabhākara takes it to be inferrable.

Both the schools hold different views regarding the problem how the study of Veda comes in. Kumārila holds that every Brāhmaṇa has to study the Veda according to the injunction *svādhyāyo'dhyetavyaḥ*. Prabhākara, on the other hand, thinks that it is the duty of the teacher to teach a boy according to the injunction *aṣṭavarṣam brāhmaṇam upanayita tam adhyāpayita* and thus the study comes as subservient to teaching.

The two schools hold different views regarding the subject matter of Mīmāṁsā. Both of them agree that Mīmāṁsā is the discussion of *dharma*. However, *dharma* according to Prabhākara means *vedārtha*, while Kumārila understands it to be anything which is imposed by the Vedic injunction for some desired benefit, viz., the ritualistic performance. According to Kumārila the acts enjoined by *nityavidhis* are to avoid sin and those enjoined by *kāmyavidhis* are to attain some desired fruit. This results in the further difference that according to Kumārila the acts imposed by Vedic injunctions are intended for some desired result while according to Prabhākara the Vedic injunctions enjoin only without any idea of the results to be achieved. Hence Prabhākara held that duty, *kārya*, *niyoga* or *apūrva* is the meaning of the Vedic *liṅ* or injunction and not the accomplished facts.

Apūrva for Prabhākara means a *kārya*, which a man should perform, while Kumārila takes it as a link in the form of the past impressions meant to connect *yāga* and heaven. Prabhākara seems to hold the views of pre-Jaimini *Ācāryas* especially Bādari and his followers, while Kumārila follows the spirit of Jaimini and Śabara.

In the analysis of categories Kumārila seems to be influenced by Sāṁkya system also, while Prabhākara is more inclined to Vaiśeṣika. The differences between the two schools are summarized in the following verses :

संविदोऽस्वप्रकाशत्वमन्यथाख्यातिसंशयौ ।
कर्मदिक्कालवियतां प्रत्यक्षज्ञानगम्यता ॥
ध्वनेर्विभुत्वद्रव्यत्वे मनसोऽस्पन्दवैभवे ।
भिन्नाभिन्नत्वमेकस्य समवायस्य नास्तिता ॥
विभुद्वयस्य संयोगो नित्यत्वं तस्य चात्मनः ।
ज्ञेयत्वं मुक्तिवेलायां नित्यानन्दानुभाविता ॥
अभावप्रकटत्वं च शक्तेरनुमेयता ।
गुणत्वमन्धकारस्य पुंगिरां स्वार्थमानता ॥
पृथिवीत्वादिसामान्यं रूपत्वाद्याश्च जातयः ।
अनन्विताभिधानं च वेदस्याकार्यमानता ॥
श्रुतार्थापत्तिरित्येषु स्थलेषु प्रतियोगिनः ।
प्राभाकरा निराकार्या भट्टमार्गानुसारिणा ॥

The Later Commentaries and Treatises

After these two great authors we come across the important works in the form of commentaries as well as some celebrated treatises from the view point of either of the above founders of the two schools. The most important writer of the Bhāṭṭa school is Maṇḍana Miśra who is traditionally considered to be a contemporary of Kumārila and Śaṁkara. He is believed to be a Mithilā Brāhmaṇa who lived at Māhiṣmatī. Tradition also equates him with Sureśvara, the great Vedāntin. He wrote *Vidhiviveka*, *Ḅhāvanāviveka*, *Vibhramaviveka*, *Mīmāṁsānukramaṇikā*, and *Sphoṭasiddhi* on Mīmāṁsā and *Brahmasiddhi*, *Naiṣkarmyasiddhi* and *Vārttikās* on the *Bhāṣya* of Śaṁkara on *Bṛhadāraṇyakopaniṣad*.

Umbeka is the earliest commentator on *Ślokavārttika*. He is sometimes wrongly identified with Maṇḍana Miśra. Umbeka also wrote a commentary on *Bhāvanāviveka* of Maṇḍana Miśra.

Then flourised the celebrated writer Pārthasārathi Miśra of the rank of Śālikanātha Miśra in Prābhākara school. He is credited with many important works. He wrote *Nyāyaratnamālā* which deals with many important topics of Mīmāṁsā school. Still more important work of Pārthasārathi Miśra is the *Śāstradipikā* which can be called an *adhikaraṇa*-wise commentary on the *Mīmāṁsāsūtra* of Jaimini. It is commented upon by many authors of great reputation like Somanātha, Campakanātha, Vaidyanātha Bhaṭṭa, Sudarśanācārya and others. He wrote a commentary on *Ślokavārttika* called *Nyāyaratnākara* and another commentary on *Ṭupṭīkā* called *Tantraratna*.

Someśvara Bhaṭṭa (12th cen.), son of Mādhava Bhaṭṭa, wrote a lengthy commentary on *Tantravārttika* named *Nyāyasudhā* and variously called *Sarvopakāriṇi*, *Sarvānavadyakāriṇi* or *Rāṇaka*. He is also supposed to have written *Tantrasāra*.

Another commentary on *Tantravārttika* of the same period is Paritoṣamiśra's *Ajitā* or *Tantraṭīkānibandhana* (unpublished).

Then we meet with the powerful authors Vedāntadeśika who wrote *Mīmāṁsāpādukā* and *Seśvaramīmāṃsā*, and Mādhavācārya the author of *Jaiminiyanyāyamālā-vistara*.

Annambhaṭṭa is also supposed to have composed many works, which are unpublished.

Another important author of sixteenth century is Appayya Dīkṣita who wrote *Vidhirasāyana* and *Vādanakṣatramālā* (and some works available only in manuscript form).

In the same period Veṅkaṭa Dīkṣita wrote an important running commentary on *Ṭupṭīkā* called *Vārttikābharaṇa*.

Another important author of 17th century is Nārāyaṇa who wrote *Tantravārttikanibandhana* and *Māna* section of the *Mānameyodaya*. Laugākṣi Bhāskara is the author of the same age. Another author Nārāyaṇa Paṇḍita of the same age completed the *Meya* section of the *Mānameyodaya*.

Kamalākara alias Dādu Bhaṭṭa is also an important author of 17th century who wrote a commentary on *Tantravārttika* called *Bhāvārtha*, a commentary on the *Śāstradīpikā* called *Āloka* and an independent commentary on the *Jaiminisūtra* called *Śāstramālā*.

Then we have *Mīmāṁsābālaprakāśa* of Śaṁkarabhaṭṭa.

A leading Mīmāṁsaka of 17th century was Viśveśvara alias Gāgā Bhaṭṭa who was a protege of the the great Chatrapati Shivājī. His treatise called *Bhāṭṭacintāmaṇi* deals with many topics from Bhāṭṭa point of view. He is also credited with a *Vṛtti* called *Kusumāñjali* on *Jaiminisūtra*. He is also credited with a completed *Śivārkodaya* which, it is believed, was left unfinished by Kumārila.

In the same age we meet with the important Mīmāṁsā teatise the *Mīmāṁsānyāyaprakāśa* of Āpadeva II. There are several commentaries on this work. One of them is the *Bhaṭṭālaṅkāra* written by Āpadeva's son Anantadeva who also wrote the *Phalasāṁkaryakhaṇḍana* and the *Smṛtikaustubha*.

In the later half of the 17th century flourished Khaṇḍadevamiśra alias Śrīdharendra who wrote the celebrated works *Mīmāṁsākaustubha* and *Bhāṭṭadīpikā*.

Gopālabhaṭṭa II wrote *Mīmāṁsāvidhibhūṣaṇa* in defence of the *Vārttika* of Kumārila against the criticism by Appayyadīkṣita's *Vidhirasāyana*. The *Vidhisvarūpavicāra* of Gadādharabhaṭṭa, *Nyāyabindu*, an adhikaraṇawise commentary on Jaiminisūtra, *Anyatvaniryukti* of Murārimiśra II, *Adhvaramīmāṁsā* and *Kutūhalavṛtti* commentaries on *Jaiminisūtra* by Vāsudeva Dīkṣita, *Bhāṭṭamīmāṁsā* of Nārāyaṇatīrtha and *Mīmāṁsāparibhāṣā* of Kṛṣṇayajvan are other important works of this period.

In the school of Prabhākara Śālikanātha Miśra occupies an important place. He quotes two verses from *Vidhiviveka* and is quoted by Vācaspati Miśra. So he should be placed before Vācaspati and after Maṇḍana Miśra. He wrote two commentaries on the commentaries of Prabhākara: *Dīpaśikhā* on *Laghvī* and *Ṛjuvimalā-pañcikā* on *Bṛhatī*. Besides his *Prakaraṇapañcikā* is a very important treatise to know the essentials of the Prābhākara school. The *Nayaviveka* of Bhavanātha Miśra also known as Bhavadeva Miśra is an important work of Prābhākara school. It is an independent commentary on *Jaiminisūtra* from Prābhākara point of view. It is also commented upon by many powerful authors, though only one commentary named *Dīpikā* is available to us in published form. Another author Gurumatācārya Candra of the same period is supposed to have written *Nyāyaratnākara*, a commentary on *Jaiminisūtra* and a treatise *Amṛtabindu*. A good compendium of Prābhākara school is the *Prabhākaravijaya* of Nandīśvara. Of the 15th century is the important commentary on *Nayaviveka* called *Dīpikā*, also known as *Arthadīpikā* or *Varadarāji* by Varadarāja. In the 18th century we come across a celebrated work *Tantrarahasya* by Rāmānuja which deals with the *meyas* and *mānas* from Prābhākara point of view.

The Murāri School

Mention should be made of Murāri school of Mīmāṁsā which is described to be different from the above two in the popular saying like *murārestṛtīyaḥ panthāḥ*. We do not have any information about the doctrines or literature of this school except some hearsays. Umeśa Miśra has published *Tripādanītinayam* which is the explanation of the first four *pādas* of the *sūtras* of Jaimini, and *Ekādaśādhyāyādhikaraṇa* which discusses a small portion of the eleventh chapter of *Jaiminisūtra*. This strengthens the possibility of the explanation of the sūtras of Jaimini from Murāri point of view. Some more information about Murāri requires further investigation.

Laugākṣi Bhāskara

We do not have sufficient information about the personal life of Laugākṣi Bhāskara, the author of *Arthasaṁgraha*. Scholars have tried to deduce a few things from his name. They think that Bhāskara was his proper name and Laugākṣi his family name, and such a name suggests that he was a resident of south India. However, such a surmise is not supported by any historical fact. The basis of the above assumption is that Laugākṣi and Bhāskara stand for two names. Laugākṣi Bhāskara may, however be a single name consisting of two units. Though the author calls himself only Bhāskara in the concluding verse, it does not necessarily mean that Bhāskara is a single name. To fulfill the need of the metre the author may call himself by a single unit of his name. Nor is there any conclusive evidence to prove that Laugākṣi is a family name. Laugākṣi is sometimes found as a proper name also as in the case of the author of the *Kātyāyana Śrautasūtra*. The fact that the author names himself as Bhāskara Śarmā at the end of his *Tarkakaumudi* strengthens the doubt.

According to A. B. Keith Laugākṣi Bhāskara was the son of Mudgala and the grandson of Rudra. In the commencement of his works Laugākṣi Bhāskara offers salutations to Vāsudeva associated with Ramā. It suggests that Laugākṣi Bhāskara was a devotee of lord Viṣṇu. The selection of the term Vāsudeva as an epithet of Viṣṇu especially found in the Pāñcarātras as meaning the supreme Lord further suggests that Laugākṣi Bhāskara was a follower of the Pāñcarātra school of Vaiṣṇavism.

A. B. Gajendragadkar suggests a further possibility that the expression *vāsudevam ramākāntam* paronomastically refers either to Laugākṣi Bhāskara's parents Vāsudeva and Ramā or to his spiritual preceptor and his wife, bearing these names. If the statement of Keith about the parents of Laugākṣi Bhāskara is considered authentic the possibility that the expression refers to the parents of Laugākṣi Bhāskara does not arise. The latter possibility is not controverted though not supported by some other external evidence as well. On the contrary, it is somewhat strengthened by the close connection of the *Arthasaṁgraha* with the *Mimāṁsānyāyaprakāśa*. The latter refers to his spiritual preceptor in the bebedictory verse and if the pattern of the two works is the same, we can conjecture that Laugākṣi Bhāskara also paronomastically refers to his preceptor and his wife. Laugākṣi Bhāskara is credited with another work *Tarkakaumudi*, a treatise dealing with the Vaiśeṣika system for beginners.

The Arthasaṁgraha

The *Arthasaṁgraha* is profound in contents, scholarly in treatment and simple and lucid in style and language. It condenses great amount of matter in pregnant language. The author aims to write the text for beginners and hence adopts simplicity and brevity in language. He successfully maintains it even in treating difficult problems briefly in a masterly style. That is why the work is held in respect by scholars as well as serves as a gateway to the system of Pūrvamīmāṁsā for the beginners. Sometimes the reader may come across some expressions which appear too big and high sounding for a beginner, for example those in the context of *bhāvanā*, but this is unavoidable in the treatment of such a subject matter. The author himself stresses the purpose and utility of the work claiming that the study of the present work would help the student in getting an easy entrance into Jaimini's doctrines.

The full name of the work as given by the author in the colophon is *Pūrvamimāṁsārthasaṁgraha* which means a compendium which deals with the topics of the Pūrvamīmāṁsā (पूर्वमीमांसायाः अर्थानाम् पूर्वमीमांसा-शास्त्रप्रतिपादितानां विषयाणां संग्रहः). The title *Arthasaṁgraha*, remarks A. B. Gajendragadkar, perhaps suggests paronomastically that by the composition of the present work the author was expecting to make some money (to pursue his studies of Pūrvamīmāṁsā system).

The striking similarity in contents and language of the *Arthasaṁgraha* with the *Mīmāṁsānyāyaprakāśa* of Āpadeva has puzzled scholars about the posteriority and priority of the two works. It finally results into the further problem as to whether the *Arthasaṁgraha* serves as a source for the other or *vice versa*. A. B. Keith, S. Radhakrishnan etc. are of the opinion that Laugākṣi seems to freely utilise the view of Āpadeva as the basis of *Arthasaṁgraha*. According to them Laugākṣi Bhāskara has summarized the contents of the *Mīmāṁsānyāyaprakāśa* avoiding some details. There is another group of scholars like Ramaswāmi Shastri, F. Edgerton, etc. who date Laugākṣi Bhāskara before Āpadeva and regard *Arthasaṁgraha* as the source of *Mīmāṁsānyāyaprakāśa*. They hold that Āpadeva found the *Arthasaṁgraha* to be too brief for thoroughly understanding it and elaborated its contents with some more details. In the absence of any conclusive evidence the matter is open for further investigation.

Dharma

The chief aim of the *Arthasaṁgraha* is to provide an introduction for an easy understanding of the system of Jaimini. The author, however, restricts the scope of *dharma*. *Dharma* according to Laugākṣi Bhāskara is briefly the ritualistic acts, and he claims that the definition is in conformity with the meaning of the term given by Jaimini. S. K. Gokhale,* however, finds the definition indefinite. He further charges Laugākṣi Bhāskara of supplying a wrong definition of the words already defined by Jaimini. He thinks that Jaimini defines *dharma* as the fundamental principles underlying the practice of ritual while Laugākṣi Bhāskara equates *dharma* with ritual and adds the word *ādi* without defining its scope.

A close study of the context in the *Arthas ımgraha*, however, leaves no scope for such a charge. Laugākṣi Bhāskara also gives such a meaning of *dharma* in the context of desire of knowing *dharma*. If ritual is correlated with the desire of its knowledge, the meaning amounts to the principles underlying ritualistic performance. As regards the scope intended by the word *ādi*, one can easily understand it to be muttering the sacred syllable (*japa*), physical austerities, charity, etc. which are practised for supra-mundane results. Thus we can briefly say that *dharma* is the act which yields supramundane results. The other good works like saluting the elders which yield the worldly result of pleasing them are not *dharma* and hence they are excluded by the word *eva*. It further signifies that the Vedas stress the improvement of man's condition after this life.

The source of *dharma* is the Veda which is defined as 'the

*S. K. Gokhale, "Laugākṣi Bhāskara's Artha-saṃgraha: an adverse criticism", *Poona Orientalist*, 25 (1960).

sentence not produced by man'. S. K. Gokhale finds the definition of Veda given by Laugākṣi Bhāskara to be unnecessary as Veda is already defined by Jaimini. He further finds it faulty firstly because it does not conform to Jaimini's statement that Veda in Mīmāṁsā is the *Mantra* and *Brāhmaṇa* literature and secondly, because it discusses the irrelevant question whether Vedas are composed by man or not. However, the definition proves an improvement upon the statement of Jaimini. Jaimini merely gives a description of Veda, while Laugākṣi Bhāskara defines it. Rāmeśvara brings out the significance of the words used in the definition. The word *apauruṣeya* excludes the works of human beings like *Mahābhārata* and the word *vākya* excludes the entities like soul which are *apauruṣeya* but not Veda. The definition implies eternity, self-evidence and perfectness of contents and non-human agency in the case of Vedas.

Laugākṣi Bhāskara discusses in detail how the Vedas enjoin *dharma*. *Dharma* is enjoined through injunctions and hence Laugākṣi Bhāskara explains the way of understanding the injunctions like *yajeta svargakāmaḥ*. The following diagram makes this manner clear.

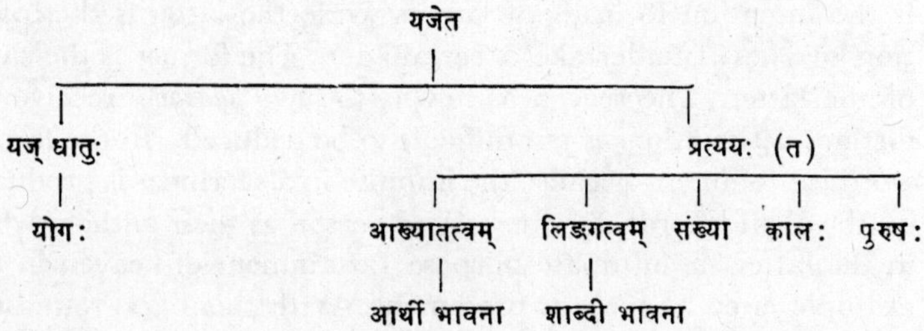

Bhāvanā

The verbal form *yajeta* consists of two grammatical elements, the root (technically called *ākhyāta*) and the suffix (*lakāra*). The latter conveys the general verbal sense or the idea of action in general, while the former restricts it to a particular action. For example, in the verbal form *pacati* the root-form *pac* denotes the particular action of cooking, while the suffix representing *lakāra* denotes action in general. The *lakāra* is replaced or represented by a suffix which further restricts the idea to the particular mood, tense and number. Thus the particular suffix is supposed to convey the idea of tense, mood and number. Both the constituent elements of the suffix convey the creative energy expressed by the technical term *bhāvanā* used by the Mīmāṁsakas. *Bhāvanā* is defined as the particular activity (*vyāpāraviśeṣaḥ*) of an agent (*bhāvayituḥ*) which is conducive to the production of that which is to come into being (*bhavituḥ*). This may be explained by the following example. Yajñadatta orders his son Devadatta—*Devadatta, gāmānaya.* Here Yajñadatta wants to produce an inclination (*pravṛtti*) to bring the cow in Devadatta. Hence, Yajñadatta is *bhāvayitṛ*, the inclination in Devadatta the *bhavitṛ* and Yajñadatta's effort (*vyāpāra*) is the *bhāvanā.* If the situation is viewed from Devadatta's point of view, the position is like this. Devadatta wants the accomplishment of the act of bringing the cow. Therefore, he is the *bhāvayitṛ*, the act of bringing the cow, the *bhavitṛ* and Devadatta's effort, the *bhāvanā.* The former is technically termed as *śābdī bhāvanā* and the latter, the *ārthī bhāvanā.* In the Vedic statements like *yajeta svargakāmaḥ* the *śābdī bhāvanā* viz., the intention that the person should be prompted for the performance of sacrifice resides in the words of the Vedas while the *ārthī bhāvanā* viz., the intention relating to the actual performance of the sacrifice resides in the sacrificer. The former is the intention to instigate others while the latter is the intention to oneself undertake a certain act. The former is the cause of the latter. The reason as to why the two *bhāvanās* receive the distinct designations is not difficult to be deduced. In the former word is prominent because the impulse in a sacrificer is produced by the Vedic words, for there is no person as their author; while in the latter the ultimate purpose (attainment of heaven in the example cited above), is prominent. With this background the definitions of the two *bhāvanās* given in *Arthasaṁgraha* become quite easy to understand.

Kinds of Vedic Texts

A division of the Veda is put forth on the basis of the variety of Vedic statements in accordance with the manner in which they refer to *dharma.* The Veda is declared to consist of five parts: injunction (*vidhi*), sacrificial formula (*mantra*), name (*nāmadheya*), prohibition (*niṣedha*) and explanatory passage (*arthavāda*).

Vidhi

Vidhi is the most important as it enjoins the acts directly. *Vidhi* is defined as 'the portion of Veda which makes known (enjoins) a matter not known by any other source of knowledge'. It is of three, kinds—(i) *pradhānavidhi* or *utpattividhi* which enjoins the principal, viz., the sacrifice itself as अग्निहोत्रं जुहुयात् स्वर्गकाम: (one desirous of heaven should offer the Agnihotra); (ii) *Guṇa-vidhi* which enjoins the subsidiary matter (in relation to the former which is already known through some other injunction) as दध्ना जुहोति (one sacrifices with curds); (iii). *viśiṣṭavidhi* which enjoins the sacrifice as well as the material with which it is performed or in other words a sacrifice characterised by material (विशिष्टस्य गुणविशिष्टस्येत्यर्थ: यज्ञादे: कर्मण: विधि:) e.g. सोमेन यजेत (one should sacrifice with *soma*).

Vidhi is again divided into four classes: originative (*utpatti-vidhi*), applicatory (*viniyogavidhi*), that of qualification (*adhikāra-vidhi*) and that of procedure (*prayogavidhi*). These four kinds of injunction respectively supply the answer to the questions: What acts are enjoined by the *śruti*? In what manner are they to be performed? Who is the person to whom different injunctions are applicable? And which is the order of succession of the subordinate acts the sum total of which leads to the one principal result. The originative injunction is that which indicates merely the nature of a rite as अग्निहोत्रं जुहोति (he offers the *Agnihotra*). The applicatory injunction is that which conveys the connection of a subsidiary with the principal, as दध्ना जुहोति (he sacrifices with curds).

There are six means to determine this relation of principal and subsidiary among various objects and acts constituting the sacrifice—the direct statement (*śruti*), indictatory mark (*liṅga*), sentence (syntactical connection or *vākya*), context (*prakaraṇa*), position (*sthāna*), and etymological sense (*samākhyā*). If two or more of these become available together (*samavāye*) the nature of being principal or subsidiary is determined on the ground of the distance which separates them from their application. Thus, the earlier is the stronger than the latter as stated by Jaimini himself: श्रुति-लिङ्ग-वाक्य-प्रकरण-स्थान-समाख्यानां समवाये पारदौर्बल्यम् अर्थविप्रकर्षात्.

The *Arthasaṁgraha* provides the full details of the matter with sufficient examples which need not be recorded here.

The injunction of qualification is that which intimates the

ownership or the state of being the enjoyer of the fruit of the action as यजेत स्वर्गकामः (one desirous of heaven should sacrifice). The two divisions of injunctions are not mutually exclusive.

Mantra

Laugākṣi Bhāskara proceeds to discuss the second part of Veda—the *mantra*. Though *mantra* refers to the original Veda, yet in view of the main purpose of Mīmāṁsā, viz., performance of sacrifices etc. it is subservient to *Vidhi* embodied in the *Brāhmaṇa* literature. The *mantras* are not merely to be uttered blindly during the performance of a ritual but they render their share in a particular way. The purpose of Veda is to remind the performer of matters connected with the performance, which implies that the *mantras* are not meaningless, and that the purpose of the study of the Veda is the understanding of their meaning and not some unseen result.

Now an objection naturally arises that such a purpose can be served by the Brāhmaṇas themselves and hence the purpose of the Veda is defeated. Here the Mīmāṁsakas come forward with a restriction that it should be done by the *mantras* only making it a case of *niyamavidhi*. Laugākṣi Bhāskara in tune with the other Mīmāṁsakas discussed casually the nature of *niyamavidhi* and *parisaṁkhyāvidhi*. The utterances of the *mantras* generates a mystic or supersensuous quality in the transcendental result of sacrifice (*apūrva*).

Nāmadheya

The third part of Veda is name (*nāmadheya*) which prompts to understand some words as names of sacrifices. For example, in the statement like *udbhidā yajeta paśukāmaḥ* (one desirous of cattle should sacrifice with *Udbhid*) *udbhid* should be understood as the name of a sacrifice.

The following reasons compel us for such an acceptance: (i) Fear of admitting an indication (*lakṣaṇā*) of possession, (ii) fear of a split in the sentence, (iii) the scriptural passages declaratory of it and (iv) designation with it. (i) In the example quoted above, the term *ubdhid* may be understood as a name of a sacrifice or the material used in a sacrifice. The second alternative compels us to consider it a case of indication of possession which is to be normally avoided if the sense is satisfactorily explained through primary sense. It, however, does not uproot the scope of *viśiṣṭa-vidhi* through the negation of acceptance of indication of possession even in the injunction like *somena yajeta* because firstly the term *soma* is better understood in the sense of the juice of a plant and hence one has to resort to the indication of possession to understand it in the sense of a sacrifice, but *udbhid* is not popularly known in the sense of a spade. Secondly, *soma* as a juice can serve as material for sacrifice but it is not so in the case of a spade. (ii) To avoid the undesirable contingency of split of as entence we have to understand *citrā* as a name of a sacrifice in the injunction *citrayā yajeta paśukāmaḥ* (the one desirous of cattle should perform citrā sacrifice). If the example is taken as a case of an injunction enjoining both the material for sacrifice and the fruit of the sacrifice, one has to resort to split of the sentence as *citrayā yāgam bhāvayeta* (one should perform a sacrifice with variegated material) and *yāgena paśum bhāvayeta* (one should get cattles with such a sacrifice). The defect can be easily avoided if the word *citrā* is understood as a name of a sacrifice. (iii) The expression 'agnihotra' in *agnihotram juhoti* should be understood in the sense of the name of a sacrifice because of the existence of a scriptural passage declaring that this is the subsidiary matter. The above expression may otherwise enjoin either the subsidiary matter fire (*agnau hotramasmin*) or the deity fire (*agnaye hotramasmin*). Both of these are, however, enjoined by some other passages; it leads to the possibility of considering *agnihotra* as a name of a sacrifice. (iv) In the expression *śyenenābhicaranyajeta* the term *śyena* is understood in the sense of a name of a sacrifice because of the designation of a rite with it (i.e. comparison with a falcon) which cannot be explained in any other way. The falcon cannot be compared with itself nor with any other thing except the sacrifice in the present context.

Niṣedha

Prohibitory sentences are the opposite of injunctions in nature insofar as these sentences turn people away from actions and imply that the prohibited acts if done lead to greater evil or highly undesirable results. This clarifies the purpose of prohibitions also.

To explain the import of a prohibitory sentence still further Laugākṣi Bhāskara discusses the further problems as to what exact constituent of the prohibitory sentence is to be construed with *na* and as to what is the sense in which this *na* is to be understood. The underlying principle is that it should negate what is prescribed by injunctions so that its opposition to the injunction may be proved and it should be construed with the principal element in the prohibitory sentence. Even though the prohibitory particle *na* is in immediate proximity to the root, it cannot be construed with the root because the root-meaning being subordinate (*upasarjana*) to *ārthi bhāvanā* cannot be construed with *na*. Therefore, what remains to be construed with *na* is the meaning of the *pratyaya* (termination). The *pratyaya* also consists of two elements—*ākhyātatva* which expresses the *ārthi bhāvanā* and the element of *liṅ* which expresses the *śābdi bhāvanā*. Here, with the application of the above general rule since the *ārthi bhāvanā* is subordinate to the *śābdi bhāvanā*, *na* is construed with the meaning of *liṅ*.

However, in two circumstances viz., (i) introduction of the prohibitory sentence under the province '*tasya vratam*' and (ii) the contingency of option, the prohibitory particle *na* is construed with the meaning of a root. The first can be exemplified as नेक्षेतोद्यन्तमादित्यम् where the ultimate sense is positive in form and which is a case of *paryudāsa* (exclusion). It is expressed in the following popular saying:

पर्युदासः स विज्ञेयो यत्र पूर्वपदेन नञ् ।
प्रतिषेधः स विज्ञेयो यत्रोत्तरपदेन नञ् ॥

The second case is illustrated as यजतिषु येयजामह करोति नानुयाजेषु. Here, if the *na* is construed with the meaning of the suffix, there arises the undesirable contingency of option (*vikalpa*) which can be alleviated through construing the particle *na* with *anuyāja*. It is again a case of *paryudāsa*. However, there is an exception to it also. In the case of नातिरात्रे षोडशिनं गृह्णाति we have to construe *na* with the suffix even admitting the undesirable contingency of option because there is no other way out. Here, *na* cannot be construed either with the noun or the meaning of the root.

Arthavāda

The fifth and the last kind of Vedic text is explanatory passage (*arthavāda*). It is a sentence which conveys praise or glorification of the thing enjoined and censure of the thing prohibited. Laugākṣi Bhāskara takes notice of the Mīmāṁsā maxim that every part of the Veda should be related with *yāga* (ritual). To apply the same to *arthavāda* he holds that it is related to ritual secondarily i.e. through *lakṣaṇā*. For example, a statement like वायुर्वै क्षेपिष्ठा देवता (*vāyu* is the swiftest deity), has to be related through *lakṣaṇā* or secondary meaning with the sacrifice of a white animal in honour of Vāyu surpassing its primary meaning. *Arthavāda* is of two types : (i) praising the thing enjoined, and (ii) censuring the thing prohibited. The example of the first kind is given above. The second kind is illustrated as सोऽरोदीत् यद् अरोदीत् तद् रुद्रस्य रुद्रत्वम्. Here is the censure of silver and when related with the sacrifice, the sentence conveys the censure of offering silver on sacrificial grass.

Arthavāda is again divided into three : (i) stating a quality (*guṇavāda*), (ii) containing a repetition (*anuvāda*) and (iii) stating the real state of affairs (*bhūtārthavāda*). The first occurs in the cases when its contents are contradicted by another means of knowledge. For example, in the sentence आदित्यो यूपः the identification of the sacrificial post with the sun being contradictory to perception, figurative sense (*lakṣaṇā*) is resorted to and the passage is understood as referring to the brilliance of the post. The second conveys a matter which is known through some other means of knowledge. For example, in the expression like अग्निर्हिमस्य भेषजम् it is the repetition of the directly known fact that fire is opposed to cold. The third kind includes the statements which can neither be contradicted nor established by any other means of knowledge, for example इन्द्रो वृत्राय वज्रमुदयच्छत्.

Laugākṣi Bhāskara concludes the treatise with the remark that if sacrifice is performed with a view to the attainment of a desired object, that object is attained, while if it is performed with the idea of dedicating it to God, it leads to liberation, though the ideas of liberation and dedication of acts to God are later developments in Mīmāṁsā.

Commentaries and Translations of the Arthasaṁgraha

The appearance of several editions of the *Arthasaṁgraha* prove its growing popularity. It was brought to light in *The Hindu Commentator* in 1873. As an aid to the understanding of the text we have some Sanskrit commentaries and translations. In Sanskrit the oldest available commentary is the *Kaumudī* by Rāmeśvarabhikṣu, also known as Rāmeśvara Śivayogī. The original name of Rāmeśvara was Kṣitikaṇṭha. He lived at Banaras in the middle of the 19th century. He was the son of Subrahmaṇya who taught him the *śāstra* in his childhood. He was a pupil of Sadāśivendra Sarasvatī. He wrote a commentary called *Subodhinī* on the *Mīmāṁsāsūtra*. Then he became a *sannyāsi*, changed his name to Rāmeśvara and wrote the *Kaumudī*. The commentary is quite extensive and useful and was printed several times.

Another important commentary is *Pratipādikā* (Calcutta, 1920) by Kṛṣṇanātha Nyāyapañcānana whose father's name was Keśava and mother's Kamalā and who lived in a village called Pūrvasthalī on the bank of Bhāgīrathī in the later half of the 19th century. Kṛṣṇanātha was a versatile scholar and wrote besides the above commentary a commentary on Vācaspati's *Tattvakaumudī*, *Āśubodhinī* commentary on *Vedāntaparibhāṣā* of Dharmarāja and *Arthadarśini* on *Mīmāṁsānyāyaprakāśa* of Āpadeva.

Mention should be made of two brief commentaries, one by J. Vidyāsāgara (Calcutta, 1875) and the other named *Amalā* by Pramathanātha Tarkabhūṣaṇa (Calcutta, 1899).

A valuable commentary named *Arthāloka* was recently written by Pattābhirāma Śāstrī, the biggest living authority on Mīmāṁsā. Several translations and explanations are also available.

In English it was translated by G. Thibaut (Benares, 1882), D.V. Gokhale (Poona, 1932) and jointly by A. B. Gajendragadkar and R. D. Karmarkar (Bombay, 1934). Out of these the last is the most helpful for the understanding of the text. The *Arthasaṁgraha* is translated and explained in Hindi by Tatambari ji Maharaj (Varanasi, 1956), Dayashankara Sastri (Meerut, 1972) and Vachaspati Upadhyaya (Delhi, 1977). Mention should be made here of the Marathi explanation by Mahadeva Paranjape (Bombay, 1927) which is very helpful in understanding the text of *Arthasaṁgraha*.

अर्थसंग्रहः

प्रथम उपोद्घातविभागः

मङ्गलश्लोकः

वासुदेवं रमाकान्तं नत्वा लौगाक्षिभास्करः।
कुरुते जैमिनिनये प्रवेशायार्थसंग्रहम् ॥ १ ॥

शास्त्रारम्भसूत्रम्

(१) अथ परमकारुणिको भगवाञ्जैमिनिर्धर्मविवेकाय द्वादशलक्षणीं प्रणिनाय[1]। तत्रादौ धर्मजिज्ञासां सूत्रयामास–'अथातो धर्मजिज्ञासा' (जै. सू. १.१.१) इति। अत्राथशब्दो वेदाध्ययनानन्तर्यवचनः। अतःशब्दो हि वेदाध्ययनस्य दृष्टार्थत्वं ब्रूते। 'स्वाध्यायोऽध्येतव्य' इत्यध्ययनविधौ तदध्ययनस्यार्थज्ञानरूपदृष्टार्थकत्वेन व्यवस्थापनात्। तथा च वेदाध्ययनानन्तरं यतोऽर्थज्ञानरूपदृष्टार्थकं

COMPENDIUM OF TOPICS

FIRST INTRODUCTORY CHAPTER

Benedictory Stanza

Having bowed to Vāsudeva, the lover of Ramā, Laugākṣi-Bhāskara composes [this] Compendium of Topics for entrance into the system or doctrine of Jaimini.

The Initial Aphorism of the Science

(1) First, the extremely compassionate divine Jaimini composed [the work consisting of] a group of twelve chapters (*lakṣaṇam*) for the discriminative comprehension of piety. There, in the beginning [he] set forth the desire to know piety in an aphorism viz. 'Then, therefore, a desire to know *dharma*.'* In this [aphorism] the word 'then' expresses immediate succession [of this desire] to the study of the Veda. For, the word 'therefore' declares that the study of the Veda has a seen or visible purpose. Because in [the discussion concerning] the injunction to study [contained in the text] 'The Veda (*svādhyāyaḥ*) should be studied,' it has been settled that the study thereof has a visible purpose in the

---

[1] 'प्रणिनीय'

*It is better to retain the original word as the concept is too complex to be expressed by a single English word, e.g. 'piety', 'duty' etc. The concept includes religious duties mainly, of course, not excluding moral duties. Hence 'piety' as the equivalent originally used by the translator has been dropped.

तदध्ययनमतो हेतोर्धर्मस्य वेदार्थस्य जिज्ञासा कर्तव्येति शेषः जिज्ञासापदस्य विचारे लक्षणा । अतो धर्मविचारशास्त्रमिदमारम्भणीयमिति शास्त्रारम्भसूत्रार्थः ।

धर्मलक्षणम्

(२) अथ को धर्मः, किं तस्य लक्षणमिति चेत् । उच्यते— यागादिरेव धर्मः । तल्लक्षणं वेदप्रतिपाद्यः प्रयोजनवदर्थो धर्म इति । प्रयोजनेऽतिव्याप्तिवारणाय प्रयोजनवदिति । भोजनादावतिव्याप्तिवारणाय वेदप्रतिपाद्य इति । अनर्थफलकत्वादनर्थभूते श्येनादावतिव्याप्तिवारणायार्थ इति ।

---

form of the knowledge of the sense [of the Veda]. And so, consequent on the study of the Veda, since the study thereof possesses a visible purpose in the form of the knowledge of the sense—for this reason, a desire to know *dharma*, [which represents] the sense of the Veda, should be entertained—this [latter expression is] to be supplied (*śeṣaḥ*). The word jijñāsā (desire to know) metaphorically indicates investigation. Hence, this science of the investigation into *dharma* should be commenced—this is the meaning of the aphorism [occurring] at the commencement of the science [of Pūrvamīmāṁsā].

Definition of *Dharma*

(2) Now if you ask (*cet*), ' What [is] piety, what [is] its definition ?', we reply (*ucyate*), ' Sacrifice and the like alone [constitute] *dharma*.' Its definition [is that it is] a desirable matter or end (*arthaḥ*), which is expounded or enjoined by the Veda [and] which has a purpose. [The expression] ' which has a purpose ' [is used in the definition] to prevent [its] unwarranted (*ati*) extension (*vyāptiḥ*) to the purpose. [The phrase] ' which is expounded by the Veda ' [is used in the definition] to prevent the unwarranted inclusion (*ativyāptiḥ*) of eating and the like [therein]. [The words] ' a desirable matter ' [serve] to prevent the unwarranted extension [of the definition] to the Śyena—[sacrifice] and the like, which have become an undesirable matter, because they [ultimately] lead to an undesirable fruit.

धर्मो वेदप्रतिपाद्यः

(३) न च ' चोदनालक्षणोऽर्थो धर्मः ' (जै. सू. १. १. २) इति सौत्रतल्लक्षणविरोधः । चोदनापदस्य विधिरूपवेदैकदेशपरत्वादिति वाच्यम् । तत्रापि चोदनाशब्दस्य वेदमात्रपरत्वात् । वेदस्य सर्वस्य धर्मतात्पर्यवत्त्वेन धर्मप्रतिपादकत्वात् ।

धर्मस्वरूपम्

(४) स च यागादिः ' यजेत स्वर्गकामः ' इत्यादिवाक्येन स्वर्गमुद्दिश्य पुरुषं प्रति विधीयते । तथा हि । ' यजेत ' इत्यत्रास्त्यंशद्वयं यजिधातुः प्रत्ययश्च । प्रत्ययेऽप्यस्त्यंशद्वयं आख्यातत्वं लिङ्त्वं च ।

Dharma is expounded by the Veda

(3) And [it] should not be objected (*vācya*) that [this definition involves] contradiction with the definition of that [*dharma*] contained in the aphorism [of Jaimini] viz. '*Dharma* [is] a matter the distinctive characteristic of which is instigation, ' because the word ' instigation ' signifies (*para*) one portion [only] of the Veda, which is of the form of injunction. For, [we urge in reply] even there [that is, in the definition contained in the aphorism], the word ' instigation ' signifies the entire (*mātra*) Veda. Since, the whole of the Veda expounds piety, because it possesses *dharma* as its purport.

Nature of *Dharma*

(4) And that [*dharma* consisting of] sacrifice and the like is enjoined by the sentence such as, ' One desirous of heaven should sacrifice, ' for a man with a view to [his attaining] heaven. For, to the same effect [point the following consideration] : In [the word] yajeta there are two constituent elements [viz.] the root yaj and the suffix. In the suffix also there are two constituent elements [viz.] verbality [that is, the general sense of the verb] and optativeness [that is, the injunctive force]. There, verbality [is] common to [all] the ten moods and tenses (*lakārah̤*), but optativeness [is exclusive] to only the optative mood.

तत्राख्यातत्वं दशलकारसाधारणं लिङ्त्वं पुनर्लिङ्मात्रे । उभाभ्यामप्यंशाभ्यां भावनैवोच्यते ।

भावनालक्षणम्

(५) भावना नाम भवितुर्भवनानुकूलो भावयितुर्व्यापारविशेषः। सा द्विधा। शाब्दी भावना आर्थी भावना चेति ।

शब्दभावनालक्षणम्

(६) तत्र पुरुषप्रवृत्त्यनुकूलो भावयितुर्व्यापारविशेषः शाब्दी भावना । सा च लिङंशेनोच्यते । लिङ्श्रवणेऽयं मां प्रवर्तयति मत्प्रवृत्त्यनुकूलव्यापारवानयमिति नियमेन प्रतीतेः। यद्यस्माच्छब्दान्नियमतः प्रतीयते तत् तस्य वाच्यम्। यथा गामानय इत्यस्मिन् वाक्ये गोशब्दस्य

Even by both the constituent elements [of the suffix in the word yajeta] creative energy [bhāvanā = lit. causing–to–come–into–being] is expressed.

Definition of Creative Energy

(5) Creative energy means a particular activity of a productive agent (*bhāvayitā*), which is conducive or favourable to the coming-into-being or production of that which is to come into being, [that is, an effect]. That [creative energy is] two-fold viz. word-creative-enery or verbal creative energy and end-creative energy or actual creative energy.

Definition of Verbal Creative Energy

(6) There verbal creative energy [represents] a particular activity of a productive agent, which is conducive or favourable to a man's exertion [that is, which has a tendency to make a man undertake the action denoted by the verb]. And it is expressed by the optative element [of the suffix]. For, on hearing an optative [form] one invariably (*niyamena*) understands, 'This [person viz. the one who uses that optative form] impels me [to action], this [person] possesses an activity which is favourable to my exertion.' What is invariably understood from a certain (*yasmāt*) word is what is expressed by that [word]. As in this sentence viz. 'Bring a cow', the word cow [expresses] cowness or cowhood or the generic character of a cow. And that parti-

गोत्वम्। स च व्यापारविशेषो लौकिकवाक्ये पुरुषनिष्ठोऽभिप्रायविशेषः। वैदिकवाक्ये तु पुरुषाभावाल्लिङादिशब्दनिष्ठ एव। अत एव शाब्दी भावनेति व्यवह्रियते।

शब्दभावनाया अंशत्रयम्

(७) सा च भावनांशत्रयमपेक्षते साध्यं साधनमितिकर्तव्यतां च, किं भावयेत् केन भावयेत् कथं भावयेदिति। तत्र साध्याकाङ्क्षायां वक्ष्यमाणांशत्रयोपेता आर्थी भावना साध्यत्वेनान्वेति, एकप्रत्ययगम्यत्वेन समानाभिधानश्रुतेः। संख्यादीनामेकप्रत्ययगम्यत्वेऽप्ययोग्यत्वान्न साध्यत्वेनान्वयः। साधनाकाङ्क्षायां लिङादिज्ञानं

---

cular activity, in [the case of] a worldly sentence, [takes the form of] the particular intention, residing in the man, [who wants to urge another to some exertion]. But in a Vedic sentence, owing to the absence of a man [who can be supposed to have uttered that sentence, the Veda being apauruseya, that particular activity] resides just in the word such as an optative [form]. Hence, indeed, [it] is spoken of as verbal creative energy.

Three Constituents of Verbal Creative Energy

(7) And that creative energy requires three elements or constituents [viz.] that which is to be accomplished [that is, the end or aim], the means or instrument [by which the bhāvanā accomplishes the end] and the mode, process or manner (*iti-kartavyatā*) [in which the accomplishment of the end is effected]. [These three elements respectively represent the answers to the three questions] namely (*iti*) what should [one] effect or bring into being, by which instrument should [one] effect [it and] how should [one] effect [it] ? There, as for the expectancy of the end, actual creative energy, endowed with the three elements to be mentioned later, is construed as the end ; because there is a common statement (*samāna-śrutiḥ*) which expresses [the ārthī bhāvanā along with the śābdī], since [the ārthī bhāvanā] is understood from one [and the same] suffix, which denotes [the śābdī as well]. Though number and others are understood from one [and the same] suffix, they are not construed as the end [for the

करणत्वेनान्वेति। तस्य च करणत्वं न भावनोत्पादकत्वेन, तत्पूर्वमपि तस्याः शब्दे सत्त्वात्। किंतु भावनाज्ञापकत्वेन शब्दभावनाभाव्यनिर्वर्तकत्वेन वा। इतिकर्तव्यताकाङ्क्षायामर्थवादज्ञाप्यप्राशस्त्यमितिकर्तव्यतात्वेनान्वेति।

अर्थभावनालक्षणम्

(८) प्रयोजनेच्छाजनितक्रियाविषयव्यापार आर्थी भावना। सा चाख्यातत्वांशेनोच्यते, आख्यातसामान्यस्य व्यापारवाचित्वात्।

अर्थभावनाया अंशत्रयम्।

(९) साप्यंशत्रयमपेक्षते साध्यं साधनमितिकर्तव्यतां च, किं

śābdī bhāvanā], because they are not fit [to be so construed]. As for the expectancy of the means [the hearer's] knowledge of [the meaning of] the optative (*liṅ*) and others is construed as the instrument. And its instrumentality [arises] not from [its] character of being the producer of the verbal creative energy, because it [namely, the verbal creative energy] is present in the word even before it [namely, the knowledge of the optative is obtained]; but from [its] character of making the verbal creative energy known or from [its] character of bringing into existence [the ārthī bhāvanā] which is to be produced by the verbal creative energy. As for the expectancy of the mode the glorification [of the rites] made known by the explanatory passages (*arthavādaḥ*) is construed as the mode.

Definition of Actual Creative Energy

(8) Actual creative energy [is] the activity [of a person], referring to [some particular] action and engendered by the desire for [some] object. And it is expressed by the element of verbality, for a verb (*ākhyātam*) in general [that is, independent of the different moods and tenses] expresses activity.

Three Elements of Actual Creative Energy

(9) It [that is, actual creative energy] also requires three elements [viz.] the end, the means and the mode. [These three elements respectively represent the answers to the three questions] namely, what should [one] effect, by

भावयेत् केन भावयेत् कथं भावयेदिति। तत्र साध्याकाङ्क्षायां स्वर्गादिफलं साध्यत्वेनान्वेति। साधनाकाङ्क्षायां यागादिः करणत्वेनान्वेति। इतिकर्तव्यताकाङ्क्षायां प्रयाजाद्यङ्गजातमितिकर्तव्यतात्वेनान्वेति।

वेदलक्षणम्

(१०) अथ को वेद इति चेदुच्यते। अपौरुषेयं वाक्यं वेदः। स च विधिमन्त्रनामधेयनिषेधार्थवादभेदात् पञ्चविधः।

---

which instrument should one effect [it and] how should [one] effect [it]? There, as regards the expectancy of the end, the fruit consisting of heaven and others is construed as the end. As regards the expectancy of the means, sacrifice and others are construed as the instrument. As regards the expectancy of the mode, the group of subsidiary rites such as the fore-sacrifices (*prayājaḥ*) is construed as the mode.

Definition of the Veda

(10) Now, if it be asked 'What [is] the Veda?', it is declared, 'The Veda is the sentence not produced by man.' And that [Veda is] of five kinds owing to [its] division into injunction (*vidhiḥ*), sacrificial formula (*mantra*), name, prohibition and explanatory passage.

द्वितीयो विधिविभागः

विधिलक्षणम्

(११) तत्राज्ञातार्थज्ञापको[1] वेदभागो विधिः । स च तादृश[2]प्रयोजनवदर्थविधानेनार्थवान् । तादृशं चार्थं प्रमाणान्तरेणाप्राप्तं विधत्ते । यथा 'अग्निहोत्रं जुहुयात् स्वर्गकाम' इति विधिर्मानान्तरेणाप्राप्तं स्वर्गप्रयोजनवद्धोमं विधत्ते । अग्निहोत्रहोमेन स्वर्गं भावयेदिति वाक्यार्थबोधः । यत्र कर्म मानान्तरेण प्राप्तं तत्र तदुद्देशेन गुणमात्रं विधत्ते । यथा 'दध्ना जुहोति' इत्यत्र होमस्य 'अग्निहोत्रं जुहुयात्' इत्यनेन प्राप्तत्वा-

---

SECOND CHAPTER DEALING WITH INJUNCTION

Definition of Injunction.

(11) There, [that] portion of the Veda, which makes known, intimates or enjoins a matter not known [before by any other means, is] injunction. And that [injunction] has a purpose or a function or a sense or derives its meaning (*arthavān*) from its enjoining such a matter having a purpose. And [it] enjoins such a matter as is not established by, or does not accrue from, [some] other means of proof or authority. For example (*yathā*), the injunction 'One desirous of heaven should offer the Agnihotra' enjoins a sacrifice, which is not established by any other means of proof and which possesses heaven for [its] purpose. '[One] should bring into existence [that is, should realise] heaven by means of the Agnihotra-sacrifice'—this [is] the meaning understood from the [above] sentence. Where a [sacrificial] rite is established by some other means of proof, there, an injunction enjoins merely a secondary or accessary matter (*guṇaḥ*) with reference to it [that is, that sacrificial rite]. For example, in this [injunction viz.]—'[One] sacrifices with curds', the sacrifice having been established by this [sentence] viz. '[One] should offer the Agnihotra,' only curds is enjoined with reference to the sacrifice in the form (*iti*) '[One] should

---

१ 'अज्ञातज्ञापकः' २ 'यादृशं'

द्धामोद्देशेन दधिमात्रविधानं दध्ना होमं भावयेदिति । यत्र तूभयमप्राप्तं तत्र विशिष्टं विधत्ते । यथा 'सोमेन यजेत' इत्यत्र सोमयागयोरप्राप्तत्वात् सोमविशिष्टयागविधानम् । सोमपदे मत्वर्थलक्षणया सोमवता यागेनेष्टं भावयेदिति वाक्यार्थबोधः ।

न चोभयविधाने वाक्यभेदः प्रत्येकमुभयस्याविधानात्, किं तु विशिष्टस्यैकस्यैव विधानात् ।

न च 'ज्योतिष्टोमेन स्वर्गकामो यजेत 'इति विधिप्राप्तयागोद्देशेन सोमरूपगुणविधानमेवास्तु, ' सोमेन यागं भावयेत् ' इति, किं मत्वर्थ लक्षणयेति वाच्यम् । तस्याधिकारविधित्वेनोत्पत्तिविधित्वासंभवात् ।

---

effect the sacrifice with curds'. But where both [the sacrificial action and the subsidiary matter] are not established [by any other means of proof], there, [the injunction] lays down [something] which is qualified or particularized or specialized. For example, in this [injunction viz.] '[One] should sacrifice with Soma', [both] the sacrifice and Soma not having been established [by any other means of proof], a sacrifice particularized by Soma [as its material] is enjoined. By means of an indication of possession (*matvartha-lakṣaṇā*) [understood] in the word Soma, the meaning conveyed by the sentence [is], '[One] should accomplish [one's] desired [object] by means of a sacrifice possessing Soma [for its material].'

And [there arises] no split of the sentence or syntactic disunity, when both [these] are enjoined; for the two are not individually or separately (*pratyekam*) enjoined; but only one as qualified [by the other] is enjoined.

And it should not be urged: 'Let there be [in the sentence Somena yajeta] just the enjoining of a secondary matter in the form of [the material] Soma, to this effect (*iti*), '[One] should accomplish the sacrifice with Soma,' with reference to the sacrifice [already] established by the injunction, '[One] who is desirous of heaven should sacrifice with the Jyotiṣṭoma'; what is the use of the indication of possession?' For, that [sentence] being an injunction of qualification, it cannot possibly be an injunction of origination.

ननु 'उद्भिदा यजेत पशुकामः' इत्यस्येव 'ज्योतिष्टोमेन' इत्यस्याप्युत्पत्त्याधिकारविधित्वमस्त्विति चेत् । न । दृष्टान्ते उत्पत्तिवाक्यान्तराभावेनान्यथानुपपत्त्या तथात्वाश्रयणात् । किं च 'ज्योतिष्टोमेन' इत्यस्योभयविधित्वेऽनेनैव यागस्तस्य फलसंबन्धोऽपि बोधनीय इति सुदृढो वाक्यभेदः । तद्वरं सोमपदे मत्वर्थलक्षणया विशिष्टविधानम् ।

चतुर्विधो विधिः

(१२) विधिश्चतुर्विधः उत्पत्तिविधिर्विनियोगविधिरधिकारविधिः प्रयोगविधिश्चेति ।

उत्पत्तिविधिः

(१३) तत्र कर्मस्वरूपमात्रबोधको विधिरुत्पत्तिविधिः । यथा

If you were to urge (*nanu-cet*): Let [the sentence] Jyotistomena etc. also be an injunction of [both] origination and qualification like the [sentence] '[One] who is desirous of cattle should sacrifice with the Udbhid,' [we reply] No. For, in the parallel instance or illustration on account of the absence of another sentence of origination it is impossible to account for [the qualification] otherwise [than by supposing the same sentence to be originative]; hence we have to admit [that sentence] to be of that kind [viz. as containing both the injunction of origination and that of qualification]. Moreover, if [the sentence] Jyotiṣṭomena etc. were to possess the character of a double injunction, the split of the sentence would be quite certain, because the same sentence would intimate the sacrifice [and] also its connection with the fruit. Therefore, it is better to have an injunction of a qualified [matter] by means of an indication of possession [understood] in the word Soma.

Four-fold Injunction

(12) Injunction [is] four-fold viz. injunction of origination or originative injunction, injunction of application or applicatory injunction, injunction of claim, qualification or competence and injunction of performance.

Injunction of Origination

(13) There, the injunction of origination [is] the injunction which indicates merely the [general] nature of a

'अग्निहोत्रं जुहोति' इति। अत्र च विधौ कर्मणः करणत्वेनान्वयः। 'अग्निहोत्रहोमेनेष्टं भावयेत्' इति।

ननु यागस्य द्वे रूपे द्रव्यं देवता च। तथा च रूपाश्रवणे 'अग्निहोत्रं जुहोति' इति कथमुत्पत्तिविधिः। अग्निहोत्रशब्दस्य तु तत्प्रख्यन्यायेन नामधेयत्वादिति चेत्। न। रूपाश्रवणेऽप्यस्योत्पत्तिविधित्वात्। अन्यथा रूपश्रवणात् 'दध्ना जुहोति' इत्ययमेवोत्पत्तिविधिः स्यात्। तथा च 'अग्निहोत्रं जुहोति' इति वाक्यमनर्थकं स्यात्।

विनियोगविधिः

(१४) अङ्गप्रधानसंबन्धबोधको विधिर्विनियोगविधिः। यथा

---

rite or action, as in '[He] offers the Agnihotra.' And in this injunction the action [expressed by the root] is construed as the instrument, [the sense of the injunction being] '[One] should bring into existence the desired [object] by means of the Agnihotra-sacrifice.'

But it may be objected (*nanu*): 'A sacrifice has two forms or aspects—the material [that is offered] and the deity [to whom it is offered]. And so, when the forms are not mentioned, how can [the sentence], "[He] offers the Agnihotra" be an injunction of origination? As regards (*tu*) the word Agnihotra, it is a [proper] name [of the sacrifice] according to the maxim [of the existence of another scriptural passage] declaratory of it.' [We reply:] 'No. Because though the forms are not mentioned, this [sentence is] an injunction of origination. Otherwise this very [sentence] viz. "[He] sacrifices with curds" would be an injunction of origination, because a form [viz. the material curds] is mentioned [therein]. And so, the sentence "[He] offers the Agnihotra" would be purposeless.'

Injunction of Application

[14] The injunction, which indicates or intimates or conveys the connection of a subsidiary with the principal [matter is] the injunction of application, as [the sentence] '[He] sacrifices with curds.' For, that [injunction] lays down the connection of curds, whose subsidiary character

'दध्ना जुहोति' इति। स हि तृतीयया प्रतिपन्नाङ्गभावस्य दध्नो होमसंबन्धं विधत्ते 'दध्ना होमं भावयेत्' इति।

गुणविधौ च धात्वर्थस्य साध्यत्वेनान्वयः। क्वचिदाश्रयत्वेनापि। यथा 'दध्नेन्द्रियकामस्य जुहुयात्' इत्यत्र 'दधिकरणत्वेनेन्द्रियं भावयेत्'। तच्च किंनिष्ठमित्याकाङ्क्षायां संनिधिप्राप्तहोम आश्रयत्वेनान्वेति।

विनियोगविधेः श्रुत्यादिषट्प्रमाणानि

(१५) एतस्य विधेः सहकारिभूतानि षट् प्रमाणानि श्रुतिलिङ्गवाक्यप्रकरणस्थानसमाख्यारूपाणि। एतत्सहकृतेनानेन विधि-

---

is understood by the instrumental case [in which the word occurs], with the sacrifice, thus (*iti*) '[One] should effect the sacrifice with curds.'

And in an injunction of a subsidiary matter (*guṇaḥ*) [that is, in an injunction of application], the sense of the root is construed as the thing to be accomplished. In some cases [it is construed] as the abode also. As in this [injunction viz.] 'For [him, who is] desirous of [the strength of] the senses, [one] should sacrifice with curds,' [the sense is] '[One] should produce [the strength of] the senses by the instrumentality of curds.' And when the expectancy as to where that [instrumentality of curds] resides arises, the sacrifice, which is found or occurs (*prāpta*) in the neighbourhood is construed as the abode.

Six Means of Proof, Direct Statement and others, of the Injunction of Application

(15) [There are] six means of proof, which have become the helpers of this injunction [of application] and which take the form of direct statement, mark or word-meaning (*liṅgam*), sentence or syntactical connection, context or interdependence (*prakaraṇam*) position or order, and name (*samākhyā*). This injunction [of application], assisted by these, intimates subsidiariness or subservience or the subsidiary relation, which consists in or takes the form of, the condition of being accomplished by the activity of [some one such as a sacrificer] who is engaged in the

नाङ्गत्वं परोद्देशप्रवृत्तकृतिसाध्यत्वरूपं पाराथ्यांपरपर्यायं ज्ञाप्यते।

श्रुतिः

(१६) तत्र निरपेक्षो रवः श्रुतिः। सा च त्रिविधा-विधात्री, अभिधात्री, विनियोक्त्री च। तत्राद्या लिङाद्यात्मिका। द्वितीया व्रीह्यादिश्रुतिः। यस्य च शब्दस्य श्रवणादेव संबन्धः प्रतीयते सा विनियोक्त्री।

त्रिविधा विनियोक्त्री श्रुतिः

(१७) सापि त्रिविधा-विभक्तिरूपा, एकाभिधानरूपा, एकपदरूपा चेति। तत्र विभक्तिश्रुत्या अङ्गत्वं यथा 'व्रीहिभिर्यजेत' इति तृतीयाश्रुत्या व्रीहीणां यागाङ्गत्वम्। तदपि पुरोडाशप्रकृतितया। यथा

---

pursuit of the highest [aim] and the other synonym (*paryāyaḥ*) of which is existence for the purpose of another or dependence.

Direct Statement

(16) There, direct statement [means or consists in] independent sound [that is, words which express their sense without any intermediate steps such as those that are required by the other means, of proof]. And that [direct statement is] three-fold [viz.] injunctive, denotative and applicatory. Among them the first consists of the optative and other [forms which directly indicate the bhāvanā]. The second [kind of direct statement is] the scriptural passage that refers to rice-grains. And the applicatory [direct statement is] that word from the mere hearing of which the connection [between the subsidiary and principal matter] is understood.

Three-fold Applicatory Direct Statement

(17) That [applicatory direct statement is] also of three kinds [viz.] of the form of a case, of the form of one [common] denotative element [of a word which has more than one such element] and of the form of one word [in the grammatical sense, which has more than one element]. There, subservience by the direct statement of a case [is illustrated] in '[One] should sacrifice with rice-grains,' [where] by the direct statement of the instrumental case the

पशोर्हृदयादिरूपहविःप्रकृतितया यागाङ्गत्वम् । 'अरुणया पिङ्गाक्ष्या एकहायन्या गवा सोमं क्रीणाति' इत्यस्मिन् वाक्ये आरुण्यस्यापि तृतीयाश्रुत्या क्रयाङ्गत्वम् । तदपि गोरूपद्रव्यपरिच्छेदद्वारा न तु साक्षात्, अमूर्तत्वात् ।

'व्रीहीन् प्रोक्षति' इति प्रोक्षणस्य व्रीह्यङ्गत्वं द्वितीयाश्रुत्या । तच्च प्रोक्षणं न व्रीहिस्वरूपार्थम्, तस्य तेन विनाप्युपपत्तेः । किंत्वपूर्वसाधनत्वप्रयुक्तम् । व्रीहीनप्रोक्ष्य यागानुष्ठानेऽपूर्वा[1]नुत्पत्तेः । एवं सर्वेष्वङ्गेष्वपूर्वप्रयुक्तमङ्गत्वं बोध्यम् । एवम् 'इमामगृभ्णन् रशनामृतस्येत्यश्वा-

---

subservience of the rice-grains to the sacrifice [is understood]. That [subservience] too [arises] on account of [their] being the original substances of the sacrificial cake (*puroḍāśaḥ*); as an animal becomes subservient to the sacrifice owing to [its] being the original substance of the oblation in the form of the heart etc. 'With a ruddy, yellow-eyed, one-year-old cow [he] purchases Soma'–in this sentence even ruddiness becomes subservient to purchase owing to the direct statement of the instrumental. That [subservience] too [becomes possible] through [its] defining or particularizing (*paricchedaḥ*) the substance in the form of the cow, but not directly, owing to its incorporeality or immateriality (*amūrtatvam*).

In '[He] sprinkles the rice-grains [with water],' the sprinkling becomes subservient to the rice-grains by the direct statement of the accusative. And that sprinkling [is] not for the purpose of [producing] the natural form of the rice-grains; because that [natural form] is accounted for even without it. But [the sprinkling] is employed as a means of [bringing into existence] the not-existent-before (*apūrvam*) [that is, the transcendental result]. If the sacrifice is performed without sprinkling the rice-grains [with water], the not-existent-before would not be produced. Thus, in all subsidiaries the subsidiariness should be understood to have been caused by, or intended for the not-existent-before or the transcendental result. Similarly, '[They] grasped this rein of truth—thus

---

१ 'अपूर्वानुपपत्तेः' इति मुद्रितपुस्तकपाठः

भिधानीमादत्ते' इत्यत्र द्वितीयाश्रुत्या मन्त्रस्याश्वाभिधान्यङ्गत्वम्।

'यदाहवनीये जुहोति' इत्याहवनीयस्य होमाङ्गत्वं सप्तमीश्रुत्या। एवमन्योऽपि विभक्तिश्रुत्या विनियोगो ज्ञेयः।

'पशुना यजेत' इत्यत्रैकत्वपुंस्त्वयोः समानाभिधानश्रुत्या कारकाङ्गत्वम्। 'यजेत' इत्याख्याताभिहितसंख्याया भावनाङ्गत्वं समानाभिधानश्रुतेरेव। एकपदश्रुत्या च यागाङ्गत्वम्।

अमूर्तमपि भावनाङ्गं भवति

(१८) न चामूर्तायास्तस्याः कथं भावनाङ्गत्वमिति वाच्यम्। कर्तृपरिच्छेदद्वारा तदुपपत्तेः। कर्ता चाक्षेपलभ्यः। आख्यातेन हि

[he] grasps the rein of the horse—here the formula (*mantraḥ*) becomes subservient to the rein of the horse by the direct statement of the accusative.

'When he sacrifices in the Āhavanīya fire'—[here] the Āhavanīya fire becomes subservient to the sacrifice by the direct statement of the locative. In this manner other application also by means of the direct statement of a case should be understood.

'[One] should sacrifice with an animal'—here singularity and masculinity, or oneness and maleness, or singular number and masculine gender, become subservient to the [particular] case relation [viz. the instrumental] on account of the direct statement in [one] common denotative element. The number, expressed by [the suffix in] the verb 'Yajeta' becomes subservient to the creative energy on account of the very direct statement in [one] common denotative element. And [it becomes] subservient to the sacrifice on account of the direct statement of one word.

Even an Incorporeal Thing can be subservient to Creative Energy

(18) And it should not be urged, 'How can that [number], which is incorporeal or immaterial, be subservient to creative energy?' Because that becomes reasonable, or is accounted for, through [its] defining the agent. And the agent is to be understood by implication.

भावनोच्यते। सा च कर्तारं विनानुपपन्नेति तमाक्षिपति।

श्रुतिर्लिङ्गादिभ्यः प्रबला

(१९) सेयं श्रुतिर्लिङ्गादिभ्यः प्रबला। लिङ्गादिषु न प्रत्यक्षो विनियोजकः शब्दोऽस्ति किंतु कल्प्यः। यावच्च तैर्विनियोजकशब्दः कल्प्यते तावत् प्रत्यक्षया श्रुत्या विनियोगस्य कृतत्वेन तेषां कल्पकत्वशक्तेर्व्याहतत्वात्। अत एवैन्द्या लिङ्गान्नेन्द्रोपस्थानार्थत्वम्। किंतु 'ऐन्द्या गार्हपत्यमुपतिष्ठते' इत्यत्र गार्हपत्यमिति द्वितीयाश्रुत्या गार्हपत्योपस्थानार्थत्वम्।

लिङ्गम्

(२०) शब्दसामर्थ्यं लिङ्गम्। यथाहुः 'सामर्थ्यं सर्वशब्दानां लिङ्गमित्यभिधीयते' इति। सामर्थ्यं रूढिरेव। तेन समाख्यातोऽस्या

For, by the verb is expressed the creative energy. And that [creative energy would become] unreasonable or impossible without an agent ; hence [it] implies him.

Direct Statement Stronger than Mark and others

(19) This direct statement here [is] stronger than mark and others. In mark and others no actual or direct (*pratyakṣa*) applicatory word is present, but [it] has to be presumed. And by the time those [mark and others] presume the applicatory word, during that time (*tāvat*) the actual direct statement will have [already] made the application; consequently their power of presumption or assumption is nullified or set aside. For this reason alone (*ata eva*) Indra's verse [is] not [used] for the the purpose of waiting upon or reverencing Indra ; but as in the sentence 'By means of Indra's verse [he] reverences the Gārhapatya fire,' there is a direct statement of the accusative viz. Gārhapatyam, [Indra's verse is used] for the purpose of reverencing the Gārhapatya fire.

Mark

(20) Mark [is] the power of words [to denote or point out something]. As [they] say, 'The power of all words is said to be the mark.' The power [is] convention itself. Hence, this [convention which forms the power] is distinguished from name. Because a word containing mark, con-

भेदः। यौगिकशब्दसमाख्यातो रूढ्यात्मकालिङ्गशब्दस्य भिन्नत्वात्। तेन 'बर्हिर्देवसदनं दामि' इति मन्त्रस्य कुशलवनाङ्गत्वं न तूलपादिलवनाङ्गत्वम्। तस्य 'बर्हिर्दामि' इति लिङ्गात् तल्लवनं प्रकाशयितुं समर्थत्वात्। एवमन्यत्रापि लिङ्गाद्विनियोगो द्रष्टव्यः।

लिङ्गं वाक्यादिभ्यो बलवत्

(२१) तदिदं लिङ्गं वाक्यादिभ्यो बलवत। अत एव 'स्योनं ते सदनं कृणोमि' इति मन्त्रस्य पुरोडाशसदनकरणाङ्गत्वं 'सदनं कृणोमि' इति लिङ्गात् न तु वाक्यात्।

वाक्यम्

(२२) समभिव्याहारो वाक्यम्। समभिव्याहारश्च साध्यत्वादिवाचकद्वितीयाद्यभावेऽपि वस्तुतः शेषशेषिवाचकपदयोः सहोच्चारणम्।

---

sisting of the conventional meaning (*rūḍhuḥ*) is different from name which consists of a word understood in its etymological or literal sense (*yaugika*). Consequently (*tena*) the formula, '[I] cut grass, the seat of the gods', becomes subservient to the cutting of the Kuśa-grass, but not to the cutting of the Ulapa and other kinds of grass. For, that [formula] is able to reveal or make known the cutting of that [grass] from the mark contained in '[I] cut the Kuśa-grass.' Similarly, in other places also, application from mark should be seen.

Mark Stronger than Sentence and others

(21) This mark here is stronger than sentence and other [means of proof]. For this reason alone the formula, 'A pleasant (*syona*) seat [I] prepare for thee,' is subservient to the making of a seat for the sacrificial cake from the mark contained in 'A seat [I] prepare,' but not from the sentence.

Sentence

(22) Sentence or syntactical connection [is] connected utterance. And connected utterance is the pronouncing together of two words expressing subsidiary and principal [things], which are really so (*vastutaḥ*) even in the absence of case-forms such as the accusative denoting the thing to

यथा 'यस्य पर्णमयी जुहूर्भवति न स पापꣳ श्लोकं शृणोति'। अत्र पर्णताजुह्वोः समभिव्याहारादेव पर्णताया जुह्वङ्गत्वम्।

न चानर्थक्यम्। अन्यथापि जुह्वाः सिद्धत्वादिति वाच्यम्। जुहूशब्देन तत्साध्यापूर्वलक्षणात्। तथा च वाक्यार्थः। पर्णतयावत्तहविर्धारणद्वारा जुह्वंपूर्वं भावयेदिति। एवं च पर्णतया यदि जुहूः क्रियते तदैव तत्साध्यमपूर्वं भवति नान्यथेति गम्यत इति न पर्णताया वैयर्थ्यम्। अवत्तहविर्धारणद्वारेति चावश्यं वक्तव्यम्। अन्यथा स्रुवादिष्वपि पर्णतापत्तेः।

सेयं पर्णता अनारभ्याधीतापि सर्वप्रकृतिष्वेवान्वेति न विकृतिषु।

---

be accomplished etc. For example, 'Whose ladle is made of parṇa-wood, he hears no evil report [about himself i. e. becomes famous]'. Here from the very connected utterance of being-made-of-parṇa-wood (*parṇatā*) and ladle, the being-made-of-parna-wood becomes subservient to the ladle.

And it should not be urged: '[There is] purposelessness [in enjoining that the ladle should be made of parṇa-wood]. For, even otherwise [than from parṇa-wood] can the ladle be made.' For, the word ladle indicates the not-existent-before or the transcendental result to be accomplished by that [viz. by the ladle made of parṇa-wood]. And so the meaning of the sentence [is]: [One] should bring into existence the not-existent-before [arising] from the ladle by means of [its] being-made-of-parṇa-wood through the holding of the cut (*avatta*) oblation [in it]. And it is understood that if the ladle is made of parna-wood, then only, the not-existent-before, which is to be accomplished by that [ladle], arises, not otherwise; hence [there is] no futilily or uselessness of being-made-of-parṇa-wood. And 'Through the holding of the cut oblation'—this must necessarily be said [in the explanation of the above sentence]. Otherwise, the being-made-of-parṇa-wood would accrue in the case of sruva and others also.

This being-made-of-parṇa-wood, though prescribed without reference to any particular sacrifice (*anārabhyādhīta*), is construed with all arche-types (*prakṛtiḥ*) only,

तत्र चोदकेनापि तत्प्राप्तिसंभवात् पौनरुक्त्यापत्तेः ।

प्रकृतिविकृत्यनारभ्यविधिलक्षणम्

(२३) यत्र समग्राङ्गोपदेशः सा प्रकृतिः । यथा दर्शपूर्णमासादिः । तत्प्रकरणे सर्वाङ्गपाठात् । यत्र न सर्वाङ्गोपदेशः सा विकृतिः । यथा सौर्यादिः । तत्र कतिपयाङ्गानामतिदेशेन प्राप्तत्वात् । अनारभ्यविधिः सामान्यविधिः ।

वाक्यं प्रकरणादिभ्यो बलवत्

(२४) तदिदं वाक्यं प्रकरणादिभ्यो बलवत् । अत एव 'इन्द्राग्नी इदं हविः' इत्यादेरेकवाक्यत्वाद्दर्शाङ्गत्वं न तु प्रकरणाद्दर्शपूर्णमासाङ्गत्वम् ।

[but] not with the modifications. For, since there is a possibility of its obtaining there [i. e. in the modifications] even by means of extended application or transfer (*atideśaḥ*), repetition would accrue (*āpattiḥ*), [if it is construed with modifications as well].

Definition of Arche-type, Modification and Detached Injunction

(23) Where there is specification or mention of all subsidiaries, that [is] the arche-type, as the new moon and full moon sacrifices and others. For, in their context all subsidiaries are mentioned. Where all subsidiaries are not specified, that [is] the modification, as the oblation to the sun (*saurya*). There some subsidiaries become available (*prāpta*) by means of extended application. An injunction without reference to any particular sacrifice [is] a general injunction [i. e. an injunction of general application].

Sentence Stronger than Context and others.

(24) This sentence here [is] stronger than context and others. Hence, indeed, (*ata eva*) the formula, '[O] Indra and Agni, this offering [you have accepted],' is subsidiary to the new moon sacrifice on account of its forming one sentence, but not subsidiary to [both] new moon and full moon sacrifices on account of context.

प्रकरणम्

(२५) उभयाकाङ्क्षा प्रकरणम्। यथा प्रयाजादिषु। 'समिधो यजति' इत्यादिवाक्ये फलविशेषस्यानिर्देशात् 'समिद्यागेन भावयेत्' इति बोधानन्तरं 'किम्' इत्युपकार्याकाङ्क्षा। दर्शपूर्णमासवाक्येऽपि 'दर्शपूर्णमासाभ्यां स्वर्गं भावयेत्' इति बोधानन्तरं 'कथम्' इत्युपकारकाकाङ्क्षा। इत्थं चोभयाकाङ्क्षया प्रयाजादीनां दर्शपूर्णमासाङ्गत्वम्।

प्रकरणं द्विविधम्

(२६) तच्च प्रकरणं द्विविधम्। महाप्रकरणमवान्तरप्रकरणं चेति।

महाप्रकरणम्

(२७) तत्र मुख्यभावनासंबन्धिप्रकरणं महाप्रकरणम्। तेन च

Context

(25) Context [means] inter-dependence, or mutual requirement or expectancy, or mutual need for compliment; as in the fore-sacrifices and others. In the sentence commencing with '[He] offers to the fire-sticks,' a special fruit is not pointed out or mentioned; hence after the sense '[One] should effect by means of the offering to the fire-sticks' is apprehended, the expectancy as to what is to be helped or effected (*upakārya*) [by the offering to the fire-sticks arises] in the form 'What ?' In the sentence [enjoining] new and full moon sacrifices also, after the sense '[One] should bring into being or realise heaven by means of new and full moon sacrifices' is apprehended, the expectancy as to what would help [the realization of heaven arises] in the form 'How ?' And thus on account of the expectancy of both, the fore-sacrifices and others become subservient to new and full moon sacrifices.

Context of Two Kinds

(26) And that context [is] of two kinds viz. great or chief or major context and intermediate or subordinate or minor context.

Great Context

(27) There the great context [is] the context which refers to or is connected with the principal creative energy.

प्रयाजादीनां दर्शपूर्णमासाङ्गत्वम्।

एतच्च प्रकृतावेव उभयाकाङ्क्षायाः संभवान्न तु विकृतौ। तत्र 'प्रकृतिवद्विकृतिः कर्तव्या' इत्यतिदेशेन कथंभावाकाङ्क्षाया उपशमेनापूर्वाङ्गानामप्युभयाकाङ्क्षया विनियोगासंभवात्। तस्मादपूर्वाङ्गानां स्थानादेव विकृत्यर्थत्वम्।

अवान्तरप्रकरणम्

(२८) अङ्गभावनासंबन्धिप्रकरणमवान्तरप्रकरणम्। तेन चाभिक्रमणादीनां प्रयाजाद्यङ्गत्वम्। तच्च संदंशेनैव ज्ञायते। तदभावे

And on account of that [great context] the fore-sacrifices and others become subservient to new moon and full moon sacrifices.

And this [great context works] in the arche-type only, because [in the arche-type] there is a possibility of expectancy [on the part] of both, but not in the modification] There [that is, in a modification] as the expectancy about the procedure (*kathaṁbhāvaḥ*) is satisfied by the extended application (*atideśaḥ*) [contained] in 'A modification should be performed like the arche-type,' even the new (*apūrva*) subsidiaries cannot possibly be applied or made subservient by means of mutual expectancy. Therefore, new subsidiaries serve the purpose of the modification through place only.

Intermediate Context

(28) Intermediate context [is] the context which is connected with the creative energy [belonging] to a subsidiary. And by means of that [intermediate context] the [rite of the] stepping near and others become subservient to fore-sacrifices and others. And that [viz. the subservience of abhikramana etc. to prayāja etc.] is known from a pair of tongs (*sandaṁśaḥ*) only. And in the absence of that [pair of tongs] there would arise the contingency of all [subsidiaries such as prayāja etc. and abhikramana etc.] being without distinction or equally (*aviśeṣāt*) covered by

चाविशेषात् सर्वेषां फलभावनाकथंभावेन ग्रहणप्रसङ्गेन प्रधानाङ्गत्वापत्तेः।

संदंशलक्षणम्

(२९) एकाङ्गानुवादेन विधीयमानयोरङ्गयोरन्तराले विहितत्वं संदंशः। यथाभिक्रमणे। तद्धि 'समानयते जुह्वाम् उपभृतस्तेजो वा' इत्यादिना प्रयाजानुवादेन किंचिदङ्गं विधाय विधीयते 'यस्यैवं विदुषः प्रयाजा इज्यन्ते प्रैभ्यो लोकेभ्यो भ्रातृव्यान् नुदते। अभिक्रामं जुहोत्यभिजित्यै' इति। तदनन्तरं 'यो वै प्रयाजानां मिथुनं वेद' इत्यादिना किंचिदङ्गं विधीयते। अतः प्रयाजाङ्गमध्ये विहितमभिक्रमणं तदङ्गम्। 'प्रयाजैरपूर्वं कृत्वा यागोपकारं भावयेत्' इति ज्ञाते 'कथमेभिरपूर्वं

[the expectancy of] the procedure referring to the creative energy of the [principal] fruit; hence it would follow (*āpattiḥ*) that they would [all] be subsidiaries of the principal [action].

Definition of a Pair of Tongs

(29) A pair of tongs consists in being enjoined in the interval of, or in between, two subsidiaries, which are enjoined in further reference (*anuvāda*) to one subsidiary, as in [the case of] the stepping near. For, after having enjoined some subsidiary in further allusion (*anuvādaḥ*) to the fore-sacrifices by [the passage] commencing with '[He] pours [ghee] in the ladle from the upabhrt pot; or lustre–,' that [viz. the rite of stepping near] is enjoined in [the passage] '[He] for whom, knowing thus, the fore-sacrifices are offered, drives far away (*pra*) [his] enemies from these worlds. Having stepped near (*abhikrāmam*) [he] sacrifices for victory.' After that some [other] subsidiary is laid down by [the passage] commencing with 'Who, indeed, knows the pair of fore-sacrifices.' Hence the [rite of] stepping near, enjoined between two subsidiaries of the fore-sacrifices, becomes subsidiary to them. For, when this viz. 'Having produced the not-existent-before by means of the fore-sacrifices, [he] should effect help to the sacrifices,'

कर्तव्यम्' इति कथंभावाकाङ्क्षायाः सत्त्वात्। सा च संदंशपठितैरभिक्रमणादिभिः शाम्यति। न चाङ्गभावनायाः कथंभावाकाङ्क्षाभावः, भावनासामान्येन तत्रापि तत्संभवात्।

प्रकरणं क्रियाया एव विनियोजकम्

(३०) तदिदं प्रकरणं क्रियाया एव साक्षाद्विनियोजकं द्रव्यगुणयोस्तु तद्द्वारा। तथा हि। 'यजेत स्वर्गकामः' इत्यत्र फलभावनायां कथंभावाकाङ्क्षायां संनिधिपठिताश्रूयमाणफलकं क्रियाजातमुपकार्याकाङ्क्षयेतिकर्तव्यतात्वेनान्वेति। क्रियाया एव लोके कथंभावाकाङ्क्षायामन्वयदर्शनात्। न हि 'हस्तेन कुठारेण च्छिन्द्यात्' इत्यत्र कथं-

---

is understood, there exists the expectancy of procedure in the form 'How should the not-existent-before be produced by these [fore-sacrifices]?' And that expectancy is satisfied by the stepping near and others that are mentioned in the pair of tongs [that is, in between matters which are subsidiary to the prayājas]. And it is not that creative energy [belonging] to a subsidiary does not possess the expectancy of procedure; for even there [that is, in the case of subsidiary creative energy] it [viz. expectancy of procedure] is possible owing to the general nature of creative energy.

Context is Applicatory of Action only

(30) This context here directly makes the application of action only; but of substance and quality [it makes the application] through that [action]. To explain (*tathā hi*): When in this [sentence], namely, '[One], desirous of heaven, should sacrifice,' the expectancy regarding how to bring into existence (*kathaṁbhāvaḥ*) arises in the case of the creative energy referring to the fruit, the group of rites, which is mentioned in [its] proximity and for which no fruit is laid down, is construed as the procedure (*itikartavyatā*) owing to its expectancy [i. e. the expectancy of this group of rite] of something which it might help (*upakārya*). For, in the world only action is seen to be connected with the expectancy of procedure (*kathaṁbhāvaḥ*) Indeed (*hi*), when here viz. in '[One] should cut by the

भावाकाङ्क्षायामुच्चार्यमाणोऽपि हस्तोऽन्वेति। किंतु हस्तेनोद्यम्य निपात्येति उद्यमननिपातने एव। हस्तश्च तद्द्वारैवान्वेतीति सार्वजनीनमेतत्।

प्रकरणं स्थानादिभ्यो बलवत्

(३१) इदं च स्थानादिभ्यो बलवत्। अत एव 'अक्षैर्दीव्यति' 'राजन्यं जिनाति' इति देवनादयो धर्मा अभिषेचनीयसंनिधौ पठिता अपि स्थानान्न तदङ्गं, किंतु प्रकरणाद्राजसूयाङ्गम्।

स्थानम्

(३२) देशसामान्यं स्थानम्। तद्द्विविधं पाठसादेश्यमनुष्ठानसादेश्यं चेति। स्थानं क्रमश्चेत्यनर्थान्तरम्। पाठसादेश्यमपि द्विविधं यथासङ्ख्यपाठः संनिधिपाठश्चेति।

---

hand with the axe,' the expectancy of procedure arises, the hand, though actually mentioned (*uccyāryamāṇa*), is not construed [as the procedure] ; but only the raising (*udyamanam*) and lowering (*nipātanam*) [are so construed], because (*iti*) having raised and lowered [the axe] with the hand [the cutting is affected]. And the hand is construed [as the procedure] through them [viz. the raising and the lowering]. This is known to all people.

Context Stronger than Position and others

(31) And this [context is] stronger than position and others. For this reason alone, characteristics (*dharmaḥ*) like gambling, laid down in '[He] plays with dice,' '[He] subdues a king,' though mentioned in the vicinity of the sprinkling rite, are not subsidiary to it through position; but [they are] subservient to the king's sacrifice through context.

Position

(32) Position [is] commonness of place or common location. That [is] of two kinds viz. commonness of place in the text and commonness of place in the performance. Position and order–these do not form a different entity [that is, mean the same thing or are synonyms]. Commonness of place in the text also [is] of two kinds viz. text according to number and text in proximity.

पाठसादेश्येन विनियोगः

(३३) तत्र 'ऐन्द्राग्नमेकादशकपालं निर्वपेत्' 'वैश्वानरं द्वादशकपालं निर्वपेत्' इत्येवं क्रमविहितेषु 'इन्द्राग्नी रोचना दिवः' इत्यादीनां याज्यानुवाक्यामन्त्राणां यथासंख्यं प्रथमस्य प्रथमं द्वितीयस्य द्वितीयमित्येवंरूपो विनियोगो यथासंख्यपाठात्। प्रथमपठितमन्त्रस्य हि कैमर्थ्याकाङ्क्षायां प्रथमतो विहितं कर्मैव प्रथममुपातिष्ठते समानदेशत्वात्। एवं द्वितीयमन्त्रस्यापि।

वैकृताङ्गानां प्राकृताङ्गानुवादेन विहितानां संदंशपतितानां[१] विकृत्यर्थत्वं संनिधिपाठात् यथा आमनहोमानाम्। तेषां हि कैमर्थ्याका-

Application according to Commonness of Place in the Text

(33) There, when [sacrificial rites] are enjoined in a [certain] order, thus, viz., ' [He] should offer [the cake prepared] in eleven potsherds in honour of Indra and Agni,' ' [He] should offer [the cake prepared] in twelve potsherds in honour of Vaiśvānara,' the application of the formulas that constitute the presenting (*yājyā*) and invoking (*anuvākyā*) verses, according to the number or respectivity (*yathāsaṁkhyam*), in this manner, viz. (*iti evaṁrupaḥ*), the first [formula belongs] to the first [rite], the second, to the second, [is made] from text according to number. For, when the expectancy of purpose (*kaimarthyam*) for the formula cited first [arises], [that] rite alone, [which is] enjoined first, first presents [itself] owing to commonness of place. Thus [in the case of the expectancy of purpose] of the second formula also.

[New] subsidiaries of the modification, [whether] enjoined in further reference to a subsidiary of the arche-type, [or] falling within a pair of tongs, serve the purpose of the modification [that is, become subservient to modification] through text in proximity, as [in the case] of the āmana-sacrifices. For, when the expectancy of purpose [arises] for them, the fruit, viz. the not-existent-before or transcendental result of the modification itself, is connected as the matter-

१ 'प्राकृताङ्गाननुवादेन विहितानां संदंशापतितानाम्' इति मीमांसान्यायप्रकाशानुसारेण कल्पितः कैश्चित् पाठः।

ङ्क्षायां फलं विकृत्यपूर्वमेव भाव्यत्वेन संबध्यते, उपस्थितत्वात्। स्वतन्त्रफलकत्वे विकृतिसंनिधिपाठानर्थक्यापत्तेः।

अनुष्ठानसादेश्येन विनियोगः

(३४) पशुधर्माणामग्नीषोमीयार्थत्वमनुष्ठानसादेश्यात्। औपवसथ्येऽह्नि अग्नीषोमीयः पशुरनुष्ठीयते। तस्मिन्नेव दिने ते धर्माः पठ्यन्ते। अतस्तेषां कैमर्थ्याकाङ्क्षायामनुष्ठेयत्वेनोपस्थितं पश्वपूर्वमेव भाव्यत्वेन संबध्यते।

स्थानं समाख्यातः प्रबलम्

(३५) तच्च स्थानं समाख्यातः प्रबलम्। अत एव शुन्धनमन्त्रः सांनाय्यपात्राङ्गं पाठसादेश्यात् न तु पौरोडाशिकमिति समाख्यया पुरोडाशपात्राङ्गम्।

---

to-be-brought-into-being, on account of [its] nearness [to those subsidiaries of the modification]. If they were to have an independent fruit, the purposelessness of [their] mention in the proximity of the modification would follow (*āpattiḥ* .

Application according to Commonness of Place in the Performance

(34) The properties of the animal serve the purpose of, or become subservient to, [the animal to be sacrificed] in honour of Agni and Soma on account of the commonness of place in the performance. On the fasting (*aupavasathya*) day the animal in honour of Agni and Soma is sacrificed. [Among the rites to be performed] on that same day, those properties are mentioned. Hence, when the expectancy of purpose [arises] for them, the not-existent-before of the animal alone, which presents [itself] as the thing to be performed, is connected as the matter-to-be-effected.

Position Stronger than Name

(35) And that position [is] stronger than name. For this reason alone the formula of purification [is] subservient to vessels of milk and curds (*sāṁnāyyam*) owing to commonness of place in the text, but not subservient to the vessels of the sacrificial cake owing to name [contained] in [the title of the section viz.] 'Concerning the sacrificial cake.'

समाख्या

(३६) समाख्या यौगिकः शब्दः। सा च द्विविधा वैदिकी लौकिकी च। तत्र होतुश्चमसभक्षणाङ्गत्वम्, होतृचमस इति वैदिक्या समाख्यया। अध्वर्योस्तत्तत्पदार्थाङ्गत्वम्, लौकिक्या आध्वर्यवमिति समाख्यया। इति संक्षेपः।

तदेवं निरूपितानि संक्षेपतः श्रुत्यादीनि षट् प्रमाणानि।

द्विविधान्यङ्गानि

(३७) एतत्सहकृतेन विनियोगविधिना 'समिदादिभिरुपकृत्य दर्शपूर्णमासाभ्यां यजेत' इत्येवंरूपेण यानि विनियुज्यन्ते तान्यङ्गानि द्विविधानि, सिद्धरूपाणि क्रियारूपाणि चेति। तत्र सिद्धानि जाति-द्रव्यसंख्यादीनि। तानि च दृष्टार्थान्येव। क्रियारूपाणि च द्विवि-

---

Name

(36) Name [means] a word understood in [its] literal or 'etymological sense. And that [name is] of two kinds [viz.] Vedic or belonging to the language of the Veda and worldly or belonging to the language of the world. There the Hotr becomes subservient to the eating of [the contents of] the cup owing to Vedic name in [the word] hotrcamasa, [which etymologically means the cup from which the Hotr drinks]. The Adhvaryu becomes subsidiary to the various things [mentioned in the ādhvaryava chapter of the Yajurveda] owing to worldly name in [the word] ādhvaryava [which etymologically means 'connected with the Adhvaryu']. Thus [ends] a short treatmeut [of name].

Thus then (*tat*) have been explained in brief the six means of proof, commencing with direct statement.

Subsidiaries of Two Kinds

(37) Those subsidiaries, which are applied or made subservient by the applicatory injunction, helped by these [means of proof] and possessing such a form viz. 'Contributing towards, or helping [them], by means of fuel-sacrifices and others, [one] should perform new moon and full moon sacrifices,' are of two kinds viz. of the form of accomplished things and of the form of actions. Of those

धानि गुणकर्माणि प्रधानकर्माणि चेति। एतान्येव संनिपत्योपकारकाणि आरादुपकारकाणीति चोच्यन्ते।

संनिपत्योपकारकाणि

(३८) कर्माङ्गद्रव्याद्युद्देशेन विधीयमानं कर्म संनिपत्योपकारकम्। यथावघातप्रोक्षणादि। तच्च दृष्टार्थम्, अदृष्टार्थं, दृष्टादृष्टार्थं चेति। तत्र दृष्टार्थमवघातादि, अदृष्टार्थं प्रोक्षणादि, दृष्टादृष्टार्थं पशुपुरोडाशादि। तद्धि द्रव्यत्यागांशेनैव अदृष्टं देवतोद्देशेन च देवतास्मरणं दृष्टं करोति।

आरादुपकारकाणि

(३९) द्रव्याद्यनुद्दिश्य केवलं विधीयमानं कर्म आरादुपकारकम्।

---

the accomplished [are] generality, substance, number and others. And those have only a visible purpose. And [those subsidiaries that are] of the form of action [are] of two kinds viz. secondary actions and primary actions. These very [subsidiaries] are called indirectly-helping and directly-helping [the general result of the sacrifice].

The Indirectly-Helping

(38) An action, which is enjoined with reference to a substance [that itself is] subservient to [some] rite [is] indirectly-helping; as beating, or husking or thrashing [of the rice-grains], sprinkling and others. And that [indirectly-helping subsidiary] has [either] a seen purpose, [or] an unseen purpose [or both] a seen and unseen purpose. There, beating [of the rice-grains] and others have a seen purpose, sprinkling and others have an unseen purpose [and] the animal, the sacrificial cake and others have [both] a seen and unseen purpose. For, that [viz. the offering of an animal or of a sacrificial cake] produces an unseen [fruit] only by [that] part [of it which consists] of the presentation (*tyāgaḥ*) of the substance and [it pro duce a seen [fruit viz.] the recollection of the deity by [its] reference to the deity.

The Directly-Helping

(39) A directly-helping [subsidiary is] an action, which is enjoined by itself (*kevalam*) without reference to [any] substance etc.; as the fore-sacrifices and others. And

यथा प्रयाजादि । आरादुपकारकं च परमापूर्वोत्पत्तावेवोपयुज्यते । संनिपत्योपकारकं तु द्रव्यदेवतासंस्कारद्वारा यागस्वरूपेऽप्युपयुज्यते । इदमेव चाश्रयिकर्मेत्युच्यते ।

तदेवं निरूपितः संक्षेपतो विनियोगविधिः ।

प्रयोगविधिः

(४०) प्रयोगप्राशुभावबोधको विधिः प्रयोगविधिः । स चाङ्गवाक्यैकवाक्यतापन्नः प्रधानविधिरेव । स हि साङ्गं प्रधानमनुष्ठापयन् विलम्बे प्रमाणाभावादविलम्बापरपर्यायं प्रयोगप्राशुभावं विधत्ते । न च तदविलम्बेऽपि प्रमाणाभाव इति वाच्यम् । विलम्बे हि अङ्गप्रधानविध्येकवाक्यतावगततत्साहित्यानुपपत्तिः । विलम्बेन क्रियमाणयोः

---

a directly-helping [subsidiary] is used in producing the highest not-existent-before only [that is, the transcendental result produced by the main sacrificial action in its totality]. But an indirectly-helping [subsidiary] is used for also the form of the sacrifice through the consecration or purification of the substance and the deity. And this [indirectly-helping subsidiary] itself is termed dependent action.

Thus then is explained in brief the injunction of application.

Injunction of Performance

(40) The injunction, which intimates speediness or promptness of performance [is] the injunction of performance. And it [is] nothing but (*eva*) the main injunction, which has formed one syntactical whole with the sentences enjoining subsidiaries. For, causing the performance of the main [action] along with [its] subsidiaries, it enjoins promptness of performance, otherwise called absence or avoidance of delay, because [there is] no authority to [make] delay. And it should not be urged that there is no authority for absence of delay in that [performance] as well. For, if there were delay, there would be the impossibility of those [namely, the subsidiaries and the main action] being performed together (*sāhityam*), which [namely, performance together] is understood from the one

पदार्थयोः 'इदमनेन सहकृतम्' इति साहित्यव्यवहाराभावात्। स चाविलम्बो नियते क्रमे आश्रीयमाणे भवति। अन्यथा हि 'किमेतदनन्तरमेतत् कर्तव्यमेतदनन्तरं वा' इति प्रयोगविक्षेपापत्तेः। अतः प्रयोगविधिरेव स्वविधेयप्रयोगप्राशुभावसिद्ध्यर्थं नियतं क्रममपि पदार्थविशेषणतया विधत्ते। अत एवाङ्गानां क्रमबोधको विधिः प्रयोगविधिरित्यपि लक्षणम्। तत्र क्रमो नाम विततिविशेषः, पौर्वापर्यरूपो वा।

क्रमे श्रुत्यादिषट्प्रमाणानि

(४१) तत्र षट् प्रमाणानि श्रुति-अर्थ-पाठ-स्थान-मुख्य-प्रवृत्त्याख्यानि।

---

syntactical whole, formed by the injunctions of the subsidiaries and the main action. When two things are being performed with delay, there can be no use of the expression (*vyavahārah*) of their having been performed together in the form (*iti*), 'This [has been] performed [along] with this.' And that absence of delay results when a fixed or definite order is resorted to. For, otherwise confusion or distraction (*vikṣepaḥ*) in the performance would arise (*āpattiḥ*) in such form as (*iti*) 'What! Should this be done after this, or after this?' Hence, the injunction of performance itself enjoins a fixed order also, as an attribute of the things [enjoined]. in order to effect speediness in the performance of what it has itself laid down. Hence, indeed, the injunction that conveys the order of subsidiaries [is] the injunction of performance—this also [is] the definition [of the injunction of performance]. There, order means a particular kind of extension or arrangement, or it takes the form of the state of one thing being first and the other later, or the relation of prior and posterior.

Six Means of Proof with reference to Order

(41) With reference to that [order i. e. in the matter of setting it, there are] six means of proof, known as direct statement, sense, text, position principal and procedure (*pravṛttiḥ*).

श्रुतिक्रमः

(४२) तत्र क्रमपरवचनं श्रुतिः । तच्च द्विविधम् । केवलक्रमपरं तद्विशिष्टपदार्थपरं चेति । तत्र 'वेदं कृत्वा वेदिं करोति' इति केवलक्रमपरं, वेदिकरणादेर्वचनान्तरप्राप्तत्वात् । 'वषट्कर्तुः प्रथमभक्षः' इति तु क्रमविशिष्टपदार्थपरम् । एकप्रसरताभङ्गभयेन भक्षानुवादेन क्रममात्रस्य विधातुमशक्यत्वात् ।

सेयं श्रुतिरितरप्रमाणापेक्षया बलवती । तेषां वचनकल्पनद्वारा क्रमप्रमाणत्वात् । अत एवाश्विनग्रहस्य पाठक्रमात्तृतीयस्थाने ग्रहणप्रसक्तौ 'आश्विनो दशमो गृह्यते' इति वचनाद्दशमस्थाने ग्रहणमित्युक्तम् ।

Order by Direct Statement

(42) There, direct statement [means] a text intimating order. And that [is] of two kinds viz. intimating mere order and intimating things particularized by that [order]. There, [the text] viz. 'Having prepared the grass-brush (*vedaḥ*) [he] prepares the altar (*vediḥ*)' intimates mere order, because the preparation of the altar etc. accrues or is enjoined (*prāpta*) by another text. But [the text] viz. 'The first draught [is] for the Vasat-maker' intimates a matter [viz. bhaksana or drinking in this case] qualified by order. For, it is impossible [for this text] to lay down merely the order by an after-statement (*anuvādaḥ*) of drinking (*bhakṣaḥ*) for fear that it would [thus] break the unity of syntactical construction (*ekaprasaratā*).

This direct statement here [is] strong in consideration of (*apekṣā*) [i. e. stronger than] other means of proof. For, they [obtain] the status of authority to [determine] order through the supposition of a direct statement. For this reason alone it is said that when there arises the contingency of taking up the cup (*grahaḥ*) of the Aśvins in the third place on account of [its] order in the text (*pāṭhaḥ*), it is [actually] taken up in the tenth place on account of the direct statement viz. '[The cup] of the Aśvins is taken up the tenth.'

अर्थक्रमः

(४३) यत्र प्रयोजनवशेन क्रमनिर्णयः सोऽर्थक्रमः। यथा 'अग्निहोत्रं जुहोति' 'यवागूं पचति' इत्यग्निहोत्रयवागूपाकयोः। अत्र हि यवाग्वा होमार्थत्वेन तत्पाकः प्रयोजनवशेन पूर्वमनुष्ठीयते।

स चायं पाठक्रमाद्बलवान्। यथापाठं ह्यनुष्ठाने क्लृप्तप्रयोजनबाधोऽदृष्टार्थत्वं च स्यात्। न हि होमानन्तरं क्रियमाणस्य पाकस्य किंचिद्दृष्टं प्रयोजनमस्ति।

पाठक्रमः

(४४) पदार्थबोधकवाक्यानां यः क्रमः स पाठक्रमः। तस्माच्च पदार्थानां क्रम आश्रीयते। येन हि क्रमेण वाक्यानि पठितानि तेनैव क्रमेणाधीतान्यर्थप्रत्ययं जनयन्ति। यथाप्रत्ययं च पदार्थानामनुष्ठा-

---

Order by Sense

(43) Where the determination or decision as regards order [is made] according to the demands or force (*vaśaḥ*) of purpose—that [is] order by, or based or founded on, sense, as [the order] of the Agnihotra and the cooking of rice-gruel, in '[He] offers the Agnihotra' [and] '[He] cooks the rice-gruel.' For here, as the rice-gruel is intended for the sacrifice, its cooking is performed before [that sacrifice] on account of the demands of the purpose [which it has to serve]

And this [order based on sense] here [is] stronger than order by text. For, if the performance [of the acts takes place] according to [their order mentioned in] the text, there would arise the sublation or annulment (*bādhaḥ*) of the established [i. e. seen] (*klṛpta*) purpose and [the performance] would be for [only] an unseen purpose. Indeed (*hi*), the cooking, performed after the sacrifice, can have no seen purpose whatsoever.

Order by Text

(44) Order by text is that which [is] the order of the sentences which intimate [certain] things. And from that [order of the sentences] the order of the things [conveyed by them] is resorted to [i. e. is settled]. For, sentences, [when] studied or read, produce the idea or apprehension of things [intimated by them], exactly in that order in which

नम्। स च पाठो द्विविधः-मन्त्रपाठो ब्राह्मणपाठश्चेति। तत्राग्नेयाग्नीषोमीययोस्तत्तद्याज्यानुवाक्यानां पाठाद् यः क्रम आश्रीयते स मन्त्रपाठात्।

स चायं मन्त्रपाठो ब्राह्मणपाठाद्बलीयान्, अनुष्ठाने ब्राह्मणवाक्यापेक्षया मन्त्रपाठस्यान्तरङ्गत्वात्। ब्राह्मणवाक्यं हि प्रयोगाद्बहिरेवेदं कर्तव्यमिति अवबोध्य कृतार्थम्। मन्त्राः पुनः प्रयोगकाले व्याप्रियन्ते, अनुष्ठानक्रमस्य स्मरणक्रमाधीनत्वात्। तत्क्रमस्य च मन्त्रक्रमाधीनत्वाद् अन्तरङ्गोऽयं मन्त्रपाठः।

प्रयाजानां 'समिधो यजति' 'तनूनपातं यजति' इत्येवंविधपाठक्रमाद् यः क्रमः स ब्राह्मणपाठक्रमात्। यद्यपि ब्राह्मणवाक्यान्यर्थे

[they are] mentioned in the text (*paṭhita*). And according to [their] apprehension [takes place] the performance of the things. And that text [is] of two kinds viz. Mantra-text and Brāhmaṇa-text. There, the order, that is resorted to for the offerings in honour of Agni and of Agni-Soma on account of the order of their respective presenting (*yājyā*) and invoking (*anuvākyā*) verses [in the Saṁhitā], [is so settled] owing to Mantra-text.

And this Mantra-text here [is] stronger than the Brāhmaṇa-text, for the Mantra-text is more intimately, closely or vitally connected (*antaraṅga*) with the performance than (*apekṣayā*) the Brāhmaṇa-text. For, a Brāhmaṇa sentence fulfils its porpose (*kṛtārtha*) after having intimated, 'This should be performed,' [while itself standing] just outside the performance. But the Mantras are used at the time of the performance, for the order of the performance depends on the order of the remembrance [of the things to be performed]. And as the order of that [remembrance] is dependent on the order of the Mantras, this mantra-text [is said to be] intimately connected [with the performance].

The order of the fore-sacrifices, which [is derived or decided] from the order of texts of this kind viz. '[He] sacrifices to the Samidhs,' '[He] sacrifices to Tanūnapāt'—that [is order] from the order in the Brāhmaṇa-text. Even though

विधाय कृतार्थानि, तथापि प्रयाजादीनां क्रमस्मारकान्तरस्याभावात्ता-न्येव क्रमस्मारकत्वेन स्वीक्रियन्ते ।

स्थानक्रमः

(४५) स्थानं नामोपस्थितिः । यस्य हि देशे योऽनुष्ठीयते तत्पूर्वतने पदार्थे कृते स एव प्रथममुपस्थितो भवतीति युक्तं तस्य प्रथममनुष्ठानम् । अत एव साद्यस्क्र अग्नीषोमीयसवनीयानुबन्ध्यानां सवनीयदेशे सहानुष्ठाने कर्तव्ये आदौ सवनीयपशोरनुष्ठानमितरयोः पश्चात् । तस्मिन् देशे आश्विनग्रहणानन्तरं सवनीयस्यैव प्रथममुपस्थितिः ।

तथा हि । ज्योतिष्टोमे त्रयः पशुयागाः–अग्नीषोमीयः, सवनीयः अनुबन्ध्यश्चेति । ते च भिन्नदेशाः—अग्नीषोमीय औपवसथ्येऽह्नि, सवनीयः सुत्याकाले, अनुबन्ध्यस्त्वन्ते । साद्यस्क्रो नाम यागविशेषः । स

Brāhmana sentences serve their purpose (*krtārtha*) after having enjoined a [certain] thing, still they themselves are accepted as reminders of order, because [in the case] of the fore-sacrifices and others [there is] no other reminder of order.

Order by Position

(45) Position means presentation or presenting oneself. For, that [thing, viz. Savanīya] alone, in the place of which something [else] (*yaḥ*) [viz. Agnīsomīya and Anubandhya] is performed, presents itself first, when the thing [viz. Āśvina-graha], which regularly precedes it (*tat-pūrvatana*), is performed; hence [it is] proper that it should be performed first. Hence alone, when in the Sādyaskra-sacrifice the Agnīṣomīya, Savanīya and Anubandhya [animals] are to be performed [i. e. sacrificed] together [i. e. in immediate consecution] in the region of the Savanīya, first the Savanīya animal is performed, the two others afterwards. In that region after the taking up of [the cup] of the Aśvins, the Savanīya alone presents itself first.

To explain : In the Jyotiṣṭoma sacrifice [there are] three animal-sacrifices viz. Agnīṣomīya, Savanīya and Anubandhya. And they are performed in different regions [i. e. on different days].—Agnīṣomīya [is performed] on the

चाव्यक्तत्वाज्ज्योतिष्टोमविकारः। अतस्ते त्रयोऽपि पशुयागाः साद्यस्क्रे चोदकप्राप्ताः। तेषां च तत्र साहित्यं श्रुतं 'सह पशूनालभेत' इति। तच्च साहित्यं सवनीयदेशे, तस्य प्रधानप्रत्यासत्तेः, स्थानातिक्रमसाम्याच्च। सवनीयदेशे ह्यनुष्ठानेऽग्नीषोमीयानुबन्ध्ययोः स्वस्वस्थानातिक्रमो भवति। अग्नीषोमीयदेशे त्वनुष्ठाने सवनीयस्य स्वस्थानातिक्रममात्रम्। अनुबन्ध्यस्य तु स्वस्थानातिक्रमः सवनीयस्थानातिक्रमश्च स्यात्। एवमनुबन्ध्यदेशेऽग्नीषोमीयस्य द्रष्टव्यः स्थानातिक्रमः।

तथा च सवनीयदेशे सर्वेषामनुष्ठाने कर्तव्ये सवनीयस्य प्रथममनुष्ठानम्। आश्विनग्रहणानन्तरं हि सवनीयदेशः। प्रकृतौ 'आश्विनं

Aupavasathya day, Savanīya at the time of the pressing of Soma (*sutyā*), but Anubandhya at the end. Sādyaskra means a particular sacrifice. And owing to [its] unmanifestness it [is regarded as] a modification of Jyotiṣṭoma. Hence all (*api*) those three animal-sacrifices accrue to Sādyaskra by transfer. And there [i. e. in the Sādyaskra sacrifice], their performance–together (*sāhityam*) is directly laid down (*śruta*) in ' [One] should slaughter the animals together. ' And that performance–together [is effected] in the region of the Savanīya, because of its [viz. of the Savanīya] proximity to the main action [viz. the pressing of Soma] and because of the equality of removal from proper place [that results from such procedure]. For, if the performance [takes place] in the region of the Savanīya, the Agnīṣomīya and Anubandhya are [each] removed from [its own] respective place. But if the performance [takes place] in the region of the Agnīṣomīya, the Savanīya is removed from just its own place. The Anubandhya on the other hand (*tu*) would be removed from its own place and would [also] be removed from the place of the Savanīya. Similar removal from place should be observed [in the case] of the Agnīṣomīya [when the performance takes place] in the region of the Anubandhya.

And so, when the performance of all is to be effected in the region of the Savanīya, the Savanīya is performed first. For, the region of the Savanīya [comes] after the taking up of [the cup] of the Aśvins. In the arche–type the Savanīya

ग्रहं गृहीत्वा त्रिवृता यूपं परिवीय आग्नेयं सवनीयं पशुमुपाकरोति' इत्याश्विनग्रहणानन्तरं सवनीयो विहित इति साद्यस्क्रेऽप्याश्विनग्रहणे कृते सवनीय एवोपस्थितो भवति। अतो युक्तं तस्य स्थानात् प्रथममनुष्ठानमितरयोस्तु पश्चादित्युक्तम्।

मुख्यक्रमः

(४६) प्रधानक्रमेण योऽङ्गानां क्रमः स मुख्यक्रमः। येन हि क्रमेण प्रधानानि क्रियन्ते तेनैव क्रमेण तेषामङ्गान्यनुष्ठीयन्ते चेत्, तदा सर्वेषामङ्गानां स्वैः स्वैः प्रधानैस्तुल्यं व्यवधानं भवति। व्युत्क्रमेणानुष्ठाने केषांचिदङ्गानां स्वैः प्रधानैरत्यन्तमव्यवधानं केषांचिदत्यन्तं व्यवधानं स्यात्। तच्चायुक्तं, प्रयोगविध्यवगतसाहित्यबाधापत्तेः। अतः प्रधानक्रमोऽप्यङ्गक्रमे हेतुः।

---

has been enjoined after the taking up of [the cup] of the Aśvins by the sentence (*iti*) 'Having taken up the cup of the Aśvins [and] having tied round the sacrificial post with a triple cord [he] leads on or offers (*upākṛ*) the Savanīya animal.' Hence (*iti*) in the Sādyaskra also, when the taking up of [the cup] of the Aśvins is effected, the Savanīya only presents itself [immediately afterwards]. Hence it is proper that it should be performed first on account of position, but the other two [should be performed] afterwards—thus has been stated [by Jaimini].

Order by Principal

(46) The order of subsidiaries [settled] according to the order of [their] principals—that [is] order by or based on principal. For, if their subsidiaries are performed exactly in the same order in which order the principals are performed, then all subsidiaries will be [separated] from their respective principals by equal interval or distance. [But] if [subsidiaries] are performed in the reverse order (*vyutkramaḥ*), some subsidiaries [would have] complete want of distance from, or extreme proximity with, their principals, [while] others would have extreme distance [from their principals]. And that [is] improper, because it would involve (*āpattiḥ*) the violation or annulment of the together-ness, or connectedness or contiguity (*sāhityam*) [of the actions], understood from the injunction of performance. Hence, even the order of principals [becomes] the cause [of determining] the order of subsidiaries.

अत एव प्रयाजशेषेणादावाग्नेयहविषोऽभिघारणं पश्चादैन्द्रस्य दध्नः, आग्नेयैन्द्रयागयोः पौर्वापर्यात्। एवं च द्वयोरभिघारणयोः स्वस्वप्रधानेन तुल्यमेकान्तरितं व्यवधानम्। व्युत्क्रमेणाघारे त्वाग्नेयहविरभिघारणाग्नेययागयोरत्यन्तमव्यवधानम्, ऐन्द्रदध्यभिघारणैन्द्रयागयोर्व्द्यन्तरितं व्यवधानम्। तच्चायुक्तमित्युक्तमेव।

स च मुख्यक्रमः पाठक्रमाद्दुर्बलः। मुख्यक्रमो हि प्रमाणान्तरसापेक्षप्रधानक्रमप्रतिपत्तिसापेक्षतया विलम्बितप्रतिपत्तिकः। पाठक्रमस्तु निरपेक्षस्वाध्यायपाठक्रममात्रसापेक्षतया न तथेति बलवान्।

Hence, indeed, [it is that] with the remainder [of the ghee] of the fore-sacrifices, first the oblation [of the cake] to Agni is sprinkled [and] afterwards the curds to Indra ; because the sacrifices to Agni and Indra are related to each other as prior and posterior. And thus the two respective acts of sprinkling are separated from their respective main action viz. the actual presentation of the [oblation] by equal distance i. e. by one intervening act. But if the sprinkling is done in the reverse order, the sprinkling of the oblation to Agni and [its] presentation (*yāgaḥ*) to Agni would have complete absence of distance [between them i. e. would be quite near each other and] the sprinkling of the curds to Indra and [its] presentation to Indra would be separated from each other by two intervening acts. And that it is improper has already been said [before].

And that order by principal [is] weaker than order by text. For, order by principal is comprehended in a delayed or retarded manner owing to [its] being dependent on the comprehension of the order of the principals, which [itself] depends on some other means of proof. But order by text [is] not like that, as it depends only on the order of the text [as found] in the Veda (*svādhyāyaḥ*) which [in itself] is [quite] independent.

स चायं मुख्यक्रमः प्रवृत्तिक्रमाद् बलवान्। प्रवृत्तिक्रमे हि बहूनामङ्गानां प्रधानविप्रकर्षात्, मुख्यक्रमे तु संनिकर्षात्।

प्रवृत्तिक्रमः

(४७) सहप्रयुज्यमानेषु प्रधानेषु सांनिपातिनामङ्गानामावृत्त्यानुष्ठाने कर्तव्ये द्वितीयादिपदार्थानां प्रथमानुष्ठितपदार्थक्रमाद् यः क्रमः स प्रवृत्तिक्रमः। यथा प्राजापत्यपश्वङ्गेषु। प्राजापत्या हि 'वैश्वदेवीं कृत्वा प्राजापत्यैश्चरन्ति' इति वाक्येन तृतीयानिर्देशात् सेतिकर्तव्यताका एककालत्वेन विहिताः। अतस्तेषां तदङ्गानां चोपाकरणनियोजनप्रभृतीनां साहित्यं संपाद्यम्। तच्च प्राजापत्यपशूनां संप्रतिपन्नदेवताकत्वेन युगपदनुष्ठानादुपपद्यते। तदङ्गानां चोपाकरणादीनां

And this order by principal [is] stronger than order by procedure. For, in the order by procedure many subsidiaries are distant from the principal; but in the order by principal [they are] near.

Order by Procedure

(47) When [several] principals are being performed together [and their] indirectly-helping subsidiaries have to be performed seriatim or one after another (*āvṛttiḥ*), the order of the second and the following things, which [is determined] by the order of the thing first performed—that [is] order by procedure; as in [the case of] the subsidiaries of the animals of Prajāpati. For, the sentence, 'Having performed the Vaiśvadevī, [they] proceed with Prajāpati's [animals],' enjoins that the animals of Prajāpati, along with [the subsidiaries which form their] procedure as pointed out (*nirdeśaḥ*) by the instrumental, are to be offered at one time. Hence, connected performance (*sāhityam*) has to be secured between them and their subsidiaries beginning with bringing near (*upākaraṇam*) and tying to the post (*niyojanam*). And that [connected performance] becomes possible by simultaneously (*yugapat*) performing [the actual presentation of the animals], since [all the] animals of Prajāpati have the [same] deity understood for them (*sampratipanna*). But (*ca*), simultaneous performance of their subsidiaries beginning with bringing near is impossible. Hence their connectedness (*sāhityam*) has to be secured by unseparated

युगपदनुष्ठानमशक्यम् । अतस्तेषां साहित्यमव्यवहितानुष्ठानात् संपाद्यम् । तच्चैकस्योपाकरणं विधायापरस्योपाकरणं विधेयम् । एवं नियोजनादिकमपि । तथा च प्राजापत्येषु कस्माच्चित् पशोरारभ्य एकं सर्वत्रानुष्ठाय द्वितीयादिपदार्थस्तेनैव क्रमेणानुष्ठेयः स प्रवृत्तिक्रमः। सोऽयं श्रुत्यादिभ्यो दुर्बलः ।

तदेवं संक्षेपतो निरूपितः षड्विधक्रमनिरूपणेन प्रयोगविधिः ।

अधिकारविधिः

(४८) कर्मजन्यफलस्वाम्यबोधको विधिरधिकारविधिः। कर्मजन्यफलस्वाम्यं कर्मजन्यफलभोक्तृत्वम्। स च 'यजेत स्वर्गकामः' इत्यादिरूपः। स्वर्गमुद्दिश्य यागं विदधतानेन स्वर्गकामस्य यागजन्यफलभोक्तृत्वं प्रतिपाद्यते। 'यस्याहिताग्नेरग्निर्गृहान् दहेत् सोऽग्नये क्षाम-

---

or uninterrupted (*avyavahita*) performance. And that [unseparated performance is secured when] after performing the bringing near of one [animal], the bringing near of another is performed. Thus tying to the post and others also [are to be performed]. And so, in [the case of] the animals of Prajāpati, commencing with some animal [and] performing one [rite] everywhere [i. e. on all animals], the second and subsequent rites (*padārthaḥ*) are to be performed in exactly the same order—that [is] order by procedure. This here [is] weaker than direct statement and others.

Thus then is treated in brief the injunction of performance by treating the six-fold order.

Injunction of Qualification

(48) Injunction of qualification [is] the injunction which intimates the ownership of the fruit to be produced by the action. The ownership of the fruit to be produced by action [means] the state of being the enjoyer of the fruit to be produced by action. And that [injunction of qualification is] of the form such as '[One] desirous of heaven should sacrifice.' This injunction, laying down a sacrifice with a view to heaven, conveys that [he] who is desirous of heaven becomes the enjoyer of the fruit to be produced by the sacrifice. 'That keeper of fire (*āhitāgniḥ*), whose house fire might burn, should offer a cake prepared

वतेऽष्टाकपालं निर्वपेत्' इत्यादिनाऽग्निदाहादौ निमित्ते कर्म विदधता निमित्तवतः कर्मजन्यपापक्षयरूपफलस्वाम्यं प्रतिपाद्यते। एवं 'अहरहः सन्ध्यामुपासीत' इत्यादिना शुचिविहितकालजीविनः संध्योपासनजन्यप्रत्यवायपरिहाररूपफलस्वाम्यं बोध्यते।

तच्च फलस्वाम्यं तस्यैव योऽधिकारविशिष्टः। अधिकारश्च स एव यद्विधिवाक्येषु पुरुषविशेषणत्वेन श्रूयते। यथा काम्ये कर्मणि फलकामना, नैमित्तिके कर्मणि निमित्तनिश्चयः, नित्ये संध्योपासनादौ शुचिविहितकालजीवित्वम्। अत एव 'राजा राजसूयेन स्वाराज्यकामो यजेत' इत्यनेन विधिवाक्येन स्वाराज्यमुद्दिश्य विदधतापि न

---

in eight potsherds to the devouring (*kṣāmavat*) fire'—this [injunction], laying down an action on an occasion (*nimittam*) like the burning by fire, states that the ownership of the fruit in the form of the destruction of sin to be produced from [that] action, belongs to [him] who is subject to such an occasion. Similarly, [the injunction] commencing with, 'Day by day [one] should wait upon the twilight,' intimates that the ownership of the fruit in the form of the avoidance of sin to be produced from the waiting upon of the twilight, belongs to [him] who is pure and leads his life, [performing all necessary acts] at the times enjoined.

And that ownership or the fruit [belongs] to him only who is characterised by the qualification. And the qualification [is] that only, which is found in injunctory sentences as a distinguishing attribute of the man. To illustrate (*yathā*): In [the case of] a rite undertaken with [some specific] desire, the desire for the friut [is the qualification], in [the case of] an occasional rite, the ascertainment of the occasion, in [the case of] an obligatory (*nitya*) [rite] such as the waiting upon of the twilight, leading a life, pure and [marked by the performance of necessary acts at] the times enjoined. Hence, indeed, this injunctory sentence viz. 'A king, who is desirous of rulership of heaven, should sacrifice with the Rājasūya,' though enjoining [the Rājasūya sacrifice] with a view to rulership of heaven, does not state that the enjoyership of the fruit of that [Rājasūya] belongs to [him]

स्वाराज्यमात्रकामस्य तत्फलभोक्तृत्वं प्रतिपाद्यते, किंतु राज्ञः सतः स्वाराज्यकामस्यैव, राजत्वस्याप्यधिकारिविशेषणत्वेन श्रवणात् ।

क्वाचित्तु पुरुषविशेषणत्वेनाश्रुतमप्यधिकारिविशेषणम् । यथाध्ययनविधिसिद्धा विद्या । क्रतुविधीनामर्थज्ञानापेक्षणीयत्वेनाध्ययनविधिसिद्धार्थज्ञानवन्तं प्रत्येव प्रवृत्तेः । एवमग्निसाध्यकर्मसु आधानसिद्धाग्निमत्ता । अग्निसाध्यकर्मणामग्न्यपेक्षत्वेन तद्विधीनामाधानसिद्धाग्निमन्तं प्रत्येव प्रवृत्तेः । एवं सामर्थ्यमपि । 'आख्यातानामर्थं ब्रुवतां शक्तिः सहकारिणी' इति न्यायात् समर्थं प्रत्येव विधिप्रवृत्तेः ।

तदेवं निरूपितो विधिः ।

---

who is merely desirous of rulership of heaven, but to [him] who being a king is desirous of rulership of heaven; for kingship also has been declared (*śravaṇam*) to be a distinguishing attribute of [one who is] to be qualified.

But in some cases, [an attribute] though not directly stated (*aśruta*) as a distinguishing attribute of the man [concerned], [becomes] a distinguishing attribute of [one who is] to be qualified; as knowledge obtained by [following] the injunction to study [the Veda]. For, [all] injunctions of sacrifice, requiring as they do the knowledge of the sense [of the Vedic texts], become applicable to [him] only who is possessed of the knowledge of the sense [of the Vedic texts] obtained by [following] the injunction to study [the Veda]. Similarly, in rites to be performed with fire, possession of fires, or the state of being provided with fires (*agnimattā*) obtained by means of [the rite of] establishing [fires], [is a distinguishing attribute of the aspirant, though not expressly stated]. For, on account of the rites to be performed with fire being dependent on the fires, injunctions with regard to them become applicable to [him] only who is possessed of the fires obtained by means of [the rite of] establishment. Similarly, capacity or capability also [is an implied qualifying attribute]. For, according to the maxim, 'For verbs, which express a meaning, power is a help-mate,' an injunction applies only to [him who is] capable [of performing the thing enjoined].

Thus then injunction has been expounded.

तृतीयो मन्त्रविभागः

मन्त्रः

(४९) प्रयोगसमवेतार्थस्मारका मन्त्राः। तेषां च तादृशार्थस्मारकत्वेनैवार्थवत्त्वम्। न तु तदुच्चारणमदृष्टार्थम्, संभवति दृष्टफलकत्वेऽदृष्टकल्पनाया अन्याय्यत्वात्। न च दृष्टस्यार्थस्मरणस्य प्रकारान्तरेणापि संभवान्मन्त्राम्नानं व्यर्थमिति वाच्यम्। मन्त्रैरेव स्मर्तव्यमिति नियमविध्याश्रयणात्।

नियमविधिः

(५०) नानासाधनसाध्यक्रियायामेकसाधनप्राप्तावप्राप्तस्यापरसाधनस्य प्रापको विधिर्नियमविधिः। यथाहुः—

THIRD CHAPTER DEALING WITH FORMULA

Formula

(49) [Sacred] formulas [are those] that call to memory matters connected with [sacrificial] performance. And their purposefulness or utility (*arthavatvam*) [arises] from just [their] character of being the reminders of matters of that nature. But their recitation [must] not [be considered to be] for the purpose of [creating] an unseen [result]; for when it is possible [for a matter] to have a seen fruit, it is unjust or unreasonable to imagine an unseen [one for it]. And it should not be urged that the recitation (*āmnānam*) of formulas is purposeless, because the visible [fruit viz.] the recollection of matters is possible in another way also. For, we have [here] to resort to an injunction of restriction or fixation viz. 'The reminding should be effected by formulas alone'.

Injunction of Restriction

(50) An injunction of restriction [is] the injunction, which establishes or makes available or enforces (*prāpaka*) another instrument which has not been established, when one instrument has been established [i. e. is likely to be adopted] in [the case of] an action which can be performed by different means. As [they] say—

'विधिरत्यन्तमप्राप्तौ नियमः पाक्षिके सति ।
तत्र चान्यत्र च प्राप्तौ परिसंख्येति गीयते ॥' इति ।

अस्यार्थः । प्रमाणान्तरेणाप्राप्तस्य प्रापको विधिरपूर्वविधिः यथा 'यजेत स्वर्गकामः' इत्यादिः । स्वर्गार्थकयागस्य प्रमाणान्तरेणाप्राप्तस्यानेन विधानात् ।

पक्षेऽप्राप्तस्य प्रापको विधिर्नियमविधिः । यथा 'व्रीहीनवहन्ति' इत्यादिः । कथमस्य पक्षेऽप्राप्तप्रापकत्वमिति चेत् । इत्थम् । अनेन ह्यवघातस्य वैतुष्यार्थत्वं न प्रतिपाद्यतेऽन्वयव्यतिरेकसिद्धत्वात् । किंतु नियमः । स चाप्राप्तांशपूरणम् । वैतुष्यस्य हि नानोपायसाध्य-

---

'A [new] injunction [takes effect] in [the case of some thing] absolutely non-established. [An injunction of] restriction [is found] when [a matter is not established] as an alternative. When the establishment is there and elsewhere simultaneously (*ca–ca*), it is sung as [i. e. declared to be] [an injunction of] exclusion. '

The meaning of this [couplet is as follows]: The injunction, which establishes [a matter which is] not established by any other means of proof [is] a new or original injunction ; as '[He] who is desirous of heaven should sacrifice' and others. For, this [injunction] lays down a sacrifice intended for [the attainment of] heaven, which [sacrifice] has not been established by any other means of proof.

The injunction, which establishes a matter, which is not established in the alternative, [is] an injunction of restriction, as '[He] pounds or thrashes the rice-grains' and others. If you ask (*iti cet*), ' How does this [injunction of restriction] establish [a matter] not established in the alternative', [we reply:] ' Thus : Indeed (*hi*), this [injunction] does not intimate that pounding [is resorted to] for the purpose of unhusking [the grains], for that is known or established (*siddha*) by positive and negative instances. But [it lays down] restriction. And that [restriction consists] in supplying or establishing (*pūraṇam*) the part not established [before]. Indeed (*hi*), as unhusking is capable of being effected or accomplished (*sādhya*) by different means, wher

त्वाद् यदा अवघातं परित्यज्य उपायान्तरं ग्रहीतुमारभते, तदा अवघातस्याप्राप्तत्वेन तद्विधानात्मकमप्राप्तांशपूरणमेवानेन विधिना क्रियते । अतश्च नियमविधावप्राप्तांशपूरणात्मको नियम एव वाक्यार्थः । पक्षेऽप्राप्तावघातस्य विधानमिति यावत् ।

परिसंख्याविधिः

(५१) उभयोश्च युगपत्प्राप्तावितरव्यावृत्तिपरो विधिः परिसंख्याविधिः । यथा–'पञ्च पञ्चनखा भक्ष्याः' इति । इदं हि वाक्यं न पञ्चनखभक्षणपरं, तस्य रागतः प्राप्तत्वात् । नापि नियमपरं, पञ्चपञ्चनखापञ्चनखभक्षणस्य युगपत्प्राप्तेः पक्षेऽप्राप्त्यभावात् । अत इदमपञ्चपञ्च-[1]

[one], abandoning pounding, proceeds to adopt another means, then, pounding not being established [i. e. not being adopted], this injunction effects the supplying or establishment of the unestablished part consisting of the laying down of that [pounding]. And hence, in an injunction of restriction the sentence-sense [is] merely restriction consisting of the supplying of a non-established part. Laying down pounding, which is not established in the alternative—this is what it amounts to (*iti yāvat*).

Injunction of Exclusion

(51) And when both [alternatives] are simultaneously established or obtain simultaneously or become simultaneously available, the injunction, which aims at (*para*) excluding one of them (*itara*), [is] the injunction of exclusion, as 'Five five-nailed animals should be eaten.' For, this sentence does not aim at [laying down] the eating of five five-nailed animals, because [it viz. such eating] obtains or is established through natural appetite (*rāgaḥ*). Not also [does this sentence] aim at restriction, because, on account of the simultaneous obtainment or establishment of the eating of five five-nailed and non-five-nailed [animals], there is no non-obtainment [of the eating of five five-nailed animals] in the alternative. Hence, this [sentence] aims at [laying down] abstention from the eating of animals other than the

१ 'अपञ्चनखभक्षणानिवृत्तिपरम्' इति केषुचिन्मुद्रितपुस्तकेषु पाठः । 'पञ्चातिरिक्तपञ्चनखभक्षणनिवृत्तिपरम्' इति मीमांसान्यायप्रकाशे ।

नखभक्षणनिवृत्तिपरमिति भवति परिसंख्याविधिः।

द्विविधः परिसंख्याविधिः

(५२) सा च द्विविधा-श्रौती लाक्षणिकी चेति। तत्र 'अत्र हि एव आवपन्ति' इति श्रौती परिसंख्या। एवकारेण पवमानातिरिक्तस्तोत्रव्यावृत्तेरभिधानात्। 'पञ्च पञ्चनखा भक्ष्याः' इति तु लाक्षणिकी। इतरनिवृत्तिवाचकपदाभावात्। अत एवैषा त्रिदोषग्रस्ता।

लाक्षणिक्याः परिसंख्याया दोषत्रयम्

(५३) दोषत्रयं च श्रुतहानिरश्रुतकल्पना प्राप्तबाधश्चेति। तदुक्तम्-

'श्रुतार्थस्य परित्यागादश्रुतार्थप्रकल्पनात्।
प्राप्तस्य बाधादित्येवं परिसंख्या त्रिदूषणा॥' इति।

---

five five-nailed [specified in it]. Thus [it] becomes an injunction of exclusion.

Two-fold Injunction of Exclusion

(52) And that [injunction of exclusion] is of two kinds viz. direct, directly stated or expressed (*śrautī*) and indirect, metaphorical or implied (*lākṣaṇikī*). There, in 'Indeed, here only [they] insert [new words]', [we have] expressed [injunction of] exclusion. For, the word 'only' expresses exclusion of laudatory stanzas (*stotram*) other than the Pavamāna. But, 'Five five-nailed animals should be eaten' —this [is] an implied [injunction of] exclusion. Hence only, this [implied injunction of exclusion] is swallowed [that is,] vitiated by three defects.

Three Defects of Implied [Injunction of] Exclusion

(53) And the three defects [are] these [viz.] abandonment of what is directly stated or the expressed sense, assumption of what has not been directly stated and contradiction, annulment or rejection of what is established or has accrued or obtains. The same is said [in] :

'On account of the abandonment of the directly-stated sense, on account of the assumption of a not-directly-stated sense [and] on account of the annulment of what is established—so thus [an implied injunction of] exclusion is possessed of three defects.'

श्रुतस्य पञ्चपञ्चनखभक्षणस्य हानात्, अश्रुताया अपञ्चपञ्चनखभक्षणनिवृत्तेः कल्पनात्, प्राप्तस्य चापञ्चपञ्चनखभक्षणस्य बाधनादिति। अस्मिंश्च दोषत्रये दोषद्वयं शब्दनिष्ठम्। प्राप्तबाधस्त्वर्थनिष्ठः। इति दिक्।

येषां तु प्रयोगसमवेतार्थस्मारकत्वं न संभवति तदुच्चारणस्यानन्यगत्या अदृष्टार्थकत्वं कल्प्यत इति नानर्थक्यमिति।

On account of the abandonment of [the sense of] the eating of the five five-nailed [animals], which [eating] is directly stated, on account of the supposition of [the sense of] the absention from the eating of animals other than the five five—nailed, which [absention] is not directly stated and on account of the annulment of the eating of [animals] other than the five five–nailed, which [eating] is established—thus [the three defects are specifically explained]. And among these three defects, the [first] two defects are stationed in [that is, belong to] word. But the annulment of what is established is stationed in sense. This [is just to show] the direction.

But [as regards those formulas] which cannot possibly be the reminders of matters connected with [sacrificial] performance—their recitation is supposed to serve an unseen purpose owing to there being no other course [left open except to make such supposition]. Hence purposelessness does not [arise in their case].

चतुर्थो नामधेयविभागः

नामधेयम्

(५४) नामधेयानां च विधेयार्थपरिच्छेदकतयार्थवत्त्वम्। तथा हि। उद्भिदा यजेत पशुकामः' इत्यत्रोद्भिच्छब्दो यागनामधेयं, तेन च विधेयार्थपरिच्छेदः क्रियते। तथा हि। अनेन वाक्येनाप्राप्तत्वात् फलोद्देशेन यागो विधीयते। यागसामान्यस्याविधेयत्वाद् यागविशेष एव विधीयते। तत्र 'कोऽसौ यागविशेषः' इत्यपेक्षायामुद्भिच्छब्दादुद्भिद्रूपो याग इति ज्ञायते। 'उद्भिदा यागेन पशुं भावयेत्' इत्यत्र सामानाधिकरण्येन नामधेयान्वयात्।

नामधेयत्वे निमित्तचतुष्टयम्

(५५) नामधेयत्वं च निमित्तचतुष्टयात्। मत्वर्थलक्षणाभयात्,

FOURTH CHAPTER DEALING WITH NAME

Name

(54) Names serve a purpose on account of their character of defining (*paricchedaḥ*) the matter to be enjoined. To explain: '[One] desirous of cattle should sacrifice with Udbhid'—thus here the word Udbhid is the name of a sacrifice and by it the defining or limiting or specifying of the matter to be enjoined is effected. To explain: By this sentence a [certain] sacrifice is enjoined with reference to the fruit, because it is not established [by any other means of proof]. As a sacrifice in general cannot be enjoined, a particular or specific sacrifice alone is enjoined. There, when this expectancy [viz.] 'Which [is] that particular sacrifice?' arises, from the word Udbhid it is known that the sacrifice is of the form of Udbhid. For, here [viz.] in 'By means of the Udbhid-sacrifice [he] should bring into being or realise cattle,' the name [Udbhid] is construed as standing in grammatical co-ordination (*sāmānādhikaranyam*) [with the word yāga, understood from the verb yajeta].

Four Reasons for [understanding a word] as Name

(55) And that [a word is] a name [is understood] from four reasons: (1) from the fear of [having to admit or understand] an indication of possession;

वाक्यभेदभयात्, तत्प्रख्यशास्त्रात्, तद्व्यपदेशात्, चेति।

मत्वर्थलक्षणाभयात् नामधेयत्वम्

(५६) तत्र 'उद्भिदा यजेत पशुकामः' इत्यत्रोद्भिच्छब्दस्य यागनामधेयत्वं मत्वर्थलक्षणाभयात्। तथा हि। न तावदनेन वाक्येन फलं प्रति यागविधानम्, तं प्रति च गुणविधानं युज्यते, वाक्यभेदापत्तेः। उद्भिच्छब्दस्य गुणसमर्पकत्वे च यागस्याप्यप्राप्तत्वात् गुणविशिष्टकर्मविधानं वाच्यम्। 'उद्भिद्वता यागेन पशुं भावयेत्' इति विशिष्टविधौ च मत्वर्थलक्षणेत्युक्तमेव।

वाक्यभेदभयात् नामधेयत्वम्

(५७) 'चित्रया यजेत पशुकामः' इत्यत्र चित्राशब्दस्य कर्मनामधे-

---

(2) from the fear of a split in the sentence [which would otherwise be caused]; (3) from a scriptural passage declaratory of it; and (4) from designation or representation (*vyapadeśaḥ*) with it.

The Character of Name [understood] from the Fear of an Indication of Possession

(56) There,–'[One] desirous of cattle should sacrifice with Udbhid'–thus here, the word Udbhid becomes the name of the sacrifice from the fear of an indication of possession. To explain: In the first place (*tāvat*) it is not proper that this sentence should enjoin a sacrifice with reference to a fruit and [also] enjoin a subsidiary (*guṇaḥ*) with reference to that [viz. the sacrifice], because [such interpretation of the sentence] would involve (*āpattiḥ*) a split in the sentence. And if the word Udbhid were to intimate or supply (*samarpaka*) an accessory [such as a spade], the sacrifice also not having been established [by any other passage], we should have to say that [the sentence] enjoins a rite characterised by an accessory. And in this qualified injunction viz. '[One] should realise cattle by means of a sacrifice, which is possessed of Udbhid,' [there exists] an indication of possession—this has already (*eva*) been stated.

The Character of Name [understood] from the Fear of a Split in the Sentence

(57) '[One] desirous of cattle should sacrifice with

यत्वं वाक्यभेदभयात्। तथा हि। न तावदत्र गुणविशिष्टयागविधानं संभवति। 'दधि मधु पयो घृतं धाना उदकं तण्डुलास्तत्संसृष्टं प्राजापत्यम्' इत्यनेन गुणस्य विहितत्वात् तद्विशिष्टयागविध्यनुपपत्तेः। यागस्य फलसंबन्धे गुणसंबन्धे च विधीयमाने वाक्यभेदः। तस्माच्चित्राशब्दः कर्मनामधेयम्। तथा च 'चित्रायागेन पशुं भावयेत्' इति सामानाधिकरण्येनान्वयान्न वाक्यभेदः। प्रकृतेष्टेरनेकद्रव्यवत्त्वेन चित्राशब्दवाच्यत्वोपपत्तिः।

तत्प्रख्यशास्त्रात् नामधेयत्वम्

(५८) 'अग्निहोत्रं जुहोति' इत्यत्राग्निहोत्रशब्दस्य कर्मनामधेयत्वं

Citrā'—thus here the word Citrā becomes the name of the rite from the fear of a split in the sentence. To explain: Here in the first place (*tāvat*), an injunction of a sacrifice qualified by an accessory [such as a variegated and feminine thing viz. an animal of this kind] is not possible. Because, as this [sentence] viz. 'Curds, honey, milk, ghee, grains, water, rice—a mixture of [all] those [constitutes the oblation] in honour of Prajāpati' enjoins the subsidiary, it is improper that [the sentence Citrayā etc.] should enjoin a sacrifice qualified by that [subsidiary]. [If it be said that in this sentence] the connection of the sacrifice with the fruit and [its] connection with the subsidiary are enjoined, [there would be] a split in the sentence. Therefore, the word Citrā [must be understood to be] the name of the rite. And so, no split of the sentence [arises] on account of the construction [of the word Citrā as standing] in grammatical co-ordination [with the word yāga culled from the verb yajeta], thus: 'By means of Citra-sacrifice [one] should realise cattle.' As the present sacrifice is possessed of various substances, it is proper that [the sacrifice be] expressed or designated by the word Citrā.

The Character of Name [understood] from a Scriptural Passage Declaratory of it

(58) '[He] offers the Agnihotra'-thus here the word Agnihotra [is understood to be] the name of the rite from a scriptural passage declaratory of it [viz. the subsidiary

तत्प्रख्यशास्त्रात। तस्य गुणस्य प्रख्यापकस्य प्रापकस्य शास्त्रस्य विद्यमानत्वात्, अग्निहोत्रशब्दः कर्मनामधेयमिति यावत्।

नन्वयं गुणविधिरेव कुतो नेति चेत्। न। यदि 'अग्नौ होत्रमस्मिन्' इति सप्तमीसमासमाश्रित्य होमाधारत्वेनाग्निरूपो गुणो विधेयस्तदा 'यदाहवनीये जुहोति' इत्यनेनैवाग्नेः प्राप्तत्वात्तद्विधानानर्थक्यम्। 'अग्नये होत्रमस्मिन्' इति चतुर्थीसमासमाश्रित्य अग्निदेवतारूपगुणोऽनेन विधीयत इति चेत्। न। तद्देवतायाः शास्त्रान्तरेण प्राप्तत्वात्।

अग्निप्रापकशास्त्रान्तरम्

(५९) किं तच्छास्त्रान्तरमिति चेत्। 'यदग्नये च प्रजापतये च सायं जुहोति' इति केचित्। अपरे तु 'अग्निर्ज्योतिर्ज्योतिरग्निः स्वाहा'

---

matter]. On account of the existence of a scriptural passage declaring [that is,] establishing that [that is,] the subsidiary matter, the word Agnihotra [is understood as] the name of the rite—this is what is meant (*iti yāvat*).

Well, if it be said, 'Why should this not [be regarded as] just (*eva*) the injunction of a subsidiary matter', [we reply,] 'No. If having resorted to a locative [Bahuvrīhi] compound in the form (*iti*) 'In this the sacrifice (*hotram*) [is] in the fire', [we were to suppose that here] the subsidiary matter of the form of the fire is laid down as the support of the sacrifice, then purposelessness of the injunction of that [fire would result] on account the fire having been already established by just this [text] viz. 'When [he] sacrifices in the Āhavanīya'. If, having resorted to a dative [Bahuvrīhi] compound in the form 'In this the sacrifice [is] for the fire,' you were to say that (*iti cet*) this [sentence] enjoins the subsidiary matter in the form of the deity Fire,' [we reply,] 'No. Because that deity has been established by another scriptural passage.'

The Other Scriptural Passage establishing Fire

(59) If you ask, 'Which is that other scriptural passage ?', [we reply :] 'When to Agni and to Prajāpati [he] sacrifices in the evening'–this [is that scriptural passage, say] some But others [say that] the wording of this

इति मन्त्रवर्ण एवाग्निरूपदेवताप्रापकः।

नन्वग्नेर्मान्त्रवर्णिकत्वे प्रजापतिदेवतया बाधः स्यात्। मन्त्रवर्णस्य चतुर्थीतो दुर्बलत्वात्। यथाहुः—

'ताद्धितेन चतुर्थ्या वा मन्त्रवर्णेन वा पुनः।
देवताया विधिस्तत्र दुर्बलं तु परं परम्॥'

इति चेत्। न। 'यदग्नये च प्रजापतये च सायं जुहोति' इत्यत्र न केवलं प्रजापतिविधानम्, किंतु मन्त्रवर्णप्राप्तमाग्निमनूद्य तत्समुच्चित प्रजापतेः। एवं च न बाधः, केवलप्रजापतिविधानाभावात्। न चात्र समुच्चितोभयविधानमेव कथं नेति वाच्यम्। समुच्चितोभयविधानापेक्षयान्यतः प्राप्तमाग्निमनूद्य तत्समुच्चितप्रजापतिमात्रविधाने लाघवात्।

---

formula itself, viz. 'Agni [is] light, light Agni, hail,' establishes the deity in the form of the Fire.

But (*nanu*) if you say: If Agni [as a deity] be established by the wording of the formula, the deity Prajāpati will annul [him]; because the wording of a formula is weaker than a dative. As [they] say:

'A deity is established or enjoined by a secondary formation, or by a dative, or again by the wording of a formula. But there each subsequent is less powerful.'

[To this we reply:] No. 'When to Agni and to Prajāpati [he] sacrifices in the evening'—thus here [there is] not the injunction of Prajāpati alone. But, having further alluded to Agni (*anūdya*), who is established by the wording of the formula, [the passage] enjoins Prajāpati in addition to him. And thus there is no annulment [of Agni by Prajāpati], owing to the absence of the injunction of Prajāpati alone. And it should not be said: How [is it that] here [we do not have] just the injunction of the two combined (*samuccata*) [deities]? For, there is greater ease or simplicity or want of laboriousness or naturalness (*lāghavam*) in enjoining Prajāpati alone as combined with that [Agni], after having further alluded to Agni who is established by another [passage], than (*apekṣayā*) in enjoining both as combined.

एवं प्रयाजेषु समिदादिदेवतानां 'समिधः समिधो अग्न आज्यस्य व्यन्तु' इत्यादिमन्त्रवर्णेभ्यः प्राप्तत्वात्, 'समिधो यजति' इत्यादिषु समिदादिशब्दास्तत्प्रख्यशास्त्रात् कर्मनामधेयम्।

तद्व्यपदेशात् नामधेयत्वम्

(६०) 'श्येनेनाभिचरन् यजेत' इत्यत्र श्येनशब्दस्य कर्मनामधेयत्वं तद्व्यपदेशात्। तेन व्यपदेशादुपमानात्, तदन्यथानुपपत्तेरिति यावत्। तथा हि। यद्विधेयं तस्य स्तुतिर्भवति। यद्यत्र श्येनो विधेयः स्यात्, तदार्थवादैस्तस्यैव स्तुतिः कार्या। अत्र 'यथा वै श्येनो निपत्यादत्ते एवमयं द्विषन्तं भ्रातृव्यं निपत्यादत्ते' इत्यनेनार्थवादेन श्येनः स्तोतुं न शक्यः, श्येनोपमानेनार्थान्तरस्तुतेः क्रियमाणत्वात्। न च श्येनो-

---

Thus, as in the fore-sacrifices the deities Samids and others are established by the wordings of the formulas beginning with 'May the fire-sticks severally, [O] Agni, partake of ghee', the words Samid and others, in [the sentences] beginning with '[He] sacrifices to Samids,' are the name of the rites on account of [another] scriptural passage declaratory of those [deities].

The character of Name [understood] from Designation with It

(60) '[One desirous of] practising hostile magic should sacrifice with the Śyena or falcon'—thus here the word Śyena is the name of the rite [and does not denote the material of the sacrifice] on account of the designation [of the rite] with it. On account of the designation [that is,] on account of the comparison with it, on account of the impossibility or otherwise [having] it [that is, the comparison]. To explain: There is praise of that which is to be enjoined. If here the falcon were [the object] to be enjoined, then the laudatory passages (*arthavādah*) would praise it only. 'As, indeed, (*vai*) a falcon, swooping down, seizes [its prey], so this, swooping down, seizes the hating enemy'—thus by this laudatory passage it is not possible to praise the falcon, because [here] praise is being offered to another entity by [its] comparison with the falcon. And it is not possible to praise that

पमानेन स एव स्तोतुं शक्यते, उपमानोपमेयभावस्य भिन्ननिष्ठत्वात्। यदा तु श्येनसंज्ञको यागो विधीयते तदार्थवादेन श्येनोपमानेन तस्य स्तुतिः कर्तुं शक्यत इति श्येनशब्दः कर्मनामधेयं तद्व्यपदेशादिति।

उत्पत्तिशिष्टगुणबलीयस्त्वात् नामधेयत्वम्

(६१) उत्पत्तिशिष्टगुणबलीयस्त्वमपि पञ्चमं नामधेयनिमित्तमिति केचित्। यथा 'वैश्वदेवेन यजेत' इत्यादौ। अत्रोत्पत्तिशिष्टाग्न्यादीनां बलीयस्त्वाद्वैश्वदेवशब्दस्य विश्वदेवदेवताभिधायकत्वं न संभवतीति कर्मनामधेयत्वम्।

वस्तुतस्तु तत्प्रख्यशास्त्रादेवास्य कर्मनामधेयत्वम्, प्रकृतयागे विश्व-

---

[falcon] itself by means of a comparison with the falcon, because the character of the standard of comparison (*upamānam*) and the object of comparison (*upameyam*) resides in different [entities]. But when [we understand that] a sacrifice, designated Śyena is enjoined [by this sentence], then it is possible to praise it by means of the laudatory passage through a comparison with the falcon. Hence, (*iti*) the word Śyena is the name of the rite from the designation [of that rite] with it.

The Character of Name [understood] from the Greater Power of the Subsidiaries taught in the Originative Injunction

(61) The greater power of the subsidiaries taught (*śiṣta*) in the originative injunction [is] also the fifth reason or criterion for name—thus [hold] some; as in '[One] should sacrifice with the Vaiśvadeva.' Here on account of the greater power of [the deities] Agni and others that are enjoined (*śiṣṭa*) in the originative injunction, the word Vaiśvadeva cannot possibly express the deity Viśvadeva. Hence (*iti*) [the word Vaiśvedeva becomes] the name of the rite.

But in reality, this [word Vaiśvadeva is understood to be] the name of the rite from just a scriptural passage declaratory of it. For, in the present sacrifice there is a

देवरूपगुणसंप्रतिपन्नशास्त्रस्यार्थवादरूपस्यैव सत्त्वात् । 'यद् विश्वेदेवाः समयजन्त तद् वैश्वदेवस्य वैश्वदेवत्वम्' इति ।

---

scriptural passage, of the form of a laudatory statement (*arthavādaḥ*) itself, which clearly establishes (*sampratipanna*) the subsidiary in the form of [of the deity] Viśvadeva. 'Because all gods sacrificed together (*sam*), therefore the rite performed by all gods (*vaiśvadeva*) [is designated] Vaiśvadeva'—thus [runs the laudatory statement].

पञ्चमो निषेधविभागः

निषेधः

(६२) पुरुषस्य निवर्तकं वाक्यं निषेधः। निषेधवाक्यानामनर्थहेतुक्रियानिवृत्तिजनकत्वेनैवार्थवत्त्वात्। तथा हि। यथा विधिः प्रवर्तनां प्रतिपादयन् स्वप्रवर्तकत्वनिर्वाहार्थं विधेयस्य यागादेरिष्टसाधनत्वमाक्षिपन् पुरुषं तत्र प्रवर्तयति, तथा 'न कलञ्जं भक्षयेत्' इत्यादिनिषेधोऽपि निवर्तनां प्रतिपादयन् स्वनिवर्तकत्वनिर्वाहार्थं निषेध्यस्य कलञ्जभक्षणस्य परानिष्टसाधनत्वमाक्षिपन् पुरुषं ततो निवर्तयति।

लिङर्थशब्दभावनाया नञर्थेनान्वयः

(६३) ननु निषेधवाक्यस्य कथं निवर्तनाप्रतिपादकत्वमिति चेत्।

FIFTH CHAPTER DEALING WITH PROHIBITION

Prohibition

(**62**) Prohibition [is] a sentence which turns away a man [from some action]; for prohibitory sentences have a purpose, just because they effect [men's] turning away from actions which are the cause of evils or undesirable results (*anarthaḥ*). To explain : As an injunction, intimating an instigation (*pravartanā*) [to do something], suggests (*ākṣipan*), in order to justify or demonstrate (*nirvāhārtham*) its character as an instigator, that the sacrifice and others, which are to be enjoined, are the means of [attaining] desired [objects], [and thus] instigates a man thereto, similarly (*tathā*) a prohibition also, such as (*ityādi*) '[One] should not eat poisoned meat (*kalañjam*), intimating negative instigation or determent (*nivartanā*), suggests, in order to justify its charactor as a negative. instigator or deterrent, that the eating of poisoned food, which is to be prohibited, is the means of the greatest evil or highly undesirable result, [and thus] turns away a man therefrom.

Construction of the Meaning of the Negative with Verbal Creative Energy which is the Sense of the Optative.

(**63**) Well, if you urge, 'How can a prohibitory sentence convey determent?', we say: Here, in the first place

उच्यते। न तावदत्र धात्वर्थस्य नञर्थेनान्वयः, अव्यवधानेऽपि तस्य प्रत्ययार्थभावनोपसर्जनत्वेनोपस्थितेः। न ह्यन्योपसर्जनत्वेनोपस्थितमन्यत्रान्वेति। अन्यथा 'राजपुरुषमानय' इत्यादावपि राज्ञः क्रियान्वयापत्तेः। अतः प्रत्ययार्थस्यैव नञर्थेनान्वयः। तत्रापि नाख्यातत्वांशवाच्यार्थभावनायाः, तस्या लिङंशवाच्यप्रवर्तनोपसर्जनत्वेनोपस्थितेः, किंतु लिङंशवाच्यशब्दभावनायाः, तस्याः सर्वापेक्षया प्रधानत्वात्।

नञ्स्वभावः

(६४) नञश्चैष स्वभावो यत् स्वसमभिव्याहृतपदार्थविरोधिबोधकत्वम्। यथा 'घटो नास्ति' इत्यादौ 'अस्ति' इतिशब्दसमभिव्याहृतो

(*tāvat*) the meaning of the root cannot be construed with the meaning of the negative; for though there is no interval [between the nañartha and the dhātvartha], it [namely, the dhātvartha or the sense of the root] exists or presents itself [there], as subordinate (*upasarjanam*) to actual creative energy [expressed] by [the ākhyātatva or verbality in] the suffix. Indeed, [something] which exists as subordinate to one is not construed with another. Otherwise, in such [sentences] as, 'Bring the king's officer,' there would be the contingency (*āpattiḥ*) of the king being connected with the action [of bringing]. Hence, the sense of the suffix alone is construed with the meaning of the negative. Even there, [it is] not the actual creative energy, which is denoted by the element of verbality, [that is connected with the meaning of the negative,] because it exists as subordinate to instigation which is expressed by the element of the optative; but [it is] the verbal creative energy expressed by the element of the optative [that is construed with the meaning of the negative]; because it is the principal in relation to all.

Nature of the Negative

(**64**) And this is the nature of the negative that it intimates the opposite of the sense of the word which is used along (*samabhivyāhṛta*) with it. For example (*yathā*), in such [sentences] as 'A jar exists not,' the negative

नञ् घटसत्त्वविरोधि घटासत्त्वं गमयति। तद्वदिह लिङ्समभिव्याहृतो नञ् लिङर्थप्रवर्तनाविरोधिनीं निवर्तनामेव बोधयति। विधिवाक्यश्रवणे 'अयं मां प्रवर्तयति' इति प्रवर्तनाप्रतीतिवत् निषेधवाक्यश्रवणे 'अयं मां निवर्तयति' इति निवृत्त्यनुकूलव्यापाररूपनिवर्तनायाः प्रतीतेः। तस्मान्निषेधवाक्यस्थले निवर्तनैव वाक्यार्थः।

प्रत्ययार्थस्य नञर्थान्वये द्विविधं बाधकम्

(६५) यदा तु प्रत्ययार्थस्य तत्रान्वये बाधकं तदा धात्वर्थस्यैव तत्रान्वयः। तच्च बाधकं द्विविधम्। 'तस्य व्रतम्' इत्युपक्रमो विकल्पप्रसक्तिश्च।

---

which is used along with the word viz. 'exists' conveys the non-existence of the jar, which is opposite to the existence of the jar. Similarly here, the negative, used along with the optative, intimates just the determent, which is the opposite of instigation, [that forms] the sense of the optative. For, as on hearing an injunctory sentence one apprehends (*pratītiḥ*) instigation in the form (*iti*) 'This [injunction] instigates me', [so] on hearing a prohibitory sentence one understands determent of the form of an activity favourable to abstention [from prohibited actions] in the form 'This [prohibition] turns me away.' Therefore, in the place of a sentence of prohibiton determent alone is the sense of the sentence.

Two-fold Obstacle to the Construction of the Sense of the Suffix with the Meaning of the Negative

(65) But when there is an obstacle or unfavourable circumstance (*bādhakam*) to the construction of the sense of the suffix with it [i. e. with the meaning of the negative], then the sense of the root itself is construed with it. And that obstacle [is] of two kinds: Introduction with 'His vow [is]' and the contingency of option.

---

१ अत्रत्यो मुद्रितपुस्तकपाठस्त्रुटितप्राय एव। स चास्माभिर्मीमांसान्यायप्रकाशानुसारेण शोधितः।

प्रथमं बाधकम्

(६६) तत्राद्यं 'नेक्षेतोद्यन्तमादित्यम्' इत्यादौ, 'तस्य व्रतम्' इत्युपक्रम्यैतद्वाक्यपाठात् । तथा चात्र पर्युदासाश्रयणम् । तथाहि-व्रतशब्दस्य कर्तव्यार्थे रूढत्वात् 'तस्य व्रतम्' इत्यत्र स्नातकस्य व्रतानां कर्तव्यत्वेनोपक्रमात् । किं तत् कर्तव्यमित्याकाङ्क्षायां 'नेक्षेतोद्यन्तम्' इत्यादिना कर्तव्यार्थ एव प्रतिपादनीयः । अन्यथा पूर्वोत्तरवाक्ययोरेकवाक्यत्वं न स्यात् । तथा च नञर्थेन न प्रत्ययार्थान्वयः, कर्तव्यार्थानवबोधात् । विध्यर्थप्रवर्तनाविरोधिनिवर्तनाया एव तादृशनञा बोधनात्, तस्याश्च कर्तव्यार्थत्वाभावात् । तस्मात् 'नेक्षेत' इत्यत्र नञा धात्वर्थविरोध्यनीक्षणसंकल्प एव लक्षणया प्रतिपाद्यते, तस्य कर्तव्यत्वसंभवात् ।

First Obstacle

(66) There, the first [occurs] in such [sentences] as '[He] should not see the rising sun'; for this sentence is stated after making the introduction with 'His vow [is]'. And so here we have to resort to exclusion (*paryudāsaḥ*). To explain: For, as the word vow conventionally means something to be performed, here viz. in 'His vow [is],' vows of a graduate-student (*snātakaḥ*) are introduced as fit to be performed or observed [by him]. When an expectancy such as (*iti*) 'What [is] that which is to be performed?' [arises], [sentences] such as '[He] should not see the rising sun' have to convey only such a matter as is fit to be performed. Otherwise, there would be no syntactical unity between the previous and subsequent sentences. And thus the sense of the suffix [namely, verbal creative energy or instigation expressed by the *liṅ* element of the suffix] cannot, be connected with the meaning of the negative, because [the passage then] would not convey a matter to be performed. For, such a negative conveys only the determent which is opposed to the instigation [that forms] the sense of the injunction; and that [determent] is not a matter to be performed. Therefore, here viz. in '[He] should not see,' the resolution (*saṁkalpaḥ*) of not seeing which is the opposite of the root-sense [viz. seeing], is conveyed by the negative by means of indication; because it [viz. the resolution] is possible to be performed [i. e. put into practice].

'आदित्यविषयकानीक्षणसंकल्पेन भावयेत्' इति वाक्यार्थः। तत्र भाव्याकाङ्क्षायाम् 'एतावता हैनसा वियुक्तो भवति' इतिवाक्यशेषावगतः पापक्षयो भाव्यतयान्वेति। एवं च पूर्वोत्तरयोरेकवाक्यत्वं निर्वहत्येव।

न च 'अत्र धात्वर्थविरोधिनः पदार्थान्तरस्यापि संभवात् कथमनीक्षणसंकल्पस्यैव भावनान्वयः' इति वाच्यम्। तस्य कर्तव्यताभावेन प्रकृते भावनान्वयायोग्यत्वात्।

द्वितीयं बाधकम्

(६७) द्वितीयं 'यजतिषु येयजामहं करोति नानुयाजेषु' इत्यादौ। अत्र विकल्पप्रसक्तौ च पर्युदासाश्रयणात्। तथा हि। यद्यत्र वाक्ये नञर्थेन प्रत्ययार्थान्वयः स्यात्,तदा अनुयाजेषु 'ये यजामहे' इति मन्त्रस्य

'By the resolution of not seeing with reference to the sun [he] should bring into existence'—this is the sense of the sentence [Nekṣeta etc]. There, on the requirement or expectancy of the end or the thing to be accomplished (*bhāvyam*), the destruction of sin, understood from the remaining portion of the passage (*vākyam*) viz. 'From just so much sin [he] becomes separated or free,' is construed as the thing to be accomplished. And thus, syntactical unity between the previous and subsequent sentences is certainly (*eva*) established.

And it should not be urged [against us]: 'How is [it that] the resolution of not seeing alone is construed with creative energy, when another thing also [such as the covering of the eyes with a piece of cloth] is possible here.' Because, as that [another thing] is not capable of being performed, it is unfit to be construed with creative energy in the present case.

Second Obstacle

(**67**) The Second [obstacle occurs] in such [cases] as 'He utters "Ye yajāmahe" in [all] sacrifices (*yajatiḥ*) [but] not in after-sacrifices'. And because here on the contingency of option exclusion has to be resorted to To explain: If in this sentence the sense of the suffix is con-

प्रतिषेधः स्यात्, 'अनुयाजेषु येयजामहं न कुर्यात्' इति। स च प्राप्ति पूर्वक एव, प्राप्तस्यैव प्रतिषेधात्। प्राप्तिश्च 'यजतिषु येयजामहं करोति' इति शास्त्रादेव वाच्या। शास्त्रप्राप्तस्य च प्रतिषेधे विकल्प एव, न तु बाधः। प्राप्तिमूलरागस्येव तन्मूलशास्त्रस्य शास्त्रान्तरेण बाधायोगात्।

न च 'पदे जुहोति' इतिविशेषशास्त्रेण 'आहवनीये जुहोति' इति शास्त्रस्येव 'नानुयाजेषु' इत्यनेन 'यजतिषु येयजामहं करोति' इत्यस्य बाधः स्यादिति वाच्यम्। परस्परनिरपेक्षयोरेव शास्त्रयोर्बा-

---

strued with the meaning of the negative, then in the after-sacrifices there would be the prohibition of the formula viz. 'Ye yajāmahe' in the form (*iti*), 'In the after-sacrifices [one] should not utter "Ye yajāmahe"'. And that [prohibition] must, indeed (*eva*), be preceded by the establishment [by some text of what is prohibited]; for only [that which is] established can be prohibited. And the establishment must be said [to proceed] from the scriptural text viz. 'In [all] sacrifices he utters "Ye yajāmahe".' And when [a matter,] established by a scriptural text is prohibited [by another], only option [can exist between the two], but not sublation or annulment [of the former by the latter]. Because another scriptural passage cannot with propriety sublate or annual the scriptural passage which is at the basis of that [establishment], as [it can annul] the passion which is at the basis of the establishment [of some such act as the slaughter of a Brāhmaṇa].

And it should not be said: As the special text '[He] sacrifices on the [seventh] foot-print' annuls the [general] text '[He] sacrifices in the Āhavanīya [fire], [so] this [text] viz. 'Not in the after-sacrifices' would annul this viz. '[He] utters "Ye yajāmahe" in [all] sacrifices'. For, only between texts which are mutually independent [can] the relation of that which is annulled and that which annuls [exist]. Indeed (*hi*), the text

ध्यबाधकभावात्। पदशास्त्रस्य हि स्वार्थविधानार्थमाहवनीयशास्त्रा-नपेक्षणान्निरपेक्षत्वम् । प्रकृते तु निषेधशास्त्रस्य निषेध्यप्रसक्त्यर्थं 'यजातिषु येयजामहम्' इत्यस्यापेक्षणान्न निरपेक्षत्वम् ।

' यजतिषु ' इत्यत्र विकल्पस्य अयुक्तत्वात् पर्युदास आश्रयणीयः

(६८) तस्माच्छास्त्रविहितस्य शास्त्रान्तरेण प्रतिषेधे विकल्प एव। स च न युक्तः । विकल्पे शास्त्रस्य पाक्षिकाप्रामाण्यापातात् । न ह्यनुयाजेषु ' ये यजामहम् ' इत्यस्यानुष्ठाने ' नानुयाजेषु 'इत्यस्य प्रामाण्यं संभवति, व्रीहियागानुष्ठाने यवशास्त्रस्येव। द्विरदृष्टकल्पना च स्यात्, विधिप्रतिषेधयोरपि पुरुषार्थत्वात् । अतो नात्र प्रतिषेधस्या-श्रयणम्, किंतु नञोऽनुयाजसंबन्धमाश्रित्य पर्युदासस्यैव । इत्थं

---

relating to the foot-print is independent, because it does not require that text relating to Āhavanīya in order to lay down its own meaning. But in the present case, the text relating to prohibition is not independent, because it requires this [text] viz. '[He utters] "Ye yajāmahe" in [all] sacrifices ', for the establishment (*prasaktiḥ*) of that which is to be prohibited.

In this [sentence] viz. 'Yajatiṣu ', Option being Improper, Exclusion should be resorted

(68) Therefore, when what is enjoined by a text is prohibited by another text, option alone [must be understood to exist between the two]. And that [option is] not proper. For, in an option there arises the contingency (*āpātaḥ*) of partial or alternative (*pākṣika*) unauthoritativeness accruing to a text. For, when in the after-sacrifices this viz. ' Ye yajāmahe ' is performed, this [text] viz. ' Not in the after-sacrifices, ' cannot possibly have authoritativeness, like the text referring to barley [which also does not possess authoritativeness], when the sacrifice is performed with rice-grains. Moreover (*ca*), the assumption of a double unseen [result] will have to be made, because even [both] injunction and prohibition are for the benefit of man. Hence here, prohibition is not to be resorted to, but only exclusion, taking our stand on (*āśritya*) the connection of the

चानुयाजव्यतिरिक्तेषु यजतिषु 'ये यजामहे' इति मन्त्रं कुर्यादिति वाक्यार्थबोधः, नञोऽनुयाजव्यतिरिक्ते लाक्षणिकत्वात्। एवं च न विकल्पः। अत्र च वाक्ये 'ये यजामहे' इति न विधीयते, 'यजतिषु ये यजामहम्' इत्यनेनैव प्राप्तत्वात्। किं तु सामान्यशास्त्रप्राप्त-येयजामह इत्यस्यानुवादेन तस्यानुयाजव्यतिरिक्तविषयकत्वं विधीयते। यत् 'यजतिषु येयजामहं करोति' तदनुयाजव्यतिरिक्तेष्विति।

पर्युदासोपसंहारयोर्भेदः

(६९) नन्वेवं सामान्यशास्त्रप्राप्तस्य विशेषे संकोचनरूपादुपसंहारात् पर्युदासस्य भेदो न स्यादिति चेत्। न। उपसंहारो हि तन्मात्रसंकोचार्थः। यथा 'पुरोडाशं चतुर्धा करोति' इति सामान्यप्राप्तच-

---

negative with the after-sacrifices. And thus the sense understood from the sentence [is] this: In sacrifices different from the after-sacrifices [one] should employ the formula 'Ye yajāmahe'; because the negative metaphorically signifies [sacrifices] different from the after-sacrifices. And thus [there is] no option. And in this sentence [viz. 'Not in the after-sacrifices'] 'Ye yajāmahe' is not enjoined, because it is established by just this [sentence] viz. 'In [all] sacrifices [he utters] "Ye yajāmahe".' But this [formula] viz. 'Ye yajāmahe', which is established by the general text [viz. Yajatisu etc.] is further referred to [in 'Nānuyājeṣu' and thus] it is laid down that [its] province [covers sacrifices] different from the after-sacrifices. When in sacrifices one recites 'Ye yajāmahe', that is in [sacrifices] different from after-sacrifices.

Distinction between Exclusion and Limitation

(**69**) Well, if you object, 'Thus exclusion would not be distinguished or would not differ from limitation (*upasaṁhāraḥ*), which consists in restricting what is established by a general text to a particular case', [we reply:] No. For, limitation serves the purpose of, or is intended for, restricting [a matter] to that only [that is, to the particular case only]. As the division into four, which is established for the generality [of cakes] by, or which is established by the general [text] viz., '[He] divides the cake into four',

तुर्धाकरणम् 'आग्नेयं चतुर्धा करोति' इति विशेषादाग्नेयपुरोडाशमात्रे संकोच्यते। पर्युदासस्तु तदन्यमात्रसंकोचार्थ इति ततो भेदः।

कुत्रचित् विकल्पप्रसक्तावपि प्रतिषेध आश्रयणीयः

(७०) कुत्रचिद्विकल्पप्रसक्तावप्यनन्यगत्या प्रतिषेधाश्रयणम्। यथा 'नातिरात्रे षोडशिनं गृह्णाति' इत्यादौ। अत्र हि 'अतिरात्रे षोडशिनं गृह्णाति' इति शास्त्रप्राप्तषोडशिग्रहणस्य निषेधाद्विकल्पप्रसक्तावपि न पर्युदासाश्रयणम्, असंभवात्। तथा हि। यद्यत्र षोडशिपदार्थेन नञर्थान्वयस्तदातिरात्रे षोडशिव्यतिरिक्तं गृह्णातीति वाक्यार्थबोधः स्यात्। स च न संभवति, 'अतिरात्रे षोडशिनं गृह्णाति' इति प्रत्यक्षविधिविरोधात्। यदि नञोऽतिरात्रपदार्थेनान्वय-

---

is restricted to only the cake of Agni on account of the special [text] viz. '[He] divides into four [the cake] belonging to Agni '. But, exclusion is intended for restricting [a matter] to only [those cases that are] different from that [viz. the specified case]. Thus [exclusion] is distinguished from that [viz. limitation].

In some cases Prohibition has to be resorted to even on the Contingency of Option

(70) In some cases, even on the contingency of option, prohibition has to be resorted to owing to there being no other alternative. As in [sentences] beginning with '[He does not take the sodaśin [which is a kind of cup to hold the Soma] in the Atirātra '. For, here, though the contingency of option arises on account of the prohibition of the taking of the ṣodaśin, which is established by the text viz. '[He] takes the sodaśin in the Atirātra,' exclusion is not resorted to on account of [its] impossibility. To explain: If, here, the meaning of the negative is connected with the sense of the word ṣodaśin, then the meaning understood from the sentence would be this : In the Atirātra [he] takes [something] different from the ṣodaśin. And that [meaning of the sentence] is not possible, because it contradicts the direct injunction viz. 'In the Atirātra [he] takes the sodaśin. And if [the meaning of the negative] is construed with the sense of the word Atirātra, then the meaning understood

स्तदातिरात्रव्यतिरिक्ते षोडशिनं गृह्णातीति वाक्यार्थबोधः स्यात्, सोऽपि न संभवति, तद्विधिविरोधात्। अतोऽत्रानन्यगत्या शास्त्रप्राप्त-षोडशिग्रहणस्यैव निषेधः। न च विकल्पप्रसक्तिस्तस्याप्यपेक्षणीयत्वात्।

विकल्पे प्रतिषिध्यमानं नानर्थहेतुः

(७१) इयांस्तु विशेषो यद्विकल्पादेकप्रतिषेधेऽपि प्रतिषिध्यमानस्य नानर्थहेतुत्वम्, विधिनिषेधोभयस्यापि क्रत्वर्थत्वात्। यत्र तु न विकल्पः, प्राप्तिश्च रागत एव, प्रतिषेधश्च पुरुषार्थः, तत्र प्रतिषिध्यमानस्यानर्थहेतुत्वम्, यथा 'न कलञ्जं भक्षयेत्' इत्यादौ कलञ्जभक्ष-

---

from the sentence would be this: In [sacrifices] different from the Atirātra [he] takes the sodaśin. That [meaning] also is not possible, because it contradicts the injunction of that [viz. the taking of the sodaśin in the Atirātra]. Hence, here, on account of there being no other alternative, the prohibition of the taking itself of the sodaśin, which is established by the text, [has to be resorted to]. And the contingency of option [should] not [here be urged against us], because that [viz. the option] has to be expected [i. e. admitted].

In an Option [the thing] which is being Prohibited is not the Cause of Undesirable Result

(71) But this much [is] the difference [between absolute prohibition such as kalañja-bhakṣaṇa and prohibition admitted on the contingency of option such as ṣodśigrahaṇa] that even though owing to option one [thing] is prohibited, the thing which is being prohibited does not become the cause of evil or disadvantage or undesirable result [for man]; because both the injunction and prohibition [in this case are] in the interest of the sacrifice [i. e. contribute to the outward form of the sacrifice]. But where [there is] no option and the establishment [is] from passion only and the prohibition [is] in the interest of man, there [the thing] which is being prohibited becomes the cause of evil ; as the eating of poisoned meat and the like [which are prohibited] in [texts] like ' [One] should not eat poison-

णादेः । तत्र भक्षणनिषेधस्यैव पुरुषार्थत्वात् ।

न च 'दीक्षितो न ददाति न जुहोति' इत्यादौ शास्त्रप्राप्तदानहोमादीनां निषेधाद्विकल्पापत्तिरिति वाच्यम् । स्वतः पुरुषार्थभूतदानहोमादीनां निषेधस्य पुरुषार्थत्वाभावेऽपि निषिध्यमानस्यानर्थहेतुत्वात्, यथा क्रतौ स्वस्त्रीगमनादेः । तन्निषेधस्य क्रत्वर्थत्वेन तस्य क्रतुवैगुण्यसंपादकत्वात् ।

---

ed meat.' Because there the prohibition of the eating itself is in the interest of man.

And it should not be urged : On account of the prohibition of gifts, sacrifices and the like, which are established by [general] texts, by such [texts] as 'The consecrated [one] gives not, sacrifices not', [there arises] the contingency of option. For, though the prohibition of gifts, sacrifices and the like, which in themselves have become beneficial to man, is not in the interest of man, the thing which is being prohibited is the cause of evil ; as the approach to one's own wife during [the course of] the sacrifice. For, its prohibition being in the interest of the sacrifice, it produces imperfection in the sacrifice.

षष्ठोऽर्थवादविभागः

अर्थवादः

(७२) प्राशस्त्यनिन्दान्यतरपरं वाक्यमर्थवादः । तस्य च लक्षणया प्रयोजनवदर्थपर्यवसानम् । तथाहि–अर्थवादवाक्यं हि स्वार्थप्रतिपादने प्रयोजनाभावाद्विधेयनिषेध्ययोः प्राशस्त्यनिन्दितत्वे लक्षणया प्रतिपादयति । स्वार्थमात्रपरत्वे आनर्थक्यप्रसङ्गात् । आम्नायस्य हि क्रियार्थत्वात् । न चेष्टापत्तिः । 'स्वाध्यायोऽध्येतव्यः' इत्यध्ययनविधिना सकलवेदाध्ययनं कर्तव्यमिति बोधयता सर्ववेदस्य प्रयोजनवदर्थपर्यवसायित्वं सूचयतोपात्तत्वेनानर्थक्यानुपपत्तेः ।

अर्थवादो द्विविधः

(७३) स द्विविधः, विधिशेषो निषेधशेषश्चेति । तत्र 'वायव्यं

SIXTH CHAPTER DEALING WITH EXPLANATORY PASSAGE

Explanatory Passage

(72) An explanatory passage [is] a sentence, which aims at either the praise or glorification, or blame or censure [of a rite]. And it ultimately leads to a matter with a purpose by indication. To explain: Indeed, a sentence [which forms] an explanatory passage conveys by indication the praise or censure of a matter to be enjoined or a matter to be prohibited, because there is no purpose or usefulness in conveying its own [literal] sense. For, if it were to aim at only its own sense, there would arise the contingency of its purposelessness. Because the Veda [is] for the purpose of action. And [you must] not [say that] the contingency [of the purposelessness of explanatory passages is] agreeable or desirable. Because it is improper or unreasonable to accept purposelessness [with regard to arthavādas], since [they are] covered by, or included in (*upātta*) this injunction to study [viz.] 'The Veda should be studied', which [injunction] teaches that the study of the entire Veda should be performed [and] which [further] suggests that the entire Veda ultimately leads to matters with a purpose.

Explanatory Passage [is] of Two Kinds

(73) It [viz. explanatory passage is] of two kinds

श्वेतमालभेत भूतिकामः ' इत्यादिविधिशेषस्य 'वायुर्वै क्षेपिष्ठा देवता' इत्यादेर्विधेयार्थप्राशस्त्यबोधकतयार्थवत्त्वम् । 'बर्हिषि रजतं न देयम्' इत्यादिनिषेधशेषस्य ' सोऽरोदीत्, यद् अरोदीत् तद् रुद्रस्य रुद्रत्वम्' इत्यादेर्निषेध्यस्य निन्दितत्वबोधकतयार्थवत्त्वम् ।

न च प्राशस्त्यादिबोधस्य निष्प्रयोजनत्वेन नार्थवादस्यार्थवत्त्वमिति वाच्यम् । आलस्यादिवशादप्रवर्तमानस्य पुंसः प्रवृत्त्यादिजनकत्वेन तद्बोधस्योपयोगात् ।

अर्थवादस्य भेदत्रयम्

(७४) स पुनस्त्रेधा । तदुक्तम्–

' विरोधे गुणवादः स्यादनुवादोऽवधारिते ।
भूतार्थवादस्तद्धानादर्थवादस्त्रिधा मतः ॥ ' इति ।

---

viz. complimentary to injunction and complimentary to prohibition. There [the explanatory passage] beginning with 'Vāyu, verily, is the swiftest deity', which is complimentary or subservient to the injunction commencing with '[One] desirous of prosperity should immolate or slaughter (*ā-labh*) a white [animal] in honour of Vāyu', possesses a purpose, because it teaches the praise of the matter to be enjoined. [The explanatory passage] beginning with 'He howled. Since he howled, therefore to Rudra belongs the character of the Howler', which is complimentary to the prohibition commencing with 'On the grass silver should not be offered', serves a purpose, because it conveys the censure or dispraise (*ninditatva*) of the matter to be prohibited.

And it should not be urged that as the knowledge of the praise and the like has no object [to serve], an explanatory passage is not possessed of a purpose. For, the knowledge of that [praise and dispraise] is useful, because it produces activity and the like [i. e. nivrtti or abstention from activity] in the case of [one who is] inactive through the force (*vaśaḥ*) of laziness and the like.

Three Divisions of Explanatory Passage

(74) That [explanatory passage is] again three-fold. The same is declared [in] :—

अस्यार्थः–प्रमाणान्तरविरोधे सत्यर्थवादो गुणवादः, यथा 'आदित्यो यूपः' इत्यादिः। यूप आदित्याभेदस्य प्रत्यक्षबाधितत्वादादित्यवदुज्ज्वलत्वरूपगुणोऽनेन लक्षणया प्रतिपाद्यते। प्रमाणान्तरावगतार्थबोधकोऽर्थवादोऽनुवादः, यथा 'अग्निर्हिमस्य भेषजम्' इति। अत्र हिमविरोधित्वस्याग्नौ प्रत्यक्षावगतत्वात्। प्रमाणान्तरविरोधतत्प्राप्तिरहितार्थबोधकोऽर्थवादो भूतार्थवादः, यथा 'इन्द्रो वृत्राय वज्रमुदयच्छत्' इत्यादिः।

उपसंहारः

(७५) एवं च 'यजेत स्वर्गकामः' इत्यादिनिखिलवेदस्य साक्षात्

In [case of] contradiction, [the Arthavāda] would state a quality; in [case of] ascertainment [it would be] a repetition; on account of the absence (*hānam*) of [both of] those [viz. contradiction and ascertainment it would] state the real state of affairs (*bhūtārthaḥ*)–[thus] an explanatory passage [is] regarded to be three-fold.

The meaning of this [couplet is]: When there is a contradiction with another means of proof, an explanatory passage states a quality, as 'The sacrificial post [is] the sun' and the like. On account of the non-difference or identity with the sun being contradicted in the sacrificial post, this [explanatory passage] conveys by indication the quality of the form of brilliance like [that of] the sun. An explanatory passage, which conveys a matter understood from another means of proof, [contains] a repetition, as 'Fire [is] a remedy against cold'. Because here the opposition of cold towards fire is understood from direct preception. An explanatory passage, which conveys a matter free from contradiction with another means of proof and [also] from establishment by that [i. e. another means of proof] [embodies] a statement of the real state of affairs, as 'Indra raised the thunderbolt for [striking] Vrtra' and the like.

Conclusion

(75) And thus [it is] established that the entire Veda comprising [sentences like] '[He] who is desirous of

परम्परया वा यागादिधर्मप्रतिपादकत्वं सिद्धम् ।

सोऽयं धर्मो यदुद्दिश्य विहितस्तदुद्देशेन क्रियमाणस्तद्धेतुः । ईश्वरार्पणबुद्ध्या क्रियमाणस्तु निःश्रेयसहेतुः । न च तदर्पणबुद्ध्यानुष्ठाने प्रमाणाभावः ।

'यत् करोषि यदश्नासि यज्जुहोषि ददासि यत् ।
यत् तपस्यसि कौन्तेय तत् कुरुष्व मदर्पणम् ॥' इति

भगवद्गीतास्मृतेरेव प्रमाणत्वात् । स्मृतिचरणे तत्प्रामाण्यस्य श्रुतिमूलकत्वेन व्यवस्थापनात् । इति शिवम् ।

बालानां सुखबोधाय भास्करेण सुमेधसा ।
रचितोऽयं समासेन जैमिनीयार्थसंग्रहः ॥ २ ॥

इति श्रीमहामहोपाध्यायलौगाक्षिभास्करविरचितपूर्वमीमांसार्थसंग्रहनामकं प्रकरणं समाप्तिमगात्

---

heaven should sacrifice' conveys piety [consisting of] sacrifice and the like either directly or indirectly. This piety here, when practised with a view to that with reference to which it is enjoined, becomes the cause of that. But when practised with the idea of dedicating [it] to God, [it becomes] the cause of the highest beatitude. And it should not be urged that there is no authority to practise piety with the idea of dedicating [it] to Him. Because the following [stanza from] the Smṛti [viz.] the Bhagavadgitā itself is an authority :

What you do, what you eat, what you sacrifice, what you give, what you practise as penance, [O] son of Kunti, that make dedicated to me.

For, in the quarter (*caraṇam*) [i. e. in Pāda 3 of Adhyāya i of Jaimini's Sūtras] dealing with Smṛti, the authoritativeness of that [Smṛti] has been established on account of [its] being rooted in Śruti. Thus [may] bliss [attend all].

For the easy comprehension of the young has this Compendium of Topics dealt with by Jaimini been prepared in brief (*samāsena*) by Bhāskara of good intelligence.

Thus has ended the work (*prakaraṇam*), named Compendium of Topics of the Pūrva–Mīmāṁsā and composed by Śrī Mahāmahopādhyāya Laugākṣi Bhāskara.

Notes

Stanza 1

It is a well-known traditional custom of Sanskrit writers to begin their works with a salutation or benediction. This is called मङ्गल. It is credited with the power of removing obstacles and leading to safe conclusion the work undertaken. Usually it takes the form of a stanza or stanzas in glorification of some favourite deity or deities. For the efficacy and desirability of the Mangala read 'माङ्गलिक आचार्यो महतः शास्त्रौघस्य मङ्गलार्थं सिद्धशब्दमादितः प्रयुङ्क्ते । मङ्गलादीनि हि शास्त्राणि प्रथन्ते वीरपुरुषकाणि भवन्ति आयुष्मत्पुरुषकाणि च अध्येतारश्च सिद्धार्था यथा स्युरिति' पतञ्जलि's महाभाष्य pp. 6–7 (Kielhorn); 'ननु मङ्गलस्य समाप्तिसाधनत्वं नास्ति । मङ्गले कृतेऽपि कादम्बर्यादौ निर्विघ्नपरिसमाप्त्यदर्शनात् । मङ्गलाभावेऽपि किरणावल्यादौ समाप्तिदर्शनात् अन्वयव्यतिरेकव्यभिचारादिति चेत् । न । कादम्बर्यादौ विघ्नबाहुल्यात् समाप्त्यभावः । किरणावल्यादौ तु ग्रन्थाद्बहिरेव मङ्गलं कृतमतो न व्यभिचारः । ननु मङ्गलस्य कर्तव्यत्वे किं प्रमाणमिति चेत् । न । शिष्टाचारानुमितश्रुतेरेव प्रमाणत्वात् । "समाप्तिकामो मङ्गलमाचरेत्" इति श्रुतेः' अन्नंभट्ट's दीपिका.

वासुदेवम्–At the commencement of his work Laugākṣi Bhāskara offers salutation to Viṣṇu in his Mangala stanza. This indicates he was a devotee of that god. Vāsudeva is the special designation, by which the supreme Lord is referred to among the Pañcarātras. Bhāskara, therefore, may have been a follower of the Pañcarātra school of the Vaiṣṇavas.

There is another reason why salutation to Viṣṇu at the beginning of a work on Mīmāṁsā is appropriate. In sacrificial literature Viṣṇu is regarded as the highest god ('अग्निर्वै देवानामवमो **विष्णुः परमः**'). He is in fact the sacrifice itself ('विष्णुर्वै यज्ञः'). Therefore, salutation to him at the commencement of a science dealing mainly with sacrificial literature is quite proper.

रमाकान्तम्—It is possible that this epithet has no special significance. For, reference to his wife in the glorification of a god is not unusual. On the other hand it is not impossible that the expression वासुदेवं रमाकान्तम् is paronomastic and contains a reference either to Bhāskara's parents, Vāsudeva and Ramā, or to his spiritual preceptor and his wife, possessing the same names.

जैमिनेः नयः सिद्धान्तः मतम् इत्यर्थः. जैमिनिनय means the doctrine or system of Jaimini viz. the Pūrva-mīmāṁsā. नीयते पुरुषः अनेन इष्टप्राप्तिं

प्राति इति नयः. By following Jaimini's doctrine a man can attain his desired object viz. heaven.

अर्थानां मीमांसाशास्त्रप्रतिपादितानां विषयाणां संग्रहः अत्र तम् or अर्थानां संग्रहः तम्. **अर्थसंग्रह** means the book, which treats of the topics (अर्थः) that are dealt with in the Pūrva-mīmāṁsā. Hence in the colophon at the end of the book Bhāskara calls it 'पूर्वमीमांसार्थसंग्रहनामकं प्रकरणम्.' He does not pretend to deal in his treatise with all the topics that Jaimini treats of in his sūtras. What he claims is that a study of his अर्थसंग्रह would secure for the student an entrance into Jaimini's doctrine. **अर्थसंग्रहं कुरुते** would perhaps suggest paronomastically that Bhāskara was expecting to make some money by the composition of this book.

Section 1

अथ is often used at the beginning of Sanskrit compositions as a mark of auspiciousness. It is sometimes looked upon as serving the purpose of a Maṅgala, when the regular one is absent. This particle, along with the mystic syllable ओम्, is said to have emanated from the throat of Brahmā. Hence their auspiciousness. Note 'ओंकारश्चाथशब्दश्च द्वावेतौ ब्रह्मणः पुरा । कण्ठं भित्त्वा विनिर्यातौ तेन माङ्गलिकावुभौ.'

करुणा शीलमस्य असौ कारुणिकः । परमश्चासौ कारुणिकश्च. **कारुणिक** means one who is habitually compassionate. Jaimini was exceedingly so. That was why with a view to enlighten ignorant people regarding the true nature of धर्म he composed his sūtras.

भगवान्—This word is primarily applicable to the highest god viz. Viṣṇu. It is applied to spiritually eminent personages like Jaimini, Vyāsa and Śaṅkarācārya only secondarily. भगः is glory, dignity, excellence or distinction भगवान्, therefore, means glorious, dignified etc. and is applicable to the highest god *par excellence.* For the meaning and use of the word read '**तदेव भगवद्वाच्यं स्वरूपं परमात्मनः** । वाचको भगवच्छब्दस्तस्य स्यादक्षयात्मनः ॥ 69... अशब्दगोचरस्यापि तस्य वै ब्रह्मणो द्विज । पूजायां भगवच्छब्दः क्रियते ह्यौपचारिकः ॥ 71 शुद्धे महाविभूत्याख्ये **परे ब्रह्मणि विद्यते** । मैत्रेय **भगवच्छब्दः** सर्वकारणकारणे ॥ 72 संभर्तेति तथा भर्ता भकारोऽर्थद्वयान्वितः । नेता गमयिता स्रष्टा गकार्थस्तथा मुने ॥ 73 ऐश्वर्यस्य समग्रस्य वीर्यस्य यशसः श्रियः । ज्ञानवैराग्ययोश्चैव षण्णां भग इतीङ्गना ॥ 74 वसन्ति तत्र भूतानि भूतात्मन्यखिलात्मनि । सर्वभूतेष्वशेषेषु वकारार्थस्ततोऽव्ययः ॥ 75 **एवमेष महाशब्दो भगवानिति सत्तम । परमब्रह्मरूपस्य वासुदेवस्य नान्यगः** ॥ 76 तत्र पूज्यपदार्थोक्तिपरिभाषासमन्वितः । शब्दोऽयं नोपचारेण **अन्यत्र ह्युपचारतः** ॥ 77 उत्पत्तिं प्रलयं चैव भूतानामागतिं गतिम् । वेत्ति विद्यामविद्यां **च स वाच्यो भगवानिति** ॥ 78 ज्ञानशक्तिबलैश्वर्यवीर्यतेजांस्यशेषतः । **भगवच्छब्दवाच्यानि** विना हेयैर्गुणादिभिः ॥ 79' विष्णुपुराण vi. 5.

जैमिनिः—This sage is regarded as the founder of the science of पूर्वमीमांसा. But as in his sūtras references to distinguished predecessors occur, it is concluded that he was not actually the founder, but the most eminent exponent of that science. Tradition traces the origin of this science to Brahmā himself and regards Jaimini as the man, who reduced the doctrine, which was up to his time being transmitted orally, to writing and embodied it in a book. Read 'ब्रह्मा प्रजापतये मीमांसां प्रोवाच, सोऽपीन्द्राय, सोऽप्यग्नये, स च वसिष्ठाय, सोऽपि पराशराय, पराशरः कृष्णद्वैपायनाय, सोऽपि **जैमिनये**, स च स्वोपदेशादनन्तरमिमं न्यायं ग्रन्थे निबद्धवान् इति । क्वचित्तु ब्रह्मा महेश्वरो वा प्रजापतये मीमांसां प्रोवाच, प्रजापतिरिन्द्राय, इन्द्र आदित्याय इत्येवमादि पाठान्तरम्' सिद्धान्तचन्द्रिका.

धर्मविवेकाय—धर्म is a term of the widest significance in Sanskrit and is almost untranslatable by a single word. It applies to duties and obligations of all kinds, both religious and profane. In the पूर्वमीमांसा it has a restricted sense and means sacrifices and other matters enjoined by the Vedas. विवेकः discrimination, discriminative knowledge or comprehension. In order to understand properly what धर्म is, it is necessary to distinguish it from अधर्म. This is विवेक.

द्वादशानां लक्षणानाम् अध्यायानां समाहारः द्वादशलक्षणी a group of twelve chapters taken together. This represents the Pūrvamīmāṁsā, constituted by the sūtras of Jaimini, which are divided in twelve chapters. These twelve chapters bear the following twelve names, which are suggestive of their subject matter :—(1) धर्मप्रमाणम्, (2) कर्मभेदः, (3) शेषशेषिभावः, (4) क्रत्वर्थपुरुषार्थभेदेन प्रयुक्तिः, (5) श्रुत्यर्थपाठनादिक्रमभेदः, (6) अधिकारः, (7) सामान्यातिदेशः, (8) विशेषातिदेशः, (9) ऊहः, (10) बाधः, (11) तन्त्रम् and (12) प्रसङ्गः. The following couplets of Mādhava give the headings of Jaimini's twelve chapters : 'धर्मो **द्वादशलक्षण्या** व्युत्पाद्यस्तत्र लक्षणैः । प्रमाणभेदशेषत्वप्रयुक्तिक्रमसंज्ञकाः ॥ अधिकारोऽतिदेशश्च सामान्येन विशेषतः । ऊहो बाधश्च तन्त्रं च प्रसङ्गश्चोदिताः क्रमात् ॥' जैमिनीयन्यायमालाविस्तर p. 5. In another place Mādhava summarises the contents of the Pūrvamīmāṁsā as follows: 'तत्र धर्मः किंलक्षणकः किंप्रमाणक इति चेत् । उच्यते । श्रूयतामवधानेन । अस्य प्रश्नस्य प्रतिवचनं प्राच्यां मीमांसायां प्रादर्शि जैमिनिना मुनिना । **सा हि मीमांसा द्वादशलक्षणी** । तत्र प्रथमेऽध्याये विध्यर्थवादमन्त्रस्मृतिनामधेयार्थकस्य शब्दराशेः प्रामाण्यम् । द्वितीये उपोद्घातकर्मभेदप्रमाणापवादप्रयोगभेदरूपोऽर्थः । तृतीये श्रुतिलिङ्गवाक्यादिविरोधप्रतिपत्तिकर्मानारभ्याधीतबहुप्रधानोपकारकप्रयाजादियाजमानचिन्तनम् । चतुर्थे प्रधानप्रयोजकत्वाप्रधानप्रयोजकत्वजुहूपर्णतादिफलराजसूयगतजघन्याङ्गाक्षद्यूतादिचिन्ता । पञ्चमे श्रुत्यादिक्रमतद्विशेषवृद्ध्यवर्धनप्राबल्यदौर्बल्यचिन्ता । षष्ठेऽधिकारितद्धर्मद्रव्यप्रतिनिध्यर्थलोपनप्रायश्चित्तसत्रदेयवह्निविचारः । सप्तमे प्रत्यक्षवचनातिदेशशेषनामलिङ्गातिदेशविचारः । अष्टमे स्पष्टास्पष्टप्रबललिङ्गातिदेशापवादविचारः । नवमे ऊहविचारारम्भसामोहमन्त्रोहतत्प्रसङ्गागतविचारः । दशमे बाधहेतुद्वारलोपविस्तारबाधकारणकार्यैकत्वसमुच्चयग्रहादि

सामप्रकीर्णनञर्थविचारः । एकादशे तन्त्रोपोद्घाततन्त्रावापतन्त्रप्रपञ्चनावापप्रपञ्चनचिन्तनानि । द्वादशे प्रसङ्गतन्त्रनिर्णयसमुच्चयविकल्पविचारः । ' सर्वदर्शनसंग्रह pp. 257-261

We have seen above that the Pūrvamīmāṁsā sūtras of Jaimini extend over twelve chapters and that the science is consequently known as द्वादशलक्षणी. There is, however, a sūtra work called संकर्षकाण्ड, which deals with sacrificial deities and runs over four chapters. Jaimini is by some believed to be the author of this संकर्षकाण्ड. This would make Jaimini's Pūrvamīmāṁsā comprise, not twelve, but sixteen chapters. In his Śrībhāṣya Rāmānuja quotes वृत्तिकार, who refers to Jaimini's system as षोडशलक्षण. खण्डदेव, the author of भाट्टदीपिका, also believes that the sūtras comprising संकर्षकाण्ड form part of the Pūrvamīmāṁsā of Jaimini. But this view is not generally accepted. Read ' तदाह **वृत्तिकारः** । वृत्तात् कर्माधिगमादनन्तरं ब्रह्मविविदिषेति । वक्ष्यति च कर्मब्रह्ममीमांसयोरैकशास्त्र्यं संहितमेतच्छारीरकं **जैमिनीयेन षोडशलक्षणेन** इति शास्त्रैकत्वसिद्धिरिति । ' श्रीभाष्य p. 2

सूत्रयामास strung i. e. set forth or expressed in a sūtra (सूत्रेण प्रतिपादयामास). The Pūrvamīmāṁsā of Jaimini, as well as the Brahmamīmāṁsā of Bādarāyaṇa, is composed in what is known as the sūtra style. A sūtra is thus defined : 'स्वल्पाक्षरमसंदिग्धं सारवद्विश्वतोमुखम् । अस्तोभमनवद्यं च सूत्रं सूत्रविदो विदुः ॥ Sūtra-knowers know [that to be a] sūtra, which contains a few syllables, is free from doubt [as to its meaning], contains substantial sense, is of universal application, is free from superfluous words and is blameless [from the grammatical or logical point of view].'

' अथातो धर्मजिज्ञासा ' is the first of Jaimini's sūtras and ' अन्वाहारे च दर्शनात् ' the last. Bhāskara now proceeds to explain the meaning of the first sūtra. The word अथ in this sūtra (अत्र=अस्मिन् ' अथातो धर्मजिज्ञासा ' इति प्रथमे सूत्रे) expresses immediate succession (आनन्तर्यम्=अनन्तरस्य भावः). This means that धर्मजिज्ञासा is to be undertaken immediately after something viz. after the study of the Veda.

In order to understand the meaning of अतः, the second word in the sūtra, we must know the exact significance of the Vedic injunction (विधिः) to study. This injunction is ' स्वाध्यायोऽध्येतव्यः. ' स्वाध्याय means literally one's own study and as the proper study of the Brāhmaṇas in ancient times was the Veda, the word स्वाध्याय became a synonym of the Veda. Now, what is meant by the adhyayana of the Veda ? One view is that the study of the Veda means learning the Veda by heart without necessarily trying to understand its meaning. Note ' प्रथमं तावत् " स्वाध्यायोऽध्येतव्यः " इत्यध्ययनेनैव

स्वाध्यायशब्दवाच्यवेदाख्याक्षरराशेर्ग्रहणं विधीयते ' ' आचार्योच्चारणानूच्चारणम**क्षरराशिग्रहणफलमध्ययन**मित्यवगम्यते ' श्रीभाष्य p. 3. But the Mīmāṁsā Śāstra has decided (व्यवस्थापनम्) that the study enjoined in अध्येतव्यः extends up to the understanding of the sense of the sacred texts, which are learnt by heart. Thus ' स्वाध्यायोऽध्येतव्यः ' means not only that the Veda should be made by heart, but that its meaning should be understood.

The meaning of the Veda, according to the Mīmāṁsakas, is धर्म or piety. Therefore, an inquiry or investigation into the nature of piety is to be undertaken. Thus the meaning of the first sūtra comes to be this: After the study of the Veda (अथ), as that study aims at understanding the meaning of the Veda, therefore (अतः), an inquiry into piety, which is the sense of the Veda, should be undertaken. It is to be noted that in order to make the sūtra complete, we have to supply the word कर्तव्या after धर्मजिज्ञासा.

अर्थज्ञान, which is the fruit of वेदाध्ययन, is here declared to be दृष्टार्थ or a seen or visible purpose. This is opposed to अदृष्टार्थ or अपूर्व or unseen fruit or the non-existent-before. Vedic injunctions have either a seen or an unseen fruit. The injunction व्रीहीन् अवहन्ति (He pounds the grains) has a seen purpose viz. making the grains huskless. But the injunction व्रीहीन् प्रोक्षति (He sprinkles the grains) does not possess any seen purpose in so far as the sprinkling of the grains with water effects no material change in them. Consequently this injunction is supposed to aim at some unseen supersensuous result, which is produced only when the grains used in the sacrifice are so sprinkled.

The general rule in the matter of the fruit of Vedic injunctions is that an unseen fruit should not be assumed, when a seen one is possible. Note ' लभ्यमाने फले दृष्टे नादृष्टफलकल्पना ' सर्वदर्शनसंग्रह p. 266. The जैमिनीयन्यायमालाविस्तर reads (p. 13) ' लभ्यमाने फले दृष्टे नादृष्टपरिकल्पना. '

Now, what kind of fruit does the present injunction viz. स्वाध्यायोऽध्येतव्यः possess? Those, who believe that अध्ययन means merely learning the Veda by heart hold that वेदाध्ययन possesses an unseen fruit. Their idea is that making the Veda by heart leads to some unseen supersensuous result, even though no attempt is made to understand the meaning or, no meaning is understood. They have to make this assumption, because the unintelligent study of the Veda, such as they believe in, produces no appreciable effect. Against this it is pointed out that in the present case a seen, appreciable and practical fruit viz. अर्थज्ञान is possible and, therefore, it is improper to hold that this injunction has an unseen fruit. The general rule explained above will not allow us to do so.

व्यवस्थापनात्—This word shows that Laugākṣi Bhāskara is referring to some work, where discussion is held about the exact meaning of the injunction 'स्वाध्यायोऽध्येतव्यः' and the decision or settlement (व्यवस्थापनम्) that वेदाध्ययन is दृष्टार्थ and that that दृष्टार्थ is अर्थज्ञान is arrived at. In a work, called पुरुषार्थानुशासन quoted in extenso by Sāyaṇa in his Introduction to the Ṛgveda-bhāṣya, this topic has been discussed and the conclusion that is arrived at is that the study has a seen purpose viz. arthajñāna and also includes the learning of the sacred texts by heart. Says Sāyaṇa 'तस्य च अध्ययनस्य दृष्टार्थत्वम् अक्षरग्रहणान्तत्वं च पुरुषार्थानुशासने सूचितम्। तानि सूत्राणि तद्वृत्तिं च उदाहरिष्यामः'. Also see जैमिनीयन्यायमालाविस्तर p. 12 'दृष्टफले अर्थज्ञाने संभवति अदृष्टस्य कल्पयितुमशक्यत्वात्'. Read also Śābarabhāṣya on I. ii. 31–53.

धर्मजिज्ञासा—The word जिज्ञासा means a desire to know (ज्ञातुमिच्छा). But this meaning is unsuitable in the present case. For what is to be undertaken (कर्तव्य) is not a desire to know, but an inquiry or investigation (विचारः). Therefore, जिज्ञासा is to be metaphorically understood in the sense of inquiry.

लक्षणा—According to Sanskrit rhetoricians a word has three powers (शक्तिः) viz. अभिधा or the power of expression, लक्षणा or the power of indication, and व्यञ्जना or the power of suggestion. In the familiar example गङ्गायां घोषः (a hamlet on the Ganges) the word गङ्गा signifies the stream of the river by means of अभिधा, because that is its primary sense. But we find that the primary sense is incompatible in the present case, as a hamlet cannot be situated on the stream of the Ganges. Therefore, लक्षणा is resorted to and the word then indicates the sense गङ्गातीर or the bank of the Ganges. Further, the purpose for which we use the expression गङ्गायां घोषः, rather than गङ्गातीरे घोषः, is to suggest that the hamlet, situated on the bank, is so near the stream that the peculiar characteristics of the stream viz. शीतत्व, पावनत्व etc. also belong to the hamlet. This idea is conveyed by the word गङ्गा by means of the third power viz. व्यञ्जना.

It will be noticed that लक्षणा comes in when the primary sense is unsuitable. In the present case the primary sense of जिज्ञासा will not do. For, a desire to know cannot be a suitable object for the injunction contained in कर्तव्या. Besides on the study of the Veda, a desire to know the meaning thereof naturally arises on account of that study itself. It need not, therefore, be specially enjoined. Hence, what is enjoined is inquiry or investigation and this sense we obtain from जिज्ञासा by means of लक्षणा.

There is another way of explaining the sūtra अथातो धर्मजिज्ञासा. In order properly to understand what धर्म is we must know अधर्म as well. For, धर्म must be distinguished from अधर्म. It is also necessary to know what अधर्म is in order that we might avoid it. Accordingly the sūtra is also split as 'अथ अतः अधर्मजिज्ञासा,' thus bringing within the scope of the inquiry laid down by it अधर्म as well. Read 'धर्मग्रहणं चोपलक्षणार्थम् । अधर्मस्यापि हानाय जिज्ञास्यत्वात् । अकारप्रश्लेषेण वा सूत्रमधर्मजिज्ञासायामपि व्याख्येयमिति निरवद्यम्' शास्त्रदीपिका.

Section 2

It has been said above that धर्म constitutes the meaning of the Veda. This paragraph defines धर्म and points out the propriety of each word in that definition.

यागादिरेव०—धर्म consists in sacrifice and the like alone. The word आदि includes जप, तपस्, दान etc., which also are enjoined by the Veda and possess a purpose. The word एव excludes such practices a offering salutation to mounds or trees, because they are not sanctioned by the Veda. Note 'यागादिरेवेत्येवकारेण चैत्यवन्दनादेर्धर्मत्वं वारयति । न चैत्यवन्दनादिर्धर्मस्तत्र प्रमाणाभावादित्यर्थः' रामेश्वर.

धर्म is defined as 'वेदप्रतिपाद्यः प्रयोजनवदर्थः.' There are really three words in the definition viz. वेदप्रतिपाद्यः, प्रयोजनवान् and अर्थः. The sentence 'स्वर्गकामः यजेत' enjoins sacrifice with a view to attain heaven. This याग is वेदप्रतिपाद्य, because it is laid down or propounded by the Veda. It is प्रयोजनवान्, because its purpose is स्वर्ग. And it is अर्थ or a desirable matter, because it leads to heaven, which is full of enjoyments. The definition of धर्म being thus fully applicable to it, याग is धर्म.

After giving the definition of धर्म, the author proceeds to point out the exact significance of the three words therein. In doing this he chooses the word प्रयोजनवत् first. There is no reason why he should do so. It only shows that he is not a very careful and systematic writer.

प्रयोजने०—This sentence establishes the necessity of the word प्रयोजनवत् in the definition of धर्म. If प्रयोजनवत् be dropped, the definition will be वेदप्रतिपाद्यः अर्थः. Now, स्वर्ग or heaven is वेदप्रतिपाद्य, because it is laid down in the Veda as the purpose of a certain sacrifice. It is अर्थ or a desirable matter, because on account of the many enjoyments to be had therein, people hanker after it. Thus, स्वर्ग would be धर्म, if वेदप्रतिपाद्यः अर्थः were its definition. The word प्रयोजनवत् excludes स्वर्ग from the province of धर्म. For, though स्वर्ग is the प्रयोजन of the sacrifice, it is not प्रयोजनवत् in itself. Hence it cannot be धर्म.

अतिव्याप्ति—According to Sanskrit logicians a definition should be free from three faults viz. अव्याप्तिः, अतिव्याप्तिः and असंभवः. (1) अव्याप्ति means non-inclusion. It makes a definition too narrow. An अव्याप्त definition does not include or extend to all the objects intended to be defined. If we were to define a Brāhmaṇa as one who is possessed of the tuft of hair and the sacred thread, this will be too narrow a definition, as it will not include saṁnyāsins, who, though Brāhmaṇas, do not wear the tuft of hair and the sacred thread. Read 'लक्ष्यैकदेशे लक्षणस्य अवर्तनम् **अव्याप्तिः** । यथा शिखासूत्रवान् ब्राह्मणः इत्यस्य संन्यासिनि अव्याप्तिः, तस्य ब्राह्मणत्वेऽपि शिखासूत्रत्वाभावात्.' (2) अतिव्याप्ति, or unwarranted inclusion or extension, makes a definition too wide. An अतिव्याप्त definition consequently becomes applicable to objects, which are not intended to be thus included. A Brāhmaṇa is a human being—this is an अतिव्याप्त or too-wide definition. For, it is applicable to a Śūdra as well. Note 'अलक्ष्ये लक्षणगमनम् **अतिव्याप्तिः** । यथा मनुष्यो ब्राह्मणः इति लक्षणस्य शूद्रेऽतिव्याप्तिः, तस्यापि मनुष्यत्वात्.' The definition 'शिखासूत्रवान् ब्राह्मणः' may also from another point of view be looked upon as अतिव्याप्त. Because it is applicable to Kṣatriyas and Vaiśyas, who also possess the tuft of hair and the sacred thread. (3) असंभवः or impossibility consists in defining an object in such a manner that the definition is not applicable to even a single individual of the class intended to be defined. A Brāhmaṇa is he who is possessed of horns—this is an instance of an impossible definition. For, no Brāhmaṇa is possessed of horns. Read 'लक्ष्ये अवर्तनम् **असंभवः** । यथा शृङ्गवान् ब्राह्मणः । न खलु शृङ्गवत्त्वं कस्मिंश्चिदपि ब्राह्मणे दृश्यते.'

In this connection vide also 'लक्ष्यैकदेशावृत्तित्वमव्याप्तिः, यथा गोः कपिलत्वम्। अलक्ष्यवृत्तित्वमतिव्याप्तिः, यथा गोः शृङ्गित्वम् । लक्ष्यमात्रावर्तनमसंभवः, यथा गोरेकशफत्वम्' अन्नंभट्ट's दीपिका.

It will thus be seen that if धर्म be defined as 'वेदप्रतिपाद्यः अर्थः', the definition will be too wide and would extend to स्वर्ग, which is really the purpose (प्रयोजनम्) of the real धर्म viz. याग. This is what is meant by the sentence 'प्रयोजने...प्रयोजनवदिति'

भोजनादौ etc-This sentence points out the significance of the word वेदप्रतिपाद्य. भोजन is प्रयोजनवत् and अर्थ, because it serves the purpose of satisfying our hunger and is much relished. It would be धर्म, if our definition were to be merely 'प्रयोजनवदर्थः धर्मः.' But भोजन is not वेदप्रतिपाद्य. भोजन is what is called रागतः प्राप्त i. e. we are inclined to eat on account of natural appetite. No injunction from the Veda is necessary to make us take our meal. So 'वेदप्रातिपाद्यः' excludes भोजन from the province of धर्म. The word आदि in भोजनादौ includes क्रीडा, for example. It is प्रयोजनवदर्थः, because everybody likes it and it serves the purpose of removing our fatigue. But as it is not वेदप्रतिपाद्य, it cannot be धर्म.

अनर्थफलकत्वात् etc—This sentence shows the propriety of 'अर्थः' in the definition of धर्म. अर्थ means a desirable matter or end. सर्वथा इष्टफलजनकत्वेन अर्थ्यते प्रार्थ्यते इति अर्थः. The Vedic sentence 'श्येनेन अभिचरन् यजेत' lays down a sacrifice, called Śyena, for him who is desirous of bringing about the destruction of his enemies by means of अभिचार or the practice of magic rites. This sacrifice is वेदप्रतिपाद्य, because it is actually propounded by the Veda. It is प्रयोजनवत्, because it possesses शत्रुवध for its purpose. But it is not अर्थ in the sense of an absolutely (सर्वथा) desirable matter, because we learn from the same Veda, which lays it down, that he, who brings about the destruction of his enemies by means of the Śyena sacrifice, himself goes to hell. श्येनयाग may be partially desirable, because it leads to शत्रुवध. But it is not wholly or absolutely desirable, since it sends the performer himself to hell. Thus, as श्येनयाग possesses an undesirable matter viz. नरकप्राप्ति as its ultimate fruit (अनर्थफलकत्वात्), it becomes an undesirable matter itself (अनर्थभूते). By the word आदि in श्येनादौ other rites, resembling magical practices, such as वज्रः and इषुः, are included.

As regards how श्येनयाग is an अनर्थ read 'श्येनफलस्य शत्रुवधस्य नरकजनकत्वेन अनर्थत्वात् श्येनोऽपि **तद्द्वारा** अनर्थ एव, तस्यापि शत्रुवधद्वारा नरकजनकत्वादिति भावः' रामेश्वर; 'यद्यपि श्येनस्य शत्रुवधः फलं न तु नरकः, तथापि तस्य वधस्य नरकहेतुत्वात् **वधद्वारा** श्येनोऽनर्थः' जै. न्या. मा. विस्तर p. 15.

A question that arises here is : If Śyena is an evil rite, how is it that it has been laid down by the Veda ? In other words, if Śyena has been enjoined by the Veda, how can it be evil ?

The answer to this is that the Veda does not lay down Śyena in the way it lays down Jyotiṣṭoma and other sacrifices. In the world we find that some people are inclined to bring about their desired objects by resorting to magical practices. To such people the Veda points out that the Śyena and such other rites are the means by which they can achieve their objects. The intention of the Veda is not to enjoin the performance of these rites, though it mentions them.

Read in this connection 'उभयमिह चोदनया लक्ष्यते, अर्थोऽनर्थश्चेति। कोऽर्थः। यो निःश्रेयसाय, ज्योतिष्टोमादिः। कोऽनर्थः। यः प्रत्यवायाय, श्येनो वज्र इषुरित्येवमादिः। तत्र अनर्थो धर्मो मा भूदिति अर्थग्रहणम् [चोदनालक्षणोऽर्थो धर्म इति धर्मलक्षणे]। कथं पुनरसौ अनर्थः। हिंसा हि सा। हिंसा च प्रतिषिद्धेति। कथं पुनरनर्थः कर्तव्यतयोपादिश्यते। उच्यते। **नैव श्येनादयः कर्तव्या विज्ञायन्ते। यो हि हिंसितुमिच्छेत् तस्यायमभ्युपाय इति हि तेषामुपदेशः।** श्येनेन अभिचरन् यजेत इति हि समामनन्ति। न आभिचारितव्यम्।' शाबरभाष्य on i. 1. 2.

'ननु एवमभिचारस्य वेदोक्तत्वात् आभिचारिके कर्मणि आस्तिकानामपि प्रवृत्तिः स्यादिति चेत्। न। **वेदोक्तोऽपि आभिचारो वेदविहितो न भवति** फलत्वात्। फलं न विधेयम्, किंतु फलमुद्दिश्य तत्साधकत्वेन कर्मैव विधेयमिति सिद्धान्तात्। अतः अभिचारस्य अविहितत्वेन प्रत्यवायजनकत्वम्।' मीमांसापरिभाषा.

'वस्तुतस्तु शत्रुवधरूपाभिचारस्य श्येनफलस्य लोकतः प्राप्तत्वात् तत्र रागतः प्रवृत्तं पुरुषं प्रति श्येनस्य तत्साधनमात्रं वेदेन बोध्यते इति न तस्य वेदप्रतिपाद्यत्वम्।' रामेश्वर.

It will be noticed that the above defence of the inclusion of the Śyena and other similar rites in the Veda is very weak. The distinction between वेदोक्त and वेदविहित, which the मीमांसापरिभाषा definitely makes and which is also suggested by Śabara, seems unsatisfactory. The truth would appear to be that these undesirable practices, such as the Śyena sacrifice, were borrowed from the followers of the Atharvaveda, which mainly deals with spells and incantations, witchcraft and magical practices, at the time when that Veda was admitted into the sacred writings of the Aryans in addition to the three Vedas, which constituted the traditional trayī vidyā. It was later on that their unsuitability to the original Aryan culture was realised and explanations like the above were invented to account for their inclusion in the Veda.

Section 3

Bhāskara has just defined धर्म as 'वेदप्रतिपाद्यः प्रयोजनवदर्थः.' But Jaimini defines it as 'चोदनालक्षणोऽर्थो धर्मः' in the second sūtra of his Pūrvamīmāṁsā. In this Section Bhāskara shows that his definition does not contradict the definition of Jaimini.

चोदना means instigation, then a sentence that instigates or enjoins an action. ('चोदनेति क्रियायाः प्रवर्तकं वचनमाहुः' शाबरभाष्य). लक्षण means a distinctive characteristic. लक्ष्यते अनेन इति लक्षणं ज्ञानजनकं प्रमाणम् इत्यर्थः. चोदना लक्षणं यस्य means that whose distinctive characteristic is instigation i. e. which is laid down by instigatory or injunctive sentences. चोदनालक्षणः means in short चोदनाप्रमाणकः or चोदनाप्रतिपाद्यः Now, as we shall learn later on in Section 10 below, वेद consists of five constituents viz. विधि, मन्त्र, नामधेय, निषेध and अर्थवाद. Out of these विधि alone is चोदना properly so called, because it actually lays down an action. So जैमिनि's definition of धर्म viz. चोदनाप्रतिपाद्यः is really equal to वेदैकदेशाविधिप्रतिपाद्यः. Consequently Bhāskara's definition वेदप्रतिपाद्यः is in conflict with this definition of Jaimini (सूत्रेण 'चोदनालक्षणोऽर्थो धर्मः' इत्यनेन सूत्रेण कृतं सौत्रम् । तस्य धर्मस्य लक्षणं तल्लक्षणम् । सौत्रं यत् तल्लक्षणं तेन विरोधः). This is the view of the Pūrvapakṣin.

Bhāskara refutes this view by saying that the word चोदना, occurring in the definition of Jaimini (तत्रापि=जैमिनिकृते सौत्रे धर्मलक्षणे अपि), stands for the entire Veda (वेदमात्रपरत्वात् इत्यत्र मात्रपदं कात्स्न्र्यबोधकम्). So the statement that चोदनाप्रतिपाद्यः is equal to वेदैकदेशाविधिप्रतिपाद्यः is incorrect. Consequently his definition does not contradict the definition of Jaimini.

वेदस्य सर्वस्य etc–It is admitted that विधि or चोदना proper lays down धर्म. It does so directly. The other constituents of the Veda such as मन्त्र, नामधेय etc. are subservient to विधि and thus they lay down धर्म indirectly through विधि. Consequently, they are said to possess धर्म for their purport (धर्मतात्पर्यवत्त्वेन), though their direct import may be something different. But they are धर्मप्रतिपादक all the same and are hence included under चोदना.

Section 4

In Section 2 above it has been declared that sacrifice and the like alone constitute piety (यागादिरेव धर्मः) and that piety is enjoined by the Veda. The author now proceeds to show how that piety is enjoined by the Veda.

The sentence 'यजेत स्वर्गकामः' lays down a certain sacrifice as a means of attaining heaven for a man who is desirous of attaining it. The question here is: How is all this viz. that the sacrifice is a means of attaining heaven and that it is enjoined by the Veda, known from the sentence 'यजेत स्वर्गकामः'? As an answer to this Bhāskara explains the Mīmāṁsaka way of understanding the meaning of injunctive sentences. This explanation begins with तथाहि and extends to the end of Section 9.

'यजेत' इत्यत्र etc—The following diagram will make our author's meaning clear.

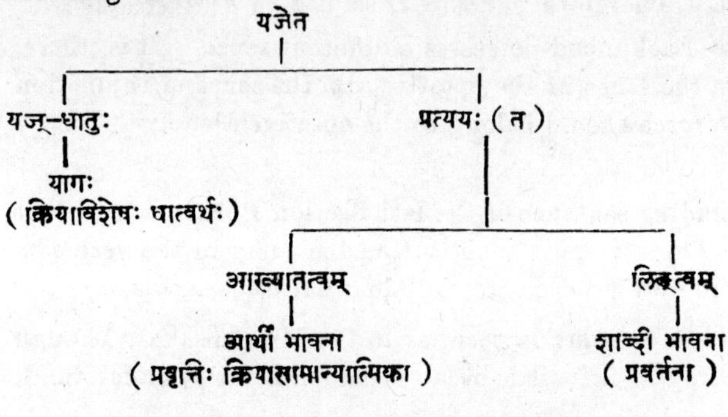

आख्यातम् is an old grammatical term for a verb. It is mentioned by Yāska, who uses it in enumerating the four classes of words viz नाम (noun), आख्यातम् (verb), उपसर्गः (preposition) and निपातः (particle). आख्यात literally means what is told or predicated. In the sentence देवदत्तः पचति, what is told about Devadatta is that he cooks and as this action is expressed by the verb पचति, the verb itself is known as आख्यातम्. आख्यातत्वम् or verbality means the general sense of the verb. In the verb पचति there is a general as well as a particular sense. पचति is equal to पाकं करोति. Here करोति represents the general sense and पाक the particular. So also in गच्छति=गमनं करोति we have a general and a particular sense. This general verbal sense or the idea of action in general is represented by the ākhyāta element of the suffix.

दशलकारसाधारणम्—According to Pāṇini's grammar verbs have six tenses and four moods. The names of all these begin with ल्. Hence they are known as दश लकाराः. The ten lakāras are as follows :—

(1) लट् or present
(2) लिट् or perfect
(3) लुट् or first future
(4) लृट् or second future
(5) लङ् or imperfect
(6) लुङ् or aorist

} These are the six tenses.

(7) लेट् or subjunctive
(8) लोट् or imperative
(9) लिङ् or optative or
potential (विधिलिङ्) and
benedictive (आशीर्लिङ्)
(10) लृङ् or conditional

} These are the four moods.

Now, verbality or the idea of action in general belongs to all these tenses and moods. Thus गच्छति=गमनं करोति, जगाम=गमनं चकार, गच्छ=गमनं कुरु etc. Therefore, आख्यातत्व is said to be दशलकारसाधारण.

लिङ्त्वं पुनः etc–Each mood possesses a different sense. It is, therefore, natural that the sense of the optative viz. the sense of injunction or the injunctive force should belong to the optative alone.

Section 5

In the concluding sentence of the last Section Bhāskara said that both verbality and optativeness constituting the suffix in the verb यजेत express भावना. He now proceeds to explain what भावना means.

The doctrine of bhāvanā is peculiar to the Mīmāṁsakas. Though somewhat confusing at first, it is by no means difficult to understand.

भावना नाम ... विशेषः—This is how Bhāskara defines bhāvanā. Let us take an illustration. Yajñadatta orders his son Devadatta to bring a cow. Consequently, the idea or inclination that he should go through certain action which would result in the bringing of the cow arises in Devadatta's mind. He then puts that inclination into practice and actually brings the cow. This incident can be looked at from two points of view, which will illustrate the two kinds of bhāvanā.

First, then Yajñadatta wants that a certain thing viz. inclination (प्रवृत्तिः) on the part of his son Devadatta should come about. Yajñadatta is, therefore, the भावयितृ, or one who makes a certain thing to happen, and Devadatta's inclination the भवितृ, or the thing that is going to happen. Now, भावना is some activity (व्यापारः) on the part of the भावयिता, which is favourable for the happening (भवनम्) of the thing which is going to happen. Such activity in the present case is the particular intention (अभिप्रायविशेषः) residing in Yajñadatta, which might be expressed by him in words such as 'देवदत्त, गामानय', or might be conveyed by him to his son in some other way. Though intention is not a physical, but is only a mental activity, it is activity all the same. Consequently, it is designated as व्यापारविशेषः. Thus, Yajñadatta's intention to make Devadatta inclined towards a certain action is the भावना from this point of view.

Now, look at the matter from another stand-point i. e. from the stand-point of Devadatta. He also wants that a certain thing viz. the bringing of the cow (गवानयन) should come about. Devadatta, therefore, is now the भावयितृ and the bringing of the cow the भवितृ. भावना here is some activity on the part of Devadatta, which would be favourable to गवानयन. And that activity is nothing but Devadatta's inclination to go through various physical actions such as getting up from his seat, moving to where the cow is tied, unfastening it and leading it on to where it is wanted, which are comprehensively called आनयन. This inclination of Devadatta with reference to the specific action of bringing the cow is then the bhāvanā from this point of view.

Thus in the present case the two भावनाs are यज्ञदत्तस्य or यज्ञदत्तनिष्ठः अभिप्रायः and देवदत्तस्य [आनयनविषया] प्रवृत्तिः. The first is known as शाब्दी भावना or शब्दभावना and the second is termed आर्थी भावना or अर्थभावना.

These two bhāvanās may further be illustrated by taking a Vedic example. The sentence 'यजेत स्वर्गकामः' wants that a certain thing viz. inclination on the part of a person desirous of attaining heaven, should come to pass. The Vedic sentence is, therefore, the भावयितृ and the inclination on the part of the person desirous of heaven the भवितृ in the present case. Now, भावना here would be the intention of the Vedic sentence. In the case of the Veda there is no person in whom this intention can be said to reside. For, the dogma is that the sentence 'यजेत स्वर्गकामः' is not uttered or composed by anybody, but is अपौरुषेय and eternal. So, the intention in the case of Vedic injunctions resides in the optative form itself (लिङादिशब्दनिष्ठ एव).

The Mīmāṁsakas are primarily concerned with Vedic injunctions. Injunctions or commands from ordinary life are used by them only as illustrations. As the first kind of bhāvanā viz. the intention resides in the case of Vedic injunctions in the word viz. the optative form only, it is called शाब्दी भावना by the Mīmāṁsakas.

The name शाब्दी भावना may be understood to be significant in the case of worldly injunctions as well. In the world we find that the intention of people, who want to issue some command, is usually conveyed by means of words. So it may be called शाब्दी भावना.

Thus, it will be seen that the intention, which constitutes the first kind of bhāvanā, is called Śābdī in the Veda, because it resides in the word. In ordinary life also it may be designated Śābdī, because it is usually expressed in words.

Now, look at the Vedic sentence 'यजेत स्वर्गकामः' from another point of view i. e. from the point of view of the person who is desirous of attaining heaven. Such a person also wants that a certain thing viz. his attainment of heaven should happen. The person desirous of heaven is, therefore, the भावयितृ and the attainment of heaven the भवितृ in the present case. Now, भावना here would be represented by that activity on the part of the person desirous of heaven, which would lead to his attainment of heaven. Such an activity is his inclination to perform the sacrifice or याग proper. Thus यागविषया प्रवृत्तिः is the भावना from this point of view.

This bhāvanā is known as आर्थी भावना. The name is significant· अर्थः प्रयोजनं स्वर्गप्राप्तिः इत्यर्थः तत्सम्बन्धिनी भावना स्वर्गकामस्य यागविषया प्रवृत्तिः आर्थी भावना.

It will thus be seen that while शाब्दी भावना represents an urge, an impulse (प्रवर्तना or प्रेरणा), instigating a person to become inclined towards a certain action, आर्थी भावना is the tendency or inclination

(प्रवृत्तिः) to undertake that action. Both शाब्दी भावना and आर्थी भावना are mental activities. Both of them can be looked upon as अभिप्रायविशेषs. But while शाब्दी भावना is the intention *to instigate another* towards a certain tendency, आर्थी भावना is the intention *to instigate oneself i.e. oneself to undertake* a certain action. शाब्दी भावना is the cause, आर्थी भावना the effect arising therefrom.

We have seen that these two bhāvanās are called शाब्दी and आर्थी respectively and that these two terms are significant. But it is possible to argue that if the terms are literally understood, they become interchangeable. Thus, the intention or impulse is called शाब्दी भावना, because it resides in the optative form, being conveyed by the लिङ् element thereof. But the आर्थी भावना also is conveyed by the आख्यात element in that optative form and has consequently every right to be designated शाब्दी. Similarly, आर्थी भावना is so called because it has reference to अर्थ or प्रयोजन. But शाब्दी भावना also has its own अर्थ or प्रयोजन viz. the production of an inclination in an agent to which it refers. So, there is no reason why it should not be designated आर्थी.

Thus, though both the भावनाs are शाब्दी and आर्थी in the literal sense of those terms, they are each designated by only one term on account of the one special characteristic appearing prominent in them. In the case of the शाब्दी भावना, the fact that the impulse in Vedic sentences is furnished by the word itself, because there is no person who can be said to do so, appears prominent. In the case of the आर्थी भावना on the other hand, the ultimate purpose viz. the attainment of heaven shines prominently. Hence the two bhāvanās receive their distinctive designations.

Section 6

शाब्दी भावना is defined as पुरुषप्रवृत्त्यनुकूलो भावयितुर्व्यापारविशेषः. It is now easy to understand this definition. Verbal creative energy then is 'a particular activity [viz. the intention] of a productive agent, which is favourable to, or productive of (अनुकूल=जनक), a man's inclination (प्रवृत्तिः) [that is, which instigates a man to become inclined towards a certain action that is denoted by the verb].'

सा च—The शाब्दी भावना or the intention to instigate is expressed by the लिङ् element of the suffix त. For, whenever we hear an optative form such as उपासीत, स्नायात् or यजेत, the idea that arises in our mind is that somebody viz. the author or user of such forms is instigating us to something. अयम्=लिङ्प्रयोजकः पुरुषः.

मत्प्रवृत्त्यनुकूलव्यापारवान् मम या प्रवृत्तिः कांचित् क्रियामधिकृत्य मनसः प्रवणता, तस्या अनुकूलः जनकः व्यापारः मानसी क्रिया अभिप्रायात्मिका, स विद्यते अस्य.

It should be noted that in the definition of भावना as well as in the definitions of शाब्दी and आर्थी भावना, the words व्यापार and प्रवृत्ति are used in the sense of mental activity. Physical activity is designated by क्रिया, which is contrasted with व्यापारः (= प्रवृत्तिः) in the definition of आर्थी भावना in Section 8 below.

यद् यस्मात् शब्दात्०—This general principle is enunciated to support the statement that the लिङ् element expresses शाब्दी भावना.

गोशब्दस्य गोत्वम्—With reference to the question as to what exactly is expressed by words primarily by means of the power called अभिधा, or where exactly the convention (संकेतः) of words is understood, whether in the individual (व्यक्तिः), or in the universal or generality (जातिः), or in the attributes of the individual (उपाधिः), five different schools were prevalent in ancient India. These were (1) केवलव्यक्तिवादिनः (नव्यनैयायिकाः), (2) जातिविशिष्टव्यक्तिवादिनः (प्राचीननैयायिकाः, whom अन्नंभट्ट, the author of the तर्कसंग्रह, follows), (3) अपोहवादिनः (सौगताः), (4 - जातिवादिनः (मीमांसकाः) and (5) जात्यादिवादिनः (वैयाकरणाः, whom rhetoricians such as Mammaṭa follow).

According to the Mīmāṁsakas, then, the primary sense of a word is जाति or generality. Thus, when one says 'गाम् आनय,' the primary sense is गोत्वमानय. But, as it is not possible to bring cow-ness, because it cannot be separated from the individual cow, an individual cow, which is characterised by cowness, is brought.

वैदिकवाक्ये तु०–This sentence is based on the doctrine that the Vedas are apauruṣeya, or not composed by any man, not even by God himself. They are eternal and exist all through the beginningless time. This doctrine of the अपौरुषेयत्व of the Vedas is admitted by the Mīmāṁsakas and the Vedāntins. On account of their apauruṣeya character the Vedas possess supreme and infallible authority. They are also self-authoritative for the same reason. They are further the fountain-head from which human writings such as the Smṛtis derive their authority.

The Naiyāyikas on the other hand believe that the Vedas are the composition of God and their supreme authority is due to this fact.

The question of the apauruṣeyatva of the Veda is discussed by Jaimini in I. i. 27–32. Read the following from the जैमिनीयन्यायमालाविस्तरः '" काठकम्, कौथुमम्, तैत्तिरीयकम् " इत्यादिसमाख्या तत्तद्वेदविषया लोके दृष्टा। तद्धितप्रत्ययश्च " तेन प्रोक्तम् " इत्यर्थे वर्तते। तथा सति " व्यासेन प्रोक्तं वैयासिकं भारतम् "

इत्यादाविव पौरुषेयत्वं प्रतीयते । किं च " विमतं वेदवाक्यं पौरुषेयं, वाक्यत्वात्, कालिदासादिवाक्यवत् " इति प्राप्ते—ब्रूमः—

अध्ययनसंप्रदायप्रवर्तकत्वेन समाख्योपपद्यते । कालिदासादिग्रन्थेषु तत्तत्सर्गावसाने कर्तार उपलभ्यन्ते । तथा वेदस्यापि पौरुषेयत्वे तत्कर्तोपलभ्येत । न चोपलभ्यते । अतो वाक्यत्वहेतुः प्रतिकूलतर्कपराहतः । तस्मादपौरुषेयो वेदः । तथा सति पुरुषबुद्धिदोषकृतस्य अप्रामाण्यस्य अनाशङ्कनीयत्वात् विधिवाक्यस्य धर्मे प्रामाण्यं सुस्थितम् । ' p. 21.

The मीमांसान्यायप्रकाश of आपदेव contains the following on this topic: 'न हि वेदः पुरुषनिर्मितः । " वेदस्याध्ययनं सर्वं गुर्वध्ययनपूर्वकम् । वेदाध्ययनसामान्यादधुनाध्ययनं यथा ॥ " इत्यादिना वेदापौरुषेयत्वस्य साधितत्वात् । " यः कल्पः स कल्पपूर्वः ' इति न्यायेन संसारस्य अनादित्वात् ईश्वरस्य च सर्वज्ञत्वात् ईश्वरो गतकल्पीयवेदमस्मिन् कल्पे स्मृत्वा उपदिशति इति एतावतैव उपपत्तौ प्रमाणान्तरेण अर्थमुपलभ्य रचितत्वकल्पनानुपपत्तेश्च ।' p. 3 (Benares).

In this connection see शाबरभाष्य on I. i. 27–32 ; सर्वदर्शनसंग्रह pp. 270–277 and सायण's ऋग्वेदभाष्योपक्रमणिका.

Our author has nothing to say on this topic except that he defines Veda as ' अपौरुषेयं वाक्यम् ' in Section 10 below.

Section 7

सा च भावना॰—The लिङ् element of the suffix त in यजेत expresses शाब्दी भावना, as we saw before. The शाब्दी भावना is an impulse or urge, which wants to bring something into existence. Now in all impulses, injunctions, or orders three questions naturally arise viz. what is it that is to be brought into existence (किं भावयेत्), by which instrument is that to be brought into existence (केन भावयेत्) and in what way or how is it to be brought into existence (कथं भावयेत्) ? These three requirements are respectively known as साध्य, साधन and इतिकर्तव्यता and the expectancy with regard to them is respectively termed साध्याकाङ्क्षा, साधनाकाङ्क्षा and इतिकर्तव्यताकाङ्क्षा.

तत्र साध्याकाङ्क्षाया...अन्वेति—Now the first question is : What is the साध्य of the शाब्दी भावना i. e. what is it that this impulse wants to bring into existence ? We have seen before that this impulse aims at producing the tendency or inclination to undertake a certain activity viz. to perform the sacrifice with a view to attain heaven. This inclination is known as आर्थी भावना, which also, even like the शाब्दी, has three elements. अंशत्रयोपेता आर्थी भावना is, therefore, the साध्य of शाब्दी भावना. Thus, to the question ' किं भावयेत् ' in the case of शाब्दी भावना, the answer is ' अंशत्रयोपेताम् आर्थीं भावनां भावयेत्. '

एकप्रत्यय...श्रुतेः—These two expressions supply the reason why आर्थी भावना is the साध्य of शाब्दी भावना.

We have seen before that both the शाब्दी and आर्थी भावनाs are conveyed (गम्य) by the suffix त. The लिङ् element of that suffix conveys the शाब्दी भावना and the आख्यात element the आर्थी भावना. Thus, the शाब्दी and आर्थी भावना are एकप्रत्ययगम्य. As they are एकप्रत्ययगम्य, it is said that there is a common Vedic statement (समानश्रुतिः), which expresses them both (अभिधान). Their एकप्रत्ययगम्यत्व makes them समानाभिधानश्रुतिक. Which is then the समानश्रुति that expresses them both? The समानश्रुति is nothing but the suffix त, which conveys both these भावनाs. श्रुति means the Veda or a Vedic statement or a Vedic passage. The Veda is of course made of all the various elements that constitute the words which go to form it. Consequently, the suffix त, which conveys both the शाब्दी and आर्थी भावना, is here referred to by the expression समानश्रुति. Read 'अर्थभावनाया एव शब्दभावनासाध्यत्वम्, अनयोः एकलिङादिप्रत्ययगम्यत्वेन एकलिङादिप्रत्ययशब्दात्मिकायाः समानाभिधानश्रुतेः सत्त्वात् ।' रामेश्वर.

Thus, the reason why आर्थी भावना is to be considered the साध्य of शाब्दी भावना is that there is a common Vedic statement, which expresses them both. And the existence of such common Vedic statement is due to the fact that both the bhāvanās are conveyed by the same suffix. आर्थी भावना शाब्द्या भावनायाः साध्यं कस्मात् भवति । समानाभिधानश्रुतेः । समानाभिधानश्रुतिश्च कस्मात् । शाब्दी भावना आर्थी भावना च एकप्रत्ययगम्ये स्तः इत्यतः ।

Now, what is it that is exactly meant when it is said that समानाभिधानश्रुति, based on एकप्रत्ययगम्यत्व, is the cause why आर्थी भावना is the साध्य of शाब्दी भावना? The meaning is as both the bhāvanās are conveyed by the same suffix, they are so near each other. Consequently, when the शाब्दी भावना wants a साध्य, it naturally adopts the आर्थी भावना, which is nearest to it.

The propriety of the expression एकप्रत्ययगम्यत्वेन as forming part of the reason why आर्थी भावना must be regarded as the साध्य of शाब्दी भावना is this: समानाभिधानश्रुतेः is the reason why आर्थी भावना is the साध्य of शाब्दी भावना. But if we look to the word यजेत, we find that याग, or the actual performance of the sacrifice, is also समानाभिधानश्रुतिक. For, the word यजेत conveys याग by means of यजधातुः, आर्थी भावना by means of आख्यातत्व and शाब्दी भावना by means of लिङ्त्व. So all those three are एकपदगम्य or एकशब्दगम्य. Consequently, the reason समानाभिधानश्रुतेः is equally applicable to याग, because याग, आर्थी भावना and शाब्दी भावना are all conveyed by the common expressive śruti viz. the word यजेत. It would thus appear that याग is also as near शाब्दी भावना as आर्थी भावना itself on account of all the three being conveyed by the same word यजेत. Why then should याग not be regarded as the साध्य of शाब्दी भावना?

This objection is removed by the expression एकप्रत्ययगम्यत्वेन. Though याग is समानाभिधानश्रुतिक, it is एकपदगम्यत्वेन समानाभिधानश्रुतिक. आर्थी भावना on the other hand is एकप्रत्ययगम्यत्वेन समानाभिधानश्रुतिक. Tathā hi: Though in the somewhat wider province of the word यजेत, याग is as near शाब्दी भावना as आर्थी भावना, in the limited sphere of the suffix त, आर्थी भावना is nearer शाब्दी भावना than याग. Hence आर्थी भावना is the साध्य of शाब्दी भावना.

संख्यादीनाम्...साध्यत्वेन अन्वयः—आर्थी भावना is declared to be the साध्य of शाब्दी भावना on the ground that it is very near शाब्दी भावना, owing to both these being एकप्रत्ययगम्य. It is now pointed out that the termination त expresses number, tense and person, besides आख्यातत्व and लिङ्त्व. This may be shown as follows :

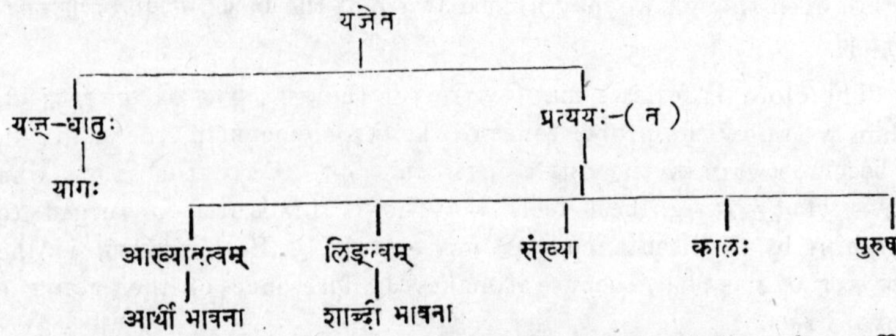

Besides verbality and optativeness or potentiality the suffix त signifies the singular number, the present tense and the third person. संख्या, काल and पुरुष, therefore, are as near शाब्दी भावना as आर्थी भावना itself. For, all these are एकप्रत्ययगम्य. Why, then, should either संख्या, काल or पुरुष not be regarded as the साध्य of शाब्दी भावना ?

This question is very easily answered. Though with reference to संख्यादि there is समानाभिधानश्रुति based upon एकप्रत्ययगम्यत्व, neither संख्या, nor काल, nor पुरुष is intrinsically fit (अयोग्यत्वात्) to be the साध्य of शाब्दी भावना. For, a साध्य must adequately answer the question ' किं भावयेत् ? ' And it is not possible to say ' संख्यां भावयेत्, ' or ' कालं भावयेत्, or ' पुरुषं भावयेत् '.

साधनाकाङ्क्षायाम्...अन्वेति—The second requirement of शाब्दी भावना is साधन. So, we want to know now ' What is the साधन of शाब्दी भावना ? [शाब्दी भावना स्वीयं साध्यं नाम आर्थीं भावनां] केन भावयेत् ? ' The answer to this is that the साधन of शाब्दी भावना is लिङादिज्ञानम्. करणत्वेन=साधनत्वेन. The words साधनम् and करणम् are used as synonyms.

तस्य च करणत्वम्...निर्वर्तकत्वेन वा-Bhāskara here shows how लिङादिज्ञान is the करण of शाब्दी भावना.

साधन or करण is of two kinds: (1) कारक or productive and (2) ज्ञापक or indicative or informative. इन्द्रियार्थसंनिकर्ष produces घटज्ञान. So this संनिकर्ष is the कारक साधन or करण (productive cause) of घटज्ञान. घटज्ञान did not exist before. It is this इन्द्रियार्थसंनिकर्ष, which produces it. On the other hand the smoke on the mountain indicates the existence of fire thereon. So धूम is the करण of वह्नि. But the smoke does not produce the fire. It only indicates its presence. Therefore, धूम is not the कारक or उत्पादक करण of वह्नि, but merely its ज्ञापक करण.

Now, what kind of करण is the लिङादिज्ञान with reference to शाब्दी भावना? Surely, लिङादिज्ञान cannot be said to have produced the शाब्दी भावना (भावनोत्पादकत्वेन = शब्दभावनाया उत्पादकत्वेन). For, the शब्दभावना exists in the लिङ् element of the suffix त in the form यजेत from time immemorial, even though we may not be aware of the fact (तत्पूर्वमपि = लिङादिज्ञानपूर्वमपि).

Therefore, it follows that लिङादिज्ञान is the ज्ञापक करण of शाब्दी भावना. When we know the proper sense of the लिङ् element in the suffix त, we become aware of the शाब्दी भावना in यजेत. Only the man, who knows what लिङ् signifies, feels that he is instigated or urged to something by such sentences as 'यजेत स्वर्गकामः'. So, लिङादिज्ञान is the ज्ञापक करण of शब्दभावना, because it makes the presence of the शब्दभावना known to us.

The करणत्व of लिङादिज्ञान with reference to शाब्दी भावना can be looked at from another point of view as well. शब्दभावना aims at producing अर्थभावना. It produces this अर्थभावना by means of लिङादिज्ञान. अर्थभावना or the प्रवृत्ति or the inclination was not in existence before. It is produced in the mind of a man on account of his knowledge of the sense of the लिङ् element. लिङादिज्ञान is thus the कारक or उत्पादक or निर्वर्तक करण of अर्थभावना. It is, however, said to be the करण of the शब्दभावना as well, even as the axe, which produces the cutting and is consequently the निर्वर्तक करण of that cutting, is regarded as the करण of the man who cuts. Read 'यथा कुठारः पुरुषसाध्यछेदनव्यापारं निर्वर्तयन् पुरुषस्य करणमित्युच्यते, एवं लिङादिज्ञानमपि शब्दभावनाभाव्यार्थभावनां निर्वर्तयत् शब्दभावनाकरणमित्युच्यते।' सारविवेचनी on आपदेव.

It will thus be seen that लिङादिज्ञान is the ज्ञापक करण of शब्दभावना, when we consider it with reference to शब्दभावना itself. When, however, we consider it with reference to the साध्य of शब्दभावना viz. अर्थभावना, it becomes उत्पादक करण.

शब्दभावनाभाव्यनिर्वर्तकत्वेन = शब्दभावनायाः भाव्यं साध्यं नाम आर्थी भावना, तस्य भाव्यस्य, तस्या अर्थभावनाया इत्यर्थः, निर्वर्तकत्वेन उत्पादकत्वेन.

The significance of the two-fold करणत्व of the लिङादिज्ञान comes to this. On account of our knowledge of the exact meaning of the लिङ् we become aware, on the one hand, of the instigation which the Veda gives us and become, on the other, inclined towards the performance of the sacrifice along with its subsidiaries with a view to the attainment of heaven.

The propriety of the word आदि in लिङादिज्ञानम् is this: In the Veda शब्दभावना is not always expressed by optative forms alone. Many a time simple present tense is used to convey injunctions e. g. दध्ना जुहोति, व्रीहीनवहन्ति, व्रीहीन् प्रोक्षति and आहवनीये जुहोति. Thus in these cases it is the लट्ज्ञान that will be the करण of शब्दभावना.

It should be noted that when the expectancy about the means (साधनाकाङ्क्षा) arises in the case of the शब्दभावना in the form 'शब्दभावना अर्थभावनां केन भावयेत्', the proper answer is 'शब्दभावना लिङादिज्ञानेन अर्थभावनां भावयेत्.' Now arises the question as to what exact part the लिङादिज्ञान plays in the production of the अर्थभावना. The answer to this is two-fold: (1) The लिङादिज्ञान makes the presence of the instigation known to us and we become inclined towards the particular sacrifice consequently. Thus, the लिङादिज्ञान is the ज्ञापककरण of शाब्दी भावना. (2) The लिङादिज्ञान produces in us the inclination to perform the sacrifice. So the लिङादिज्ञान is the कारक करण of आर्थी भावना and as आर्थी भावना is the साध्य of शाब्दी, लिङादिज्ञान is said to be the करण of शाब्दी as well.

It has been said above that the लिङादिज्ञान is the ज्ञापक करण of शाब्दी भावना. But it is possible to look at the matter from a slightly different point of view. Though it is true that the लिङादिज्ञान does not produce शब्दभावना, it produces the शब्दभावनाज्ञान all right. So, with reference to the शब्दभावनाज्ञान the लिङादिज्ञान is the कारक करण, even as धूम is the कारक करण with reference to वह्निज्ञान.

इतिकर्तव्यता...अन्वेति—The third expectancy is इतिकर्तव्यताकाङ्क्षा. The word इतिकर्तव्यता is thus explained: इति अनेन प्रकारेण, कर्तव्यं साध्यम् उत्पादनीयम्, इति इतिकर्तव्यम्, तस्य भावः इतिकर्तव्यता the thus-should-be-done-ness i. e. the mode or procedure by which a certain thing should be accomplished. (2) कर्तव्यस्य इति (=प्रकारः) इतिकर्तव्यम्, तस्य भावः इतिकर्तव्यता। इतिशब्दः प्रकारवाची. इतिकर्तव्यम् thus means the manner of doing a certain thing.

The distinction between साधन and इतिकर्तव्यता should be noted. Both of them belong to the same class. Both signify the instrument by which a certain thing is brought about. But while साधन signifies an instrument in general, इतिकर्तव्यता specifies it by adding details which go to make it effective. The distinction will be clear from the following illustration.

With reference to the sentence ओदनकामः तण्डुलान् पचेत्, the साध्याकाङ्क्षा (किं भावयेत्) is satisfied by 'ओदनं भावयेत्' and the साधनाकाङ्क्षा (केन भावयेत्) is fulfilled by '[तण्डुलानां] पाकेन ओदनं भावयेत्.' But still the expectancy as to how exactly the cooking is to be done remains unfulfilled. Hence arises the इतिकर्तव्यताकाङ्क्षा or कथंभावाकाङ्क्षा in the form 'कथं पाकेन ओदनं भावयेत्.' The answer to this is 'इन्धनफूत्काराद्युपकृतेन पाकेन ओदनं भावयेत्.' Thus, इन्धनफूत्काराद्युपकृतत्व forms the इतिकर्तव्यता in the present case. And इन्धनफूत्काराद्युपकृतत्व is nothing but the specification of details which make the पाक effective.

Now, in the Vedic example under discussion the साध्य and साधन are thus stated: शब्दभावना लिङादिज्ञानेन अर्थभावनां भावयेत्. But in the case of many people the लिङादिज्ञान is not enough to produce in them the requisite inclination (अर्थभावना). Some more inducement to make them thus inclined is necessary. And that inducement is supplied by those Vedic passages, which glorify the particular rite by either describing the glory or the greatness of the result that is to follow, or by praising the deity through whose favour the final fruit is obtained. The glorification of the rites (प्राशस्त्यं कर्मप्राशस्त्यमित्यर्थः) then is the additional inducement that helps the लिङादिज्ञान to generate the required inclination. This glorification, therefore, constitutes the इतिकर्तव्यता for the शब्दभावना.

अर्थवादः (अर्थस्य वादः) means primarily the statement of a thing or a fact. This term is applied to those passages in the Veda, which do not lay down any action, but either glorify or condemn certain rites. अर्थवाद in the present case means glorificatory or laudatory passages. For, from these arthavādas the glorification is known. अर्थवादैः स्तुतिपरैः वाक्यैः ज्ञाप्यं यत् प्राशस्त्यम्.

The sentence 'ज्योतिष्टोमेन स्वर्गकामो यजेत' lays down the ज्योतिष्टोम sacrifice for one who is desirous of heaven. The ज्योतिष्टोम sacrifice is rendered more acceptable by the passage 'यस्मिन्नोष्णं न शीतं नार्तिः', which describes the pleasures of heaven. This passage, therefore, is the अर्थवाद bringing out the प्राशस्त्य of ज्योतिष्टोम.

To take another instance. 'वायव्यं श्वेतमालभेत भूतिकामः' lays down the slaughter of a white animal in honour of Wind. The passage 'वायुर्वै क्षेपिष्ठा देवता, वायुमेव स्वेन भागधेयेन उपधावति, स एव एनं भूतिं गमयति' glorifies Wind by telling us 'क्षिप्रगामी वायुः स्वोचितेन भागेन तोषितो भागप्रदाय ऐश्वर्यं प्रयच्छति.' This passage, therefore, is the अर्थवाद, which makes the offering to

Wind more desirable. The ultimate idea from these विधि and अर्थवाद passages is 'यतः क्षिप्रगामिस्वभावतया शीघ्रफलप्रदो वायुरस्य पशोर्देवता, ततः प्रशस्तमिमं वायव्यं पशुमालभेत ।' जैमिनीयन्यायमालाविस्तर p. 23.

We have thus seen what the three elements required by verbal creative energy are. These may be illustrated by the following diagram :

शाब्दी भावना

साध्यम्	साधनम्	इतिकर्तव्यता
(किं भावयेत्)	(केन भावयेत्)	(कथं भावयेत्)
अंशत्रयवतीम् आर्थीं भावनां भावयेत्	लिङादिज्ञानेन भावयेत्	कर्मप्राशस्त्यविशिष्टेन लिङादिज्ञानेन भावयेत्

Section 8

प्रयोजनेच्छा...व्यापारः is the definition of आर्थी भावना. It means 'the [mental] activity [of a person] referring to [some particular] action which is engendered by the desire for [some] object.'

प्रयोजनं स्वर्गः, तस्य इच्छा अभिलाषः, तया जनिता या क्रिया यागरूपा, सा विषयः यस्य, ईदृशः व्यापारः मानसी प्रवृत्तिः इत्यर्थः.

रामेश्वर explains this compound in a slightly different manner as follows : प्रयोजनस्य स्वर्गादिरूपफलस्य या इच्छा रागविशेषः तेन च रागविशेषेण जनितो यो यागादिक्रियाविषयः पुरुषस्य व्यापारविशेषः सा आर्थी भावना.

According to रामेश्वर, जनित qualifies व्यापारः. But जनित as a qualification of क्रिया is preferable. For, it is better to hold that the actual physical action of performing the sacrifice was caused by the desire of attaining heaven than to say that the mental inclination was generated by such desire. Because the direct cause of the attainment of heaven is the sacrifice and not the mental inclination.

आख्यात...वाचित्वात्—आख्यातसामान्यम् is the same as आख्यातत्वम् (verbality) of Section 4 above. It expresses activity or the idea of action in general, both mental and physical.

Section 9

The three requirements of आर्थी भावना would be clearly seen from the following diagram :

आर्थी भावना

साध्यम्	साधनम्	इतिकर्तव्यता
(किं भावयेत्)	(केन भावयेत्)	(कथं भावयेत्)
स्वर्गादि फलं भावयेत्	यागादिना भावयेत्	प्रयाजाद्यङ्गजातोपकृतेन यागादिना भावयेत्

स्वर्गादि फलं साध्यत्वेन—आर्थी भावना, we have seen, is the inclination to undertake a certain action with a view to attain a certain end. The question 'आर्थी भावना किं भावयेत्' seeks to find out the साध्य of the आर्थी भावना. The साध्य is nothing but the कर्म or the object of the verb भावयेत् (=कुर्यात् or जनयेत्). To the above question two answers are possible viz. स्वर्गादिफलं भावयेत् and यागं भावयेत्. Which of these two viz. स्वर्गादिफल and याग, then, is the proper साध्य or कर्म of the आर्थी भावना? A कर्म or object is defined as 'कर्तुरीप्सिततमं कर्म' (पाणिनि i. 4. 49) and out of these two स्वर्गादिफल is of course the most desired. For, while स्वर्गादिफल is full of pleasures and enjoyments, याग entails quite a lot of trouble for the performer. Nobody likes a troublesome thing in preference to one bringing delight So स्वर्गादिफल is the साध्य of आर्थी भावना. Read 'दुःसाध्यात्मकस्य यागस्य ईप्सिततमत्वरूपकर्मत्वायोगात्, स्वर्गस्य तु आनन्दात्मत्वेन ईप्सिततमतया कर्मत्वेन अन्वययोग्यत्वात्' मीमांसापरिभाषा.

We must here understand what is exactly meant by स्वर्गादिफलभावना or the effecting or bringing into existence or production of the fruit viz. the heaven. The man, who is desirous of heaven, is certainly not going to produce or create heaven. For, heaven exists there from time beginningless. What he actually does by means of his sacrifice is to make that heaven available to him. Only in this sense must the स्वर्गभावना be understood as the साध्य of the आर्थी भावना in यजेत.

यागादिः करणत्वेन--As the sacrifice is the means of attaining heaven, it is natural that यागादि becomes the means of the आर्थी भावना.

Here the following difficulty arises : A man desirous of heaven commences the necessary sacrifice to-day. The sacrifice lasts for some time and is then finished. But the man does not obtain heaven immediately afterwards. He has to wait till his death for going to heaven. How then can the sacrifice, between which and heaven a long period intervenes, be said to be the means of heaven? For, a means must immediately precede the fruit to which it leads (फलायोगव्यवच्छिन्नं करणम्).

To escape from this difficulty the Mīmāṁsakas developed the doctrine of अपूर्व or the not-existent-before. What they mean is this :

The performance of the sacrifice creates a certain power, which was not in existence before and which consequently is known as अपूर्व. This Apūrva resides in the performer of the sacrifice till his death and leads him to heaven afterwards. So the proper means of attaining heaven is this Apūrva. But as it is produced by the sacrifice, the sacrifice itself is called the means.

It should be noted that though the Mīmāṁsakas invented the term Apūrva, the idea underlying it is common to all systems. A man performs a charitable deed here and expects to get his reward for it after his death. The charitable deed is the cause of the reward. But between the deed and the reward a long period of time may elapse. So it is believed that the charitable deed gives rise to some invisible power, called variously प्रारब्धकर्म, धर्म, अदृष्ट and पुण्य, which really secures for the man the expected reward after his death. Read 'यागादिजन्यः स्वर्गादिजनकः कश्चन गुणविशेषः। तं गुणविशेषम् **अपूर्वम्** इति मीमांसका वदन्ति। **प्रारब्धकर्म** इति वेदान्तिनः। **धर्माधर्मौ** इति नैयायिकाः। **अदृष्टम्** इति वैशेषिकाः। **पुण्यपापे** इति पौराणिकाः।' न्यायकोश p. 60

We saw above that the साधन of शाब्दी भावना viz. लिङादिज्ञान was regarded as possessing a double characteristic. It was ज्ञापक with reference to the शाब्दी भावना itself and कारक with reference to the आर्थी भावना, which was produced by the शाब्दी. यागादि, which is the साधन of आर्थी भावना, also possesses this two-fold character. When Devadatta begins to perform a sacrifice, we naturally conclude that he must have been so inclined. याग thus makes the presence of the आर्थी भावना in Devadatta known to us. It is thus the ज्ञापक करण of the आर्थी भावना. On the other hand याग secures for us the enjoyment of heaven through the अपूर्व which it generates. It is thus the कारक करण of स्वर्ग' And as heaven is what the आर्थी भावना aims at producing, याग is regarded as the करण of the आर्थी भावना as well.

इतिकर्तव्यताकाङ्क्षायाम्...अन्वेति–The requirement of इतिकर्तव्यता in the case of the आर्थी भावना is fulfilled by the group (जातम्) of subsidiary rites (अङ्गम्) such as प्रयाजाः. The word आदि shows that other rites such as अनुयाजाः are also included in the अङ्गजातम्.

The terms प्रयाजाः and अनुयाजाः occur now and then and require explanation. The sentence 'दर्शपूर्णमासाभ्यां यजेत स्वर्गकामः' lays down new (दर्शः) and full-moon (पूर्णमासः) sacrifices for a person desirous of obtaining heaven. The दर्शपूर्णमास thus constitutes the principal sacrifice (अङ्गी यागः), in which oblations are offered to अग्नि, विष्णु, अग्नीषोमा and इन्द्राग्नी, who are its principal deities. प्रयाज and अनुयाज are subsidiary or subordinate offerings that precede and follow the principal oblations. The Prayājas or fore-sacrifices are laid down by the sentence 'प्रयाजाः कर्तव्याः.' These are five in number and are mentioned in 'समिधो यजति (He sacrifices to the fire-sticks) तनूनपातं यजति, इडो यजति, बर्हिर्यजति, स्वाहाकारं यजति.' The Prayājas are offered with आज्य or clarified butter or ghee and precede the principal oblations to Agni, Viṣṇu etc., which consist of pieces of the Puroḍāśa or the sacrificial cake. After the principal oblations follows an offering to विश्वे देवाः or All-gods, which is known as स्विष्टकृत्. After this are offered the अनुयाजाः or the after-sacrifices, which are laid down in 'पृषदाज्येन अनुयाजान् यजेत'. These are three in number and consist of पृषदाज्य or speckled ghee. Thus, the order of the sacrifices in the दर्शपूर्णमास is पञ्च प्रयाजाः, अग्न्यादिचतुर्भ्यः मुख्या यागाः, स्विष्टकृत् and अनुयाजाः.

The याग is the साधन of आर्थी भावना and this याग consists of several details such as अग्न्यन्वाधान, अवघात, प्रयाजs and अनुयाजs. Therefore, these details, comprehensively called अङ्गजातम्, constitute the इतिकर्तव्यता of आर्थी भावना.

The ultimate meaning of the आर्थी भावना in 'यजेत स्वर्गकामः' is thus expressed: 'तथा च "यजेत स्वर्गकामः" इत्यत्र अग्न्यन्वाधानावघातप्रयाजादिभिरुपकारं संपाद्य यागेन स्वर्गं भावयेत् स्वर्गं कुर्यात् इति वाक्यार्थः।' रामेश्वर.

Putting the senses of the शाब्दी and the आर्थी भावना together the meaning that we derive from the sentence 'यजेत स्वर्गकामः' is this: By means of the knowledge of लिङ् (शब्दभावनायाः साधनम्), helped by the glorification of the rite (शब्दभावनायाः इतिकर्तव्यता), the Vedic intention conveyed by the लिङ् element in यजेत (शब्दभावना) produces the tendency or inclination (शब्दभावनायाः साध्यम् = अर्थभावना) that by means of the sacrifice (अर्थभावनायाः साधनम्), helped by its various subsidiaries (अर्थभावनायाः इतिकर्तव्यता), one should secure heaven (अर्थभावनायाः साध्यम्). The whole ponderous meaning reduces itself plainly to this that the Veda urges that one should secure heaven by means of the sacrifice.

So far Bhāskara has elaborated the Mīmāṁsaka theory of understanding the meaning from injunctive sentences. This theory represents their method of what is called शाब्दबोध. In this they attach greater importance to the suffix in the form यजेत. They are consequently known as प्रत्ययार्थविशेष्यकशाब्दबोधवादिनः. As opposed to them are the Naiyāyikas and the Vaiyākaraṇas, who are respectively designated कर्तृमुख्यविशेष्यकशाब्दबोधवादिनः and धात्वर्थमुख्यविशेष्यकशाब्दबोधवादिनः.

Section 10

It will be remembered that we started with the first aphorism of the Mīmāṁsakas, which laid down that investigation into piety should be undertaken. Piety was then defined as 'वेदप्रतिपाद्यः प्रयोजनवदर्थः.' We then learnt that piety consists in sacrifice, which is enjoined by such sentences as 'यजेत स्वर्गकामः' and we further saw the elaborate way in which Vedic sentences enjoin piety. Now arises the question 'What is this Veda that enjoins piety?' The rest of the Arthasamgraha consists of an answer to this question.

'अपौरुषेयं वाक्यं वेदः' is the definition of the Veda, according to the Mīmāmsakas. Both the words in the definition are significant. The word अपौरुषेय excludes from the province of the Veda such a work as the Mahābhārata, which is known to be the work of a human being viz. Vyāsa. The word वाक्य is also necessary. Otherwise entities like the Soul, which are अपौरुषेय would be the Veda. Read 'वेद इति लक्ष्यनिर्देशः । तत्र भारतादौ अतिव्याप्तिवारणाय अपौरुषेयम् इति विशेषणम् । आत्मादौ तद्दोषवारणाय वाक्यमिति विशेष्यम् । ' रामेश्वर.

Sāyaṇa in the Introduction to his Ṛgbhāṣya defines the Veda as 'मन्त्रब्राह्मणात्मकः शब्दराशिर्वेदः'.

पञ्चविध :—The five divisions of the Veda represent its analysis from the point of view of the Mīmāmsakas i. e. from the point of view of its ability to enjoin piety.

It should be noticed that this five-fold division of the Mīmāmsakas is practically the same as the two-fold division of Sāyaṇa. For, Brāhmaṇa, mentioned in Sāyaṇa's definition, covers विधि, नामधेय, निषेध and अर्थवाद.

The following five chapters of the Arthasamgraha deal with these five divisions of the Veda.

Section 11

अज्ञातार्थ०—The essence of a Vedic injunction lies in conveying to us a matter that was not known before. Such a matter should further have a purpose. The justification (अर्थवत्त्वम्) of an injunction lies just in this that it enjoins a matter that was not known before and that has a purpose. Take, for example, the sentence 'अग्निहोत्रं जुहुयात् स्वर्गकामः'. This sentence enjoins the performance of the Agnihotra with a view to attain heaven. Now, Agnihotra is a matter not known before. For, neither perception, nor inference, nor any other means of proof can give us any information about the Agnihotra. It is known only from this sentence of the Veda. Being thus an अज्ञातार्थ, it is a प्रयोजनवदर्थ as well. For, its purpose is heaven. As the sentence 'अग्निहोत्रं जुहुयात् स्वर्गकामः' thus lays down अग्निहोत्र, which is an अज्ञात and प्रयोजनवद् अर्थ, that sentence becomes a proper विधिः.

The correct Mīmāṁsist meaning that we obtain from the sentence 'अग्निहोत्रं जुहुयात् स्वर्गकामः' is 'अग्निहोत्रहोमेन स्वर्गं भावयेत्.'. Here a question arises: The word अग्निहोत्र occurs in the accusative in the original sentence, but is understood in the sense of the instrumental in the meaning that is understood therefrom. How is this possible? The answer to this is that the Agnihotra unites in itself the characteristics of both a साध्य (द्वितीया) and a साधन (तृतीया) Till the sacrifice is actually performed, it is a साध्य. Only when it is completed, it becomes a साधन. So there is nothing objectionable if the Veda refers to the Agnihotra in the accusative and we understand it as the means of attaining heaven. Read 'अनुष्ठानादूर्ध्वं धात्वर्थस्य सिद्धत्वाकारेण करणत्वेऽपि ततः पूर्वं साध्यत्वाकारं वक्तुम् "अग्निहोत्रम्" इति द्वितीयाया युक्तत्वात्।' जैमिनीयन्यायमालाविस्तर pp. 45–46.

नादृष्ट means अज्ञात and is further explained as प्रमाणान्तरेण अप्राप्त, which does not accrue from any other means of proof. The number of Pramāṇas admitted by different systems varies. Mīmāṁsakas admit five or six pramāṇas. Followers of Prabhākara recognise प्रत्यक्ष, अनुमान, उपमान, शब्द and अर्थापत्ति as the five pramāṇas. The Bhāṭṭa Mīmāṁsakas (followers of Kumārila-bhaṭṭa) admit अनुपलब्धि as a sixth pramāṇa.

The sentence 'अग्निहोत्रं जुहुयात् स्वर्गकामः' contains what is known as उत्पत्तिविधिः or प्रधानविधिः. As this is the injunction from which the Agnihotra originates, it is called उत्पत्तिविधिः. As the Agnihotra as a sacrifice is principal in relation to such subsidiary matters as the material with which the sacrifice is performed, the injunction which lays it down is known ar प्रधानविधिः.

अग्निहोत्रम्—This is the name of two rites, which are performed every morning and evening in honour respectively of the Sun and Fire. The duty of performing the Agnihotra is life-long ('यावज्जीवमग्निहोत्रं जुहोति'). Note 'अग्निसूर्यदेवताकस्य सायंप्रातःकालयोर्नियमेन अनुष्ठेयस्य कर्मणः "अग्निहोत्रम्" इति यौगिकं नामधेयम्।' जैमिनीयन्यायमालाविस्तर p. 45.

यत्र कर्म मानान्तरेण०—Sometimes it so happens that an injunction lays down only the material with which a sacrifice is performed, the sacrifice itself (कर्म=यज्ञकर्म) having been enjoined by some other sentence. Take, for example, the sentence 'दध्ना जुहोति'. Here only a secondary matter (गुणः) viz. the material with which the sacrifice is to be performed is laid down. The sacrifice in which this material viz. curds is to be used is enjoined by another sentence viz 'अग्निहोत्रं जुहुयात्'. Therefore, the injunction in 'दध्ना जुहोति' is understood to prescribe only the curds with reference to the sacrifice which is enjoined in 'अग्निहोत्रं जुहुयात्'. The sentence 'दध्ना जुहोति' then yields the sense 'दध्ना होमं भावयेत्'

Such an injunction is called गुणविधिः, because it lays down merely a secondary or subsidiary matter, as opposed to प्रधानविधिः, which enjoins the sacrifice itself, regarded as principal in relation to its subsidiaries.

यत्र तूभयमप्राप्तम्०—Sometimes the sacrifice as well as the material with which it is offered are both enjoined by one and the same sentence; e. g. 'सोमेन यजेत'. This sentence looks very much like 'दध्ना जुहोति'. But there is a great difference between the two. While 'दध्ना जुहोति' refers to a sacrifice, which is already laid down in 'अग्निहोत्रं जुहुयात्', 'सोमेन यजेत' is not connected with any sacrifice enjoined elsewhere. Consequently, 'सोमेन यजेत' must be understood to lay down the sacrifice as well as the material with which it is performed. Or to speak more correctly from the technical point of view, 'सोमेन यजेत' enjoins a sacrifice characterised by Soma. The injunction in this sentence is, therefore, known as विशिष्टविधिः (विशिष्टस्य गुणविशिष्टस्य इत्यर्थः यागादेः कर्मणः विधिः).

Thus, the sense that we obtain from 'सोमेन यजेत' is 'सोमवता सोमविशिष्टेन वा यागेन इष्टं भावयेत्'. Here a question arises: How can सोमेन mean सोमवता? The answer to this is that the primary sense of सोमेन is unsuitable to the present context. For, 'सोमेन यागेन इष्टं भावयेत्' makes no sense. Therefore, the word सोमेन should be understood to be metaphorical in the sense of सोमवता. Such metaphor is not uncommon. In 'कुन्ताः प्रविशन्ति' we understand 'कुन्ताः' in the sense of 'कुन्तवन्तः पुरुषाः', because कुन्ताः in its primary sense cannot well be construed with प्रविशन्ति. Similarly, सोमेन should metaphorically be taken in the sense of सोमवता.

मत्वर्थलक्षणया—The power by which सोमेन is understood in the sense of सोमवता is technically known as उपादानलक्षणा, because in the sense ultimately understood from the word the primary sense is included. It is also designated अजहल्लक्षणा, because the indicated sense does not abandon the primary sense. Bhāskara calls it मत्वर्थलक्षणा or indication of possession, because the indicated sense of the word is an entity, which is possessed of the primary sense.

The word मत्वर्थलक्षणा is thus explained: मतोः अर्थः यस्याः, ईदृशी च असौ लक्षणा च. मतु or मतुप् is the technical form of the termination मत्, which denotes possession.

The difficulty in the sentence **'सोमेन यागेन इष्टं भावयेत्'** was that the word **सोमेन** could not properly be canstrued with **यागेन** in its primary sense. The help of **मत्वर्थलक्षणा** was, therefore, sought. Grammar would solve the difficulty in another manner viz. by understanding the word **सोमेन** as being equal to **सोमवता**, thus: **सोमः अस्ति अस्य असौ सोमः । 'अर्शआदिभ्योऽच्'** (पा० 5.2.127) **इत्यनेन मत्वर्थीयः अच् प्रत्ययः ।** The peculiarity of this possessive termination **अच्** is that it works no change whatsoever in the word to which it is applied.

Another way to surmount the difficulty is to take **सोमेन** as an instance **उपलक्षणे तृतीया. सोमेन** will then be equal to **सोमेन विशिष्टेन**, which makes the sentence quite intelligible.

न चोभयविधाने०—We have seen that the **विशिष्टविधि** or qualified injunction in '**सोमेन यजेत**' really lays down two things viz. the sacrifice and its material. The one sentence **सोमेन यजेत** is thus equal to two viz. **सोमेन यागं भावयेत्** and **यागेन इष्टं भावयेत्**. Consequently, we are landed in what is known as 'a split of the sentence' in so far as we are reduced to the expedient of splitting one sentence and understanding it as being equal to two (**वाक्यभेदः भिन्ने वाक्ये इत्यर्थः**).

Now, it is well known that in the case of a real **वाक्यभेद**, the two sentences lay down two independent things and as it is not possible to go in for both of them simultaneously, we understand an option (**विकल्पः**) as existing between them. '**व्रीहिभिर्यजेत यवैर्वा**' is a case of a real **वाक्यभेद**. For, this sentence is equal to two viz. **व्रीहिभिर्यजेत** and **यवैर्यजेत**, and lays down two kinds of material viz. rice-grains (**व्रीहिः**) and barley-grains (**यवः**). It is not possible to perform a sacrifice with both rice-grains and barley-grains simultaneously. Consequently an option is here understood and the sacrificer is left free to choose either rice or barley as the material for his sacrifice.

It is further known that an option leads to eight faults and should, therefore, be avoided as far as possible. Thus, **वाक्यभेद** leads to **विकल्प** and **विकल्प** involves eight faults. Consequently, **वाक्यभेद** is also to be avoided. Therefore, if we interpret '**सोमेन यजेत**' in such a way as to have two things enjoined, **वाक्यभेदः**, **विकल्पः** and **अष्टदोषाः** would follow. So, it is not correct to understand '**सोमेन यजेत**' as laying down both the sacrifice and its material.

This objection is refuted as follows: The **वाक्यभेद**, which leads to option and the eight faults, occurs in that case only where the two things laid down by the two sentences are independent and cannot, therefore, be accepted simultaneously. But in the present case **याग** and **सोम** are not independent. One is subordinate to the other and the two can, therefore, be accepted simultaneously. Hence, it is not necessary to resort to option here and consequently the eight faults do not arise. In fact, in 'सोमेन यजेत' there is not that kind of वाक्यभेद which leades to option and the eight faults. For, the two things are not here individually or separately (प्रत्येकम्) laid down (अविधानात्), but one viz. याग, qualified by the other viz. सोम, is enjoined.

For the eight faults arising from a split of the sentence read '**यत्र वाक्यभेदस्तत्र अष्टदोषप्रसङ्गात्** । तथा हि । "व्रीहिभिर्यजेत यवैर्वा" इत्यत्र । तत्र च प्रथमप्रयोगे व्रीह्यनुष्ठाने (1) यवशास्त्रप्रामाण्यस्य स्वार्थानुष्ठापकत्वरूपस्य परित्यागः। (2) स्वार्थाननुष्ठापकत्वरूपस्य अप्रामाण्यस्य च स्वीकारो भवति । ततो द्वितीयप्रयोगे यवानुष्ठाने तु (3) पूर्वपरित्यक्तस्य यवशास्त्रप्रामाण्यस्य स्वीकारः (4) स्वीकृतस्य च तदप्रामाण्यस्य परित्यागश्चेति यवशास्त्रे चत्वारो दोषा भवन्ति । तथा प्रथमप्रयोगे यवानुष्ठाने (5) व्रीहिशास्त्रप्रामाण्यस्य स्वार्थानुष्ठापकत्वलक्षणस्य परित्यागः । (6) स्वार्थाननुष्ठापकत्वस्वरूपस्य चाप्रामाण्यस्य स्वीकारः । ततो द्वितीयप्रयोगे व्रीह्यनुष्ठाने तु (7) व्रीहिशास्त्रप्रामाण्यस्य पूर्वं परित्यक्तस्य स्वीकारः (8) स्वीकृतस्य च तदप्रामाण्यस्य परित्यागश्चेति व्रीहिशास्त्रे चत्वारो दोषा भवन्ति । इति **अष्टदोषदुष्टो विकल्पो यथा व्रीहियववाक्ये प्रसिद्धः** तथा अत्रापि स्यात् । ' सोमेश्वर.

न च 'ज्योतिष्टोमेन०—The point discussed in this paragraph is as follows: Why should 'सोमेन यजेत' not be regarded as a गुणविधि, laying down the material Soma for a sacrifice, which is enjoined in 'ज्योतिष्टोमेन स्वर्गकामो यजेत'? 'ज्योतिष्टोमेन...यजेत' would then be an उत्पत्तिविधि or a प्रधानविधि and 'सोमेन यजेत' a गुणविधि with reference to it, even as 'अग्निहोत्रं जुहुयात्' was an उत्पत्तिविधि, for which 'दध्ना जुहोति' served as a गुणविधि. Such interpretation would have this advantage viz. that we would not be required to understand the word सोमेन in a metaphorical sense. To give up the primary sense of a word and to understand it in a metaphorical sense is after all a defect. It is a पददोष. If we could avoid it by understanding 'सोमेन यजेत' as a गुणविधि, why should we not do so?

The answer to this is that the sentence 'ज्योतिष्टोमेन...यजेत' does not lay down a sacrifice at all. It does not contain a प्रधानविधि or an उत्पत्तिविधि. Its purpose is to lay down the qualification of a man, who is entitled to obtain heaven. That qualification is स्वर्गकामत्व. The sentence 'ज्योतिष्टोमेन...यजेत' is, therefore, an instance of अधिकारविधि.

The distinction between उत्पत्तिविधि or प्रधानविधि and अधिकारविधि is as follows: उत्पत्तिः साधनस्वरूपं तद्बोधको विधिः उत्पत्तिविधिः. An injunction of origination lays down a sacrifice, which is the means of attaining something. Sentences like 'अग्निहोत्रं जुहोति' 'सोमेन यजेत' are instances of उत्पत्तिविधि. अधिकारविधिः on the other hand tells us with whom the fruit of the rite laid down by उत्पत्तिविधि is connected i. e. tells us who is qualified to perform that rite. अधिकारः फलसंबन्धः तद्बोधको

विधिः अधिकारविधिः. Sentences like 'अग्निहोत्रं जुहुयात् स्वर्गकामः' 'ज्योतिष्टोमेन स्वर्गकामो यजेत,' 'दर्शपूर्णमासाभ्यां स्वर्गकामो यजेत' 'दध्ना इन्द्रियकामस्य जुहुयात्' 'सौर्यं चरुं निर्वपेद् ब्रह्मवर्चसकामः' are all instances of अधिकारविधि. For उत्पत्तिविधि and अधिकारविधि see below Sections 13 and 48 respectively.

Read in this connection 'ननु 'सोमेन यजेत' इत्यस्य गुणविधित्वमेव अस्तु, सोमयागस्वरूपविधिस्तु 'ज्योतिष्टोमेन स्वर्गकामो यजेत' इत्ययमेव भवतु । ततश्च 'ज्योतिष्टोमेन' इत्यादिना प्राप्ते कर्मणि गुणविधायकत्वेनापि सोमवाक्यस्य उपपत्तौ मत्वर्थलक्षणा पददोषरूपत्वेन अस्वीकर्तव्या । इति चेत् । न । 'ज्योतिष्टोमेन' इत्ययमधिकारविधिरेव । तेन न तस्य उत्पत्तिविधित्वमपि । **कर्मस्वरूपमात्रबोधकस्यैव विधेरुत्पत्तिविधित्वं व्यवह्रियते । उत्पत्तिविधिविहितस्य कर्मणः फलविशेषण सह संबन्धमात्रमधिकारविधिः करोति ।** यथा 'आग्नेयोऽष्टाकपालो भवति' इति उत्पत्तिविधिविहितस्य कर्मणः स्वर्गरूपफलविशेषेण संबन्धो 'दर्शपूर्णमासाभ्यां स्वर्गकामो यजेत' इत्यनेन विधिना क्रियते इति तस्य अधिकारविधित्वमेव, नोत्पत्तिविधित्वम् । तद्वदस्यापि अधिकारविधेर्नोत्पत्तिविधित्वं संभवति ।' रामेश्वर with a little addition.

ज्योतिष्टोम—This is one of the Soma sacrifices. अश्वमेध and राजसूय also belong to the same class. The main idea in Soma sacrifices is the pressing (सवनम्) of the Soma at three times of the day viz. the morning, the mid-day and the evening. These pressings are collectively known as त्रिषवण, comprising प्रातःसवन, माध्यन्दिनसवन and सायंसवन.

Soma sacrifices fall into three groups according to the length of time required for their performance. These are एकाह, अहीन and सत्र. एकाह sacrifices extend over just one day, as the name itself shows. अहीन group comprises those that take from two to eleven days for their performance. सत्र includes all those sacrifices that may last from twelve days up to a thousand years.

ज्योतिष्टोम is an एकाह Soma sacrifice. In it all the three pressings of Soma are performed on one day. It is the प्रकृति or arche-type for all Soma sacrifices. It possesses seven varieties viz. (1) अग्निष्टोम, (2) अत्यग्निष्टोम, (3) उक्थ, (4) षोडशिन्, (5) अतिरात्र, (6) अप्तोर्याम and (7) वाजपेय.

The sentence 'सोमेन यजेत' constitutes the उत्पत्तिविधि or प्रधानविधि with reference to all Soma sacrifices. It lays down Soma sacrifices in general. It is also their गुणविधि, because it enjoins in addition the material viz. Soma with which they are performed.

ननु 'उद्भिदा यजेत'—Another objection against considering 'सोमेन यजेत' as a विशिष्टविधि is being considered in this paragraph.

It is stated above that it is not possible to regard 'ज्योतिष्टोमेन स्वर्गकामो यजेत' as an instance of an उत्पत्तिविधि in addition to an अधिकारविधि, which it properly is. This means in general that one and the same sentence cannot be both an आधिकारविधि and an उत्पत्तिविधि. But against this principle the Mīmāṁsakas hold that 'उद्भिदा यजेत पशुकामः' is both an अधिकारविधि and an उत्पत्तिविधिः. That the sentence is an अधिकार-विधि is clear from the occurrence therein of the word पशुकामः, which establishes फलसंबन्ध or the connection of the fruit viz. cattle with one who is desirous of it.

That the sentence 'उद्भिदा etc' is an उत्पत्तिविधि as well is indicated by Jaimini's sūtra I. iv. 2. There, it has been settled that the word उद्भिद् is a proper name and means a sacrifice which secures for the performer abundance of cattle ('उद्भिद्यते पशुफलमनेन यागेन' इति निरुक्त्या नामत्वमुद्भित्पदस्य उपपद्यते). Now, this sacrifice called उद्भिद् is laid down by this very sentence. So, it becomes an उत्पत्तिविधि for that sacrifice उद्भिद्. Thus, on account of the occurrence of the word पशुकामः in it and on account of the fact that 'उद्भिद् is a proper name, the sentence 'उद्भिदा यजेत पशुकामः' becomes both an अधिकारविधि and an उत्पत्तिविधि.

Why, then, should 'ज्योतिष्टोमेन स्वर्गकामो यजेत' also not be regarded as both an अधिकारविधि and an उत्पत्तिविधि ?

This objection is refuted as follows: The sentences 'उद्भिदा...पशुकामः' and 'ज्योतिष्टोमेन...यजेत' are not on all fours. Therefore, what is true in one case cannot be true in the other. The difference between the two sentences is this : In the case of 'उद्भिदा...पशुकामः' there is no other sentence which can serve as an उत्पत्तिवाक्य. This means that no other sentence except this lays down the sacrifice called उद्भिद्. Thus, there being no other alternative (अन्यथानुपपत्त्या) we are obliged to regard the sentence 'उद्भिदा...पशुकामः' as both an अधिकारविधि and an उत्पत्तिविधि.

But in the case of 'ज्योतिष्टोमेन...यजेत' no such necessity exists. For, 'सोमेन यजेत,' which lays down Soma sacrifices in general, can serve as an उत्पत्तिवाक्य with regard to it. Consequently, it is not proper to consider 'ज्योतिष्टोमेन...यजेत' as an उत्पत्तिविधि also.

किं च 'ज्योतिष्टोमेन' इत्यस्य उभयविधित्वे०—Another objection against holding 'ज्योतिष्टोमेन... यजेत' as both an उत्पत्तिविधि and an अधिकारविधि is being pointed out here. If this sentence were to lay down both the sacrifice (उत्पत्तिविधिः) and the connection with the fruit (अधिकारविधिः), it would really be doing the work of two sentences. वाक्यभेद would consequently follow and we have seen before that वाक्यभेद should be avoided as far as possible.

But it might be urged that 'उद्भिदा यजेत पशुकामः', when understood as both an उत्पत्तिविधि and an अधिकारविधि, also involves वाक्यभेद. The answer to this is that 'उद्भिदा... पशुकामः' has to be understood as an उभयाविधि inspite of the वाक्यभेद् involved, because there is no other alternative. The case of 'ज्योतिष्टोमेन... यजेत' is not so bad. So, it is not necessary to understand it as an उभयाविधि.

Now, why is all this trouble of understanding 'ज्योतिष्टोमेन...यजेत as an उत्पत्तिविधि as well being taken ?

It is simply to avoid the indication of possession (मत्वर्थलक्षणा) in the word सोमेन. For, if 'ज्योतिष्टोमेन...यजेत' were to be an उत्पत्तिविधि, 'सोमेन यजेत' could be taken to be merely a गुणविधि, supplying the material for the sacrifice enjoined in 'ज्योतिष्टोमेन...यजेत.' It would then not be necessary to take सोमेन=सोमवता. The मत्वर्थलक्षणा would thus be avoided.

So the position ultimately comes to this: If 'ज्योतिष्टोमेन...यजेत' is regarded as an उभयाविधि, वाक्यभेद् results. If it is considered as only an अधिकारविधि, मत्वर्थलक्षणा has to be admitted in 'सोमेन यजेत'. Both of them are evils no doubt. We must, therefore, choose the lesser one.-

Now, मत्वर्थलक्षणा is a पददोष, while वाक्यभेद् constitutes a वाक्यदोष' Between the two पददोष is to be preferred. Consequently, it is better (तद् वरम्) to admit मत्वर्थलक्षणा and understand the sentence 'सोमेन यजेत as an instance of विशिष्टविधि.

Read 'न च 'सोमेन यजेत' इत्यस्य उत्पत्तिविधित्वे यद्यपि न वाक्यभेदः, तथापि मत्वर्थ' लक्षणा स्यादेव इति वाच्यम् । तस्याः स्वीक्रियमाणत्वात् । **लक्षणातो वाक्यभेदस्य जघन्यत्वात्'** लक्षणा हि पददोषः, वाक्यभेदस्तु वाक्यदोषः । पदवाक्ययोर्मध्ये पद एव दोषकल्पनाया उचितत्वात् । आपदेवी.

It will thus be seen that Section 11 deals with three kinds of विधि viz.

(1) प्रधानाविधिः or उत्पत्तिविधिः e. g. अग्निहोत्रं जुहुयात् स्वर्गकामः
(2) गुणाविधिः e. g. दध्ना जुहोति
(3) विशिष्टविधिः e. g. सोमेन यजेत

Section 12

In the previous Section injunctions were divided into three kinds according as the thing enjoined was principal (उत्पत्तिविधिः), or subordinate (गुणविधिः), or a principal qualified by a subordinate (विशिष्टविधिः). A further division of injunctions is being given in this Section. The basis of this division is the help which each of these new varieties of injunction gives to the actual performance of the sacrifice. The two divisions are by no means mutually exclusive.

According to this new divison injunctions are of four kinds, which are as follows :—

(1) उत्पत्तिविधिः or injunction of origination e. g. अग्निहोत्रं जुहोति

(2) विनियोगविधिः or injunction of application e. g. दध्ना जुहोति
This injunction is helped by six means of proof viz. श्रुति, लिङ्ग, वाक्य, प्रकरण, स्थान and समाख्या.

(3) अधिकारविधिः or injunction of qualification e. g. यजेत स्वर्गकामः

(4) प्रयोगविधिः or injunction of performance e. g. वेदं कृत्वा वेदिं करोति
This injunction determines the order of subsidiaries by means of श्रुति, अर्थ, पाठ, स्थान, मुख्य and प्रवृत्ति.

Section 13

तत्र=तेषु चतुर्षु विधिषु

The injunction of origination is defined as the injunction, which conveys (बोधक) only the nature of the rite or action that is laid down. The word मात्र or only is significant. It serves to exclude the other three injunctions, which also may contain, in addition to their proper feature viz. गुण (विनियोगविधिः), फल (अधिकारविधिः) and क्रम (प्रयोगविधिः), a reference to the nature of the rite. 'दध्ना जुहोति' is, as we shall presently see, an example of विनियोगविधिः, because it lays down the connection of the subsidiary दधि with the principal viz. the sacrifice. Now, the sentence 'दध्ना जुहोति' is also कर्मस्वरूपबोधक, because it conveys the nature of the sacrifice by means of the word जुहोति. But it is not कर्मस्वरूपमात्रबोधक, inasmuch as besides कर्मस्वरूप it conveys गुणस्वरूप by means of the word दध्ना. 'अग्निहोत्रं जुहोति' on the other hand conveys only the nature of the sacrifice. Hence it is a proper example of उत्पत्तिविधि.

The sentence 'उद्भिदा यजेत पशुकामः' is recognised to be an instance of both अधिकारविधि and उत्पत्तिविधि. The presence of the word पशुकामः, which establishes फलसंबन्ध, makes it an अधिकारविधि all right. But the sentence is not कर्मस्वरूपमात्रबोधक. For, it intimates both कर्मस्वरूप (यजेत) and फलसंबन्ध (पशुकामः). How can it then be regarded as an उत्पत्तिविधि consistently with our definition thereof ?

The answer to this objection is that 'उद्भिदा यजेत पशुकामः' is primarily an अधिकारविधि only. But as we do not possess any other sentence, which can be regarded as containing the उत्पत्तिविधि thereof, the same sentence is secondarily looked upon as an उत्पत्तिविधि as well.

Note '" उद्भिदा यजेत पशुकामः " इति विधेस्तु श्रौतमधिकारविधित्वमेव। उत्पत्तिविधित्वं तु कर्मस्वरूपबोधकविध्यन्तराभावेन आर्थिकमेव।' रामेश्वर

अत्र च विधौ०—A peculiarity of an उत्पत्तिविधि is being explained in this sentence. An injunction of origination lays down a certain rite कर्म). That rite is laid down with a view to the attainment of some desired object. Naturally therefore, in interpreting the injunction of origination, the rite is construed as the means or instrument (करणत्वेन) of attaining that desired object. Thus ' अग्निहोत्रं जुहोति ' means ' अग्निहोत्रहोमेन इष्टं भावयेत्. '

The author thinks it necessary to explain this peculiarity of an उत्पत्तिविधि for the following reason. In the sentence ' अग्निहोत्रं जुहोति ' the sacrifice that is laid down viz. अग्निहोत्र occurs in the accusative and is the grammatical object of जुहोति. A grammatical object is usually the साध्य (' कर्तुरीप्सिततमं कर्म ' पा. 1. 4. 49). It is, therefore, likely that some may look upon अग्निहोत्र as the साध्य. So the author points out that अग्निहोत्र is merely the instrument and that the साध्य is something else.

But one may urge no mention of the साध्य, expressed by ' इष्टम् in the sentence ' अग्निहोत्रहोमेन इष्टं भावयेत् ,' is made in ' अग्निहोत्रं जुहोति '. Why then should we understand it in interpreting that sentence ? The answer to this is that as the Veda has laid down the Agnihotra, it is proper to presume that it must have intended some साध्य for it. We, therefore, infer that साध्य and express it in a general way by ' इष्टम् '. As a matter of fact the साध्य in the present case is स्वर्ग. We have further to remember that the अग्निहोत्र itself cannot be the इष्ट साध्य. For, the sacrifice is a troublesome affair and nobody would desire it for its own sake. It is only desired as an instrument to heaven, which, being full of bliss, is the proper साध्य.

कर्मणः—This word means the sacrificial rite such as अग्निहोत्र, that is laid down in originative injunctions. It is possible to take कर्मणः in the sense of the grammatical object. For, in sentences like ' अग्निहोत्रं जुहोति,' the sacrifice viz. अग्निहोत्र forms the grammatical object. But such is not always the case. In sentences like ' श्येनेन अभिचरन् यजेत ' ' सोमेन यजेत ' ' उद्भिदा यजेत पशुकामः ', the sacrifice is mentioned in the instrumental. It is, therefore, better to take the word कर्मणः in the sense of the rite or action, which, as we shall see below, is the same as धात्वर्थ or the meaning of the root.

On this subject viz. that the rite is to be construed as the instrument in originative injunctions read ' उत्पत्तिविधौ च कर्मणः करणत्वेनैव अन्वयः ' होमेन

इष्टं भावयेद्' इति । न तु 'होमं कुर्याद्' इति साध्यत्वेन । तथा सति साध्यस्य साध्यान्तरान्वयायोगेन अधिकारवाक्यावगतफलसंबन्धो न स्यात् । करणत्वेन तु अन्वये 'होमेन इष्टं भावयेत्' 'किं तदिष्टम्' इत्याकाङ्क्षायां फलविशेषसंबन्धो घटते ।

न च उत्पत्तिविधौ इष्टवाचकपदाभावेन 'कर्मणा इष्टं भावयेद्' इति कथं वाक्यार्थ इति वाच्यम् । विधिश्रुतेरेव इष्टबोधकत्वात् । सा हि पुरुषार्थे पुरुषं प्रवर्तयन्ती कर्मणः फलसंबन्धमात्रं बोधयति । तस्माद् युक्तमुत्पत्तिविधौ कर्म करणत्वेन अन्वेति इति । ' आपदेवी

ननु यागस्य द्वे रूपे०—An originative injunction is defined above as an injunction which indicates the स्वरूप of a rite. An objection is now being raised against this definition.

A sacrifice has two रूपs or forms viz. the material which is offered and the deity to whom it is offered. In the sentence 'अग्निहोत्रं जुहोति' neither of these two forms is mentioned. For, here neither the material with which the Agnihotra is performed, nor the deity in whose honour it is performed, is stated. How then can this sentence be regarded as an injunction of origination ?

Bhāskara's answer to this objection is two-fold. First, he seems to hold that express mention of one or the other or both the forms of sacrifice is not necessary for a sentence to become an उत्पत्तिविधि. Even when these forms are not mentioned (रूपाश्रवणेऽपि), a sentence can be an उत्पत्तिविधि. For, if the forms are not directly stated, they can be easily inferred or imagined.

Further, distinction should be made between the स्वरूप or the proper general nature and the रूप or the form, of a sacrifice. What is necessary for an उत्पत्तिविधि is the स्वरूप of the rite. That स्वरूप is supplied by verbs like जुहोति, यजेत etc., which show that a होम or याग in general is enjoined. The रूप or form of the होम or याग can then be inferred.

Read in this connection ' यद्यपि अत्र [' अग्निहोत्रं जुहोति ' इत्यस्मिन् वाक्ये] कर्मणो रूपं **न श्रूयते**, तथापि विध्यन्यथानुपपत्त्या **तत् कल्प्यते** । तच्च सामान्यतः कल्प्यमानं द्रव्यदेवतात्मकं कर्मणो रूपं विशेषाकाङ्क्षया गुणविधिमन्त्रवर्णाभ्यां विशेषेण चावगम्यमानमत्र संभवति । ततश्च ' अग्निहोत्रं जुहोति ' इत्यत्र द्रव्यदेवतात्मकस्य **कर्मरूपस्य** श्रवणाभावेऽपि अस्य होमरूपकर्म**स्वरूप**मात्रबोधकत्वरूपमुत्पत्तिविधित्वं संभवति । ' रामेश्वर

Secondly, Bhāskara points out an undesirable result, which would follow if we were to insist that mention of the रूप of the sacrifice is necessary for an उत्पत्तिविधि. In that case ' दध्ना जुहोति ', which is recognised as a विनियोगविधि or गुणविधि with reference to ' अग्निहोत्रं जुहोति ', would itself be an उत्पत्तिविधि, because one of the forms of the sacrifice viz. the material curds is mentioned here. Consequently, ' अग्निहोत्रं

जुहोति ' will have no purpose to serve and that sentence will, therefore, be redundant. This is a highly undesirable result from the Mīmāṁsaka's point of view.

अग्निहोत्रशब्दस्य...नामधेयत्वात्–In stating his objection against the definition of उत्पत्तिविधि, the पूर्वपक्षिन् urged that in the sentence ' अग्निहोत्रं जुहोति ' neither the material nor the deity of the sacrifice is mentioned. Against this a counter-objector points out that the word अग्निहोत्रम् contains the name of the deity. For, अग्निहोत्रम् means अग्नये होत्रम् (a sacrifice to Fire). We thus have here one of the forms of the sacrifice viz. the deity, who is Fire in the present case. It is, therefore, not correct to urge that neither of the two forms of the sacrifice is mentioned in ' अग्निहोत्रं जुहोति. '

The sentence under explanation is directed against this counter-objector. The पूर्वपक्षिन् points out that according to the view of the सिद्धान्तिन्, as embodied in the तत्प्रख्यन्याय, the word अग्निहोत्र does not contain the name of the deity, but is merely the proper name of the sacrifice. So it is quite correct to say that neither of the two forms of the sacrifice is mentioned in ' अग्निहोत्रं जुहोति.'

तत्प्रख्यन्यायः–This maxim is based on Jaimini's sūtra ' तत्प्रख्यं चान्यशास्त्रम् (and there is another passage declaring that)' I. iv. 4, which constitutes an अधिकरण by itself. Here तत् = गुणो देवतारूपः and प्रख्यम् = वाचकम्.

In this अधिकरण with reference to the sentence ' अग्निहोत्रं जुहोति' the पूर्वपक्षिन् urges that the word अग्निहोत्रम्, explained as अग्नौ होत्रम् or अग्नये होत्रम् lays down a subordinate matter of the sacrifice viz. the deity Fire (अग्निदेवतारूपो गुणोऽनेन दर्विहोमे विधीयते). To this the सिद्धान्तिन् replies by saying that there is another injunctory passage (अन्यशास्त्रम्) viz. ' अग्निर्ज्योतिर्ज्योतिरग्निः स्वाहेति सायं जुहोति, सूर्यो ज्योतिर्ज्योतिः सूर्यः स्वाहेति प्रातः,' which declares (प्रख्य) that अग्नि and सूर्य are the deities of this rite, which is offered evening and morning. Thus, the word अग्निहोत्र in the sentence 'अग्निहोत्रं जुहोति' is merely a technical name for that rite, which is performed in honour of अग्नि and सूर्य every evening and morning.

Read ' " अग्निर्ज्योति...प्रातः" इति विहितेन मन्त्रेण प्राप्तत्वात् देवता न विधेया। ततो-ऽग्निसूर्यदेवताकस्य प्रातःसायंकालयोर्नियमेन अनुष्ठेयस्य **कर्मणः 'अग्निहोत्रम्' इति यौगिकं नामधेयम्**। योगश्च बहुव्रीहिणा दर्शितः । [अग्नौ होत्रं यस्मिन् इति]।' जैमिनियन्यायमाला-विस्तर p. 45

Section 14

This Section deals with the second kind of injunction viz. viniyoga-vidhi or the injunction of application. It consists in the conveying of the connection of a subsidiary with its principal. 'दध्ना जुहोति' is an example of a विनियोगविधि. Here the word दधि occurs in the instrumental case. The usual sense of the instrumental is करण or instrument or means and a means is subordinate to its principal. Thus, the subordinate character (अङ्गभावः) of दधि is here understood (प्रतिपन्न = ज्ञात) from the instrumental case in which the word दधि occurs. The principal with reference to दधि in the present case is होम or sacrifice, which is conveyed by जुहोति. The sentence दध्ना जुहोति thus lays down that the subordinate curds is connected with the principal sacrifice and means ultimately 'दध्ना होमं भावयेत्.'

गुणविधौ... अन्वयः— It will be remembered that in dealing with उत्पत्तिविधि the author told us that in that injunction कर्म or the sacrificial rite that is laid down is construed as the instrument (p. 11, l. 1). He now informs us that in विनियोगविधि the sacrificial rite is construed as साध्य or the thing to be accomplished. And this is quite natural. For, the purpose of a विनियोगविधि is to convey that a certain thing is subsidiary to a sacrifice. Naturally therefore, the sacrifice is here regarded as the साध्य, for which the material mentioned serves as the साधन.

गुणविधौ— The author uses the word गुणविधि as a synonym for विनियोगविधि. गुणविधि means an injunction, which lays down a subsidiary matter with reference to its principal.

धात्वर्थस्य—This represents the paraphrase of कर्मणः used above (p. 11, l. 1). The sense of the root means here the sacrifice. This paraphrase shows incidentally that the word कर्मणः, previously used, means not the grammatical object, but the sacrificial rite expressed by the root.

क्वचिदाश्रयत्वेनापि०—Bhāskara has just declared that in a विनियोगविधि or गुणविधि, the sense of the root or the sacrifice is construed as the साध्य. Now he tells us that sometimes the धात्वर्थ is construed as the abode or substratum (आश्रयः) in which the गुण or the subsidiary matter that is enjoined resides. This is explained by the following illustration :

'दध्ना इन्द्रियकामस्य जुहुयात्' is a गुणविधि, which lays down curds as the material for a sacrifice intended to secure power of senses (इन्द्रियम् इन्द्रियबलमित्यर्थः). The फल or ultimate fruit aimed at in this injunction is इन्द्रिय, even as the फल in 'ज्योतिष्टोमेन स्वर्गकामो यजेत' is स्वर्ग. Therefore, just as 'ज्योतिष्टोमेन स्वर्गकामो यजेत' means 'ज्योतिष्टोमेन स्वर्गं भावयेत्,' even so 'दध्ना इन्द्रियकामस्य जुहुयात्' means 'दध्ना इन्द्रियं भावयेत्' or 'दधिकरणत्वेन इन्द्रियं भावयेत्.'

Now, the question is: Where does this instrumentality of curds reside (तत् दधिकरणत्वं किंनिष्ठम्)? That is, how or in what way does curds become the means of producing the power of senses? It is of course not correct to say that partaking of curds at the time of our daily meals brings about this result. For, if it were so, दधिभक्षण, being रागतः प्राप्त, would not have been laid down by the Śruti. The proper answer, therefore, is that curds becomes the means of producing the power of senses, when it is used as a material for performing the sacrifice. The दधिकरणत्व thus resides in the होम. The होम or sacrifice is thought of as the आश्रय of the दधिकरणत्व, because the होम, conveyed by the word जुहुयात्, is in the neighbourhood of दधि (संनिधिप्राप्त). What is meant by this is that दधि as a means is connected with the sacrifice, because दधि occurs in the company of जुहुयात् in the sentence 'दध्ना इन्द्रियकामस्य जुहुयात्'. The ultimate meaning, obtained from the sentence under discussion, is thus 'होमाश्रयदधिकरणत्वेन होमनिष्ठदधिकरणत्वेन वा इन्द्रियं भावयेत्.'

In plain words the sentence 'दध्ना इन्द्रियकामस्य जुहुयात्' means that दधि is the instrument by which one can achieve इन्द्रिय i. e. इन्द्रियबल and that this दधि resides in the होम.

To say that दधि resides in the होम appears to us somewhat strange. We, therefore, venture to suggest another, and perhaps a better, way of understanding the sentence 'दध्ना इन्द्रियकामस्य जुहुयात्.'

Bhāskara told us that in an उत्पत्तिविधि the कर्म or धात्वर्थ is construed as करण, while in a विनियोगविधि or गुणविधि it is construed as साध्य. He further said that in some cases the धात्वर्थ is construed as आश्रय also in a गुणविधि. Instead of this we would say that in some cases the धात्वर्थ is construed as साधन or करण also in a गुणविधि and proceed to prove this as follows:

'जुहुयात् स्वर्गकामः' means 'होमेन स्वर्गं भावयेत्'. Similarly 'इन्द्रियकामस्य जुहुयात्' means 'होमेन इन्द्रियं भावयेत्'.

Now, arises the expectancy as to what kind of sacrifice is this that secures the strength of senses. That expectancy is satisfied by the word दध्ना, which means that the sacrifice is to be performed with curds as its material. Thus, the ultimate meaning we obtain from 'दध्ना इन्द्रियकामस्य जुहुयात्' is 'दधिविशिष्टेन दधिवता वा होमेन इन्द्रियं भावयेत्'. Here we find that the धात्वर्थ is construed as साधन or करण.

The word दध्ना may be understood as a case of मत्वर्थलक्षणा, or of मत्वर्थीय अच्, or simply as an उपलक्षणे तृतीया.

The general rule then that we deduce in the case of a गुणविधि is that here the धात्वर्थ is usually construed as साध्य. But in cases where along with the गुण or subsidiary matter the फल or the ultimate fruit is also mentioned, the धात्वर्थ is construed as a साधन or करण.

Thus following Bhāskara's terminology we might express ourselves as follows :

गुणविधौ च धात्वर्थस्य साध्यत्वेन अन्वयः। क्वचित् करणत्वेनापि । यथा 'दध्ना इन्द्रियकामस्य जुहुयात्' इत्यत्र 'होमेन इन्द्रियं भावयेत्' इति । तत्र च किंविशिष्टः स होमः इत्याकाङ्क्षायां संनिधिप्राप्तं दधि विशेषणत्वेन अन्वेति । तेन 'दधिविशिष्टेन होमेन इन्द्रियं भावयेत्' इति फलितम् ।

'दध्ना इन्द्रियकामस्य जुहुयात्' has evidently been quoted by our author as an instance of गुणविधि. But it appears to be an अधिकारविधि, even as 'ज्योतिष्टोमेन स्वर्गकामो यजेत' was declared to be an अधिकारविधि. 'दध्ना... जुहुयात्' is, however, something more than a mere अधिकारविधि. For, unlike 'ज्योतिष्टोमेन...यजेत' it lays down the material with which the sacrifice is to be performed. Therefore, 'दध्ना इन्द्रियकामस्य जुहुयात्' should be regarded as a mixture of गुणविधि and अधिकारविधि. Such sentences are also known as 'फलाय गुणवाक्यानि' or sentences in which subsidiaries are laid down with a view to the ultimate fruit.

Now, we can say that in all cases of the mixture of गुणविधि and अधिकारविधि, the धात्वर्थ is construed as an आश्रय, according to Bhāskara's way of interpretation, or as a साधन, according to our suggested interpretation.

Section 15

The purpose of a viniyoga-vidhi is to convey the relation of subordinate and principal i. e. to declare which is subordinate to which. In this task it is helped by six means of proof, which are श्रुति, लिङ्ग, वाक्य, प्रकरण, स्थान and समाख्या.

अङ्गत्वम् is paraphrased by परोद्देशप्रवृत्तकृतिसाध्यत्वम्. This latter is explained in three ways : (1) परम् (उत्कृष्टं साध्यं स्वर्गादिरूपम्) तस्य उद्देशेन (तत्प्राप्त्यर्थमित्यर्थः) प्रवृत्तः (क्रियावान् यः स्वर्गकामः पुरुषः), तस्य कृत्या व्यापारेण साध्यत्वं कार्यत्वम्. परम् means the highest goal viz. heaven. A man is engaged (प्रवृत्त) in the pursuit of heaven. He is, therefore, परोद्देशप्रवृत्त. His activity (कृतिः) accomplishes such rites as प्रयाज, अनुयाज, अवघात and प्रोक्षण. Consequently, such rites are known as अङ्ग or subsidiaries. They are of course subsidiary to दर्शपूर्णमास, which represents the principal sacrifice. (2) परः (नाम मुख्यः यः दर्शपूर्णमासरूपः यागः) तस्य उद्देशेन (तस्य करणार्थमित्यर्थः) प्रवृत्तः etc. Here पर is taken to mean the principal sacrifice viz. दर्शपूर्णमास. A man, who is engaged in performing this sacrifice, accomplishes प्रयाज, अनुयाज etc. These rites consequently become the subsidiaries. (3) परं (नाम स्वेतरं किंचित्, स्वर्गादिरूपमुत्कृष्टं साध्यम् दर्शपूर्णमासरूपो मुख्यो यागो वा) तस्य उद्देशेन प्रवृत्ता (प्रारब्धा अङ्गीकृता) कृतिः क्रिया तया साध्यम् तस्य भावः Here, पर just means another, other than itself, and प्रवृत्त is taken as an adjective qualifying कृति. A certain activity is undertaken with a view to स्वर्ग or दर्शपूर्णमास. That activity embraces such rites as प्रयाज and अनुयाज. These rites, therefore, become subsidiaries.

पारार्थ्य is given as a synonym of अङ्गत्वम्. पारार्थ्य signifies existence for the purpose of पर (परार्थस्य भावः) and the word पर means here one of the three things noted above. The usual sense of पारार्थ्य of course is existence for the purpose of another i. e. dependence.

Read the following from रामेश्वर is this connection: परं स्वर्गादिरूपमुत्कृष्टं साध्यं फलं तदुद्देशेन संकलनया मनसि सिद्धवत्करणेन तत्साधनयागादिषु प्रवृत्तस्य पुरुषस्य कृतिसाध्यत्वरूपकृतिव्याप्यत्वरूपत्वम् । तथा च स्वर्गफलोद्देशेन दर्शादिषु प्रवृत्तपुरुषकृतिव्याप्यत्वं प्रयाजानुयाजावघातप्रोक्षणादीनां सुप्रसिद्धमिति तेषां शेषत्वम् । यद्वा परशब्दो दर्शादिपरः । तथा च तदुद्देशेन प्रवृत्तपुरुषकृतिव्याप्यत्वं प्रयाजादीनां भवतीति तेषां तत्त्वम् । दर्शादिस्तु प्रयाजाद्युद्देशेन प्रवृत्तपुरुषकृतिव्याप्यत्वाभावान्न तत्रातिव्याप्तिः । केवलप्रयाजाद्युद्देशेन कस्याचिदपि पुरुषस्य प्रवृत्त्यभावादिति ध्येयम् ।

Section 16

श्रुति or direct statement is the first of the six means of proof, which help the applicatory injunction in deciding which is subordinate to which. श्रुति is defined as independent sound i. e. words. The emphasis is on the word निरपेक्ष or independent. We shall see later on that the other helpers of विनियोगविधि such as लिङ्ग themselves depend upon, or require the assistance of, something else in carrying out their task of rendering help to विनियोगविधि. They are thus सापेक्ष. For instance, लिङ्ग becomes a सहकारि of विनियोगविधि through श्रुति, वाक्य through लिङ्ग and श्रुति and so on. Hence, the word निरपेक्ष in the definition 'निरपेक्षो रवः श्रुतिः' serves to distinguish श्रुति from the other pramāṇas.

सा च त्रिविधा०–The word श्रुति is a synonym of वेद. The Veda is called Śruti, because the belief is that the Veda was not composed by the various seers, with whose names it is connected, but was merely heard by them from some mysterious source and in some mysterious manner.

विधात्री, अभिधात्री and विनियोक्त्री represent three broad divisions of the Śruti or Veda in general i. e. of the words, which constitute it. विधात्री श्रुतिः includes optative and other forms, occurring in Vedic sentences, which lay down something. Thus in 'ज्योतिष्टोमेन स्वर्गकामो यजेत' and 'अग्निहोत्रं जुहोति,' यजेत and जुहोति are examples of विधात्री श्रुतिः, because these optative and present forms enjoin the Jyotiṣṭoma and the Agnihotra respectively.

अभिधात्री (अभिधया स्वार्थं प्रतिपादयित्री) श्रुतिः means those words in Vedic sentences, which do not lay down anything, but merely denote or convey something e. g. the word व्रीहीन् in the sentences 'व्रीहीन् अवहन्ति' and 'व्रीहीन् प्रोक्षति'. Here व्रीहीन् merely denotes rice-grains.

विनियोक्त्री श्रुतिः comprises those words which, even as they are heard, convey the relation of the subsidiary and the principal matter. Examples of विनियोक्त्री श्रुतिः will be seen in the following Section.

Note that in the sentence 'यस्य च शब्दस्य श्रवणादेव संबन्धः प्रतीयते सा विनियोक्त्री', सा=सः (शब्दः). स शब्दो विनियोक्त्री श्रुतिरित्यर्थः. The demonstrative pronoun takes the feminine form, instead of the masculine, owing to the influence of the predicate विनियोक्त्री श्रुतिः, on the analogy of 'शैत्यं हि यत् सा (=तत् शैत्यम्) प्रकृतिर्जलस्य' रघुवंश 5.54.

It should be noted that the topic here is विनियोक्त्री श्रुतिः, as we are dealing with विनियोगविधि. Reference to विधात्री and अभिधात्री श्रुति is, therefore, somewhat irrelevant. But here, as in many other places, our author is borrowing verbatim from Āpadeva. The commentory सारविवेचनी on Āpadeva's मीमांसान्यायप्रकाश makes the following remarks on this point : 'यद्यपि अत्र विनियोगप्रस्तावे विधात्र्यभिधात्र्योः निरूपणं नातीव संगतम्, तथापि श्रुतिप्रसङ्गाद् तयोः विधिसहकारित्वाच्च तन्निरूपणमिति बोध्यम् ।'

Section 17

विनियोक्त्री श्रुतिः or applicatory direct statement is of three kinds viz. विभक्तिरूपा, एकाभिधानरूपा and एकपदरूपा. Of these विभक्तिरूपा is explained in the first three paragraphs of this Section. The last paragraph deals with the other two.

'व्रीहिभिर्यजेत' is an example, where subservience is indicated directly by means of a case. व्रीहिभिः is in the instrumental case and the sense of the instrumental is the means or instrument of accomplishing something. So the word व्रीहिभिः at once shows that rice-grains are the means with which the sacrifice is performed. Consequently, rice-grains become subservient to the sacrifice.

तदपि०—We have just seen that rice-grains are subservient to the sacrifice, because they are the material with which the sacrifice is performed. But we know that rice-grains as such are not used in the sacrifice. A sacrificial cake (पुरोडाशः पुरः देवतानामग्रे दाश्यते दीयते असौ पुरोडाशः । स एव पुरोडाशः) is prepared from the flour of rice-grains and that cake is used as an oblation in the sacrifice. So the subservience (तदपि=व्रीहीणां यागाङ्गत्वमपि) of rice-grains to the sacrifice arises from the fact that the rice-grains are the material or original substance

(प्रकृतिः) from which the sacrificial cake is prepared. Rice-grains are thus not directly (साक्षात्) subservient to the sacrifice, but indirectly (परंपरया) so, through the cake of which they are the cause.

यथा पशोः०—A parallel instance of indirect subservience is being pointed out in this sentence. 'पशुना यजेत' lays down an animal-sacrifice. The instrumental पशुना shows that the animal is a यागाङ्ग. But the animal as a whole is not sacrificed. It is killed first and portions from various parts of its body such as the heart, the tongue, the chest are cut in accordance with the instruction 'हृदयस्य अग्रे अवद्यति, अथ जिह्वायाः, अथ वक्षसोऽवद्यति, दोष्णोरवद्यति, पार्श्वयोरवद्यति' and it is these portions that are offered as oblations (हविः). As the animal forms the source (प्रकृतिः) from which these oblations, represented by portions from the heart etc. are derived, the animal itself is indirectly (परंपरया) regarded as a यागाङ्ग. Vide in this connection जै. सू. X. vii. 1–2.

It has been said above that the animal as a whole is not sacrificed but that portions, cut from various parts of its body, are offered. There is, however, an exception to this general practice viz. the पात्नीवतयाग or the sacrifice in honour of त्वष्टा, who is called पत्नीवत्, because he has many wives. This sacrifice is laid down by 'त्वाष्ट्रं पात्नीवतमालभेत'. In this after the rite of waving fire round the animal (पर्यग्निकरणम्) is performed, the whole animal, even while alive, is sacrificed.

Note 'क्वचित्तु साक्षात् पशोरेव यागाङ्गत्वम् । यथा पात्नीवतयागे । तत्र हि पशोराग्नेयस्य जीवत एवोत्सर्गः क्रियते 'पर्यग्निकृतं पात्नीवतमुत्सृजति' इति वाक्यात् ।' रामेश्वर

'अरुणया पिङ्गाक्ष्या'०–One more illustration of indirect subservience (परंपरया अङ्गत्वम्) is being given. The sentence 'अरुणया...क्रीणाति' lays down the purchase of Soma by means of a ruddy, yellow-eyed, one-year-old cow. Here, the instrumental गवा shows that a cow is subservient to the purchase of Soma. This is quite understandable, because one can barter a cow for Soma.

But the instrumental case of the other words of the sentence equally signifies that the things denoted by them are also subservient to the purchase. Thus अरुणया denotes आरुण्य or redness (अरुणाशब्दः अरुणिमानं गुणमाचष्टे ।...तस्य च अरुणिमगुणस्य तृतीयाश्रुत्या सोमक्रयसाधनत्वं प्रतीयते ।). Now, redness is an incorporeal or immaterial (अमूर्त) entity. It cannot, therefore, be an instrument of purchase directly or by itself (साक्षात्). It becomes so, however, because it defines or specifies (परिच्छेदः) the substance viz. a cow. Thus, it is क्रयाङ्ग only indirectly (परम्परया).

Read 'यद्यपि [आरुण्यम्] अमूर्तो गुणः, तथापि हायनवदक्षिवच्च गोद्रव्यमवच्छिनत्ति। तच्च द्रव्यं साधनमिति तद्द्वारा गुणस्य क्रयेण अन्वयो भवति । ... गुणस्यैवात्र तृतीयाश्रुत्या

साधनत्वमुच्यते । तच्च द्रव्यद्वारमन्तरेण न संभवतीति अर्थापत्त्या द्रव्यावच्छेदकत्वं कल्प्यते ।' जै. न्या. मा. वि. p. 113

The difference between this illustration and the two previously given should be noted. All three are cases of परंपरया अङ्गत्वम्. But while rice-grains and the animal are subservient to the sacrifice, redness is subservient to purchase. Secondly, while rice-grains and the animal are substances (द्रव्यम्), redness is a quality (द्रव्यम्). Thirdly, while rice-grains and the animal become subservient, because they form the material or source from which the principal subsidiaries viz. the cake and the portions cut, are derived (प्रधानाङ्गप्रकृतितया), redness becomes subservient, because it defines the principal subsidiary viz. the cow (प्रधानाङ्गपरिच्छेदद्वारा). And fourthly, while rice-grains and the animal are corporeal (मूर्त), redness is incorporeal (अमूर्त).

मूर्त is a term from Nyāya. It means corporeal, having a body, having limited dimensions. It is a characteristic of some of the substances. Out of the nine substances only five are corporeal viz पृथिवी, आप्, तेजस्, वायु and मनस्. मूर्तत्व is variously defined as 'परिच्छिन्नपरिमाणवत्त्वम्' (तर्कदीपिका), 'वेगवत्त्वं क्रियावत्त्वं वा' (न्यायबोधिनी), or 'इयत्तावच्छिन्नपरिमाणयोग: '. The following couplet enumerates the five corporeal substances and their characteristics : 'क्षितिर्जलं तथा तेजः पवनो मन एव च । परापरत्वमूर्तत्वक्रियावेगाश्रया अमी ।'

It will be seen from the above that मूर्तत्व can belong to substances only. Qualities and actions are अमूर्त or incorporeal.

'व्रीहीन्... श्रुत्या—' In the three illustrations given above subservience is indicated by the instrumental case. Now the author quotes an illustration where subservience is shown by the accusative.

'व्रीहीन् प्रोक्षति' lays down the sprinkling of rice-grains. The accusative व्रीहीन् shows that sprinkling is subservient to rice-grains.

Here one may ask : Why should rice-grains be not regarded as subservient to sprinkling, even as they were regarded as subservient to sacrifice in 'व्रीहिभिर्यजेत'? The answer to this is that the instrumental case invariably shows that the entity expressed by the word, which occurs in it, is subsidiary to something else. Not so the accusative, however. The accusative represents the साध्य, which is the principal. Consequently, wherever we have an applicatory accusative (विनियोक्त्री द्वितिया), the entity expressed by it is to be regarded as the principal, to which something else becomes subordinate. Hence in 'व्रीहीन् प्रोक्षति' the accusative shows that sprinkling is subservient to rice-grains.

तच्च प्रोक्षणं...अपूर्वानुत्पत्तेः—Now what is this sprinkling intended for? The sprinkling does not produce the natural form of rice-grains; for even without the sprinkling (तेन विना=तेन प्रोक्षणेन विना) rice-grains are rice-grains all right. Sprinkling produces no appreciable change in rice-grains. It has, therefore, no visible purpose. Consequently, we have to suppose that sprinkling is resorted to (प्रयुक्त) for the purpose of producing some transcendental result. The idea is only when rice-grains, which are sprinkled over with holy water, are used in a sacrifice, अपूर्व or the transcendental result follows. If they are not so sprinkled, अपूर्व does not arise.

A similar case of such अपूर्व is the following: A Brāhmana boy is to commence the study of the Veda after the उपनयन ceremony. But even if no Upanayana is performed, the Vedic study is in no way affected. Why should we then perform the Upanayana ceremony? The answer to this is that the Upanayana is intended for अपूर्व. Only an उपनयनपूर्व वेदाध्ययन produces this अपूर्व. Note 'अनुपनीतानुष्ठितवेदाध्ययनस्य अपूर्वाजनकत्ववत् व्रीहीणां प्रोक्षणं न कृत्वा तैरनुष्ठितस्य यागस्य अपूर्वाजनकत्वम्।'

एवं सर्वेषु...बोध्यम्—सर्वेषु अङ्गेषु means all subsidiaries *of a similar nature.* The idea is wherever subsidiaries are observed to produce no tangible result in their principal, their subsidiariness must be considered to have been intended for अपूर्व. Another illustration of this type is 'आज्यमवेक्षते'. Here अवेक्षण produces no visible result on the ghee. It must, therefore, be considered to have been intended for अपूर्व. Read 'यत्र दृष्टार्थता न संभवति, तादृशाङ्गेषु केवलापूर्वप्रयुक्तत्वम्। यत्र तु दृष्टार्थता, तत्र नियमापूर्वप्रयुक्तत्वमित्यर्थः।' सारविवेचनी

एवम् 'इमामगृभ्णन्...अश्वाभिधान्यङ्गत्वम्—This gives another example of subservience by the accusative. The passage has reference to the rite of building the sacrificial altar, called चयन. For this purpose bricks (इष्टका) are necessary. In order to prepare them clay is to be brought. A horse and a donkey are employed for bringing this clay. The passage 'इमाम्...आदत्ते' lays down that the mantra 'इमामगृभ्णन् रशनामृतस्य' is to be recited at the time of grasping the rein (अश्वः अभिधीयते बध्द्वा धार्यते यया रशनया सेयमश्वाभिधानी–सायण) of the horse. Thus, this mantra is subservient to the rein of the horse and this is known from the accusative case of अश्वाभिधानीम्.

This is also a case of 'अपूर्वसाधनत्वप्रयुक्तमङ्गत्वम्.' What happens is this: The priest recites 'इमामगृभ्णन् रशनामृतस्य' and grasps the rein of the horse. The recitation has no visible effect on the horse's rein which he grasps. Even if he did not recite the formula, he would be able to grasp the rein and guide the horse all right. The formula is, therefore, regarded as having been intended for producing अपूर्व.

It will be noticed that in the previous illustrations substances like rice-grains and an animal and a quality like redness were the subsidiaries. In these two examples of subservience by the accusative an action (प्रोक्षणम्) and a formula (मन्त्रः), both incorporeal (अमूर्त), become the subsidiaries.

'यदाहवनीये...श्रुत्या—This is an example where subservience is shown by the locative. The sense of the locative is अधिकरण or location or place, where something takes place. Naturally the location is subservient to that which is located on it. Here sacrifice (होमः) takes place in the Āhavanīya, which consequently is known to be subservient to the sacrifice.

आहवनीय is one of the three sacrificial fires, the other two being दक्षिण and गार्हपत्य. This fire is taken from the house-holder's perpetual fire and its place on the sacrificial altar is in the east. Read 'गार्हपत्यादाहवनीयं ज्वलन्तमुद्धरेत् । पिता वा एषोऽग्नीनां यद्दक्षिणः, पुत्रो गार्हपत्यः, पौत्र आहवनीयः' आश्वलायन; 'पिता वै गार्हपत्योऽग्निर्माताग्निर्दक्षिणः स्मृतः । गुरुराहवनीयस्तु साग्नित्रेता गरीयसी ॥' मनुस्मृति 2.231

एवमन्योऽपि...ज्ञेयः—The author has given us examples of subservience by the instrumental, the accusative and the locative. Other examples are the following : 'मैत्रावरुणाय दण्डं प्रयच्छति'—Here the dative shows that मैत्रावरुण is subservient to दण्डप्रदान. मैत्रावरुण is the name of one of the officiating priests at a sacrifice. He is the first assistant of the Hotṛ and is also called Praśāstṛ. 'मध्यात् पूर्वार्धाच्च हविषोऽवद्यति'—Here the ablative shows that हविर्मध्य and हविःपूर्व are subservient to अवदान or cutting. 'वासिष्ठानां नाराशंसः' or 'यजमानस्य याज्या'—Here the genitive indicates that Vāsiṣṭhas and Yajamāna are subservient to Nārāśaṁsa and Yājyā.

Thus, we have seen subservience indicated by the accusative, instrumental, dative, ablative, genitive and locative. It will be noticed that except in the case of the accusative, the entities expressed by words occurring in the various other cases become subservient to something else. The entities, denoted by the accusative on the other hand, are the principal to which something else stands in the relation of subservience.

'पशुना यजेत' इति...कारकाङ्क्षत्वम्—So far we saw examples of 'विभक्तिरूपा विनियोक्त्री श्रुतिः'. Now the author gives two examples of the second variety of 'विनियोक्त्री श्रुतिः' viz. एकाभिधानरूपा. It should be noted that in this paragraph Bhāskara uses the term समानाभिधान instead of एकाभिधान. Having used the term एकाभिधान at the time of classifying 'विनियोक्त्री श्रुतिः' he should have stuck to it. His paraphrase of the term by समानाभिधान only shows that he is not a very careful writer.

The following diagram will help to make the meaning of our author clear:

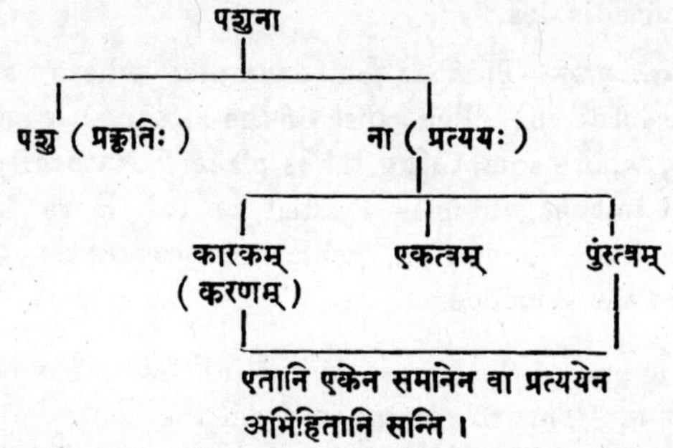

Before we proceed, the term कारक must be explained. कारक is a technical term in grammar and signifies the relation existing between a noun and a verb in a sentence. This relation is of six kinds, which belong to the first seven cases except the genitive. The genitive does not denote any special relation, but signifies relation in general (संबन्धसामान्यम्). Thus, there are six kārakas, which are enumerated in 'कर्ता कर्म च करणं संप्रदानं तथैव च । अपादानाधिकरणमित्याहुः कारकाणि षट् ॥'

'पशुना यजेत' lays down an animal sacrifice. The word पशुना is made of two elements viz. the crude form पशु and the termination ना. The termination ना signifies कारक, which in this case is करण, एकत्व and पुंस्त्व. These three are, therefore, एकाभिहित or समानाभिहित, because they are expressed by one or common element viz. the termination ना. Thus, with regard to these three there is an एकाभिधानश्रुति or समानाभिधानश्रुति, the श्रुति of course being the termination ना. This may be expressed as follows: त्रयाणां कारकैकत्वपुंस्त्वानामेकेन समानेन वा प्रत्ययेन अभिहितत्वात् तत्संबन्धिनी 'ना' इत्येतत्प्रत्ययात्मिका एकाभिधानरूपा समानाभिधानरूपा वा श्रुतिः वर्तते ।

Out of these three senses of the termination ना, कारक is the principal, because it represents the relation of the noun with the verb in the sentence. The other two viz एकत्व and पुंस्त्व are subservient to कारक and this subservience of theirs arises from एकाभिधानरूपा or समानाभिधानरूपा श्रुतिः.

'यजेत इत्याख्याता...श्रुतेरेव–This sentence gives another example of समानाभिधानश्रुत्या अङ्गत्वम्. We have seen before (p. 89 *supra*) that the suffix त in the verb यजेत expresses आख्यातत्व, लिङ्त्व, संख्या, काल and पुरुष. All these are, therefore, समानाभिहित. Thus, with reference to them there is a समानाभिधानश्रुति ('त' इत्येतत्प्रत्ययात्मिका).

Now out of these five things denoted by the suffix त, आर्थी भावना, expressed by आख्यातत्व, is the principal, because it is the साध्य of शाब्दी भावना, which is expressed by लिङ्त्व. Consequently, the other things are subordinate to आर्थी भावना. Among these संख्या is included. संख्या is, therefore, subservient to आर्थी भावना and this subservience arises from ('त' इत्येतत्प्रत्ययरूपा) समानाभिधानश्रुति.

It should be noted that Bhāskara is guilty of an inexactitude in his wording here. He speaks of आख्याताभिहितसंख्या, meaning apparently that number is expressed by verbality. But this is not correct. Number is not expressed by आख्यात, but by the suffix त. Bhāskara himself has definitely said so before ('संख्यादीनामेकप्रत्ययगम्यत्वे p. 5).

It is difficult to account for this lapse. The author should have said ''यजेत' इत्यत्र प्रत्ययाभिहितसंख्यायाः etc.' Thibaut cuts the Gordian knot by translating आख्याताभिहित by 'expressed by the verbal termination.' Our way out of the difficulty is to explain 'यजेत' इत्या...संख्यायाः as 'यजेत' इति आख्याते अभिहिता प्रत्ययाभिहिता इत्यर्थः या संख्या तस्याः.

एकपदश्रुत्या च यागाङ्गत्वम्—This sentence gives an illustration of the third variety of 'विनियोक्त्री श्रुतिः' viz. एकपदरूपा. The sentence, when properly expanded, would run as follows: 'यजेत' इत्याख्याताभिहितसंख्यायाः एकपदश्रुत्या च यागाङ्गत्वम्।

In order to understand this we must once more look to the diagram on p. 89. It will be seen from this that while आख्यात (आर्थी भावना), संख्या and others are समानाभिहित in the limited sphere of the termination त, if we look to the wider province of the word (पद) यजेत, याग (यज्धातुः) and संख्या, along with others such as आख्यात, are all एकपदाभिहित, being expressed by the one word viz. यजेत. Thus, with reference to them there is एकपदरूपा श्रुतिः or एकपदश्रुतिः. Now between याग and संख्या, याग is of course the principal, because it is the means of attaining the final end viz. heaven. संख्या is thus subservient to याग on account of एकपदश्रुति.

If we apply the same reasoning to एकत्व and पुंस्त्व of the previous illustration, we can say that while एकत्व and पुंस्त्व are कारकाङ्ग by समानाभिधान श्रुति, they are पश्वङ्ग or पशुद्रव्याङ्ग by एकपदश्रुति. Further, एकत्व and पुंस्त्व become यागाङ्ग through पशु. All this may be expressed as follows: 'पशुना यजेत' इत्यत्र एकत्वपुंस्त्वयोः समानाभिधानश्रुत्या कारकाङ्गत्वम्। तयोरेव

एकत्वपुंस्त्वयोः एकपदश्रुत्या पशुद्रव्याङ्गत्वं भवति । एकत्वपुंस्त्वयोः यागाङ्गत्वं तु पशुद्वारेण, न तु एकपदश्रुत्या । एकेन 'पशुना' इति पदेन यागस्यापि अनभिहितत्वात् ।

The distinction between एकाभिधानश्रुति or समानाभिधानश्रुति and एकपदश्रुति should be clearly understood. In एकाभिधानश्रुति or समानाभिधानश्रुति one element of a word, which has more than one element, denotes two or more things between which the relation of principal and subsidiaries exists. In एकपदश्रुति on the other hand one word, or पद in the grammatical sense of that term, expresses two or more things, which are related to one another as principal and subordinates. एकाभिधान or समानाभिधान looks on the face of it more general than एकपदाभिधान. As a matter fact it is more restricted.

Section 18

न च अमूर्तया...तदुपपत्तेः--It has been declared above that संख्या or number is subsidiary to भावना by समानाभिधानश्रुति and to याग by एकपदश्रुति. Here a doubt arises. संख्या is a गुण and as such is incorporeal (अमूर्त). How can it then be subsidiary to भावना and याग ('भावनाङ्गत्वम्' इत्यत्र भावनाशब्दो यागमपि उपलक्षयति) ?

The reply to such doubt had already been given, when the author discussed the sentence 'अरुणया पिङ्गाक्ष्या etc'. There it was pointed out that the quality redness became subsidiary to purchase owing to its defining the substance viz. the cow. Similarly, in the present case संख्या becomes subsidiary to भावना and याग on account of its defining the agent (कर्तृपरिच्छेदः) of that भावना and that याग. What is meant is that in the sentence 'पशुना यजेत', the word यजेत shows that the agent of that action is one.

कर्ता च...आक्षिपति—संख्या was declared to be subsidiary to भावना, because it defined the agent. But one may ask : Where does the agent come in here from ? यजेत is made of यज्धातु and the suffix त, which consists of आख्यातत्व and लिङ्त्व But none of these, viz. यज्धातु, आख्यातत्व and लिङ्त्व, expresses कर्ता. How can संख्या then define the agent?

The answer to this is that the agent is understood by implication (आक्षेपलभ्यः । आक्षेपः अनुमानमर्थापत्तिर्वा । तेन लभ्योऽनुमेयः कल्प्यो वा). The element आख्यात expresses (आर्थी) भावना. भावना is an activity (mental) and no activity is possible without an agent. Thus an agent is implied.

The passage 'कर्ता च...आक्षिपति' is really directed against the grammarians, who hold that आख्यात *expresses* the कर्ता or agent. As against them the Mīmāṁsakas believe that आख्यात *expresses* भावना and that the कर्ता is merely *implied* therefrom.

Section 19

In Section 15 above six pramāṇas are enumerated as helpers of the injunction of application viz. श्रुति, लिङ्ग, वाक्य, प्रकरण, स्थान and समाख्या. The order of their enumeration is significant. In this series each subsequent pramāṇa is weaker or less powerful than the preceding. Thus, लिङ्ग is less powerful than श्रुति, वाक्य less powerful than श्रुति and लिङ्ग, प्रकरण less powerful than श्रुति, लिङ्ग and वाक्य and so on. To put this the other way round one can say that श्रुति is stronger than लिङ्ग and others, लिङ्ग stronger than वाक्य and others, वाक्य stronger than प्रकरण and others.

The reason for this comparative strength of the six pramāṇas is this : The object of all of them is to convey विनियोग or application. श्रुति conveys this application directly and independently without the help of any other pramāṇa. The other pramāṇas on the other hand require the help of the preceding pramāṇa or pramāṇas to denote the application. Thus, लिङ्ग denotes the application through श्रुति, वाक्य through लिङ्ग and श्रुति, प्रकरण through वाक्य, लिङ्ग and श्रुति and so on. Examples to illustrate all this are given by the author below.

The question of the comparative strength of the pramāṇas arises when two or more of them become available together (समवाये) in any particular case. And this question is decided on the ground of the distance which separates them from their final goal viz. the application (अर्थविप्रकर्षात् अर्थात् विनियोगरूपात् प्रयोजनात् विप्रकर्षः दूरस्थत्वं तस्मात्). The greater the distance that separates a pramāṇa from the application, the weaker it is.

Jaimini has expressed all this in his sūtra ‘ श्रुतिलिङ्गवाक्यप्रकरणस्थान-समाख्यानां समवाये पारदौर्बल्यम् अर्थविप्रकर्षात् ’ III. iii. 14.

In this Section 19 Bhāskara tells us that श्रुति is more powerful than लिङ्ग and others, gives reason for this greater strength of श्रुति and quotes an illustration to show how श्रुति is more powerful than लिङ्ग. He does the same in the case of the other pramāṇas as well.

This is fundamentally an unsystematic procedure. We have learnt so far what श्रुति is. We have yet to know the nature of लिङ्ग. How then shall we be able to understand the superiority of श्रुति to लिङ्ग ? The correct procedure for the author to follow would have been to tell us at the end of his treatment of लिङ्ग, ‘ तदिदं लिङ्गं श्रुतेर्दुर्बलम् ’, and give the illustration, which proves the superiority of श्रुति to लिङ्ग. Or, he should have reserved the question of the comparative strength of the pramāṇas till he finished with their treatment. But here also our author is merely adopting Āpadeva almost varbatim.

Jaimini is quite systematic, however. His sūtra 'श्रुतिलिङ्ग... विप्रकर्षात्' comes after his treatment of application by all the pramāṇas.

सेयं श्रुतिः... व्याहतत्वात्—In this passage Bhāskara tells us that श्रुति is stronger than लिङ्ग and others and gives the reason for this greater strength of श्रुति.

विनियोग requires some direct applicatory word such as we have in श्रुति. Such word is absent in लिङ्ग and others. We have, therefore, to presume or imagine it in their case. But by the time we imagine this प्रत्यक्ष विनियोजक शब्द in the case of लिङ्ग and others, श्रुति will have already pointed out the विनियोग and rendered null and void (व्याहत) the power of presumption (कल्पकत्वशक्तिः) of लिङ्गादि. For, when विनियोग is conveyed by श्रुति, the कल्पकत्वशक्ति by which the प्रत्यक्ष विनियोजक शब्द is presumed by लिङ्गादि has no occasion for functioning. श्रुति is, therefore, stronger than लिङ्गादि. What is meant is that श्रुति conveys the विनियोग directly and independently. लिङ्गादि require the help of प्रत्यक्ष विनियोजक शब्द i. e. श्रुति. Hence, they are inferior to श्रुति.

अत एव ऐन्द्र्या...स्थानार्थम्—This gives an illustration to prove that श्रुति is more powerful than लिङ्ग.

'कदाचन स्तरीरसि नेन्द्र सश्चसि दाशुषे' is one half of a Ṛgvedic stanza (viii. 51. 7). Its meaning is : भो इन्द्र, कदाचन स्तरीः (barren, harmful) न असि कदापि घातको न भवासि । किन्तु दाशुषे आहुतिं दत्तवते यजमानाय सश्चसि (cling to, be pleased with) प्रीयसे ।

Now, let us try to determine the विनियोग of this stanza by means of लिङ्ग. First, then, we find out what the stanza means. Secondly, we must see what the power of the words in the stanza indicates. Now, there is the word इन्द्र in this stanza. Its power shows that the stanza is ऐन्द्री or addressed to Indra. This means the stanza is to be used in some rite where Indra is the principal deity. We do not know what this rite is. Therefore, thirdly, we imagine a Śruti passage such as 'अनेन मन्त्रेण इन्द्रमुपतिष्ठते'. Fourthly, this imagined Śruti passage gives us the viniyoga or application of the stanza viz. in the upasthāna or the rite of waiting upon or reverencing Indra.

The determination of application by लिङ्ग thus involves four stages viz. (1) स्वाभिधेयप्रतिपादन, (2) सामर्थ्यनिरूपण, (3) श्रुतिकल्पना and (4) विनियोग. It will be seen that in this process the कल्पकत्वशक्ति of लिङ्ग is exercised. On account of this power of imagination the passage 'अनेन मन्त्रेण इन्द्रमुपतिष्ठते' is presumed and the application of the stanza is determined.

But it is not necessary to take all this trouble in the case of the stanza 'कदाचन स्तरी...दाशुषे.' For, with reference to this stanza we have a real, not an imaginary, Śruti passage viz. 'ऐन्द्र्या गार्हपत्यमुपतिष्ठते.', which means '' कदाचन स्तरीरासि ' इत्यनया इन्द्रप्रकाशिकया ऋचा गार्हपत्यसंज्ञकमग्निमुपतिष्ठते पूजयति '. Here the accusative गार्हपत्यम् directly and independently lays down that the particular ऐन्द्री stanza is to be used for गार्हपत्योपस्थान.

Thus, in this determination of application by श्रुति (' गार्हपत्यामिति द्वितीयाश्रुत्या ') there are only two stages viz. (1) स्वाभिधेयप्रतिपादन and (2) विनियोग.

The position now is this : लैङ्गिक विनियोग shows that the stanza ' कदाचन ..दाशुषे ' is to be used for इन्द्रोपस्थान. श्रौत विनियोग on the other hand signifies that it is to be employed for गार्हपत्योपस्थान. Now, as श्रुति is more powerful than लिङ्ग, it stultifies (बाधयति) लिङ्ग and the final decision in the matter, therefore, is that the stanza ' कदाचन...दाशुषे ' is to be utilized for गार्हपत्योपस्थान.

The above explanation of the लैङ्गिक and श्रौत विनियोग with reference to ' कदाचन...दाशुषे ' must have made it quite clear how श्रुति is more powerful than लिङ्ग. In the case of श्रुति, स्वाभिधेयप्रतिपादन at once leads to विनियोग. But in the case of लिङ्ग, two intermediate stages are necessary. That is exactly why लिङ्ग is weaker than श्रुति.

Read in this connection ' श्रुतिराशु विनियुङ्क्ते । लिङ्गं तु विलम्बेन विनियुङ्क्ते । तथा हि । तत्र प्रथमं मन्त्रपदानि स्वाभिधेयार्थं प्रतिपादयन्ति, तत ऊर्ध्वं मन्त्रस्य वस्तुप्रकाशनसामर्थ्यं निरूप्यते, तत ऊर्ध्वं च तत्सामर्थ्यवशात् साधनत्ववाचिनी प्रधानत्ववाचिनी च श्रुतिः कल्प्यते । कल्पिता च श्रुतिः पश्चात् ' एन्द्रमन्त्रेण इन्द्रमुपतिष्ठेत ' इति विनियुङ्क्ते इति मन्त्रपदाभिधेयप्रतिपादनविनियोगयोर्मध्यवर्तिनौ सामर्थ्यनिरूपणश्रुतिकल्पनव्यापारौ भवतः । प्रत्यक्षश्रुतिविनियोगपक्षे तु मन्त्रपदाभिधेयप्रतिपादनमात्रेण तस्या विनियोजकत्वसंभवात् न तौ मध्यवर्तिनौ व्यापारौ भवतः इति श्रुतेः प्राबल्यात् तया लिङ्गं बाध्यते । ' रामेश्वर

लिङ्गादिभ्यः प्रबला—Bhāskara says here that श्रुति is more powerful than लिङ्ग *and others.* But the example that he has quoted shows that श्रुति is stronger than लिङ्ग only. He does not definitely establish the superiority of श्रुति to the others viz. वाक्य, प्रकरण etc. This is because he will tell us later on that लिङ्ग is more powerful than वाक्य, प्रकरण etc. If then श्रुति is shown to be stronger than लिङ्ग, it naturally follows that it is stronger than the others, which are weaker than श्रुति.

This procedure is according to what is known as the प्रधानमल्लनिबर्हणन्याय or the maxim of the defeat or demolition of the principal wrestler. If one defeats the प्रधानमल्ल, one is as good as having defeated all others, who are inferior to the प्रधानमल्ल.

This maxim is followed in modern days in arranging sports. The champion in a tennis tournament, for example, is he who defeats the competitor, who has come up to the final. Though the champion does not defeat all other competitors individually, he is supposed to have done so, because he defeats the most powerful.

Bhāskara follows the same procedure in the case of the other pramāṇas, as will be seen from below. Thus in Section 21 *infra* he says that लिङ्ग is more powerful than वाक्य *and others,* but establishes the superiority of लिङ्ग to वाक्य only. Similarly, in Section 24 he remarks that वाक्य is stronger than प्रकरण *and others,* but actually proves that it is superior to प्रकरण only.

It has been decided above that on account of the द्वितीया श्रुति in 'ऐन्द्र्या गार्हपत्यमुपतिष्ठते' the stanza 'कदाचन...दाशुषे' is to be employed for गार्हपत्योपस्थान. But one may here naturally ask: 'How can the word इन्द्र in the stanza be made applicable to the Gārhapatya fire?' The answer to this is that it is true the word इन्द्र primarily signifies the god of that name, but secondarily it can go with गार्हपत्य in the sense of 'supreme' or 'sovereign.' This represents the literal sense of the word इन्द्र, which is derived from the root इद् to be of supreme power (इदि परमैश्वर्ये). The word ऐन्द्र्या in 'ऐन्द्र्या गार्हपत्यमुपतिष्ठते' thus really means a stanza, which appears to belong to Indra.

Read 'गार्हपत्योपस्थाने विनियुज्यमानो मन्त्रोऽर्थं प्रकाशयन् मुख्यमिन्द्रं प्रकाशयति। मुख्यश्चेन्द्रः स्वर्गाधिपतिः सहस्राक्षः, तत्र इन्द्रशब्दस्य रूढत्वात्। गौणस्तु इन्द्रो गार्हपत्यः। तस्य ऐश्वर्यगुणयोगेन यज्ञसाधनत्वेन वा मुख्येन्द्रसदृशत्वात्।' जैमिनीयन्यायमालाविस्तर pp. 122-123

The question of the comparative strength of pramāṇas arises, when two of them become available (प्राप्त) simultaneously (समवाये). One of them is then stultified (बाधित) and the other conveys the correct application. But in the present case there is no conflict between श्रुति and लिङ्ग at all. For, the direct statement in 'ऐन्द्र्या गार्हपत्यमुपतिष्ठते' at once lays down that the stanza 'कदाचन...दाशुषे' is to be employed in गार्हपत्योपस्थान. There is no opportunity or occasion for लिङ्ग to function in this case. How is it then that our author gives this ऐन्द्री ऋक्, as an illustration, where लिङ्ग is stultified (बाधित) by श्रुति, which consequently gives the correct application?

The answer to this is that stultification is of two kinds viz. stultification of something, which has actually accrued (प्राप्तबाधः), and stultification of something, which has not actually accrued (अप्राप्तबाधः), but is possible. The present is a case of the latter kind of stultification. With reference to the present ऐन्द्री ऋक् it is possible for some

one to regard it as subservient to इन्द्रोपस्थान on account of the इन्द्रलिङ्ग present therein. This possibility is set aside by the passage 'ऐन्द्र्या गार्हपत्यमुपतिष्ठते.'

Section 20

लिङ्ग is the next pramāṇa, which helps the injunction of application. Etymologically the word is explained as 'लिङ्ग्यते ज्ञायते विनियोगः अनेन तत् लिङ्गम्.'

लिङ्ग is defined as the power of words to denote something. For this definition Bhāskara cites the authority of Kumārilabhaṭṭa from whose Tantravārtika the line 'सामर्थ्यं सर्वशब्दानां लिङ्गमित्यभिधीयते' is quoted. Power is nothing but convention. So the pramāṇa लिङ्ग consists in the conventional meaning of a word, the meaning which is expressed by अभिधा.

It is pointed out that the word शब्द in the definition 'शब्दसामर्थ्यं लिङ्गम्' is significant. For, if we were to define लिङ्गम् as 'सामर्थ्यं लिङ्गम्.' any power such as that of a seed to develop into a sprout would fall within the province of लिङ्ग. Read 'लिङ्गमिति लक्ष्यनिर्देशः । सामर्थ्यं लिङ्गमित्युक्ते अङ्कुरादिजननानुकूलबीजादिसामर्थ्ये तत्प्रसङ्गः स्यात्, तद्वारणाय शब्देति विशेषणम् ।' रामेश्वर

We have seen above (p. 76) that words have three powers (शक्तयः) viz. अभिधा, लक्षणा and व्यञ्जना. By equating सामर्थ्य with रूढि **Bhāskara** shows that the Mīmāṁsakas restrict the word सामर्थ्य or शक्ति **to** only one of these powers viz. अभिधा, which expresses the conventional meaning.

तेन समाख्यातो...भिन्नत्वात्—By means of these two sentences Bhāskara distinguishes लिङ्ग from समाख्या, which is the last of these prāmaṇas. The first sentence just points out that because सामर्थ्य is equal to रूढि, therefore it is distinguished from समाख्या. The second makes this distinction clear by pointing out the nature of समाख्या and रूढि.

Words are of three kinds viz. यौगिक or etymological, रूढ or conventional and योगरूढ or यौगिकरूढ or etymologico-conventional.

यौगिक words are those that convey a meaning, which is the same as is denoted by their individual etymological constituents (अवयवशक्त्या अर्थप्रतिपादकाः). यौगिक words, in short, convey their literal or etymological sense. योगः means etymology (निरुक्तिः निर्वचनं वा). पाचकः, हारकः, **कारकः and** लावकः are examples of यौगिक words, because they all signify **a meaning,** which is the same as is denoted by their respective root **and the termination** अक, which is कर्तृवाचक. पाचकः thus means one **who cooks** and so on.

रूढ words are those that convey their meaning without reference to etymology. गौः, अश्वः, पुरुषः, and हस्ती are words of this type. They convey the senses of bull, horse, man and elephant, not because etymology warrants them, but because a general convention that these words should have these senses exists in society from the beginning of language. Such words thus convey their meaning, not by the power of their etymological constituents taken individually, but by the power of their constituents taken as a whole (समुदायशक्त्या अर्थप्रतिपादकाः).

योगरूढ or यौगिकरूढ words are those that denote a sense, which is both etymological and conventional. पङ्कजम् and नीरजम् are examples of such words. Literally they signify mud-born and water-born. But not all those that are mud-born and water-born are denoted by those words. A frog and a fish are respectively mud-born and water-born. But the words पङ्कज and नीरज are not applicable to them. These words mean a lotus. As a lotus is mud-born and water-born, पङ्कज and. नीरज are यौगिक words. Then again as these words are restricted to only one of the many things that are mud-born and water-born, they partake of the characteristics of रूढ words as well. गिरिजा may be regarded as another example of a योगरूढ word. It means born of a mountain. Not all things that are born of a mountain are called गिरिजा. A stone (दृषद् *f.*) is born of a mountain. But it is not called गिरिजा. Only Pārvatī, who is a daughter of the mountain Hīmālaya, is known by that epithet.

According as ·words are of three kinds, even so the senses conveyed by them are known as यौगिकार्थ, रूढार्थ and योगरूढार्थ.

Now, समाख्या means a यौगिक शब्द or a word used in its etymological sense, while लिङ्ग is a रूढ शब्द or a word used in its conventional sense. The two, therefore, are easily distinguished.

अस्याः = अस्याः रूढेः, सामर्थ्यस्य लिङ्गस्य इति यावत्. यौगिकशब्दसमाख्यातः = यौगिकशब्दरूपा समाख्या (मध्यमपदलोपी समासः) तस्याः.

तेन ' बर्हिर्देवसदनं...समर्थत्वात्—These two sentences illustrate ' लिङ्गाद् विनियोगः.' Here we have the sentence ' बर्हिर्देवसदनं दामि (I cut the grass, the seat of the gods).' Now, we want to know what the विनियोग of this sentence is. We have, therefore, to go through all the four stages mentioned before (p. 122). Thus, first, we find out what the meaning of this sentence is. This is स्वाभिधेयप्रतिपादन. Then we go to सामर्थ्यनिरूपण The power of the word दामि shows that this mantra is to be used in cutting. What is it in cutting which this mantra is to be employed?

The answer is बर्हिस्. Now, the word बर्हिस् primarily denotes the Kuśa-grass by means of लिङ्ग, सामर्थ्य, रूढि or अभिधा. Secondarily बर्हिस् indicates some other kinds of grass such as उलप, that resemble बर्हिस्. The लिङ्ग in बर्हिर्दामि, however, restricts the employment of the sentence to कुशलवन. The mantra, therefore, must not be used for उलपादिलवन. This finishes सामर्थ्यनिरूपण. Then we go to श्रुतिकल्पना. Having decided that the sentence 'बर्हि...दामि' is subservient to the cutting of the Kuśa grass, we try to see if there is any Śruti to that effect. We find there is none. So we presume some such Śruti as 'अनेन मन्त्रेण कुशलवनं कर्तव्यम्.' This is श्रुतिकल्पना. Lastly, this कल्पित श्रुति gives us the विनियोग viz. अस्य मन्त्रस्य कुशलवनाङ्गत्वम्.

It will thus be seen that in conveying the विनियोग, लिङ्ग requires the help of Śruti.

Read ' 'बर्हिर्देवसदनं दामि' इति लवनप्रकाशको मन्त्र आम्नातः । तत्र लवनप्रकाशनसामर्थ्यलक्षणेन लिङ्गेन अयं मन्त्रो लवनक्रियायां विनियुज्यते । लवितव्यं च बर्हिर्द्विविधम् । मुख्यं गौणं च । मुख्यं कुशकाशादिदशविधदर्भरूपम् । गौणं तु तत्सदृशं तृणान्तरम् । तस्मिन् बर्हिःशब्दस्य माणवके अग्निशब्दवत् गुणयोगेन प्रवृत्तत्वात् । तथा सति मुख्यवद् गौणस्यापि शब्दार्थत्वेन दर्भस्य तृणान्तरस्य च लवने मन्त्रविनियोगः—इति प्राप्ते—

ब्रूमः । मुख्यस्य शीघ्रप्रतीतत्वेन मुख्ये मन्त्रं विनियुज्य चरितार्थं लिङ्गं विलम्बप्रतीततया गौणप्रतीक्षां न करोति । तस्मात् मुख्यस्यैव लवने मन्त्रो नियम्यते ।' जैमिनीयन्यायमालाविस्तर p. 122

एवमन्यत्रापि...द्रष्टव्यः–Another case of लैङ्गिक विनियोग is the following: 'अग्नये जुष्टं निर्वपामि (I present the desired offering to Fire)' is a sentence the application of which we want to understand. The power of the word निर्वपामि shows that the sentence is to be employed in presenting the particular offering to Fire. 'अनेन मन्त्रेण निर्वापः कर्तव्यः' is the Śruti that we then presume and this कल्पित श्रुति gives us the विनियोग viz. 'अस्य मन्त्रस्य निर्वापाङ्गत्वम्.'

Section 21

This Section tells us that लिङ्ग is stronger than वाक्य and others and quotes an example to prove how लिङ्ग prevails against वाक्य, when both of them become available in one passage.

The relevant passage runs as follows: 'स्योनं ते सदनं कृणोमि, घृतस्य धारया सुशेवं कल्पयामि । तस्मिन् सीद, अमृते प्रतितिष्ठ व्रीहीणां मेध, सुमनस्यमानः ।'

This is thus commented upon: 'भोः पुरोडाश, ते तव स्योनं समीचीनं सदनं स्थानमासनमित्यर्थः कृणोमि करोमि । तच्चासनं घृतस्य धारया सुशेवं सुष्ठु सेवितुं योग्यं कल्पयामि । भो व्रीहीणां मेध व्रीहिसारभूत, त्वं सुमनस्यमानः समाहितमनस्कः सन् तस्मिन् अमृते समीचीने स्थाने सीद उपविश । प्रतितिष्ठ तत्र स्थिरो भव ।'

स्योन सदनम् a pleasant seat. सुशेवम् agreeable or lovely. मेधः sap, pith, essence.

Now, the demonstrative pronoun तस्मिन् occurring at the commencement of the second half of this passage shows that the two halves form one complete sentence. Consequently, from the वाक्यप्रमाण we learn that this whole sentence, made of the two halves, must be used in some rite or rites. लिङ्ग, or the power of words, shows that the first half refers to the rite of सदनकरण and the second to that of पुरोडाशस्थापन. The वाक्यप्रमाण would then lay down that this whole mantra is to be used either for सदनकरण or for पुरोडाशस्थापन or for both. Some such Śrutis as 'सर्वेण अनेन मन्त्रेण सदनं कर्तव्यम्' and 'सर्वेण अनेन मन्त्रेण तत्र पुरोडाशः स्थापनीयः' will, therefore, have to be presumed. After this the विनियोग would follow. Thus in understanding the विनियोग by means of वाक्यप्रमाण, we have to go through these three stages viz. (1) वाक्य, (2) लिङ्ग and (3) श्रुति.

If we follow this विनियोग by means of वाक्यप्रमाण, what happens is this: The first half, which has nothing to do with पुरोडाशस्थापन, will have to be used for that rite. Similarly, the second half, which has nothing to do with सदनकरण, will have to be employed at the time of preparing the seat. In order to avoid this undesirable contingency लिङ्ग steps in and rules that the first half, which by means of the सामर्थ्य of the words 'सदनं कृणोमि' is known to refer to सदनकरण, is to be employed for that rite i. e. is पुरोडाशसदनकरणाङ्ग. Similarly, the second half, लिङ्ग would further lay down, which is understood to refer to पुरोडाशस्थापन from the सामर्थ्य of the words 'तस्मिन् सीद...प्रतितिष्ठ,' is to be used for that rite. The requisite Śrutis such as ''स्योनं ते सदनं कृणोमि' इत्यनेन मन्त्रेण सदनं कर्तव्यम्' and ''तस्मिन् सीद' इत्यनेन मन्त्रेण पुरोडाशः स्थापनीयः' will then be imagined and they will give the विनियोग, finally. It will thus be seen that in this लैङ्गिक विनियोग there are only two steps viz. (1) लिङ्ग and (2) श्रुति. वाक्य, as we saw before, involves three steps and is consequently removed further from विनियोग to that extent (अर्थविप्रकर्षः). वाक्य is, therefore, weaker than लिङ्ग.

Read 'ततश्च लिङ्गकल्पनव्यवधानेन वाक्यं श्रुतिं प्रति विप्रकृष्यते । प्रत्यक्षं तु लिङ्गद्वयं तां श्रुतिं प्रति न विप्रकृष्यते । तथा सति लिङ्गेन वाक्यस्य बाधात् मन्त्रस्य अर्धद्वयं सदनकरणपुरोडाशस्थापनयोर्व्यवस्थितम् ।' रामेश्वर

'[अस्मिन् मन्त्रे] पूर्वार्धं सदनं प्रकाशयति, उत्तरार्धं तु सादनम् । यद्यपि 'तस्मिन्' इति उत्तरार्धस्थतच्छब्दस्य पूर्वार्धसापेक्षत्वात् एकवाक्यत्वं परिकल्प्यते तदा उभयोरेकवाक्यत्वात् उभयोरपि अर्धयोः सदने सादने उभयत्र वा विनियोगः स्यात् । तद् बाधित्वा लिङ्गेन पूर्वार्धस्य सदनाङ्गत्वमेव ।' सारविवेचनी on आपदेव

न तु वाक्यात्—The idea is the mantra 'स्योनं ते सदनं कृणोमि' is to be पुरोडाशसदनकरणाङ्ग on account of लिङ्ग and not on account of वाक्य. For, if वाक्य were to make the mantra पुरोडाशसदनकरणाङ्ग, it would make the whole of the mantra, consisting of the two halves, so subservient to पुरोडाशसदनकरण, and not merely the first half thereof. This is undesirable, as we have seen. Therefore, the विनियोग here must be understood to be due to लिङ्ग.

Section 22

वाक्य is the third pramāṇa. It is defined as समभिव्याहारः (from सम् + अभि + वि + आ + हृ) or connected utterance. The idea, suggested by the word समभिव्याहार, or सहोच्चारण by which it is paraphrased in the next sentence, is the same as is conveyed by the word आसत्ति in विश्वनाथ's definition of a वाक्य as 'वाक्यं स्यात् योग्यताकाङ्क्षासत्तियुक्तः पदोच्चयः' साहित्यदर्पण ii. 1, or by the word संनिधि in केशवमिश्र's 'वाक्यं तु आकाङ्क्षायोग्यतासंनिधिमतां पदानां समूहः' तर्कभाषा. And that idea is that the various words, which constitute a sentence, must be uttered in a connected manner and must not be separated by any very great interval of time. 'पर्णमयी जुहूः' is an example of वाक्य given below. But if we were to utter the word पर्णमयी to-day and the word जुहूः to-morrow, the two would not constitute a sentence. This is the significance of the preposition सम् in समभिव्याहार, or the particle सह in सहोच्चारण.

समभिव्याहारश्च...सहोच्चारणम्—This gives the definition of समभिव्याहार and the definition has purposely been so framed as to suit the particular example of वाक्य, quoted below, viz. पर्णमयी जुहूः. समभिव्याहार means utterance together of two words, which express a subsidiary (शेषः) and a principal (शेषी), which are really so (वस्तुतः). In the sentence 'यस्य पर्णमयी...शृणोति', the two words पर्णमयी and जुहूः are uttered together. Of these पर्णमयी is शेषवाचक and जुहूः is शेषिवाचक. Therefore, on account of वाक्य or connected utterance पर्णता becomes subservient to जुहूः.

पर्णमयी means made of parṇa–or palāśa–wood (पलाशवृक्षनिर्मिता) Note 'पलाशः किंशुकः पर्णो याज्ञियो रक्तपुष्पकः'. जुहूः (हूयते अनया) means a ladle. श्लोकः (from श्लोक् श्लोकते to praise) means praise. पापं श्लोकम् means evil praise i. e. infamy. The idea in the sentence 'यस्य... शृणोति' is that he, who uses a ladle made of palāśa-wood becomes famous. The sentence thus lays down the material parṇa for the ladle. पर्णता or being-made-of-parṇa hence becomes subsidiary to the ladle.

साध्यत्वादिवाचकद्वितीयाद्यभावेऽपि—This part of the definition of समभिव्याहार we have so far left out. Its propriety is as follows: In an ordinary sentence such as 'कुम्भकारः मृत्तिकया घटं करोति,' there are words in various cases. Thus, घटम् is in the accusative, which expresses the साध्य or the thing to be accomplished. The accusative shows that what the potter wants to produce is the jar. Then, again the instrumental मृत्तिकया shows the साधन or the means or material out of which the jar is to be fashioned.

But the वाक्यप्रमाण of the Mīmāṁsakas does not always require words in the accusative etc. to be in it. 'पर्णमयी जुहूः' is a case of a वाक्य, according to the Mīmāṁsakas. And this sentence does not possess any word in the accusative, which would express the साध्य. The expression साध्यत्वादि...द्यभावेऽपि shows that वाक्य, according to the Mīmāṁsakas, is possible even in the absence of words in the accusative etc.

The force of अपि in ०द्यभावेऽपि is this : For the वाक्य of the Mīmāṁsakas it is not absolutely necessary that there should be साध्यत्वादिवाचकद्वितीयाद्यभाव. The Mīmāṁsaka वाक्य is possible, also when words in the accusative etc. are present in it. For example, in the last section we have seen that the passage 'स्योनं ते सदनं कृणोमि etc' is an example of वाक्य and it is possessed of words in the accusative. अपि thus shows that words in the accusative etc. are not necessary for वाक्य. The वाक्य of the Mīmāṁsakas is possible even in their absence, as it is when they are present.

It must be remarked that Bhāskara's definition of वाक्य is not satisfactory. The two examples of वाक्य that we know from this and the preceding Section are 'पर्णमयी जुहूः' and 'स्योनं ते सदनम् etc.' Bhāskara should have framed his definition in such a way as to include both these examples. But he seems to have only 'पर्णमयी जुहूः' before him, when he prepared his definition.

Then, again, the word वस्तुतः in the definition is superfluous. It serves no purpose at all. The dual in शेषशेषिवाचकपदयोः, though necessary when we have only 'पर्णमयी जुहूः' in view, must be pronounced as non-significant (द्वित्वमविवक्षितम्). For, in the other illustration of वाक्य viz. the passage 'स्योनं ते सदनं कृणोमि etc.' there is the utterance together of several words and not merely of two.

न चानर्थक्यम्०—This paragraph discusses a new topic viz. the sacrificial necessity of पर्णता for the ladle.

We have seen above that the sentence 'यस्य पर्णमयी...शृणोति' lays down that the ladle should be made of parṇa-wood. But one may urge it is useless to enjoin parṇa-wood for the ladle (आनर्थक्यं पर्णतायाः

आनर्थक्यमित्यर्थः). For, the ladle can be prepared from any other wood also and such ladle will serve the purpose which the parṇa-ladle serves, equally well. What is then the propriety of laying down the being-made-of-parṇa-wood for the ladle ?

The answer to this is that the word जुहूः in 'पर्णमयी जुहूः' indicates the transcendental result or the not-existent-before (अपूर्वम्), which is to be accomplished by means of a parṇa-ladle. What is meant is this : As no visible purpose can be assigned for the injunction that the ladle should be made of parṇa-wood, an invisible purpose (अदृष्टार्थः) viz. the apūrva is presumed therefor. Such apūrva will arise only when the sacrificer uses a parṇa-ladle, not otherwise. Hence, the injunction about पर्णता is not useless.

तत् in 'जुहूशब्देन तत्साध्यापूर्वलक्षणात्' means पर्णमयी जुहूः. तया पर्णमय्या जुह्वा साध्यं यत् अपूर्वं तत् जुहूशब्दो लक्षयति.

Thus, the correct Mīmāṁsist meaning of the injunction contained in 'यस्य पर्णमयी...शृणोति' is 'पर्णतया अवत्तहविर्धारणद्वारा जुह्वपूर्वं भावयेत्.' अवत्त means cut, from अव + दो द्यति to cut or divide.

अवत्तहविर्धारण...पर्णतापत्तेः—Bhāskara here points out that the expression अवत्तहविर्धारणद्वारा (through the holding of the cut oblation) is necessary in the ultimate meaning derived from the sentence 'यस्य ...शृणोति.' For, otherwise पर्णता would become necessary for स्रुव and others also.

What is meant is this: The word जुहूः in its etymological sense viz. हूयते अनया may signify स्रुव, स्रुच्, उपभृत् and ध्रुवा, which are some other kinds of ladle or spoon used in sacrifices. From the sentence 'यस्य पर्णमयी जुहूर्भवति' पर्णता would accrue to all these kinds of ladle viz. जुहू, स्रुव and others, because etymologically speaking they are all included in 'जुहूः'. But the expression अवत्तहविर्धारणद्वारा restricts पर्णता to जुहू only. For, out of these five kinds of ladle only जुहू is used for holding the oblation, which has been cut by means of the अवदान rite. स्रुव (स्रवति घृतादिकमस्मात्) on the other hand is used for cutting the oblation (स्रुवेण अवद्यति), which is then held by जुहू. Thus, only जुहू is to be made of parṇa-wood.

Note the following couplet, which enumerates the different kinds of wood that are used for preparing these various ladles : 'वैकङ्कती ध्रुवा प्रोक्ता आश्वत्थी चोपभृन्मता । जुहूः पलाशकाष्ठस्य खादिरस्य स्रुवो मतः ।।'

सेयं पर्णता...पौनरुक्त्यापत्तेः—In this passage Bhāskara discusses another new topic viz. the scope or province of the injunction that the

Juhū-ladle should be made of parna-wood. In these two sentences he uses four technical terms, three of which are defined in the next Section. We shall first see the meaning of these four terms.

अनारभ्याधीत (अन् + आरभ्य + अधीत) means prescribed without commencing any particular sacrifice, mentioned with reference to no particular sacrifice, laid down by means of a disconnected or detached injunction. There are two methods of giving rules or injunctions in the Veda. Sometimes the topic of a particular sacrifice is commenced and in that connection certain rules are laid down. Those rules are known as आरभ्यविधिs or they are said to be आरभ्याधीत. When such rules are quoted for discussion, they are introduced by some such formula as ' दर्शपूर्णमासप्रकरणे श्रूयते,' ' ज्योतिष्टोमे श्रूयते ' or ' राजसूये दशपेयनामके यागे श्रूयते.'

Then, again, certain rules are given without reference to any particular sacrifice. They are अनारभ्यविधिs, or are said to be अनारभ्याधीत. An अनारभ्यविधि is a general injunction or an injunction of general application (सामान्यविधिः). When such injunctions are quoted for discussion, they are prefaced by ' अनारभ्य श्रूयते '. Examples of अनारभ्यविधिs from ordinary life are ' नानृतं वदेत्, ' ' न हिंस्यात् सर्वाणि भूतानि ' and ' न परधनं कामयेत्', which embody precepts of universal application.

प्रकृतिः—Sacrifices are of two kinds viz. प्रकृति or an archetype or a model sacrifice and विकृति or a modification or a derivative. प्रकृति means that sacrifice with reference to which specification or mention (उपदेशः) of all its subsidiaries is made, or instruction (उपदेशः) about all its subsidiaries is given (यत्र समग्राङ्गोपदेशः सा प्रकृतिः) in the relevant sacrificial literature, where we consequently find a full description of such a sacrifice. दर्शपूर्णमास is a standard example of an archetype. Other model sacrifices are अग्निहोत्र and ज्योतिष्टोम.

विकृतिः—This means a derivative sacrifice or a modification. Here instruction about all the details is not given (यत्र न सर्वाङ्गोपदेशः सा विकृतिः). Only those points in which it differs from the model are mentioned. Other necessary details are derived from the model sacrifice on account of the general rule which says that a modification should be performed like the model (प्रकृतिवद् विकृतिः कर्तव्या). Examples of modifications are सौर्य (' सौर्यं चरुं निर्वपेत् '), वायव्य ('वायव्यं श्वेतमालभेत'), श्येन and ऐन्द्राग्न.

The word उपदेश, which occurs in the definitions of प्रकृति and विकृति in the next Section is defined in the जैमिनीयन्यायमालाविस्तर, thus : यत्र अपेक्षितस्य अर्थजातस्य प्रतिपादका ग्रन्थसन्दर्भाः पठ्यन्ते स उपदेशः ।

प्रकृति and विकृति are thus distinguished by कपर्दिस्वामी in his भाष्य on आपस्तम्बसूत्र 31 : 'येषां प्रधानानां श्रुत्याद्यवगतशेषत्वैः पदार्थैः कल्पित उपकारः कथमंशपूरकस्ताः प्रकृतयः । ततश्च विकृतयः कथमंशपूरकमुपकारं गृह्णीयुः । विकृत्यपेक्षं हि प्रकृतित्वम् । येषां च अविहितेतिकर्तव्यतानामन्यत्र विहितेनोपकारेण कथमंशः पूर्यते ता विकृतयः । ...एवं च काश्चित् प्रकृतय एव अग्निहोत्रदर्शपूर्णमासज्योतिष्टोमाः । काश्चिद् विकृतयः प्रकृतयश्च यथा वैश्वदेवाग्नीषोमीयपशुप्रमयनिकाय्यद्वादशाहादयः । काश्चिद् विकृतय एव यथा कुण्डपायिनामयने अग्निहोत्रसौर्यवायव्यपश्वाद्विन्पौण्डरीकादयः ।'

चोदकः—चोदक literally means a directing sentence or passage (चोदकं वाक्यं चोदको ग्रन्थो वा). The direction, given by such passage, is 'प्रकृतिवद् विकृतिः कर्तव्या', the general rule we saw before. This general rule is otherwise called अतिदेशः or extended application or transfer. Details are given in an archetype. The rule by which they become available in, or are transferred to a derivative, is called चोदक or अतिदेश. अतिदेश is thus defined : 'अन्यत्रैव प्रणीतायाः कृत्स्नाया धर्मसंहतेः । अन्यत्र कार्यतः प्राप्तिरतिदेशः स उच्यते ॥' शबर explains the term अतिदेश in his भाष्य on जैमिनिसूत्र VII. i. 12 as follows : 'अतिदेशो नाम ये परत्र विहिता धर्मास्तमतीत्य अन्यत्र तेषां देशः । यथा, देवदत्तस्य भोजनविधिं कृत्वा 'शालिसूपमांसापूपैर्देवदत्तो भोजयितव्य' इति तमेव विधिं यज्ञदत्तेऽतिदिशति 'देवदत्तवद् यज्ञदत्तो भोजयितव्य' इति । श्लोकमपि उदाहरन्ति । प्रकृतात् कर्मणो यस्मात् तत्समानेषु कर्मसु । धर्मप्रदेशो येन स्यात् सोऽतिदेश इति स्थितिः ॥'

Now the rule about पर्णता is given without reference to any particular sacrifice. It is thus an अनारभ्यविधिः or सामान्यविधिः. The question then is whether it should be followed in models, or in modifications, or in both. The prima facie view is that as it is a general rule, it should apply to both models and modifications. Against this Bhāskara points out that पर्णता is to be primarily construed only with models and not with modifications. This does not mean that in modifications the rule about पर्णता is not to be followed. In modifications पर्णता becomes available by चोदक i. e. by means of the general rule, which says that a modification should be performed like a model. If पर्णता were made applicable to modifications primarily, it would once more be available there by means of चोदक and thus repetition of its applicability would arise.

Read 'पर्णवाक्यात् पर्णताया यावत्क्रतुप्रवेशे जुहूद्वारम् । सा च जुहूः प्रकृतावेव विहिता विकृतिषु सर्वत्र अतिदिश्यते ।' जैमिनीयन्यायमालाविस्तर p. 201

Section 24

In this Section Bhāskara proves that वाक्य is stronger than प्रकरण or context.

In the chapter on दर्शपूर्णमास there is a Section (अनुवाकः), called सूक्तवाक. This section is used for offering into the fire a handful of Darbha-grass (प्रस्तरः) in accordance with the injunction 'सूक्तवाकेन प्रस्तरं प्रहरति.' The reason why this Section is called सूक्तवाक is that Fire is thus addressed therein : 'त्वं सूक्तवागसि.'

In this Section the following mantra occurs :

अग्नीषोमौ, इदं हविरजुषेताम् , अवीवृधेताम् , महो ज्यायोऽक्राताम् । इन्द्राग्नी इदं हविरजुषेताम्, अवीवृधेताम् , महो ज्यायोऽक्राताम् ।

[O] Agni and Soma, this offering [you two] have accepted, [this offering you two] have made to thrive, great eminence [you two] have displayed. [O] Indra and Agni, this offering etc.

दर्श and पूर्णमास are two sacrifices, which are performed on the new–moon (दर्शः) and full–moon (पूर्णमासः) day. दर्श is so called, because on that day the moon is observed to stay with the sun and consequently it is not visible in the sky. Note 'एकत्रस्थितचन्द्रार्कदर्शनात् दर्श इति उच्यते ।' 'दर्श इति सूर्याचन्द्रमसोः परः संनिकर्षः अभिधीयते ।' दर्श is also known as अमावास्या, because the sun and the moon live together on that day. See 'अमाशब्दः सहार्थे । यस्मिन् काले सूर्याचन्द्रमसोः सहवासः स कालः अमावस्या ।' Note 'अमावास्या त्वमावस्या दर्शः सूर्येन्दुसंगमः' अमरः.

पूर्णमास is so called, because the moon is full on that day. Note 'मास इति चन्द्रमसः आख्या । पूर्णो मासो यस्मिन् काले स पूर्णमासः ।'

It has been settled, on the ground of लिङ्ग, that इन्द्र and अग्नि are the deities of दर्श, because the moon is not visible on that day. Similarly, on the same ground, अग्नि and सोम are determined to be the deities of पूर्णमास, because the moon is full on that day. Vide मी. सू. III. iii. 15–18.

Now with reference to the mantra in question the Pūrvapakṣa view is that as the passage occurs in the context of दर्शपूर्णमास, the whole of the passage must be used for both दर्श and पूर्णमास sacrifices. But, while using it for दर्श, we should drop the word अग्नीषोमौ, because these are not the deities of दर्श. Similarly, while using it for पूर्णमास, we should omit the word इन्द्राग्नी, because these deities have nothing to do with पूर्णमास. This we do on the ground of प्रकरणप्रमाण and only if we were to do so, the fact that the passage occurs in दर्शपूर्णमासप्रकरण would receive its due significance.

Against this the Siddhāntin points out that the two sentences form each a complete sentence (एकवाक्यम्) in itself. From the वाक्यप्रमाण, therefore, we learn that the first sentence is in honour of

अग्नीषोमौ and is consequently to be used for the पूर्णमास sacrifice. Similarly, the same pramāṇa tells us that the second sentence is in honour of इन्द्राग्नी and is, therefore, to be used in the दर्शयाग. As वाक्य is more powerful than प्रकरण, the sentence 'इन्द्राग्नी, इदं हविः etc.,' Bhāskara points out, becomes subservient to दर्श on account of its forming one complete sentence (एकवाक्यत्वात्), and not subservient to both दर्श and पूर्णमास on account of प्रकरण.

The reason why वाक्य is stronger than प्रकरण is as follows: In deciding विनियोग by means of प्रकरण what we do is this: We first drop the word अग्नीषोमौ from the first sentence. Then, in order to construe the remaining part of that sentence viz. 'इदं हविः ... अक्राताम्' with इन्द्राग्नी we presume that it forms one syntactical whole with the second sentence (' इदं हविः ' इत्यादिकस्य अवशिष्टप्रथमवाक्यस्थशब्दसमूहस्य ' इन्द्राग्नी ' इत्यादिना द्वितीयवाक्येन सह एकवाक्यताकल्पनम्). For the śruti does not specifically connect this part of the first sentence with the second. Afterwards through लिङ्ग and श्रुति, विनियोग is reached. Thus in 'प्रकरणाद् विनियोगः' we have the following stages viz. (1) प्रकरणम्, (2) वाक्यम्, (3) लिङ्गम्, (4) श्रुतिः and (5) विनियोगः. In वाक्याद् विनियोगः, on the other hand, there are only four stages viz. (1) वाक्यम्, (2) लिङ्गम्, (3) श्रुतिः and (4) विनियोगः. प्रकरण, being thus more विप्रकृष्ट from विनियोग than वाक्य, it is weaker than वाक्य.

Read 'सूक्तवाके श्रूयते—"अग्नीषोमाविदं हविरजुषेताम्, अवीवृधेताम्, महो ज्यायोऽक्राताम्। इन्द्राग्नी इदं हविरजुषेताम्, अवीवृधेताम्, महो ज्यायोऽक्राताम्।" इति। तत्र देवतावाचकमग्नीषोमादिपदं पौर्णमास्यादिकाले यथादेवतं विभज्य प्रयोक्तव्यम् इति पूर्वपादे निर्णीतम्। यत्तु "इदं हविः" इत्यादिकमवशिष्टं पदजातं, तदग्नीषोमीयमन्त्रगतमपि अमावास्यायाम् अग्नीषोमपदपरित्यागेन पठनीयम्। एवम् इन्द्राग्निमन्त्रगतमपि पौर्णमास्याम् इन्द्राग्निपदपरित्यागेन पठनीयम्। तथा सति एषां मन्त्रभागानां सर्वशेषत्वबोधको दर्शपूर्णमासप्रकरणपाठोऽनुगृह्यते। इति प्राप्ते—

ब्रूमः। अग्नीषोममन्त्रशेषस्य इन्द्राग्निपदान्वयाश्रवणात्। प्रकरणेन प्रथमं तदन्वयरूपं वाक्यं कल्पनीयम्। तेन च वाक्येन इन्द्रादिप्रकाशनसामर्थ्यरूपं लिङ्गं कल्प्यते। तच्च लिङ्गम् 'अनेन मन्त्रभागेन इन्द्राग्निविषयक्रिया अनुष्ठेया' इति विनियोजिकां तृतीयाश्रुतिं कल्पयति। ततः प्रकरणविनियोगयोर्मध्ये त्रिभिर्व्यवधानं भवति। अग्नीषोमपदान्वयरूपं तु वाक्यं श्रूयमाणत्वात् लिङ्गश्रुतिभ्यामेव व्यवधीयते। तस्माद् वाक्येन प्रकरणस्य बाधितत्वात् तच्छेषस्तत्रैव व्यवतिष्ठते।' जैमिनीयन्यायमालाविस्तर on III. iii. 14.

Section 25

प्रकरण or context is the next विनियोजक प्रमाण. It is defined as expectancy on the part of two i. e. two sentences. Other definitions of प्रकरण are 'अङ्गप्रधानोभयवाक्यगता आकाङ्क्षा प्रकरणम्' 'वाक्यैकवाक्यता प्रकरणम्' 'अङ्गवाक्यसापेक्षं प्रधानवाक्यं प्रकरणम्' 'कर्तव्यस्य इतिकर्तव्यताकाङ्क्षस्य वचनं प्रकरणम्.' When two sentences are found to be complimentary of each other, they constitute प्रकरणं. Here is an example.

The sentence, commencing with 'समिधो यजति,' lays down the five fore-sacrifices (प्रयाजाः). Vide pp. 95-96 above. The Mīmāṁsist meaning of this sentence is 'समिद्यागेन भावयेत्.' On hearing this the expectancy as to what is it that is to be brought into existence by समिद्याग arises in our mind. For, in the sentence 'समिधो जयति,' the particular fruit to which समिद्याग is to be subservient is not mentioned.

उपकार्याकाङ्क्षा is the same as फलाकाङ्क्षा. The फल is उपकार्य, because it is helped by the समिद्याग in its rise. The सामिद्याग is then known as उपकारक.

Secondly, the sentence 'दर्शपूर्णमासाभ्यां स्वर्गकामो यजेत' yields the sense 'दर्शपूर्णमासाभ्यां स्वर्गं भावयेत्' Here the उपकार्य or फल viz. स्वर्ग is mentioned. But, कथंभाव, or the expectancy as to how exactly heaven is to be achieved by the new and full moon sacrifices, is not satisfied by any word in the sentence. The sentence is thus उपकारकसाकाङ्क्ष.

These two sentences are thus साकाङ्क्ष and the expectancy of one is satisfied by the other. 'सामिधो यजति' requires फल or उपकार्य, which is supplied by 'दर्शपूर्णमासाभ्यां स्वर्गकामो यजेत' by pointing out that the fruit of सामियाग is स्वर्ग. Similarly, 'दर्शपूर्ण...यजेत' requires इतिकर्तव्यता or उपकारक. That is supplied by 'सामिधो यजति,' which shows that सामिद्याग or प्रयाजाः form the इतिकर्तव्यता of दर्शपूर्णमास. The two sentences, therefore, form प्रकरण.

Which of these two sentences is the principal and which the subordinate ? As 'दर्शपूर्णमासाभ्यां स्वर्गकामो यजेत' lays down the main sacrifice, which is the means of attaining heaven, it naturally attains to the position of the principal (उपकार्य, शेषिन्, अङ्गिन्). 'समिधो यजाति', supplying as it does, the details of the means, consequently becomes the subordinate.

The mutual expectancy of the two sentences in प्रकरण is satisfied according to what is known as नष्टाश्वदग्धरथन्याय. One man's horses were lost and another's chariot was burnt. The former had the expectancy of horses and the latter of a chariot. They, therefore, came together and supplied each other's deficiency. This is what happens in the case of प्रकरण. In Marāṭhī this न्याय takes the form of 'सटवाईला नाहीं नवरा आणि म्हसोबाला नाहीं बायको.'

Section 27

We have seen that the two sentences 'दर्शपूर्णमासाभ्यां स्वर्गकामो यजेत (दर्शपूर्णमासाभ्यां स्वर्गं भावयेत्)' and 'समिधो यजति (सामिद्यागेन भावयेत्)' express भावना. As the sentence 'दर्श...यजेत is principal, the भावना connected with it is known as मुख्य. The sentence 'समिधो यजाति' is subordinate.

Because it lays down the प्रयाजs, which are subsidiaries (अङ्गानि) of the दर्शपूर्णमास. The भावना, connected with that sentence is, therefore, called अङ्गभावना.

महाप्रकरण or great context is connected with मुख्यभावना, while अवान्तरप्रकरण or intermediate context is connected with अङ्गभावना.

What is exactly meant by महाप्रकरण being connected (संबन्धिन्) with मुख्यभावना ? When certain rites are determined to be subsidiary to मुख्यभावना by means of प्रकरण, that प्रकरण is said to be connected with मुख्यभावना. Thus, in the case of the two sentences 'दर्शपूर्णमासाभ्यां स्वर्गकामो यजेत' and 'समिधो यजति,' the fore-sacrifices laid down by 'समिधो यजति' are known to be subservient to the मुख्यभावना in 'दर्श...यजेत' on account of प्रकरण. This प्रकरण is, therefore, connected with मुख्यभावना and is consequently महाप्रकरण.

This meaning of 'being connected with' must be specially noted. For, as the present prakaraṇa deals with both the sentences viz. 'दर्श...यजेत' (मुख्यभावना) and 'समिधो यजति' (अङ्गभावना), it might as well be said that it is connected with अङ्गभावना also. But we saw in the previous paragraph that connection of a प्रकरण with भावना means the laying down, by that prakaraṇa, of the subservience of some rites to that भावना. And as the present prakarana does not lay down the subservience of any rites to the अङ्गभावना in 'समिधो यजति,' it cannot be regarded as 'अङ्गभावनासंबन्धि प्रकरणम्'.

प्रकरण also means a chapter, a section or any small division of a book. When two sentences occur in a chapter dealing with मुख्यभावना and the अङ्गाङ्गिभाव or मुख्यप्रधानभाव between them is determined by प्रकरण, that प्रकरण will be महाप्रकरण. Similarly, when two sentences occur in a chapter dealing with अङ्गभावना and the relation of principal and subordinate between them is determined by प्रकरण, that प्रकरण will be अवान्तरप्रकरण. This meaning of प्रकरण will also do.

There is another way of explaining the expression मुख्यभावनासंबन्धि viz. मुख्यभावनया [तदीयाङ्गानां प्रयाजादीनां] संबन्धः, स अस्ति अस्मिन् तत् wherein there is the connection [of subsidiaries such as the fore-sacrifices] with the principal creative energy. Similarly, अङ्गभावनासंबन्धि can be explained as 'अङ्गभावनया [तदीयाङ्गानां अभिक्रमणादीनां] संबन्धः, स अस्ति अस्मिन् तत्.'

एतच्च...विकृत्यर्थम्—This paragraph points out the province of प्रकरणप्रमाण viz. the arche-type or model sacrifice.

एतच्च = एतत् प्रकरणं च. रामेश्वर paraphrases एतच्च by महाप्रकरणं च. Context seems to show that एतत् means महाप्रकरण. But this is not correct. By एतत् the author means प्रकरण in general and not the महाप्रकरण only. This will be seen from the following.

प्रकरण determines the अङ्गाङ्गिभाव and विनियोग between two sentences, which are mutually expectant (परस्परसाकाङ्क्ष). The subsidiary sentence is फलाकाङ्क्ष and the principal sentence is कथंभावाकाङ्क्ष. For example, ' समिधो यजति ' is फलाकाङ्क्ष, while ' दर्शपूर्ण...यजेत ' is कथंभावाकाङ्क्ष. Such double expectancy is possible only in an arche-type and hence prakaraṇa works in an arche-type only.

Now, take the case of a derivative (विकृतिः). सौर्यं चरुं निर्वपेद् ब्रह्मवर्चसकामः is a derivative, whose model is दर्शपूर्णमास. ' सौर्यचरुणा ब्रह्मवर्चसं भावयेत् ' is the meaning we get from this sentence. Then, as soon as the expectancy ' सौर्यचरुणा कथं ब्रह्मवर्चसं भावयेत् ' arises, it is at once satisfied by the extended application (अतिदेशः), which embodies the general rule that a derivative should be carried out like the arche-type (प्रकृतिवद् विकृतिः कर्तव्या). Thus, there is no कथंभावाकाङ्क्षा on the part of the principal sentence. The subsidiaries in a derivative are taken over from the arche-type. So here subsidiary sentences simply do not exist. Consequently, there is no फलाकाङ्क्षा as well. Thus both the expectancies not being there, prakaraṇa has no scope in a derivative.

Now, it may so happen that in a derivative there are some new subsidiaries (अपूर्वाङ्गानि = पूर्वं प्रकृतौ अपठितानि), which are not found in its arche-type. These will certainly have फलाकाङ्क्षा and it will be satisfied by the principal sentence, which lays down the derivative. Will not the derivative have कथंभावाकाङ्क्षा with regard to these new subsidiaries at least? If so, the principal sentence would have कथंभावाकाङ्क्षा with regard to these new subsidiaries and thus both the expectancies being there, prakaraṇa would step in.

Let us take the previous illustration viz. ' सौर्यं चरुं निर्वपेद् ब्रह्मवर्चसकामः'. Now, in this सौर्ययाग there are certain subordinate oblations, known as उपहोम and others, which are not found in the arche-type दर्शपूर्णमास. So these oblations have फलाकाङ्क्षा in the form ' उपहोमादिभिः किं भावयेत्.' It is satisfied by उपहोमादिभिर्ब्रह्मवर्चसं भावयेत्. Now, if we were to suppose that the सौर्य याग has कथंभावाकाङ्क्षा at least with regard to उपहोम and others, the second expectancy would be there and prakaraṇa would come in.

Against this view it is pointed out that though उपहोम and others may have फलाकाङ्क्षा, the सौर्ययाग cannot have कथंभावाकाङ्क्षा with regard to them. For, the कथंभावाकाङ्क्षा of the सौर्ययाग is satisfied by 'प्रकृतिवद् विकृतिः कर्तव्या.' The सौर्ययाग is thus simply unaware of the existence of these new subsidiaries and consequently cannot entertain any expectancy with regard to them.

So the position comes to this: In a derivative when there are new subsidiaries, those new subsidiaries have फलाकाङ्क्षा, which is satisfied by the principal sentence. But the derivative itself does not possess कथंभावाकाङ्क्षा with regard to these new subsidiaries. Thus, there being only one आकाङ्क्षा viz. फलाकाङ्क्षा on the part of the new subsidiaries, prakaraṇa, which requires two, has no scope here.

But, then, how will the new subsidiaries be subservient to the derivative, if not by prakaraṇa ? The answer is that they become so by means of स्थान or place (for which see below Sections 32–35).

It will thus be seen that in a derivative प्रकरण as such has no scope on account of the absence of the double expectancy which is necesary for it. If the word एतत् at the beginning of the paragraph be paraphrased by महाप्रकरण, it will suggest that in a derivative अवान्तरप्रकरण may have scope. But as we have seen above, no prakaraṇa, whether great or intermediate, can operate in a derivative owing to the absence of its essential condition viz. double expectancy. Therefore, Rāmeśvara's paraphrase of एतत् by महाप्रकरणम् is inaccurate.

Read in this connection 'यद्यपि उपहोमादीनाम् अपूर्वाङ्गानाम् "उपहोमादिभिर्भावयेत्" "किं भावयेत्" इति अस्ति आकाङ्क्षा, तथापि सौर्यादिविकृतियागस्य अतिदेशवाक्यप्राप्तप्राकृताङ्गैरेव नैराकाङ्क्ष्येण न अपूर्वाङ्गानामपि उपहोमादीनाम् उभयाकाङ्क्षया विनियोगः संभवति ।' रामेश्वर

'**विकृतौ तु न प्रकरणं संभवति** ।...तत्र च यानि अपूर्वाणि अङ्गानि पठ्यन्ते उपहोमादीनि, तेषां न प्रकरणं विनियोजकम् । तत्र यद्यपि तेषां 'किं भावयेत्' इति अस्ति आकाङ्क्षा, तथापि प्रधानस्य न कथंभावाकाङ्क्षास्ति, प्राकृतैरेवाङ्गैर्निराकाङ्क्षत्वात् ।...अन्यतराकाङ्क्षारूपस्थानादेव अपवर्गग्रहणम् ।' आपदेव

How subsidiaries of the arche-type and also new subsidiaries become available in a derivative will be clear from the following diagram :—

विकृतियागः

प्राकृताङ्गानि (चोदकप्राप्तानि) — अपूर्वाङ्गानि (स्थानात् प्राप्तानि)

(उभयाकाङ्क्षाविरहात् प्रकरणाप्राप्तानि) — (कथंभावाकाङ्क्षाविरहात् प्रकरणाप्राप्तानि)

Section 28

अङ्गभावना...प्रयाजाद्यङ्गत्वम्—अवान्तरप्रकरण is that prakaraṇa, which is connected with अङ्गभावना i. e. which lays down the subservience of some rite or rites to subsidiary creative energy. 'प्रयाजाः कर्तव्याः' lays down the performance of the five fore-sacrifices enumerated in 'समिधो यजति etc.' 'प्रयाजैर्भावयेत्' is the Mīmāṁsist meaning of this sentence. As the fore-sacrifices are subsidiary to दर्शपूर्णमास, the भावना which this sentence expresses is अङ्गभावना. This अङ्गभावना possesses कथंभावाकाङ्क्षा in the form 'प्रयाजैः कथं भावयेत्'.

Now, in connection with this topic of the fore-sacrifices occurs the injunction of a rite called अभिक्रमण or stepping near. This rite has फलाकाङ्क्षा in the form 'अभिक्रमणेन किं भावयेत्'.

Thus here we have two sentences which are परस्पराकाङ्क्ष. One wants कथंभाव and the other wants फल. प्रकरण, therefore, brings them together and shows that अभिक्रमण is subsidiary to प्रयाजs. The कथंभावाकाङ्क्षा of प्रयाजs is then satisfied by 'अभिक्रमणोपकृतैः प्रयाजैर्भावयेत्'. Similarly, the फलाकाङ्क्षा of अभिक्रमण is fulfilled by 'अभिक्रमणेन प्रयाजोपकारं भावयेत्'.

As प्रकरण here determines that अभिक्रमण is subservient to प्रयाजs, which represent an अङ्गभावना, this prakaraṇa is an अवान्तरप्रकरण.

The word आदि in अभिक्रमणादीनाम् refers to some other rite, which by means of अवान्तरप्रकरण, is subservient to some other अङ्गभावना expressed by the word आदि in प्रयाजाद्यङ्गत्वम्.

तच्च (i e. अभिक्रमणादीनां प्रयाजाङ्गत्वम्) संदंशेनैव ज्ञायते—A peculiarity of अवान्तरप्रकरण is here being pointed out. अवान्तरप्रकरण, we have just seen, determines the subservience of a rite to अङ्गभावना. We are now told that this rite, whose subservience to अङ्गभावना is to be established by अवान्तरप्रकरण, must occur in the text between two others, which are definitely known to be subsidiary to that अङ्गभावना. Such occurrence is called संदंश, or a pair of tongs, or a texual clasp. The two definite subsidiaries, between which the doubtful one occurs, represent as though the two limbs of a pair of tongs. That is why this phenomenon is called संदंश.

अवान्तरप्रकरण, then, establishes the subservience of a rite to अङ्गभावना, only when helped by a pair of tongs.

In the present illustration the pair of tongs duly exists. For, अभिक्रमण, which is here established as subservient to प्रयाजs, occurs between घृतानयन and मिथुनवेदन, which are definitelv known to be the subsidiaries of the fore-sacrifices.

तदभावे (संदंशाभावे)...प्रधानाङ्गत्वापत्तेः—This sentence gives the reason why a pair of tongs is necessary for अवान्तरप्रकरण.

अवान्तरप्रकरण deals with अङ्गभावना, such as is represented by the प्रयाजs. The प्रयाजs occur in a context the main purpose of which is the satisfaction of the कथंभावाकाङ्क्षा of the मुख्यभावना contained in 'दर्शपूर्णमासाभ्यां स्वर्गं भावयेत्'. The प्रयाजs themselves are फलाकाङ्क्ष and that expectancy of theirs is satisfied by the दर्शपूर्णमास sentence. All this we have seen before in dealing with मुख्यप्रकरण.

Now, what happens is this : Near about the place, where the प्रयाजs are mentioned, occurs the आभिक्रमण sentence. The आभिक्रमण, even like the प्रयाजs, is फलाकाङ्क्ष. So, it is just likely that as the प्रयाजs are covered by the कथंभावाकाङ्क्षा of the फलभावना (स्वर्गफलभावना मुख्यभावना इत्यर्थः), even so the similarly-situated अभिक्रमण would also be so covered and all of them viz. प्रयाजs and आभिक्रमण would be subsidiaries of the principal sacrifice viz. दर्शपूर्णमास (प्रधानाङ्गत्वापत्तेः प्रधानस्य दर्शपूर्णमासस्य अङ्गत्वापत्तेः).

This contingency is averted by the pair of tongs. As आभिक्रमण is sandwiched between घृतानयन and मिथुनवेदन, which are definitely known to be subsidiaries of प्रयाजs, it cannot be subservient to दर्शपूर्णमास, but becomes, like घृतानयन and मिथुनवेदन, by which it is compassed round, a subsidiary of प्रयाजs. Thus, in the absence of the pair of tongs अभिक्रमण would have become a subsidiary of दर्शपूर्णमास. Vide in the this connection मी. सू. III. i. 19-20.

Section 29

Bhāskara begins this Section by giving a definition of संदंश. It is 'एकाङ्गानुवादेन विधीयमानयोः अङ्गयोः अन्तराले विहितत्वम्.' This may be thus explained: एकाङ्गस्य दर्शपूर्णमासाङ्गस्य प्रयाजरूपस्य अनुवादेन पुनरुल्लेखेन विधीयमानयोः अङ्गयोः धृतानयनमिथुनवेदनरूपयोः प्रयाजाङ्गयोः अन्तराले मध्ये विहितत्वम् ।

The प्रयाजs are laid down by 'प्रयाजाः कर्तव्याः'. They are further alluded to (अनुवादेन) by the sentence 'समिधो यजति, तनूनपातं यजति, इडो यजति, बर्हिर्यजति, स्वाहाकारं यजति.' The first three प्रयाजs viz. समिद्याग, तनूनपाद्याग and इड्याग are offered with the ghee in the ladle called जुहू. For the remaining two प्रयाजs viz. बर्हिर्याग and स्वाहाकारयाग ghee is to be poured into the जुहू ladle (जुह्वाम् *loc. sing.*) from the उपभृत् pot. This rite of pouring the ghee from the upabhṛt into juhū is called घृतानयन and is laid down by the sentence 'समानयते जुह्वामुपभृतः। तेजो वा-'. Here supply आज्यम् as the object of समानयते. 'तेजो वा-' is followed in the original by आज्यम् and means 'or lustre [is ghee]'.

After this occurs the sentence 'यस्यैवं विदुषः... अभिजित्यै', which lays down the rite called अभिक्रमण. Here एवं विदुषः means 'ते देवाः प्रयाजैरेभ्यो लोकेभ्योऽसुरान् प्राणुदन्त' इति ज्ञातवतः. प्र in प्रैभ्यः goes with नुदते, which then means 'drives far away.' अभिक्रामम् is a gerund in णमुल् and means अभिक्रम्य or अभिक्रमणं कृत्वा. अभिक्रमण is explained as 'प्रतिप्रयाजं किंचिदन्तरम् आहवनीयसमीपदेशं प्रति पदप्रक्षेपणम्।' सारविवेचिनी, or 'अभिक्रामम् अभिक्रम्य अभिक्रम्य अदूरे स्थित्वा प्रथमं हुत्वा पादं पुरतः प्रक्षिप्य द्वितीयं जुहुयात्। एवमुत्तरत्र। तदेतदभिक्रमणम्।' सायण, अभिजित्यै for victory or conquest.

तद् in तद् हि 'समानयते etc. means अभिक्रमणम् and is to be construed with विधीयते.

After the अभिक्रमण sentence occurs 'यो वै प्रयाजानां मिथुनं वेद', which lays down मिथुनवेदन.

Thus, the three rites occur in the order of घृतानयन, अभिक्रमण and मिथुनवेदन. Out of these घृतानयन is specially intended for the last two prayājas and is, therefore, a प्रयाजाङ्ग, certainly. मिथुनवेदन occurs in a sentence, which looks like an अर्थवाद. But as the word प्रयाजानाम् is found therein, मिथुनवेदन is also known to be definitely a subsidiary of prayājas. Thus, between these two known प्रयाजाङ्गs occurs अभिक्रमण. Consequently, by means of अवान्तरप्रकरण, helped by संदंश, अभिक्रमण is established as a प्रयाजाङ्ग.

Two things deserve note in this discussion. First, the author does not tell us by which pramāṇa घृतानयन and मिथुनवेदन become the subsidiaries of the fore-sacrifices. That they are so is almost taken for granted. We must, however, decide the point and it appears to us that घृतानयन and मिथुनवेदन are प्रयाजाङ्गs by means of लिङ्गप्रमाण. The plain meaning of the words (शब्दसामर्थ्यम्) in those two sentences viz. 'समानयते...तेजो वा' and 'यो वै...वेद' shows that the rites laid down by them viz. घृतानयन and मिथुनवेदन are प्रयाजाङ्गs.

Secondly, the author seems to assume that the विनियोग of अभिक्रमण here is doubtful and therefore अवान्तरप्रकरण, helped by संदंश, determines that अभिक्रमण is a प्रयाजाङ्ग. To us this assumption appears incorrect. For, the word 'प्रयाजाः' occurs in this sentence, which lays down अभिक्रमण, and consequently, अभिक्रमण, can by लिङ्गप्रमाण be easily understood to be a प्रयाजाङ्ग.

The pair of tongs and the subsidiaries of the prayājas will be clearly seen from the following diagram :—

प्रयाजाङ्गानि

घृतानयनम्	अभिक्रमणम् (सदंशपातितम्)	मिथुनवेदनम्
(लिङ्गप्रमाणेन प्रयाजाङ्गम्)	(अवान्तरप्रकरणेन संदंशोपकृतेन् प्रयाजाङ्गम्)	(लिङ्गप्रमाणेन प्रयाजाङ्गम्)

'प्रयाजैरपूर्वं...शाम्यति—This passage points out the technical way by which अभिक्रमण becomes a प्रयाजाङ्ग. The Mīmāṁsist meaning of 'प्रयाजाः कर्तव्याः' is 'प्रयाजैरपूर्वं कृत्वा यागोपकारं भावयेत्'. When this is known, कथंभावाकाङ्क्षा in the form 'कथमेभिरपूर्वं कर्तव्यम्' arises for the prayājas. That कथंभावाकाङ्क्षा is satisfied by अभिक्रमण and other rites in this manner viz. 'अभिक्रमणाद्युपकृतैः प्रयाजैरपूर्वं कृत्वा यागोपकारं भावयेत्.'

It may be noted that the expression 'संदंशपतितैरभिक्रमणादिभिः' is inaccurate. It should be 'संदंशपतितेन अभिक्रमणेन.' For, we know that only अभिक्रमण is संदंशपतित. The other subsidiaries viz. घृतानयन and मिथुनवेदन are not in the textual clasp. The author should really have said 'सा च संदंशपतितेन अभिक्रमणेन घृतानयनमिथुनवेदनाभ्यां च शाम्यति।'

न च अङ्गभावनायाः....तत्संभवात्—This is directed against the view of the followers of Prabhākarabhaṭṭa, who hold that इतिकर्तव्यताकाङ्क्षा or कथंभावाकाङ्क्षा is the monopoly of फलभावना or मुख्यभावना. अङ्गभावना, such as we find in प्रयाजs, is अफल. कथंभावाकाङ्क्षा is really connected with फल, because it tells us how that fruit is to be brought about. प्रयाजs, which satisfy the कथंभावाकाङ्क्षा of दर्शपूर्णमास and are अफल, cannot themselves have कथंभावाकाङ्क्षा.

Note 'अत्र प्रधानभावनानामेव इतिकर्तव्यताकाङ्क्षा, तासामेव फलसाधनत्वेन कथमिति आकाङ्क्षोदयात्, न अङ्गभावनानाम्, तासामफलत्वात् इति वदतां **प्राभाकराणां मतमनुवदति।**' सारविवेचनी

The answer to this view is that अङ्गभावना is भावना all the same and as such it is possible for it to have कथंभावाकाङ्क्षा. The following syllogism may be noted in this connection: प्रयाजाद्यङ्गभावना कथंभावसाकाङ्क्षा भावनात्वात्, दर्शादिमुख्यभावनावत्।

Section 30

तदिदं प्रकरणं...अन्वेति—We have seen before that श्रुति establishes the subservience of all sorts of things viz. a द्रव्य like व्रीहि, a गुण like आरुण्य, a क्रिया like प्रोक्षण, a मन्त्र like 'इमामगृभ्णन् etc.', a fire like आहवनीय and even immaterial things like एकत्व and पुंस्त्व. लिङ्ग makes विनियोग of mantras only as in the case of 'बर्हिर्देवसदनं दामि' and 'स्योनं ते सदनं कृणोमि'. वाक्य lays down the subsidiariness of a quality such as पर्णता in 'यस्य पर्णमयी जुहूर्भवति' and a mantra as in 'इन्द्राग्नी इदं हविः etc.'

Now, the author tells us that प्रकरण is directly applicatory of action only. It may establish the application of substance and quality indirectly through action. This can be easily seen.

In a महाप्रकरण the आर्थी भावना or फलभावना or मुख्यभावना in 'यजेत स्वर्गकामः' is कथंभावाकाङ्क्ष. Near about the place, where the sentence 'यजेत

स्वर्गकामः ' occurs, are mentioned (संनिधिपठित) a group of actions or rites (क्रियाजातम्) such as प्रयाजs, for which no fruit is laid down (अश्रूयमाणफलक). This group, therefore, wants something which it should serve (उपकार्यम्). It is, in other words, उपकार्याकाङ्क्ष or फलाकाङ्क्ष. It is consequently construed as the इतिकर्तव्यता of ' यजेत स्वर्गकामः ', whose कथंभावाकाङ्क्षा it satisfies and from which it receives an उपकार्य or फल for itself.

In an अवान्तरप्रकरण the कथंभावाकाङ्क्षा of the अङ्गभावना of the प्रयाजs is satisfied by such rites as अभिक्रमण, which are themselves फलाकाङ्क्ष and whose फलाकाङ्क्षा is fulfilled by the प्रयाजs.

Thus, in a महाप्रकरण the प्रयाजs are established as subsidiary and in an अवान्तरप्रकरण the subservience of अभिक्रमण is laid down. Both the प्रयाजs and अभिक्रमण are क्रिया or action. The author, therefore, rightly says that a प्रकरण is applicatory of action only.

Now, in carrying out the prayājas and abhikramaṇa certain substances and qualities would be necessary. These also would be subsidiary to the मुख्यभावना or अङ्गभावना as the case may be. But their subsidiariness arises through action for which they are directly useful.

Though the author gives an example of महाप्रकरण only in proving that a प्रकरण is applicatory of action alone, his remark ' तादृशं प्रकरणं क्रियाया एव साक्षाद्विनियोजकं द्रव्यगुणयोस्तु तद्द्वारा (क्रियाद्वारा) ' is applicable to both महाप्रकरण and अवान्तरप्रकरण. For, both these prakaranas, as we have just seen, are applicatory of action alone.

क्रियाया...सार्वजनीनमेतत्—The main topic in a prakaraṇa is the satisfaction of the कथंभावाकाङ्क्षा of either the मुख्यभावना or अङ्गभावना. कथंभावाकाङ्क्षा means expectancy about the procedure of carrying out a certain rite. Procedure naturally consists of action. Therefore, the statement 'प्रकरणं क्रियाया एव साक्षाद्विनियोजकम्' is quite correct.

Even in ordinary life the expectancy about procedure is satisfied by action alone. ' कुठारेण वृक्षं छिन्द्यात् ' is an instance of an injunction from ordinary life. Here the साध्य is वृक्षच्छेदः and the साधन is कुठारः. The third आकाङ्क्षा viz. कथंभावाकाङ्क्षा in the form ' कथं कुठारेण छिन्द्यात् ' is satisfied by ' हस्तेन कुठारेण छिन्द्यात् '. Here, though the word ' हस्तः ' is actually mentioned (उच्चार्यमाणोऽपि) in the sentence purporting to satisfy the कथंभावाकाङ्क्षा, the hand as such does not satisfy that expectancy. What satisfies the expectancy about procedure in this case is the raising (उद्यमन) and lowering (निपातन) of the axe by means of the hand. So it is उद्यमन and निपातन that are construed with the कथंभावाकाङ्क्षा of छेदन.

The hand is construed through those actions (तद्द्वारा तयोः उद्यमननिपातनयोः द्वारा इत्यर्थः). This is known to all people (सार्वजनीनम् । सर्वेषु जनेषु भवम् । सर्वेषु जनेषु प्रसिद्धमित्यर्थः). The correct answer to satisfy the expectancy of कथंभाव in this case, therefore, is ' हस्तकृताभ्याम् उद्यमननिपातनाभ्यामुपकृतेन कुठारेण छिन्द्यात्.'

Read in this connection 'कथंभावाकाङ्क्षा नाम करणगतप्रकाराकाङ्क्षा, थमुनः प्रकारत्वाचित्वात् । सामान्यस्य भेदको विशेषः प्रकारः, सामान्यं च क्रियारूपमेव आख्यातेनोच्यते । 'यजेत स्वर्गकामः' इत्यस्य हि अयमर्थः । यागेन तथा कर्तव्यं यथा स्वर्गो भवतीति । क्रियासामान्यस्य च विशेषः क्रियैव भवति । न हि ब्राह्मणविशेषः परिव्राजकादिरब्राह्मणो भवति । एवं च करणगतक्रियाविशेषाकाङ्क्षापरनामधेयायां कथंभावाकाङ्क्षायां क्रियैव अन्वेति इति युक्तम् ।' रामेश्वर

Section 31

This Section proves the superiority of प्रकरण to स्थान. The plural स्थानादिभ्यः is unwarranted. For, प्रकरण is stronger than स्थान and समाख्या, which are only two and not many. स्थानादिभ्यः is really equal to स्थानसमाख्याभ्याम्. रामेश्वर seems to read स्थानादितः, which is certainly better.

The illustration to prove the greater strength of प्रकरण in comparison with स्थान is taken from the ceremonies that form the राजसूय sacrifice. The राजसूय consists of many sacrifices of different kinds such as animal sacrifices, Soma sacrifices and sacrifices with other cooked or baked oblations consisting of various grains. For a description of the Rājasūya vide Keith's The Religion and Philosophy of the Veda and the Upaniṣads Vol. II § 14. pp. 340-343.

अभिषेचनीय (Concerning Coronation) is one of the Soma sacrifices that constitute the Rājasūya. Near about the place where अभिषेचनीय is enjoined occurs the sentence 'अक्षैर्दीव्यति, राजन्यं जिनाति, शौनःशेपमाख्यापयति,' which means ' He plays with dice, subdues or overpowers a king and makes [the priest] recite the story of Śunahśepa. ' राजन्य is a synonym of a क्षत्रिय (' मूर्धाभिषिक्तो राजन्यो बाहुजः क्षत्रियो विराट् ' अमरः), meaning a king. The word is a case of collective singular (समूहेकवचनम्). जिनाति is from ज्या I P and means overpowers or conquers.

Now, the question here is whether those rites viz. देवन, ज्यान and आख्यापन, are subservient to अभिषेचनीय or to राजसूय i. e. to all the sacrifices that collectively form राजसूय. The पूर्वपक्षिन्'s view is that on account of स्थानप्रमाण i. e. on account of the fact that अभिषेचनीय and these धर्मs (characteristics or rites) are mentioned in one place, देवन, ज्यान and आख्यापन become subservient to अभिषेचनीय.

The सिद्धान्तिन्'s reply to this is that the मुख्यभावना in ' राजा स्वाराज्यकामो राजसूयेन यजेत (राजसूयेन यागेन स्वाराज्यं भावयेत्) ' is कथंभावाकाङ्क्षा. The rites देवन, ज्यान and आख्यापन occur in a section the object of which is to satisfy this कथंभावाकाङ्क्षा. These rites themselves are उपकार्याकाङ्क्ष or फलाकाङ्क्ष.

The two sentences viz. 'राजा स्वाराज्यकामो...यजेत' and 'अक्षैः...ख्यापयति' being thus परस्परसाकाङ्क्ष, the rites देवन, ज्यान and आख्यापन are naturally construed with राजसूय as its इतिकर्तव्यता on account of महाप्रकरण.

The natural consequence of this decision is this: राजसूय consists of more than one sacrifice, which include अभिषेचनीय. The rites देवन, ज्यान and आख्यापन are subservient to राजसूय i.e. to all the sacrifices that constitute it. This means that these rites are subservient to अभिषेचनीय along with the other sacrifices that go to make up the राजसूय.

If we had followed स्थानप्रमाण, देवनादयो धर्माः would have been subservient to अभिषेचनीय only. प्रकरण प्रमाण makes them subsidiary to all the sacrifices, including अभिषेचनीय, that constitute राजसूय. As प्रकरण is stronger than स्थान, the decision given by प्रकरण prevails.

The reason why प्रकरण is more powerful than स्थान is that स्थान is one step further removed from विनियोग than प्रकरण. This can be seen from the following.

अभिषेचनीय is a modification or derivative from ज्योतिष्टोम. The rule 'प्रकृतिवद् विकृतिः कर्तव्या' is applicable in its case. This being so, अभिषेचनीय has no कथंभावाकाङ्क्षा. Consequently, देवन, ज्यान and आख्यापन, though mentioned near it (संनिधौ पठिता अपि), cannot be construed with अभिषेचनीय as its इतिकर्तव्यता.

If some one were to say that as अभिषेचनीय and देवनादि occur in the same place (स्थानप्रमाणम्), we should suppose that अभिषेचनीय is कथंभावाकाङ्क्ष and construe देवनादि as satisfying that expectancy. This is exactly how स्थानप्रमाण works. But then this means that स्थान requires the help of प्रकरण. So, the steps in the case of स्थान are (1) स्थान, (2) प्रकरण, (3) वाक्य, (4) लिङ्ग, (5) श्रुति and (6) विनियोग. In the case of प्रकरण on the other hand there are only five steps, the first step स्थान being absent. Thus प्रकरण is stronger than स्थान.

Read in this connection '**राजसूये** पश्चिष्टिसोमयागा बहवः प्रधानभूताः । तत्र अभिषेचनीयाख्यः कश्चित् सोमयागः । तस्य संनिधौ देवनादयः श्रूयन्ते 'अक्षैर्दीव्यति, राजन्यं जिनाति, शौनःशेपमाख्यापयति' इति । जिनाति जयति । बह्वृचब्राह्मणे समाम्नातं शुनःशेपविषयमुपाख्यानं शौनःशेपम् । तत्र संनिधिबलात् देवनादयोऽभिषेचनीयाङ्गम्—इति चेत्—

मैवम् । राजसूयस्य कथंभावाकाङ्क्षायामनुवृत्तायां विहिता देवनादयः प्रकरणेन राजसूयशेषाः । राजसूयश्च बहुयागात्मक इति तत्रत्यसर्वयागशेषत्वम् । न च अभिषेचनीयस्य काचिदाकाङ्क्षा देवनादिषु अस्ति । ज्योतिष्टोमविकृतित्वेन अतिदिष्टैः प्राकृताङ्गैरेव तदाकाङ्क्षानिवृत्तेः ।

संनिधिबलादाकाङ्क्षा उत्थाप्यते इति चेत् । अत एव आकाङ्क्षारूपमवान्तरप्रकरणमादौ परिकल्प्य तद्द्वारा वाक्यलिङ्गश्रुतिकल्पनया संनिधिर्विप्रकृष्यते । राजसूयाकाङ्क्षारूपं तु महाप्रकरणं कल्प्यत्वादेकया कक्षया संनिकृष्यते । तस्मात् प्रकरणेन संनिधिबाधात् सर्वशेषा देवनादयः ।' जैमिनीयन्यायमालाविस्तर p. 145

Also note 'तदिदं [प्रकरणं] स्थानादिप्रमाणाद् बलवत् । यत्र हि स्थानादङ्गत्वं तत्र अन्यतरस्य प्रकारान्तरेण निराकाङ्क्षत्वम् । न च साकाङ्क्षं निराकाङ्क्षेण संबद्धुं योग्यं विना आकाङ्क्षोत्थापनेन । अतश्च अन्यतराकाङ्क्षया यावदुभयाकाङ्क्षारूपप्रकरणकल्पनद्वारा वाक्यादि कल्पयितुमारभ्यते, झटिति तावत् प्रकरणेन वाक्यादिकं कल्पयित्वा विनियोगः क्रियते इति स्थानात् प्रकरणस्य बलीयस्त्वम् ।

अत एव विदेवनादयो धर्मा अभिषेचनीयसंनिधौ पठिता अपि नाभिषेचनीयस्य अङ्गम् । तेषां तदङ्गत्वं भवत् स्थानाद् भवेत्, न तु प्रकरणात् । अभिषेचनीयस्य अव्यक्तचोदनाचोदितत्वेन ज्योतिष्टोमविकारत्वात् प्राकृतैरेव धर्मैर्निराकाङ्क्षत्वात् । किन्तु प्रकरणाद् राजसूयाङ्गम् ।' आपदेव's मीमांसान्यायप्रकाश

Section 32

स्थान is the fifth प्रमाण, which helps विनियोग. स्थान means commonness of place. When two things are found together in a common place and become on that ground related to each other as principal and subordinate, this relationship is said to arise from स्थानप्रमाण.

This commonness of place is possible in two ways. Sometimes certain mantras occur in a common Section of the Veda or the Brāhmaṇa. This is known as commonness of place in a text (पाठसादेश्यम्). Sometimes mantras, occurring different places in the text, are brought together in the performance of some rite. This is called commonness of place in the performance (अनुष्ठानसादेश्यम्). स्थान is thus of two kinds.

पाठसादेश्य again has two varieties. Sometimes certain things are mentioned in the text in a particular order. Then in another text other things are enumerated in exactly the same order with reference to these things mentioned first. This is known as यथासंख्यपाठः (संख्यामनतिक्रम्य यथा स्यात् तथा पाठः) or mention or text according to number or respectivity. Then again, mantras may occur in the text together without there being any idea of respectivity connected with them. This is called संनिधिपाठ.

These divisions of स्थान would be clear from the following :

स्थानम्
- पाठसादेश्यम्
  - यथासंख्यपाठः
  - संनिधिपाठः
- अनुष्ठानसादेश्यम्

सादेश्य and देशसामान्य mean the same thing. सादेश्य is explained as समानः देशः येषां ते समानदेशाः सदेशाः वा । समानदेशानां सदेशानां वा भावः समानदेशत्वं सदेशत्वं सादेश्यं वा । Thus देशसामान्य, सादेश्य, सदेशत्व and समानदेशत्व mean one and the same thing. All these convey the sense एकदेशविहितत्वम् or being enjoined in one place

स्थान क्रमश्चेति अनर्थान्तरम्–अर्थान्तरम् (अन्योऽर्थः) means a different entity. अनर्थान्तरम्, therefore, signifies not a different entity i. e. synonymous. Bhāskara wants to tell us here that स्थान and क्रम are synonyms. This information seems somewhat un-called for. The explanation of this solicitude to convey irrelevant information is, however, to be found in Āpadeva's wording in his मीमांसान्यायप्रकाश, which our author has adopted not only slavishly, but also unintelligently.

After giving the two-fold division of स्थान into पाठसादेश्य and अनुष्ठानसादेश्य Āpadeva adds 'यथाहुः । "तत्र क्रमो द्विधैवेष्टो देशसामान्यलक्षणः । पाठानुष्ठानसादेश्यात् विनियोगस्य कारणम् ॥ " स्थानं क्रमश्चेत्यनर्थान्तरम् । '

Āpadeva here quotes a couplet from कुमारिलभट्ट's तन्त्रवार्तिक to support his two-fold division of स्थान. In this couplet occurs the word क्रम. Āpadeva, therefore, naturally thinks it necessary to tell his readers that स्थान mentioned by him and क्रम used by कुमारिलभट्ट in his कारिका are one and the same thing. Our author does not quote कुमारिलभट्ट's couplet, but merely adds the line 'स्थानं क्रमश्चेति अनर्थान्तरम्.' This is certainly not only slavish, but also blind adoption of Āpadeva.

Section 33

The first paragraph of this Section gives an illustration of यथासंख्यपाठ. Before we go to it, a few things must receive comment and explanation.

क्रमविहितेषु requires यागेषु to be supplied after it as a substantive for it to qualify. आपदेव's expression is क्रमविहितेष्टिषु. Bhāskara has unnecessarily dropped the syllable ष्टि.

याज्यानुवाक्यामन्त्राणाम् requires explanation. याज्या (इज्यते अनया) is a verse of sacrifice, or a presenting or sacrificing verse, which is intended for the consecration of the offering and which is recited by the Hotṛ at the time of its actual presentation. अनुवाक्या (अनूच्यते अनया) is an invoking verse, which is recited by the Hotṛ or the Maitrāvaruṇa priest and by which the deity is invoked to partake of the offering presented to him.

For these two words see 'शब्दितामनपशब्दमुच्चकैर्वाक्यलक्षणविदोऽनुवाक्यया । याज्यया यजनकर्मिणोऽत्यजन् द्रव्यजातमपदिश्य देवताम् ॥' शिशुपालवध IX. 20 and Mallinātha's commentary thereon.

Now to turn to the illustration of यथासंख्यपाठ. In the मैत्रायणी संहिता two sacrificial rites, one in honour of Indra and Agni and the other in honour of Vaiśvānara, are enjoined by the sentences 'ऐन्द्राग्न... निर्वपेत्' and 'वैश्वानरं... निर्वपेत्.' These yāgas are mentioned in the order of ऐन्द्राग्न and वैश्वानर. Later on in the same Saṁhitā occur two pairs of presenting (याज्या) and invoking (अनुवाक्या) verses, one pair commencing with 'इन्द्राग्नी रोचना दिवः (Indra and Agni are the illuminators of heaven)' and the other with 'वैश्वानरोऽजीजनत् (Vaiśvānara created)' in this same order. Now, the question here is which pair of mantras is subordinate to which rite. Then, from यथासंख्यपाठ we decide that the pair of mantras first mentioned is subservient to the rite, which is first enjoined, and the pair of mantras mentioned second to the rite enjoined second.

The reason why we do so is this: When the expectancy as to whose purpose it has to serve (कैमर्थ्याकाङ्क्षा), or to which it is to be subservient, arises in the case of the pair of mantras occurring first, the rite mentioned first naturally comes forward (उपतिष्ठते) as the claimant for the services of this first pair of mantras. Because both these belong to the same place viz. the first place in the order of their occurrence in the text (समानदेशत्वात् यथासंख्यपाठरूपसमानदेशत्वात् उभयोः प्रथमपठितत्वेन प्राथम्यरूपैकदेशस्थत्वादित्यर्थः). Similar is the case with the second pair of mantras and the second rite.

प्रथमस्य प्रथमम् = प्रथमस्य मन्त्रस्य प्रथमं कर्म. कैमर्थ्याकाङ्क्षा = कः अर्थः यस्य स किमर्थः, तस्य भावः कैमर्थ्यम्, तस्य आकाङ्क्षा.

यथासंख्यपाठाद् विनियोगः in the present case may be represented a follows :—

मैत्रायणी संहिता

यागयोः प्रधानभूतयोः अनुक्रमः	याज्यानुवाक्यामन्त्राणामङ्गभूतानामनुक्रमः
(1) ऐन्द्राग्नम्	(1) 'इन्द्राग्नी रोचना दिवः'
(2) वैश्वानरम्	(2) 'वैश्वानरोऽजीजनत्'

In connection with this विनियोग by यथासंख्यपाठ the following point is likely to arise: In the two pairs of verses, which are here established as being subservient to the two rites mentioned first, the words इन्द्राग्नी and वैश्वानर occur. लिङ्गप्रमाण, therefore, would show that these pairs are to be respectively used as subservient to rites in honour of

इन्द्राग्नी and वैश्वानर. Why should this then not be regarded as a case of लौङ्गिक विनियोग ? What special propriety is there in regarding this as an instance of 'यथासंख्यपाठाद् विनियोगः' ?

The answer to this is that if we were to regard the present mantras as a case of लैङ्गिक विनियोग, these mantras would be subservient to whatever rites are performed in honour of Indra-Agni and Vaiśvānara. But the Śrutī wants to restrict the use of these mantras to the particular yāgas laid down by 'ऐन्द्राग्न...निर्वपेत्' and 'वैश्वानरं...निर्वपेत्.' Therefore, this must be regarded as a case of यथासंख्यपाठाद् विनियोगः'.

Another good illustration of यथासंख्यपाठाद् विनियोगः is given in the जैमिनीयन्यायमालाविस्तर under III. iii. 12. In the दर्शपूर्णमास chapter there are two Sections called आध्वर्यव काण्ड and याजमान काण्ड. In the आध्वर्यव काण्ड three sacrifices known as (1) आग्नेय, (2) उपांशुयाज and (3) अग्नीषोमीय याग are mentioned one after the other. In the याजमान काण्ड occur three mantras in the order of (1) 'अग्नेरहं देवयज्यया अन्नादो भूयासम् (May I be the eater of food through the divine sacrifice to Agni),' (2) 'दब्धिरसि, अदब्धो भूयासम्, अमुं दभेयम् (A fatal weapon art thou, uninjured may I be, him i. e. my enemy may I injure)' and (3) 'अग्नीषोमयोरहं देवयज्यया वृत्रहा भूयासम् (Through the divine sacrifice to Agni and Soma may I be the killer of Vṛtra).'

Now, लिङ्गप्रमाण shows that the first and the third mantras are respectively subservient to आग्नेय and अग्नीषोमीय याग, because the words अग्ने and अग्नीषोमयोः occur therein. The question of the second mantra is settled by यथासंख्यपाठ. As the mantra 'दब्धिरसि etc.' occurs second in order, it is subservient to उपांशुयाज, whose order in the enumeration is also second.

Read 'दर्शपूर्णमासयोराध्वर्यवे काण्डे आग्नेय-उपांशुयाज-अग्नीषोमियियागाः क्रमेण आम्नाताः। याजमाने च काण्डे आग्नेयादिविषयाः तेनैव क्रमेण मन्त्रा आम्नाताः । 'अग्नेरहं देवयज्यया अन्नादो भूयासम्' 'दब्धिरसि, अदब्धो भूयासम्, अमुं दभेयम्' 'अग्नीषोमियियोरहं देवयज्यया वृत्रहा भूयासम्' इति । तत्र आद्यन्तयोः आग्नेयाग्नीषोमीययोः कर्मणोः आद्यन्तौ मन्त्रौ, मध्यमस्य च उपांशुयाजस्य कर्मणो मध्यमो 'दब्धिरसि, अदब्धो भूयासम्, अमुं दभेयम्' इति मन्त्रोऽङ्गम् । तस्य च ब्राह्मणवाक्यमेवमाम्नायते 'एतया वै दब्ध्या देवा असुरान् दभ्नुवन्, तयैव भ्रातृव्यं दभ्नोति' इति । दब्धिर्घातुकमायुधमित्यर्थः । न च आग्नेय-अग्नीषोमीययोरपि अनिष्टनिवारकत्वेन साधारण-लिङ्गेन दब्धिमन्त्रस्य अङ्गत्वं किं न स्यादिति वाच्यम् । यथा वाक्यद्वयानुसंधानेन संपन्नप्रकरणं पृथक्प्रमाणं तथा प्रकरणद्वयानुसंधानसंपन्नेन क्रमप्रमाणेन उपांशुयाजे तस्य मन्त्रस्य विनियोगात् । न च क्रमस्य प्रकरणेऽन्तर्भाव इति वाच्यम् । द्वयोर्वाक्ययोरिव प्रकरणयोरेकवाक्यत्वाभावात् । तस्मात् क्रमप्रमाणेन मध्यवर्तिन उपांशुयाजस्य मध्यवर्ती मन्त्रोऽङ्गं समानदेशत्वात् ।' रामेश्वर

वैकृताङ्गानां...आनर्थक्यपत्तेः—In this paragraph Bhāskara gives us an illustration of application by संनिधिपाठ, which is the second variety of पाठसादेश्य.

The sentence 'वैश्वदेवीं सांग्रहणीं निर्वपेद् ग्रामकामः' lays down a विकृतियाग (modification or derivative), called सांग्रहणी, of which the प्रकृति (arche-type or model) is दर्शपूर्णमास. This derivative is called सांग्रहणी or a sacrifice of conciliation, because it involves conciliation or winning over (मनसा परस्परमैकमत्येन सम्यक् स्वीकारः संग्रहणम्। तद् यस्याम् इष्टौ अस्ति सा सांग्रहणी — सायण). A man, who is hankering after a village, must naturally secure the conciliation of the inhabitants thereof.

In close proximity with the सांग्रहणीयाग occurs the sentence 'आमनम् अस्य आमनस्य देवा इति तिस्र आहुतीर्जुहोति,' which lays down three sacrificial rites called आमनहोमाः (संगृहीतं मनोऽस्मिन् इति आमनम्। छान्दसोऽन्त्यलोपः। — भट्टभास्कर) or rites of conciliation.

No special fruit is mentioned for these आमनहोमs. They are thus फलाकाङ्क्ष or require something to which they would be subordinate. Therefore, by means of संनिधिपाठ, or mention or text in proximity, the आमनहोमs become subordinate to the derivative सांग्रहणी, according to the rule 'फलवत्संनिधौ अफलं तदङ्गम्.'

Prakaraṇa can have no scope here, because though the आमनहोमs are फलाकाङ्क्ष, सांग्रहणी is not कथंभावाकाङ्क्ष. For, its कथंभावाकाङ्क्षा is satisfied by चोदक or अतिदेश viz. 'प्रकृतिवद् विकृतिः कर्तव्या.' सांग्रहणी would get all the प्राकृताङ्गs by means of this अतिदेश. The आमनहोमs, however, are new subsidiaries and their subsidiariness arises from स्थान, of which संनिधिपाठ is a variety. Vide paragraph beginning with 'एतच्च प्रकृतौ एव' on p. 21 above.

वैकृताङ्गानाम् of the paragraph under discussion thus means 'of *new* subsidiaries of the derivative.' It is the same as अपूर्वाङ्गानाम् of line 4 on p. 21.

फलवत्संनिधौ अफल तदङ्गम्—This is a well-known maxim from the Mīmāṁsāśāstra. It means that when a rite, having no independent fruit of its own (अफलम्=अश्रूयमाणफलं कर्म), is mentioned in the vicinity of another which has a fruit, the fruit-less rite becomes subservient to the fruit-ful one. दर्शपूर्णमास are sacrifices whose fruit is heaven. In their vicinity are mentioned rites like प्रयाजs, which have no fruit of their own. प्रयाजs, therefore, become दर्शपूर्णमासाङ्ग according to this maxim.

Read 'स्वर्गादिफलवतो दर्शपूर्णमासादेः संनिधाने श्रुतं प्रयाजादि स्वतो विफलं तदङ्गम्-इति अङ्गीक्रियते [सोऽयं फलवत्संनिधौ अफलं तदङ्गमिति न्यायः]' आनन्दगिरि on शाङ्करभाष्य on II. i. 14.

सांग्रहणी and आमनहोमs form the subject of an अधिकरण of जैमिनि (IV. iv. 7). There the पूर्वपक्ष view is that आमनहोमs and सांग्रहणी should all be considered as being equally principal, even as the six sacrifices constituting दर्शपूर्णमास, or the many sacrifices constituting राजसूय, are all regarded as being equally principal. To this the सिद्धान्तिन् points out that the cases of सांग्रहणी–आमनहोमs and the sacrifices that constitute दर्शपूर्णमास or राजसूय are not similar. The sacrifices that form दर्शपूर्णमास are all सफल or connected with the fruit viz. heaven. Similarly, all the sacrifices comprising राजसूय are connected with the fruit viz. universal sovereignty. But आमनहोमs have no fruit. Therefore, they have to be subservient to सांग्रहणी, according to the maxim 'फलवत्संनिधौ अफलं तदङ्गम्.'

Read 'काम्येष्टिकाण्डे श्रूयते—" वैश्वदेवीं सांग्रहणीं निर्वपेद् ग्रामकामः " इति । तत्र आमनहोमाः श्रुताः । " आमनस्य आमनस्य देवाः—इति तिस्र आहुतीर्जुहोति " इति ।

त एते आमनहोमा सांग्रहण्या इष्ट्या सह समप्रधानभूताः । न हि तेषां मुख्यत्वे कश्चिद्विरोधोऽस्ति । दृष्टं हि आग्नेयादिषु [दर्शपूर्णमासयागेषु] अनुमत्यादिषु [राजसूययागेषु] च बहूनमुख्यत्वम् । इति चेत्—

मैवम् । " दर्शपूर्णमासाभ्यां स्वर्गकामः " इति वाक्येन " स्वाराज्यकामो राजसूयेन " इति वाक्येन च यथा बहूनां फलसंबन्धावगमः, न तथा आमनहोमानाम् । फलसंबन्धाभावे सति प्राधान्यायोगात् । "सांग्रहणीं निर्वपेद् ग्रामकामः" इति वाक्यं तु सांग्रहण्या एव फलसंबन्धं बोधयति, न तु आमनहोमानाम् । तस्मात् फलवत्याः सांग्रहण्याः संनिधौ आम्नाता अफला आमनहोमा तदङ्गम् ।' जैमिनीयन्यायमालाविस्तर p. 257

So far we have seen the meaning of 'वैकृताङ्गानां (विकृतियागस्य अपूर्वाणां नवीनानां प्राकृतेतराणामित्यर्थः अङ्गानां) विकृत्यर्थत्वं संनिधिपाठात् यथा आमनहोमानाम्.' We have left out of consideration the words प्राकृताङ्गानुवादेन विहितानां संदंशपतितानाम्. We shall leave them for the present and return to them later on.

तेषां हि कैमर्थ्याकाङ्क्षायां...उपस्थितत्वात्—This sentence gives us the reason why आमनहोमs are considered subservient to सांग्रहणी.

आमनहोमs, we have seen, are फलाकाङ्क्ष (which is the same as कैमर्थ्याकाङ्क्ष), because no fruit is mentioned for them. 'आमनहोमैः किं भावयेत्' or 'किमर्थाः आमनहोमाः' is the expectancy that arises with regard to them. 'आमनहोमैः विकृत्यपूर्वं भावयेत्' or 'आमनहोमाः विकृत्यर्थाः' is the answer to this question. विकृत्यपूर्व means the transcendental result, which would be produced by the derivative सांग्रहणी and which would give to the performer of सांग्रहणी mastery over a village. This विकृत्यपूर्व is connected with the आमनहोमs as its fruit, because it is so near them (उपस्थितत्वात्). For, the sentences 'वैश्वदेवीं......ग्रामकामः' and 'आमनस्य...जुहोति' occur in the vicinity of each other.

It should be noted that it is not quite correct to say that विकृत्यपूर्व is the भाव्य of आमनहोमs. For, the आमनहोमs are not going to produce विकृत्यपूर्व directly. विकृत्यपूर्व will be generated by the विकृति itself viz. सांग्रहणी. आमनहोमs only help the विकृति in producing the अपूर्व. So, properly speaking the कैमर्थ्याकाङ्क्षा of आमनहोमs is fulfilled by 'आमनहोमैः विकृत्युपकारं भावयेत्'.

स्वतन्त्रफलकत्वे...आनर्थक्यापत्तेः—This small sentence is full of meaning and is intended to refute a possible objection against the arrangement arrived at above viz. that आमनहोमs are subordinate to सांग्रहणी.

The objection is thus stated:–The sentence 'विश्वजिता यजेत' is अश्रूयमाणफल i. e. no fruit is laid down for the विश्वजित् sacrifice. The पूर्वपक्ष view in the matter is that either no fruit should be imagined for this sacrifice, or that any fruit should be regarded as its fruit. Against this the सिद्धान्तिन् establishes that heaven as being the highest kind of pleasure and as being liked by all should be regarded as the fruit of the विश्वजित् sacrifice. This arrangement is known as विश्वजिन्न्याय. Stated in general terms the विश्वजित् maxim means that when no fruit is mentioned for a sacrifice, heaven should be regarded as its fruit.

Relying on the विश्वजिन्न्याय the objector here urges that as the आमनहोमs are अश्रूयमाणफलक, heaven should be regarded as their fruit. It is not right to regard them as subservient to सांग्रहणीयाग and assign its अपूर्व as the भाव्य or फल for the आमनहोमs.

To this the answer is that it आमनहोमs are considered to possess an independent fruit viz. heaven, their mention (पाठः) in the vicinity of the derivative सांग्रहणी would be purposeless. What is meant is this: The fact that the आमनहोमs are mentioned in the neighbourhood of the सांग्रहणीयाग must be regarded as significant. And that significance is this viz. that the अफल आमनहोमs are to be regarded as subservient to the सफल सांग्रहणीयाग, whose fruit becomes consequently the fruit of the आमनहोमs as well.

This means in short that two conditions must be satisfied before विश्वजिन्न्याय becomes applicable viz. (1) the rite must be fruit-less and (2) it must not occur in the vicinity of a fruitful one. Though the first condition is satisfied in the case of the आमनहोमs, the second is not. Therefore, the maxim of the विश्वजित् sacrifice is not applicable in their case.

Read 'फलवत्कर्मसंनिधौ पठितस्य एव अश्रूयमाणफलस्य विश्वजिन्न्यायेन स्वतन्त्रफलं कल्प्यते। अफलस्य फलवत्संनिधौ पाठस्तु तदङ्गत्वायैव। तदभावे अनर्थकत्वमेव तस्य आपद्येत इति भावः।' रामेश्वर

प्राकृताङ्गानुवादेन विहितानां संदंशपतितानाम्—We now come to the explanation of these two expressions, which had been left out before.

It should be noted that the omission of these two adjectives of वैकृताङ्गानाम् would not in any way affect the main topic here. They are by no means necessary to illustrate 'संनिधिपाठाद् अङ्गत्वम्,' which is the purpose of the paragraph under discussion.

Bhāskara, however, uses these apparently unnecessary expressions in order to controvert a view of Āpadeva. According to Āpadeva there are two exceptions to the general rule that अपूर्वाङ्ग of विकृति become subservient to it by means of स्थान. These two exceptions are: (1) First, when a new subsidiary is laid down for a derivative in further reference to a subsidiary of the arche-type, this new subsidiary becomes subservient to the derivative by प्रकरण and not by स्थान. (2) Secondly, when a new subsidiary is found in a pair of tongs (संदंशपतित), it becomes subservient to the modification by प्रकरण and not by स्थान.

The following are the illustrations of these two exceptions, according to आपदेव.

(1) The sentence 'सोमापौष्णं त्रैतमालभेत पशुकामः' lays down a derivative (विकृतियागः), called सोमापौष्ण, which is offered in honour of सोम and पूषन्. In close proximity with this sentence occurs the direction 'औदुम्बरो यूपो भवति'. Now यूप or the sacrificial post is a प्राकृताङ्ग and accrues to the विकृति सोमापौष्ण by means of अतिदेश. But in further reference to this subsidiary of the arche-type (प्राकृताङ्ग) viz. यूप, औदुम्बरत्व or being-made-of-Udumbara-wood is enjoined by the sentence 'औदुम्बरो यूपो भवति' for the विकृतियाग in contradistinction from the प्रकृतियाग, where a खादिर यूप is used. According to Āpadeva this औदुम्बरत्व becomes a subsidiary of the derivative by प्रकरण, because औदुम्बरत्व is प्राकृताङ्गानुवादेन विहित.

Āpadeva holds that the कथंभावाकाङ्क्षा of the विकृतियाग सोमापौष्ण is not satisfied by the अतिदेश of यूप merely, but requires औदुम्बरत्व as well. Thus, उभयाकाङ्क्षा being present viz. फलाकाङ्क्षा on the part of औदुम्बरत्व and कथंभावाकाङ्क्षा on the part of the विकृतियाग सोमापौष्ण, प्रकरण steps in and decides that औदुम्बरत्व is subsidiary to सोमापौष्ण.

(2) The second exception which Āpadeva quotes is the अभ्यन्होमs. These sacrifices are, as we saw before, mentioned in the proximity of the सांग्रहणी याग. With regard to them the passage 'यत् प्रयाजानां पुरस्तात् जुहुयात् बहिरात्मानं सजातानां दध्यात्, यदनुयाजानामुपरिष्टात् जुहुयात् स्वर्गं लोकमपक्रामेत्,

मध्ये जुहोति, मध्य एव सजातानामात्मानं धत्ते' lays down that they viz the आमनहोमs should be offered in between प्रयाजs and अनुयाजs. The आमनहोमs thus fall within a pair of tongs formed by प्रयाजs and अनुयाजs. Consequently, according to Āpadeva, the आमनहोमs become subservient to the विकृतियाग सांग्रहणी by प्रकरण and not by स्थान.

The following extracts from the मीमांसान्यायप्रकाश will make the view of आपदेव clear:

'यत्तु विकृतौ प्राकृताङ्गानुवादेन विधीयते यथा 'औदुम्बरो यूपो भवति' इति यूपानुवादेन औदुम्बरत्वं तत् प्रकरणाद् गृह्यते।'

'यत्तु विकृतावपि प्राकृतधर्मानुवादेन विधीयमानयोः धर्मयोः अन्तराले अपूर्वमपि अङ्गं केवलं पठ्यते तदपि प्रकरणेन विनियुज्यते। यद्यपि विकृतेः कथंभावाकाङ्क्षा प्राकृतैरेवाङ्गैः शाम्यति, तथापि यत्र प्राकृताङ्गानुवादेन धर्मविधानं तत्र तद्विधानं यावद् भवति तावत् कथंभावाकाङ्क्षा न निवर्तते। अतो विकृतेराकाङ्क्षावत्त्वात् अन्तराले विहितस्यापि अपूर्वाङ्गस्य भाव्याकाङ्क्षासत्त्वात् युक्तं तस्य प्रकरणाद् विकृत्यर्थम्, यथा आमनहोमेषु। ते हि प्राकृताङ्गानुवादेन विधीयमानयोर्धर्मयोरन्तराले विधीयन्ते इति उक्तं तन्त्ररत्नावल्यादौ।'

Āpadeva believes, as we saw before, that the rule 'अपूर्वाङ्गानां स्थानाद् विकृत्यर्थत्वम्' has the two above-explained exceptions. When, therefore, he wanted to illustrate 'संनिधिपाठाद् विकृत्यर्थत्वम्,' he made reference to these two exceptions in the following manner: 'यानि तु वैकृतानि अङ्गानि **प्राकृताङ्गाननुवादेन** विहितानि **संदंशापतितानि** तेषां विकृत्यर्थत्वं संनिधिपाठात्।'

Bhāskara on the other hand does not believe, and for good reasons too, that the rule 'अपूर्वाङ्गानां स्थानाद् विकृत्यर्थत्वम्' has any exceptions. He, therefore, wanted to include Āpadeva's exceptions in the province of 'संनिधिपाठाद् विकृत्यर्थत्वम्.' To do this he adopted Āpadeva's own expressions, but dropped therefrom the negative particles अन् and अ and said 'वैकृताङ्गानां **प्राकृताङ्गानुवादेन** विहितानां **संदंशपतितानां** विकृत्यर्थत्वं संनिधिपाठात् यथा आमनहोमानाम्।' If we add 'वा' after संदंशपतितानाम्, Bhāskara's meaning would be clearer. His view is that new subsidiaries of the derivative, whether enjoined in further reference to a subsidiary of the arche-type or falling within a pair of tongs, become all subservient to the derivative through mention or text in proximity (संनिधिपाठात्).

All printed editions of the Arthasaṃgraha, the edition of Thibaut (1882), the edition in the Kashi-Sanskrit-Series (1915) and the Nirṇayasāgara edition, read here 'प्राकृताङ्गानुवादेन विहितानां संदंशपतितानाम्'. We have just seen that the purpose of these expressions is to indicate difference of opinion from Āpadeva and to include in the province of 'संनिधिपाठाद् विकृत्यर्थत्वम्' the two exceptions mentioned by him. But the late Mr. S. M. Paranjpe missed this purpose of Bhāskara. He was thus unable to get any meaning from 'प्राकृताङ्गानुवादेन विहितानां संदंशपतितानाम्'. Consequently, he thought that these expressions were misprints and, taking his cue from Āpadeva, bluntly changed Bhāskara's words into 'प्राकृताङ्गाननुवादेन विहितानां संदंशापतितानाम्'.

Having changed Bhāskara's words into what was found in the Mīmāṁsānyāyaprakāśa Paranjpe had to admit that the passage was difficult to understand, because the two exceptions, which were supposed to be referred to therein, were not mentioned by Bhāskara before.

But all this was unnecessary. The truth is that Bhāskara refuses to follow Āpadeva in this matter. Once at least he shows the courage to differ from him. In this connection the following points deserve note.

(1) Bhāskara has definitely said before that *even* the new subsidiaries of a modification (अपूर्वाङ्गानामपि p.21, l. 4) become subservient to it through place *alone* (स्थानादेव p. 21, l. 5). The words अपि and एव show that Bhāskara admits no exceptions to the general rule viz. 'अपूर्वाङ्गानां स्थानाद् विकृत्यर्थत्वम्.'

Āpadeva on the other hand has very elaborately explained the two exceptions, which in his opinion this rule has. If we were to adopt here the reading from the मीमांसान्यायप्रकाश, we should have to suppose that Bhāskara tacitly admits these two exceptions. But this is not fair. If Bhāskara had believed that the general rule 'अपूर्वाङ्गानां स्थानाद् विकृत्यर्थत्वम्' had any exceptions, he would have mentioned them at the proper place. He would not have tacitly and indirectly admitted their existence in the manner he is supposed to have done by Paranjpe.

(2) Bhāskara has further declared that प्रकरण directly lays down the application of action only. If we change his words so as to make him admit the two exceptions mentioned by Āpadeva, we shall have to understand 'क्रियाया एव' in the sentence 'तदिदं प्रकरणं क्रियाया एव साक्षाद् विनियोजकम्' with a reservation. For, औदुम्बरत्व, which, as an exception. is regarded as प्रकरणविनियुक्त, is not a क्रिया, but a गुण.

(3) By quoting the rule 'प्रकृतिवद् विकृतिः कर्तव्याः' Bhāskara has definitely stated that a modification has no कथंभावाकाङ्क्षा. If प्रकरण were to have scope in a modification in the case of the two exceptions, we

should have to admit that a modification *has* कथंभावाकाङ्क्षा in the case of at least these two exceptions. But to restrict the अतिदेश in this manner is not proper.

(4) आमनहोमs form the decisive test for the correctness of Bhāskara's reading here. Bhāskara definitely says that आमनहोमs become subservient to the विकृतियाग सांग्रहणी through संनिधिपाठ. Āpadeva on the other hand has stated with equal definiteness that आमनहोमs form an exception to the general rule of 'अपूर्वाङ्गानां स्थानाद् विकृत्यर्थत्वम्' and consequently they become subservient to the derivative through प्रकरण. If in the present passage we were to adopt the reading found in Āpadeva viz. 'प्राकृताङ्गाननुवादेन विहितानां संदंशापतितानाम्', it would be tantamount to Bhāskara's tacitly admitting the two exceptions so elaborately explained by Āpadeva. That makes Bhāskara blow hot and cold in the same breath. For, his tacit admission of the two exceptions means his assent to the view that the आमनहोमs are subservient to सांग्रहणी through प्रकरण. But his express statement is that the आमनहोमs are विकृत्यर्थ through संनिधिपाठ.

The only logical and reasonable conclusion under the circumstances is that Bhāskara did not admit the two exceptions mentioned by Āpadeva. He wanted to suggest this definitely and therefore read 'प्राकृताङ्गानुवादेन विहितानां संदंशापतितानाम्,' which shows that the two exceptions of Āpadeva are included by Bhāskara in the province of 'संनिधिपाठाद् विकृत्यर्थत्वम्.'

It must here be pointed out that पार्थसारथिमिश्र (शास्त्रदीपिका) and सोमेश्वर (न्यायसुधा) are on the side of Bhāskara in holding that आमनहोमs are स्थानविनियुक्त, while a work called तन्त्ररत्न is appealed to by Āpadeva for his opinion that आमनहोमs are प्रकरणविनियुक्त.

(5) With regard to the statement of Āpadeva that आमनहोमs are संदंशपतित, it must be noted that strictly speaking they do not fall within a pair of tongs. It is true that they are mentioned within two प्राकृताङ्गs. But the technical संदंश requires that an अङ्ग should be mentioned between two अङ्गs of an अङ्ग e g. अभिक्रमण, which is mentioned between घृतानयन and मिथुनवेदन, which are the अङ्गs of प्रयाजs, themselves an अङ्ग of दर्शपूर्णमास. Vide Section 29 above.

The subservience of subsidiaries to the arche-type and the derivative would be clear from the following diagram :—

यज्ञः

प्रकृतिः — विकृतिः

अङ्गानि are made subservient to प्रकृति through प्रकरण, because there is उभयाकाङ्क्षा.

(विकृतिः →) प्राकृत–अङ्गानि — वैकृत or अपूर्व अङ्गानि

(प्राकृत–अङ्गानि:) These are made subservient to विकृति through अतिदेश.

(वैकृत or अपूर्व अङ्गानि →)

(1) प्राकृताङ्गानुवादेन विहितमपूर्वमङ्गम् e. g. औदुम्बरत्वम्. This is स्थानविनियुक्त or made subservient to विकृति through स्थान, i. e. through संनिधिपाठ, which is a division of स्थान.

(2) प्राकृतधर्मसंदंशपातितमपूर्वमङ्गम् e. g. आमनहोमाः. These also are made subservient to विकृति through संनिधिपाठ i. e. through स्थान.

(3) एतद्द्वयेतरद् अपूर्वाङ्गम् e. g. उपहोमः. This is also स्थानविनियुक्त in the same manner.

All these three kinds of अपूर्व or वैकृत अङ्गs are made subservient to the derivative by means of स्थान i. e. संनिधिपाठ, according to our author.

Āpadeva on the other hand believes that the first two are प्रकरणविनियुक्त, because they form exceptions to the general rule that new subsidiaries become subservient to the derivative through place and that the third only is स्थानविनियुक्त. Bhāskara does not mention the first and the third. They are found in Āpadeva's book.

Section 34

Having dealt with यथासंख्यपाठ and संनिधि, the two varieties of पाठसादेश्य, the author now proceeds to explain अनुष्ठानसादेश्य, which represents the other main division of स्थान. Vide p. 147 above.

पशुधर्माणा...सादेश्यात्—This sentence gives an illustration of अनुष्ठानसादेश्य द् विनियोगः.

There are three main classes of sacrifices, known as पाकयज्ञसंस्था, हविर्यज्ञसंस्था and सोमयज्ञसंस्था. Each of these comprises seven sacrifices, which thus number 21. ज्योतिष्टोम is a सोमयाग and is the प्रकृति or archetype for all Soma-sacrifices.

In normal Soma-sacrifices, of which ज्योतिष्टोम is the model, three animals, known as अग्नीषोमीय, सवनीय and अनुबन्ध्य, are sacrificed on three successive days called औपवसथ्य, सौत्य and अवभृथ respectively. Thus the अग्निषोमीय animal is sacrificed on the औपवसथ्य day, which is so called, because the sacrificer observes a fast on that day along with certain other vows. See आपस्तम्ब सूत्र I. iv. 14. 15 'एतत् कृत्वा उपवसति', on which the Bhāṣya runs as follows: 'अन्वाधानादिपरिस्तरणान्तं कर्म कृत्वा अग्निसमीपे नियमविशिष्टो वास उपवासः।' The सवनीय animal is slaughtered on the सौत्य day, which receives its name from the fact that the Soma is pressed on that day (सुत्या सवनं तस्या अयं सौत्यः). And lastly, the अनुबन्ध्य animal is immolated on the अवभृथ day, whose appellation arises from the final purificatory bath (अवभृथः), indicating the close of the sacrifice which takes place on that day.

These three animals viz. अग्नीषोमीय, सवनीय and अनुबन्ध्य are metioned in the chapter dealing with the ज्योतिष्टोम sacrifice. In the same chapter are mentioned certain rites such as उपाकरण, पर्यग्निकरण and यूपनियोजन. उपाकरण consists in touching the animal with two Vedic stanzas viz. 'प्रजापतेर्जायमानाः' and 'इमं पशुम्.' पर्यग्निकरण is the waving of burning darbhas three times round the animal, commencing from the right. यूपनियोजन means the tying of the animal to the sacrificial post.

Now, the question here is whether these rites belong or are subservient to all the three animals or to only one of them. The Pūrvapakṣin holds that as the three animals and the rites are mentioned in the same chapter and as there is nothing to restrict them to any one of the animals, the rites primarily belong to all the three animals.

Against this the Siddhāntin points out that these rites are mentioned at a place, where the performances to be gone through on the औपवसथ्य day are described. The अग्नीषोमीय animal is also sacrificed on the औपवसथ्य day, according to the direction contained in 'स एष द्विदेवत्यः पशुः औपवसथ्ये अहनि आलब्धव्यः।' When, therefore, the expectancy as to what these rites are intended for arises, the not-existent-before of the अग्नीषोमीय animal, which is present (उपस्थित) there as the thing to be produced, is connected with these rites as their भाव्य or the matter to be effected. Consequently, the rites become subservient to the अग्नीषोमीय animal primarily.

What is meant is this : 'एभिर्धर्मैः किं भाव्यम्' or 'एते धर्माः किमर्थाः' is the expectancy that arises in the case of the rites उपाकरण etc. They want a फल, in short. Now, these rites are performed on the औपवसथ्य day. On the same day the अग्नीषोमीय animal is offered. So the place of performance (अनुष्ठानदेशः) of the rites and the अग्नीषोमीय animal is the same. Therefore, on account of अनुष्ठानसादेश्य the rites become sub servient to this animal. Thus, the expectancy referred to above is satisfied by 'एभिर्धर्मैः अग्नीषोमीयपशुपूर्वं भाव्यम्' or 'एते धर्मा अग्नीषोमीयपश्वर्थाः'.

Strictly speaking the former answer to the expectancy is not quite correct. For, the rites do not produce the पश्वपूर्व directly. The correct answer is 'एभिर्धर्मैः अग्नीषोमीयपश्वपूर्वोपकारः भाव्यः।'.

It should be noted here that though the rites and [the sacrifice of] the अग्नीषोमीय animal are performed on the same day, their mention occurs in different places i. e. though between the rites and the animal अनुष्ठानसादेश्य exists, there is no पाठसादेश्य between them. For, while the rites are mentioned among the performances of the औपवसथ्य day, the अग्नीषोमीय animal is mentioned earlier viz. near the place where the purchase of Soma is enjoined.

Thus, the rites उपाकरण and others belong primarily to the अग्नीषोमीय animal. This does not, however, mean that they are not to be performed on the other animals. In the case of the other animals they become available by अतिदेश.

The mutual relation of the rites, animals and days will be clear from the following :—

दिनत्रयात्मकः सोमयागः

- (1) औपवसथ्यदिनः
  - (1) अग्नीषोमीयपशुः
  - (2) पशुधर्माः:
    - (a) उपाकरणम्
    - (b) पर्यग्निकरणम्
    - (c) यूपनियोजनम्

  एतेषामनुष्ठानसादेश्यं वर्तते। तस्मादनुष्ठानसादेश्यात् पशुधर्माणामग्नीषोमीयार्थत्वम्।
- (2) सौत्यादिनः
  - (2) सवनीयपशुः
- (3) अवभृथदिनः
  - (3) अनुबन्ध्यपशुः

  एतयोः पशुधर्मा अतिदेशप्राप्ताः।

Read 'अग्नीषोमीयः सवनीयः अनुबन्ध्यः इत्येते त्रयः पशवो ज्योतिष्टोमप्रकरणे समाम्नाताः। पशुधर्माश्च उपाकरणपर्यग्निकरणादयः तत्र आम्नाताः। 'प्रजापतेर्जायमानाः' 'इमं पशुम्' इत्याभ्यामृग्भ्यां **पशोरुपस्पर्शनमुपाकरणम्**। दर्भज्वालया त्रिः प्रदक्षिणीकरणं **पर्यग्निकरणम्**। त एते धर्मास्त्रिषु अपि पशुषु साधारण्येन विधीयन्ते। त्रयाणामपि ज्योतिष्टोमप्रकरणपाठसाम्यात्।...[एते धर्माः] अविशेषतः त्रिषु अपि पशुषु अवतिष्ठन्ते। **इति प्राप्ते**—

ब्रूमः। अस्ति अत्र विशेषः संनिधिलक्षणः। सौत्यनामकादह्नः प्राचीने औपवसथ्यनाम्नि आह्नि धिष्ण्यनिर्माणादूर्ध्वमेते धर्मा आम्नाताः। अग्नीषोमीयस्यापि तदेव स्थानम्। सवनीयस्तु सौत्येऽहनि श्रूयते—'आश्विनं ग्रहं गृहीत्वा त्रिवृता यूपं परिवीय आग्नेयं सवनीयं पशुमुपाकरोति' इति। अनुबन्ध्यश्च अवभृथान्ते समाम्नातः। ततः संनिधिना ते धर्मा अग्नीषोमीये संबध्यन्ते, सवनीयानुबन्ध्ययोस्तु चोदकाद् अतिदिश्यन्ते।' जैमिनीयन्यायमालाविस्तर pp. 183—184

Section 35

This Section proves the superiority of स्थान over समाख्या.

In the literature relating to दर्शपूर्णमास there is a chapter, which the Yājñikas (priests or ritualists) name पौरोडाशिक 'Concerning the sacrificial cake (पुरोडाशस्य इदं पौरोडाशिकं काण्डमित्यर्थः),' because here all the injunctions referring to the sacrificial cake are given (अत्र पुरोडाशोपयोगिनः विधयः श्रूयन्ते). In this chapter are mentioned certain vessels such as कुम्भी, शाखापवित्रम्, अभिधानी and दोहनपात्रम्, which are used for the purpose of sacrificial milk and curds (सान्नाय्यं दधिपयसी, तस्य पात्राणि) and also certain others such as उलूखल, मुसल, कृष्णाजिनम्, दृषदुपले and जुहू, which are used for preparing the पुरोडाश or the sacrificial cake. These two sets of vessels are respectively known as सांनाय्य vessels and पुरोडाश vessels. This chapter also contains the mantra or formula 'शुन्धध्वं दैव्याय कर्मणे', which means 'हे पात्राणि, देवयज्यात्मने दैव्याय कर्मणे शुन्धध्वं शुद्धानि भवत। Be pure for a rite in honour of the gods,' and which is employed at the time of cleansing the vessels.

Now the question is whether this formula of purification (शुन्धनमन्त्रः) viz. 'शुन्धध्वं दैव्याय कर्मणे' is applicable to both the सांनाय्य vessels and the पुरोडाश vessels, or to any one of these two sets. The Pūrvapakṣin holds that as the heading of the chapter is पौरोडाशिक, the formula occurring in it should be made applicable not only to सांनाय्य vessels but also to पुरोडाश vessels. This will be application on account of the etymological sense of the word पौरोडाशिक i. e. समाख्यया विनियोगः.

Against this the Siddhāntin points out that the formula and the सांनाय्य vessels are mentioned in the chapter near each other. On account of संनिधिपाठ, which is a division of पाटसादेश्य, the mantra, therefore, becomes subservient to सांनाय्य vessels.

The position now is this: समाख्याविनियोग makes the mantra subservient to both सांनाय्य vessels and पुरोडाश vessels. संनिधिपाटविनियोग, which is the same as पाटसादेश्यविनियोग or स्थानविनियोग on the other hand, makes the formula applicable to सांनाय्य vessels only. As स्थान is stronger than समाख्या, the final decision in the matter is that the formula is subordinate to सांनाय्य vessels only.

The reason why स्थान is stronger than समाख्या is that even in making the application by means of समाख्या, the help of स्थान is necessary. For, in the journey from समाख्या to विनियोग, the next step is स्थान. What is meant is that after having realised the etymological meaning of पौरोडाशिकम्, we have to consider the fact that the two sets of vessels and the formula are mentioned in one and the same chapter

i. e. they possess देशसामान्य or स्थान. Then, we think of the mutual expectancy of the vessels and the formula i. e. we seek the help of प्रकरण and so on with reference to the other pramāṇas till we reach विनियोग through the further stages of वाक्य, लिङ्ग and श्रुति. Thus, as समाख्या requires the help of स्थान in determining application, स्थान is stronger than समाख्या.

In order to understand the exact place where the सांनाय्य vessels are mentioned, it is necessary to have some more information. The दर्श sacrifice is performed on the new-moon day. Preparations for it, however, begin on the day preceding. On this day three rites are performed viz. वत्सापकरण, इध्माबर्हिःसंपादन and दोहन or the milking of the sacrificial cow. Of these दोहन is performed at night and for दोहन the सांनाय्य vessels are mentioned. On the new moon day the sacrificial cake (पुरोडाश:) is prepared and offered and three rites viz. व्रीहिनिर्वाप, व्रीह्यवहनन and पुरोडाशहवन are performed in that connection. The पुरोडाश vessels such as उलूखल, मुसल, कृष्णाजिनम्, दृषदुपले and जुहू are mentioned with reference to व्रीह्यवहनन and पुरोडाशहवन.

The order of rites to be performed in the दर्श sacrifice is thus as follows: (1) वत्सापकरण, (2) इध्माबर्हिःसंपादन, (3) दोहन, (4) व्रीहिनिर्वाप, (5) व्रीह्यवहनन and (6) पुरोडाशहवन. The सांनाय्य vessels are mentioned in connection with दोहन and the पुरोडाश vessels in connection with व्रीह्यवहनन and पुरोडाशहवन.

Now, the mantra 'शुन्धध्वं दैव्याय कर्मणे' occurs in connection with सांनाय्य vessels and in between the mantras referring to इध्माबर्हिःसंपादन and व्रीहिनिर्वाप. Thus, not only on account of संनिधिपाठ, but also on account of यथासंख्यपाठ, the शुन्धनमन्त्र becomes subsidiary to सांनाय्य vessels. As regards the पुरोडाश vessels they are far too removed from the mantra, which consequently cannot be subservient to them.

All this will be clear from the following diagram:—

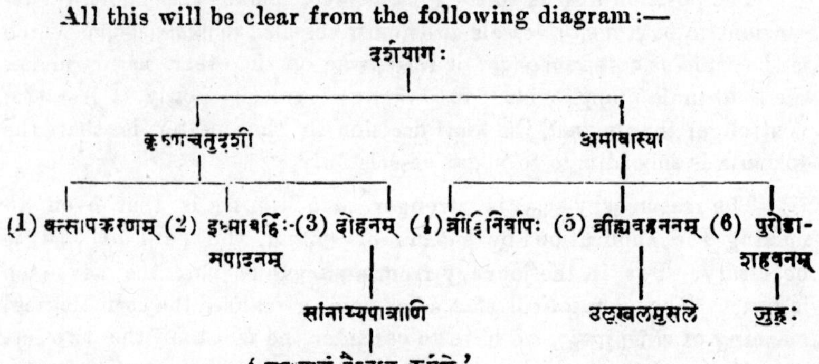

Read in this connection 'शुन्धध्वं दैव्याय कर्मणे' इत्ययं मन्त्रः 'पौरोडाशिकम्' इति याज्ञिकैः समाख्याते काण्डे पठितत्वात् पुरोडाशकाण्डोक्तानाम् उलूखलजुह्वादीनामपि शोधने अङ्गम् इति चेत्—

मा एवम्। 'पौरोडाशिकम्' इति समाख्यायां प्रकृतिः पुरोडाशमात्रमभिधत्ते, तद्धितप्रत्ययश्च काण्डम्। न चैतावता कृत्स्नपुरोडाशपात्राणां मन्त्रसंनिधिः प्रत्यक्षो भवति। किन्तु अर्थापत्त्या कल्प्यते—यदि उक्तसंनिधिर्न स्यात्, तदा मन्त्रप्रतिपादकग्रन्थस्य पौरोडाशिकसमाख्या न स्यात्। तस्मात् काण्डसमाख्यया **संनिधिं परिकल्प्य** तत्संनिध्यन्यथानुपपत्त्या परस्पराकाङ्क्षारूपं कृत्स्नं पात्रप्रकरणं कल्पयित्वा तद्द्वारा वाक्यलिङ्गश्रुतीः कल्पयित्वा तया श्रुत्या विनियोगः इति समाख्याया विप्रकर्षः। **सांनाय्यपात्राणां शोधने मन्त्रसंनिधिस्तु प्रत्यक्षः**। इध्माबर्हिःसंपादनस्य मुष्टिनिर्वापस्य च अन्तरालं सांनाय्यपात्राणां देश उक्तः। मन्त्रश्च इध्माबर्हिर्निर्वापविषययोः मन्त्रानुवाकयोः मध्यमे अनुवाके पठ्यते। तेन च प्रत्यक्षसंनिधिना प्रकरणादीनां चतुर्णामेव कल्पनात् संनिधिः संनिकृष्यते। तस्मात् क्रमेण (=स्थानेन) समाख्यां बाधित्वा 'सांनाय्यपात्रशोधनशेषो मन्त्रः' इत्ययं चरमः पक्षोऽभ्युपेयः।' जैमिनीयन्यायमालाविस्तर p. 146

Section 36

समाख्या is the last of the six pramāṇas that help the विनियोगविधि in determining the application. समाख्या means, as we saw before (p. 126), a word understood in its literal sense. Sometimes the literal sense of a word serves to indicate the relation of principal and subordinate existing between two things.

समाख्या is of two kinds—Vedic and worldly. 'प्रतु होतुश्चमसः, प्र ब्रह्मणः प्र उद्गातॄणाम्' is a Vedic sentence. It lays down that होता, along with ब्रह्मा and उद्गाता, is to drink the Soma-juice contained in the cup called चमस. This is known from the plain literal sense of the expression 'होतुश्चमसः', which means the cup of the Hotṛ i. e. the cup from which the Hotṛ drinks the Soma-juice. The समाख्या 'होतुश्चमसः' thus tells us that the Hotṛ drinks from the cup.

'होतुश्चमसः' denotes two things viz. the Hotṛ and his drinking from the cup (चमसभक्षणम्=चमसस्थितसोमपानम्). Out of these, drinking, being an action, is principal and Hotṛ is subordinate. Thus from the समाख्या 'होतुश्चमसः' we understand that the Hotṛ is subservient to drinking from the cup (होतुश्चमसभक्षणाङ्गत्वम्).

Read 'भक्षणस्य क्रियात्मकत्वेन प्राधान्यात् तत्कर्तुः होतुः भवति तदङ्गत्वम्।' रामेश्वर.

चमसः is derived from चम्-चमति, चमोति-to sip or drink and means a sacrificial cup from which the Soma is drunk by some particular priests (चम्यते पीयते सोमः अत्र स्थितः इति चमसः). From the same root the Marāṭhī word चमचा (a spoon) is derived.

'होतुश्चमसः' is an instance of Vedic समाख्या, because the expression 'होतुश्चमसः' occurs in a passage from the Veda.

It should be noted that our author uses the expression 'होतृचमसः' in illustrating वैदिकी समाख्या. This is inaccurate, because 'होतृचमसः' does not occur in the Veda. 'होतृचमसः' may represent correct paraphrase of 'होतुश्चमसः,' but unless the expression actually occurs in the Veda, it cannot be an instance of वैदिकी समाख्या. Bhāskara's 'होतृचमसः' is either due to carelessness or is only a corruption from the original 'होतुश्चमसः.'

Then again, in 'चमसभक्षणाङ्गत्वम्' भक्षण is not a very happy word. The cup holds the Soma juce. But to speak of भक्षण with regard to it is not proper. पान is the correct word. But here our author seems to follow well-known Vedic use, according to which भक्ष् is the root employed in such connection.

अध्वर्योस्तत्तत्...इति समाख्यया—This sentence gives an illustration of लौकिकी समाख्या.

The Ṛgveda, the Yajurveda and the Sāmaveda are required for the performance of the various sacrifices. The Ṛgveda supplies the presenting verses (याज्या) and the invoking verses (अनुवाक्या or पुरोनुवाक्या). In the Yajurveda are mentioned the various mechanical rites such as गोदोहन and व्रीहिनिर्वाप. From the Sāmaveda chants such as आज्यस्तोत्र and पृष्ठस्तोत्र are taken.

The question now is: Which of the various officiating priests is to go through the rites connected with these three Vedas? The Pūrvapakṣin holds that as there is nothing to assign the various rites to particular priests, any priest may go through any rites.

Against this the Siddhāntin points out that the terms हौत्रम्, आध्वर्यवम् and औद्गात्रम् are current among the Yājñikas and that they refer to the Ṛgveda, the Yajurveda and the Sāmaveda respectively. The literal meaning of these terms is useful in dividing these rites among the three priests. आध्वर्यवम् means literally 'अध्वर्युसंबद्धमिदम्' or 'अध्वर्योः कर्म.' Thus, the literal meaning of the term आध्वर्यवम्, which is applied by the Yājñikas to the Yajurveda, shows that the priest अध्वर्यु is to go through all the rites laid down by the Yajurveda. Similarly, the terms हौत्रम् and औद्गात्रम् indicate that the priests होतृ and उद्गातृ are connected with the rites mentioned in the Ṛgveda and the Sāmaveda respectively.

The समाख्या 'आध्वर्यवम्' thus shows that अध्वर्यु is connected with those various things (तत्तत्पदार्थाः) occurring in the Yajurveda. As these things are actions such as गोदोहन, the समाख्या 'आध्वर्यवम्' indicates that अध्वर्यु is subservient to these things.

This is an example of लौकिकी समाख्या, because the term आध्वर्यवम्, as also the two others, occurs nowhere in the Veda. These terms are invented by the priests for their convenience.

It should be noted that both वैदिकी and लौकिकी समाख्या have reference to Vedic matters connected with the sacrifice. But the difference between the two is that while the expression 'होतुश्चमसः', which represents वैदिकी समाख्या, actually occurs in the Veda, आध्वर्यवम्, which is an instance of लौकिकी समाख्या, is not found in the holy text, but is a term invented by the priests for their convenience.

Section 37

So far we have seen how the six means of proof help the injunction of application in determining the relation of principal and subordinate existing between various matters. Now the author wants to tell us something about those matters, which are thus determined to be subordinate. Such matters then, which are called अङ्गानि, are of two kinds viz. सिद्धरूप and क्रियारूप.

सिद्धरूप can be explained as either those that possess the form of accomplished things (सिद्धस्य सिद्धवस्तुनः इत्यर्थः रूपमिव रूपं येषाम्), or those that possess an accomplished form (सिद्धं रूपं येषाम्). Both these ways of dissolving the compound ultimately convey the same idea. सिद्धरूप अङ्गs are those that exist independently of us. It is not neccessary for us to do anything in order to bring them into existence. They are कर्तृप्रयत्नासाध्य and are consequently accepted exactly as they are. Examples of सिद्धरूप अङ्गs are जाति, द्रव्य, संख्या etc. In 'पशुना यजेत' पशुत्व and पुंस्त्व, even like संख्या एकत्व, are subservient to the sacrifice. पशुत्व-पुंस्त्व (जातिः) and एकत्व (संख्या) exist in the animal inherently. We do not produce them. They are, therefore, सिद्धरूप. Similarly, in 'व्रीहिभिर्यजेत' the substance व्रीहि, which is accepted for sacrificial purposes, exists there independently of ourselves. Consequently, it is सिद्धरूप. The word आदि in 'जातिद्रव्यसंख्यादीनि' includes such things as a गुण viz. आरुण्य, which is subsidiary to purchase, as understood from 'अरुणया... गवा सोमं क्रीणाति'. The red colour in the cow is not the result of any activity on our part. It is, therefore, सिद्धरूप. Similarly आदि may include a mantra such as 'इमाम्... ऋतस्य', which, we have seen, is subservient to the rein of the horse (अश्वाभिधानी). For, the mantra exists there eternally and is as such सिद्धरूप.

तानि च दृष्टार्थानि एव–This sentence points out a peculiarity of सिद्धरूप अङ्गs. Subsidiaries of accomplished form serve a purpose which is visible. सिद्धरूप अङ्गs, such as the animal and the rice-grains, are used for performing the sacrifice. We can actually see how the animal and rice-grains form the libations which are thrown into the fire. The purpose of सिद्धरूप अङ्गs is in short the याग or the sacrifice and the sacrifice can be seen in its various details. Therefore, सिद्धरूप अङ्गs are declared to be दृष्टार्थ. Note 'तैः सिद्धरूपैः अङ्गैः क्रियानिर्वृत्तिरूपदृष्टप्रयोजनस्यैव जननात् तेषां दृष्टार्थत्वम्' सारविवेचनी with additions.

दृष्टार्थान्येव—The word एव here serves to distinguish सिद्धरूप अङ्गs from क्रियारूप अङ्गs, some of which latter are अदृष्टार्थ, as we shall see later on.

क्रियारूपाणि अङ्गानि, as their name suggests, are subsidiaries which are of the form of actions. As we perform these actions and thus bring them into existence, क्रियारूप अङ्गs are कर्तृप्रयत्नसाध्य. They are also said to be साध्यरूप as opposed to the others which are सिद्धरूप. क्रियारूप अङ्गs are of two kinds viz. secondary actions (गुणकर्माणि) and primary or principal actions (प्रधानकर्माणि). Secondary actions are known as संनिपत्योपकारकाणि and primary actions as आरादुपकारकाणि.

These terms are significant. Of these संनिपत्योपकारकाणि is thus explained : संनिपत्य द्रव्यादिषु संबध्य उपकुर्वन्ति तानि those that help the general result of the sacrifice after coming into contact with i. e. through substance and others. संनिपत्योपकारक अङ्गs thus help the sacrifice indirectly through substance and others. आरादुपकारकाणि on the other hand help the sacrifice directly. This term means 'आरात् समीपतः साक्षादित्यर्थः, द्रव्यादिसंबन्धमनपेक्ष्य इति यावत्, ('आराद् दूरसमीपयोः' अमरः) उपकुर्वन्ति तानि.'

Section 38

This Section deals with संनिपत्योपकारक अङ्गs. An indirectly helping subsidiary is that action, which is enjoined with reference to substance and others that are themselves subservient to some rite. दर्शपूर्णमास is a rite (कर्म). व्रीहि is a substance, which is its अङ्ग. With reference to this व्रीहि actions such as अवघात (thrashing) and प्रोक्षण (sprinkling) are enjoined. अवघातप्रोक्षणादि कर्म is thus कर्माङ्गद्रव्याद्युद्देशेन विधीयमान. It is, therefore, a गुणकर्म or a संनिपत्योपकारक कर्म. Thrashing and sprinkling are गुणकर्मन्s, because they belong to rice-grains, which are subsidiary (गुणः) to the principal sacrifice दर्शपूर्णमास. They are संनिपत्योपकारक, because they help the दर्शपूर्णमासयाग indirectly through the rice-grains.

तच्च दृष्टार्थं...दृष्टं करोति—These sentences tell us that indirectly-helping subsidiary actions can further be divided into three classes according, as their fruit is seen, or unseen, or both seen and unseen.

अवघात or thrashing is an indirectly-helping action, which is laid down by 'व्रीहीन् अवहन्ति'. It has a seen purpose viz. the unhusking of the grains, or the separation of the chaff from the grains (तुषविमोकः). Thrashing has to be continued till the chaff is separated from the grains. For, only the unhusked grains are used for making flour from which the sacrificial cake is prepared. अवघात is, therefore, दृष्टार्थ,

The sentence 'व्रीहीन् प्रोक्षति' lays down sprinkling. Sprinkling produces no visible effect on the rice-grains. It is, therefore, regarded as having an unseen fruit (अदृष्टार्थ).

An example of दृष्टादृष्टार्थ संनिपत्योपकारक कर्म is पशुपुरोडाशादि. Note that पशुपुरोडाशादि stands for पशुपुरोडाशादियाग or the presentation of an animal and a sacrificial cake. For, mere पशुपुरोडाशादि would not be a proper example of क्रियारूप अङ्ग. It would rather represent सिद्धरूप अङ्ग.

When an offering of a substance such as an animal or a cake is presented to a deity, it is accompanied by the formula 'इन्द्राय स्वाहा। इन्द्राय इदम्। न मम।' Here इन्द्राय and इन्द्राय इदम् stand for the deity to whom the offering is presented. These expressions constitute the reference or address to the deity (देवतोद्देशः). The words स्वाहा and न मम on the other hand represent the actual presentation of the substance (द्रव्यत्यागांशः).

In a case of this kind द्रव्यत्यागांश is अदृष्टार्थ. For, what is actually produced by the presentation of the offering to the particular deity is not seen by us. The presentation as a matter of fact gives rise to the अपूर्व, which ultimately secures us the desired fruit. And this अपूर्व is अदृष्ट.

देवतोद्देश on the other hand is दृष्टार्थ or has a seen fruit, because the words इन्द्राय and इन्द्राय इदम् serve to remind us of the deity इन्द्र to whom the sacrifice is offered.

पशुपुरोडाशादि or पशुपुरोडाशादियाग is thus दृष्टादृष्टार्थ.

It will be noticed that the sentence 'तद्धि द्रव्यत्यागांशेनैवादृष्टं...दृष्टं करोति' speaks of two parts of such a rite as पशुपुरोडाशयाग. As a matter of fact such rites have three parts viz. मन्त्रपाठः, द्रव्यप्रक्षेपः and देवतोद्देशेन त्यागः. Of these मन्त्रपाठ consists of the recitation of appropriate stanzas and formulas in order to invite the deity and corresponds to what is here called देवतोद्देश. Its purpose is देवतास्मरण. द्रव्यप्रक्षेप is the actual throwing of the oblation into the fire. Its purpose is द्रव्यसंस्कार. द्रव्यत्याग is the presentation of the oblation to the deity. Its purpose is अदृष्ट, viz. the production of the अङ्गापूर्व or अवान्तरापूर्व.

The difference between द्रव्यप्रक्षेप and द्रव्यत्याग is this: प्रक्षेप is a physical act and consists in the actual throwing of the oblation into the fire. त्याग is a mental operation and consists in relinquishing one's ownership of the article (स्वत्वनिवृत्तिः), indicated by 'न मम' and dedicating it to the deity (स्वाहा).

Bhāskara does not mention द्रव्यप्रक्षेप.

Read 'कर्मण एकत्वे अपि अंशभेदात् प्रयोजनभेदो न विरुध्यते। मन्त्रपाठः, द्रव्यप्रक्षेपः, देवतोद्देशेन त्यागश्च इति त्रयोंऽशाः। तत्र त्यागेन परमापूर्वोपयुक्तम् अवान्तरापूर्वमुत्पद्यते। जैमिनीयन्यायमालाविस्तर p. 224

Note also the following couplets: 'मन्त्रेण देवसंस्कारः प्रक्षेपाद् द्रव्यसंस्कृतिः। त्यागादपूर्वमुत्पन्नं प्रधानापूर्वगं च तत्॥' 'देवतास्मरणं मन्त्रात् प्रक्षेपाद् द्रव्यसंस्कृतिः। त्यागांशस्य तु नादृष्टादृते किंचित् प्रयोजनम्॥'

आपदेव gives another division of संनिपत्योपकारक अङ्ग viz. उपयोक्ष्यमाणार्थ and उपयुक्तार्थ. Those actions, which have reference to articles that are yet to be used in the sacrifice, are उपयोक्ष्यमाणार्थ. अवघात and प्रोक्षण are thus उपयोक्ष्यमाणार्थ, because they are performed on the rice-grains, which have yet to be used in the sacrifice.

An example of उपयुक्तार्थ is the following: The sentence 'कृष्णविषाणया कण्डूयते' occurs in connection with the ज्योतिष्टोम sacrifice. It lays down that the sacrificer should scratch his body with the horn of a black antelope, if after the initiation he feels any itching sensation. For this purpose he carries the horn in his hand. Further, the sentence 'नीतासु दक्षिणासु चात्वाले [=गर्ते] कृष्णविषाणां प्रास्यति' enjoins that the horn of the black antelope should be thrown in a pit after the completion of the sacrifice. Here the rite of चात्वालप्रासन or throwing into the pit refers to the horn, which had been used in the course of the sacrifice. This rite is, therefore, उपयुक्तार्थ.

Section 39

This Section deals with आरादुपकारक अङ्ग or directly-helping subsidiaries. A directly-helping subsidiary is one that is laid down without reference to any substance. This definition is quite simple. If a subsidiary is laid down with reference to a substance, it would help the sacrifice through that substance and would consequently be संनिपत्योपकारक. All those actions, which are independently laid down as subsidiaries are, therefore, आरादुपकारक अङ्ग.

An illustration of an आरादुपकारक अङ्ग is the subordinate sacrifices known as प्रयाजस. Prayājas are performed before the main sacrifice

(प्रधानयागात् पूर्वम् इज्यन्ते यैः ते प्रयाजाः) and are five in number, as we have seen before (pp. 95–96). As they are directly subordinate to the main sacrifice, they help it directly and are, therefore, आराद्दुपकारक. The word आदि in प्रयाजादि includes such sacrifices as अनुयाज or after-sacrifices (प्रधानयागादनु पश्चाद् इज्यन्ते यैः ते अनुयाजाः), which are also directly-helping for the same reason.

आराद्दुपकारकं च...यागस्वरूपे अपि उपयुज्यते–These two sentences explain how the आराद्दुपकारक and संनिपत्योपकारक अङ्ग्s help the general result of the sacrifice. It will be seen that the characteristics of these अङ्ग्s, which are mentioned here, follow from their very nature. The distinction between them, which is here pointed out, is based on the kind of अपूर्व that they help to produce.

परमापूर्वम्–We have seen before that the performance of a sacrifice such as the दर्शपूर्णमास or the ज्योतिष्टोम creates some transcendental result, designated अपूर्व by the Mīmāṁsakas, which secures for the sacrificer the desired fruit such as heaven after his death. See pp. 94–95 above. The Mīmāṁsakas distinguish between various kinds of अपूर्व. Of these परमापूर्व (the highest not-existent-before), otherwise called फलापूर्व (the firuit–securing not–existent–before), is that अपूर्व, which represents the result of the whole sacrifice, consisting of many subordinate rites taken together, and which is the direct cause of the sacrificer's attainment of the desired fruit. As the आराद्दुपकारक अङ्ग्s, as their very name shows, directly help the general result of the sacrifice, it naturally follows that they are used in producing the परमापूर्व, which is just this general result.

संनिपत्योपकारकं तु...यागस्वरूपेऽपि उपयुज्यते—This sentence shows how the indirectly–helping subsidiaries are used in the sacrifice.

अवघात and प्रोक्षण are some of these संनिपत्योपकारक अङ्ग्s. अवघात and प्रोक्षण are used for the purification and consecration of the substance viz. rice grains (द्रव्यसंस्कारः).

Recitation of proper stanzas for invoking the various deities, which constitutes देवतावाहन, and the utterance of formulas like इन्द्राय इदम्, which represents देवतोद्देश, are also संनिपत्योपकारक अङ्ग्s. Such संनिपत्योपकारक अङ्ग्s are used for देवतासंस्कार. Remember that संस्कार means 'कार्यान्तरयोग्यताकरणम्' (श्रीभाष्य). देवतावाहन and देवतोद्देश make the deities fit for receiving the sacrificial oblations. Therefore, they are said to produce देवतासंस्कार.

संनिपत्योपकारक अङ्ग्s are thus useful for द्रव्यसंस्कार and देवतासंस्कार. द्रव्य and देवता constitute the form of the sacrifice, as we saw before (p.

11, l. 3). Therefore, Bhāskara says that संनिपत्योपकारक अङ्गs are used for यागस्वरूप through द्रव्यदेवतासंस्कार.

Read 'द्रव्यसंस्कारकत्वम् अवघातप्रोक्षणादीनाम् । देवतासंस्कारकत्वं देवतावाहनपशुपुरोडाशयागीयोद्देशांशादीनामिति विवेकः।' सारविवेचनी. 'यागस्य देवतोद्देशेन द्रव्यत्यागस्वरूपत्वात् द्रव्यदेवते खलु यागस्वरूपम्।' रामेश्वर

परमापूर्वोत्पत्तौ एव–The force of एव here is that the आरादुपकारक अङ्गs are used for the production of the highest apūrva only and *not* for the production of the यागस्वरूप through the consecration of द्रव्य and देवता. For, the आरादुपकारक अङ्गs are not enjoined with reference to द्रव्य and देवता (द्रव्याद्यनुद्दिश्य केवलं विधीयमानम्) and have consequently nothing to do with them, but are used for the production of the apūrva only.

Note 'अत्र 'परमापूर्वोत्पत्तौ एव' इति एवकारेण द्रव्यदेवतागतसंस्कारजननद्वारा यागस्वरूपोपयोगित्वम् आरादुपकारकाणां निरस्यते।' रामेश्वर

यागस्वरूपे अपि—The word अपि is also significant here. It shows that संनिपत्योपकारक अङ्गs are used not only for the production of some अपूर्व, even like the आरादुपकारक अङ्गs, but *also* for यागस्वरूप.

Bhāskara does not tell us what kind of अपूर्व the संनिपत्योपकारक अङ्गs produce. In order to understand what it is we must know a little more of the apūrva theory of the Mīmāṁsakas.

According to the Mīmāṁsakas simple sacrifices have only one apūrva viz. the one that produces the fruit. Complicated sacrifices on the other hand have usually four kinds of apūrva viz. (1) फलापूर्व or परमापूर्व, (2) समुदायापूर्व, (3) उत्पत्त्यपूर्व and (4) अङ्गापूर्व. The following diagram, which represents the apūrvas in the दर्शपूर्णमास sacrifice, will make these four kinds of apūrva clear.

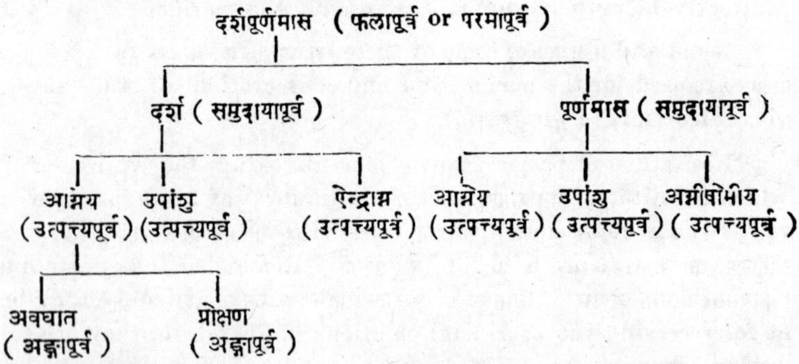

The दर्शपूर्णमास sacrifice is made of two principal sacrifices known as दर्श and पूर्णमास, each of which consists of three minor rites called आग्नेय, उपांशु etc., as shown above. The अपूर्व, which is created by the

दर्शपूर्णमास as a whole and which is responsible for the sacrificer's attainment of heaven is known as फलापूर्व or परमापूर्व. This अपूर्व is made of the अपूर्वs produced by दर्श and पूर्णमास, which are called समुदायापूर्व each. The समुदायापूर्व in its turn represents the total of the अपूर्वs produced by the rites, which make the दर्श and the पूर्णमास sacrifices These constituents of the दर्श and the पूर्णमास such as आग्नेय and उपांशु each produce its own अपूर्व, which is designated उत्पत्त्यपूर्व. Now these constituents have also their own subsidiaries such as अवघात and प्रोक्षण, which give rise to what is termed अङ्गापूर्व.

It will thus be seen that संनिपत्योपकारक अङ्गs such as अवघात and प्रोक्षण, besides producing their own special अपूर्व viz. अङ्गापूर्व, are also used for the form of the sacrifice through the saṃskāra of the material and the deity. This is what is suggested by the word अपि in यागस्वरूपे अपि.

Read ' यागस्वरूपे अपि इति अपिना संनिपत्योपकारकाणां द्रव्यदेवतासंस्कारद्वारा **यागोत्पत्त्यपूर्वे** अपि उपकारकत्वं समुच्चीयते । अत्र च व्रीह्यादीनां पिष्टद्वारा पुरोडाशनिवर्तकत्वं तद्द्वारा **यागशरीरतदुत्पत्त्यपूर्वजनकत्वं** च भवति । याज्यानुवाक्यादेः देवतासंस्कारद्वारा यागोत्पत्त्यपूर्वादौ उपयोगित्वं देवतायाश्च साक्षाद् यागशरीरनिर्वर्तकत्वं तद्द्वारा तदुत्पत्त्यपूर्वनिष्पादकत्वं च भवति ।' रामेश्वर

Regarding the different kinds of अपूर्व read ' तर्हि यागजन्या काचिच्छक्तिरपूर्वमस्तु । शक्तिव्यवधानेऽपि यागस्य साधनत्वमविरुद्धम् । औष्ण्यव्यवहितेऽपि अग्नौ दाहकत्वाङ्गीकारात् । यथा अङ्गारजन्यमौष्ण्यं शान्तेषु अपि अङ्गारेषु जले अनुवर्तते, तथा यागजन्यमपूर्वं नष्टेऽपि यागे कर्तरि आत्मनि अनुवर्तताम् । तस्मादस्ति अपूर्वम् । तद्विशेषस्तु संप्रदायसिद्धयागप्रक्रियया अवगन्तव्यः ।

तथा हि । प्रक्रिया पूर्वाचार्यैरित्थं दर्शिता । प्रथमं तावत् फलवाक्येन करणः फलसाधनता बोध्यते ' यागेन स्वर्गं कुर्यात् ' इति । ' कथं विनश्वरेण फलं कर्तव्यम्' इत्यपेक्षायाम् ' अपूर्वं कृत्वा' इति उच्यते । ' कथमपूर्वं क्रियते ' इत्यपेक्षायां ' यागानुष्ठानप्रकारेण ' इति ।

तच्च अपूर्वं दर्शपूर्णमासयोरनेकविधम् । **फलापूर्वम्, समुदायापूर्वम्, उत्पत्त्यपूर्वम्, अङ्गापूर्वं** च इति । येन स्वर्ग आरभ्यते तत् **फलापूर्वम्** । अमावास्यायां त्रयाणां यागानामेकः समुदायः, पौर्णमास्यामपरः । तयोर्भिन्नकालवर्तिनोः संहत्य फलापूर्वारम्भायोगात् तदारम्भाय **समुदायद्वयजन्यमपूर्वद्वयं** कल्पनीयम् । तयोरेकैकस्य आरम्भाय एकैकसमुदायवर्तिनां त्रयाणां यागानां भिन्नक्षणवर्तित्वेन संघातापत्त्यभावात् यागत्रयजन्यानि त्रीणि **उत्पत्त्यपूर्वाणि** कल्पनीयानि । तेषां च अङ्गोपकारमन्तरेण अनिष्पत्तेः अङ्गानां च अनेकक्षणवर्तिनां संघातासंभवात् **अङ्गापूर्वाणि** कल्पनीयानि । ' जैमिनीयन्यायमालाविस्तर p. 65

इदमेव च आश्रयि कर्म इति उच्यते—This sentence has somehow been misplaced in all the printed editions of the Arthasaṃgraha. It should come towards the end of Section 38. In the आपदेवी it is rightly found at the end of the paragraph that treats of संनिपत्योपकारक अङ्गs.

The copy of the Arthasaṁgraha, which रामेश्वर commented upon. also read this sentence in the wrong place. For, रामेश्वर observes 'इदमेव चेति । संनिपत्योपकारकमेव च, न तु आराडुपकारकमित्यर्थः ।'

What the sentence does is to tell us that the संनिपत्योपकारक अङ्ग itself (इदमेव) is also known by the term आश्रयि कर्म.

आश्रयि (dependent) कर्म is a significant epithet. संनिपत्योपकारक अङ्गs, such as अवघात, प्रोक्षण and पशुपुरोडाशयाग depend upon द्रव्य and देवता for their usefulness in sacrifice. In fact, they serve the sacrifice, as we saw before, through द्रव्य and देवता. Consequently, they are properly called 'dependent actions.'

Note 'द्रव्यदेवतादिरूपः आश्रयः अस्य अस्ति इति आश्रयि । पारिभाषिकी वा आश्रयि कर्म इति संज्ञा ।' रामेश्वर

It is thus clear that इदम्=संनिपत्योपकारकम् and we have just seen that the term आश्रयि कर्म is applicable to all the three kinds of संनिपत्योपकारक. But पार्थसारथिमिश्र evidently holds that the term आश्रयि कर्म is to be applied to only the third kind of संनिपत्योपकारक viz. दृष्टादृष्टार्थ. We see no reason why this term should be restricted to only the third kind of संनिपत्योकारक, when it is literally applicable to all the three. Nor does पार्थसारथिमिश्र furnish any reasons for such restriction.

Read 'दृष्टादृष्टार्थं च किंचित् कर्म । यद् आश्रयिशब्दाभिधानीयकं भजते । यथा पशुपुरोडाशयागः । स हि त्यागांशेन अदृष्टम्, उद्देशांशेन च दृष्टं देवतास्मरणं करोति–इति उभयार्थः ।' न्यायरत्नमाला of पार्थसारथिमिश्र p. 121

The term संनिपत्योपकारक has been translated above by 'indirectly-helping', because such action helps the sacrifice through substance etc., with which it is directly connected. Similarly, आराडुपकारक is explained as 'directly-helping', because such action helps the sacrifice directly, without the intervention of the substance etc., by producing the अपूर्व. Here the basis of directness is the absence of contact with substance etc. आराडुपकारक has no contact with substance etc. It is, therefore, 'directly-helping.' संनिपत्योकारक, on the other hand, first comes in contact with substance etc. and through substance helps the sacrifice. It is, therefore, 'indirectly-helping.'

There is, however, another way of looking at the help rendered to the sacrifice by these two kinds of action. The sacrifice means द्रव्य and देवता (यागस्य द्वे रूपे । द्रव्यं देवता च). Whatever is directly concerned with these helps the sacrifice directly. Thus संनिपत्योपकारक is 'directly-helping.' आराडुपकारक has no connection with substance etc. It is, therefore, 'indirectly-helping.' The dictionary-sense of आराद् viz.

either near or distant ('आराद् दूरसमीपयोः') is favourable to this twofold interpretation of the term.

The following extract from the मीमांसापरिभाषा will be found to be helpful in understanding संनिपत्योपकारक and आरादुपकारक अङ्गs:

'तानि अङ्गानि द्विविधानि । संनिपत्योपकारकाणि आरादुपकारकाणीति चेति । यानि अङ्गानि साक्षात् परंपरया वा प्रधानयागशरीरं निष्पाद्य तद्द्वारा तदुत्पत्त्यपूर्वोपयोगीनि तानि **संनिपत्योपकारकाणि।** यथा व्रीह्यादिद्रव्याणि तत्संयुक्तावहननप्रोक्षणादीनि अग्न्यादिदेवतातत्संयुक्तयाज्यानुवाक्यावचनानि । अत्र प्रोक्षणादेर्व्रीहिगतातिशयद्वारा अवहननादेस्तुषविमोकादिरूपदृष्टद्वारा व्रीह्यादीनां पिष्टद्वारा पुरोडाशनिष्पादकत्वं तद्द्वारा यागशरीरतदुत्पत्त्यपूर्वहेतुत्वं च । याज्यानुवाक्यादेर्देवतासंस्कारद्वारा देवतायाश्च साक्षाद्यागशरीरनिवर्तकत्वं तद्द्वारा तदुत्पत्त्यपूर्वोपयोगित्वं च । यागस्य देवतोद्देशन द्रव्यत्यागरूपत्वात् । द्रव्यदेवते हि यागस्वरूपमिति सिद्धान्ताच्च । एतान्येव सामवायिकानीत्युच्यन्ते ।

आत्मसमवेतापूर्वजनकानि **आरादुपकारकाणि** । यथा प्रयाजाज्यभागानुयाजादीनि । एतानि द्रव्यगतं देवतागतं वा संस्कारं न जनयन्ति । किन्तु आत्मगतमदृष्टं जनयन्तीति आरादुपकारकाणि । मीमांसापरिभाषा pp. 11-12

Section 40

From this Section Bhāskara commences the treatment of प्रयोगविधि which continues till the end of Section 47. It will be noticed that in enumerating the four kinds of विधि in Section 12 above the author mentioned them in the order of उत्पत्तिविधि, विनियोगविधि, अधिकारविधि and प्रयोगविधि. In accordance with this order he should have dealt with अधिकारविधि before going to प्रयोगविधि.

But there is a reason why he treats प्रयोगविधि first. विनियोगविधि, we have seen, deals with the relation of principal and subordinates. It tells us in short which rites are principal and which subordinate. Now, the province of प्रयोगविधि is to secure the performance of all these rites in a particular order. प्रयोगविधि is thus more vitally connected with विनियोगविधि than अधिकारविधि. It is, therefore, natural that the treatment of प्रयोगविधि should come after the treatment of विनियोगविधि.

It would, however, appear that Bhāskara's enumeration of the विधिs in the order found in Section 12 represents a scribe's mistake. There are two indications which lead us to believe that in Section 12 the original reading must have been 'उत्पत्तिविधिर्विनियोगविधिः प्रयोगविधिराधिकारविधिश्चेति ।' First, आपदेव, whom our author generally follows, has this order in his book and there is no reason why Bhāskara should depart from it. Secondly, when Rāmeśvara commences his commentary on the portion of the Arthasaṁgraha dealing with अधिकारविधि, he prefaces it with the remark, 'इदानीं **क्रमप्राप्त**मधिकारविधिं निरूपयति.' This shows that in the text which Bhāskara had before him the order of अधिकारविधि was after that of प्रयोगविधि.

प्रयोगप्राशुभाव...विधत्ते—This passages gives the definition of प्रयोगविधि or the injunction of performance and points out its general nature. प्रयोगविधि is that which intimates the speediness or promptness (आशु or प्राशु =quick, prompt) of performance. What प्रयोगविधि then lays down is just this that the whole sacrifice along with its subsidiaries should be performed quickly without unnecessary delay. The sacrifice has to be performed without delay, because there is no authority for making delay (विलम्बे प्रमाणाभावात्) in its performance.

It will thus be seen that प्रयोगविधि does not lay down anything very new. In fact, it is not a new and independent विधि at all. It is the same as प्रधानविधि or उत्पत्तिविधि, which enjoins the principal action, forming a syntactical whole (एकवाक्यता) with sentences that lay down subsidiaries. When प्रधानविधि and गुणविधि, or उत्पत्तिविधि and विनियोगविधि, are combined together so as to form one complete sentence, we get प्रयोगविधि. Now, this one complete sentence, formed by the combination of प्रधानविधि and गुणविधि would naturally make it incumbent on us to perform the main action along with its subsidiaries (साङ्गं प्रधानमनुष्ठापयन्). This is exactly what प्रयोगविधि does.

The expression अविलम्बापरपर्यायम् (अविलम्बः अपरः पर्यायः यस्य) just paraphrases the word प्राशुभाव. For, अविलम्ब is a synonym of प्राशुभाव.

न च तदाविलम्बेऽपि...साहित्यव्यवहाराभात्—It is said above that because there is no authority for making delay, the sacrifice along with its subsidiaries has to be performed without delay. But some one may here object that there is also no authority for avoiding delay (अविलम्बेऽपि) i. e. for performing the sacrifice with promptness. The answer to this is that when the प्रधानविधि and the गुणविधि or अङ्गविधि form one syntactical whole, it naturally follows that the main action and the subsidiaries have to be performed together. Otherwise they would cease to be related to each other as principal and subordinate. For, if delay were to occur between the performance of the main action and the subsidiaries, their togetherness or performance together (तत्साहित्यम् =तेषामङ्गप्रधानानां साहित्यं सहभावः सहानुष्ठानमित्यर्थः) would be impossible. Because, when two things are performed with an interval between them (विलम्बेन), nobody ever says that the one is performed with the other.

स च अविलम्बो...पदार्थविशेषणतया विधत्ते—We have seen so far that the purpose of प्रयोगविधि is to secure promptness of performance. This promptness is assured when a definite or fixed (नियत) order is followed. Otherwise i. e. in the absence of a definite order (अन्यथा—

नियतस्य क्रमस्य अभावे) one would not know which rite is to be performed when or after which. Consequently, confusion (विक्षेपः) in the performance would result. Therefore, the injunction of perf[illegible]nce itself enjoins a fixed order as an attribute of the various things enjoined in order to secure promptness of performance, which is its aim.

पदार्थविशेषणतया—It has just been said that प्रयोगविधि enjoins some definite order. Now, order is an abstract idea and does not form a proper object of injunction. Besides, if we were to say that प्रयोगविधि enjoins प्राशुभाव and पदार्थानां नियतक्रम, वाक्यभेद with all its attendant evils would follow. Therefore, Bhāskara uses the expression पदार्थविशेषणतया. Though an abstract idea, order is enjoined as an attribute of concrete things. Hence, the objection that order is not a proper object of injunction does not arise. Secondly, as order is not enjoined as an independent thing but only as a qualification of other matters, वाक्यभेद does not result.

अत एव...लक्षणम्—The fore going explanation of the definition of प्रयोगविधि tells us that it lays down a definite order for the various matters that constitute the sacrifice with a view to secure promptness of performance, which is its proper विधेय. Therefore, 'अङ्गानां क्रमबोधको विधिः' is another definition of प्रयोगविधिः. For, it enjoins the order in which the subsidiaries are to be performed and thus secures speediness of performance.

It will thus be seen that the order which प्रयोगविधि enjoins refers to the subsidiaries. Consequently, पदार्थविशेषणतया, occurring above, is equal to अङ्गविशेषणतया.

तत्र क्रमो...वा—In the second definition of प्रयोगविधि viz. 'अङ्गानं क्रमबोधको विधिः' the word क्रम occurs. The author now gives two paraphrases of the word क्रम.

वितातिविशेषः means a particular kind of extension or arrangement. This particular kind consists in arranging or performing the subsidiaries in some fixed order. विताति is from तन् तनोति-तनुते to stretch or extend, with वि. तन् and वितन् are often used in the sense of 'to perform or accomplish as a sacrifice.' Read 'इति क्षितीशो नवतिं नवाधिकां महाक्रतुनां महनीयशासनः । समारुरुक्षुर्दिवमायुषः क्षये ततान सोपानपरंपरामिव॥' रघुवंश 3.69; 'यज्वभिः संभृतं हव्यं विततेष्वध्वरेषु सः । जातवेदोमुखान्मायी मिषतामाच्छिनत्ति नः ॥' कुमारसंभव 2. 46. वितानः-नम् is actually used in the sense of a sacrifice. Note 'वितानेष्वप्येवं तव च मम सोमे विधिरभूत्' वेणीसंहार 6. 30.

पौर्वापर्यरूपो वा—This is another paraphrase of क्रम. Supply वितानः after पौर्वापर्यरूपः. So the whole sentence becomes क्रमो नाम पौर्वापर्यरूपः

वितानः. This is rather clumsy. It would have been enough if Bhāskara had said ' क्रमो नाम विततिविशेषः, पौर्वापर्यं वा. ' But here, as in so many other places, Bhāskara is merely plagiarizing from Āpadeva.

पूर्वं च अपरं च पूर्वापरे, तयोः भावः पौर्वापर्यम्, तस्य रूपं यस्य सः पौर्वापर्यरूपो वितानः. Order means some arrangement wherein one rite comes first (पूर्वं) and another follows (अपर).

A question, which is here sometimes discussed, is this: Is क्रम or order the characteristic of all the rites which it covers, or is it the characteristic of the subsequent rite only? Two views are held in this matter. According to one, क्रम is a characteristic of both the prior (पूर्व) and posterior (अपर) rite. The terms prior and posterior are relative. A rite is said to be prior only with reference to some other, which is posterior. Therefore, पौर्वापर्य or क्रम belongs to both. The second view is that the prior rite has no expectancy as to which rite is going to follow it. It never says ' मदुत्तरं कः पदार्थः कर्तव्यः '. Once it is performed, it is finished. But the subsequent rite has the expectancy ' कस्मादुत्तरमहं कर्तव्यः '. Therefore, क्रम is a characteristic of the अपर or उत्तर or subsequent rite only.

Section 41

This Section enumerates the six means of proof by which the order of subsidiaries is settled.

Section 42

Out of the six proofs, which help the determination of the order in which the subsidiaries are to be performed, श्रुति or direct statement is the first. श्रुति means a passage, which actually conveys (पर) the order. Such passages fall under two groups. One group conveys the order merely, while the other intimates a matter or a rite (पदार्थः) as qualified by the order. श्रुति is thus of two kinds according as it conveys mere order, or a matter pariticularized by the order.

' वेदं कृत्वा वेदिं करोति ' is a sentence, which enjoins mere order. वेद means a small brush prepared from Darbha-grass for the purpose of cleaning the altar (वेदो नाम संमार्जनार्थो दर्भमुष्टिविशेषः). वेदि represents a particular part of the altar in between the places of the Āhavanīya and the Gārhapatya fire, four aṅgulas in depth and used for depositing the oblations (वेदिः आहवनीयगार्हपत्ययोर्मध्ये चतुरङ्गुलं निखातं भूतलं हविर्निधानस्थानविशेषरूपम्).

In the above sentence the word which directly conveys the order is the indeclinable past participle कृत्वा. For, indeclinable past participles or gerunds are used to denote the prior of two actions that have the same agent, according 'समानकर्तृकयोः पूर्वकाले' पाणिनि 3.4.21 (समानकर्तृकयोर्धात्वर्थयोः पूर्वकाले विद्यमानाद्धातोः क्त्वा स्यात्। भुक्त्वा व्रजाति। सि. का.). Read 'क्त्वाप्रत्ययः पूर्वकालवाची' 'क्त्वाप्रत्ययस्य पूर्वकालतार्थः' 'क्त्वाप्रत्ययेन क्रमोऽभिधीयते.' Other words which directly intimate order are अथ, ततः, पश्चात् etc.

कृत्वा of the above sentence, therefore, denotes that वेदिकरण comes after वेदकरण. It gives us the क्रम of वेदि. As पूर्वकाल is the sense of the indeclinable past participle termination, the sentence is directly expressive of order. The sentence lays down order merely, because the preparation of the वेदि, to which the order belongs, has already been enjoined by some other sentence. Read 'दर्शपूर्णमासयोर्हविरभिवासनोत्तरं वेदिकरणविधिवाक्येन एव वेदिकरणस्य प्राप्तत्वात् तदनुवादेन क्त्वाप्रत्ययोक्तक्रममात्रमत्र विधीयते।' रामेश्वर

'वषट्कर्तुः प्रथमभक्षः' is a sentence which illustrates the second kind of श्रुतिक्रम viz. the one in which a matter (पदार्थः) qualified by order is conveyed. Here प्रथम is the word that directly expresses the order. The matter, which is enjoined, is भक्ष. It is qualified by प्राथम्य or first-ness, as shown by the Karmadhāraya compound प्रथमभक्षः. Hence 'वषट्कर्तुः प्रथमभक्षः' is क्रमविशिष्टभक्षपदार्थपर.

वषट्कर्तुः—वषट्कर्तृ is a designation of the priest होतृ. The term has reference to sacrificial procedure. When an offering is to be presented to a deity, the Adhvaryu issues an instruction (प्रैषः) such as 'अग्नये अनुब्रूहि.' On hearing this the Hotṛ recites the relevant invoking stanza (अनुवाक्या अनूच्यते आहूयते देवता अनया, also called पुरोऽनुवाक्या, because it is recited by the Hotṛ before the actual presentation of the offering), which is intended to invite the deity to partake of the offering to be presented to him. After this the Adhvaryu gives a second instruction such as 'अग्निं यज.' On hearing this the होतृ recites the sacrificing or presenting stanza (याज्या) in honour of that deity, at the end of which he utters the exclamation वषट्, in accordance with 'याज्याया अधि वषट् करोति.' वषट् is joined with the name of the deity, which is put in the dative e. g. अग्नये वषट्. Then the Adhvaryu throws the oblation into the fire and thus the presentation is complete. As in this procedure the Hotṛ utters the exclamation वषट्, he is designated वषट्कर्तृ.

वषट् is supposed to be a derivative from the root वह्. इन्द्राय वषट् is really equal to अग्निः इन्द्राय हविर्वहतु. Other exclamations derived from वह् for a similar purpose are वट् and वौषट्.

The following definitions of याज्या and पुरोऽनुवाक्या or अनुवाक्या have reference to this procedure: 'अध्वर्युणा 'यज' इति प्रैषे कृते होत्रा यो मन्त्रः पठ्यते सा याज्या 'अनुब्रूहि' इति प्रैषानन्तरमन्त्रः पुरोऽनुवाक्या।' रत्नप्रभा on शाङ्करभाष्य on ब्रह्मसूत्र 3.3.43. Rāmeśvara seems to believe that याज्या and अनुवाक्या are recited by Brahman and not by Hotṛ. See his definitions: ' 'यज' इति प्रैषानन्तरमृग् या ब्रह्मणा समुच्चार्यते सा याज्या इति उच्यते। 'अनुब्रूहि' इति प्रैषानन्तरमृग् या तेनैव समुच्चार्यते सा अनुवाक्या इति उच्यते।'

The आज्यभागब्राह्मण defines पुरोऽनुवाक्या and याज्या in a different manner. पुरोऽनुवाक्या is a stanza which contains the name of the deity or a characteristic thereof in its first half. It is recited by the Hotṛ before the actual presentation for the purpose of invoking the deity on the instruction अनुब्रूहि, issued by the Adhvaryu. याज्या, on the other hand, is a stanza which contains the name of the deity or a characteristic thereof in its second half. With the याज्या the oblation is actually offered. That is why it is so called and also why it is preceded by the instruction यज.

Read 'पुरस्ताल्लक्ष्मा पुरोऽनुवाक्या। उपरिष्टाल्लक्ष्मा याज्या। ...यस्या ऋचः पूर्वार्धे देवतालिङ्गं सा **पुरोऽनुवाक्या**। उत्तरार्धे तल्लिङ्गं चेद् **याज्या** सा भवति। ... पुरोऽनुवाक्या यागात् पुरस्तात् देवताह्वानाय अध्वर्युप्रैषमनु होत्रा वक्तव्यत्वात्। 'इन्द्राग्निभ्यामनुब्रूहि' इति एतादृशोऽध्वर्युप्रैषः। द्वितीयो मन्त्रो याज्या। इज्यते अनया इति तद्व्युत्पत्तिः। अत एव अत्र 'यज' इति प्रैषः पठ्यते।'

प्रथमभक्षः (प्रथमश्चासौ भक्षश्च) first fill or draught. This also has reference to some sacrificial procedure. In the ज्योतिष्टोम sacrifice after the Soma has been offered to the various deities, the remainder is partaken of by the priests. In this connection 'वषट्कर्तुः प्रथमभक्षः' lays down that the Hotṛ takes the first draught.

The difference between 'वेदं कृत्वा वेदिं करोति', which is केवलक्रमपर, and 'वषट्कर्तुः प्रथमभक्षः,' which is क्रमविशिष्टपदार्थपर, is this: In 'वेदं कृत्वा वेदिं करोति' वेदिकरण is merely अनूदित or mentioned again, or further referred to, because it has actually been laid down somewhere else. What is enjoined by the sentence is, therefore, merely the order of वेदिकरण, which is after वेदकरण. In 'वषट्कर्तुः प्रथमभक्षः', on the other hand, वषट्कर्तृभक्ष is nowhere else laid down. That is why we cannot regard 'वषट्कर्तुः प्रथमभक्षः' as केवलक्रमपर by supposing that भक्ष is here merely referred to as an अनुवाद or after-mention and that what is actually laid down is प्राथम्य belonging to that भक्ष (भक्षानुवादेन क्रममात्रस्य विधातुमशक्यत्वात्).

एकप्रसरताभङ्गभयेन—This expression embodies the reason why 'वषट्कर्तुः प्रथमभक्षः' cannot be regarded as केवलक्रमपर. It is capable of three interpretations. (1) प्रसरः means वाक्यम्. एकप्रसरता = एकवाक्यता. एकप्रसरताभङ्गः = एकवाक्यताभङ्गः = वाक्यभेदः. If we were to suppose that 'वषट्कर्तुः प्रथमभक्षः lays down क्रम only, and not क्रमविशिष्ट पदार्थ, we should have to admit that it enjoins drinking on the part of the वषट्कार in addition. For, भक्ष is nowhere else laid down. Thus 'वषट्कर्तुः प्रथमभक्षः' would really be equal to 'वषट्कारो भक्षयति, वषट्कारो प्रथमं भक्षयति च.' This involves वाक्यभेद or the splitting of one sentence into two, which is a defect. Therefore, we must suppose that 'वषट्कर्तुः प्रथमभक्षः' lays down क्रमविशिष्ट-भक्षण. The वाक्यभेद that arises in a case like this is known as आवृत्त्यात्मको वाक्यभेदः. (2) एकप्रसरता is paraphrased by संभूय विशिष्टार्थप्रतिपादकत्वम् or the quality of jointly denoting a qualified thing. The compound प्रथमभक्षः is a कर्मधारय and as such denotes भक्ष as qualified by प्राथम्य, even as नीलोत्पल expresses a lotus as qualified by blueness. Now, if we were to suppose that the sentence lays down प्राथम्य alone, we should have to interpret the compound as 'यो वषट्कर्तुः भक्षः स प्रथमः'. Here भक्ष is उद्देश्य and प्रथम is विधेय. उद्देश्य usually comes first and विधेय afterwards. But in our compound प्रथम comes first and भक्ष afterwards. This shows that the two words jointly express a qualified thing. But if क्रम be understood to have been laid down independently, this एकप्रसरता or एकस्मिन्नेव विशिष्टे अर्थे पदयोः प्रसरणम् would be violated. (3) Explain एकप्रसरता as एकस्यां वृत्तौ समासरूपायां प्रसरः पदयोः उद्देश्यविधेयभावेन प्रवेशः, तस्य भावः एकप्रसरता, तस्याः भङ्गः अभावः असंभवः इत्यर्थः, तस्य भयेन । एकस्मिन्नेव कर्मधारयरूपे समासे उद्देश्यविधेयवाचकपदयोः प्रवेशासंभवात् इति यावत्. If क्रम be supposed to have been independently laid down here, we shall have to admit that भक्ष is उद्देश्य and प्रथम is विधेय. But it is impossible that उद्देश्य and विधेय should form a कर्मधारय compound such as प्रथम and भक्ष have formed in the present case. If they were to do so, the fault known in poetics as अविमृष्टविधेयांश would arise.

सेयं श्रुतिः... बलवती—This sentence establishes the superiority of श्रुति or direct statement over the other means of proof such as अर्थ, पाठ, स्थान etc. As in the case of the six helpers of विनियोगविधि (for which vide Section 15 above), even so in the case of these six pramāṇas helping the determination of order, each preceding pramāṇa is stronger than those that follow. Thus श्रुति is more powerful than अर्थ and the four others that follow, अर्थ is stronger than पाठ and the three others that come after it and so on.

तेषा वचनः ...प्रमाणत्वात्—This sentence embodies the reason why श्रुति is stronger than the other means of proof. तेषाम्=इतरेषां प्रमाणानाम्. वचनकल्पनद्वारा—वचनं क्रमपरं श्रुतिसंज्ञं वचनम्, तस्य कल्पनं तस्य द्वारा. The reason why श्रुति is stronger than the other pramāṇas is that the other pramāṇas determine order by presuming or assuming a suitable श्रुति or direct statement. In fact the other pramāṇas will not be able to determine क्रम without the help of श्रुति. Hence they are weaker than श्रुति.

Read 'पाठादिस्थलेषु न प्रत्यक्षवचनमस्ति, येन क्रमो विधीयेत। पौर्वापर्यरूपेण पाठान्यथानुपपत्त्या तु 'एतदन्तरमेतत् कर्तव्यम्' इति कल्पनीयं क्रमबोधकं वचनम्। यावच्च तैः कल्पयितुमारभ्यते ततः पूर्वमेव प्रत्यक्षेण क्लृप्तेन वचनेन क्रमे बोधिते न तेषां प्रवृत्तिरिति दौर्बल्यं तेषामिति भावः।' सारविवेचिनी

अत एव...इत्युक्तम्—This sentence gives an example to prove the superiority of श्रुतिक्रम over पाठक्रम. In a section of the ज्योतिष्टोम sacrifice occurs the sentence 'ऐन्द्रवायवं गृह्णाति, मैत्रावरुणं गृह्णाति, आश्विनं गृह्णाति. This has reference to the taking up of the cups (ग्रहः) sacred to the various deities. These cups are taken up in order to offer to the deities the contents thereof. Now, if here we rely on the order mentioned in the text (पाठक्रमः), आश्विनग्रहग्रहण or the taking up of the cup of the Aśvins comes third. For, in accordance with the पाठक्रम, we presume a श्रुति such as 'आश्विनस्तृतीयो गृह्यते.' But an actual existing direct statement viz. आश्विनो दशमो गृह्यते tells us that the order for the taking up of the cup of the Aśvins is the tenth. Therefore, tenth is the proper order for आश्विनग्रहग्रहण, because श्रुतिक्रम is more powerful than पाठक्रम, which has to depend on a कल्पितश्रुति in order to convey the order.

Read 'पाठो हि न क्रमस्य अभिधायकः। किन्तु अन्यथानुपपत्त्या क्रमं कल्पयति। 'दशमः' इत्येषा श्रुतिस्तु साक्षादेव क्रममभिधत्ते। ततः पाठादपि श्रुतिः प्रबला।' रामेश्वर

इति उक्तम्—This evidently refers to जैमिनिसूत्र 5.4.1, which lays down the superiority of श्रुति and अर्थ over पाठ. Vide जैमिनीयन्यायमालाविस्तर p.296.

It should be noted that according to the procedure followed in the case of the helpers of विनियोगश्रुति, Bhāskara should have here established the superiority of श्रुतिक्रम over अर्थक्रम, which stands next on the list. Instead he shows here that श्रुतिक्रम is more powerful than पाठक्रम. The reason for this is that as अर्थक्रम depends entirely on श्रुति, there is no likelihood of opposition between them. Hence श्रुतिक्रम is here declared to be stronger than पाठक्रम.

Read 'यद्यप्यत्र प्रथमतः श्रुत्यर्थयोः प्राबल्यदौर्बल्यनिरूपणमेव कर्तुमुचितं तथापि यथाश्रुत्यैव प्रयोजनस्य कल्पनीयत्वेन तयोर्विरोधस्यैव असंभवात् तत् परित्यज्य श्रुतिपाठयोः प्राबल्य-

चौर्बल्योदाहरणमुक्तमिति वेदितव्यम् । तथा हि उक्तम् । श्रुत्यर्थयोर्विरोधस्तु नैवं वचनसंभवे । यथाश्रुत्यैव हि न्याय्यमर्थस्य परिकल्पनम् ॥ इति ' सारविवेचिनी

Section 43

The second pramāṇa for determining order is अर्थ or sense. अर्थक्रम or order by sense occurs there where order is determined according to the force (वशः) of purpose. The following is an illustration of अर्थक्रमः—

In the chapter dealing with अग्निहोत्र occur the sentences ' अग्निहोत्रं जुहोति ' and ' यवागूं पचति ' in this same order. Here, the question is: What is the order of अग्निहोत्रहोम and यवागूपाक ? The question is answered by taking into consideration the purpose for which ' यवागू' or the rice-gruel is intended. From the sentence ' यवाग्वा अग्निहोत्रं जुहोति ' we know that rice-gruel is required for अग्निहोत्रहोम (यवाग्वाः होमार्थत्वम्). Therefore, in accordance with this purpose of the rice gruel यवागूपाक is prepared first and then अग्निहोत्रहोम is performed, though the sentence यवागूं पचति occurs after अग्निहोत्रं जुहोति.

यवागू is derived from यु to mix. It means gruel prepared from rice or barley.

स चायं...प्रयोजनमस्ति–This paragraph proves the superiority of अर्थक्रम over पाटक्रम. This is done by describing the undesirable results, which would follow if we were to accept पाठक्रम here. According to पाठक्रम the order of these two rites is अग्निहोत्रहोम and यवागूपाक. If we were to resort to this order, the seen purpose, which the rice-gruel is meant to serve viz. to become the material for the होम, as understood from ' यवाग्वा अग्निहोत्रं जुहोति, ' would be violated (क्लृप्तं दृष्टं यत् प्रयोजनं यवाग्वाः होमार्थत्वं तस्य बाधः). For, if the होम be performed before यवागूपाक, यवागू can obviously not be used for the होम. [We must of course suppose in this alternative that the होम is performed with some other material.] Secondly, there can be no seen purpose for यवागू, if it be prepared after the होम. We shall, therefore, have to suppose an unseen purpose for it. And this we know is against the Mīmāṁsist principle that an unseen purpose should not be presumed, when a seen one is possible. Compare ' लभ्यमाने फले दृष्टे नादृष्टफलकल्पना ' quoted above on p. 75.

Read ' द्रव्यमन्तरेण होमासंभवात् । द्रव्यनिष्पत्त्यै पाकस्यैव प्राथमिकत्वावश्यंभावत्वात् । होमद्रव्यत्वं च यवाग्वाः " यवाग्वा अग्निहोत्रं जुहोति " इति तृतीयया अवगम्यते । तस्मात् पाटक्रमं बाधित्वा अर्थतः क्रमोऽत्र अभ्युपगन्तव्यः । ' जैमिनीयन्यायमालाविस्तर p. 265

The name अर्थक्रम or order by sense arises from the fact that the purpose, which determines the order here, is understood only after the sense is grasped. अर्थक्रम can also mean order by purpose or end. For, अर्थ is a synonym of प्रयोजन. Note 'अर्थो विषयार्थनयोर्धनकारणवस्तुषु । अभिधेये च शब्दानां निवृत्तौ च प्रयोजने ॥' मेदिनी.

Section 44

The third pramāṇa for determining order is पाठ. There is a certain order in which sentences or words ('वाक्यानाम्' इति पदानामपि उपलक्षणम्), that lay down sacrificial matters (पदार्थः), occur in the holy texts.

From that order the order of those sacrificial matters is settled. The reason for such settlement is this. We study the sentences in the order in which they occur in the texts. The comprehension of the matters laid down arises according to the order of the study of the sentences that enjoin them. And the performance of those matters follows the order of their comprehension. Thus पाठक्रमानुसारेण अध्ययनक्रमः, अध्ययनक्रमानुसारेण अर्थप्रत्ययक्रमः, अर्थप्रत्ययक्रमानुसारेण पदार्थानामनुष्ठानम्. Therefore, the order of performance ultimately depends on the order of the matter-enjoining sentences in the texts.

The Veda, in which sacrificial matters are mentioned, consists of Mantra or Saṁhitā and Brāhmaṇa. Consequently, पाठ is of two kinds–मन्त्रपाठः and ब्राह्मणपाठः.

तत्राग्नेयाग्नीषोमीययोः ... मन्त्रपाठात्–This sentence gives an illustration of मन्त्रपाठ and proves at the same time the superiority of मन्त्रपाठ over ब्राह्मणपाठ.

आग्नेय and अग्नीषोमीय are two of the oblations that constitute the पूर्णमास sacrifice of the दर्शपूर्णमास. Vide p.170 above. In the तैत्तिरीय ब्राह्मण, अग्नीषोमीय is mentioned first and आग्नेय afterwards. But in the तैत्तिरीय संहिता the sacrificing and invoking stanzas (याज्यानुवाक्ये) of the आग्नेय oblation occur first and those of the अग्नीषोमीय afterwards. Thus, according to ब्राह्मणपाठ the order of these oblations is अग्नीषोमीय and आग्नेय, while according to मन्त्रपाठ, as understood from the order of the respective याज्याs and अनुवाक्याs, the order is आग्नेय and अग्नीषोमीय. As मन्त्रपाठ is more powerful than ब्राह्मणपाठ the order that is actually resorted to in the पूर्णमास sacrifice is आग्नेय and अग्नीषोमीय, based on the order of their याज्याs and अनुवाक्याs occurring in the Saṁhitā.

Read in this connection '**अग्नीषोमीययागस्**तैत्तिरीयब्राह्मणे पञ्चमप्रपाठके द्वितीयानुवाके समाम्नातः—' ताभ्यामेत**मग्नीषोमीयमे**कादशकपालं पूर्णमासे प्राच्छेत् ' इति । **आग्नेययागस्तु** षष्ठप्रपाठके तृतीयानुवाके समाम्नातः ' **यदाग्नेयो**ऽष्टाकपालोऽमावास्यायां **पौर्णमास्यां** च अच्युतो भवति ' इति । तत्र अनुष्ठानस्य ब्राह्मणोक्तविध्यधीनत्वाद् अग्नीषोमीयस्य प्रथममनुष्ठानम् । **इति प्राप्ते**—

ब्रूमः । मन्त्रकाण्डे पूर्वं पठिता आग्नेयमन्त्राः । तथा हि । हौत्रकाण्डे आज्यभागमन्त्रानुवाकादुत्तरस्मिन्ननुवाके प्रथमम् ' अग्निर्मूर्धा— ' इत्यादिके आग्नेय्यौ याज्यानुवाक्ये आम्नाते । ततः ' प्रजापते न त्वदेतानि ' इत्यादिके प्राजापत्ये । ततः ' अग्नीषोमा सवेदसा ' इत्यादिके अग्नीषोमीये । आध्वर्यवकाण्डेऽपि 'अग्नये जुष्टं निर्वपामि ' ' अग्नीषोमाभ्याम्–' इति **आग्नेयः पूर्वमाम्नातः** । याजमानकाण्डेऽपि ' अग्नेरहं देवयज्यया अन्नादो भूयासम् ' इत्याम्नाय पश्चात् ' अग्नीषोमयोरहं देवयज्यया वृत्रहा भूयासम् ' इति आम्नायते । **मन्त्रक्रमश्च प्रबलः** मन्त्रैः स्मृत्वा पश्चादनुष्ठेयत्वात् । ब्राह्मणं तु अप्राप्तपदार्थविधिनापि चारितार्थम् । अतोऽनुष्ठानस्मरणादेव उत्पन्नत्वात् मन्त्रान् बाधितुं नालम्—इति **मन्त्रक्रमेण आग्नेयस्यैव प्रथममनुष्ठानम्** । ' जैमिनीयन्यायमालाविस्तर p. 270

स चायं मन्त्रपाठो...अन्तरङ्गोऽयं मन्त्रपाठः—This paragraph gives the reason why मन्त्रपाठ is more powerful than ब्राह्मणपाठ. The reason is just this that the Mantras are nearer to, or more closely connected with (अन्तरङ्ग), the performance of the sacrifice than the Brāhmaṇas. This would be clear if we were to take into consideration the part which the Mantras and Brāhmaṇas play in the performance of a sacrifice.

Brāhmaṇa sentences like ' उद्भिदा यजेत पशुकामः ' ' दध्ना इन्द्रियकामस्य जुहुयात् ' ' व्रीहीन् प्रोक्षति ' and ' यदाहवनीये जुहोति ' lay down various rites. When once we become inclined towards these rites on account of the injunctions contained in the Brāhmaṇa sentences, the Brāhmaṇa sentences have served their purpose. They have no further use when the rites are actually commenced. They just point out from outside the performance (प्रयोगाद् बहिरेव) that such and such a rite should be performed. With the performance proper they have no connection.

Mantras, on the other hand, are used (व्याप्रियन्ते) at the time of, and during, the performance itself. The performance consists of various rites, which are gone through one after another in a certain order. This order of performance depends on the order of the remembrance of the various rites. And the order of the remembrance depends on the order of the Mantras, wherein these various rites are mentioned. Hence Mantras are said to be more vitally connected with (अन्तरङ्ग) the performance. Consequently, मन्त्रपाठ is stronger than ब्राह्मणपाठ.

What is meant is this : Brāhmaṇas lay down various sacrifices. In the actual performance of these sacrifices Mantras are used. For, by means of Mantras we remember the various matters, which are to be performed. Mantras have also to be recited during the performance. Hence, Mantras are nearer the performance than Brāhmaṇas. Therefore, मन्त्रपाट is more powerful than ब्राह्मणपाट.

प्रयाजानां...ब्राह्मणपाटक्रमात्--This sentence gives an illustration of order determined by the Brāhmaṇa-text. It will be noticed that symmetry requires that ब्राह्मणपाटक्रमात् should be read as ब्राह्मणपाठात्, for in the case of order determined by the Mantra-text the author has said above '...यः क्रम आश्रीयते स **मन्त्रपाठात्.**'

The five fore-sacrifices are laid down by 'प्रयाजाः कर्तव्याः.' They are referred to in a Brāhmaṇa-text as follows : 'समिधो यजति, तनूनपातं यजति, इडो यजति, बर्हिर्यजति, स्वाहाकारं यजति.' The question now is: In which order are these five fore-sacrifices to be performed ? It will be noticed that in the Brāhmaṇa-text, which refers to them by name, there is neither a gerund ending in त्वा, nor a word like ततः or पश्चात्, which would have directly shown the order of these sacrifices. Nor again is it possible to say that order here can be established through the force of purpose as was done in the case of 'यवागूपाक' and 'अग्निहोत्रहोम.' For, it is possible to perform तनूनपाद्याग even without first performing समिद्याग. Under these circumstances the Brāhmaṇa-text itself is regarded as determining the order i. e. the order of the fore- sacrifices is determined to be the same as is mentioned in the Brāhmaṇa passage.

यद्यपि...स्वीक्रियन्ते —It has been pointed out in the above paragraph that Brāhmaṇa-sentences serve their purpose, when they enjoin certain sacrificial matters (अर्थः). How can the Brāhmaṇa sentences then be regarded as laying down order ? The answer to this objection is that in the present case viz. that of the fore-sacrifices, there is no other passage, which lays down their order (क्रमस्मारकान्तरस्य अभावः). Especially, there is no Mantra-text, which can be regarded as enjoining the order of the Prayājas. Therefore, the Brāhmaṇa-passage itself is accepted as laying down order (क्रमस्मारकत्वेन) in the case of the Prayājas.

It has been said above that in the case of the Prayājas there is no Mantra-text, which lays down order. Therefore, the Brāhmaṇa passage itself is accepted as enjoining order. Against this commentators point out that the following passage from the तैत्तिरीयसंहिता 2. 6. 1 viz. 'समिधो यजति । वसन्तमेव ऋतूनामवरुन्धे । तनूनपातं यजति । ग्रीष्ममेवा-

वरुन्धे। इडो यजति। वर्षा एवावरुन्धे। बर्हिर्यजति। शरदमेवावरुन्धे। स्वाहाकारं यजति। हेमन्तमेवावरुन्धे।' can be regarded as laying down order in the case of the Prayājas. Similarly, the प्रयाजमन्त्रs commencing with 'समिधोऽग्न आज्यस्य व्यन्तु' also refer to the Prayājas in the same order. These can also be considered as laying down the order of the Prayājas. Therefore, the illustration of ब्राह्मणपाठात् क्रमः given by Bhāskara viz. प्रयाजानां क्रमः is not happy. Under these circumstances our author's illustration should be regarded as intimating just this that whenever there is no Mantra-text, conveying order, a Brāhmaṇa-text should be accepted as doing it. This happens particularly in the case of those rites, which are performed silently without the accompaniment of the recital of Mantras.

Read 'वस्तुतस्तु प्रयाजक्रमो न ब्राह्मणपाठक्रमात् स्वीक्रियते' समिधोऽग्न आज्यस्य व्यन्तु-इत्यादिभिः क्रमप्रकरणप्राप्तैर्मन्त्रैर्देवता गुणत्वेन समर्प्यन्ते इति नवमतन्त्ररत्नविरोधात्।... ब्राह्मण' पाठक्रमात् क्रमस्तु यत्र अर्थस्मारका मन्त्रा न सन्त्येव तेषामेव, यथा तूष्णीं विहितानां कर्मणां क्रमो ब्राह्मणपाठक्रमाद् भवति, तत्र तेषामेव प्रयोगसमवेतार्थस्मारकत्वात्।' रामेश्वर

'एवं च यत्र कर्माङ्गभूतो मन्त्रः समस्ति तत्र मन्त्रपाठक्रमादेव क्रमः। यत्र स नास्ति, तत्र ब्राह्मणपाठस्यापि अगत्या क्रमबोधकत्वमङ्गीकरणीयमिति भावः।' साःविवेचिनी

Section 45

This Section deals with the fourth pramāṇa for determining order viz. स्थान or position. स्थान is defined as existence near (उपस्थितिः) or being present or presenting oneself. The general nature of this presentation of oneself is explained in the sentence 'यस्य हि देशे... अनुष्ठानम्.' This sentence is formed by the use of pronouns and looks at first sight somewhat confusing. But when we understand the illustration, the sentence will become very easy.

The general nature of स्थान is as follows: Many things are to be performed together in the place of one. The question is which is to be performed first. The answer is that the thing, in the place of which all these things are being performed, presents itself first, when the time for the performance of them all arrives. Therefore, that thing, which thus presents itself first, is performed first. All this will be clear from the following illustration.

ज्योतिष्टोम is a Soma sacrifice in which, as we saw before (vide pp. 158–159), three animals viz. अग्नीषोमीय, सवनीय and अनुबन्ध्य are sacrificed on three successive days. Thus, the अग्नीषोमीय is offered on the औपवसथ्य day, the सवनीय on the सौत्य day (सुत्याकाले = सवनकाले at the time of the pressing of Soma, which is done on the second day, called सौत्यदिन) and the अनुबन्ध्य on the अवभृत day at the end (अन्ते) of the purificatory bath.

साद्यस्क is a sacrifice, which is a derivative (विकारः) from ज्योतिष्टोम. Here the three animals of the arche-type accrue by transfer (चोदकप्राप्ताः). But a peculiarity of साद्यस्क is that all the three animals are here slaughtered together i. e. on one and the same day, in accordance with the injunction 'सह पशून् आलभते,' instead of on three successive days as in ज्योतिष्टोम. लभ् with आ means to kill or slaughter. Note 'आलम्भपिञ्जविशरघातोन्माथवधा अपि' अमरः.

Two questions arise in connection with the साद्यस्क sacrifice viz. (1) On which of the three days for which साद्यस्क lasts are the three animals offered? (2) Which is the animal that is offered first? Only the second of these questions is decided by स्थानप्रमाण. The first is settled by other considerations.

The other considerations, which decide the first question are two viz. प्रधानप्रत्यासत्ति and स्थानातिक्रमसाम्य. On account of these it is settled that in साद्यस्क the three animals are sacrificed in the region of the सवनीय animal (सवनीयदेशे).

प्रधानप्रत्यासत्ति means proximity to the main action. The main action in a Soma sacrifice is of course the pressing of Soma (सुत्या सवनं वा). This pressing in done on the second day i. e. the day of सवनीय.

If, therefore, the three animals are sacrificed on the Savanīya day, they would be close to the main action viz. सुत्या. That is why it has been settled that in साद्यस्क the three animals are sacrificed on the सवनीय day.

The second reason why the three animals are offered on the Savanīya day in साद्यस्क is स्थानातिक्रमसाम्य or equality of removal from proper place. This will be clear from the following diagram :—

पशवः		दिनानि
(1) अग्नीषोमीयः	... ...	(1) औपवसथ्यम् अहः
(2) सवनीयः	... ...	(2) सौत्यादिनम् or सुत्याकालः
(3) अनुबन्ध्यः	... ...	(3) अवभृथादिनम् or अन्तः

If the three animals are offered on the Savanīya day, अग्नीषोमीय and अनुबन्ध्य leave their own place and go to सवनीय. अग्नीषोमीय takes as it were a step downwards, while अनुबन्ध्य takes a step up. Thus, both अग्नीषोमीय and अनुबन्ध्य have to go through one स्थानातिक्रम each and this is what is exactly meant by स्थानातिक्रमसाम्य.

Now see what happens if any other day is chosen for the performance of these three animals together. If the animals are offered on the अग्नीषोमीय day, सवनीय will take one step up, but अनुबन्ध्य will have not only to leave its own place, but also to cross over the place of सवनीय i. e. अनुबन्ध्य will have to take two steps up. Thus, if अग्नीषोमीय day is chosen for the performance of the three animals together, सवनीय is involved in one स्थानातिक्रम and अनुबन्ध्य in two. Consequently स्थानातिक्रमवैषम्य results.

Similarly, if अनुबन्ध्य day is selected for the simultaneous sacrifice of these three animals, अग्नीषोमीय will have to go through two स्थानातिक्रमs and सवनीय only one. Here also स्थानातिक्रमवैषम्य follows.

Therefore, as the selection of the सवनीय day leads to स्थानातिक्रमसाम्य, all the three animals are offered on the Savaniya day.

Thus, on the grounds of प्रधानप्रत्यासत्ति and स्थानातिक्रमसाम्य all the three animals are sacrificed on the सवनीय day in साद्यस्क्र, instead of on three successive days as in ज्योतिष्टोम.

The second question must now be answered. Which of these three animals is offered first ? The order, that is laid down in the arche-type, is अग्नीषोमीय, सवनीय and अनुबन्ध्य. Is this the order that is to be followed in the derivative also ? 'No,' says the स्थानप्रमाण. 'In साद्यस्क्र, सवनीय is offered first, अग्नीषोमीय and अनुबन्ध्य afterwards.' The reason for this decision regarding the प्राथम्य of सवनीय by स्थान is as follows :

In the arche-type i. e. in ज्योतिष्टोम it is laid down that after taking up the cup of the Aśvins at the time of the प्रातःसवन (the pressing of Soma in the morning) on the सौत्य day, the सवनीय animal is to be offered. Thus, in ज्योतिष्टोम the region of सवनीय is after the taking up of the cup of the Aśvins on the सौत्य day (आश्विनग्रहणानन्तरं हि सवनीयदेशः). When, therefore, in साद्यस्क्र, the cup of the Aśvins is taken up, the सवनीय animal first presents itself (उपस्थितो भवति) for offer, following the procedure in ज्योतिष्टोम. This presenting of itself after आश्विनग्रहण by सवनीय is स्थान or उपस्थितिः, on account of which the सवनीय animal is performed first (तस्य स्थानात् प्रथममनुष्ठानम्) and the two others afterwards.

Now, out of the two animals which are to be offered afterwards अग्नीषोमीय is offered first and अनुबन्ध्य after it. For, there is no reason why their order, as found in the arche-type, should be abandoned. Read 'तयोरपि [अग्नीषोमीयानुबन्ध्ययोरपि] मध्ये कस्य प्रथममनुष्ठानमिति चिन्तायां तत्र प्रकृतिदृष्टक्रमस्य परित्यागे प्रमाणाभावेन प्रथमतोऽग्नीषोमीयस्य अनन्तरमानुबन्ध्यस्य इत्येव क्रमो बोद्धव्यः ।' सारविवेचिनी. Thus, the order of the performance of these three animals in साद्यस्क्र is सवनीय, अग्नीषोमीय and अनुबन्ध्य.

We shall now be able to understand clearly the general sentence at the commencement of this Section, which explains the nature of

स्थान or उपस्थिति viz. यस्य हि देशे यो अनुष्ठीयते तत्पूर्वतने पदार्थे कृते स एव प्रथममुपस्थितो भवति. This can be thus paraphrased : यस्य हि नाम यस्य सवनीयस्य हि देशे यः नाम अग्नीषोमी-[illegible]य–अनुबन्ध्यात्मकः पदार्थः अनुष्ठीयते तत्पूर्वतने नाम सवनीयपूर्वतने पदार्थे आश्विनग्रहग्रहणरूपे कृते स एव नाम सवनीय एव प्रथममुपस्थितो भवति.

साद्यस्क्र as the name of the sacrifice is derived from सद्यः + क्री and means a sacrifice which is performed with recently purchased Soma (साद्यस्क्रो नाम सद्यःसोमक्रयविशिष्टः सोमयागविशेषः). The sacrifice is also sometimes called साद्यस्कः, which epithet arises from the fact that in this sacrifice everything is performed quickly (सद्यः) i. e. on one and the same day ('सद्यो दीक्षयन्ति' 'सद्यः सोमं क्रीणन्ति' इत्यादि श्रुत्युक्तप्रकारेण सर्वमङ्गजातं यत्र सद्य एवानुष्ठीयते स एकदिनानुष्ठेयो यागविशेषः **साद्यस्क**शब्दवाच्यः).

भिन्नदेशाः (भिन्नः देशः येषां ते) of different regions. देश is a technical term in sacrificial literature and means the day or the time of the performance of a certain rite in the course of a sacrifice.

अव्यक्तत्वात्—This represents the reason why साद्यस्क्र is regarded as a modification of ज्योतिष्टोम. The अव्यक्तत्व or unmanifestness of साद्यस्क्र lies in this that no deity in honour of whom साद्यस्क्र is to be offered is mentioned. Consequently, the deity accrues to this sacrifice by transfer from the arche-type ज्योतिष्टोम.

Note 'अव्यक्तत्वात् स्वार्थचोदितदेवतारहित्यत्वादित्यर्थः' रामेश्वर; 'का अव्यक्तता । द्रव्यदेवतस्य अभावः । द्रव्यदेवतेन हि यागः अभिव्यज्यते ।' शाबरभाष्य; 'यत्र तद्धितचतुर्थीमन्त्रवर्णैर्यागार्थतयैव देवता विनियुक्ता तद् व्यक्तम् । इतरत्तु अव्यक्तम् ।' शास्त्रदीपिका

आश्विनग्रहणानन्तरम्—Here आश्विन (अश्विनोः अयम् आश्विनः) stands for आश्विनग्रह or the cup of the Asvins, according to Vāmana's famous dictum 'विशेषणमात्रप्रयोगो विशेष्यप्रतिपत्तौ ।' काव्यालंकारसूत्र 5. 1. 10.

त्रिवृता = त्रिगुणया रज्ज्वा with a triple cord. परिवीय (परितः संवेष्ट्य) gerund from परि + वी वेति to go round, encircle, surround. उपाकरोति performs the उपाकरण ceremony on, offers.

इति उक्तम्—This expression refers to पूर्वमीमांसा V. i. 13, which discusses this topic of the order of the performance of the three animals in साद्यस्क्र.

Read 'साद्यस्क्रनामकः कश्चित् सोमयागः । तत्र श्रूयते 'सह पशून् आलभते' इति । प्रकृतौ अग्नीषोमीयः पशुः औपवसथ्ये पूर्वदिने आलभ्यते, सवनीयपशुः सुत्यादिने प्रातःसवने आश्विनग्रहादूर्ध्वमालभ्यते, अनुबन्ध्यपशुरवभृथादूर्ध्वमालभ्यते । इह त्रयोऽपि पशवः सह आलब्धव्याः । सोऽयं सहालम्भः सुत्यादिने आश्विनग्रहादूर्ध्वं सवनीयस्थाने भवति इत्येतत् अवश्यमभ्युपेयम् । तथा सति **प्रधानसोमप्रत्यासत्तिलाभात् ।**

तेषु त्रिषु पशुषु अग्नीषोमीयस्य प्रथममुपाकरणम् । कुतः । प्रकृतौ तत्प्राथम्यस्य अपेक्षितत्वात इति चेत् ।

मैवम् । सवनीयो हि स्वस्थान एव वर्तते । आश्विनग्रहसामीप्यस्य सवनीयस्थानत्वात् । **आश्विने गृहीते सति सवनीय एव बुद्धिस्थो भवति**, प्रकृतौ तदानन्तर्यस्य क्लृप्तत्वात् । ततः **सवनीयस्य प्राथम्ये स्थानान्निश्चिते सति** स्थानभ्रष्टयोरग्नीषोमीयानुबन्ध्ययोः प्रकृतौ इव पूर्वोत्तरभावो द्रष्टव्यः । ' जैमिनीयन्यायमालाविस्तर p. 268

Section 46

This Section deals with the fifth pramāṇa for determining order viz. मुख्य. मुख्यक्रम means the order of subsidiaries as determined by the order of their principals. There are some principal rites, which have to be performed in a certain order. There are also subordinate rites which refer to these principals. The order of the principals has been fixed. The question is : Which is going to be the order of the subsidiaries ? Under these circumstances the order of the subsidiaries is determined by the already fixed order of the principals. This is known as मुख्यक्रम.

The reason why the order of the subsidiaries is determined by the order of the principals is as follows : प्रयोगविधि lays down promptness or speediness (प्राशुभावः) of performance. This is secured if the principals are performed along with their subsidiaries. This साहित्य or togetherness of the principals and the subsidiaries must always be maintained. This means that there should be no unnecessary interval between the principals and the subsidiaries.

When there are several principal rites to which one or more subsidiaries belong, it is not possible to perform the principals and the subsidiaries absolutely together without the least interval between them. Some interval (व्यवधानम्) between the principal and its subsidiary is inevitable. Under these circumstances what we must do is to perform the subsidiaries in such a manner as to secure equal interval (तुल्यं व्यवधानम्) between the several principals and their subsidiaries. And this equal interval is secured by performing the subsidiaries in the same order as the order of the principals.

If the order of the principals is not followed in the case of the subsidiaries, what would happen is that there would be absolutely no interval (अत्यन्तमव्यवधानम्) between some principal and its subsidiary, while some other principal would be far too removed (अत्यन्तं व्यवधानम्) from its subsidiary. This of course is improper, because it would involve the violation of the togetherness (साहित्यबाधः) of the principal and its subsidiary that is understood from the injunction of performance (प्रयोगविधिः). Therefore, the order of the principals also becomes a reason for determining the order of the subsidiaries.

All this will be clear from the following illustration : In the दर्श sacrifice of the दर्शपूर्णमास two of the principal rites are known as आग्नेय and ऐन्द्र. The आग्नेय oblation is made of a cake prepared in eight potsherds (अष्टाकपालः पुरोडाशः अष्टसु कपालेषु संस्कृतः पुरोडाशः इत्यर्थः), while the ऐन्द्र oblation consists of curds, according to ' यदाग्नेयोऽष्टाकपालोऽमावास्यायां भवति, ऐन्द्रं दधि—' (तैत्तिरीयसंहिता II. v. 3). The order of these oblations is आग्नेय and ऐन्द्र and it is fixed on the authority of the order of their याज्याs and अनुवाक्याs. The आग्नेय and ऐन्द्र oblations are offered after the performance of the प्रयाजs and it is laid down in ' प्रयाजशेषेण हवींषि अभिघारयति (besprinkles) ' that these oblations should be sprinkled over with the ghee, remaining after the प्रयाजs are performed, before they are actually presented. Thus, अभिघारण or sprinkling with ghee is a subordinate rite, which belongs to the आग्नेय and ऐन्द्र oblations. The question now is: In what order is the अभिघारण to be performed on these two oblations ? And this question is decided on the authority of मुख्यक्रम, which tells us that the order of the subsidiary rite अभिघारण with reference to the two oblations must be the same as the order of the principal rites viz. आग्नेययाग and ऐन्द्रयाग. Thus, the order of अभिघारण is आग्नेयहविरभिघारण and ऐन्द्रदध्यभिघारण.

When this order is followed, equal distance is secured between the principal rite and its subsidiary. But, if a reverse order (व्युत्क्रमः = विरुद्धः क्रमः) is accepted for the अभिघारण, आग्नेयहविरभिघारण and आग्नेययाग would be too close to each other, while ऐन्द्रदध्यभिघारण and ऐन्द्रयाग would be far too removed from each other. This will be clearly seen from the following diagram:—

मुख्यक्रमेण अभिघारणस्य अनुष्ठाने	व्युत्क्रमेण अभिघारणस्य अनुष्ठाने
(1) आग्नेयहविरभिघारणम् (अङ्गम्)	(1) ऐन्द्रदध्यभिघारणम् (अङ्गम्)
(2) ऐन्द्रदध्यभिघारणम् (अङ्गम्)	(2) आग्नेयहविरभिघारणम् (अङ्गम्)
(3) आग्नेय यागः (प्रधानम्)	(3) आग्नेययागः (प्रधानम्)
(4) ऐन्द्रयागः (प्रधानम्)	(4) ऐन्द्रयागः (प्रधानम्)

It will be seen from above that in the case of मुख्यक्रमेण अनुष्ठाने, the interval between the principal rite and its subsidiary is just one. आग्नेययाग and आग्नेयहविरभिघारण are separated by just ऐन्द्रदध्यभिघारण. Similarly ऐन्द्रयाग and ऐन्द्रदध्यभिघारण are also separated by just आग्नेययाग. On the other hand in the case of व्युत्क्रमेण अभिघारणे, आग्नेययाग and आग्नेयहविरभिघारण are too close, while ऐन्द्रयाग and ऐन्द्रदध्यभिघारण are too far away, being separated by two (व्यन्तारितं व्यवधानम्) viz. आग्नेयहविरभिघारण and आग्नेययाग.

तच्च अयुक्तमिति उक्तमेव—The reference in 'उक्तमेव' here is to 'तच्च अयुक्तम्, प्रयोगविध्यवगतसाहित्यबाधापत्तेः ।', occurring at the end of the last paragraph.

The expression मुख्यक्रमः is somewhat confusing. It does not mean मुख्यानां कर्मणां क्रमः. It is really a मध्यमपदलोपी समासः and is explained as मुख्यनिर्णीतः क्रमः, मुख्यैः कर्मभिः निर्णीतः क्रमः, मुख्यानां कर्मणां क्रमेण निर्णीतः क्रमः इत्यर्थः. The commentary सारविवेचिनी explains मुख्यक्रमः as मुख्यानां क्रम इव क्रमः मुख्यक्रमः. Such a dissolution of the compound is incorrect from the grammatical point of view.

The expression प्रधानक्रमः possesses the natural sense of प्रधानानां कर्मणां क्रमः

स च मुख्यक्रमः...बलवान्—This paragraph proves that मुख्यक्रम is weaker than पाठक्रम. मुख्यक्रम means the order of subsidiaries as determined by the order of the principal rites. मुख्यक्रम thus depends on the comprehension (प्रतिपत्तिः) of the प्रधानक्रम. For, unless we know what प्रधानक्रम is, we cannot arrive at मुख्यक्रम. प्रधानक्रम in its turn depends on another means of proof (प्रमाणान्तरम्) viz. पाठक्रम. For, प्रधानक्रम is determined from the order in which the principal rites are mentioned in the Brāhmaṇas, or from the order in which the याज्याs and अनुवाक्याs of the principal rites occur in the Mantra—or Saṁhitā-text. Thus, in order to determine मुख्यक्रम we must first know पाठक्रम and प्रधानक्रम. The comprehension of मुख्यक्रम is in this manner delayed or retarded (विलम्बित) by the comprehension of पाठक्रम and प्रधानक्रम.

But पाठक्रम is more quickly comprehended. For, it depends only on the order of the mention (पाठक्रम) of the particular rites in the Veda (स्वाध्यायः=वेदः), which is independent of anything else.

It will thus be seen that the ground on which पाठक्रम is established to be stronger than मुख्यक्रम is that पाठक्रम is more quickly grasped than मुख्यक्रम. In order to understand what पाठक्रम is we have merely to look to the order in which the particular rites occur in the holy texts. Thus स्वाध्यायपाठ directly leads to पाठक्रम.

But मुख्यक्रम requires the knowledge of one further step. From पाठक्रम we go to प्रधानक्रम and प्रधानक्रम helps us to determine मुख्यक्रम. मुख्यक्रम thus takes a longer time to understand than पाठक्रम. मुख्यक्रम is consequently weaker than पाठक्रम. This will be clear from the following:

पाठक्रमप्रतिपत्तिः	मुख्यक्रमप्रतिपत्तिः
(1) स्वाध्यायपाठः	(1) स्वाध्यायपाठः
|	|
(2) पाठक्रमः	(2) पाठक्रमः
	|
	(3) प्रधानक्रमः
	|
	(4) मुख्यक्रमः

It should be noticed that Bhāskara need not have brought in here the question of विलम्बितप्रतिपत्ति. He should have merely stated that मुख्यक्रम is weaker than पाठक्रम, because it depends on पाठक्रम. But here, as in many other places, भास्कर is merely following आपदेव.

प्रमाणान्तरसापेक्षप्रधानक्रमप्रतिपत्तिसापेक्षतया = प्रमाणान्तरेण ब्राह्मणपाठक्रमेण याज्यानुवाक्याक्रमेण वा सापेक्षः, तस्मिन् प्रमाणान्तरे अवलम्बमानः इत्यर्थः, यः प्रधानक्रमः प्रधानानां कर्मणां क्रमः, तस्य या प्रतिपत्तिः ज्ञानं तया सापेक्षः तस्य भावः तया.

निरपेक्षस्वाध्यायपाठक्रममात्रसापेक्षतया = निरपेक्षः प्रमाणान्तरनिरपेक्षः इत्यर्थः यः स्वाध्यायः वेदः तस्मिन् यो पाठः पठनं तस्य क्रमः, स एव ०क्रममात्रम्. तेन सापेक्षः तस्य भावः तया.

In this paragraph Bhāskara merely states that पाठक्रम is more powerful than मुख्यक्रम. But he gives no illustration to prove his statement. That illustration is supplied by पूर्वमीमांसासूत्र V. i. 15. It is as follows:

उपांशु and अग्नीषोमीय are two of the याजs that constitute the पूर्णमास sacrifice of the दर्शपूर्णमास. Vide p. 170 above. The material for उपांशुयाज is आज्य or clarified butter and that for अग्नीषोमीय is पुरोडाश or a cake. There are certain subordinate rites such as उत्पवन and चतुर्गृहीतत्व, which have to be performed for the आज्य. Then again, there are certain others such as निर्वाप and अवघात, which belong to the पुरोडाश. The question now is: Which of these subordinate rites are to be performed first, the rites of the आज्य or the rites of the पुरोडाश?

The answer, according to मुख्यक्रम प्रमाण, is that आज्यधर्मs are to be performed first and पुरोडाशधर्मs afterwards, because the order of the principal rites, to which these धर्मs refer through their material आज्य and पुरोडाश, is उपांशु first and अग्नीषोमीय afterwards. Thus following मुख्यक्रम the order for the subsidiaries is (1) आज्यधर्माः and (2) पुरोडाशधर्माः.

But in the holy texts we find that the characteristics of the पुरोडाश such as निर्वाप and अवघात are mentioned first and the characteristics of the आज्य afterwards. According to पाठक्रम the order, therefore, is (1) पुरोडाशधर्माः and (2) आज्यधर्माः. As पाठक्रम is stronger than मुख्यक्रम, this order has to be followed.

Read 'दर्शपूर्णमासयोः उपांशुयाजोऽग्नीषोमीयश्च इत्येतदुभयं पौर्णमास्यामाम्नातम्। तत्र उपांशुयाजस्य आज्यं द्रव्यम्। आज्यधर्मा उत्पवनचतुर्गृहीतत्वादयः। अग्नीषोमीयस्य पुरोडाशो द्रव्यम्। तस्य धर्मा निर्वापावघातादयः। तत्र मुख्यौ यागौ उपांशुयाजाग्नीषोमीयौ पूर्वोत्तरभाविनौ। तथा सति पूर्वन्यायेन धर्मक्रमस्य मुख्यक्रमाधीनत्वात् आज्यधर्माणाम् अनुष्ठाने प्राथम्यम् **इति प्राप्ते**—

ब्रूमः। औषधधर्माः (properties of the rice-grains which are obtained from plants and from which the cake is prepared) निर्वापादयः पूर्वम् आम्नाताः। पश्चादाज्यधर्माः। तत्र मुख्यक्रमप्रयुक्तमाज्यधर्माणां प्राथम्यं बाधित्वा पाठक्रमानुसारेण औषधधर्मा एव

प्रथममनुष्ठेयाः । पाटक्रमो हि वैदिकैः शब्दैः सहसा प्रतीयते । मुख्यक्रमानुसारी तु क्रम उपपत्त्या कल्पनीयः । तस्मात् अग्नीषोमीयपुरोडाशार्थेभ्यः औषधधर्मेभ्य ऊर्ध्वमाज्यधर्मा अनुष्ठेयाः ।' जैमिनीयन्यायमालाविस्तर pp. 269-270

आपदेव refers to this illustration in the following sentences: 'अत एव आग्नेयोपांशुयाजाग्नीषोमीयाणां क्रमेण अनुष्ठीयमानानामपि उपांशुयाजाज्यनिर्वापो मुख्यक्रमान्न पूर्वमनुष्ठीयते, तस्य दुर्बलत्वात् । पाटक्रमात्तु पश्चादनुष्ठीयते, तस्य प्रबलत्वात् ।'

स चायं मुख्यक्रमः...संनिकर्षात्—In this paragraph Bhāskara states that मुख्यक्रम is more powerful than प्रवृत्तिक्रम. The reason is that if we were to follow प्रवृत्तिक्रम, many subsidiaries would be unduly removed from their principal, but if we follow मुख्यक्रम, they are placed near it.

It will be noticed that here also Bhāskara gives no illustration to prove that मुख्यक्रम is more powerful than प्रवृत्तिक्रम. आपदेव gives such an illustration, however. We shall, therefore, explain it after him.

But first we must know what प्रवृत्तिक्रम is. It is defined and explained in the next Section. Its general nature is as follows:

प्रयोगविधि, we have seen, aims at promptness of performance. In order to secure this promptness it lays down a definite order for the performance of the subsidiaries. When several subsidiaries have to be performed, their order is fixed by प्रवृत्तिक्रम. In fixing this order the object aimed at is to secure साहित्यम् or togetherness of these subsidiaries. प्रवृत्तिक्रम thus tells us that all subsidiaries should be performed together without any unnecessary interval between them. अङ्गानां साहित्यम् or प्रत्यासत्तिः is what प्रवृत्तिक्रम is anxious to secure.

आग्नेय and उपांशु are two of the rites that constitute the दर्श sacrifice of the दर्शपूर्णमास. Vide p. 170 above. The उपांशुयाग is offered with सांनाय्य i. e. with milk and curds and is, therefore, known as सांनाय्ययाग. There are certain subsidiaries such as अवदान (cutting or dividing), अभिघारण (sprinkling with ghee) and हविरासादन (bringing near the oblation), which belong to आग्नेय. They are known as आग्नेयधर्माः. There are others, which are designated सांनाय्यधर्माः and which include शाखाहरण, वत्सापकरण and दोहन, as also अवदान, अभिघारण and हविरासादन. सांनाय्यधर्माः fall in two groups, शाखाहरण, वत्सापकरण and दोहन forming one and अवदान, अभिघारण and हविरासादन constituting another. Of these, शाखाहरण, वत्सापकरण and दोहन have necessarily to be performed on the previous day i. e. on कृष्णचतुर्दशी. For, unless we milk the cow on the previous day after removing the calf from it with the help of a Palāśa branch, we cannot have the curds for sacrifice on दर्श. The others viz. अवदान, अभिघारण and हविरासादन are to be performed on the दर्श day at the time of the actual presentation of the oblation.

We have seen before that प्रवृत्तिक्रम is anxious to see that all subsidiaries are performed together. If we were to follow प्रवृत्तिक्रम in the case of these properties of milk and curds (सांनाय्यधर्माः), we should have to perform all these सांनाय्यधर्मs together. Then, we would go through आग्नेयधर्मs, after which we would offer the आग्नेययाग and last the सांनाय्ययाग. Thus, the order of performance, according to प्रवृत्तिक्रम, would be (1) सर्वे सांनाय्यधर्माः, (2) आग्नेयधर्माः, (3) आग्नेययागः and (4) सांनाय्ययागः.

Herein we find that the many subsidiaries of सांनाय्य are far too removed from their principal viz. the सांनाय्ययाग (बहूनामङ्गाना सांनाय्यधर्माणामित्यर्थः प्रधानविप्रकर्षात् प्रधानात् सांनाय्ययागात् विप्रकर्षात् विशेषेण दूरस्थितत्वात्). For, between them come आग्नेयधर्माः and आग्नेययागः. On the other hand आग्नेयधर्माः and आग्नेययागः are far too close.

Now, see what happens when we follow मुख्यक्रम, which tells us that the order of subsidiaries is the same as the order of the principals. The first three सांनाय्यधर्मs must in any case be performed first i. e. on the previous day for the reason stated above. After these are performed, मुख्यक्रम steps forward and decrees that the subsidiaries should be performed in the same order in which the principals are performed. Now, the order of the principal yāgas is fixed viz. आग्नेय and सांनाय्य. So the subsidiaries have also to be performed in the order of आग्नेयधर्माः and सांनाय्यधर्माः. Thus, according to मुख्यक्रम, the order of performance is (1) शाखाहरणादयः त्रयः सांनाय्यधर्माः, (2) आग्नेयधर्माः, (3) अवदानादयः अवशिष्टाः सांनाय्यधर्माः, (4) आग्नेययागः and (5) सांनाय्ययागः.

Here we see that सांनाय्यधर्माः are brought a little nearer to सांनाय्ययागः than before (मुख्यक्रमे तु संनिकर्षात् = मुख्यक्रमे तु बहूनामङ्गानाम् अवदानादीनां सांनाय्यधर्माणामित्यर्थः स्वप्रधानस्य सांनाय्ययागस्य संनिकर्षो वर्तते, प्रवृत्तिक्रमापेक्षया न्यूनं व्यवधानं वर्तते इत्यतः) and equal distance between आग्नेयधर्माः and आग्नेययागः, and सांनाय्यधर्माः and सांनाय्ययागः is secured.

This is the reason why मुख्यक्रम is more powerful than प्रवृत्तिक्रम.

The विप्रकर्षः and संनिकर्षः (= तुल्यं व्यवधानम्), which form the reason of the superiority of मुख्यक्रम over प्रवृत्तिक्रम, will be clear from the following comparative table:—

प्रवृत्तिक्रमेण अनुष्ठाने	मुख्यक्रमेण अनुष्ठाने
(1) सर्वे सांनाय्यधर्माः	(1) शाखाहरणादयस्त्रयः सांनाय्यधर्माः
(2) आग्नेयधर्माः	(2) आग्नेयधर्माः
(3) आग्नेययागः	(3) अवशिष्टाः सांनाय्यधर्माः
(4) सांनाय्ययागः	(4) आग्नेययागः
	(5) सांनाय्ययागः

It should be noted that the sentence 'प्रवृत्तिक्रमे हि बहूनामङ्गानां प्रधानविप्रकर्षात्, मुख्यक्रमे तु संनिकर्षात्' is not very happily worded. It does not bring out the author's meaning clearly. But, for this clumsy phraseology also Bhāskara is indebted to his master Āpadeva. A more careful writer would perhaps have expressed himself somewhat as follow: 'प्रवृत्तिक्रमे हि केषांचिदङ्गानां (सांनाय्यधर्माणां) स्वप्रधानेन अत्यन्तं व्यवधानम्, केषांचित् (आग्नेयधर्माणाम्) अत्यन्तमव्यवधानं स्यात्। मुख्यक्रमे तु अङ्गानां तुल्यं व्यवधानं भवति।'

The word सांनाय्य has occurred before. Vide p. 161 above. It means curds and milk (दधिपयसी). The तैत्तिरीयसंहिता II. v. 3 relates a story, which contains an etymological explanation of the name सांनाय्य and from which we know that सांनाय्य originally meant milk. We quote the following from Sāyaṇa's commentary on the passage with a few changes to make the story read well: 'इंद्रो वृत्रवधेन भीतो दूरे पलायमानः स्वकीयेन सामर्थ्येन वियुक्तोऽभूत्। तदिन्द्रसामर्थ्यं विविधरूपेण पृथिवीं प्राप्नोत्। तत्र तद् ओषधीनां वीरुधां च रूपेण पर्यणमत्। ततः स इन्द्रः स्वसामर्थ्यस्य ओषध्यादिरूपेण परिणामं प्रजापतेरग्रे कथितवान्। स च प्रजापतिः 'एतद् इन्द्रियसामर्थ्यमिन्द्रार्थं सम्यक् प्रापयत' इति पशूनब्रवीत्। तत् सामर्थ्यं पशव ओषधीभ्यः सकाशादानीय स्वशरीरे सम्यक् स्थापितवन्तः। पुनः स्वनिष्ठं तद् वीर्यं क्षीरादिरूपमिन्द्रं प्रति दुग्धवन्तः। **यस्मात् पशवः समनयंस्तस्मात् सांनाय्यस्य गोरसस्य 'सम्यगानयनेन संपन्नम्' इति व्युत्पत्त्या सांनाय्यनाम भवति।'**

The following quotation from the मीमांसान्यायप्रकाश of आपदेव will make the point of the superiority of मुख्यक्रम over प्रवृत्तिक्रम clear:

'स चायं मुख्यक्रमः प्रवृत्तिक्रमाद् बलवान्। प्रवृत्तिक्रमे हि आश्रीयमाणे बहूनामङ्गानां प्रधानविप्रकर्षो भवति, अस्मिंस्तु आश्रीयमाणे संनिकर्षः। तद्यथा।

दर्शपूर्णमासयोरादौ आग्नेयानुष्ठानम्, ततः सांनाय्यस्य। तद्धर्माश्च केचित् [शाखाहरणादयः] पूर्वमनुष्ठीयन्ते। **तत्र यदि प्रवृत्तिक्रममाश्रित्य तद्धर्माः सर्वे पूर्वमनुष्ठीयेरन्**, तत आग्नेयधर्माः, तत आग्नेयानुष्ठानम्, ततः सांनाय्यानुष्ठानम्, तदा तद्धर्माणां स्वप्रधानेन सह द्वाभ्यामाग्नेयधर्मतदनुष्ठानाभ्यां विप्रकर्षः स्यात्।

यदा तु सांनाय्यधर्माणां केषांचित् पूर्वमनुष्ठानेऽपि **अन्ये सर्वे मुख्यक्रममाश्रित्य आग्नेयधर्मानुष्ठानानन्तरमनुष्ठीयन्ते**, तदा सर्वेषामाग्नेयधर्मसांनाय्यधर्माणामेकैकेन विजातीयेन व्यवधानं भवति। आग्नेयधर्माणां स्वप्रधानेन सह सांनाय्यधर्मैर्व्यवधानात्, सांनाय्यधर्माणां च स्वप्रधानेन सह आग्नेयानुष्ठानेन व्यवधानात्, इति न विप्रकर्षः। तस्मात् मुख्यक्रमः प्रवृत्तिक्रमाद् बलवान्।'

Section 47

This Section defines and illustrates the last of the six pramāṇas that determine order viz. प्रवृत्ति or procedure. The general nature of प्रवृत्तिक्रम is as follows:

There are several principal rites which are performed together. There are also some subsidiaries, which belong to these several principal rites and which also have to be performed together. It is physically impossible to perform these subsidiaries together with reference to all the principal rites. Under these circumstances प्रवृत्तिक्रम steps in and points out the method by which साहित्य or togetherness of the subsidiaries is secured. This method consists in performing the subsidiaries in such a manner as to maintain equal distance between one subsidiary and another.

What is done is this: The principal rites are arranged in a certain order, which in the first instance is fixed according to our own sweet will, for the performance of the first subsidiary on them. When the time for the performance of the second subsidiary arrives, it is performed on the principals in exactly the same order as was observed in the case of the first subsidiary. By following the, identical order in the case of the second and subsequent subsidiaries equal distance between one subsidiary and another is maintained. If we change the order of the principals when we come to perform the second subsidiary, we shall find that in some cases of the performance of the second subsidiary, the distance is increased, while in others it is lessened. Therefore, the same order, as was at random fixed for the performance of the first subsidiary, must be followed in the case of the second and the subsequent subsidiaries. This order of the second and subsequent subsidiaries, which is fixed by the procedure (प्रवृत्तिः) that we followed in the case of the first subsidiary, is known as प्रवृत्तिक्रम. Consequently, the essential part of Bhāskara's definition of प्रवृत्तिक्रम is contained in 'द्वितीयादिपदार्थानां प्रथमानुष्ठितपदार्थक्रमाद् यः क्रमः स प्रवृत्तिक्रमः ।'

The remaining part of the definition viz. 'सहप्रयुज्यमानेषु प्रधानेषु संनिपातिनामङ्गानामावृत्त्यानुष्ठाने कर्तव्ये' explains the two circumstances in which प्रवृत्तिक्रम operates.

सहप्रयुज्यमानेषु (= युगपदनुष्ठीयमानेषु) प्रधानेषु—This represents the first of these circumstances viz. that there should be many principals, which are to be performed together. This circumstance rules out the possibility of the operation of मुख्यक्रम. For, मुख्यक्रम requires that there should be many principals, which are to be performed, not simultaneously, but in some fixed order.

संनिपातिना...कर्तव्ये—Attached to these several principals which are to be simultaneously performed, are certain subsidiary rites, which are here referred to as संनिपातीनि अङ्गानि. They are the same as संनिपत्योपकारकाणि of Section 38 above. As their principals are to be simultaneously performed, they also must be performed simultaneously. But the simultaneous performance of these indirectly help.

ing subsidiaries with reference to several principals is a physical impossibility. Therefore, the subsidiaries are to be performed in succession or one after another (आवृत्त्या). So, the second circumstance, which makes it possible for प्रवृत्तिक्रम to operate, is that owing to the inherent impossibility of their simultaneous performance, the subsidiaries are to be performed in succession.

Under these circumstances प्रवृत्तिक्रम decides in which order and by which method the subsidiaries are to be performed so as to secure whatever साहित्य may be possible in their performance.

So far we have seen the general nature of प्रवृत्तिक्रम. For this read 'यत्र बहूनां प्रधानानामेककालकर्तव्यता प्राप्ता, तत्र तदङ्गानामपि संनिपत्योपकारकाणां युगपदनुष्ठानं प्राप्तम् । तच्च अशक्यम् इति एकैकस्मिन् प्रधाने अङ्गावृत्त्यामवश्यंभाविन्यां तत्र यत्प्रधानमारभ्य येन क्रमेण प्राथमिकाङ्गानुष्ठानं कृतं तेनैव क्रमेण तदेव प्रधानमारभ्य द्वितीयाङ्गानुष्ठानमिति यः क्रमः स प्रवृत्तिक्रमः' सारविवेचिनी

It will thus be seen that the word प्रवृत्ति in प्रवृत्तिक्रम means the procedure that we follow in the case of the first subsidiary and that प्रवृत्तिक्रम signifies the order of the second and subsequent subsidiaries as determined by the procedure or order followed in the case of the first.

यथा प्राजापत्यपश्वङ्गेषु— This gives us an illustration of प्रवृत्तिक्रम. The remaining part of the paragraph is devoted to the elaboration of this illustration.

In the Vājapeya sacrifice occurs the sentence 'सप्तदश प्राजापत्यान् पशून् आलभेत', which lays down the sacrifice of seventeen animals in honour of Prajāpati. Another sentence 'वैश्वदेवीं कृत्वा प्राजापत्यैश्चरन्ति' tells us, by the use of the gerund कृत्वा, that the time for these प्राजापत्य sacrifices is after the performance of the वैश्वदेवी rite. As all these seventeen animals are to be sacrificed in honour of one deity and as the time for their presentation is the same viz. after the performance of the वैश्वदेवी, it follows that they are to be simultaneously offered (एककालत्वेन विहिताः). The simultaneous performance (युगपदनुष्ठानम्) of the sacrifice of the seventeen animals is possible; for we can cook the marrow (वपा) of the seventeen animals together and throw it into the fire at one and the same time.

These प्राजापत्य यागs are then the principal rites (प्रधानम्) and their simultaneous performance in the manner stated above is the सह प्रयोग, that are referred to in 'सह प्रयुज्यमानेषु प्रधानेषु.'

Now, these प्राजापत्य यागs are accompanied by certain subsidiary rites such as उपाकरण and नियोजन, which form their procedure (इतिकर्तव्यता). This is pointed out by the instrumental प्राजापत्यैः (तृतीयानिर्देशात्) in 'वैश्वदेवीं कृत्वा प्राजापत्यैश्चरन्ति.' For, the instrumental प्राजापत्यैः

shows that the प्राजापत्य यागs are the instrument or means for achieving a certain end and an instrument cannot achieve its end unless it is fully equipped with all its subsidiaries.

'तृतीयानिर्देशात् सेतिकर्तव्यताकाः' is a clumsy expression borrowed from Āpadeva. What is intended to be conveyed is 'तृतीयया [प्राजापत्याः] सेतिकर्तव्यताका निर्दिष्टाः.'

About the significance of the instrumental read 'यत्र हि तृतीयानिर्देशः तत्र तृतीयाप्रकृत्यर्थस्य करणत्वमवगम्यते, तच्च करणत्वं फलजनकत्वरूपम्, तच्च न प्रधानमात्रस्य संभवतीति अङ्गविशिष्टस्यैव तद्वाच्यम्।' सारविवेचनी

So far we have seen that seventeen animals are to be simultaneously sacrificed in honour of Prajāpati after their subsidiaries are carried out. As the animals are to be performed together, it naturally follows that their subsidiaries have also to be performed together (तेषां तदङ्गानां च... साहित्यं संपाद्यम्).

The simultaneous performance of the animals is possible, as we noted before. But it is obviously impossible for one and the same person to perform the subsidiaries such as उपाकरण and नियोजन all at once with reference to the seventeen animals (तदङ्गानां चोपाकरणादीनां युगपदनुष्ठानमशक्यम्). Therefore, their togetherness or connectedness (साहित्यम्) is to be secured by performing them in an uninterrupted manner (अव्यवहितानुष्ठानात्). That uninterrupted manner consists in first performing the उपाकरण on the various animals one after another and then the नियोजन and others in the same way, so that उपाकरण, नियोजन and others follow one another without interval.

At this stage प्रवृत्तिक्रम steps in and points out the exact way by which अव्यवधान or absence of interval i. e. absence of undue or unnecessary interval i. e. equal interval is secured between one subsidiary of a particular animal and another.

What प्रवृत्तिक्रम wants us to do is this: In performing उपाकरण on the seventeen animals sacred to Prajāpati, we should commence from some particular animal and perform it on all the seventeen one after another. We shall thus have followed a certain order among the seventeen animals for the performance of उपाकरण. We should then perform नियोजन on the seventeen animals in exactly the same order as had been followed in the case of उपाकरण. This order followed for the second subsidiary, which is really the same as that followed for the first, is what is known as प्रवृत्तिक्रम.

It would thus be found that if we were to follow for नियोजन the same order among the animals that we adopted for उपाकरण,

the interval between the उपाकरण and the नियोजन of all the animals in the series would be uniformly maintained at sixteen padārthas or rites. But if we disturb the order, the interval would be increased in the case of some and lessened in the case of others. As नियोजन is undertaken immediately after the completion of उपाकरण, अव्यवहित अनुष्ठान or uninterrupted performance is secured.

The uniform interval maintained between the उपाकरण and the नियोजन of the various animals in the series and the disturbance in the same will be clear from the following diagram :

(I) प्रवृत्तिक्रमेण उपाकरणनियोजनयोरनुष्ठाने	(II) व्युत्क्रमेण उपाकरणनियोजनयोरनुष्ठाने
उपाकृत पशु 1	उपाकृत पशु 1
उपाकृत पशु 2	उपाकृत पशु 2
उपाकृत पशु 3	उपाकृत पशु 3
उपाकृत पशु 4	उपाकृत पशु 4
उपाकृत पशु 5	उपाकृत पशु 5
... ...	... ...
उपाकृत पशु 17	उपाकृत पशु 17
नियोजित पशु 1	नियोजित पशु 17
नियोजित पशु 2	... ...
नियोजित पशु 3	नियोजित पशु 5
नियोजित पशु 4	नियोजित पशु 4
नियोजित पशु 5	नियोजित पशु 3
... ...	नियोजित पशु 2
नियोजित पशु 17	नियोजित पशु 1

A glance at the above diagram will show that when प्रवृत्तिक्रम is followed in the performance of the subsidiaries, the interval between the उपाकरण and the नियोजन of animal No. 1 is represented by 16 उपाकरणs performed on animals Nos. 2 to 17. Similarly, the interval between the उपाकरण and the नियोजन of, say, animal Nos. 5 is 12 उपाकरणs of animals from 6 to 17 and 4 नियोजनs of animals from 1 to 4 i. e. 16 padārthas or rites altogether. This uniform interval of 16 padārthas is maintained between the उपाकरण and नियोजन of all the animals in the series, when प्रवृत्तिक्रम is followed.

Now, see what happens in the case of the second series above, where नियोजन is supposed to have been performed in exactly the reverse of the order followed for उपाकरण. Here, while there is no interval whatsoever between the उपाकरण and the नियोजन of animal No. 17, the उपाकरण and the नियोजन of animal No. 1 are separated by as many as 32 padārthas i. e. 16 उपाकरणs of animals from 2 to 17

and 16 नियोजनs of others from 17 to 2. Similarly, between the उपाकरण and नियोजन of animal No. 5, 24 padārthas viz. 12 उपाकरणs of animals from 6 to 17 and 12 नियोजनs of animals from 17 to 6 intervene. Thus, it will be seen that if we do not follow for the second subsidiary the same order as was followed for the first, the distance between the उपाकरण and नियोजन of the various animals in the series is not kept uniform.

It should here be noted that what प्रवृत्तिक्रम fixes is not so much the order of the subsidiaries of Prajāpati's animals as the order of the animals themselves on which these subsidiaries are performed. For, the order of the subsidiaries उपाकरण, नियोजन and others has already been fixed by their पाठक्रम. But प्रवृत्तिक्रम is said to fix the order of the subsidiaries in so far as these are performed on the animals arranged in that particular order. Or, we may say that the उपाकरणs and नियोजनs of seventeen animals form as it were 34 different padārthas or rites. प्रवृत्तिक्रम fixes the order of the 17 नियोजनs on the basis of the order followed in the case of the 17 उपाकरणs. Thus, प्रवृत्तिक्रम fixes the order of the subsidiaries viz. the 17 नियोजनs.

उपाकरणनियोजनप्रभृतीनाम्—उपाकरण is the formal dedication of an animal to a certain deity by touching it with two blades of Darbha grass and a twig of the Plaksa tree to the accompaniment of the recital of two Vedic stanzas. नियोजन is the tying of the animal to the sacrificial post.

Read "प्रजापतेर्जायमानाः' 'इमं पशुं पशुपते' इति मन्त्रद्वयेन बर्हिर्भ्यां प्लक्षशाखया च पशोरुपस्पर्शनपूर्वकं देवतार्थत्वेन संकल्पन**मुपाकरणम्** । यूपे पशोर्बन्धनं **नियोजनम्** ।' सारविवेचिनी. Also vide pp. 159–160 above.

संप्रतिपन्नदेवताकत्वेन—This expression embodies the reason why connected performance (तच्च = तत् साहित्यं च) of the seventeen animals is possible. The reason is that all the seventeen animals have but one deity viz. Prajāpati. Hence it is possible to throw the marrow of the seventeen animals into the fire together in honour of that one deity with some such expression as 'प्रजापतये स्वाहा.' It appears to us that संप्रतिपन्नदेवताकत्वेन is some scribe's mistake for संप्रतिपन्नैकदेवताकत्वेन. Further, the second reason which makes the simultaneous performance of the seventeen animals possible viz. that they are to be offered at the same time, is not mentioned in this sentence. We, therefore, hazard a further conjecture that संप्रतिपन्नदेवताकत्वेन is really a scribe's mistake for संप्रतिपन्नैकदेवताकालत्वेन (संप्रतिपन्ना ज्ञाता एका देवता एकः कालश्च येषां तद्भावस्तेन). This second conjecture is not altogether without a foundation. For, रामेश्वर notes a variant here viz. संप्रतिपन्नदेवताकालत्वेन, which can easily be supposed to be a corruption from the original संप्रतिपन्नैकदेवताकालत्वेन.

द्वितीयादिपदार्थः—The word पदार्थः means धर्मः or संस्कारः i. e. a rite

For the simultaneous performance of the seventeen animals of Prajāpati read ' वाजपेये सप्तदशसु प्रजापतिदेवताकेषु पशुषु तद्भेदानुसारेण वसाहोमो भिद्यते इति चेत् । न । **प्रजापतिरेक एव सप्तदशानां पशूनां देवता** । तथा पाकोऽपि सहैव क्रियते । प्रदानस्यापि पाक उपलक्षणम् । प्रदानेऽपि साहित्यमस्ति **कालश्चैकः** .... । **शक्यते च सहहोमः** । ' जैमिनीयन्यायमालाविस्तर p. 632

सोऽयं श्रुत्यादिभ्यो दुर्बलः—प्रवृत्ति is the last of the series of the pramāṇas mentioned in Section 41 above. प्रवृत्तिक्रम is consequently the weakest of all the kramas. At the end of the last Section मुख्यक्रम was shown to be more powerful than प्रवृत्तिक्रम. This means all the preceding kramas are stronger than प्रवृत्तिक्रम. That also establishes प्रवृत्तिक्रम to be the weakest of the lot.

In expounding the comparative strength of the six pramāṇas that determine the order of subsidiaries Bhāskara has followed no definite method. Thus, following the practice which he adopted in the case of the six helpers of विनियोगविधि, he should have established that श्रुतिक्रम is more powerful than अर्थक्रम. He does not do this. But, having remarked that श्रुति is more powerful than other pramāṇas, he actually establishes the superiority of श्रुतिक्रम over पाठक्रम. In the case of अर्थक्रम only he follows the old method correctly and proves that it is more powerful than पाठक्रम, which is next on the list. In the Section on पाठक्रम, he should have proved that पाठक्रम is stronger than स्थानक्रम. But instead of this he establishes that out of the two varieties of पाठक्रम, मन्त्रपाठ is more powerful than ब्राह्मणपाठ. In dealing with स्थानक्रम he does not enter into the question of its relative strength at all. As a matter of fact he should have shown that स्थानक्रम is more powerful than मुख्यक्रम or weaker than पाठक्रम. In the case of मुख्यक्रम Bhāskara rightly points out that it is stronger than प्रवृत्तिक्रम. But before doing this he shows that मुख्यक्रम is weaker than पाठक्रम. If the weakness of मुख्यक्रम was at all to be shown, it should have been shown to be weaker than स्थानक्रम, which is just above it in the list. In the case of प्रवृत्तिक्रम Bhāskara just remarks that it is the weakest of all.

It would not be just to hold Bhāskara responsible for this unsystematic and unmethodical treatment. For, in all this he has faithfully followed his master Āpadeva !

Section 48

This Section treats of अधिकारविधि, the last of the four divisions of विधि. Vide Section 12 above. अधिकारविधि is defined as the injunction which intimates the ownership of the fruit to be produced by the action and the ownership of the fruit means being the enjoyer of that fruit. Therefore, a sentence which tells us who is going to be the enjoyer of the fruit of the action laid down therein becomes an अधिकारविधि.

'यजेत स्वर्गकामः' is an instance of an अधिकारविधि. This sentence lays down a sacrifice with a view to the attainment of heaven. It also intimates that the enjoyer of the fruit of the sacrifice viz. heaven is the one who is desirous of it and who is referred to by the word स्वर्गकामः. Therefore, this sentence is an अधिकारविधि.

A practical way of determining which sentence is an अधिकारविधि is to see if there is in that sentence a word ending in कामः, which qualifies the performer of the sacrifice. Thus all those sentences, wherein words like स्वर्गकामः, पशुकामः, भूतिकामः and ब्रह्मवर्चसकामः occur, are cases of अधिकारविधि. For, these adjectives ending in कामः show which people are hankering after the fruit and which consequently are going to be the enjoyers thereof. Such sentences may sometimes be some other kind of विधि in addition. But they are अधिकारविधिs in the first instance. Thus 'उद्भिदा यजेत पशुकामः' is an उत्पत्तिविधि in addition to being an अधिकारविधि. Vide p. 10 above.

It will thus be seen that the sentence 'अग्निहोत्रं जुहुयात् स्वर्गकामः', which our author gives as an example of प्रधानविधि or उत्पत्तिविधि (Vide Section 11, pp. 10 and 104), is really not a प्रधानविधि or उत्पत्तिविधि, but an अधिकारविधि. Our author borrows this incorrect illustration from Āpadeva. On it the सारविवेचिनी remarks 'यद्यपि **नेदमुत्पत्तिवाक्यमग्निहोत्रहोमस्य**, तथापि फलाविधेयत्वस्य चतुर्थे साधयिष्यमाणत्वात् **अधिकारवाक्येऽपि** फलोद्देशेन कर्मण एव विधानात् स्पष्टतया फलवत्त्वज्ञापनार्थमिदमुक्तम्।'

Though it is true that all those sentences, in which adjectives ending in कामः occur, are अधिकारविधिs, it is not necessary that all अधिकारविधिs should have such adjectives. For, the idea of being the enjoyer of the fruit of the action, which is the main thing in an अधिकारविधि, can be brought out in other ways also. For example:

The sentence 'यस्य आहिताग्नेः अग्निः गृहान् दहेत् सः अग्नये क्षामवते अष्टाकपालं निर्वपेत्' lays down a sacrifice in honour of Kṣāmavat Fire, called क्षामवती इष्टिः, in the interest of that maintainer of fire (आहिताग्निः), whose house may have been burnt by fire. The idea underlying this injunction is that some sin must have been committed by the sacrificer, which has resulted in his house being burnt by fire. The destruction of that sin (पापक्षयः) is to be achieved. It is effected by means of the क्षामवती इष्टिः (कर्मजन्य). The destruction of the sin then is the fruit of the sacrifice in honour of Kṣāmavat Fire. The ownership of this fruit belongs to him, whose house has been burn (निमित्तवतः गृहदाहरूपं निमित्तं विद्यते अस्य तस्य). Thus, as this sentence tells us that the ownership of the fruit viz. पापक्षय, of the action or rite viz. क्षामवती इष्टि, belongs to him whose house is burnt, it is an अधिकारविधि. In this sentence an adjective ending in कामः does not occur. But the idea that a certain person is hankering after the fruit and will be the enjoyer thereof is brought out by describing the occasion (निमित्तम्) viz. the burning of the house, which necessitates this sacrifice. Therefore, it is an अधिकारविधि.

आहिताग्नेः—आहिताः अग्नयः येन सः तस्य one who keeps or maintains fires, which have been kindled according to the आधान or अग्न्याधान rite. आहिताग्नि by the way is a well known word in Sanskrit grammar. It stands at the head of a group of Bahuvrīhi compounds, wherein the order of the words can optionally be reversed. Thus, आहिताः अग्नयः येन सः may be either आहिताग्निः or अग्न्याहितः.

गृहान्—The word गृह is usually neuter, but when used in the masculine it always takes the plural. गृहान्, therefore, does not mean 'houses' but 'a house'. Note 'गृहाः पुंसि च भूम्न्येव' अमरः. Compare 'इमे नो गृहाः' मुद्राराक्षस i.

क्षामवते—Sāyaṇa paraphrases this word by क्षुधायुक्ताय (hungry or devouring). क्षाम is a past passive participle from क्षै क्षायति to become emaciated or lean. क्षामं क्षैण्यं क्षयः इत्यर्थः । नपुंसके भावे क्तः । तदस्ति अस्य तस्मै । One who is emaciated or reduced for want of food is usually hungry. Thus क्षामवते = क्षुधायुक्ताय. Other explanations can also be offered. Thus, क्षामं क्षयः गृहदाहरूपः तद्वते येन गृहदाहरूपः क्षयः आहिताग्नेः कृतः तस्मै who has inflicted destruction on the sacrificer by burning his house. A third explanation is as follows : क्षमते क्षाम्यति वा असौ क्षमः, क्षम एव क्षामः । क्षाम एव क्षामत्वं क्षमाशीलता इत्यर्थः । भावप्रधानो निर्देशः । तद्वते । Thus क्षामवते means merciful or forgiving.

अष्टाकपालम् = अष्टसु कपालेषु मृत्तिकानिर्मितेषु द्व्यङ्गुलोच्छ्रितेषु पात्रविशेषेषु संस्कृतं पुरोडाशम् a cake prepared in eight potsherds.

कर्मजन्यपापक्षयरूपफलस्वाम्यम् = कर्मणा क्षामवत्या इष्ट्या जन्यः उत्पाद्यः यः पापक्षय आहिताग्निकृतदुरितनाशः तद्रूपं यत् फलं तस्य स्वाम्यं भोक्तृत्वम्.

A third example of अधिकारविधि is supplied by ' अहरहः सन्ध्यामुपासीत.' Performance of the Saṁdhyā-adoration is an obligatory duty for all twice-borns. Its performance brings in no religious merit (पुण्यम्). But its omission entails sin, which is technically known as प्रत्यवाय. Avoidance of this sin is the fruit of the rite of सन्ध्योपासन that is enjoined by ' अहरहः सन्ध्यामुपासीत. ' This fruit belongs to him who is qualified to perform the Saṁdhyā. Such a person is referred to by the expression शुचिविहितकालजीविनः, which means one who is pure i. e. one who is not contaminated by any impurity (अशौचम्) such as arises from birth or death in the family and who performs the rites that are enjoined at stated periods. Thus, the sentence ' अहरहः सन्ध्यामुपासीत ' intimates that the ownership of the fruit of the rite of सन्ध्योपासन, enjoined by it, belongs to him who is pure and pious. Therefore, this sentence is an अधिकारविधि.

It should be noted that in the sentence ' अहरहः सन्ध्यामुपासीत ' no mention in any manner whatsoever is made of him to whom the fruit viz. avoidance of sin belongs. The form in which this sentence is usually quoted is ' अहरहः स्नात्वा सन्ध्यामुपासीत '. Here स्नान or bath, referred to in स्नात्वा, may be regarded as an उपलक्षण and may thus point to a pure and pious man, as owner of the fruit viz. प्रत्यवायपरिहार. As the sentence stands in the text we must suppose that शुचिविहितकालजीवित्वम् is an implied qualification of the performer in the case of all obligatory duties. Or we may somehow regard ' अहरहः ' as forming a sort of adjectival expression for the performer and suggesting the idea of शुचिविहितकालजीविन्.

It will thus be seen that though no adjective, ending in ' कामः ' occurs in the sentence ' अहरहः सन्ध्यामुपासीत,' it intimates in an implied manner that the fruit of सन्ध्योपासन belongs to a शुचिविहितकालजीविन्. Therefore, this sentence is an अधिकारविधि.

शुचिविहितकालजीविनः—This is a clumsy expression. It means शुचिः जननमरणाद्यशौचहीनः, विहितानि कर्माणि तेषु तेषु उचितेषु कालेषु कुर्वन् जीवितुं शीलमस्य one who is pure and who is habituated to perform at the proper time all the rites enjoined. The adjective has reference to the prohibition of the performance of religious rites during the अशौच period.

प्रत्यवायः means sin arising from failure to perform an obligatory duty. It should be distinguished from पापम् which is sin emanating from the performance of a forbidden act. प्रत्यवाय is a sin of omission, while पाप is a sin of commission.

अधिकारविधि is otherwise known as फलविधि, because it intimates the connection of the fruit with the rite to be performed. Read ' उत्पन्नस्य

कर्मणः फलाकाङ्क्षायां फलसंबन्धबोधको विधि **फलविधिः**। यथा 'अग्निहोत्रं जुहुयात् स्वर्गकामः' इति। अत्र 'यः स्वर्गं कामयते स तत्साधनत्वेन अग्निहोत्रनामकं होमं भावयेत् कुर्यात्' इति अग्निहोत्रवाक्योत्पन्नस्य कर्मणः फलसंबन्धो बोध्यते इति **फलवाक्यमिदम्**।' मीमांसापरिभाषा

The three instances of अधिकारविधि given in the text tell us incidentally that actions or rites are of three kinds viz. नित्य, नैमित्तिक and काम्य. नित्य or obligatory actions are those which every pious man must perform e. g. अग्निहोत्र which is enjoined as a life-long duty on all house-holders, सन्ध्यावन्दन etc. Performance of obligatory actions brings no merit, but failure to perform them involves one in sin. नैमित्तिक or occasional rites are those which have to be performed, when their proper occasion arises. Certain rites are enjoined on such occasions as birth, marriage or death. All these are नैमित्तिक कर्मs. A sacrifice called पथिकृदिष्टि is enjoined for a man, who has failed to perform the दर्शपूर्णमास sacrifice in time. क्षामवती इष्टि, we know, is to be performed by one whose house is burnt by fire. Both these are instances of नैमित्तिक कर्मs. Performance of these occasional rites means also no positive gain. But omission to perform them brings in प्रत्यवाय. काम्य or optional rites are those which are performed with a desire for a specific object e. g. दर्शपूर्णमास or ज्योतिष्टोम for heaven and पुत्रेष्टि for a son. Optional rites are further divided into three kinds according as the fruit to be gained belongs either to this world or the next or to both.

Read the following is this connection : 'अर्थकर्म त्रिविधम् नित्यनैमित्तिककाम्यभेदात्। तत्र 'यावज्जीवमग्निहोत्रं जुहोति' 'सायं जुहोति' 'प्रातर्जुहोति' इति जीवता पुरुषेण सायंप्रातःकालयोर्नियमेन कर्तव्यतया अवगतमग्निहोत्रादिकं **नित्यम्**। 'अग्नये पथिकृते पुरोडाशमष्टाकपालं निर्वपेत्' इति दर्शपूर्णमासातिपत्तिनिमित्तकपथिकृदिष्ट्यादिकं **नैमित्तिकम्। नित्यनैमित्तिकयोरकरणे प्रत्यवाय एव**। कृते फलं नास्तीति केचित्। अन्ये तु दुरितनिवृत्तिः फलमस्ति 'नित्यनैमित्तिकैरेव कुर्वाणो दुरितक्षयम्' इत्यादिवाक्यैः प्रत्यवायनिवृत्तेः फलत्वेन श्रूयमाणत्वात्। न चैवं तयोरपि काम्यत्वापत्तिः फलवत्त्वादिति वाच्यम्। फलकामनापूर्वकानुष्ठानाभावात्। तत्तद्विधिवाक्ये फलकाममुद्दिश्य तदर्थसाधनत्वेन विधानाभावाच्च काम्यत्वानुपपत्तिः। **काम्यमपि कर्म त्रिविधम्**। केवलमैहिकफलकम्, आमुष्मिकफलकम्, ऐहिकामुष्मिकफलकं चेति। तत्र आद्यं यथा कारीर्यादि। तत्तत्समयवर्तिशुष्यत्सस्यसंजीवनहेतुवृष्टिकामिना क्रियते। न कालान्तरभाविवृष्टिकामेन जन्मान्तरीयवृष्टिकामेन वा। केवलामुष्मिकफलकं यथा स्वर्गाद्यर्थं दर्शपूर्णमासादिकम्। स्वर्गस्य इहलोकभोग्यत्वाभावात्। ऐहिकामुष्मिकसाधारणफलकं यथा 'वायव्यं श्वेतमालभेत भूतिकामः' इत्यादि भूत्यादिफलकम्।' मीमांसापरिभाषा

तच्च फलस्वाम्यं...श्रवणात्—This paragraph gives further explanation of 'the ownership of the fruit,' which forms the central idea of an अधिकारविधि. The ownership of the fruit then naturally belongs to him who possesses the necessary qualification (अधिकारः). And qualification is represented by whatever forms a distinguishing attribute (विशेषणम्) of the performer in injunctory sentences.

Here the word विशेषण is to be understood in a broad sense. It does not mean a grammatical adjective merely. It certainly includes that, but denotes something more. Thus, in all optional rites the desire for fruit forms the qualification. This desire is usually conveyed by a grammatical adjective ending in कामः. In occasional rites the qualification consists in the definite knowledge that the occasion has arisen. This knowledge does not necessarily arise from a grammatical adjective. It may spring from an adjectival clause, which consequently forms the विशेषण. In the case of obligatory rites the qualification is represented by the habit of leading a pure and pious life. This is quite natural. For, obligatory rites can have force only for those, who are pure and pious. The qualification in the case of obligatory rites is usually presumed. Generally, it does not find expression by means of an adjective or an adjectival clause in the injunctive sentences themselves. Thus, we find that in 'अहरहः सन्ध्यामुपासीत' and 'यावज्जीवमग्निहोत्रं जुहोति', which lay down obligatory rites, शुचिविहितकालजीवित्व, which forms the qualification of the performer, is not expressed in so many words. It has, therefore, to be presumed.

अत एव०—It was remarked above that in optional rites qualification is represented by the desire for fruit, which is usually expressed by a grammatical adjective ending in कामः. Bhāskara now wants to tell us that the desire for fruit does not in some cases exhaust the qualification. Sometimes other words in injunctive sentences, which qualify the performer, also represent the qualification. Thus, in the sentence 'राजा राजसूयेन स्वाराज्यकामो यजेत', फलकामना or the desire for fruit is represented by स्वाराज्यकामः one who is desirous of rulership of heaven (स्वर् = स्वर्गः + राज्यम् = राज्ञः कर्म. स्वाराज्यम् = स्वर्गाधिपतित्वम्). This would mean whoever is desirous of rulership of heaven is qualified to perform the Rājasūya sacrifice. But that is not correct. The word राजा is also a qualification of the performer and राजा means one who being a Kṣatriya is a king. Thus, a Brāhmaṇa king, who may be desirous of rulership of heaven, is not qualified for the performance of the Rājasūya, because the word राजन् primarily signifies the Kṣatriya caste (राजशब्दो जातिपरः).

अत एव = विधिवाक्येषु पुरुषविशेषणत्वेन श्रूयमाणस्य अधिकारत्वादेव because qualification consists in whatever occurs in injunctive sentences as attributes of the performer.

राजसूयः (राजा सोमो सूयते अत्र असौ)—This sacrifice is so called, because King Soma is pressed therein. The Rājasūya consists of many sacrifices, but as the Soma sacrifice is the most prominent of them all, it is called राजसूय, according to 'प्राधान्येन व्यपदेशा भवन्ति' Vide p. 145 above.

स्वाराज्यमात्रकामस्य is a clumsy expression for स्वाराज्यकाममात्रस्य.

In connection with the question of the qualifications for the Rājasūya read 'अत्र हि राजशब्देन क्षत्रिय एवोच्यते, न तु राज्यसंबन्धमात्रेण तदन्योऽपि । तेन **क्षत्रियस्यैव राजसूयेऽधिकारः**, न तु तदन्यस्य ब्राह्मणादेः ।' रामेश्वर

'**राजशब्द क्षत्रियजातौ रूढः**, न तु राज्ययोगस्तस्य प्रवृत्तिनिमित्तम् । प्रत्युत राज्यशब्दस्य राजयोगः प्रवृत्तिनिमित्तम्, 'राज्ञः कर्म' इति विगृह्य राजप्रातिपदिकस्योपरि प्रत्ययविशेषविधानात् । ब्राह्मणवैश्ययोः प्रजापालनेन राज्यशब्द उपचरितः ।' जैमिनीयन्यायमालाविस्तर p. 94

' राजा प्रभौ च नृपतौ **क्षत्रिये** रजनीपतौ । यक्षे शक्रे च पुंसि स्यात्' मेदिनी

क्वचित्तु०—So far we have seen three kinds of qualifications viz. फलकामना, निमित्तनिश्चय and शुचिविहितकालजीवित्व with reference to काम्य, नैमित्तिक and नित्यकर्मs respectively. These qualifications were actually mentioned (श्रुत) in the sentences that enjoined their respective rites. Thus, फलकामना was mentioned in 'स्वर्गकामः,' निमित्तनिश्चय in 'यस्या...दहेत्' and शुचिविहितकालजीवित्व in 'अहरहः.'

Now, Bhāskara wants to tell us that sometimes an attribute, though not actually occurring, or directly stated (अश्रुतमपि), in injunctive sentences, has to be understood as a qualification of the performer. Three such qualifications are mentioned in this paragraph viz. अध्ययनविधिसिद्धा विद्या, आधानसिद्धा अग्निमत्ता and सामर्थ्य. These three then are examples of अश्रुत पुरुषविशेषणs, which become qualifications inspite of their not having been specifically mentioned in injunctive sentences.

अध्ययनविधिसिद्धा विद्या—This means knowledge of the sense of the Vedic texts obtained by following the injunction to study. Before a man becomes qualified to perform Vedic sacrifices, it is necessary that he should study the Veda in the prescribed manner and understand the meaning of the sacred texts. For, sacrificial injunctions (क्रतुविधि.) presuppose such knowledge on the part of the performer and thus they become applicable only to him who possesses such knowledge. And this is quite natural. For, unless one has studied and understood the Veda, one would not be able to grasp the meaning of even the sacrificial injunctions.

अध्ययनविधिसिद्धा—The propriety of this expression is that the knowledge of the sacred texts, which qualifies a man for the performance of Vedic sacrifices, must have been derived by following the injunction about study. This injunction is found in such sentences as ‘ स्वाध्यायोऽध्येतव्यः ’ and ‘ अष्टवर्षं ब्राह्मणमुपनयीत तमध्यापयेत् ’. Vedic study is preceded by उपनयन, which is laid down by such sentences as ‘ अष्टवर्षं ब्राह्मणमुपनयीत । एकादशवर्षं राजन्यम् । द्वादशवर्षं वैश्यम् ’ and ‘ वसन्ते ब्राह्मणमुपनयीत । ग्रीष्मे राजन्यम् । शरदि वैश्यम् ।’ Thus as उपनयन and वेदाध्ययन are restricted to only the first three classes viz. ब्राह्मण, क्षत्रिय and वैश्य, they alone are qualified for Vedic sacrifices. Śūdras are not qualified for them.

क्रतुविधीनाम् goes both with अर्थज्ञानापेक्षणीयत्वेन and प्रवृत्तेः.

एवमग्निसाध्य…आग्निमत्ता—Another qualification, not specified (अश्रुत) in injunctive sentences, is represented by possession of fires (अग्निमत्ता). This applies specially to those rites that are to be performed with fire (अग्निसाध्य). For, such rites presuppose possession of fires by the performer. And this is also natural. For, how can अग्निसाध्य rites be carried out without the performer possessing the necessary fires? Consequently, all injunctions regarding rites to be performed with fires become applicable (प्रवृत्तिः) to him only who possesses fires obtained according to the rite of establishment (आधानम्).

आधानसिद्ध०—The propriety of this adjective is the same as that of अध्ययनसिद्ध above. The ceremony of establishing fires is laid down by ‘ वसन्ते ब्राह्मणोऽग्नीनादधीत । ग्रीष्मे राजन्यः । शरदि वैश्यः । ’ This ceremony is also restricted to the first three classes (त्रैवर्णिकः). Consequently, only the first three varṇas, not the Śūdras, are qualified for the performance of Vedic sacrifices.

एवं सामर्थ्यमपि—Capacity or capability or the physical power to do the things enjoined (सामर्थ्यम्) is the third unmentioned qualification to be dealt with in this paragraph. This qualification is not based on any Vedic injunction as the two previous ones are, but it arises from sound common sense. That common sense consists in the fact that all injunctions become applicable only to those who are capable of following them (समर्थं प्रत्येव प्रवृत्तेः). Thus, an injunction to jump has application only in the case of those who can jump. Similarly, Vedic injunctions, which require, on the part of the performer, the use of his eyes, tongue and ears, are not applicable to the blind, the dumb and the deaf.

This rule, based on common sense, is embodied in the maxim ‘ आख्यातानामर्थं ब्रुवतां शक्तिः सहकारिणी. ’ This maxim is found in Śabara's bhāṣya on Jaimini-sūtra I. iv. 30 and in the Jaiminīya-nyāya-mālā-vistara of Mādhava on the same sūtra. Śabara's reading is ‘ आख्यातशब्दानाम् ’ instead of ‘ आख्यातानाम् ’, which is found in Mādhava.

The general meaning of the maxim is that when verbs (आख्यातम् lay down certain things, it is presumed that they are laid down for those who are able to perform them. Thus, this ability (शक्तिः) to perform the things enjoined is the helpmate (सहकारिणी) of verbs in all injunctions. Consequently, ability is regarded as an unmentioned qualification of the performer in the case of all rites.

The maxim 'आख्यातानां...सहकारिणी' is deduced from the discussion which centres round the sentences 'स्रुवेण अवद्यति,' 'स्वधितिना अवद्यति,' 'हस्तेन अवद्यति.' Here it is pointed out that these three instruments of अवदान (cutting or dividing) are to be used in those cases, where they have power to cut or divide. Thus, स्रुव or a ladle is used for portioning a liquid like ghee, स्वधिति or an axe for cutting a solid substance like flesh and हस्त or a hand for breaking such things as a cake. The verb अवद्यति lays down cutting. But ability to cut is presumed in the case of all the three instruments with which the cutting is to be effected. That is why the three instruments are restricted to three different kinds of substances.

In ordinary life also we often presume ability as a helpmate for verbs, which express certain things. Thus, in 'कटे भुङ्क्ते' and 'कांस्यपात्र्यां भुङ्क्ते' कटे and कांस्यपात्र्याम्, according to the above maxim, mean respectively 'कटे आसीनः' and 'कांस्यपात्र्यामोदनं निधाय.' Similarly, in 'अञ्जलिना नमस्करोति' अञ्जलि means the two hands folded together, such as we have in saluting, without any hollow between them. But in 'अञ्जलिना पिबति' अंञ्जलि signifies the two hands folded together so as to form a cavity or hollow between them.

Read "स्रुवेण अवद्यति' 'स्वधितिना अवद्यति' 'हस्तेन अवद्यति' इति श्रूयते। तत्र अवदेयेषु आज्यमांसपुरोडाशेषु हविःषु अमी स्रुवाद्या अवदानहेतवः संकीर्णाः। कुतः। व्यवस्थापकस्य शब्दस्य अभावात् इति चेत्।

मैवम्। शक्तेर्व्यवस्थापकत्वात्। 'आख्यातानामर्थं ब्रुवतां शक्तिः सहकारिणी' इति न्यायात्। 'कटे भुङ्क्ते' 'कांस्यपात्र्यां भुङ्क्ते' इत्यत्र लौकिकास्तत्तद्वस्तुशक्त्यनुसारेण व्यवस्थां कल्पयन्ति–'कटे आसीनः' 'कांस्यपात्र्यामोदनं निधाय' इति। वेदेऽपि 'अञ्जलिना सक्तून् प्रदाय जुहुयात्' इत्यत्र यद्यपि द्विहस्तसंयोगोऽञ्जलिः, तथापि गुरुदेवतादिप्रसादनार्थाञ्जलिवत् निच्छिद्रसंयोगो न भवति। तादृशेऽञ्जलौ सक्तूनामवकाशाभावात्। अतः सामर्थ्यात् संयुक्तप्रसृतिद्वयात्मको मध्यगतावकाशोपेतोऽञ्जलिर्गृहीतः। एवमत्रापि द्रवद्रव्यस्य आज्यस्य स्रुवो योग्यः, छेदनीयमांसस्य शस्त्रविशेषः स्वधितिः, संहतस्य पुरोडाशस्य हस्तः, इत्यनेन प्रकारेण स्रुवाद्या व्यवस्थिताः।' जैमिनीयन्यायमालाविस्तर p. 60

The different kinds of qualifications, which are dealt with in this Section on अधिकारविधि, may be set forth by means of the following diagram :

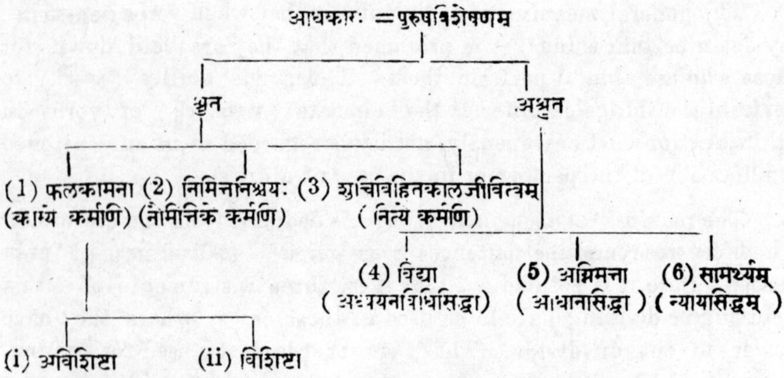

e. g. स्वर्गकामो यजेत. e. g. राजा (= क्षत्रियत्वे सति) स्वाराज्यकामो यजेत.

Qualifications of the performer of Vedic sacrifices form an interesting topic of discussion in the Mimāmsā Śāstra. Thus, we have seen that Śūdras are not qualified for sacrifice, because they are not allowed to study the Vedas and maintain the sacred fires. See जै. सू. VI. i. 25–38. **But there are two exceptions to this rule. The chief of the mountaineers or hunters (**निषादस्थपतिः**) is allowed to perform the** रौद्रयाग **in accordance with '**एतया निषादस्थपतिं याजयेत्, **which occurs in connection with '**वास्तुमयं रौद्रं चरुं निर्वपेत्. **' Vide** जै. सू. **VI. i. 51–52. Similarly, a carpenter (**रथकारः**), who is not included among the first three varṇas or classes, is allowed to maintain the holy fires, in accordance with '**वर्षासु रथकारः [अग्नीन्] आदधीत. **' Note** जै. सू. VI. i. 44–50.

The question as to whether women are qualified to perform sacrifices is discussed in जै. सू. VI. i. 6–21 **and the conclusion arrived at is that they are qualified to perform sacrifices, but only in cooperation with their husbands. So in Mīmāmsā the old rule of Manu** ' न स्त्री स्वातन्त्र्यमर्हति ' **is applicable in the sense that women cannot undertake sacrifices independently.**

Read in this connection ' ननु एवं स्त्रिया अधिकारो न स्यात् । तस्या अध्ययनप्रतिषेधेन तद्विधिसिद्धज्ञानाभावात् । न च ' नास्त्येव ' इति वाच्यम् । ' यजेत स्वर्गकामः ' इत्यादौ स्वर्गकामपदस्य उद्देश्यसमर्पकत्वेन पुंस्त्वस्य उद्देश्यविशेषणत्वात् ग्रहैकत्ववत् अविवक्षितत्वेन स्त्रिया अधिकारस्य साधितत्वात्–इति चेत् । सत्यम् । **अधिकारः साधितः न तु स्वातन्त्र्येण, ' न स्त्री स्वातन्त्र्यमर्हति ' इत्यादिना तस्य निषिद्धत्वात्,** स्वातन्त्र्येण कर्तृत्वे प्रयोगद्वयस्यापि वैगुण्यापत्तेश्च । यजमानप्रयोगे पत्नीकर्तृकाज्यावेक्षणादिलोपात्, पत्नीप्रयोगे च यजमानकर्तृकाज्यावेक्षणादिलोपात् । **अतो दम्पत्योः सहाधिकारः** । सहाधिकारत्वेन यजमानविद्ययैव पत्न्या अपि कार्यसिद्धेः न ज्ञानं विना तस्या अधिकारानुपपत्तिः । ' मीमांसान्यायप्रकाश

One Adhikaraṇa (जै. सू. VI. i. 4-5), discusses the question of **those who are unfit and hence unqualified for performing sacrifices. From this we understand that the lower animals (तिर्यक्) and physically unfit persons like the blind, the lame, the deaf and dumb are not qualified for the performance of sacrifices.**

Read ' [अन्धादीनां] केषुचिदङ्गेषु शक्तिर्नास्ति । तथा हि । अन्धो न आज्यमवेक्षितुं क्षमः । पङ्गुर्विष्णुक्रमेषु अशक्तः । बधिरो नाध्वर्युप्रोक्तं शृणोति । ततः ' क्लृप्तीर्वाचयति ' इति विहितस्यानुष्ठानं न सिध्येत् । मूकोऽनुमन्त्रणादावशक्तः । तिर्यञ्चो बहुष्वशक्ताः ।......**तस्मादशक्तस्य नास्त्यधिकारः ।**'

तदेवं निरूपितो विधिः—In Section 10 above (p. 7) we saw that the **Veda is divided into five kinds.** Of **these** विधि **or injunction is the first and the treatment of injunction is brought to a close with Section 48.**

Commentators of the Mīmāṁsānyāyaprakāśa seem to believe that the book is divided in two Parts and that the First Part comes to an end with the treatment of vidhi. Rāmeśvara, the commentator of the Arthasaṁgraha, has added a stanza at the end of his commentary on vidhi, which seems to indicate that he believed that the Arthasaṁgraha also consisted of two Parts, the First Part concluding with the treatment of vidhi. But as far as the texts of both the Mīmāṁsānyāyaprakāśa and the Arthasaṁgraha are concerned, there is not the slightest evidence that their authors intended their works to be divided into two such Parts.

Commentators' idea that the **First Part** of these books **ends with the treatment of vidhi may perhaps have arisen from the following considerations : Vidhi is the most important of the five divisions of the Veda. Most of the difficult topics of the Mīmāṁsā have been dealt with in the Introductory Chapter and the Chapter on vidhi. As far as mere mass is concerned, this portion covers more than half the book.** The conclusion of the treatment of vidhi was **perhaps regarded as a good breathing place for both the preceptor and the pupil before they entered upon the study of the remaining portion of the book. These considerations probably induced preceptors and commentators to regard this portion of the book as the Pūrvārdha and the remaining portion the Uttarārdha.**

But we have noted before that in the text of both these books there is no evidence to regard them as divided into two such Parts. That is why we have ignored this division of the commentators and divided our text into six natural chapters.

Section 49

This and the following four Sections deal with Mantra, which is the second of the five divisions of the Veda. Vide Section 10 above.

Mīmāṁsā works do not give a satisfactory definition of Mantra. In fact it is not very easy to formulate a definition which would cover all literature that is included under the term Mantra. A few indications of Mantra from the Mīmāṁsist point of view can be found in the जैमिनीयन्यायमालाविस्तर under जै. सू. II. i. 32 'तच्चोदकेषु मन्त्राख्या', which contains Jaimini's definition of Mantra.

Mantra includes what are known as the Saṁhitās of the three Vedas, Ṛc, Sāman and Yajus. The Ṛgveda, which is metrical in form, is to be recited. The Sāmaveda, also in metre, is to be sung. The Yajurveda, generally in prose, is to be muttered in a low tone, except the formulas called Nigadas, which are uttered aloud ('उपांशु यजुषा, उच्चैर्निगदेन'). See जै. सू. II. i. 36–37.

Veda is defined as 'मन्त्रब्राह्मणात्मकः शब्दराशिः.' Vide p. 97 above. Out of these two broad divisions of the Veda Mantra is, from the strict Mīmāṁsist point of view, of really no use. For, Mīmāṁsā primarily deals with विधि or चोदना or injunction and the Mantra portion of the Veda contains no injunctions. It is the Brāhmaṇas, with their divisions of विधि, नामधेय, निषेध and अर्थवाद, that are of importance to the Mīmāṁsā.

But the Mīmāṁsakas dared not openly declare the uselessness of Mantra. They had, therefore, to find out some purpose for it. Consequently, they made Mantra subservient to sacrifice and said that the purpose of Mantra was to remind (स्मारक) the performer of matters connected with sacrificial performance (प्रयोगसमवेत). Thus, 'अग्निमीळे पुरोहितम्' and 'इन्द्रस्य नु वीर्याणि प्रवोचम्' are of use to the sacrifice, because they serve to remind the sacrificer of the deities Agni and Indra, to whom oblations are to be offered. Similarly, the Mantra 'इमामगृभ्णन् रशनामृतस्य,' which makes reference to the grasping of 'the rein of truth,' was made subservient to the grasping of the rein of the horse by the Mīmāṁsakas, who said that it serves to remind us of the grasping of the rein of the horse.

Mantras then have a purpose (अर्थवत्त्वम्) in the Mīmāṁsist scheme of things, because they serve to call to our mind matters connected with sacrificial performance (तादृशार्थ=प्रयोगसमवेतार्थ).

This purpose of Mantras viz. प्रयोगसमवेतार्थस्मारकत्वम् presupposes that we understand the meaning thereof. But one school of thinkers, called Yājñikas or ritualists, of whom the celebrated Kautsa referred to by Yāska in his Nirukta i. 15, was a representative, holds that we need not trouble ourselves with understanding the meaning of the Mantras. What, then, is the purpose, according to this school, of reciting the Mantras in sacrifices? The ritualists hold that the recitation of the Mantras (तदुच्चारणं तेषां मन्त्राणामुच्चारणम्) serves the purpose of creating some unseen transcendental result (अदृष्टार्थम्). The Mīmāṁsakas refute this view by pointing out that when a seen fruit is possible, it is unjust or unreasonable (अन्याय्य) to imagine (कल्पना) that an unseen one exists. Compare 'लभ्यमाने फले दृष्टे नादृष्टफलकल्पना' quoted above on p. 75.

The Mīmāṁsist position is now attacked from another side. If the seen fruit अर्थस्मारण is necessary, it is possible to have this अर्थस्मारण or recollection of sacrificial matters in another way also (प्रकारान्तरेणापि). For instance, a sacrificer can employ an additional priest to remind him that oblations have to be offered to Agni and Indra, or that the rein of the horse has to be grasped. Similarly, even Brāhmaṇa sentences can produce this अर्थस्मारण. For example, it is held that the Mantras 'इमामगृभ्णन् रशनामृतस्य' and 'उरुप्रथा उरु प्रथस्व' respectively serve to remind the priests of the rite of grasping the rein of the horse and of the rite of spreading the oblation wide. But, it is pointed out that this reminding can as well be effected by the Brāhmaṇa sentences 'इमामगृभ्णन् रशनामृतस्येति अश्वाभिधानीमादत्ते' and 'उरुप्रथा उरु प्रथस्वेति पुरोडाशं प्रथयति' respectively. Thus, it is argued that as it is possible to produce the recollection of sacrificial matters in other ways also, the recitation of Mantras (मन्त्राम्नानं मन्त्राणाम् आम्नानं पाठः इत्यर्थः) in sacrifices is useless.

Thus, the position is this: Mantras, according to the Mīmāṁsakas, serve the purpose of reminding us of sacrificial matters and that is why they are recited in sacrifices. But, this reminding can be effected by other ways also. So, the question here is when a thing can be done in more ways than one, why should we be restricted to only one of these?

The answer to this is that the rule 'मन्त्रैरेव स्मर्तव्यम्' restricts us to Mantras alone in the matter of the recollection of sacrificial matters. Such a rule is technically known as नियमविधि or an injunction of restriction. On account of this rule we ignore other ways of reminding and resort to Mantras only for putting us in mind of sacrificial matters.

मन्त्राम्नानम्—This expression has been explained above as मन्त्राणाम् आम्नानं पाठः recitation of Mantras in sacrifices. The expression may also mean मन्त्राणाम् आम्नानं विधानम् इत्यर्थः the laying down or prescription of Mantras as reminders of sacrificial matters.

'मन्त्रैरेव स्मर्तव्यम्'—It looks as if this is some Vedic quotation containing an injunction of restriction. In the जैमिनिर्नीयन्यायमालाविस्तर this sentence occurs in the form 'मन्त्रेणैवानुस्मरणीयम्.' The quotation cannot be traced.

As regards the purpose of the recitation of Mantras read ''उरु प्रथस्व' इत्ययं कश्चिन्मन्त्रः। तस्यायमर्थः—'भोः पुरोडाश, त्वमुरु विपुलता यथा भवति तथा प्रथस्व' इति। एवमादयो मन्त्रा यागप्रयोगेषु उच्चार्यमाणा अदृष्टमेव जनयन्ति। न तु अर्थप्रकाशनाय तदुच्चारणम्। पुरोडाशप्रथनलक्षणस्य अर्थस्य ब्राह्मणवाक्येनापि भासनात्। 'उरु प्रथस्वेति पुरोडाशं प्रथयति' इति हि ब्राह्मणवाक्यम्। इति चेत्।

नैतद्युक्तम्। अर्थप्रत्यायनस्य दृष्टप्रयोजनस्य संभवे सति केवलादृष्टस्य कल्पयितुमशक्यत्वात् तस्माद् दृष्टार्थानुस्मरणमेव यागप्रयोगे मन्त्रोच्चारणस्य प्रयोजनम्। ब्राह्मणवाक्येनापि अर्थानुस्मरणसंभवे 'मन्त्रेणैवानुस्मरणीयम्' इति यो नियमः, तस्य दृष्टासंभवाददृष्टं प्रयोजनमस्तु।' जैमिनिर्नीयन्यायमालाविस्तर p. 26

'तत्र वेदो द्विविधः। मन्त्ररूपो ब्राह्मणरूपश्च। तत्र **प्रयोगकालीनार्थस्मरणहेतुतया मन्त्राणामुपयोगः** ... ... मन्त्राणामपि अध्ययनविधिना कृत्स्नस्वाध्यायस्य सफलत्वावगमात् फलवदर्थज्ञानार्थत्वमेव, न तु अदृष्टार्थत्वम्। दृष्टे संभवति अदृष्टकल्पनायोगात्। प्रयोगकाले कर्मज्ञानं विना कर्मानुष्ठानायोगात् **कर्मौपयिकमर्थज्ञानं मन्त्रैः क्रियते**। न च उपदेष्टृवचनादिनापि अर्थस्मरणसंभवादनुष्ठानोपपत्तिरिति वाच्यम्। मन्त्रैरेव अर्थं स्मृत्वा अनुष्ठाने सति फलं संभवति, न अन्यथा, इति नियमाङ्गीकारात्। नियमेन अदृष्टस्य अङ्गीकारात्। तदभावे तज्जन्यादृष्टलोपे तन्मूलकं फलं न सिद्ध्यतीति कल्पनात्।' मीमांसापरिभाषा

In this connection read also शाबरभाष्य on मन्त्रलिङ्गाधिकरण, constituted by जै. सू. I. ii. 31-53.

Section 50

In the preceding section it is pointed out that the sentence 'मन्त्रैरेव स्मर्तव्यम्' contains a नियमविधि or an injunction of restriction, which lays down that the recollection of sacrificial matters must be effected by Mantras alone. This Section now proceeds to explain what is meant by नियमविधि.

This and the following Section really give us another division of विधि, according to which विधि is of three kinds viz. विधि or अपूर्वविधि, नियम or नियमविधि and परिसंख्या or परिसंख्याविधि. We now proceed to see the nature of these three varieties of injunction.

विधि (injunction) or अपूर्वविधि (new or original injunction) lays down a thing, which is absolutely or totally non-established (अत्यन्तमप्राप्तौ = विधेयस्य अत्यन्तम् अप्राप्तौ सत्याम्), i. e. a thing which is not established by any other means of proof (प्रमाणान्तरेण अप्राप्त). For example, the sentence 'यजेत स्वर्गकामः' lays down a sacrifice for the purpose of attaining heaven. Now, स्वर्गार्थकयाग is a matter, which is not known from any other source. 'यजेत स्वर्गकामः', which lays down such a matter, is, therefore, an example of विधि or अपूर्वविधि. Such injunction is called अपूर्वविधि, because it enjoins a matter which was not known before (अपूर्वस्य पूर्वमज्ञातस्य विधिः). A विधि or अपूर्वविधि thus enjoins a matter for the first time.

Another example of विधि or अपूर्वविधि is 'व्रीहीन् प्रोक्षति.' Here sprinkling of the rice-grains, which are to be used for the preparation of the sacrificial cake in the दर्शपूर्णमास sacrifice, is laid down. Such sprinkling is known from no other source. Therefore, 'व्रीहीन् प्रोक्षति' is a विधि or अपूर्वविधि.

It should be noted that the विधि or अपूर्वविधि, mentioned here, is the same as the विधि or प्रधानविधि or उत्पत्तिविधि, dealt with in Section 11 above. About that विधि it was said 'तादृशं च अर्थं **प्रमाणान्तरेण अप्राप्तं** विधत्ते ।'

नियमः (restriction) or नियमविधिः (injunction of restriction) is that injunction, which restricts us to a particular way of accomplishing a thing, when we are likely to resort to some other, in a case where the thing can be accomplished in more than one way. नियम works in the following circumstances: There is an action or matter, which can be accomplished in different ways or by different means or instruments (नानासाधनसाध्यक्रिया). We seem to favour one of these instruments for accomplishing it (एकसाधनप्राप्तौ). But that is really not the proper instrument to choose. Therefore, नियम steps in here and asks us to adopt another instrument, which we were not going to adopt before (अप्राप्तस्य अपरसाधनस्य प्रापकः).

An example of नियम is 'व्रीहीन् अवहन्ति'. Here the result to be accomplished is वैतुष्यम् or निस्तुषीकरणम् or the unhusking of the rice-grains. This unhusking can be effected in two ways viz. by separating the chaff from the grains by means of our nails (नखविदलनम्) and by pounding or thrashing the rice-grains (अवघातः). वैतुष्य is thus नानासाधनसाध्यक्रिया or नानोपायसाध्य. When, therefore, we think of effecting the unhusking by means of our nails (एकसाधनप्राप्तौ एकस्य साधनस्य नखविदलनात्मकस्य प्राप्तौ), the sentence 'व्रीहीन् अवहन्ति' steps in and asks us to accomplish the unhusking by means of pounding. It should be noted that

10

when we think of adopting नखविदलन for unhusking, नखविदलन is प्राप्त and other means such as अवघात are अप्राप्त. 'व्रीहीन् अवहन्ति', which enforces अवघात, is, therefore, अप्राप्तस्य अपरसाधनस्य अवघातात्मकस्य प्रापकः.

Another example of नियमविधि is 'समे देशे यजेत'. When a sacrifice is to be performed, it can be performed either on even or on uneven ground. The performance of the sacrifice is thus नानासाधनसाध्यक्रिया. When we think of performing it on uneven ground i.e. when one of the means viz. विषमप्रदेश becomes प्राप्त, the sentence 'समे देशे यजेत' steps in and lays down समदेश, which was अप्राप्त, as the साधन for the performance of the sacrifice. 'समे देशे यजेत' is, therefore, a नियमविधि.

यथाहुः—Supply कुमारिलभट्टाः तन्त्रवार्तिककाराः as the subject of आहुः. The couplet 'विधिरत्यन्तमप्राप्तौ...गीयते' is quoted from Kumārila's Tantravārtika on I. ii. 34 and contains good definitions of विधि, नियम and परिसंख्या.

'अत्यन्तमप्राप्तौ विधिः' is Kumārila's definition of विधि. It has been paraphrased by Bhāskara by 'प्रमाणान्तरेण अप्राप्तस्य प्रापको विधिः'. We have already seen the meaning of this.

'पाक्षिके सति नियमः' is Kumārila's definition of नियम. 'पाक्षिके सति' is equal to विधेयस्य अप्राप्तत्वे पाक्षिके सति. Bhāskara paraphrases this definition by 'पक्षे अप्राप्तस्य प्रापको विधिः नियमविधिः.' A नियमविधि lays down something, which is non-established in the alternative.

नियमस्य पक्षे अप्राप्तप्रापकत्वम्—How नियम establishes a matter which is non-established in the alternative is thus explained.

'व्रीहीन् अवहन्ति' is an example of नियम. We have seen that वैतुष्य can be effected either by नखविदलन or by अवघात. Thus, there are two alternative courses, which may be adopted for effecting वैतुष्य. When we adopt नखविदलन, अवघात is naturally अप्राप्त. Thus, नखविदलनप्राप्तिपक्षे अवघातस्य अप्राप्तत्वम्. Here 'व्रीहीन् अवहन्ति' takes effect and enforces अवघात.

If, however, we choose अवघात for accomplishing वैतुष्य, 'व्रीहीन् अवहन्ति' has no scope. It does not operate at all. For, in this case अवघात is already प्राप्त, since we are adopting it, and नियम enforces only that which is अप्राप्त. So in this alternative नियम remains उदासीन or indifferent.

It will thus be seen that नियम works when a wrong alternative, or an alternative other than the one which it wants to lay down, is chosen. When the proper alternative is chosen, नियम does not work, but remains indifferent.

Read in this connection 'अत्यन्ताप्राप्तप्रापणं विधिः । यथा 'अग्निहोत्रं जुहुयात्' 'अष्टकाः कर्तव्याः' इति । पक्षे प्राप्तस्य अप्राप्तपक्षान्तरप्रापणं नियमः । यथा 'समे देशे

यजेत'। 'दर्शपूर्णमासाभ्यां यजेत' इति यागः कर्तव्यतया विहितः। स च देशमन्तरेण कर्तुमशक्य इति अर्थाद् देशः प्राप्तः। स च द्विविधः समो विषमश्च। **यदा यजमानः समे यियक्षते तदा 'समे यजेत' इति वचनमुदास्ते**। स्वार्थस्य प्राप्तत्वात्। यदा तु विषमे यियक्षते तदा 'समे यजेत' इति स्वार्थं विधत्ते। स्वार्थस्य तदानीमप्राप्तत्वात्। विषमदेशे निवृत्तिस्तु आर्थिकी। चोदितदेशेनैव यागनिष्पत्तेः। अचोदितदेशोपादानेन यथाशास्त्रं यागो नानुष्ठितः स्यादिति।' मिताक्षरा on याज्ञवल्क्य i. 81.

On 'पक्षे अप्राप्तस्य' सारविवेचिनी remarks 'पक्षे अप्राप्तस्य कदाचित् प्राप्तस्य कदाचिदप्राप्तस्य इत्यर्थः। वितुषीभावरूपं प्रयोजनं हि अवहननेन नखविदलनेन अश्मकुट्टनादिना वा इत्यनेकैरुपायैः साधयितुं शक्यते। तत्र नखविदलनादिभिः वितुषीभावं यदा संपादयितुमारभते, तदा अवहननस्य प्राप्त्यभावात् अस्ति तस्य कादाचित्की प्राप्तिः। तस्यां च दशायां या अप्राप्तिः तदंशेऽपि अवघातप्रापको यो विधिः स नियमविधिरित्यर्थः।'

स च अप्राप्तांशपूरणम्—This sentence points out the import of नियम, which consists in supplying or establishing (पूरणं विधानमित्यर्थः) the part viz. अवघात, which was not established before. सः = नियमः restriction.

अतश्च नियमविधौ अप्राप्तांशपूरणात्मको नियम एव वाक्यार्थः—This sentence is just a corollary of what has been said above about the function of नियमविधि. वाक्यार्थः (sentence-sense) means import. The import of नियमविधि is restriction (नियमः), consisting of establishing the part viz. अवघात not established before. Note that नियमः here has the general sense of restriction and not the technical sense of injunction of restriction.

पक्षे अप्राप्तावघातस्य विधानमिति यावत्—This represents a paraphrase in specific terms of the general statement contained in 'अप्राप्तांशपूरणात्मको नियमः'.

अनेन हि अवघातस्य ...किन्तु नियमः—These two sentences point out the difference between विधि and नियम.

Somebody may object that 'व्रीहीन् अवहन्ति' is really an अपूर्वविधि and not a नियमविधि. For, it lays down that अवघात or pounding leads to वैतुष्य or unhusking. In other words it establishes the कार्यकारणभाव or साध्यसाधनभाव between वैतुष्य and अवघात.

The answer to this is that the कार्यकारणभाव between वैतुष्य and अवघात, or the fact that pounding leads to unhusking is not अत्यन्तमप्राप्त or प्रमाणान्तरेण अप्राप्त. For, we know from our ordinary experience (लोकव्यवहारः) that if we pound the rice, they are unhusked (अन्वयः) and that if we do not, they are not (व्यतिरेकः). These positive and negative instances (अन्वयव्यतिरेकौ) thus make the कार्यकारणभाव between वैतुष्य and अवघात known to all. The कार्यकारणभाव being thus अन्वयव्यतिरेकसिद्ध, it cannot form the import of व्रीहीन् अवहन्ति, which consequently cannot be regarded as an अपूर्वविधि. For, an अपूर्वविधि has for its import a matter which is प्रमाणान्तरेण अप्राप्त.

The distinction between विधि and नियम may thus be stated : Both विधि and नियम enjoin things, which are अप्राप्त. But while विधि enjoins a matter, which is अत्यन्तमप्राप्त or प्रमाणान्तरेण अप्राप्त (not known from any other source), नियम lays down a matter, which is only पक्षे अप्राप्त (not established in the alternative). Secondly, विधि represents an injunction, pure and simple, of a matter not known from any other source; नियम on the other hand asks us to perform a thing, already known from another source, in some special manner. Thirdly, विधि performs a single function viz. enjoining a thing unknown before; but नियम performs two really, because it restricts us to one of the many alternatives and excludes the others.

Here a question may be asked : What is the propriety of insisting that अवघात or अवहनन must be adopted for effecting वैतुष्य ? Whether we adopt नखविदलन, or अश्मकुट्टन, or अवघात, the final result viz. वैतुष्य would be the same. All the three ways would bring about वैतुष्य without any distinction. Why should we then choose अवघात in preference to the other methods ?

The answer to this is as follows : As no visible purpose can be assigned to अवघात as the means of निस्तुषीकरण, we must suppose that it has an unseen purpose. This means that if we unhusk the rice-grains by अवघात, some अपूर्व, technically known as नियमापूर्व, is produced. This नियमापूर्व would not be produced, if we were to unhusk the grains by नखविदलन or अश्मकुट्टन. That is why अवघात must be adopted for effecting वैतुष्य.

The following quotation from मीमांसापरिभाषा would make all these points about विधि and नियम clear :

'पुनरपि विधिस्त्रिविधः । अपूर्वविधिर्नियमविधिः परिसंख्याविधिश्चेति । तत्र **यो विधिरत्यन्ताप्राप्तमर्थं प्रापयति सः अपूर्वविधिः** । यथा दर्शपूर्णमासप्रकरणे 'व्रीहीन् प्रोक्षति' इति । एतद्विध्यभावे दर्शपूर्णमासीयव्रीहिषु प्रोक्षणं कथमपि न प्राप्नोति । एतद्विधिसत्त्वे तु तत्संबन्धिव्रीहिषु प्राप्नोत्येव इति अत्यन्ताप्राप्तप्रोक्षणप्रापकत्वाद् अयमपूर्वविधिः ।

यश्च पक्षेऽप्राप्तमर्थं नियमति स नियमविधिः । यथा तत्रैव 'व्रीहीन् अवहन्ति' इति । एतद्विध्यभावे दार्शपूर्णमासिकेषु उत्पत्तिवाक्यावगतपुरोडाशोपयोगितण्डुलनिष्पत्त्यनुकूलवैतुष्यकार्याय अवहननवत् कदाचित् नखविदलनमपि प्राप्नुयादिति तस्मिन् पक्षे अवहननस्य प्राप्तेरभावात् कार्यान्यथोपपत्तेरवहननस्य पाक्षिकी प्राप्तिः स्यात् । सति तु अस्मिन् विधौ अवहननेनैव वैतुष्यं कार्यमिति नियमे सति विदलनं सर्वात्मना निवर्तते इति नियमविधिरयम् ।

न च वैतुष्यस्य नखविदलनेनापि संभवाद् अवहननियमो व्यर्थः प्रयोजनाभावादिति वाच्यम् । **अवघातेनैव वैतुष्यकरणे किंचिद् अदृष्टं जन्यते इति नियमादृष्टाङ्गीकारात्** । नियमेन

दृष्टकार्यालाभेऽपि अदृष्टस्योत्पत्तेः । तच्चापूर्वं यागोत्पत्त्यपूर्वद्वारा फलापूर्वे उपयुज्यते, तेन नियमापूर्वाभावे फलापूर्वमेव नोत्पद्यते इति कल्पनान्नियमापूर्वस्य न वैय्यर्थ्यम् । '

Read जैमिनीयन्यायमालाविस्तर under IV. ii. 23–24, where many श्रौत examples of नियमविधि would be found.

Section 51

This Section deals with परिसंख्याविधि. The main idea is this injunction is exclusion. The name परिसंख्याविधि is significant. परिशब्दोऽत्र वर्जनार्थः । 'अपपरी वर्जने' (पा. 1. 4. 88)। 'परेर्वर्जने' (8. 1. 5) च इति पाणिनिस्मृतेः । संख्या बुद्धिः । परिसंख्या वर्जनबुद्धिः । परिसंख्याजनकः विधिः परिसंख्याविधिः ।

When two alternatives become simultaneously available, the rule, which excludes one of them, is the injunction of exclusion. The standard example of परिसंख्याविधि is 'पञ्च पञ्चनखा भक्ष्याः (Five five-nailed animals should be eaten)'. When we feel hungry, we can satisfy our hunger by eating the flesh of any of these five five-nailed animals *as well as* the flesh of any other animals i. e. of five-nailed animals other than the five allowed and also of animals which are not five-nailed. For, we can include in our menu bits of the flesh of different kinds of animals and thus arrange to satisfy the inner man. Thus, क्षुधाशमन can be effected by both पञ्चपञ्चनखभक्षण and by अपञ्चपञ्चनखभक्षण or पञ्चपञ्चनखेतरभक्षण. पञ्चपञ्चनखभक्षण and अपञ्चपञ्चनखभक्षण are, therefore, युगपत्प्राप्त. Under these circumstances what the परिसंख्याविधि in 'पञ्च पञ्चनखा भक्ष्याः' does is to exclude अपञ्चपञ्चनखभक्षण. This means पञ्चपञ्चनखभक्षण is allowed.

We have said above that the import of परिसंख्याविधि is exclusion. The exact significance of this must be understood. It is this: 'पञ्च पञ्चनखा भक्ष्याः' does not make it obligatory for us to eat the flesh of these five five-nailed animals. What the sentence actually does is to exclude अपञ्चपञ्चनख-भक्षण i. e. it forbids us to eat the flesh of पञ्चपञ्चनखेतर animals i. e. of animals which are not five-nailed and of five-nailed animals other than the five allowed. This means if at all we desire to make use of meat to satisfy our hunger, we must choose the flesh of these five five-nailed animals only. As far as the eating of flesh is concerned, परिसंख्याविधि is only permissive and not positive.

'पञ्च पञ्चनखा भक्ष्याः'—It is interesting to note that Mīmāṁsā writers do not feel any scruples in giving this as an illustration, when holy sacrificial matters are being discussed. Meat-eating was evidently not looked upon with such great disfavour as now.

The five five-nailed animals that are allowed are enumerated in a couplet from the Rāmāyaṇa, wherein the monkey chief Vālin tells Rāma 'पञ्च पञ्चनखा भक्ष्या ब्रह्मक्षत्रेण भारत । शशकः शल्यको गोधा खड्गी कूर्मोऽथ पञ्चमः ॥' किष्किन्धाकाण्ड 17. 39. शशकः hare. शल्यकः porcupine. गोधा alligator. खड्गी rhenoceros. कूर्मः tortoise. A similar stanza is found in देवलस्मृति as well: 'पञ्च पञ्चनखा भक्ष्या धर्मतः परिकीर्तिताः । गोधा कूर्मः शशः खड्गी शल्यकश्चेति ते स्मृताः ॥' Manu and Yājñavalkya also make references to these five-nailed animals that can be eaten. Note 'श्वाविधं शल्यकं गोधां खड्गकूर्मशशांस्तथा । भक्ष्यान् पञ्चनखेष्वाहुरनुष्ट्रांश्चैकतोदतः ॥' मनुस्मृति; v.18; 'भक्ष्याः पञ्चनखाः सेधागोधाकच्छपशल्यकाः ।' याज्ञवल्क्यस्मृति i. 177. Also read 'पञ्चनखाः शशशल्यकश्वाविद्गोधाखड्गकच्छपाः' गौतम xvii; 'श्वाविच्छल्यकशशकच्छपगोधाः पञ्चनखानां भक्ष्याः ।' वसिष्ठ xiv. 39.

Another example of परिसंख्या, drawn from ordinary life, is 'एकादश्यां फलाहारं कुर्यात्.' This does not enjoin the eating of fruit on the ekādaśī day. As everybody knows, निराहारः or a complete fast is what is to be observed on the ekādaśī. But, if some people cannot do this and want to eat something, they should eat fruit. This is what is meant. The sentence thus excludes फलेतराहार. It does not enjoin फलाहार. If at all we want to have any आहार, we should indulge in फलाहार. Thus, this sentence is quite on a par with 'पञ्च पञ्चनखा भक्ष्याः.'

Kumārila's definition of परिसंख्या is 'तत्र चान्यत्र च प्राप्तौ परिसंख्या'. Bhāskara's paraphrase of 'तत्र चान्यत्र च प्राप्तौ' is 'उभयोश्च युगपत्प्राप्तौ'. 'Establishment or availability there and elsewhere' means simultaneous establishment. The two चs in Kumārila's definition also express simultaneity.

इदं हि वाक्यं...रागतः प्राप्तत्वात्—This sentence points out why 'पञ्च पञ्चनखा भक्ष्याः' cannot be an instance of अपूर्वविधि. If it were an अपूर्वविधि, it would lay down पञ्चपञ्चनखभक्षण. But there is no necessity of enjoining this भक्षण, because we are led to it by natural appetite (रागः). In other words पञ्चपञ्चनखभक्षण is not अत्यन्तमप्राप्त or प्रमाणान्तरेण अप्राप्त. Therefore, 'पञ्च पञ्चनखा भक्ष्याः' cannot be an instance of अपूर्वविधि.

नापि नियमपरं...पक्षेऽप्राप्त्यभावात्—This sentence tells us why 'पञ्च पञ्चनखा भक्ष्याः' cannot be a नियमविधि. We have seen before that नियम requires its विधेय to be पक्षे अप्राप्त. In the present case पञ्चपञ्चनखभक्षण and अपञ्चपञ्चनख-भक्षण are युगपत्प्राप्त or simultaneously available in the manner we noted before. Therefore, 'पञ्च पञ्चनखा भक्ष्याः' cannot be a नियमविधि.

It should be noted that the word 'पञ्च' is dropped from each of these two sentences. The correct reading is: इदं हि वाक्यं न पञ्चपञ्चनख-

भक्षणपरं, तस्य रागतः प्राप्तत्वात् । नापि नियमपरं, पञ्चपञ्चनखापञ्चपञ्चनखभक्षणस्य युगपत्प्राप्तेः पक्षेऽप्राप्त्यभावात् ।

अतः ... परिसंख्याविधिः—This sentence points out what the exact significance of परिसंख्याविधि is. As 'पञ्च पञ्चनखा भक्ष्याः' can be neither an अपूर्वविधि nor a नियमविधि, its purpose is to forbid the eating of animals which are not five-nailed and of all five-nailed animals other than the five enumerated.

Though the technical names of these three rules are अपूर्वविधि, नियमविधि and परिसंख्याविधि, they are usually referred to as विधि, नियम and परिसंख्या. Let us briefly review the characteristics of these three.

विधिः, नियमः and परिसंख्या

विधि lays down something which is new, something which is not known from any other source. नियम restricts us to one of the two or more mutually exclusive alternatives. परिसंख्या excludes one of the two alternatives, which become simultaneously available.

The import of विधि is injunction or the positive laying down of something, that of नियम restriction and that of परिसंख्या exclusion.

विधि asks us to do something which otherwise we would not have done. नियम requires that we do this thing, which has already been enjoined by विधि, in one particular way out of the many in which it is possible to accomplished it. परिसंख्या does not make it obligatory on us to do anything positively, but excludes one of the two alternatives which can be simultaneously adopted, leaving it to our option to resort to the other unexcluded or unprohibited alternative.

'पञ्च पञ्चनखा भक्ष्याः' is a स्मार्त example of परिसंख्या. A श्रौत example is furnished by 'इमामगृभ्णन् रशनामृतस्य इति अश्वाभिधानीमादत्ते ।' A rite called चयन or अग्निचयन is performed at the commencement of a sacrifice proper. It consists in the building of the sacrificial altar by the use of bricks. These bricks are prepared from clay, which is brought in sacks tied on the backs of a horse and a donkey.

Now, in order to guide these animals their reins have to be held. In this connection the Vedic Mantra 'इमामगृभ्णन् रशनामृतस्य' is to be recited. लिङ्गप्रमाण would show that the Mantra is subservient to the grasping of a rein. It is possible to grasp the reins of both the horse and the donkey simultaneously and repeat the stanza at the time. But the Brāhmaṇa sentence 'इमामगृभ्णन्...अश्वाभिधानीमादत्ते' excludes the grasping of the rein of the donkey. The rein of the donkey is to be grasped silently without reciting any Vedic Mantra.

So, as the purport of the sentence 'इमामगृभ्णन्...अश्वाभिधानीमादत्ते' is to exclude गर्दभरशनादान, it becomes an instance of परिसंख्या.

It should be noted that this illustration is not quite on a par with 'पञ्च पञ्चनखा भक्ष्याः'. It is true that in both the idea of exclusion is prominent. 'पञ्च पञ्चनखा भक्ष्याः' excludes अपञ्चपञ्चनखभक्षण, while 'इमा...मादत्ते' excludes गर्दभरशनादान. But 'पञ्च...भक्ष्याः' does not make पञ्चपञ्चनखभक्षण necessary. If we at all want to eat flesh, we should eat the flesh of these five five-nailed animals. That is the import of this परिसंख्या. But such interpretation would not do in the case of 'इमामगृभ्णन्...मादत्ते'. We cannot say that if we at all want to make use of this Mantra, we must use it in holding the rein of the horse. The truth is that the Mantra must be recited at the time of grasping the rein of the horse. But as the idea of excluding गर्दभरशनादान is more prominent here and as the grasping of the reins of both these is युगपत्प्राप्त, the sentence is regarded as an example of परिसंख्या.

Read 'द्वयोः समुच्चित्य प्राप्तौ इतरनिवृत्तिफलको विधिः परिसंख्याविधिः । यथा चयनप्रकरणे 'इमामगृभ्णन् रशनामृतस्य इति अश्वाभिधानीमादत्ते' इति अश्वरशनाग्रहणाङ्गत्वेन मन्त्रविधिः। एतद्विध्यभावे हि रशनाग्रहणप्रकाशको मन्त्रो रशनादानप्रकाशनरूपात् लिङ्गाद् अश्वरशनादान इव गर्दभरशनादानेऽपि प्राप्नुयात् । सति अस्मिन् विधौ अनेन मन्त्रेण अश्वरशनामेवाददीत न तु गर्दभरशनाम्, सा तु तूष्णीमेव ग्राह्या, इति गर्दभरशनायां मन्त्रनिवृत्तिर्भवति. इति द्वयोः समुच्चित्य प्राप्तौ इतरनिवृत्तिफलकत्वाद् अयं परिसंख्याविधिः ।' मीमांसापरिभाषा

'एकस्य अनेकत्र प्राप्तस्य अन्यतो निवृत्त्यर्थमेकत्र पुनर्वचनं परिसंख्या। तद्यथा 'इमामगृभ्णन् रशनामृतस्येत्यश्वाभिधानीमादत्ते' इत्ययं मन्त्रः स्वसामर्थ्याद् अश्वाभिधान्या गर्दभाभिधान्याश्च रशनाया ग्रहणे विनियुक्तः पुनः 'अश्वाभिधानीमादत्ते' इत्यनेन अश्वाभिधान्यां विनियुज्यमानो गर्दभाभिधान्या निवर्तते । यथा 'पञ्च पञ्चनखा भक्ष्याः' इत्यत्र हि यदृच्छया शशादिषु श्वादिषु च भक्षणं प्राप्तं पुनः शशादिषु श्रूयमाणं श्वादिभ्यो निवर्तते इति ।' मिताक्षरा on याज्ञवल्क्य i. 81.

It must be pointed out that the nature of परिसंख्या, as understood from these two illustrations viz. 'पञ्च...भक्ष्याः' and 'इमामगृभ्णन्...आदत्ते' is not uniform. From 'पञ्च पञ्चनखा भक्ष्याः' it would appear that परिसंख्या is merely permissive in form and does not positively lay down anything at all. For, 'पञ्च...भक्ष्याः' does not enjoin पञ्चपञ्चनखभक्षण. But from 'इमामगृभ्णन्...आदत्ते' we learn that while the Mantra is excluded from गर्दभाभिधानी, it is at the same time enjoined for अश्वाभिधानी. So, the परिसंख्या in 'इमामगृभ्णन्...आदत्ते' not only forbids us to recite the Mantra at the time of grasping the rein of the donkey, but also enjoins us to recite it at the time of holding the rein of the horse. Thus, this परिसंख्या contains both a विधि and a निषेध, the विधि of अश्वाभिधान्यादान and the निषेध of गर्दभाभिधान्यादान.

Under these circumstances it may be asked what exactly is the difference between a नियम and a परिसंख्या. For, a नियम also contains both a विधि and a निषेध, the विधि of समदेश and the निषेध of विषमदेश.

The answer to this question is that though नियम and परिसंख्या resemble in this that they both contain a विधि and a निषेध, the distinction between them lies in the fact that while the alternatives in नियम are mutually exclusive, those in परिसंख्या are युगपत्प्राप्त or such as can be simultaneously adopted. Thus, it is not possible to perform a sacrifice on both even and uneven ground simultaneously. But it is possible to hold the reins of the donkey and the horse simultaneously and repeat the Mantra at that time. Thus, it is 'युगपत्प्राप्तिः' that distinguishes परिसंख्या from नियम, which is characterized by 'पक्षेऽप्राप्तिः'.

Section 52

परिसंख्या is of two kinds — direct (श्रौती) and implied (लाक्षणिकी). A sentence is said to contain direct Exclusion, when the particle एव, which expresses the idea of the exclusion of things other than those mentioned, occurs in it. If the exclusion is not directly expressed by एव, but is merely implied, that sentence becomes an example of indirect Exclusion.

'अत्र हि एव आवपन्ति' is an example of श्रौती परिसंख्या, because the particle एव, expressive of exclusion, occurs in it.

आवपन्ति—आवापः means addition or insertion (प्रक्षेपः, समुच्चयः) of some new words and उद्वापः means omission or deletion (उद्धारः, निवृत्तिः) of some existing words. Now, the question is whether these आवाप and उद्वाप are to be practised in the case of stanzas occurring in all rites or in the case of only a few. Under these circumstances the sentence 'त्रीणि ह वै यज्ञस्य उदराणि यद् गायत्री बृहती अनुष्टुभ् । अत्र हि एव आवपन्ति, अत एव उद्वपन्ति,' occurring in connection with the पवमान rite tells us that आवाप and उद्वाप are to be performed in the पवमान rite and in the case of stanzas in the गायत्री, बृहती and अनुष्टुभ् metres. The word एव in the above passage expresses the exclusion of rites other than पवमान and of stanzas in metres other than those specified from the sphere of आवापोद्वाप. Hence, this sentence is an example of श्रौती परिसंख्या.

In 'पञ्च पञ्चनखा भक्ष्याः' there is no word which would express the exclusion of animals other than the five five-nailed (इतरनिवृत्तिवाचकपदाभावात् इतरेषाम् अपञ्चपञ्चनखानां पञ्चपञ्चनखेतरेषामित्यर्थः या निवृत्तिः तद्वाचकं यत् पदं तस्य अभावात्). Hence, this is an example of लाक्षणिकी परिसंख्या. इतरनिवृत्तिपदाभाव is the reason why the परिसंख्या is लाक्षणिकी.

In the sentence ‘अत्र हि एव आवपन्ति ’ Rāmeśvara adopts the reading आवयन्ति ’ and explains it as ‘ अवजानन्तीत्यर्थः, गायन्तीति यावत् ’. From the sentence quoted above it will be noticed that आवपन्ति, not आवयन्ति, is the correct reading.

Read in this connection जैमिनीयन्यायमालाविस्तर on X. iv. 21–22.

अत एव एषा त्रिदोषग्रस्ता — अत एव = इतरनिवृत्तिवाचकपदाभावादेव । एषा = लाक्षणिकी परिसंख्या.

As the indirect injunction of exclusion does not contain a word, expressive of the idea of exclusion, it is vitiated by three defects.

Section 53

This Section deals with the three defects of लाक्षणिकी परिसंख्या. These are श्रुतहानि or the abandonment of what is directly stated or the expressed sense, अश्रुतकल्पना or the assumption of what has not been directly stated and प्राप्तबाध or the contradiction or rejection of what has accrued.

These three faults will be clear when we see them with reference to the stock example viz. ‘पञ्च पञ्चनखा भक्ष्याः ’. Ordinarily, this sentence would seem to enjoin पञ्चपञ्चनखभक्षण, even as ‘प्रयाजाः कर्तव्याः ’ lays down प्रयाजकरण, or ‘स्वाध्यायोऽध्येतव्यः ’ enjoins स्वाध्यायाध्ययन. But the import of ‘पञ्च पञ्चनखा भक्ष्याः ’ is, as we have seen, अपञ्चपञ्चनखभक्षणनिवृत्ति. So its श्रुतार्थ or directly-stated sense viz. पञ्चपञ्चनखभक्षण is abandoned. Consequently, the defect श्रुतहानि arises. Secondly, अपञ्चपञ्चनखभक्षणनिवृत्ति, which is the ultimate sense we obtain from ‘पञ्च पञ्चनखा भक्ष्याः’, is not expressed by any word in that sentence, but has to be assumed or presumed. Thus, the defect अश्रुतकल्पना arises. Thirdly, the परिसंख्या in ‘पञ्च पञ्चनखा भक्ष्याः ’ prevents us from eating the flesh of animals other than the specified five five-nailed. Had it not been for this sentence, we would have made use of the flesh of these other animals along with the flesh of the specified five five-nailed animals in order to satisfy our hunger. पञ्चपञ्चनखभक्षण as well as अपञ्चपञ्चनखभक्षण are रागतः प्राप्त. But the परिसंख्या in ‘पञ्च पञ्चनखा भक्ष्याः ’ forbids us to eat the flesh of अपञ्चपञ्चनख. Hence, he have प्राप्तबाध.

It should be noted that both पञ्चपञ्चनखभक्षण and अपञ्चपञ्चनखभक्षण, which are रागतः प्राप्त, are in a way बाधित by the परिसंख्या in ‘पञ्च पञ्चनखा भक्ष्याः ’. श्रुतहानि does not make पञ्चपञ्चनखभक्षण obligatory. So it is as good as बाधित. प्राप्तबाध positively forbids अपञ्चपञ्चनखभक्षण. So it is really बाधित. But there is a difference between these two kinds of बाध.

While we can never indulge in अपञ्चपञ्चनखभक्षण, we can, if we like, resort to पञ्चपञ्चनखभक्षण.

अस्मिंश्च... अर्थनिष्ठः—Bhāskara is here telling us that out of these three defects of a लाक्षणिकी परिसंख्या, two belong to word and the third to matter (अर्थः). श्रुतिहानि and अश्रुतकल्पना are said to belong to word, because they consist in abandoning the direct meaning of words and assuming some other in its stead. प्राप्तबाध on the other hand has nothing to do with words and their meaning, but it consists in the rejection of a matter (अर्थः अपञ्चपञ्चनखभक्षणरूपः) that is established by, say, appetite. That is why it is called अर्थनिष्ठ.

इति दिक्—This is just to show the direction. This expression is used when the author wants to intimate that the subject has not been treated exhaustively, but only in such a manner as to show the student the direction, in which it should be studied.

इति दिक् may here be taken in the sense of 'This is by the way.' It will be remembered that this discussion about विधि, नियम and परिसंख्या arose out of the author's remark that an injunction of restriction is to be resorted to in the sentence 'मन्त्रैरेव स्मर्तव्यम्'. The proper topic of this Chapter is Mantra. Treatment of विधि, नियम and परिसंख्या is here, therefore, only by way of digression. That is what is indicated by the expression इति दिक्.

The three faults श्रुतहानि, अश्रुतकल्पना and प्राप्तबाध belong to लाक्षणिकी परिसंख्या. But श्रौती परिसंख्या is not entirely free from defects. It is vitiated by प्राप्तबाध. The sentence 'अत्र हि एव आवपन्ति' excludes आवाप and उद्वाप from stanzas other than those in the three specified metres and from rites other than those relating to पवमान. Ordinarily, आवाप and उद्वाप would have been resorted to in the case of all stanzas and all rites. Thus, आवाप and उद्वाप, which were प्राप्त, are बाधित. Hence, we have प्राप्तबाध in the case of this श्रौती परिसंख्या.

As regards श्रुतहानि and अश्रुतकल्पना these can have no scope in a श्रौती परिसंख्या. For, व्यावृत्ति or निवृत्ति, which is the import of a परिसंख्या, is here directly expressed (श्रुत) by the particle एव. So there is no necessity of abandoning the directly expressed sense and of presuming a sense not directly expressed. श्रुतहानि and अश्रुतकल्पना thus do not arise.

The following quotation supports the statement that श्रौती परिसंख्या suffers from प्राप्तबाध only :

'न च परिसंख्यायास्त्रिदोषत्वम् । एवकारेण तस्या एव श्रुतत्वात् ।' शास्त्रदीपिका on X. iv. 21–22, on which the commentary remarks 'श्रुतत्वादेव, स्वार्थत्याग-

परार्थस्वीकारलक्षणदोषद्वयाप्रसङ्गान्न त्रयोऽपि दोषाः, किन्तु प्राप्तबाधलक्षण एक एवेति नात्यन्तदुष्टा परिसंख्येति भावः।'

With reference to these three defects of a लाक्षणिकी परिसंख्या one or two things must be pointed out. First, it should be noted that the three defects have been conceived with special reference to the sentence 'पञ्च पञ्चनखा भक्ष्याः'. As we saw before, 'इमामगृभ्णन्... आदत्ते' is also an example of लाक्षणिकी परिसंख्या. Here there is really no स्वार्थहानि. For, the sentence positively enjoins that the Mantra 'इमा... ऋतस्य' is to be repeated at the time of grasping the rein of the horse. If we were to ignore this fact and concentrate our attention on the exclusion of गर्दभरशना, then only could it be said that there is some kind of स्वार्थहानि in so far as the स्वार्थ is not regarded as the main idea.

Secondly, it should be noted that the word प्राप्त in प्राप्तबाध means really 'which would have accrued in the absence of the परिसंख्या under discussion.' Thus, in the case of 'पञ्च पञ्चनखा भक्ष्याः' प्राप्तबाध arises from 'प्राप्तस्य अपञ्चपञ्चनखभक्षणस्य बाधनम्.' But 'अपञ्चपञ्चनखभक्षण' is really not प्राप्त, when the sentence 'पञ्च पञ्चनखा भक्ष्याः' is there. Thus, प्राप्त in प्राप्तबाध does not mean 'which has accrued', but 'which would have accrued if the परिसंख्या had not been there'. Similarly, 'इमामगृभ्णन्... आदत्ते' excludes गर्दभरशनादान. But गर्दभरशनादान is really not प्राप्त in the presence of the sentence 'इमा...आदत्ते'. It would be प्राप्त, if the sentence had not been there. Hence, some people regard अप्राप्तबाध as a more correct name for the third defect of a लाक्षणिकी परिसंख्या. Their view may thus be stated:

'वस्तुतोऽत्र प्राप्तस्य निवारणं न भवति, अप्राप्तस्यैव निवारणं भवति। तथा हि। 'इमामगृभ्णन् रशनामृतस्य' इत्ययं मन्त्रः अर्थसामर्थ्यात् रशनादाने प्राप्तः। ततः कस्य रशना इत्यपेक्षायां 'इत्यश्वाभिधानीमादत्ते' इति ब्राह्मणवाक्यम् 'अश्वस्य रशना' इति प्रत्यक्षमेव कथयति। तेन गर्दभरशनाप्राप्तेरवसर एव नास्ति। एवमप्राप्तैव गर्दभरशना। तस्या निवारणे जाते न प्राप्तबाधः, किन्तु अप्राप्तबाध एव।'

The main idea in a परिसंख्या is exclusion. That exclusion may either be directly expressed by the particle एव, or may have to be implied. In any case the things, which are excluded, are never expressed by the sentence, which is understood to contain a परिसंख्या. In a परिसंख्या the expressed sense is either altogether abandoned or subordinated. This gives rise to the three faults in a लाक्षणिकी परिसंख्या and to one fault in a श्रौती परिसंख्या. परिसंख्या sentences thus do not intend what they mean. This is rather awkward. For, a man or a sentence must ordinarily be supposed to intend what he or it means. Owing to this peculiarity of a परिसंख्या i. e. owing to its containing either one or three defects Mīmāṁsakas are generally unwilling to interpret a sentence as a परिसंख्या. This unwillingness is also noticeable among commentators on Dharma-texts, who also do not like to understand a doubtful text as containing a परिसंख्या as far as possible.

येषां तु... नानर्थक्यमिति— After having completed the more or less irrelevant treatment of विधि, नियम and परिसंख्या, the author now turns to the main topic of the Chapter viz. Mantra. It was pointed out that Mantras have a purpose in so far as they serve to remind the sacrificer of matters connected with the performance. This presupposes that Mantras have an intelligible meaning. But there are certain Mantras such as 'कवचाय हुम्' 'नेत्रत्रयाय वौषट्' and 'अस्त्राय फट्,' from which no intelligible sense can be derived. These Mantras obviously do not possess the characteristic of being reminders of matters connected with the performance. Are these then to be regarded as purposeless (अनर्थक)?

No, replies the Mīmāṁsaka. As these Mantras can have no seen fruit, they must be supposed to serve an unseen purpose (अदृष्टार्थकत्वम्). This we do, because there is no other alternative left open to us (अनन्यगत्या) except to make such a supposition. The idea is the injunction 'स्वाध्यायोऽध्येतव्यः' covers the entire Veda. The whole of the Veda including these apparently meaningless sentences has to be made by heart. It is axiomatic with the Mīmāṁsakas that no part of the Veda can be purposeless. If, therefore, the recitation (उच्चारणम्) of these meaningless formulas can have no seen purpose such as प्रयोगसमवेतार्थस्मारकत्वम्, it must be presumed to have an unseen purpose. Thus, such formulas do serve some purpose and cannot, therefore, be regarded as purposeless.

Section 54

This and the following seven Sections deal with Nāmadheya, which is the third of the five divisions of the Veda. Vide Section 10 above.

This Nāmadheya division of the Veda is somewhat peculiar. While the other four divisions viz. Vidhi, Mantra, Niṣedha and Arthavāda are constituted by complete sentences, this division comprises proper names only. Discussion about Nāmadheya usually centres round the four sentences 'उद्भिदा यजेत पशुकामः', 'चित्रया यजेत पशुकामः', 'अग्निहोत्रं जुहोति' and 'श्येनेन अभिचरन् यजेत', though sentences laying down well-known sacrifices such as 'दर्शपूर्णमासाभ्यां यजेत' and 'ज्योतिष्टोमेन यजेत' are also legitimate examples of Nāmadheya.

How this division which comprises only a few proper names came first to be formed cannot be easily explained. Keith (The Karma-Mīmāṁsā p. 80) conjectures that it arose from the necessity of finding out the meaning of a few obscure sacrificial terms such as Udbhid and Citrā and was later on extended into a wider area so as to include all proper names.

According to the theory of Mīmāṁsakas every portion of the Veda must subserve dharma or yāga or sacrifice. Only as being subservient to sacrifice can it be said to have a purpose (अर्थवत्) in the Mīmāṁsakas' scheme of things? In what way then are names useful to sacrifice? Names are useful to sacrifice, because they define or specify (परिच्छेदकतया) the matter to be enjoined (विधेयार्थः). To illustrate: 'उद्भिदा यजेत पशुकामः' lays down a certain sacrifice with a view to obtain cattle (फलोद्देशेन पशुरूपफलोद्देशेन). The knowledge of this sacrifice can be had from nowhere else. The sacrifice is thus अप्राप्त or non-established and is being enjoined by this sentence for the first time.

'यजेत पशुकामः' is, according to the Mīmāṁsakas' way of interpretation, equal to 'यागेन पशुं भावयेत्'. Now this refers to a sacrifice in very general terms. A sacrifice in general (यागसामान्यम्) cannot be enjoined (अविधेय). You must state which particular sacrifice is meant. A teacher, for example, cannot ask his pupils to read a book. He must tell them which particular book is to be read. When, therefore, the expectancy (आकाङ्क्षा) as to which particular sacrifice is to be performed for the purpose of obtaining cattle arises, it is fulfilled by the term उद्भिदा. We now learn that the sacrifice which a man must perform for getting cattle is called उद्भिद्. Thus, the word उद्भिद्, which represents the name of the sacrifice (यागनामधेयम्) defines the matter viz. the sacrifice which is to be enjoined (विधेयार्थपरिच्छेदः).

उद्भिदा यागेन...नामधेयान्वयात् — This sentence explains how the word उद्भिदा in 'उद्भिदा यजेत पशुकामः' is to be grammatically construed in the final meaning that we obtain from that sentence, according to the Mīmāmsakas. As उद्भिदा is the proper name of the sacrifice, it must naturally be in apposition (सामानाधिकरण्यम्) with याग. But the word याग as such does not occur in the original sentence. When, however, following the usual Mīmāṁsist method, we explain यजेत as यागेन पशुं भावयेत्, the name उद्भिदा is easily construed with (नामधेयान्वयः) with यागेन, as both of them are in the same case viz. the instrumental.

सामानाधिकरण्यम् means literally the state of having the same abode (समानम् अधिकरणं येषां तेषां भावः). In grammar the term means being in apposition with, or in the same case relation with, or in grammatical coordination with. Read 'पदयोरेकार्थाधायित्वं **समानविभक्तिकत्वं** वा सामानाधिकरण्यम् । यथा नीलो घटः इत्यादौ नीलपदघटपदयोः सामानाधिकरण्यम् ।' वैयाकरणभूषणसारदर्पणः

Section 55

This Section enumerates the four reasons which make it necessary for us to understand a particular word in a Vedic sentence as a proper noun. The four reasons are (1) मत्वर्थलक्षणाभय, (2) वाक्यभेदभय, (3) तत्प्रख्यशास्त्र and (4) तद्व्यपदेश. These are explained *seriatim* in the following Sections.

Section 56

'उद्भिदा यजेत पशुकामः' is a sentence where the word उद्भिदा is understood to be the proper name of the sacrifice from the fear of an indication of possession (मत्वर्थलक्षणाभयात्). The word उद्भिद् is then explained as 'उद्भिद्यते पशुफलमनेन (by which the fruit of the sacrifice viz. cattle is brought up or given),' or better still as 'उद्भिद्यते पशुफलमस्मात् (from which the fruit viz. cattle arises or bursts up or is produced)'. How मत्वर्थलक्षणाभय compels us to understand उद्भिदा here as a proper name is thus explained :

The sentence 'उद्भिदा यजेत पशुकामः' looks very much like 'दध्ना जुहोति' and 'व्रीहिभिर्यजेत'. These two latter sentences are examples of गुणविधि (Vide pp. 98–99 above), where the words in the instrumental viz. दध्ना and व्रीहिभिः represent the material with which the sacrifice is to be performed. Similarly, why should we not regard उद्भिदा also as representing a गुण or a secondary matter, which is useful in the performance of the sacrifice ? Etymologically उद्भिद् yields the sense of a spade or a pick–axe (उद्भिद्यते भूमिरनेन इति उद्भिद् खनित्रमित्यर्थः). Thus 'उद्भिदा यजेत पशुकामः' would be a गुणविधि, laying down the material spade, which is to be used in the sacrifice.

Against this it is pointed out that 'उद्भिदा यजेत पशुकामः,' though in appearance similar to 'दध्ना जुहोति' and 'व्रीहिभिर्यजेत', is not exactly like them. 'दध्ना जुहोति' and 'व्रीहिभिर्यजेत' lay down materials for a sacrifice, which has been enjoined by another sentence viz. 'अग्निहोत्रं जुहुयात्'. But there is no other sentence laying down a sacrifice for the attainment of cattle, to which 'उद्भिदा यजेत पशुकामः' can be regarded as subservient. Therefore, if we want to regard the sentence 'उद्भिदा यजेत पशुकामः' as laying down a गुण such as a spade, we must suppose that it does so in addition to enjoining the principal sacrifice for the attainment of cattle. For, such a sacrifice has not been laid down anywhere else (यागस्यापि अप्राप्तत्वात्).

The position now is this: The sentence 'उद्भिदा यजेत पशुकामः' enjoins, according to our supposition, a sacrifice for the attainment of the fruit (फलं प्रति यागविधानम् = पशुरूपफलोद्देशेन यागस्य विधानम्) as well as the material for the performance of that sacrifice (तं च प्रति गुणविधानम् = तं च यागं प्रति गुणस्य उद्भिद्रूपस्य खनित्रस्येत्यर्थः विधानम्). Thus, the one sentence 'उद्भिदा यजेत पशुकामः' lays down two things and is, therefore, really equal to two sentences viz. 'उद्भिदा (= खनित्रेण) यागं भावयेत्' and 'यागेन पशुं भावयेत्.' This means that in interpreting the sentence in the manner stated above, we become involved in a split of the sentence (वाक्यभेदापत्तिः). See pp. 100–101 above. Therefore, the above interpretation with उद्भिद् meaning खनित्र cannot be accepted.

But, it is urged, the split in the sentence can be avoided by understanding 'उद्भिदा यजेत पशुकामः' as an example of विशिष्टविधि, such as we have in 'सोमेन यजेत.' In the case of this latter sentence we have seen that though it enjoins two things, वाक्यभेद does not arise, because the two things are not separately enjoined, but only one as qualified by the other is enjoined. Vide above p. 9, ll. 5–6. Thus, 'उद्भिदा यजेत पशुकामः' would enjoin a sacrifice qualified by an accessory (गुणविशिष्टकर्मविधानम् = गुणेन उद्भिदा खनित्रेणेत्यर्थः विशिष्टं यत् कर्म यागरूपं तस्य विधानम्). Here the word उद्भिद् signifies an accessory viz. a spade (गुणसमर्पकत्वम् = गुणस्य खनित्ररूपस्य समर्पकः अभिधायकः तस्य भावः). The sentence 'उद्भिदा यजेत पशुकामः' would then yield the sense 'पशुकामः उद्भिद्वता खनित्रवता इत्यर्थः यागेन पशुं भावयेत्,' even as 'सोमेन यजेत' yields the sense 'सोमवता यागेन इष्टं भावयेत्.'

But such a procedure involves the understanding of the word उद्भिदा in a metaphorical sense i. e. in the sense of उद्भिद्वता, which we can only do by supposing that मत्वर्थलक्षणा or an indication of possession is present in that word. Vide p. 99 above.

Thus, if उद्भिदा is taken to mean a secondary matter such as a spade and 'उद्भिदा यजेत पशुकामः' is understood to be an instance of विशिष्टविधि, we become involved in a मत्वर्थलक्षणा, which evidently is a defect. Therefore, in order to avoid this मत्वर्थलक्षणा we take उद्भिदा to be the proper name of the sacrifice. 'उद्भिदा यजेत पशुकामः' is thus an example, where a word viz. उद्भिदा is understood to be a proper name from the fear of an indication of possession (मत्वर्थलक्षणाभयात्).

'उद्भिदा यागेन [i. e. उद्भिन्नामकेन यागेन] पशुं भावयेत् पशुकामः' is then the ultimate sense we obtain from 'उद्भिदा यजेत पशुकामः.' Here उद्भिदा and यागेन are in the same case relation (समानाधिकरण) and this their grammatical equation (सामानाधिकरण्यम्) is quite justifiable, because both the words signify the same entity, one being the proper name of the other. A similar sentence is 'विष्णुना देवेन अनुगृहीतं जगत्,' where विष्णुना and देवेन are समानाधिकरण, because one represents the proper name of the other.

But if on the contrary उद्भिदा were to signify a spade, the grammatical equation उद्भिदा यागेन in 'उद्भिदा यागेन पशुं भावयेत् पशुकामः' would not be understandable. The assumption of मत्वर्थलक्षणा would then be necessary. That is why 'उद्भिदा यजेत पशुकामः' is an example of 'मत्वर्थलक्षणाभयात् नामधेयत्वम्.'

But one may here ask: What is the exact difference between 'सोमेन यजेत' and 'उद्भिदा यजेत पशुकामः'? If you can understand 'सोमेन यजेत' as an example of विशिष्टविधि inspite of the मत्वर्थलक्षणा involved in it, why should we not do so in the case of 'उद्भिदा यजेत पशुकामः' as well? Or to ask the same question from another point of view: If उद्भिदा is to be understood as a नामधेय in 'उद्भिदा यजेत पशुकामः' from मत्वर्थलक्षणाभय, why should सोमेन also not be undertsood as a नामधेय in 'सोमेन यजेत' for exactly the same reason?

The Mīmāṁsaka answers this question by pointing out the essential difference between the two words सोम and उद्भिद्. While सोम is well known to possess the sense of the juice of a plant of that name, उद्भिद् is not known to possess the sense of a spade. It is, therefore, better to understand सोम in its well known sense of the juice rather than regard it as a proper name of obscure signification. Similarly, it is better to consider the obscure word उद्भिद् as a proper name rather than give it a meaning which it is not known to possess.

Another answer to the question may also be suggested. सोम in its well known sense of a juice is capable of serving as a material for a sacrifice. But उद्भिद् even in its obscure etymological sense of a spade can hardly be regarded as an accessory of the sacrifice. That is why सोम is to be understood in its proper sense and उद्भिद् taken as a name.

This whole topic of मत्वर्थलक्षणाभयात् नामधेयत्वम् is discussed in the जैमिनीयन्यायमालाविस्तर under I. iv. 2, from which the following will be read with advantage :—

"'उद्भिदा यजेत पशुकामः' इत्यत्र तृतीयान्तेन उद्भित्पदेन योऽर्थो विवक्षितः सोऽयं यागे कश्चिद् गुणः स्यात्। 'दध्ना जुहोति' इत्यनेन गुणविधिना समानत्वात्। अथोच्येत–दधिशब्दार्थो लोकप्रसिद्धः, उद्भिच्छब्दार्थस्तु अप्रसिद्ध इति। तन्न। रूढ्यभावेऽपि अवयवार्थनिरुक्त्या तत्प्रसिद्धेः। 'उद्भिद्यते भूमिरनेन' इति व्युत्पत्त्या खनित्रवाची असौ शब्दः।...तस्मात् गुणविधिरिति **प्राप्ते**—

ब्रूमः। 'पशुकामो यजेत' इत्यस्य पदद्वयस्य अयमर्थः–'पशुरूपं फलं यागेन कुर्यात्' इति। तत्र केन यागेन इत्यपेक्षायाम् 'उद्भिदा' इति तृतीयान्तं पदं यागनामत्वेन अन्वेति। 'उद्भिद्यते

पशुफलमनेन यागेन ' इति निरुक्त्या नामत्वमुद्भित्पदस्य उपपद्यते । एवमपि गुणविधिनामधेयत्वयोः शब्दनिर्वचनसाम्यान्न निर्णय इति चेत् । मैवम् । सामानाधिकरण्यस्य निर्णायकत्वात् । 'उद्भिन्नामकेन यागेन फलं कुर्यात् ' इत्युक्ते सामानाधिकरण्यं लभ्यते । गुणत्वे तु ' खनित्रेण साध्यो यो यागः,तेन—' इत्येवं वैयधिकरण्यं स्यात् । यदि **'खनित्रवता यागेन ' इति सामानाधिकरण्यं योज्येत, तदा मत्वर्थलक्षणा प्रसज्येत । तस्मादुद्भिदादिपदं नामधेयम् ।**

' दध्ना जुहोति ' ' व्रीहिभिर्यजेत ' इत्यादिषु द्रव्यविशेषे दध्यादिशब्दानामत्यन्तरूढतया यागनामत्वासंभवादगत्या गुणत्वमाश्रितम् । ' सोमेन यजेत ' इत्यत्रापि ' अप्रसिद्धार्थनामधेयत्वकल्पनातो वरं प्रसिद्धार्थद्वारेण लक्षणाश्रयणम् ' इत्यभिप्रेत्य ' सोमद्रव्यवता यागेन ' इति मत्वर्थलक्षणा स्वीकृता । उद्भिच्छब्दस्य तु लोकप्रसिद्धार्थाभावादुक्तरीत्या नामत्वं युक्तम् । प्रयोजनं तु नाम्नः सर्वत्र व्यवहारएव । न हि अन्तरेण नामधेयमुत्विग्वरणादिषु ' अनेनाहं यक्ष्ये ' इत्याख्यानोपायो लघुः कश्चिदस्ति । तस्माद् उद्भिदादिकं नामधेयम् । ' pp. 41–42

Also read ' न चैवं 'सोमेन यजेत' इत्यत्रापि सोमपदस्य यागनामधेयत्वापातः, गुणविधित्वे मत्वर्थलक्षणापत्तेरिति वाच्यम् । सोमपदस्य लतायां रूढत्वेन यागनामधेयत्वानुपपत्तेरगत्या लक्षणाश्रयणात् । उद्भिच्छब्दस्य तु नैवं वाच्योऽर्थः कश्चित् प्रसिद्धः । उद्भिद्यते अनेन इति योगस्य तु गुणे [खनित्ररूपे] इव यागेऽपि फलोद्भेदकारिणि उपपत्तेः । ' मीमांसान्यायप्रकाश

Section 57

' चित्रया यजेत पशुकामः ' represents an illustration where from the fear of a split in the sentence we understand the word चित्रा as the proper name of the sacrifice. This sentence looks very much like ' उद्भिदा यजेत पशुकामः '. ' उद्भिदा यजेत पशुकामः ' was regarded as a case where the word उद्भिदा was taken to be the proper name of the sacrifice from the fear of an indication of possession. Why should we then not take ' चित्रया यजेत पशुकामः ' also as an illustration of ' मत्वर्थलक्षणाभयात् नामधेयत्वम् ' ?

In order to answer this question the two sentences must be clearly distinguished. It will be remembered that when we tried to take उद्भिद् in the sense of an axe, which was supposed to be an accessory of the sacrifice (गुणः), we were first landed in वाक्यभेद. In order to get rid of this वाक्यभेद, we proposed to take ' उद्भिदा यजेत पशुकामः ' as an example of a विशिष्टविधि and as this विशिष्टविधि involved मत्वर्थलक्षणा, we decided to understand उद्भिद् as a proper name in order to avoid it. Thus ' उद्भिदा यजेत पशुकामः ' became an example of ' मत्वर्थलक्षणाभयात् नामधेयत्वम् '.

Why should we then not regard ' चित्रया यजेत पशुकामः ' as an example of a विशिष्टविधि ? If we were to do so, the word चित्रा would mean a speckled or variegated female animal, which would represent the material for the performance of a sacrifice with a view to obtain cattle. ' चित्रया यजेत पशुकामः ' would thus lay down a sacrifice as qualified by its material viz. a variegated female animal for the purpose of obtaining cattle.

Bhāskara tells us that this is not possible (न तावदत्र गुणविशिष्टयाग-विधानं संभवति). For, a विशिष्टविधि arises, only when both the sacrifice and the material are अप्राप्त or not laid down by any other sentence Compare ' यत्र तुभयमप्राप्तं तत्र विशिष्टं विधत्ते । यथा ' सोमेन यजेत ' इत्यत्र सोमयागयोर-प्राप्तत्वात् सोमविशिष्टयागविधानम् ' p. 9. *supra*). But in the present case another sentence viz. ' दधि मधु पयो... प्राजापत्यम् ' lays down the गुण or material viz. curds, honey etc., as also the deity प्रजापति, of the sacrifice in question (—अनेन गुणस्य विहितत्वात्). Therefore, ' चित्रया यजेत पशुकामः ' cannot be regarded as laying down a sacrifice qualified by the material (तद्विशिष्टयागविध्यनुपपत्तेः).

What is meant is this : The sentence ' चित्रया यजेत पशुकामः ' is neither a प्रधानविधि or an उत्पत्तिविधि, nor a गुणविधि. For, it contains neither of the two forms of sacrifice viz. material and deity (See ' यागस्य द्वे रूपे द्रव्यं देवता च ' p. 11 *supra*). It is only a फलवाक्य, or an अधिकारविधि. The sentence ' दधि मधु पयो... प्राजापत्यम् ' lays down a sacrifice in honour of Prajāpati, which is to be performed with such material as curds, honey etc. But that sentence does not tell us which fruit is aimed at by the performance of this sacrifice in honour of Prajāpati. That fruit is supplied by ' चित्रया यजेत पशुकामः '. Thus, as the sentence ' चित्रया यजेत पशुकामः ' lays down only the fruit for the sacrifice enjoined in ' दधि मधु... प्राजापत्यम् ', it cannot be regarded as a विशिष्टविधिः laying down a sacrifice as qualified by the material.

If, however, in spite of all this we were to consider that this sentence lays down a variegated material such as curds, honey etc. in addition to the fruit (यागस्य फलसबन्धे गुणसंबन्धे च विधीयमाने = फलं प्रति यागविधानं तं प्रति च गुणविधानम्), a split in the sentence would result. For, the one sentence would then be equal to two viz. ' यागेन पशुं भावयेत् (अत्र यागस्य फलसंबन्धो विहितः) ' and ' चित्रया दध्यादिचित्ररूपेण गुणेन यागं भावयेत् (अत्र यागस्य गुणसबन्धो विहितः). ' Therefore, in order to avoid वाक्यभेद, which constitutes a defect, we must take चित्रा as the proper name of the sacrifice (तस्माच्चित्राशब्दः कर्मनामधेयम्) The word चित्रा is then construed as being in grammatical equation with याग, which is extracted from the word यजेत (सामानाधिकरण्येन अन्वयात् = चित्राशब्दस्य यागशब्देन सह सामानाधि-करण्येन अन्वयात्) and, therefore, the split in the sentence does not arise.

प्रकृतेष्टेः ...वाच्यत्वोपपत्तिः—This sentence explains the significance of the name चित्रा given to the sacrifice in question. चित्र means various, of different kinds. As the sacrifice is performed with materials of different kinds such as curds, honey, milk etc, it is known as चित्रा or the Various.

We are now in a position to understand clearly the distinction between the sentences 'उद्भिदा यजेत पशुकामः' and 'चित्रया यजेत पशुकामः'. Both involve वाक्यभेद, if we try to understand the words उद्भिदा and चित्रया in the sense of a गुण. But while in the case of 'उद्भिदा यजेत पशुकामः' it is possible to get rid of this वाक्यभेद by another supposition viz. that the sentence is an instance of विशिष्टविधि, we cannot do so in case of 'चित्रया यजेत पशुकामः'. This is because in addition to being a फलवाक्य or अधिकारविधि, 'उद्भिदा यजेत पशुकामः' is an उत्पत्तिविधि or प्रधानविधि. For, no other sentence lays down the sacrifice to which 'उद्भिदा यजेत पशुकामः' can be regarded as a फलवाक्य. Further, as no other sentence enjoins the material for the sacrifice mentioned in 'उद्भिदा यजेत पशुकामः' it is possible to suppose that उद्भिदा might represent that material. But 'चित्रया यजेत पशुकामः' stands on a different footing. It is not an उत्पत्तिवाक्य, but only a फलवाक्य. Besides the material with which the sacrifice mentioned in 'चित्रया यजेत पशुकामः' is to be performed is laid down by the sentence 'दधि मधु पयो...प्राजापत्यम्'. So, it is not possible to assume that चित्रया might represent that material.

There is another point of distinction between the two sentences. The word उद्भिद् does not possess a well-known conventional sense. Hence it is easier to regard it as a proper name. But चित्रा has a definite conventional sense viz. variegatedness and femininity. Therefore, it becomes easier to hypothesize that it might specify the material such as an animal which would then have to be a female and variegated.

For these reasons 'उद्भिदा यजेत पशुकामः' illustrates 'मत्वर्थलक्षणाभयात् नामधेयत्वम्' and 'चित्रया यजेत पशुकामः' exemplifies 'वाक्यभेदभयात् नामधेयत्वम्'.

The sentence 'दधि मधु पयो... तत्संसृष्टं प्राजापत्यम्' requires some explanation. धानाः means grains in general, or barley (यवाः), or rice (तण्डुलाः). Here it means barley, because rice are separately mentioned. तत्संसृष्टं प्राजापत्यम् is explained in three ways: (1) तैर्द्रव्यैः संसृष्टं मिश्रितं प्राजापत्यं प्रजापतिर्देवताकं हविः. (2) तत्संसृष्टं प्रजापतिर्देवताकं कर्म. (3) तत्संसृष्टं तत्संसर्गः तत्समूह इत्यर्थः। नपुंसके भावे क्तः। प्राजापत्यं प्रजापतिर्देवताकः। The collection of those materials belongs to Prajāpati.

In this sentence seven things are enumerated as being sacred to Prajāpati. With reference to this Rāmeśvara remarks that in the Sruti only six are mentioned and that the word उदक has crept in the sentence through mistake. Rāmeśvara supports his remark by pointing out that Mādhava in his जैमिनीयन्यायमालाविस्तर speaks of only six things. Read 'अत्र दध्यादिवाक्ये दध्यादीनि षडेव द्रव्याणि श्रुतावाम्नातानि, उदकपदं

तु प्रमादादायातम्, श्रुतितात्पर्यज्ञैर्माधवाचार्यैस्तथैवास्य वाक्यस्य व्याख्यातत्वात्। तथा च तद्वचनं 'दध्यादीनि विचित्राणि प्रदेयद्रव्याणि षडाम्नातानि' इति।'

In this connection it has to be noted that the sentence as quoted by Mādhava in his न्यायमालाविस्तर drops 'पयः' and 'उदकम्' and adds 'आपः'. Thus, the number of things in the sentence becomes six. But in all other works where this sentence occurs the number of ingredients is seven. That the word उदक is not 'प्रमादादायातम्' is clear from जैमिनि's sūtra VIII. i.40 'मधूदके द्रवसामान्यात् पयोविकारः स्यात्,' where the word उदक actually occurs. Rāmeśvara's remark does not, therefore, seem to be correct. Mādhavā's quotation must also be pronounced as being inaccurate.

The sentence 'चित्रया यजेत पशुकामः' forms the topic of discussion under I. iv. 3 in the न्यायमालाविस्तर, where the पूर्वपक्षी argues that it prescribes 'variegatedness' and 'femininity' with reference to the animal whose slaughter in honour of Agni and Soma is laid down by 'अग्नीषोमीयं पशुमालभेत.' The conclusion is that through the fear of a split in the sentence the word चित्रा must be understood as a proper name.

Read 'चित्रया यजेत पशुकामः' इत्याम्नायते। तत्र चित्राशब्दो न उद्भिच्छब्दवत् यौगिकः, किन्तु रूढया चित्रत्वं स्त्रीत्वं चाभिधत्ते। ततो न पूर्वन्यायेन नामत्वम्। तथा सति 'अग्नीषोमीयं पशुमालभेत' इति विहितं पशुयागमात्रं 'यजेत' इत्यनेन पदेन अनूद्य तस्मिन् पशौ चित्रत्वस्त्रीत्वे गुणौ विधीयेते। इति **प्राप्ते**

ब्रूमः। चित्रत्वं स्त्रीत्वं चेति द्वावेतौ गुणौ, तयोर्द्वयोर्विधाने वाक्यं भिद्येत। तथा चोक्तम्— 'प्राप्ते कर्मणि नानेको विधातुं शक्यते गुणः। अप्राप्ते तु विधीयन्ते बहवोऽप्येकयत्नतः॥' इति। अथ वाक्यभेदपरिहाराय गुणद्वयविशिष्टं पशुद्रव्यरूपं कारकं विधीयते तदा गौरवं स्यात्। तस्माच्चित्राशब्दः पूर्ववद् यजिसामानाधिकरण्येन यागनामधेयं भवति। चित्रत्वं तु तस्य विलक्षणद्रव्यद्वारेणोपपद्यते। 'दधि, मधु, घृतम्, आपः, धानाः, तण्डुलाः, तत्संसृष्टं प्राजापत्यम्' इति दध्यादीनि विचित्राणि प्रदेयद्रव्याणि षडाम्नातानि। तदेतत् चित्रानामकस्य यागस्योत्पत्तिवाक्यम्। यागस्वरूपभूतयोर्दध्यादिद्रव्यप्रजापतिदेवतयोरत्रोपदिश्यमानत्वात्। उत्पन्नस्य तस्य यागस्य 'चित्रया यजेत पशुकामः' इत्येतत् फलवाक्यम्। एवं सति प्रकृतार्थो लभ्यते। अग्नीषोमीयपश्वनुवादेन गुणविधाने प्रकृतहान्यप्रकृतप्रक्रिये प्रसज्येयाताम्। लिङ्प्रत्ययस्यान्वानुवादकत्वाङ्गीकारान्मुख्यो विध्यर्थो बाध्यते। तस्माच्चित्रापदं नामधेयम्।' जैमिनीयन्यायमालाविस्तर pp. 42–43

The following quotation from the सारविवेचिनी distinguishes the province of 'मत्वर्थभयात् नामधेयत्वम्' from that of 'वाक्यभेदभयात् नामधेयत्वम्':—

'ननु गुणविशिष्टयागविधानाङ्गीकारेऽपि चित्रापदे मत्वर्थलक्षणाङ्गीकारापत्त्या ततो नामधेयत्वाङ्गीकरणस्यैव युक्तत्वात् पूर्वोक्तविषयत्वमेव अस्य आपतितमिति कथं ततः पृथगुक्तिरिति चेत्। न। ये शब्दाः क्वचिदप्यर्थविशेषे न रूढाः, उभयत्र तुल्यवद्वृत्तिकाः, त एव पूर्वोदाहरणविषयाः, न तु अर्थविशेषे रूढाश्चित्रादिशब्दाः, अत एव सोमादिशब्दानामर्थविशेषे रूढत्वादेव अगत्या मत्वर्थलक्षणामप्यङ्गीकृत्य विशिष्टविधिरेवाश्रितः, अतश्च युक्तैव पृथगुक्तिः।'

Section 58

This Section deals with the third reason for considering a word as a proper name viz. तत्प्रख्यशास्त्र. Bhāskara himself explains the expression तत्प्रख्यशास्त्र as तस्य गुणस्य प्रख्यापकस्य प्रापकस्य शास्त्रम् i. e. a scriptural passage which declares i. e. establishes that viz. a subsidiary matter. The general nature of this third reason is as follows: If the word under discussion be not a proper name, we shall have to suppose that it lays down some subsidiary sacrificial matter. But it may so happen that this subsidiary matter has already been enjoined by some other scriptural passage (तस्य गुणस्य प्रख्यापकस्य शास्त्रस्य विद्यमानत्वात्). Under these circumstances we cannot suppose that the same subsidiary matter is being laid down by the word in question. For, such supposition would involve the fault of पुनरुक्तता or superfluity. Consequently, we conclude that the word must be a proper name.

'अग्निहोत्रं जुहोति' is an example where the word अग्निहोत्र is to be understood as the proper name of the rite from तत्प्रख्यशास्त्र i. e. because there is a passage which lays down the subsidiary matter which, we shall have to suppose, the word अग्निहोत्र otherwise enjoins.

If the word अग्निहोत्र be not a proper name, it will have to lay down some subsidiary matter. 'अग्निहोत्रं जुहोति' would then be just an injunction of a subsidiary matter (गुणविधिर्गेत्र) What is the subsidiary matter that it will thus enjoin? The word अग्निहोत्रम् is capable of a two-fold interpretation viz. (1) अग्नौ होत्रमस्मिन् and (2) अग्नये होत्रमस्मिन्. According to the first interpretation अग्निहोत्रम् will enjoin the element fire as the support of the sacrifice i. e. it will tell us that the oblations are to be offered in the fire. The element fire is thus the subsidiary matter that it will lay down. But the sentence 'यदाहवनीये जुहोति' has already told us that the oblations in this sacrifice are to be offered in the fire known as आहवनीय. If 'अग्निहोत्रं जुहोति' were to enjoin the same subsidiary matter, the injunction would be purposeless (तद्विधानानर्थक्यम् = तस्य अग्नेः अग्निरूपगुणस्य वा विधानस्य आनर्थक्यम् विफलता). According to the second interpretation अग्निहोत्रम् will enjoin the subsidiary matter viz. the deity Fire (अग्निदेवतारूपगुणः), in whose honour the sacrifice is to be offered. But that deity has already accrued (प्राप्त) from another scriptural passage.

Thus both the subsidiary matters viz. the element fire and the deity Fire, which the word 'अग्निहोत्रम्' can possibly be supposed to lay down, having been declared or established by other scriptural passages, there is no other course left open to us but to regard the word अग्निहोत्र as the proper name of the rite.

Section 59

This Section discusses the question : 'Which is the other scriptural passage, that enjoins the deity Fire, who is supposed to have been laid down according to the second interpretation of the word अग्निहोत्र ?' In this matter there are two views. According to Śabara the sentence which lays down the deity Fire in this case is 'यदग्नये... जुहोति.' Pārthasārathimiśra and others on the other hand hold that the relevant sentence is 'अग्निर्ज्योति... स्वाहा.' Thus केचित् refers to Śabara and अपरे to Pārthasārathimiśra and others. Rāmeśvara points that the use of the word केचित् shows Bhāskara's disapprobation or dissatisfaction (अस्वरसः) of the view of Śabara. अपरे on the other hand indicates that Bhāskara likes the view of Pārthasārathimiśra and others. अपरे means न परे स्वीया इत्यर्थः. मन्त्रवर्णः means the letters or wording of the Mantra or formula. It just means मन्त्रः.

Read in this connection : 'अत्र 'अग्निर्ज्योतिः' इत्यादिमन्त्रवर्णप्राप्तमग्नि-मनूद्य तत्समुच्चितप्रजापतिमात्रविधाने लाघवम्, तदुभयसमुच्चितस्यैवात्र विधाने गौरवम्, इति न समुच्चितोभयविधानं 'यदग्नये च प्रजापतये च सायं जुहोति' इत्यत्र स्वीकर्तव्यमिति **अस्वरसबीजं 'केचित्' इत्यनेन सूचितम्।'** रामेश्वर

The reason why Bhāskara and others do not approve of the view that 'यदग्नये च प्रजापतये च सायं जुहोति' is the sentence which lays down Fire as the deity (देवतारूपो गुणः) for the evening sacrifice is this. The sentence contains two words in the dative viz. अग्नये and प्रजापतये. अग्नि and प्रजापति, therefore, appear to be the two deities enjoined for the evening sacrifice by this sentence. Now if we were to explain one sentence as laying down two deities, our explanation would involve the fault of गौरव or cumbrousness. If on the other hand we take that sentence as prescribing only one deity, we secure लाघव or simplicity or conciseness. It is a recognised principle of interpretation that the meaning which secures लाघव is to be preferred to that which involves गौरव. Therefore, what we do in the present case is as follows :

We find that the sentence 'अग्निर्ज्योतिर्ज्योतिरग्निः स्वाहा इति सायं जुहोति' has already laid down अग्नि as the deity for the evening sacrifice. Therefore, we suppose that 'यदग्नये च प्रजापतये च सायं जुहोति' really enjoins प्रजापति as the deity and that it refers to Agni as having been already laid down by some other sentence. Thus, 'यदग्नये...जुहोति' contains a विधि or injunction about प्रजापति and only an अनुवाद or subsequent or further allusion about अग्नि. As 'यदग्नये...जुहोति' is not in this manner regarded as enjoining the deity Agni primarily, it cannot be considered as the शास्त्रान्तर necessary for laying down the देवतारूप गुण for अग्निहोत्र. Therefore, the proper शास्त्रान्तर in the present case is ' अग्निर्ज्योतिर्ज्योतिरग्निः स्वाहा. '

ननु अग्नेर्मान्त्रवर्णिकत्वे...इति चेत् । न । This passage contains an objection against the view that the Mantra ' अग्निर्ज्योति...स्वाहा ' lays down Agni as the deity for the evening sacrifice. The deity for a sacrifice, an oblation or a Mantra is enjoined (देवताया विधिः) in three ways viz. by means of a तद्धित formation, a dative and the wording of a formula (मन्त्रवर्णः). And it has been settled that out of these three each subsequent is less powerful than its predecessor. Thus, मन्त्रवर्ण is less powerful than चतुर्थी and चतुर्थी less powerful than तद्धित.

तद्धित is a technical term in Pāṇini's grammar and means a derivative from a noun. Pāṇini's sūtra ' सा अस्य देवता ' 4.2.24 (इन्द्रो देवता अस्येति ऐन्द्रं हविः । पाशुपतम् । बार्हस्पत्यम् । **त्यज्यमानद्रव्ये उद्देश्यविशेषो देवता, मन्त्रस्तुत्या च** । ऐन्द्रो मन्त्रः । सि. कौ.) lays down that a derivative can be formed from names of deities in the sense of ' having that as the deity ' Thus, आग्नेय, ऐन्द्र, पाशुपत etc. are all तद्धित formations, meaning ' having Agni, Indra, Paśupati as deity.' As a तद्धित derivative is formed in the special sense of ' सा अस्य देवता,' it enjoins the deity directly and as such prevails against the two other ways of laying down the deity viz. चतुर्थी and मन्त्रवर्ण.

Pāṇini lays down the dative in the sense of संप्रदान according to ' चतुर्थी संप्रदाने ' 2. 3. 13. He defines संप्रदान as ' कर्मणा यमभिप्रैति स संप्रदानम् ' 1. 4. 32 (दानस्य कर्मणा यमभिप्रैति स संप्रदानसंज्ञः स्यात् । सि. कौ.). The deity or person, whom we have in view when we make an offering or gift, is known as संप्रदान and is put in the dative case. Though the dative thus shows for whom the offering or gift is intended, it does not possess the power of directly conveying the fact that the deity or person put in the dative case is technically the deity of that particular offering or gift. This fact becomes known to us when we reflect that the deity for whom an offering is intended must naturally be the deity of that offering. Thus, the dative conveys the sense of ' सा अस्य देवता ' only indirectly. As a तद्धित does this directly, it is more powerful than the dative.

Note " सास्य देवता ' इति तद्धितप्रत्ययस्य देवतात्वे स्मरणवत् **चतुर्थी न देवतात्वे स्मर्यते.** ' संप्रदाने चतुर्थी ' इति संप्रदानमात्रे तस्याः स्मरणात् ' रामेश्वर

मन्त्रवर्ण means just a passage from the Veda, where a certain deity is mentioned. This would at best indicate the presence of that deity at the sacrifice in question. But there is nothing here to show either directly or indirectly, that that deity is the deity of the sacrifice. We have to make this supposition by simple inference. There fore, मन्त्रवर्ण from which the sense 'सा अस्य देवता' is only inferred is less powerful than चतुर्थी, which conveys this sense at least indirectly.

All this has been expressed in the couplet 'ताद्धितेन चतुर्थ्या वा' etc, which comes from Kumārilabhaṭṭa's Tantravārtika 2. 2. 23, where it reads slightly differently as 'ताद्धितेन चतुर्थ्या वा मन्त्रवर्णेन चेष्यते । देवतासंगतिस्तत्र दुर्बलं च परं परम् ॥'

The objector now applies these general principles to the matter in hand. Here we have two passages viz. 'यदग्नये च प्रजापतये च सायं जुहोति' and 'अग्निर्ज्योतिर्ज्योतिरग्निः स्वाहा', both purporting to give the deity for the अग्निहोत्र. Of these 'अग्निर्ज्योति......स्वाहा' falls under the category 'मन्त्रवर्ण' and 'यदग्नये......जुहोति' under 'चतुर्थी.' We have seen before that चतुर्थी is stronger than मन्त्रवर्ण. The objector, therefore, points out that the deity Prajāpati, who has been enjoined by the dative प्रजापतये in 'यदग्नये च **प्रजापतये** च सायं जुहोति' is more powerful than the deity Agni, who is laid down by the formula (मन्त्रवर्णेन विहितः मान्त्रवर्णिकः) 'अग्निर्ज्योति...स्वाहा'. Prajāpati thus sets aside or annuls (बाधः) Agni. Therefore, the passage 'अग्निर्ज्योति...स्वाहा' cannot be said to enjoin Agni, as Agni mentioned therein is annulled (बाधित) by Prajāpati enjoined by 'प्रजापतये च सायं जुहोति'. Consequently, 'अग्निर्ज्योति...स्वाहा' cannot be the शास्त्रान्तर laying down the deity for the अग्निहोत्र.

The deity for the Agnihotra, according to the objector, would thus be Prajāpati. The name Agnihotra would then have to be made applicable to this rite somehow by interpreting Agni in the sense of an active or agile deity. It should be remembered here that the objector is for the present conveniently ignoring the fact that in the sentence, which according to him, lays down Prajāpati as the deity for Agnihotra, annulling Agni who is supposed to have been enjoined by 'अग्निर्ज्योति...स्वाहा,' the word अग्नये occurs along with the word प्रजापतये.

The answer to the objection raised by the objector is as follows: The sentence 'यदग्नये च...जुहोति' does not lay down Prajāpati alone as the deity for the Agnihotra. What it does is to refer to Agni, who has been established as the deity for this sacrifice by the formula 'अग्निर्ज्योति...स्वाहा' (मन्त्रवर्णप्राप्त), by way of further or subsequent allusion (अनूद्य), and to enjoin Prajāpati in addition to this thus subsequently alluded Agni. Thus, there is no annulment (बाधः) of Agni by Prajāpati, for it is not Prajāpati alone who has been laid down as the deity for the Agnihotra in this passage.

What is meant is this: The idea of Prajāpati annulling Agni as the deity of the Agnihotra is apparently based on the supposition that the Agnihotra has only one deity. As a matter of fact it has two viz. Agni and Prajāpati. Of these Agni has been laid down by the sentence 'अग्निर्ज्योति...स्वाहा' and Prajāpati by 'यदग्नये च प्रजापतये च सायं जुहोति.' This latter sentence, besides enjoining Prajāpati as the deity for the Agnihotra, makes a further reference to Agni as the second deity for the same rite.

न चात्र समुच्चितोभयविधान...लाघवात्—If Agni and Prajāpati are both the deities of the Agnihotra, why should the sentence 'यदग्नये...जुहोति' not be regarded as laying them down conjointly? Why should we consider that 'यदग्नये... जुहोति' contains the विधान of Prajāpati and only the अनुवाद of Agni? Why should it not contain the विधान of both Agni and Prajāpati? The answer to a question of this kind is that there is greater simplicity or ease (लाघवम्) in holding that 'यदग्नये... जुहोति' enjoins Prajāpati as combined (समुच्चित) with Agni, who has been established by some other passage (अन्यतः प्राप्त), than in supposing that it enjoins both of them conjointly.

The ideas underlying this argument about लाघव-गौरव are really two. First, it is better to assign to one sentence only one task. If the sentence 'यदग्नये...जुहोति' were to lay down two deities, it would be doing the work of two. This would overburden the sentence and would lead to गौरव. Secondly, if both Agni and Prajāpati be supposed to have been laid down by 'यदग्नये जुहोति', the sentence 'अग्निर्ज्योति...स्वाहा' will be superfluous and hence निरर्थक and the Mīmāṁsaka must not allow any Vedic sentence to become purposeless. That is why he regards 'अग्निर्ज्योति...स्वाहा' as enjoining Agni and 'अग्निर्ज्योति... जुहोति' as laying down Prajāpati, but referring to Agni only by way of अनुवाद. Thus, both the sentences serve a purpose.

एवं प्रयाजादिषु... कर्मनामधेयम्— This paragraph supplies another example of 'तत्प्रख्यशास्त्रात् नामधेयत्वम्'. We have seen before (pp. 95-96 above) that the sacrifices, called Prayājas, are laid down by the sentence 'प्रयाजाः कर्तव्याः' and that they are mentioned in 'समिधो यजति, तनूनपातं यजति, इडो यजति, बर्हिर्यजति, स्वाहाकारं यजति.' The question now is whether the words समिधः, तनूनपातम्, इडः etc. represent the deities of the sacrifices or the proper names thereof. It is then pointed out that the deities of the Prayājas are established (प्राप्त) by the scriptural passage 'समिधः समिधो अग्ने etc'. This passage, therefore, is the तत्प्रख्यशास्त्र with reference to the Prayājas. Consequently, the words समिधः, तनूनपातम्,

इड: etc., occurring in 'समिधो यजति etc', are the proper names of those rites (कर्मनामधेयत्वम्).

It will be noticed that in view of the above decision the correct translation of the sentence 'समिधो यजति' is 'He performs the Samids' and not 'He sacrifices to the fire-sticks' (see p. 96 above).

For the subject-matter of this Section read ''अग्निहोत्रं जुहोति' 'आघारमाघारयति' इत्यत्र अग्निहोत्रशब्दस्य कर्मनामत्वे द्रव्यदेवतयोरभावाद् यागस्य स्वरूपमेव न सिध्येत् । तस्मादग्निदेवतारूपो गुणोऽनेन दर्विहोमे विधीयते । आघारशब्दश्च 'घृ क्षरणदीप्त्योः' इत्यस्माद् धातोरुत्पन्नः क्षरद् घृतमाचष्टे । तस्मिंश्च घृते द्वितीयाविभक्त्या संस्कार्यत्वं प्रतीयते । तच्च संस्कृतं घृतमुपांशुयागे द्रव्यं भवति । तस्माद् अग्निहोत्राघारशब्दौ गुणसंस्कारयोर्विधायकौ इति **प्राप्ते**—

ब्रूमः । 'अग्निर्ज्योतिर्ज्योतिरग्निः स्वाहेति सायं जुहोति, सूर्यो ज्योतिर्ज्योतिः सूर्यः स्वाहेति प्रातः' इति विहितेन मन्त्रेण प्राप्तत्वात् देवता न विधेया । **ततोऽग्निसूर्यदेवताकस्य सायंप्रातःकालयोर्नियमेन अनुष्ठेयस्य कर्मणः 'अग्निहोत्रम्' इति यौगिकं नामधेयम् । योगश्च बहुव्रीहिणा दर्शितः** । 'चतुर्गृहीतं वा एतदभूत्तस्य आघारमाघार्य' इत्यनेनैव आज्यद्रव्यस्य प्राप्ततया क्षरद्घृतसंस्कारस्य अविधेयत्वादाधारशब्दोऽपि यौगिकं कर्मनामधेयम् । यस्मिन् कर्मणि नैर्ऋतीं दिशमारभ्य ऐशानीं दिशमवधिं कृत्वा संतत्या घृतं क्षार्यते तस्य कर्मण एतन्नाम ।

ननु नामधेयत्वे सति 'उद्भिदा यजेत' 'ज्योतिष्टोमेन यजेत' इत्यादौ इव धात्वर्थेन करणेन सामानाधिकरण्याय 'अग्निहोत्रेण जुहोति' 'आघारेण आघारयति' इति तृतीयया भवितव्यम् । नैष दोषः । अनुष्ठानादूर्ध्वं धात्वर्थस्य सिद्धत्वाकारेण करणत्वेऽपि ततः पूर्वं साध्यत्वाकारं वक्तुम 'अग्निहोत्रम्' 'आघारम्' इति द्वितीयाया युक्तत्वात् । न चात्र द्वितीयानुसारेण 'व्रीहीन् प्रोक्षति' इत्यादाविव संस्कारः शङ्कनीयः । व्रीहिशब्दवदग्निहोत्राघारशब्दयोः प्रसिद्धद्रव्यवाचकत्वाभावेन क्रियावाचित्वाभ्युपगमात् । तस्माद् अग्निहोत्राघारशब्दौ दर्विहोमोपांशुयाजयोर्गुणसंस्कारविधायिनौ न भवतः, किंतु कर्मान्तरयोर्नामनी ।' जैमिनीयन्यायमालाविस्तर on 'तत्प्रख्यं चान्यशास्त्रम्' I. iv. 4, pp. 45-46.

'दशपूर्णमासयोः प्रयाजपञ्चकमाम्नातम् 'समिधो यजति' इत्यादिना । तत्र यथा 'विष्णुं यजति' 'वरुणं यजति' इत्यादौ द्वितीयानिर्दिष्टा विष्ण्वादयो देवताः, तथा समिदादीनां देवतात्वम् । ततो यागैर्देवताः संस्क्रियन्ते, इति दृष्टार्थत्वलाभः । इति **चेत्**

मैवम् । सर्वत्र चतुर्थ्या तद्धितेन वा देवता निर्दिश्यन्ते । तद्यथा । 'यदग्नये सायं जुहुयात्' 'आग्नेयोऽष्टाकपालः' इति । न चात्र समिदादिषु चतुर्थीतद्धितौ विद्येते । तादर्थ्यप्रतीतौ देवता भवति । न च द्वितीयया तादर्थ्यं प्रतीयते, किन्तु ईप्सिततमत्वम् । तच्च कर्मनामत्वे उपपद्यते । 'अग्निहोत्रं जुहोति' इत्यादौ तद्दर्शनात् । यथा 'पाकं पचति' इति उक्ते पाकक्रियायाः कर्तव्यता प्रतीयते । तथा 'समिधो यजति' इति उक्ते समिद्यागः कर्तव्य इति अर्थो भवति । 'विष्णुं यजति' इत्यादौ तादर्थ्यमुपचर्यते । प्रयाजमन्त्रेषु 'समिधो अग्न आज्यस्य व्यन्तु' इत्यादिषु समिदादिशब्दैर्बहुवचनैकवचनान्तैर्देवता निर्दिष्टाः । तदेव निमित्तीकृत्य तादृशैरेव शब्दैरिह यागा अभिधीयन्ते 'समिधो यजति, तनूनपातं यजति, इडो यजति, बर्हिर्यजति, स्वाहाकारं यजति' इति । तस्मान्नात्र देवतासंस्कारविधिः । किन्तु केवला यागा विधीयन्ते । तेषां च श्रुत्यादिभिः कार्यविशेषानवगमात् प्रकरणेन आरादुपकारकत्वम् । पञ्चमप्रयाजस्य तु वक्ष्यमाणाज्यभागादिदेवतासंस्कारत्वं दशमे अभिधास्यते ।' जैमिनीयन्यायमालाविस्तर on IX. ii. 59-60, p. 454.

Section 60

This Section deals with the last reason for understanding a word to be a name viz. तद्व्यपदेश. An example of तद्व्यपदेशात् नामधेयत्वम् is ' श्येनेन अभिचरन् यजेत. ' Here on account of तद्व्यपदेश we understand the the word श्येनेन to be the name of the sacrifice.

तद्व्यपदेशात् is explained in two ways: (i) तेन श्येनेन उपमानभूतेन व्यपदेशात् प्रस्तुतकर्मणो निर्देशात्, प्रस्तुतं कर्म श्येनेन उपमीयते इत्यतः. व्यपदेशः means designation. तद्व्यपदेशात् means on account of the designation [of the rite] with it i. e. on account of the fact that the rite is designated as a falcon i. e. is compared with a falcon. This explanation follows Śabara, who paraphrases the sūtra ' तद्व्यपदेशं च ' जै. I. iv. 5 by ' तेन श्येनादिना प्रसिद्धेन यस्य व्यपदेशः तच्च कर्मनामधेयम्'. (ii) विशब्दो भिन्नार्थकः । अपदेशः निर्देशः कथनमिति यावत् । तस्मात् श्येनादेः प्रस्तुतकर्मणो व्यपदेशात् भिन्नत्वेन कथनात्. On account of the rite having been designated as different from that i. e. from such things as a falcon. This explanation is in accordance with Somanātha's Mayūkhamālikā on Pārthasārathimiśra's Śāstradīpikā on I. iv. 5, where he says ' तच्छब्देन यस्मिन् गुणोपदेश इति प्रकृतो गुणो निर्दिश्यते । विशब्दश्च भिन्नार्थकः । ततश्च तस्माद् विधेयत्वाभिमताद् गुणाद् व्यपदेशः भेदेन निर्देशः '.

Bhāskara paraphrases तद्व्यपदेशात् by ' तेन व्यपदेशात् उपमानात् '. This shows he follows the first explanation. Note that उपमान here means ' comparison ' and not ' the standard of comparison'. तदन्यथानुपपत्ते means उपमानान्यथानुपपत्तेः on account of the impossibility or impropriety of otherwise having it i.e. of otherwise having the comparison i.e. because it would not be possible to have the comparison if we were to suppose that श्येनेन represented the sacrificial material viz. a falcon.

The question now is this: What does the word ' श्येनेन ' in the sentence ' श्येनेन अभिचरन् यजेत ' mean ? ' श्येनेन यजेत ' resembles ' दध्ना जुहोति ' and it looks as if श्येनेन represents, even like दध्ना, the material viz. a falcon, with which the sacrifice is to be performed. Against this it is pointed out that there is an arthavāda or a laudatory passage viz. ' यथा वै श्येनो......आदत्ते ', wherein what has been laid down in ' श्येनेन अभिचरन् यजेत ' is compared with a falcon. A falcon cannot be compared with itself. For, the standard of comparison (उपमानम्) and the object of comparison (उपमेयम्) must be different (उपमानोपमेयभावस्य भिन्ननिष्ठत्वात्). What the arthavāda really does is to praise some other thing or entity (अर्थान्तरम्) by comparing it with a falcon (श्येनोपमानेन). Therefore, we cannot suppose that ' श्येनेन अभिचरन् यजेत ' lays down the material viz. a falcon. But, if we were to suppose that this sentence enjoins a sacrifice called Śyena, then it would be possible for the arthavāda to praise it by comparing it with a falcon. Therefore, we decide that on account of तद्व्यपदेश, the word श्येन in 'श्येनेन अभिचरन् यजेत' is a proper name of the rite enjoined by that sentence.

अभिचरन् practising magic with a view to bring about a desired, object such as the death of an enemy. अभिपूर्वकचरधातोर्वैरिमरणानुकूलो व्यापारोऽर्थः.—The word अयम् in 'एवमयं द्विषन्तं भ्रातृव्यं निपत्याद्त्ते' apparently means अयं श्येनसंज्ञको यागः, as is clear from the sentence 'यदा तु श्येनसंज्ञके यागो विधीयते'. But from the trend of the sentence it seems more natural that अयम् should mean the sacrificer (अयमाभिचारकर्ता यजमानः) rather than the sacrifice. For, the sentence compares अयम् with a falcon and declares that 'अयम्' swoops down like a falcon and seizes the enemy. It is of course more natural that this action should belong to an animate entity, such as the sacrificer rather than to an inanimate one like the sacrifice.—भ्रातृव्यः (भ्रातुः पुत्रः) really means a brother's son, a nephew. In Hindu society with its joint family system it often happens that nephews not only cease to have any regard for their uncle but also become actually enemical towards him, especially when the question of the division of ancestral property arises. That is why a word which signifies a near relative comes to mean an enemy. Note 'भ्रातृव्यो भ्रातृजद्विषौ' अमरः.

This illustration of 'तद्व्यपदेशात् नामधेयत्वम्' is open to the following criticism. We are told that 'श्येनेन' in 'श्येनेन अभिचरन् यजेत' cannot be taken as representing the sacrificial material viz. a falcon, because of the arthavāda. In this arthavāda something, which has been laid down by 'श्येनेन......यजेत', has been compared with a falcon. And if 'श्येनेन' were to mean a falcon, the comparison in the arthavāda would not be possible, as a falcon could not be compared with itself. For, the general rule is that the upamāna and the upameya should be different.

This argument appears to us to have been based upon a misunderstanding about the exact meaning of both the उत्पत्तिवाक्य and the अर्थवाद. What the उत्पत्तिवाक्य lays down is a certain sacrifice. Whether this sacrifice is श्येनसंज्ञकः or श्येनद्रव्यकः is the point at issue. But there is no doubt about the fact that the विधेय in 'श्येनेन अभिचरन् यजेत' is a याग.

Now we fail to understand why this विधेय viz. the sacrifice cannot be compared with a falcon, even though it is श्येनद्रव्यक. Thus, श्येनद्रव्यक

याग is the उपमेय, श्येन is the उपमान and निपत्य आदान is the common property. Here the उपमान and the उपमेय are quite different. Further, such a comparison would appear to be quite appropriate. Just as a falcon swoops down on its prey and seizes it, even so the sacrifice, wherein a falcon is offered, swoops down on the enemy of the sacrificer and captures him. When a falcon is offered in the sacrifice, that becomes the greater reason why the sacrifice should be compared with it. For, the sacrifice may be regarded as developing the characteristics of its material.

Secondly, it is not correct to take अयम् in the sense of यागः. अयम् in that arthavāda sentence really stands for the sacrificer, as is clear from the common property निपत्य आदान, which belongs to animate beings. With this interpretation there would not be the slightest difficulty for the comparison. अयं यजमानः is the उपमेय, श्येनः the उपमान and निपत्य आदान the common property. Here the उपमान and उपमेय are quite different.

Then there is another consideration. The whole foundation of तद्व्यपदेशात् नामधेयत्वम् is the supposition that the उपमान and the उपमेय must be different. But students of rhetoric know that in the figure, called अनन्वय and instanced in 'गगनं गगनाकारं सागरः सागरोपमः । रामरावणयोर्युद्धं रामरावणयोरिव,' one and the same thing forms the उपमान and the उपमेय. So even if we suppose that a falcon is laid down as the sacrificial material by the sentence 'श्येनेन अभिचरन् यजेत' and that it is referred to by अयम् in the arthavāda, there should be no difficulty in the interpretation of the sentence 'यथा वै श्येनो...आदत्ते'. For, what we should do is to take this arthavāda as embodying an अनन्वय.

This point struck Somanātha, who rules out the possibility of understanding an अनन्वय in this arthavāda as follows: An अनन्वय requires the sameness of property. Here मत्स्याद्यादान is the property in the उपमान sentence and भ्रातृव्यादान in the उपमेय. So we cannot have अनन्वय. Note 'न च अत्र अनन्वयालङ्कारः शङ्क्यः । अनन्वये हि धर्मैक्यमावश्यकम् । इह तु मत्स्याद्यादानभ्रातृव्यादानरूपधर्मभेदेन अनन्वयाप्रसक्तेः' । मयूखमालिका on जै. I. iv. 5. Also see तन्त्रवार्तिक on the same sūtra.

It should be noted that Somanātha's reply is not satisfactory. The common property in the arthavāda must be taken to be निपत्यादान and it is certainly one. If there be धर्मभेद, such as Somanātha supposes, between the उपमान and the उपमेय sentences, even an ordinary उपमा would not be possible. For, an उपमा also requires धर्मैक्य. In 'चन्द्र इव आल्हादकं मुखम्' आल्हादकत्व represents the धर्मैक्य, which makes the comparison possible.

Regarding this topic of तद्व्यपदेशात् नामधेयत्वम् the following should be read :

' ' श्येनेन अभिचरन् यजेत ' इत्यत्र तद्व्यपदेशात् श्येनपदं यागनामधेयं न तु यागाङ्गत्वेन श्येनपक्षिरूपगुणविधिः । ' यथा वै श्येनो निपत्यादत्ते, एवमयं द्विषन्तं भ्रातृव्यं निपत्यादत्ते यमभिचरति श्येनेन' इत्युपमानोपमेयव्यपदेशानुपपत्तिप्रसङ्गात् । 'श्येनपक्षी यथा पक्ष्यन्तरं निपत्यादत्ते,एवमयमपि श्येन-नामकः कर्मविशेषो भ्रातृव्यं शत्रुं निपत्यादत्ते ' इति व्यपदेशः कर्मनामत्वपक्ष एव युज्यते । यागाङ्ग-तया श्येनपक्षिविधौ तु स्वस्य स्वेनैवोपमानोपमेयभावः स्यात् । स चायुक्तः । तस्माच्छ्येनेन तुल्यता-व्यपदेशाच्छ्येनपदं कर्मनामधेयम् । ततश्च ' अभिचरन् शत्रुवधकामः श्येननामकेन यागेन अभिचारं भावयेत् ' इति वाक्यार्थः । ' मीमांसापरिभाषा

' ' श्येनेनाभिचरन् यजेत ' इत्यत्र कर्मनामत्वे द्रव्यदेवतयोरभावाद् यागस्वरूपमपि न सिद्ध्येत् । ततः सोमयागे नित्यं सोमद्रव्यं बाधित्वा सोमस्य स्थाने पक्षिद्रव्यरूपो गुणः काम्यो विधीयते । तथा सति श्येनशब्दस्य पक्षिणि लोकसिद्धा रूढिरनुगृह्यते । न च गुणविधित्वे चित्रायामिव वाक्यभङ्ग आपादयितुं शक्यः । चित्रत्वस्त्रीत्ववद् गुणद्वयाभावादिति प्राप्ते--

ब्रूमः । ' यथा वै श्येनो निपत्यादत्ते, एवमयं द्विषन्तं भ्रातृव्यं निपत्यादत्ते यमभिचरति श्येनेन ' इति वाक्येन उक्त उपमानोपमेयभावः पक्षिण्येकस्मिन् न युज्यते । तस्मात् पक्षिण उपमानस्य गुण उपमेये कर्मणि अस्ति इति श्येनशब्दस्य अभिचारकर्मनामधेयत्वम् ।

' संदंशेनाभिचरन् यजेत ' ' गवा अभिचर्यमाणो यजेत ' इत्यत्र संदंशगोशब्दयोर्नामत्वं श्येनशब्दवद् द्रष्टव्यम् । ' यथा संदंशेन दुरादानमादत्ते' 'यथा गावो गोपायन्ति' इति वाक्यशेषाभ्यामु-पमानोपमेयभावाभिधानात् । ' जैमिनीयन्यायमालाविस्तर on जै. सू. I. iv. 5, pp. 46–47.

Section 61

The four reasons for understanding a word to be a name that were mentioned in Section 55 above have been explained so far. In this Section the author deals with what by some is regarded as a fifth reason for नामधेयत्व and shows that it is nothing but तत्प्रख्यशास्त्र.

The fifth reason is उत्पत्तिशिष्टगुणबलीयस्त्व, where उत्पत्तिः = उत्पत्तिविधिवाक्यम् the sentence that lays down a certain rite for the first time. शिष्ट = विहित enjoined and गुणः = देवता. Thus, उत्पत्तिशिष्टगुणबलीयस्त्वम् = उत्पत्ति-विधिवाक्यविहितदेवताबलीयस्त्वम् the greater power of the subsidiaries viz. the deities enjoined in the injunction of origination. The बलीयस्त्व consists in the various deities being directly and specifically mentioned in the injunction of origination.

' वैश्वदेवेन यजेत ' is an example where, according to these people the word वैश्वदेव is a name of the rite on account of उत्पत्तिशिष्टगुणबलीयस्त्वम्.

The sacrifice called चातुर्मास्य has four parts viz. वैश्वदेवः, वरुणप्रघासः, साकमेधः and शुनासीरीयः. In the first of these parts eight sacrifices are enjoined by 'आग्नेयमष्टाकपालं निर्वपति, सौम्यं चरुम्, सावित्रं द्वादशकपालम्, सारस्वतं चरुम्, पौष्णं चरुम्, मारुतं सप्तकपालम्, वैश्वदेवीमामिक्षाम्, द्यावापृथिव्यमेककपालम्'. This sentence thus forms the उत्पत्तिविधि for these eight oblations.

Near about the place where these eight sacrifices are enjoined occurs the sentence 'वैश्वदेवेन यजेत'. The question now is: What does the word 'वैश्वदेवेन' in the sentence 'वैश्वदेवेन यजेत' exactly mean? Does it represent a subsidiary matter (गुणः) viz. the deities for the previously mentioned eight sacrifices, or is it merely a proper name for the entire sacrifice which is made of these eight sub-sacrifices?

The pūrvapakṣa-view is that in the sentence 'वैश्वदेवेन यजेत' the previously mentioned eight sacrifices are subsequently referred to (अनुवादः) by the word 'यजेत' and that विश्वे देवाः or All-gods, are laid down by the word 'वैश्वदेवेन' as the deities for these eight sacrifices. Thus, as this sentence 'वैश्वदेवेन यजेत' enjoins a subsidiary matter (गुणः) viz. the deities, it becomes a गुणविधि.

The pūrvapakṣin anticipates two objections to this view of his viz. (1) In the expression 'वैश्वदेवीमामिक्षाम्' All-gods are already enjoined as the deities in honour of whom आमिक्षा (a mixture of boiled milk and curds—'तप्ते पयसि दधि आनयति, सा वैश्वदेवी आमिक्षा भवति') is to be offered. How then can you say that 'वैश्वदेवेन यजेत' enjoins All-gods as the deities of these *eight* sacrifices? For, in the case of one of them viz. the āmikṣā-sacrifice the All-gods have already been established (प्राप्त) as deities by the previous sentence. (2) In the case of all these eight sacrifices different deities such as Agni, Soma and Savitṛ have already been enjoined by words like आग्नेयम्, सौम्यम् and सावित्रम्. How then can you say that 'वैश्वदेवेन यजेत' lays down All-gods as the deities for all these eight sacrifices?

The pūrvapakṣin's reply to these objections is as follows: (1) If All-gods have been already laid down as the deities of the āmikṣā-sacrifice, 'वैश्वदेवेन यजेत' should be regarded as enjoining them in the case of the remaining seven only. (2) If different deities have already been established for all the eight sacrifices, the All-gods should be regarded as optional deities. For, when two deities become established (प्राप्त) for the same rite, there is no other alternative except to admit option (विकल्पः) between them.

The pūrvapakṣin further points out that if वैश्वदेवेन be regarded as representing a proper name, the injunction in 'वैश्वदेवेन यजेत' will be purposeless. For, the sentence will then not have any reference in it to either of the two forms of the sacrifice viz. the material and the deity and the sacrifice itself will thus be impossible.

The view of the pūrvapakṣin thus boils down to this that the sentence 'वैश्वदेवेन यजेत' is a गुणविधि and that it enjoins All-gods as the optional deties for seven of the previously mentioned eight sacrifices.

Against this the siddhāntin holds that the sentence 'वैश्वदेवेन यजेत' is an example of नामधेय. In it the word यजेत contains a subsequent allusion (अनुवादः) to the previously mentioned eight sacrifices and the word वैश्वदेवेन represents the proper name of the group constituted by them.

The opposition here is really between उत्पत्तिशिष्टगुण or उत्पत्तिवाक्य-विहितदेवता and उत्पन्नशिष्टगुण or उत्पन्नकर्मविषयक-गुणविधिवाक्यविहितदेवता. उत्पत्ति here is represented by 'आग्नेयमष्टाकपाल... एककपालम्', because this sentence enjoins the eight sacrifices for the first time. उत्पन्न means the sentence 'वैश्वदेवेन यजेत', because this sentence is supposed to supply deities to the eight rites which have already come into existence (उत्पन्न = प्राप्त) and of which it contains only an anuvāda in the word यजेत. उत्पत्तिशिष्टगुणः = अग्न्यादयो देवताः and उत्पन्नशिष्टगुणः = विश्वे देवाः. The question now is which deities are to be preferred, Agni and others, who are उत्पत्तिशिष्ट, or All-gods, who are उत्पन्नशिष्ट. The answer is as उत्पत्तिशिष्टगुण is more powerful than उत्पन्नशिष्टगुण, Agni and others must be regarded as the deities of these eight sacrifices.

The reasons why उत्पत्तिशिष्टगुण is more powerful than उत्पन्नशिष्टगुण are these: (1) In the उत्पत्तिवाक्य Agni and others are directly enjoined (प्रत्यक्षश्रुत), by means of तद्धित formations such as आग्नेय, as the deities of अष्टाकपाल and others. The deities for these eight sacrifices being thus प्राप्त, the sentence is निराकाङ्क्ष or complete as regards the deities. Therefore, All-gods, who are mentioned in the उत्पन्नवाक्य or अनुवाद-वाक्य, have really no scope in these eight sacrifices, the places of deities therein having already been occupied by Agni and others (गुणान्तरावरुद्ध). (2) In the उत्पत्तिवाक्य both the forms of the sacrifice viz. the deity and the material, such as अग्नि and अष्टाकपाल, and सोम and चरु, are mentioned. In the उत्पन्नवाक्य on the other hand, though वैश्वदेव is also a तद्धित formation and as such would point to विश्वे देवाः as the deities, there is no mention of the sacrificial material with which All-gods are to be connected. What we, therefore, have to do is to construe the sentence 'वैश्वदेवेन यजेत' with 'आग्नेय-मष्टाकपालम् ...एककपालम्' and then establish the connection of All-gods with the oblations mentioned therein. Thus, while अग्न्यादयो देवताः are श्रुतिप्राप्त, विश्वे देवाः are प्रकरणप्राप्त. And as श्रुति is more powerful than प्रकरण, Agni and others must be regarded as the deities of अष्टाकपाल and others.

Thus it is held that on account of उत्पत्तिशिष्टगुणबलीयस्त्व the word वैश्वदेवेन in 'वैश्वदेवेन यजेत' is the proper name of the sacrifice.

12

From this it follows that the reply given by the pūrvapakṣin to the two anticipated objections can be easily set aside. First, as अग्न्यादयो देवताः are more powerful than विश्वे देवाः, विश्वे देवाः simply do not accrue (अप्राप्त) as the deities of अष्टाकपाल and others. Hence the question of understanding विश्वे देवाः, as the deities of only seven out of the eight previously mentioned sacrifices does not arise at all. Secondly, as regards the assertion that option should be understood between अग्न्यादयो देवताः and विश्वे देवाः, it is to be noted that this is impossible. Option can exist between things which are equally powerful Here अग्न्यादयो देवताः are more powerful than विश्वे देवाः. No option between them is, therefore, possible, for अग्न्यादयो देवताः prevail against विश्वे देवाः.

As regards the pūrvapakṣin's contention that if वैश्वदेवेन be regarded as a name, the sentence 'वैश्वदेवेन यजेत' will be purposeless, it is pointed out that this will not be the case. What the sentence does is to establish that वैश्वदेव is the name of the group of the eight sacrifices enjoined in the first sentence. And this nomenclature has a purpose. We have sentences like 'प्राचीनप्रवणे वैश्वदेवेन यजेत' and 'वसन्ते वैश्वदेवेन यजेत'. Here by the word वैश्वदेवेन we understand the group o these eight sacrifices. This we are enabled to do, because we have decided that वैश्वदेवेन represents a proper name in the sentence 'वैश्वदेवेन यजेत.'

So far we have seen the view of those who believe that उत्पत्तिशिष्टगुणबलीयस्त्व is a fifth reason for understanding a word as a name. But Bhāskara does not agree with this view. His opinion is that what is regarded as a case of 'उत्पत्तिशिष्टगुणबलीयस्त्वात् नामधेयत्वम्' is covered by 'तत्प्रख्यशास्त्रात् नामधेयत्वम्.'

Bhāskara's argument may be stated as follows. In 'वैश्वदेवेन यजेत' वैश्वदेवेन is regarded by the pūrvapakṣin as laying down a subsidiary viz. the deity All-gods for the eight sacrifices mentioned in 'आग्नेय... एककपालम्.' But that subsidiary viz. the deity All-gods (विश्वदेवरूपगुणः) has already been established (संप्रतिपन्न) by the arthavāda passage 'यद् विश्वेदेवाः...वैश्वदेवत्वम्.' This arthavāda thus becomes the तत्प्रख्यशास्त्रान्तर enjoining the deity All-gods. Consequently, वैश्वदेवेन cannot be regarded as laying down the subsidiary viz. the deity All-gods, but must be considered as representing the proper name of the sacrifice. Thus, on account of तत्प्रख्यशास्त्र we here decide that वैश्वदेवेन is a name. No fifth reason such as उत्पत्तिशिष्टगुणबलीयस्त्वम् is, therefore, necessary.

While we agree with Bhāskara in holding that cases of 'उत्पत्तिशिष्टगुणबलीयस्त्वात् नामधेयत्वम्' fall under 'तत्प्रख्यशास्त्रात् नामधेयत्वम्' and that it is, therefore, not necessary to regard उत्पत्तिशिष्टगुणबलीयस्त्व as a fifth reason for नामधेयत्व, we cannot see eye to eye with him in believing that the तत्प्रख्यशास्त्रान्तर in the present case is the arthavāda passage 'यद् विश्वेदेवाः ...वैश्वदेवत्वम्. ' We think in fact that Bhāskara has committed a blunder in pointing out this arthavāda as the तत्प्रख्यशास्त्रान्तर here. This blunder is traceable to the influence of Āpadeva.

There are two reasons why it is not possible to regard the arthavāda 'यद्.. वैश्वदेवत्वम् ' as the तत्प्रख्यशास्त्रान्तर in this case. First; this arthavāda does *not* lay down All–gods as the deities for the group of sacrifices that go under the name वैश्वदेव. How then can it be regarded as the शास्त्रान्तर enjoining the subsidiary viz. the deity All–gods ? What the arthavāda really does is to offer an etymological explanation as to why these sacrifices are called वैश्वदेव. Because विश्वे देवाः (All–gods) performed these sacrifices, therefore, they are known as वैश्वदेव (belonging to All–gods). This is a typical piece of etymology which is often met with in the Brāhmaṇas. Secondly, if the arthavāda 'यद्...वैश्वदेवत्वम् ' be regarded as the तत्प्रख्यशास्त्रान्तर, All–gods would be the deity of the sacrifices included in वैश्वदेव. But we know that out of the eight sacrifices that form this group, only one viz the āmikṣā–sacrifice possesses All–gods as its deity.

With reference to this second reason it may perhaps be urged that though only one of the eight sacrifices possesses All–gods as its deity, all the eight may be spoken of as having All–gods as their deities by what is known as छत्रिन्याय. A crowd of people is going along the road. Many of them are possessed of umbrellas. But in referring to the whole crowd we often use the expression 'छत्रिणो यान्ति '. Here though some of the crowd may not have umbrellas, they are called छत्रिणः inspite of that fact. Similarly, though only āmikṣā–sacrifice is विश्वेदेवदेवताक, the others also may be spoken of as possessing All–gods for their deities, though they really are not विश्वेदेवदेवताक.

It will be noticed that this objection has no force. The छत्रिन्याय is properly applicable to those cases where a majority being possessed of a certain characteristic, that characteristic is applied to the whole i.e. even to those who possess it not. In the present case the maxim has no application. For, out of the eight sacrifices only one has All–gods for its deity. That characteristic cannot, therefore, with propriety be transferred to the seven others, which are offered in honour of other deities.

Thus, for the two reasons above stated we hold that it is wrong to regard the arthavāda passage ‘ यद्...वैश्वदेवत्वम् ’ as the तत्प्रख्य-शास्त्रान्तर for ‘वैश्वदेवेन यजेत’.

According to our view the तत्प्रख्यशास्त्रान्तर in the present case is the उत्पत्तिवाक्य ‘आग्नेयमष्टाकपालं...एककपालम्.’ As soon as we think of interpreting वैश्वदेवेन as establishing the subsidiary viz. the deity All-gods, the sentence ‘ आग्नेय...एककपालम् ’ steps forward and points out that the deities for the eight sacrifices have already been enjoined by itself. Thus, वैश्वदेवेन has no occasion to lay down the deity. Therefore, वैश्वदेवेन must be regarded as a name.

The reason why Bhāskara does not consider the उत्पत्तिवाक्य ‘ आग्नेयमष्टाकपालं...एककपालम् ’ as the तत्प्रख्यशास्त्रान्तर here is probably this. Following Āpadeva he evidently believes that the तत्प्रख्यशास्त्रान्तर must enjoin *the same deity* as is supposed to have been enjoined by the word which is ultimately decided to be a name. Here वैश्वदेवेन is such a word. It is supposed to lay down the deity All-gods. The तत्प्रख्यशास्त्र in the present case must, therefore, be a passage which enjoins All-gods as the deity. As ‘ आग्नेय... एककपालम् ’ does not enjoin All-gods *alone* as the deity of all the eight sacrifices, Bhāskara refuses to consider it as the तत्प्रख्यशास्त्रान्तर.

This view of तत्प्रख्यशास्त्र is in our opinion incorrect. The question really is what is exactly meant by तत् in तत्प्रख्यशास्त्र. We believe तत् means स गुणः. Under ‘ स गुणः ’ may be included one detiy or more as the case may be. वैश्वदेवेन was supposed to supply a गुण or a subsidiary viz. a deity. The passage ‘आग्नेय...एककपालम्’ already supplies that subsidiary (गुणः) viz. the deity for each of the eight sacrifices mentioned therein. Therefore, that passage is quite a legitimate तत्प्रख्यशास्त्र in the present case.

Apadeva and Bhāskara evidently hold that तत् means सा देवता. And as the passage ‘ आग्नेय...एककपालम् ’ does not enjoin *that same deity* for *all* the sacrifices mentioned therein, they refuse to regard it as the तत्प्रख्यशास्त्र.

This interpretation of तत् appears to us to be incorrect. Even in the standard illustration of ‘ तत्प्रख्यशास्त्रात् नामधेयत्वम् ’ this interpretation is not found to be true. There the discussion centres round the word अग्निहोत्र. It is supposed to lay down a subsidiary viz. the deity Fire. But it is pointed out that another passage enjoins that subsidiary. Therefore, अग्निहोत्र must be regarded as a name.

Now, two passages are here quoted as representing the तत्प्रख्य-शास्त्रान्तर. Both these not only enjoin Agni but also another deity viz.

either Prajāpati or Sūrya. So it is not correct to say that the तत्प्रख्यशास्त्रान्तर must enjoin *only that deity* which is supposed to have been laid down by the word under discussion.

Further, even if the sense which Āpadeva and Bhāskara assign to तत् be accepted, we might, by having resort to छत्रिन्याय, regard all the eight sacrifices as विश्वदेव-देवताक.

All this will go to show that there is no objection to regard 'आग्नेय...एककपालम्' as the तत्प्रख्यशास्त्रान्तर in this case.

केचित्—This word refers to Someśvara, the author of the Nyāyasudhā or Rāṇaka, which is a commentary on the Tantravārtika of Kumārilabhaṭṭa. Someśvara holds that उत्पत्तिशिष्टगुणबलीयस्त्वम् is a fifth reason for नामधेयत्व. As against him Pārthasārathimiśra opines that the word वैश्वदेव is a name on account of तत्प्रख्यशास्त्र. Note 'तत्र च यद्वृत्तयोगेन एकदेशदेवतात्वेन वा विश्वेषां देवानां समवायात् **तत्प्रख्यन्यायेन नामधेयं वैश्वदेवशब्दः** ।' शास्त्रदीपिका on I. iv. 13.

Āpadeva in his Mīmāṁsānyāyaprakāśa notes both these views. In stating the view of Someśvara he declares that 'वैश्वदेवेन यजेत' cannot be covered by any of the four reasons for name that he has mentioned before. The following quotation wherein Āpadeva proves that वैश्वदेवेन cannot be considered as a name on account of तत्प्रख्यशास्त्र will be found interesting, in view of the fact that Bhāskara holds exactly the opposite opinion:

'उत्पत्तिशिष्टगुणबलीयस्त्वमपि पञ्चमं केचिन्नामधेयत्वे निमित्तमाहुः । 'वैश्वदेवेन यजेत' इत्यत्र वैश्वदेवशब्दस्य कर्मनामधेयत्वमुत्पत्तिशिष्टगुणबलीयस्त्वात् । **उक्तमत्वर्थलक्षणादिप्रकारचतुष्टयासंभवात् । ...नापि तत्प्रख्यशास्त्रान्नामधेयत्वम्** । यत्र हि विधित्सितो गुणोऽन्यत प्राप्तः तत्र तत्प्रख्यशास्त्रान्नामधेयत्वम्, यथा अग्निहोत्रशब्दे । अत्र च अग्न्यादयोऽष्टौ यागाः प्रकृताः । तत्र आमिक्षायागे यद्यपि विश्वे देवाः प्राप्ताः 'वैश्वदेवी आमिक्षा' इति, तथापि समस्तु तेषामप्राप्तत्वात् 'वैश्वदेवेन यजेत' इत्यनेन तत्र तद्विधाने न तत्प्रख्यशास्त्रमन्यत् येन तद्वशान्नामत्वं स्यात् ।'

The following quotation contains Āpadeva's exposition of the other view with which Bhāskara agrees :

'अन्ये त्वाचार्या आहुः । यः शब्दो यत्र कर्मणि यद्गुणसबन्धं बोधयति स चेत् संबन्धः शास्त्रान्तरप्रतिपन्नः तदा तस्य शब्दस्य तन्नामधेयत्वं तत्प्रख्यशास्त्रात् । तच्च शास्त्रान्तरं विधिर्वा अथवादो वा इत्यनादरः । तत्र अग्निहोत्रशब्देऽग्निसंबन्धबोधकं शास्त्रान्तरं विधिरेव । वैश्वदेवशब्दश्च विश्वदेवसंबन्धं कर्मणि बोधयति । विश्वदेवसंबन्धश्च अष्टसु यागेषु 'यद् विश्वे देवाः समयजन्त तद् वैश्वदेवस्य वैश्वदेवत्वम्' इत्यर्थवादादवगतः ।

न च विधिरेव तत्प्रख्यशास्त्रं नार्थवाद इत्यत्र किंचित् प्रमाणमस्ति । अत एव 'ज्योतिष्टोमेन स्वर्गकामो यजेत' इत्यत्र ज्योतिष्टोमशब्दः 'एतानि वाव तानि ज्योतींषि य एतस्य स्तोमाः' इत्यर्थ-

वाद्यावगतं ज्योतिस्संबन्धं निमित्तीकृत्य सोमयागे प्रवर्तमानस्तत्प्रख्यशास्त्रान्नामधेयं भवति । एवं प्रकृतेऽपि द्रष्टव्यम् । **पञ्चमप्रकारकल्पने प्रमाणाभावात्**। अत एव वैश्वदेवाधिकरणे वार्तिककारैरेवमुपसंहृतम् ' तत्प्रख्यतयैव सर्वेषां नामधेयत्वम् ' इति । यच्चोत्पत्तिशिष्टगुणबलीयस्त्वमुक्तं तद् गुणविध्यसंभवे युक्त्यभ्युच्चयमात्रम् । तत् सिद्धं तत्प्रख्यशास्त्राद् वैश्वदेवशब्दस्य कर्मनामधेयत्वम्।'

Also read the following 'चातुर्मास्ययागस्य चत्वारि पर्वाणि—वैश्वदेवः, वरुणप्रघासः, साकमेधः, शुनासीरीयश्चेति । तत्र प्रथमे पर्वणि अष्टौ यागा विहिताः—' आग्नेयमष्टाकपालं निर्वपति, सौम्यं चरुम्, सावित्रं द्वादशकपालम्, सारस्वतं चरुम्, पौष्णं चरुम्, मारुतं सप्तकपालम्, वैश्वदेवीमामिक्षाम्, द्यावापृथिव्यमेककपालम् ' इति । तेषामष्टानां यागानां संनिधाविदमाम्नायते ' वैश्वदेवेन यजेत ' इति । तत्र आग्नेयादीन् यागान् ' यजेत ' इत्यनूद्य वैश्वदेवशब्देन देवतारूपो गुणस्तेषु विधीयते । यद्यपि वैश्वदेव्यामिक्षायां विश्वे देवाः प्राप्ताः, तथापि आग्नेयादिषु सप्तसु यागेषु अप्राप्तत्वाद् विधीयन्ते । तेषु अपि अग्न्यादिदेवताः सन्तीति चेत्, तर्हि गत्यभावात् तेषु देवता विकल्प्यन्ताम् । नामधेयत्वे तु नाममात्रस्य अभिधेयत्वाद् द्रव्यदेवतयोरभावेन यागस्य अत्र स्वरूपासंभवाद् श्रूयमाणो विधिरनर्थकः स्यात् । तस्माद् गुणविधिरिति **प्राप्ते**—

ब्रूमः—उत्पत्तिवाक्यैर्विहितानाग्नेयादीनष्टौ यागान् ' यजेत ' इत्यनूद्य **अष्टानां संघे वैश्वदेवशब्दो नामत्वेनोपवर्ण्यते** । न च विधित्वासंभवेऽपि नामोपदेशवैयर्थ्यम्, ' प्राचीनप्रवणे वैश्वदेवेन यजेत ' इत्यादिषु वैश्वदेवशब्देन एकेनैव अष्टानां संभवस्य व्यवहर्तव्यत्वात् । **नामप्रवृत्तिभूता निरुक्तिस्तु** द्विधा । आमिक्षायागे विश्वेषां देवानामिज्यमानतया तत्सहचरितार्थानां सर्वेषां छत्रिन्यायेन वैश्वदेवत्वम् । अथवा विश्वे देवा अष्टानां कर्तारः इति वैश्वदेवत्वम् । तथा च ब्राह्मणम् ' यद् विश्वे देवा समयजन्त, तद् वैश्वदेवस्य वैश्वदेवत्वम् ' इति । देवताविकल्पस्तु समानबलत्वाभावान्न युज्यते । अग्न्यादय उत्पत्तिशिष्टत्वात् प्रबलाः, विश्वे देवा उत्पन्नशिष्टत्वाद् दुर्बलाः । तस्माद् वैश्वदेवशब्दः कर्मनामधेयम् । ' जैमिनीयन्यायमालाविस्तर p. 52

The following extracts from the Śābarabhāṣya and the Tantravārtika may also be read with advantage :

' चातुर्मास्येषु प्रथमे पर्वणि वैश्वदेवे संदेहः । ' वैश्वदेवेन यजेत ' इति किं वैश्वदेवशब्दो गुणविधिः, उत कर्मनामधेयम् । इति यदि संदेहो न संदेहः । वैश्वदेवे विकल्पः । गुणविधिर्वैश्वदेवशब्दः । गम्यते हि गुणविधानम् । विश्वे देवा विधीयन्ते आग्नेयादिषु यागेषु । तत्र अग्न्यादीनां वैश्वदेवैर्विकल्पः । एवं प्रसिद्धिरर्थवती भविष्यति ।

नैतदेवम् । **प्रत्यक्षश्रुतिविहिता अग्न्यादयस्तेषां यागानाम्, विश्वे देवा वाक्येन प्रकरणात्** तेनैव नान्येनेति गम्यते । **न चायं विषमशिष्टो विकल्पो भवितुमर्हति । न हि प्रकरणं श्रुतस्य द्रव्यस्य बाधने समर्थम्** । तस्मात् कर्मनामधेयम् । ' शाबरभाष्य pp. 346–347 (आनन्दाश्रम)

' अत्रोच्यते । नायं प्रकृतेषु गुणविधिरुपपद्यते । कथम् । गुणान्तरावरुद्धत्वान्नावकाशो गुणोऽपरः । विकल्पोऽपि न वैषम्यात् तस्मान्नामैव युज्यते ॥ **अग्न्यादयो हि उत्पत्तिवाक्ये तद्धितश्रुत्या अष्टाकपालादीनां देवताः, विश्वे देवा वाक्येन** । ...... न तावद् वैश्वदेवेनेति प्रकृतमप्रकृतं वा द्रव्यं देवतासंबन्धि श्रूयते । ... ... न हि ' वसन्ते वैश्वदेवेन ' ' प्राचीनप्रवणे वैश्वदेवेन ' इत्यादि विधानं परस्परसहितानामष्टानां हविषां समुदायपदादृतेऽवकल्पते । तस्मादेकदेशस्थैरपि विश्वेदेवैरुपलक्षितानां छत्रिन्यायेन **तत्प्रख्ययैव सर्वेषां नामधेयत्वम्** । ' तन्त्रवार्तिक p. 347 (आनन्दाश्रम)

From the above quotations it will be seen that while Śabara's view is nearer to that of those who believe that वैश्वदेव is a name owing to उत्पत्तिशिष्टगुणबलीयस्त्व, Kumārila thinks that वैश्वदेव is a name of all the eight sacrifices on account of तत्प्रख्यशास्त्र.

The purpose of नामधेय passages is thus stated by Rāmeśvara : 'नामधेयस्य प्रयोजनं तु सर्वत्र व्यवहार एव । न ह्यन्तरेण नामधेयमृत्विग्वरणादिषु 'अनेन अहं यक्ष्ये' इत्याख्यानोपायो लघुः कश्चिदस्ति ।'

विश्वदेवरूपगुणसंप्रतिपन्नशास्त्रस्य—This compound has become somewhat clumsy on account of the word संप्रतिपन्न having been misplaced. The sense is संप्रतिपन्नः सम्यक्तया ज्ञातः प्राप्तः इत्यर्थः विश्वदेवरूपगुणः यस्मात्, तादृशं यद् शास्त्रम्. This should ordinarily yield संप्रतिपन्नविश्वदेवरूपगुणशास्त्रस्य. As it is the compound should be included in the आहिताग्न्यादि class. Or संप्रतिपन्न should be bluntly put equal to संप्रतिपादक.

Section 62

Sections 62–71, forming the fifth Chapter of the Arthasaṁgraha, deal with Niṣedha, which is the fourth of the five parts into which the Veda is divided according to the Mīmāṁsakas. Vide Section 10 above.

Section 62 defines Niṣedha and shows what purpose it serves in the Mīmāṁsist scheme of things by instituting a comparison between it and Vidhi.

Niṣedha means prohibition. A sentence, which prohibits a man from doing something, or turns him away (निवर्तक) from some action, constitutes the technical Niṣedha of the Mīmāṁsakas. Such prohibitory sentences have a purpose in so far as they produce or bring about (जनक) the turning away (निवृत्तिः) of people from actions which are the cause of evils or undesirable results (अनर्थः).

It will thus be seen that Niṣedha does not produce any positive result such as heaven or plenty of cattle, as Vidhi does. It serves a useful purpose all the same, because it saves a man from being involved in sin or evil, which otherwise would have been his lot. 'न कलञ्जं भक्षयेत् न लशुनं न गृञ्जनम्' is an example of Niṣedha. This sentence turns a man away from the eating of the prohibited things. Had it not been for this probihition, one would have partaken of these articles and would have had to suffer the evil arising therefrom.

यथा विधिः ...निवर्तयति—This sentence institutes a comparison between the working of Vidhi and Niṣedha. While a vidhi or an injunction conveys an instigation, stimulation or exhortation

(प्रवर्तना), a niṣedha or a prohibition intimates exactly the opposite of this viz. a negative instigation or determent (निवर्तना). As an injunction, in order to justify (निर्वाहः) its character as an instigator, suggests that the thing which it wants to enjoin (विधेयम्) is a means of obtaining one's desired object such as heaven and thus instigates a man to it, in the same way a prohibition, in order to justify its character as a deterrent (निवर्तकत्वम्), suggests that the thing which it wants to prohibit (निषेध्यम्), is a means of an extremely undesired result such as hell and thus turns a man away from it.

कलञ्जम्— This word is variously explained. Its usual sense is the meat of an animal or a bird killed with a poisoned arrow. Note ' विषसंपृक्तबाणेन हतौ यौ मृगपक्षिणौ । तयोर्मांसं **कलञ्जं** स्याद् भुक्त्वा चान्द्रायणं चरेत् ॥ ' Its other senses are (2) red garlic, (3) tobacco, or (4) fermented food.

निषेध्यस्य कलञ्जभक्षणस्य—This expression should really be निषेध्यस्य कलञ्जभक्ष**णादेः**. For, at the उपक्रम or commencement of the sentence we have '**इत्यादिनिषेधोऽपि.**' Symmetry also requires कलञ्जभक्षणादेः on the analogy of विधेयस्य यागादेः, occurring above.

परानिष्टसाधनत्वमाक्षिपन्—There is no propriety for the adjective पर (extremely) here. अनिष्टसाधनत्वम् would have been quite enough. Some interpret पर in the sense of other-worldly (परानिष्टम् = पारलौकिकनरकादिरूपमनिष्टम्). Even with this sense the adjective is unnecessary. Simple अनिष्टसाधनत्वम् conveys all the intended sense.

Section 63

In the preceding Section we have been told that a prohibition or a prohibitory sentence conveys निवर्तना or determent. This and the following Sections explain how it does so.

A prohibitory sentence contains the negative particle न. With reference to this न two questions arise : (1) What exact constituent of the prohibitory sentence is to be construed with this न ? (2) What is the sense in which this न is to be understood ? The answers to these two questions will decide what the import of a prohibitory sentence is going to be. The first question is answered in Section 63 and the second in 64.

The pūrvapakṣin's view in this matter is as follows: In sentences like ' कलञ्जं न भक्षयेत् ' ' ब्राह्मणो न हन्तव्यः ' the negative particle न is immediately or without any interval (अव्यवधानम्) followed by the root-element in भक्षयेत् and हन्तव्यः. It is, therefore, natural that the root-element should be construed with the negative particle in prohibitory sentences. This means that the meaning of the root (धात्वर्थः) is to be construed with the meaning of the negative particle (नञर्थः).

Now, the usual meaning of नञ् or the negative particle is अभावः (absence or negation). When, therefore, the धात्वर्थ such as भक्षण and हनन is construed with नञर्थ, the meaning that we obtain is भक्षणाभाव and हननाभाव. भक्षयेत् and हन्तव्यः are potential forms. From a potential form such as यजेत the meaning that we obtain is धात्वर्थकर्तव्यता. Similarly, from न भक्षयेत् and न हन्तव्यः the meaning that we shall get is धात्वर्थाभावकर्तव्यता or धात्वर्थवर्जनकर्तव्यता, in some such form as भक्षणाभावः कर्तव्यः and हननाभावः कर्तव्यः.

Now, this meaning looks very much like प्रवर्तना or instigation. For, as indicated by the potential participle कर्तव्यः, we are here directed to do something. How then can you say that a prohibition or a prohibitory sentence conveys निवर्तना or determent ?

Such is the position of the pūrvapakṣin, who has tried to show that a niṣedha cannot convey determent by construing the root-element with the negative particle and interpreting the latter in the sense of absence. Read the following in this connection :

कथं निषेधानां निवर्तनाप्रतिपादकत्वम् । यावता ‘न भक्षयेत्’ ‘न हन्तव्यः’ इत्येवमादौ **अव्यवधानेन नञर्थस्य अभावस्य धात्वर्थेन अन्वये धात्वर्थवर्जनकर्तव्यतैव सर्वत्र वाक्यार्थः प्रतीयते ।** ततश्च यथा ‘यजेत’ इत्यादौ यागकर्तव्यता वाक्यार्थः, एवं निषेधेषु तत्तद्धात्वर्थवर्जनकर्तव्यता वाक्यार्थः, न निवर्तना—’ मीमांसान्यायप्रकाश

‘सर्वत्र हि लिङ्घटितवाक्यस्यैव नञ्युक्तत्वे **निषेध**व्यवहारः । लिङश्च प्रवर्तनायामेव शक्तिरनुशासनसिद्धा, न निवर्तनायामपि । **नञश्च अभावे शक्तिः तस्य च येन सह संबन्धः तदभावबोधकत्वं प्रसिद्धम् ।** अतश्च यदि स धात्वर्थेन संबध्नीयात् तदा तदभावं बोधयेत्, तस्य च धात्वर्थस्य लिङर्थेन अन्वये धात्वर्थवर्जनकर्तव्यतैव प्रतीयते । यदि च लिङर्थेन, तदापि प्रवर्तनाभाव एव बोध्येत, न निवर्तना, इति तद्बोधकपदाभावेन कथं निषेधवाक्यतो निवर्तनाप्रतीतिः इत्याशङ्क्य पूर्वपक्षी प्रत्यवतिष्ठते ।’ सारविवेचनी

‘ननु निषेधवाक्यानां निवर्तनाप्रतिपादकत्वं न संभवति, ‘न भक्षयेत्’ ‘न हन्तव्यः’ इत्येवमादौ अव्यवधानेन नञर्थस्य अभावस्य धात्वर्थेन अन्वये सति धात्वर्थवर्जनकर्तव्यताया एव सर्वत्र वाक्यार्थत्वेन प्रतीयमानत्वात् । तथा च यथा ‘यजेत’ इत्यादौ यागकर्तव्यता वाक्यार्थो भवति, तथा ‘न कलञ्जं भक्षयेत्’ ‘ब्राह्मणो न हन्तव्यः’ इत्यादौ अपि तत्तद्धात्वर्थवर्जनकर्तव्यतैव वाक्यार्थो, न निवर्तना —’ रामेश्वर

The siddhāntin refutes the pūrvapakṣin's position by pointing out that the answer of the pūrvapakṣin to both the questions connected with the negative particle न are incorrect. According to the siddhāntin the root-element cannot be construed with the negative particle. Only the लिङ् element can be so construed.

Further, न must not be understood in the sense of अभाव or absence, but in that of विरोध or opposition. Thus, when लिङ्, which means प्रवर्तना, is construed with नञ्, which means opposition, the sense that we obtain is the ite of प्रवर्तना viz. निवर्तना. Hence, it is quite correct to say that prohibitory sentences convey निवर्तना.

The negative particle is in Sanskrit used in no less than six senses, which are enumerated in the following couplet: तत्सादृश्यम**भाव**श्च तदन्यत्वं तदल्पता। अप्राशस्त्यं **विरोधश्च** नञर्थाः षट् प्रकीर्तिताः॥ Out of these the Mimāṁsakas consider विरोध to be the natural sense, as we shall see from the next Section.

The reason why the siddhāntin says that only the लिङ् element can be construed with the negative particle in 'न भक्षयेत्' is as follows :—

The only ground on which the pūrvapakṣin construes the root-element with the negative particle is their extreme proximity. If we split the expression न भक्षयेत् into its component parts, we get न + भक्ष्–धातुः + आख्यातत्वम् + लिङ्त्वम्. Here as the root-element भक्ष् immediately (अव्यवधानम्) follows न, it is natural, the pūrvapakṣin thinks, that it should be construed with that negative particle. But the siddhāntin points out that this cannot be done. भक्षयेत् means, according to the Mimāṁsaka's method of interpretation, भक्षणेन इष्टं भावयेत्. Here भावयेत् represents the sense of the अर्थभावना expressed by the आख्यातांश of the termination त (प्रत्ययार्थभावना). Vide p. 89 above. We have seen before (p. 94) that the धात्वर्थ is the साधन of the अर्थभावना. It is hence subordinate (उपसर्जनम्) to it. Thus, in the present case the धात्वर्थ भक्षण, being present as subordinate to the अर्थभावना (अर्थभावनोपसर्जनत्वेन उपस्थितिः), is naturally connected with it. It cannot, therefore, be further construed with anything else such as the negative particle न in this case. For, the rule is that when something is subordinate to one, it is naturally connected with it and cannot further be construed with another (न हि अन्योपसर्जनत्वेन उपस्थितमन्यत्र अन्वेति). even though that another be proximate to it. That is why the siddhāntin points out that the meaning of the root cannot be construed with the meaning of the negative (न तावदत्र धात्वर्थस्य नञर्थेन अन्वयः).

The general rule on the strength of which the siddhāntin says we cannot construe the धात्वर्थ with the नञर्थ may be illustrated by the following examples. In 'राजपुरुषमानय' राजन् is an उपसर्जन or subordinate of पुरुष. Its purpose is finished when it is connected with पुरुष, who is consequently distinguished, defined or specified. राजन्, therefore, cannot further be construed with आनय. Otherwise the sentence

'राजपुरुषमानय' would mean that the king is also to be brought. Similarly, in the sentence 'अरुणया एकहायन्या गवा सोमं क्रीणाति' एकहायन्या cannot be construed with आरुण्य, though it immediately follows अरुणया, because एकहायन्या is subordinate to the action क्रय.

Thus, धात्वर्थ being an उपसर्जन or subordinate of अर्थभावना, cannot be construed with न. Therefore, it is only the प्रत्ययार्थ that can be so construed (अतः प्रत्ययार्थस्यैव नञर्थेन अन्वयः).

The प्रत्यय or termination consists of two elements, the element of आख्यातत्व, which expresses अर्थभावना, and the element of लिङ्, which expresses शब्दभावना. Now, the question is which of these two भावनाs can be construed with the negative particle. Here we apply the same general rule. We then find that अर्थभावना is the उपसर्जन or distinguishing or determining attribute of शब्दभावना or प्रवर्तना, which is expressed by the लिङ् element (लिङंशवाच्यप्रवर्तनोपसर्जनत्वेनोपस्थितिः), because it is its साध्य (p. 93 above). Hence it cannot be construed with न. So शब्दभावना, which is expressed by the लिङ् element, alone remains capable of being construed with न, because it is the principal among all the three elements of भक्षयेत्.

Thus, we see that it is not the धात्वर्थ, but the लिङर्थ that must be construed with न in the sentence ' न भक्षयेत्. ' The लिङर्थ is of course प्रवर्तना. When it s construed with न, which expresses विरोध, the meaning that we obtain is the opposite of प्रवर्तना viz. निवर्तना. So it is proved that a prohibitory sentence conveys निवर्तना.

प्रत्ययार्थभावनोपसर्जनत्वेन—This is a very compressed and somewhat confusing expression. What it really means is प्रत्ययस्य यः आख्यातत्वांशः तेन वाच्या या अर्थभावना तस्या उपसर्जनत्वेन.—उपसर्जनम् is a technical term in Sanskrit grammar and occurs half a dozen times in Pāṇini's sūtras. It means a word which either by composition or by derivation loses its original independent character, while at the same time determines the sense of another word. For example, in पाणिनीय a pupil of Pāṇini, पाणिनि is उपसर्जन, and in राजपुरुषः, राजन् is उपसर्जन. आचार्योपसर्जनश्च अन्तेवासी is an example of the use of the word उपसर्जन. From these examples it will be seen that उपसर्जन means something which serves as a distinguishing or defining attribute to another, and being thus connected with it, appears as subordinate or subservient to it. It should be noted that though उपसर्जन is usually translated as subservient or subordinate, the sense expressed by the word, which is उपसर्जन, need not actually be subordinate to the sense of the other word. Thus, in आचार्योपसर्जन: अन्तेवासी, आचार्य is उपसर्जन of अन्तेवासी, because the pupil is defined or specified as the pupil of such and such a preceptor. This does not of course mean that the preceptor is subordinate to the pupil. That is why in the present case धात्वर्थ, which is the साधन of अर्थभावना, and अर्थभावना, which is the साध्य of शब्दभावना, are both regarded as उपसर्जन of अर्थभावना and शब्दभावना respectively.

न हि अन्योपसर्जनत्वेन उपस्थितमन्यत्र अन्वेति — The application of this general rule to the special instance under discussion would be as follows: अर्थभावनोपसर्जनत्वेनोपस्थितो धात्वर्थः नञर्थे न अन्वेति। तथा च शब्दभावनोपसर्जनत्वेनोपस्थिता अर्थभावनापि नञर्थे न अन्वेति. It should be noted that this general rule can also be stated in the form 'न हि अन्योपसर्जनत्वेन उपस्थितेन अन्यदन्वेति.' In this case we can say that आनय cannot be construed with राजन्, because राजन्, is पुरुषोपसर्जनत्वेन उपस्थित. Similarly, नञ् cannot be construed with धात्वर्थ and अर्थभावना, because they are respectively अर्थभावनोपसर्जनत्वेन उपस्थित and शब्दभावनोपसर्जनत्वेनोपस्थित.

अन्यथा......राज्ञः क्रियान्वयापत्तेः—This sentence has thus been paraphrased by रामेश्वरः—अन्यविशेषणत्वेनोपस्थितस्यापि अन्यत्र विशेषणत्वेन अन्वयस्वीकारे पुरुषोपसर्जनत्वेनोपस्थितस्य राज्ञोऽपि क्रियोपसर्जनत्वेन अन्वयापत्तेः।

One more point is mentioned by Āpadeva in connection with the construction of the negative particle in prohibitory sentences such as 'न कलञ्जं भक्षयेत्'. It is this that न cannot be construed with word like कलञ्ज, because these words are उपसर्जन of कारकs such as कर्म. Note 'नापि कलञ्जादिपदार्थैरन्वयः। तेषामपि कारकोपसर्जनतया उपस्थितत्वेन भिन्नपदस्य नञोऽर्थेन अन्वयायोगात् एकहायन्या इव आरुण्येन।'

For the topic dealt with in this Section read: 'अनारभ्य श्रूयते—'न कलञ्जं भक्षयेत्, न लशुनम्, न गृञ्जनम्' इति। तत्र 'न भक्षयेत्' इति संनिधिवशाद् नञ्धातोरन्वये सति अभक्षणम् इति पर्युदासः संपद्यते। तथा सति 'नेक्षेतोद्यन्तमादित्यम्' इत्यादाविव संकल्पो विधेयः। तस्य च अभक्षणसंकल्पस्य विश्वजिन्न्यायेन स्वर्गः फलत्वेन कल्पनीयः। इति चेत्—

मैवम्। पदैकदेशस्य धातोः पदान्तरेण अन्वेतुमशक्यत्वाद् विधायकपदस्य नञ्पदेन अन्वये सति रागप्राप्तां भक्षणप्रवृत्तिमनूद्य निषेधस्य विधेयत्वात्। न च निषेधो व्यर्थः नरकपातनिवारकत्वात्। एवं च सति अश्रुतं न किमपि कल्पनीयम्। त्वत्पक्षे तु अश्रुतः संकल्पः कल्पनीयः इति तदर्थं भक्षणपदे लक्षणा आश्रयितव्या। तस्मात् स्वर्गगामिनो नात्राधिकारः। किं तु नरकाद् भीतस्य।' जैमिनीयन्यायमालाविस्तर p. 314

Some of the words in this quotation will be clear when we go to the end of Section 66.

Section 64

This Section just tells us what the nature or natural sense (स्वभावः) of a negative particle is. The natural sense of a negative particle is to convey the opposite of the sense of the word which is used along with it (स्वसमभिव्याहृत – स्वान्वित or स्वसंबद्ध). अस्ति means existence. When अस्ति is connected with न, नास्ति signifies the opposite of existence viz. non-existence. In the present case we have seen that the लिङ् element is to be construed with the negative particle. The sense of the लिङ् is प्रवर्तना. Therefore, when न is conjoined with the लिङ्, it conveys the opposite of प्रवर्तना viz. निवर्तना. When we hear an injunctory sentence, we get the apprehension of instigation (प्रवर्तनाप्रतीतिः) i. e. the idea that some one is instigating us. Similarly, when we hear a prohibitory sentence, we get the apprehension of determent. i. e. the idea that somebody is turning us away. That is why we say that determent is the import of a prohibitory sentence.

निवृत्त्यनुकूलव्यापाररूपनिवर्तनायाः—This expression describes what निवर्तना is like. It is of the form of a mental activity (व्यापारः) which is favourable to absention. What is meant is that when we hear a prohibition; the necessary mental inclination to abstain from prohibited things arises in us. This inclination is exactly what is meant by determent.

There is evident corruption in the third and fourth sentences of this Section, as they occur in the printed editions of the Arthasaṁgraha. We have restored the text to what must have been its original form, as judged by the readings in the Mīmāṁsānyāyaprakāśa.

Section 65

In the preceding Sections it has been laid down that as a general rule the meaning of the suffix (प्रत्ययार्थः) is to be construed with the meaning of the negative particle (नञ् – नञर्थ) in prohibitory sentences. But sometimes on account of some obstacle or unfavourable circumstance (बाधकम्) it may not be possible to construe the प्रत्ययार्थ with the नञर्थ. In those cases the धात्वर्थ or the sense of the root itself is construed with नञर्थ.

Such obstacle is two-fold viz. (1) introduction of the prohibitory sentence with the words 'तस्य व्रतम्' and (2) the contingency of option. These two circumstances then form the exceptions to the general rule about the construction of the प्रत्ययार्थ with the नञर्थ. Section 66 deals with the first exception and Sections 67 and 68 with the second.

प्रत्ययार्थस्य—This is really equal to प्रत्ययैकदेशलिङंशार्थस्य. नञ् – नञर्थ. बाधकम् a circumstance unfavourable to the construction of लिङंशार्थ with नञर्थ. व्रतम्—This must be understood to be जात्येकवचनम् or समूहैकवचनम् or collective singular.

It should be noted that Bhāskara's statement in the first sentence of this Section is not quite correct. Therein he tells us that when there is an obstacle to the construction of प्रत्ययार्थ with the नञर्थ, the धात्वर्थ itself is construed with the नञर्थ. He then says that such obstacle is two-fold. This means that in the case of both these बाधकs or obstacles, the धात्वर्थ is construed with the नञर्थ. But this is not true. For, from the following Sections we shall see that only in the case of the first बाधक, the धात्वर्थ is construed with the नञर्थ. In the case of the second बाधक it is not the धात्वर्थ, but the noun अनुयाजेषु, that is construed with the नञर्थ.

For this inaccurate statement Bhāskara is indebted to Āpadeva, who says 'यदा तु तदन्वये किंचिद् बाधकम् तदा अगत्या धात्वर्थेन अन्वयः। तच्च बाधकं द्विविधम्। 'तस्य व्रतम्' इत्युपक्रमो विकल्पप्रसक्तिश्च।'

What Bhāskara should really have said is 'यदा तु प्रत्ययार्थस्य नत्रान्वये बाधकं तदा न प्रत्ययार्थस्य तत्रान्वयः। किन्तु धात्वर्थस्य नाम्नो वा कस्यचित्।'

Section 66

This Section deals with the first obstacle or unfavourable circumstance or exception to the construction of लिङ् with न. But before we proceed to see what the nature of this exception is, we must know the meaning of the word पर्युदास, which has been used by Bhāskara in the second sentence of this Section.

We have seen before that when लिङ् is construed with न, न conveys निवर्तना. निषेध, प्रतिषेध and निवर्तना all mean the same thing viz. prohibition or determent. Now our author tells us that in the case of the two exceptions न conveys पर्युदास. What is then the distinction between निषेध and पर्युदास? The distinction is thus stated:

Both निषेध or prohibition and पर्युदास (from परि + उद् + आस्) or exclusion ultimately convey the same idea. But while निषेध is negative in form, पर्युदास, though negative in sense, is positive in form. Secondly, निषेध has its province in those cases where the suffix i.e. the लिङ् element thereof is construed with न. पर्युदास on the other hand occurs when a धात्वर्थ or a noun is connected with न.

Note '**पर्युदासः** स विज्ञेयो यत्र पूर्वपदेन [i. e. धात्वर्थेन] नञ्। **प्रतिषेधः** स विज्ञेयो यत्रोत्तरपदेन [i. e. प्रत्ययोत्तरपदेन लिङंशेन] नञ्॥ नामधात्वर्थयोगी तु नैव नञ् प्रतिषेधकः। वदत्यब्राह्मणाधर्मावन्यमात्रविरोधिनौ॥'

It will thus be seen that पर्युदास is of two kinds viz. (1) where a धात्वर्थ is construed with न, as in 'नेक्षेतोद्यन्तमादित्यम्' and (2) where a noun is construed with न, as in 'यजतिषु येयजामहं करोति नानुयाजेषु'.

These two sentences form the illustrations of the two exceptions to the general rule about the construction लिङ् with न, as we shall presently see.

Now we proceed to see what the first exception is. The illustration of this is 'नेक्षेतोद्यन्तमादित्यम्.' This sentence comes from a section which begins with 'तस्य व्रतम्.' Therefore, in this sentence the धात्वर्थ viz. ईक्षण, and not the लिङ् element, is to be construed with न. This gives rise to पर्युदास, which as we saw before, occurs when the धात्वर्थ is construed with न. The reason why in 'नेक्षेतोद्यन्तमादित्यम्' we cannot construe लिङ् with न is as follows :

The primary or conventional sense (रूढोऽर्थः) of the word व्रत is a vow or an observance i. e. something which is to be performed (कर्तव्यार्थः).The expression 'तस्य व्रतम्', occurring at the commencement (उपक्रमः) of a passage, section or chapter, shows that that passage, section or chapter contains vows or observances for some one to practise. 'तस्य व्रतम्' in the present case introduces (उपक्रमः) the vows which are to be observed by a स्नातक or a graduate-student. In connection with these vows occurs the sentence 'नेक्षेतोद्यन्तमादित्यम्.' Context thus shows that 'नेक्षेतोद्यन्तमादित्यम्' must lay down something which has to be observed or performed (कर्तव्यार्थः). Otherwise i. e. if 'नेक्षेतोद्यन्तमादित्यम्' were not to lay down a कर्तव्यार्थ, but were to be an ordinary निषेध, syntactical unity (एकवाक्यत्वम्) between the previous sentence viz. 'अथ व्रतम्' and the subsequent sentence viz. 'नेक्षेतोद्यन्तमादित्यम्' would not be secured. For, 'अथ व्रतम्' shows, as we saw before, that in what follows we have कर्तव्यार्थs. But if 'नेक्षेतोद्यन्तमादित्यम्' were not to lay down a कर्तव्यार्थ, its purport would be inconsistent with the उपक्रम or commencement viz. 'अथ व्रतम्'. Syntactical unity between the two sentences would thus be violated. So on the ground of the context i. e. the introduction with the expression 'अथ व्रतम्' it is settled that 'नेक्षेतोद्यन्तमादित्यम्' must convey a कर्तव्यार्थ.

Now if, following the general rule of prohibitory sentences, we were to construe the लिङ् element in ईक्षेत with न (प्रत्ययार्थान्वयः = प्रत्ययैकदेशलिङ्यान्वयः), the sentence would not convey a matter to be performed (कर्तव्यार्थानवगमात्). For न, connected with लिङ्, which means प्रवर्तना, would intimate the opposite of प्रवर्तना viz. निवर्तना or determent. And determent is not a thing to be performed. Therefore, we must construe the धात्वर्थ viz. ईक्षण with न in this sentence.

When the धात्वर्थ ईक्षण is construed with न, न will convey the opposite of ईक्षण viz. ईक्षणाभाव or अनीक्षण. But this sense also is incompatible or unsuitable in the present case. For, अनीक्षण, being merely an अभाव or negation, is not a कर्तव्यार्थ. We must, therefore, resort to लक्षणा and obtain through its help a sense, which being धात्वर्थविरोधी or ईक्षणविरोधी, would be कर्तव्यार्थ in addition. Such a sense is अनीक्षणसंकल्पः or the resolution of not seeing, in some such form as 'उद्यन्तमादित्यं नेक्षिष्ये'.

संकल्प is defined as 'संकल्पः कर्म मानसम्'. Resolution is thus a mental act and as such is a कर्तव्यार्थ.

The position now is thus: The construction of the धात्वर्थ with नञर्थ in नेक्षेत gives us the sense ईक्षणाभाव or अनीक्षण. This sense is unsuitable to the present case, where we require a कर्तव्यार्थ, which अनीक्षण is not. Thus we get मुख्यार्थबाध, which is the first condition of resorting to लक्षणा. लक्षणा then yields the sense अनीक्षणसंकल्प, which is a कर्तव्यार्थ.

Let us clearly understand our author. According to him the वाच्यार्थ or मुख्यार्थ of धातु + न is ईक्षणाभाव or अनीक्षण, which not being a कर्तव्यार्थ is unsuitable to the present case. लक्षणा is, therefore, resorted to. The लक्ष्यार्थ of धातु + न then is अनीक्षणसंकल्प, which being धात्वर्थविरोधी and कर्तव्यार्थ is suitable.

Here we desire to point out that our author does not seem to possess a clear conception of what the requirements of a लक्षणा are. The three conditions of लक्षणा, as laid down in 'मुख्यार्थबाधे तद्युक्तो ययान्योऽर्थः प्रतीयते । रूढेः प्रयोजनाद्वासौ लक्षणा शक्तिरर्पिता' साहित्यदर्पण II. 5, are मुख्यार्थबाध, तद्योग and रूढिप्रयोजनान्यतरत्व. Our author seems to have misunderstood the second condition. His words create an impression that according to him the लक्ष्यार्थ must be धात्वर्थविरोधी. The wording of the first line of the last paragraph of this section confirms this impression.

Now we desire to point out that **धात्वर्थविरोधित्व** is a characteristic of the वाच्यार्थ or मुख्यार्थ. If the लक्ष्यार्थ is also to be धात्वर्थविरोधी, it would be the same as वाच्यार्थ. What the second condition requires is that the लक्ष्यार्थ should be तद्युक्त i. e. वाच्यार्थयुक्त or connected with the expressed sense in some way. Here the वाच्यार्थ of धातु + न is धात्वर्थविरोध्यनीक्षण and धात्वर्थविरोध्यनीक्षणसंकल्प is connected with धात्वर्थविरोध्यनीक्षण by the relation of विषयिन् and विषय. For, the संकल्प possesses for its object the अनीक्षण. In this way धात्वर्थविरोध्यनीक्षणसंकल्प will be the लक्ष्यार्थ all right. But what we are objecting to is Bhāskara's suggestion that the लक्ष्यार्थ must be धात्वर्थविरोधी.

As a matter of fact we think that it is not necessary to resort to लक्षणा here at all. When we construe the root-element with the negative particle, the sense we obtain is ईक्षणाविरोधि किंचित्. This then is the वाच्यार्थ of धातु + न. But this sense is very general. There are lots of things which are ईक्षणाविरोधिन्. From among these we have to choose one which would serve our purpose.

ईक्षणाभाव or अनीक्षण is one of the things opposed to ईक्षण. But as it is not a कर्तव्यार्थ, we reject it. अनीक्षणसंकल्प is another of the ईक्षणविरोधि things. It is a कर्तव्यार्थ and consequently suits our purpose. So we adopt it. But we must note that अनीक्षणसंकल्प is nothing but the वाच्यार्थ viz. ईक्षणाविरोधि किंचित् in a particularized form. To it धात्वर्थविरोधित्व, which is a characteristic of वाच्यार्थ, legitimately belongs. No recourse to लक्षणा is necessary in order to derive this particularized form of वाच्यार्थ from its general form.

Leaving aside this criticism of Bhāskara, what we have come to so far is that in नेक्षेत the construction of धात्वर्थ with नञ् gives us the sense अनीक्षणसंकल्प. We must now see what the sense of 'नेक्षेतोद्यन्तमादित्यम्' is. We know that according to the Mīmāṁsist way of interpretation यजेत means यागेन भावयेत्. So ईक्षेत will mean ईक्षणेन भावयेत्. But in our sentence the धात्वर्थ is connected with न, which together with the धात्वर्थ signifies अनीक्षणसंकल्प. नेक्षेत, therefore, means अनीक्षणसंकल्पेन भावयेत्. Taking then the whole sentence together our meaning will be आदित्यविषयकानीक्षणसंकल्पेन भावयेत्. Now arises the question : What is it that is to be brought into existence (भाव्यम्) or achieved by means of this आदित्यविषयकानीक्षणसंकल्प? Answer to this question is supplied by another sentence occurring in the same context viz. 'एतावता हैनसा वियुक्तो भवति,' which lays down the fruit viz. पापक्षय, for the observance of the various vows enjoined for the snātaka. The complete sense of the sentence under discussion then becomes 'आदित्यविषयकानीक्षणसंकल्पेन पापक्षयं भावयेत्.' The resolution not to look at the sun frees the snātaka from the sin which he otherwise would have incurred by looking at it. Thus syntactical unity between the previous and subsequent sentences is established. Here पूर्वोत्तरवाक्ये mean the sentences 'नेक्षेतोद्यन्तमादित्यम्' and 'एतावता हैनसा वियुक्तो भवति.' Syntactical unity exists between these two, because the second supplies the साध्य (पापक्षयः) for the साधन (आदित्यविषयकानीक्षणसंकल्पः), which is mentioned in the first. It will thus be seen that the second sentence is syntactically connected with the first and the third with the second. In this way all three are syntactically connected. For, 'तस्य व्रतम्' introduces the vow 'नेक्षेत...त्यम्' explains the nature of that vow and 'एतावता...भवति' mentions the fruit to be achieved by its observance.

It should be noted here that our author's words, 'तस्य **व्रतमित्युपक्रम्य**' and '**वाक्यशेषावगतः** पापक्षयः' show that the three passages quoted viz. 'तस्य व्रतम्', 'नेक्षेतोद्यन्तमादित्यम्' and 'एतावता हैनसा वियुक्तो भवति' come from the same book. The same conclusion is confirmed by his endeavour to establish syntactical unity between these three sentences But no work where all these three passages occur exists. The sentence 'नेक्षेतोद्यन्तमादित्यम्' is Manusmṛti iv. 37, which reads thus: 'नेक्षेतोद्यन्तमादित्यं नास्तं यन्तं कदाचन। नोपसृष्टं न वारिस्थं न मध्यं नभसो गतम् ॥' It is true that in the fourth Chapter of Manu the duties of a snātaka are laid down, but Manu's उपक्रम ('अतोऽन्यतमया वृत्त्या जीवंस्तु **स्नातको** द्विजः। स्वर्गायुष्ययशस्यानि **व्रतानीमानि धारयेत्** ॥ iv. 14') and उपसंहार ('अनेन विप्रो वृत्तेन वर्तयन् वेदशास्त्रवित्। **व्यपेतकल्मषो** नित्यं ब्रह्मलोके महीयते ॥ iv. 260') are not the same as 'तस्य व्रतम्' and 'एतावता हैनसा वियुक्तो भवति'. While 'तस्य व्रतम्' seems to be a quotation from some गृह्यसूत्र, 'एतावता...भवति' has all the appearance of a Brāhmaṇa passage. Under these circumstances it is by no means easy to say whether Bhāskara took these three sentences from three different works and joined them together so as to form a syntactical whole, or whether he knew of some work, which is not known to us at present, but wherein these three passages occurred in the स्नातकप्रकरण. But it is really no use trying to probe into Bhāskara's mind. For he has evidently taken the three sentences from his master Āpadeva!

न च 'अत्र...भावनान्वयायोगात्—We have seen above that in the sentence 'नेक्षेतोद्यन्तमादित्यम्' the धात्वर्थ is to be construed with न and that the sense that we thus obtain is धात्वर्थविरोधि किंचित्. ईक्षणाभाव or अनीक्षण, though धात्वर्थविरोधि, was found unsuitable for our purpose, because it was not a कर्तव्यार्थ. We then obtained the sense अनीक्षणसंकल्प, which being both धात्वर्थविरोधी and कर्तव्यार्थ served our purpose. An objector now urges that there is another thing also viz. पटादिना चक्षुषोः पिधानम्, which is equally धात्वर्थविरोधि and कर्तव्यार्थ. Why should then अनीक्षणसंकल्प alone be construed with the भावना in ईक्षेत? Why should we not take पटादिना चक्षुषोः पिधानम् as the sense of धातु + न and understand from नेक्षेत the meaning 'पटादिना चक्षुषोः पिधानेन भावयेत्'?

The answer to this objection is that though 'पटादिना चक्षुषोः पिधानम्' is both धात्वर्थविरोधि and कर्तव्यार्थ and as such seems suitable for our purpose, we cannot accept it as the meaning of धातु + न, because it goes against the general trend or spirit of the passage. The passage opens with the words 'तस्य व्रतम्.' This shows that it aims at laying down some mental activity. For व्रतम् or a vow represents a mental resolve. Note 'मानसः संकल्पो व्रतमुच्यते' मेधातिथि on Manu iv. 13. The same expression further indicates that 'नेक्षेत etc' cannot have been intended to enjoin a prohibition. Thus, from the sentence under discussion we want a meaning which, in addition to being धात्वर्थविरोधि and कर्तव्यार्थ, would refer to mental activity. Such a meaning is अनीक्षणसंकल्प and hence it is construed with the भावना. A purely physical act such as covering the eyes with a piece of cloth cannot have been intended to have been laid down (कर्तव्यताभावेन) and hence is unfit to be construed with the भावना.

Notes on a few words and expressions in this Section are necessary.—स्नातकः (l. 3) means literally one who has had a bath (स्नातं स्नानमस्ति अस्य असौ स्नातः । अर्शआदित्वादच् मत्वर्थीयः । स एव स्नातक.). The word stands for a student who has performed the ceremony of ablution, which marks the conclusion of the period of his study or his vows. Such a bath is laid down by याज्ञवल्क्य in 'गुरवे तु वरं दत्वा **स्नायीत** तदनुज्ञया । वेदं व्रतानि वा पारं नीत्वा ह्युभयमेव वा ॥ ' आचाराध्याय 51. There are three kinds of स्नातक viz. विद्यास्नातक, व्रतस्नातक and विद्याव्रतस्नातक. Read यः समाप्य वेदान्, असमाप्य व्रतानि, समावर्तते स **विद्यास्नातकः** । यः समाप्य व्रतानि, असमाप्य वेदान्, समावर्तते स **व्रतस्नातकः** । उभयं समाप्य यः समावर्तते स **विद्याव्रतस्नातकः** ।' हारीत. स्नातक thus means a student who has completed his education and is about to enter life by marriage.—विध्यर्थप्रवर्तना० (l. 7) means लिङर्थप्रवर्तना. —धात्वर्थविरोध्यनीक्षणसंकल्पः (l. 9) should be dissolved as धात्वर्थविरोधी यः अनीक्षणसंकल्पः and not as धात्वर्थविरोधि यद् अनीक्षणं तस्य संकल्पः. — तस्य कर्तव्यताभावेन (l. 16) = तस्य पदार्थान्तरस्य पटादिना चक्षुषोः पिधानरूपस्य कर्तव्यतायाः अभावेन. It should be noted that पटादिना चक्षुषोः पिधानम् is here declared to be not कर्तव्य or a कर्तव्यार्थ, because it cannot have been the intention of the sentence to lay down a mere physical act such as this. कर्तव्यताभावेन is thus really equal to कर्तव्यत्वेन विवक्षितत्वासंभवेन. —भावनान्वयायोग्यत्वात् (l. 17). In this expression भावना means अर्थभावना. The reason why a purely physical act such as पटादिना चक्षुषोः पिधानम् cannot with propriety be construed with भावना in some such form as 'पटादिना चक्षुषोः पिधानेन पापक्षयं भावयेत्' is that the sentence 'नेक्षेत…… आदित्यम्' could not have been meant to lay down a single physical act like the covering of the eyes with a piece of cloth as a means of averting sin. It looks more proper and reasonable that a mental act such as a resolve should be regarded as a means of escape from sin and should consequently be construed with the अर्थभावना in नेक्षेत.

For the discussion centering round the sentence 'नेक्षेतोद्यन्तमादित्यम्' read :

'अनारभ्य श्रूयते—' नेक्षेतोद्यन्तमादित्यं नास्तं यन्तं कदाचन ' इति । **अत्र नञ्पदमभिधावृत्त्या प्रतिषेधं ब्रूते**, न तु पर्युदासम् । प्रतिषेधश्च प्राप्तिपूर्वकः । प्राप्तिश्च वैदिकस्य निषेधस्य वैदिकी प्रत्यासन्ना । तथा सति क्रतौ यत्र आदित्येक्षणं विहितम्, तत्रायं निषेध उदयास्तमयोर्दर्शन

प्रवर्तते । एवं च सति फलं न कल्पनीयम् । पर्युदासमाश्रित्य पुरुषार्थत्वाङ्गीकारे अधिकारसिद्धये फलं कल्पनीयं स्यात् । तस्मात् क्रत्वर्थो निषेधः—इति प्राप्ते—

ब्रूमः । 'तस्य व्रतम्' इत्युपक्रम्य 'नेक्षेतोद्यन्तमादित्यम्' इत्याम्नानत्वाद् अनीक्षणरूपं किंचिदनुष्ठेयम् । तच्च पर्युदासे सति अवकल्पते । **ईक्षणस्य अभावः प्रतिषेधपक्षे नञर्थः । पर्युदासपक्षे तु ईक्षणादितरः संकल्पो नञ्पदेन लक्ष्यते । स च संकल्पोऽत्र अनुष्ठेयव्रतत्वेन विधीयते ।**

यद्यपि ईक्षणादितरे बहवो व्यापारा अनुष्ठानयोग्याः सन्ति, तथापि कायिकवाचिकव्यापारविशेषस्य अप्रतीयमानत्वात्, मानसव्यापारस्य अवर्जनीयत्वाच्च संकल्प एव परिशिष्यते । संकल्पनीयश्चार्थः प्रत्यासत्त्या धात्वर्थनिषेधः । तथा सति 'उद्यन्तम्, अस्तं यन्तं च आदित्यं नेक्षिष्ये' इत्येवंरूपः संकल्पोऽत्र अनुष्ठेयत्वेन विधीयते ।

न च तस्य संकल्पस्य क्रत्वङ्गत्वम्, तद्बोधकश्रुतिलिङ्गादिप्रमाणाभावात् । न च पुरुषार्थत्वेऽपि प्रमाणाभावः, 'एतावता हैनसा मुक्तो भवति' इत्यनेन वाक्येन ईक्षितुः पुरुषस्य प्रत्यवायसंबन्धमुपन्यस्य तत्प्रत्यवायनिवारणफलकस्य अनीक्षणसंकल्पस्य विधानेन पुरुषार्थत्वावगमात् । क्रत्वङ्गत्वविवक्षायां तु क्रतुवैकल्यरूपो विपक्षबाध उपन्यस्येत । तस्माद् अनीक्षणसंकल्पादीनि प्रजापतिव्रतानि पुरुषार्थानि ।' जैमिनीयन्यायमालाविस्तर pp. 220–221

Section 67

In Sections 63 and 64 it has been stated as a general rule that in prohibitory sentences लिङर्थ is to be construed with नञर्थ and that the sense that we obtain from such construction is निवर्तना. Section 65 mentions two exceptions to this general rule. The first exception was dealt with in Section 66, where we saw that in 'नेक्षेतोद्यन्तमादित्यम्' the धात्वर्थ was construed with न, thus giving rise to the first kind of पर्युदास. Section 67 commences the treatment of the second exception.

The second exception (द्वितीयं बाधकमित्यर्थः) is विकल्पप्रसक्तिः or the contingency of option. Its illustration is 'यजतिषु येयजामहं करोति नानुयाजेषु.' In this sentence if we were to construe the प्रत्ययार्थ with न, we should have to admit विकल्प or option. But option does not find favour with the Mīmāṁsakas, because it has certain defects such as making a text alternately unauthoritative. Therefore, in order to get rid of option, we construe the noun अनुयाजेषु with न and obtain therefrom the sense अनुयाजव्यतिरिक्तेषु. The things, which are excluded, are here construed with न. This is the second kind of पर्युदास, which, as we see, is found in a sentence that contains exceptions to a general rule.

In order to understand the discussion that centres round the sentence 'यजतिषु.. नानुयाजेषु', which illustrates the second exception, we must know the sacrificial procedure that is referred to therein. When everything is ready for the commencement of the sacrifice, the Adhvaryu or the ministering priest issues an instruction (प्रैषः)

to the Hotṛ or the invoking priest with the words 'अग्निं यज', 'इन्द्रं यज' or 'सोमं यज', according to the deity to whom the oblation is to be made. The word यज in this instruction means 'याज्यां पठ.' Thereupon the Hotṛ recites the appropriate याज्याs or presenting or sacrificing stanzas in honour of that particular deity, preceded by the formula 'ये यजामहे', which means 'ये वयं होतारः अध्वर्युणा प्रेषितास्ते वयं याज्यां पठामः'. After the recital of the याज्याs the Hotṛ repeats the word वषट् which means 'हविर्दीयेत'. We have seen before (p. 177 *supra*) that the Hotṛ is known as वषट्कर्तृ on account of his utterance of वषट् at the end of the याज्याs.

The question now is the proper interpretation of the sentence 'यजतिषु येयजामहं करोति नानुयाजेषु.' यजतिषु means यागेषु. यजति, which is the third person singular from यज to sacrifice, is treated as a noun and means a याग or sacrifice in general. In all sacrifices the Adhvaryu issues the instruction 'यज', that is mentioned in the above paragraph. यजतिषु is, therefore, paraphrased by '"यज" इति अध्वर्युप्रैषानन्तरं क्रियमाणेषु यागेषु'. येयजामहं करोति is equal to '"ये यजामहे" इति मन्त्रमुच्चारयति'. The formula 'ये यजामहे' is shortened into the noun येयजामहः.

The sentence 'यजतिषु येयजामहं करोति नानुयाजेषु' is really constituted by two viz. 'यजतिषु येयजामहं करोति' and 'अनुयाजेषु येयजामहं न करोति'. There is no trouble whatsoever about the first sentence, which contains a general injunction that in all sacrifices one should recite the formula 'ये यजामहे.' The second sentence is the proper illustration of the second exception to the general rule about the construction of न in negative sentences viz. that the negative particle is to be construed with the प्रत्यय. We shall now see how on account of विकल्पप्रसक्ति we cannot construe न with प्रत्यय in this sentence, but must construe it with the noun अनुयाजेषु.

'अनुयाजेषु येयजामहं न करोति' has all the appearance of an ordinary निषेधवाक्य. If, therefore, following the general rule about the construction of the negative particle in prohibitory sentences, we were to connect the प्रत्ययार्थ or the meaning of the suffix i.e. the meaning of the लिङ् element therein (प्रत्ययार्थान्वयः = प्रत्ययैकदेशलिङर्थान्वयः) with the नञर्थ or the meaning of the negative particle, the sense that we would obtain would be निवर्तना or निषेध or प्रतिषेध or prohibition of the use of the formula 'ये यजामहे' in the Anuyājas in some such form as 'अनुयाजेषु येयजामहं न कुर्यात्'. It should be noted here that though करोति is a form of the present tense, it is practically equal to the potential form कुर्यात्, because the present is many a time used in the Veda to enjoin things and has in such cases the sense of the potential. Vide above p. 91, paragraph 2.

स च प्राप्तिपूर्वक...बाधः—Now it is a rule of common sense that when a prohibition is laid down, it must be preceded by the establishment (प्राप्तिः) of the thing prohibited. We cannot prohibit an impossible thing. Nobody, for example, would frame a rule like 'नेक्षेत भास्करं रात्रौ.' For, it is not possible to see the sun at night. Therefore, when 'अनुयाजेषु येयजामहं न करोति' is interpreted as containing the prohibition of the use of the formula 'ये यजामहे' in the Anuyājas, we must suppose that the formula had accrued (प्राप्त) in the Anuyājas. Such प्राप्ति or establishment of the formula in the Anuyājas must be declared to proceed from the sentence 'यजतिषु येयजामहं करोति,' which refers to all sacrifices in general.

The position now is this: 'यजतिषु येयजामहं करोति' enjoins the use of the formula 'ये यजामहे' in all sacrifices including the Anuyājas. But 'अनुयाजेषु येयजामहं न करोति' prohibits its use in the Anuyājas. So here is a case of the prohibition by one scriptural passage of a thing which has been established by another. We cannot say that the second passage of prohibition annuls or renders nugatory (बाधः) the first. For, both being scriptural passages are of equal strength and the relation of बाध्य and बाधक cannot be admitted to exist between them. Therefore, in this case option has to be accepted. Thus, if in 'अनुयाजेषु येयजामहं न करोति' प्रत्ययार्थ is construed with नञर्थ, we have to admit an option between this sentence and 'यजतिषु येयजामहं करोति.' This is the विकल्पप्रसक्ति that makes it impossible for us to connect the negative particle with the suffix and forms the second exception to the general rule regarding the construction of the negative particle in prohibitory sentences.

प्राप्तिमूलरागस्य इव...बाधायोगात्—This sentence supplies a negative illustration for the assertion that the निषेध in 'अनुयाजेषु येयजामहं करोति' cannot annul or set aside the प्राप्ति or establishment of येयजामह in the Anuyājas, because such प्राप्ति proceeds from another scriptural passage. Out of some evil passion a man is inclined to commit the murder of a Brāhmaṇa. Passion (रागः) is thus the basis or root of ब्राह्मणहननप्राप्ति. The prohibition 'ब्राह्मणो न हन्तव्यः' rightly annuls the passion and sets aside the possibility of a Brāhmaṇa-murder. Here the opposition is between राग or passion, which is ब्राह्मणहननप्राप्तिमूल, and शास्त्र viz. ब्राह्मणो न हन्तव्यः, which is निषेधमूल. As शास्त्र is stronger than राग, it properly annuls राग. But in the case under discussion the opposition is between two शास्त्र viz. 'यजतिषु येयजामहं करोति,' which enjoins the formula 'ये यजामहे' in all sacrifices, and 'अनुयाजेषु येयजामहं न करोति', which forbids it in the case of the Anuyājas. Both being तुल्यबल, one cannot with propriety annul (बाधायोगः) the other. Option between the two has thus to be admitted.

'ब्राह्मणो न हन्तव्यः'—This sentence occurs in the मीमांसान्यायप्रकाश of आपदेव and looks like a quotation from some Smṛti. But it cannot be traced anywhere. Apparently, Āpadeva has framed it himself, relying upon '**न जातु ब्राह्मणं हन्यात्** सर्वपापेष्वपि स्थितम्। राष्ट्रादेनं बहिः कुर्यात् समग्रधनमक्षतम् ॥ 380 न ब्राह्मणवधाद् भूयानधर्मो विद्यते भुवि। तस्मादस्य वधं राजा मनसापि न चिन्तयेत् ॥ 381' मनुस्मृति viii.

न च 'पदे जुहोति' इति०—It was stated above that as in the present case the opposition lay between two scriptural passages, one could not with propriety annul the other. An objector now points out a case where one scriptural passage annuls another and asks why the same should not analogously happen in the present instance as well.

In the Jyotiṣṭoma sacrifice Soma is to be purchased with a ruddy, yellow-eyed, one-year-old cow. There the sacrificial procedure is that when the cow starts from the stable for the place of purchaser, the purchaser viz. the sacrificer follows her for six steps, planting his foot on the foot-print of the cow. Then on the seventh foot-print of the cow he deposits some gold and offers an oblation. This is enjoined in 'सप्तमे पदे जुहोति,' which is known as पदशास्त्र. But the general rule about हवन is 'आहवनीये जुहोति.' This is known as आहवनीयशास्त्र and lays down that all oblations are to be offered in the Āhavanīya fire. Under these circumstances it has been decided in what is known as आहवनीयबाधाधिकरण (जै. सू. X. viii. 16) that the general rule (सामान्यशास्त्रम्) 'आहवनीये जुहोति' is annulled by the special rule (विशेषशास्त्रम्) 'सप्तमे पदे जुहोति', which serves as an exception to it.

Similarly, why should we not hold, asks the objector, that the special rule 'अनुयाजेषु येयजामहं न करोति' annuls the general rule 'यजतिषु येयजामहं करोति'? Thus, बाध or annulment having been admitted, the contingency of option (विकल्पप्रसक्तिः) between the two passages would be obviated.

परस्परनिरपेक्षयोरेव०—This passage contains Bhāskara's reply to the above objection. He points out that the relation of बाध्य and बाधक can exist between those passages only, which are independent of each other (परस्परनिरपेक्ष). The passage 'सप्तमे पदे जुहोति' (पदशास्त्रम्) does not depend upon, or require (अनपेक्षणम्), the passage 'आहवनीये जुहोति' (आहवनीयशास्त्रम्) in order to enjoin its own meaning (स्वार्थविधानार्थम्). What is meant is that 'सप्तमे पदे जुहोति' has not necessarily to presuppose the existence of 'आहवनीये जुहोति' in order to lay down its sense. It is thus independent of 'आहवनीये जुहोति' and can consequently annul it. But in the present case (प्रकृते तु) the passage 'अनुयाजेषु येयजामहं न करोति,' which contains a prohibition (निषेधशास्त्रम्), has necessarily to depend upon the passage 'यजतिषु येयजामहं करोति' for the establishment of what it prohibits (निषेध्यप्रसक्त्यर्थम् = निषेध्यप्राप्त्यर्थम्). The निषेधशास्त्र, therefore, is not independent of the येयजामहशास्त्र. Consequently, the former cannot annul the latter.

The idea is this: One cannot prohibit a thing which has not accrued. The निषेधशास्त्र in the present case prohibits the use of the formula 'ये यजामहे' in the Anuyājas. The प्राप्ति of 'ये यजामहे' in the Anuyājas proceeds from the येयजामहशास्त्र. The निषेधशास्त्र thus depends upon the येयजामहशास्त्र, which it consequently cannot annul.

From the above discussion it follows that two conditions are necessary for the existence of बाध्यबाधकभाव between two scriptural passages. First, they must be related to each other as सामान्यशास्त्र and विशेषशास्त्र. Secondly, they must be independent of each other. Both these conditions are satisfied in the case of the आहवनीयशास्त्र and the पदशास्त्र. That is why the आहवनीयशास्त्र is annulled by the पदशास्त्र. But in the case of the येयजामहशास्त्र and the निषेधशास्त्र, the second condition is not satisfied, though the first is. That is why the निषेधशास्त्र cannot annul the येयजामहशास्त्र.

Another point to be noted in this connection is that in the दृष्टान्त case the बाधकवाक्य 'सप्तमे पदे जुहोति' lays down something positive. It can, therefore, do so independently of the बाध्यवाक्य. But in the प्रकृत case the sentence 'अनुयाजेषु येयजामहं न करोति,' which is sought to be made out as a बाधकवाक्य, does not enjoin anything positive. It has only a negative force. It is hence dependent upon 'यजतिषु येयजामहं करोति'. It cannot annul this, therefore.

Read in this connection:

'शास्त्रयोर्हि तत्र बाध्यबाधकभावो यत्र परस्परनिरपेक्षता। न हि पदशास्त्रस्य स्वार्थविधानार्थमाहवनीयशास्त्रापेक्षास्ति। निषेधशास्त्रस्य तु प्रसक्त्यर्थं 'यजतिषु येयजामहं करोति' इति विधेरस्ति अपेक्षा।' मीमांसान्यायप्रकाश

'अनारभ्य श्रूयते–'यदाहवनीये जुह्वति तेन सोऽस्याभीष्टः प्रीतः' इति। ज्योतिष्टोमे श्रूयते—'पदे जुहोति, वर्त्मनि जुहोति' इति। राजसूये श्रूयते—'वल्मीकवपायामुत्सृज्य जुहोति' इति। तथा अन्यत्र श्रूयते—'गार्हपत्ये पत्नीसंयाजान् जुहोति' इति। तत्र अनारभ्यवादे होमसामान्यमनूद्य

आहवनीयो विहितः । प्रकरणानियमितैः पदादिवाक्यैस्तदनुबद्धा विशिष्टहोमा विहिताः । गार्हपत्य-वाक्येन होममनूद्य गार्हपत्यो विहितः । तत्र पदादिहोमेषु सामान्यशास्त्रेण प्राप्त आहवनीयो विशेष-शास्त्रप्राप्तैः पदादिभिः सह विकल्प्यते । कुतः । उभयोः प्रत्यक्षवचनयोः क्रत्वर्थत्वेन समानबलत्वात् ।

ननु 'ऐन्द्र्या गार्हपत्यमुपतिष्ठते' इत्यत्र यथा श्रुत्या लिङ्गं बाध्यते । यथा वा चोदकातिदिष्टानां कुशानामुपदिष्टैः शरैर्बाधः । तथा सामान्यस्य विशेषेण बाधोऽस्तु । इति चेत् । न । वैषम्यात् । लिङ्ग विलम्बितत्वाद् दुर्बलम् । चोदकश्चानुमेयतया दुर्बलः । न तु एवं सामान्यशास्त्रं विलम्ब्यते, नाप्य-नुमीयते । अतो दौर्बल्याभावाद् विकल्पः । इति प्राप्ते—

ब्रूमः । होमसामान्यस्य अनुवादकं यच्छास्त्रं तत् सामान्ये मुख्यत्वाद् होमविशेषानुवादे लाक्ष-णिकतया दुर्बलम् । विशेषशास्त्रं तु व्यावृत्त्या विधायकत्वात् प्रबलम् । न च पदादिशास्त्रमपि होम-सामान्यमेवानूद्य पदादिविधायकत्वेन समानबलं स्याद् इति शङ्कयम् । प्रकरणनियमितत्वेन विशिष्ट-विधायकस्य सामान्यानुवादकत्वायोगात् । तस्मात् **प्रबलेन विशेषेण सामान्यं बाध्यते** ।'
जैमिनीयन्यायमालाविस्तर pp. 606–607

Section 68

So far we have seen that if we were to construe the negative particle न in 'अनुयाजेषु येयजामहं न करोति' with the धात्वर्थ so as to make the sentence a निषेधवाक्य, we should have to admit विकल्प or option between this sentence and 'यजातिषु येयजामहं करोति.' For, the निषेधवाक्य cannot, as we saw in the last paragraph, annul the येयजामहवाक्य. In this Section Bhāskara points out that option cannot properly be admitted (स च न युक्तः) between the two sentences under discussion, because option leads to two faults viz. पाक्षिकाप्रामाण्य and द्विरदृष्टकल्पना. We must, therefore, give up the idea of construing the negative particle with the धात्वर्थ and must construe it with the noun अनुयाजेषु. 'न अनुयाजेषु' would then yield the sense 'अनुयाजव्यतिरिक्तेषु यजातिषु'. This makes the sentence 'न अनुयाजेषु येयजामहं करोति' an example of पर्युदास and not of निषेध, which it would have been, if we had construed न with करोति.

विकल्पे...प्यापातात्—The first fault, which arises from the adoption of option is alternative unauthoritativeness (पाक्षिकं यद् अप्रामाण्यं तस्य आपातः प्रसक्तिः इत्यर्थः). The standard instance of विकल्प is 'व्रीहिभिर्यजेत यवैर्वा [यजेत]'. If we perform the sacrifice with rice-grains (व्रीहिः), the sentence 'यवैर्यजेत' becomes अप्रमाण or unauthoritative, because we are not following it. Similarly, if we carry out the sacrifice with barley-grains (यवः), 'व्रीहिभिर्यजेत' ceases to be प्रमाण or authoritative, because we are disregarding it. Thus, both the sentences become alternatively unauthoritative.

In the present case the same thing would happen. If we were to adopt the formula 'ये यजामहे' in the Anuyājas, the sentence

'न अनुयाजेषु येयजामहं करोति' would not be authoritative. If on the other hand we drop the use of that formula in the Anuyājas, the sentence 'यजातिषु येयजामहं करोति' would be अप्रमाण. Thus, पाक्षिक अप्रामाण्य follows the adoption of option. The result of this is the eight faults to which option is liable, as we saw before (p. 101).

द्विरदृष्टकल्पना च स्यात्—The second fault to which option leads is the necessity of having to admit a double unseen result. The idea is this: The adoption or otherwise of the formula 'ये यजामहे' ('ये यजामहे' इत्यस्य अनुष्ठानमननुष्ठानं वा) produces no visible result as far as the sacrifice is concerned. We must, therefore, suppose that both the adoption and non-adoption of the formula lead to some unseen transcendental result (अदृष्टम्). Further, we must assume that there are really two kinds of such unseen results, one proceeding from the adoption of the formula and the other arising from its non-adoption. For, both the adoption and non-adoption are enjoined by scriptural passages and as they have no seen fruit, they must be assumed to lead to an unseen one.

विधि...... पुरुषार्थत्वात्–In the Mīmāṁsā distinction is often made between things which are पुरुषार्थ (for the benefit of man) and those that are क्रत्वर्थ (for the benefit of the sacrifice). Rites or acts, which produce no visible fruit, are regarded as पुरुषार्थ. पुरुषार्थ things lead to unseen result. For example, sacrifices like ज्योतिष्टोम and दर्शपूर्णमास are पुरुषार्थ, because they produce no visible fruit. They are, therefore, regarded as producing some unseen result, technically known as अपूर्व, which secures heaven for their performer on his death. Similarly, संस्कारs or purificatory rites like उपनयन, are पुरुषार्थ. No visible change is produced in a boy who is उपनीत. उपनयन is, therefore, regarded as giving rise to some unseen result. On the other hand things, which have a visible fruit, are supposed to be क्रत्वर्थ e. g. अवहनन, which produces a seen fruit viz. unhusking. क्रत्वर्थ things do not lead to अदृष्ट or अपूर्व.

In the present case as both the adoption (विधिः) and the non-adoption or prohibition (प्रतिषेधः = निषेधः) of the formula 'ये यजामहे' leads to no visible fruit, they are regarded as पुरुषार्थ. Consequently, they give rise to two different kinds of अदृष्ट.

For the distinction of पुरुषार्थ and क्रत्वर्थ read 'तत्र वेदादिप्रमेयोऽर्थस्त्रिविधः–क्रत्वर्थः, पुरुषार्थः, उभयार्थश्चेति। तत्र प्रयाजादिकं केवलं क्रत्वर्थः। फलं तत्करणं च पुरुषार्थः। यथा स्वर्गादिर्ज्योतिष्टोमादिश्च। दध्यादि तु उभयरूपम्। 'दध्ना जुहोति' इति फलासंयुक्तवाक्येन क्रत्वर्थत्वात्। 'दध्ना इन्द्रियकामस्य जुहुयात्' इत्यनेन फलाय विधानात् पुरुषार्थत्वात्।' मीमांसापरिभाषा

अतो नात्र......पर्युदासस्यैव—This sentence embodies the result of the whole discussion. It is this that we cannot resort to प्रतिषेध or निषेध or prohibition in the sentence 'अनुयाजेषु येयजामहं न करोति.' This means that in the sentence under discussion we must not construe the negative particle with the धात्वर्थ. What we must, therefore, do is to resort to पर्युदास or exclusion by construing न with अनुयाजेषु (नञोऽनुयाज-संबन्धमाश्रित्य).

इत्थं च...लाक्षणिकत्वात्—This sentence gives us the ultimate meaning that we obtain from 'अनुयाजेषु येयजामहं न करोति', when we construe न with अनुयाजेषु and adopt पर्युदास.

The negative particle, as we saw in Section 64 above, conveys the opposite of the sense of the word with which it is connected. 'न अनुयाजेषु' would, therefore, intimate अनुयाजाभाव or अनुयाजासत्त्व. This sense is clearly unsuitable in the present context (मुख्यार्थबाधः). We, therefore, resort to लक्षणा and thereby obtain from 'न अनुयाजेषु' the sense 'अनुयाजेतरेषु अनुयाजव्यतिरिक्तेषु वा यजतिषु.'

It should be noted that it is really not necessary to resort to लक्षणा here. For, तदन्यत्वम् is one of the legitimate senses of the negative particle. Thus, 'न अनुयाजेषु' would naturally or primarily convey 'अनुयाजान्येषु अनुयाजव्यतिरिक्तेषु वा,' even as अब्राह्मणः means ब्राह्मणेतरः.

एवं च न विकल्पः—The final meaning that we obtain from 'अनुयाजेषु येयजामहं न करोति' is 'अनुयाजव्यतिरिक्तेषु यजतिषु येयजामहं करोति.' This meaning does not in any way conflict with the sense of 'यजतिषु येयजामहं करोति.' Therefore, the possibility of there being option between the two sentences does not simply arise.

अत्र च वाक्ये...व्यतिरिक्तेषु इति—This passage is intended to refute a possible objection, which may be thus stated:

You have decided, says the objector, that the sentence 'अनुयाजेषु येयजामहं न करोति' conveys the sense अनुयाजव्यतिरिक्तेषु यजतिषु येयजामहं करोति.' According to your interpretation the sentence under discussion really enjoins two things viz. (1) येयजामहं कुर्यात् and (2) तं च येयजामहम् अनुयाजव्य-तिरिक्तेषु यजतिषु कुर्यात्. Thus, as one sentence contains the विधि of two things, वाक्यभेद results. And वाक्यभेद is a serious defect. Your interpretation is, therefore, not acceptable.

Against this Bhāskara points out that in the sentence 'अनुयाजेषु येयजामहं न करोति' (अत्र च वाक्ये = अस्मिन् 'नानुयाजेषु' इति वाक्ये) we do not have the विधि or injunction of the formula 'ये यजामहे', as the objector thinks. For, the formula has been enjoined (प्राप्तत्वात् = विहितत्वात्) by the another sentence viz. यजतिषु येयजामहं करोति. What the sentence ' अनुयाजेषु येयजामहं न करोति ' really does is to refer by way of an अनुवाद or subsequent allusion to the formula ' ये यजामहे, ' which has been enjoined by the general rule (सामान्यशास्त्रम्) 'यजतिषु येयजामहं करोति', and to lay down that its province is all sacrifices except the Anuyājas. What it thus means is that when in sacrifices we are enjoined to use the formula ' ये यजामहे ', we have to use it in all sacrifices other than the Anuyājas (यद् यजतिषु येयजामहं करोति तदनुयाजव्यतिरिक्तेषु). So the sentence contains only one विधि viz. that regarding the limitation of the province of the formula ' ये यजामहे ', which has been laid down by ' यजतिषु येयजामहं करोति ' as a general rule. Hence, no वाक्यभेद is involved in our interpretation. In a word what the sentence ' अनुयाजेषु येयजामहं न करोति does is to limit the province of rule of general application contained in ' यजतिषु येयजामहं करोति. '

Read in this connection : ' ननु ' नानुयाजेषु येयजामहं करोति ' इत्यत्र ' ये यजामहे ' इति मन्त्रविधौ, तस्य अनुयाजव्यतिरिक्तविषयत्वविधौ च वाक्यभेदः स्यात् । [इति चेत् न ।] ' यजतिषु येयजामहं करोति ' इति याजिसामान्ये तद्विधायकशास्त्रप्राप्तमेव ' ये यजामहे ' इति मन्त्रम**नूद्य** ' नानुयाजेषु येयजामहं करोति ' इत्यत्र **तस्य अनुयाजव्यतिरिक्तविषयता विधीयते** इत्यर्थः । तथा च ' यजतिषु ' इत्यादिसामान्यशास्त्रस्य विशेषापेक्षिणो ' नानुयाजेषु ' इत्यादिविशेषशास्त्रेण अनुयाजव्यतिरिक्तविषयसमर्पणाद् अनुयाजव्यतिरिक्तयागेषु ' ये यजामहे ' इति मन्त्रः कर्तव्यतया प्राप्तः । अनुयाजेषु तु तस्य कर्तव्यत्वेन अप्राप्तत्वाद् अप्रतिषिद्धत्वाच्च नात्र विकल्पप्रसङ्गोऽपि संभवति । लक्षणया अनुयाजव्यतिरिक्तविषयसमर्पणाच्च न ' नानुयाजेषु ' इत्यादिवाक्यस्य अप्रमाण्यमपि भवति । तस्मात् पर्युदासाश्रयणे बाधकाभावात् स एव स्वीकर्तव्य इति भावः । ' रामेश्वर

Here ends the discussion about पर्युदास or exclusion, which forms an exception or obstacle (बाधकम्) to निषेध. Let us briefly recapitulate what we have learnt. In prohibitory sentences the negative particle is generally construed with the लिङ् element of the suffix. लिङ् means प्रवर्तना. Joined with the negative particle, it conveys the sense of the opposite of प्रवर्तना viz. निवर्तना or निषेध.

This general rule about the construction of the negative particle with the suffix has two exceptions viz. (1) When the prohibitory sentence occurs under the heading ' तस्य व्रतम् '. (2) When there is a contingency of option. In both these cases we understand पर्युदास instead of निषेध. पर्युदास is thus of two kinds viz. (1) the one in which the negative particle is construed with the धात्वर्थ, as in the first exception, and (2) the second in which the negative particle is construed with the things excluded or excepted, as in the second exception.

For the discussion centring round the sentence 'नानुयाजेषु येयजामहं करोति' read the following:

'महापितृयज्ञे चोदकप्राप्तं वरणं प्रति श्रूयते-' न आर्षेयं वृणीते, न होतारम्' इति। तथा अनारम्यवादः श्रूयते—' आ श्रावय ' इति चतुरक्षरम्, ' अस्तु श्रौषट्' इति चतुरक्षरम्, ' यज ' इति द्व्यक्षरम्, ' ये यजामहे ' इति पञ्चाक्षरम्, द्व्यक्षरो वषट्कारः, एष वै सप्तदशः प्रजापतिर्यज्ञमन्वायत्तः ' इति। तत्रोक्तम्—' नानुयाजेषु येयजामहं करोति ' इति। तत्र वरणस्य विधिप्रतिषेधौ चोदकप्रत्यक्षवचनाभ्यां प्रतीयेते। ' ये यजामहे ' इति मन्त्रस्य तु द्वाभ्यां प्रत्यक्षवचनाभ्यां विधिप्रतिषेधप्रतीतिः। तत्र विधायकप्रतिषेधकयोर्द्वयोः प्रमाणयोरवैयर्थ्यार्थं विकल्पः। इति प्राप्ते —

ब्रूमः—**अष्टदोषग्रस्तत्वाद् विकल्पो न न्याय्यः**। ननु परस्परविरुद्धयोर्विधिप्रतिषेधयोः समुच्चयस्यापि अभावात् का गतिरत्र इति चेत्। उच्यते। निषेधत्वेन प्रतीयमानमिदं ' न ' इत्यनेन शब्देन उपेतं वाक्यं विधिवाक्यस्य अंशो भविष्यति। तथा हि। यदि ' न ' इत्ययं शब्दः करोतिना संबध्यते, तदा ' येयजामहं न करोति ' इत्येवं प्रतिषेधः स्यात्। यदि ' वृणीते ' इति आख्यातप्रत्ययेन संबध्यते, तदा ' वरणं न कर्तव्यम् ' इति निषिध्येत। न तु एवं संबध्यते, किन्तु अनुयाजपदेन वृञ्धातुना च संबध्यते। तथा सति ' **अनुयाजव्यतिरिक्तेषु यागेषु येयजामहः कर्तव्यः** ' ' वरणव्यतिरिक्तमङ्गजातमनुष्ठेयम् ' इति **येयजामहवरणपर्युदासेन** विधेरेव विशेषितत्वे सति प्रतिषेधवाक्यस्य कस्यचिदभावाद् न विकल्पः शङ्कितुमपि शक्यः।' जैमिनीयन्यायमालाविस्तर p.600

Section 69

Towards the end of the last Section it was pointed out that what the पर्युदास or exclusion in the sentence ' अनुयाजेषु येयजामहं न करोति ' really does is to restrict (संकोचनम्) the formula ' ये यजामहे ', which accrues from a general text (सामान्यशास्त्रप्राप्त), to a particular area (विशेषः). Now, such restriction is also done by what is known as उपसंहारः or limitation. What is then the distinction between पर्युदास and उपसंहार? In this Section Bhāskara explains this distinction.

' सामान्यशास्त्रप्राप्तस्य विशेषे संकोचनम्' is a description which is applicable to both पर्युदास and उपसंहार. पर्युदास or exclusion and उपसंहार or limitation resemble each other in so far as the nature of both is to restrict what has accrued from a general rule to particular cases. But the following are the points of distinction between them: (1) While पर्युदास restricts what has been established by a general rule to cases other than those specified (तदन्यमात्रसंकोचः—तस्मात् विशेषात् स्वशब्देनोपात्ताद् अन्यमात्रे संकोचः), उपसंहार restricts it to a specified case (तन्मात्रसंकोचः—विशेषमात्रसंकोच।). (2) पर्युदास mentions the cases which are excluded from the operation of the general rule. उपसंहार on the other hand names the case where the general rule is to be followed. (3) पर्युदास is negative in form i.e. a sentence containing पर्युदास possesses a negative particle in it. This is not the case with उपसंहार, whose form is positive.

Other definitions of पर्युदास and उपसंहार are 'स्वमात्रे व्यवस्थापन**मुपसंहारः**। स्वेतरस्मिन् व्यवस्थापनं **पर्युदासः**।' ' स्वस्मिन् स्वेतरस्मिंश्च प्राप्तं विषयं स्वेतरस्माद् व्यावर्त्य स्वमात्रेऽवस्थापन**मुपसंहारः**। तथैव प्राप्तं विषयं स्वस्माद् व्यावर्त्य स्वेतरस्मिन् व्यवस्थापनं **पर्युदासः**।'

'आग्नेयं चतुर्धा करोति' is an example of उपसंहार. In the दर्शपूर्णमास there are three cakes known as आग्नेय, अग्नीषोमीय and ऐन्द्राग्न, because they are sacred to Agni, Agni and Soma, and Indra and Agni respectively. After the offering, called स्विष्टकृत्, is presented, a cake has to be divided into four for the purpose of being distributed among the four officiating priests. In this connection the general rule 'पुरोडाशं चतुर्धा करोति' makes quadruplication, or division into four, available for all the three cakes.

But the special rule 'आग्नेयं चतुर्धा करोति' restricts quadruplication to the cake of Agni only. As here we have restriction of the quadruplication, established by the general rule, to the case specified viz., the cake of Agni, 'आग्नेयं चतुर्धा करोति' becomes an example of उपसंहार.

We have already seen that 'अनुयाजेषु येयजामहं न करोति' is an example of पर्युदास. Here येयजामह is established by the general rule 'यजतिषु येयजामहं करोति' for all sacrifices. But the sentence 'अनुयाजेषु येयजामहं न करोति' restricts येयजामह to sacrifices other than the specificed Anuyājas. As 'अनुयाजेषु येयजामहं न करोति' thus restricts येयजामह to sacrifices other than the specified (तदन्यमात्रसंकोचः), it becomes an example of पर्युदास.

For the illustration of उपसंहार, given in the text, read: 'दर्शपूर्णमासयो श्रूयते—'आग्नेयं चतुर्धा करोति' इति । तत्र आग्नेयवद् ऐन्द्राग्नाग्नीषोमीययोरपि पुरोडाशयोरग्निसंबन्धाद् आग्नेयशब्देन पुरोडाशत्रयमुपलक्ष्यते । ततस्त्रयाणां शेष इति चेत् ।

मैवम् । न हि 'आग्नेयः' इत्ययं तद्धितः संबन्धमात्रे विहितः, किन्तु देवतासंबन्धे । अग्निश्च केवलो द्विदैवत्ययोः पुरोडाशयोर्न देवता । ततो देवतैकदेशेन कृत्स्नदेवतोपलक्षणत्वाद् आग्नेयत्वं तयोर्नमुख्यमिति मुख्ये एव आग्नेये चतुर्धाकरणं व्यवतिष्ठते ।' जैमिनीयन्यायमालाविस्तर p. 121

It will be noticed that in the above passage the conclusion about the restriction of quadruplication to the cake of Agni only is arrived at in a manner slightly different from that in our text.

Section 70

In Sections 67 and 68 the second exception to the general rule regarding the construction of the negative particle with the suffix in prohibitory sentences was dealt with. That exception made it clear that we must not construe the negative particle with the suffix and understand निषेध or प्रतिषेध or prohibition in the sentence, if such construction were to land us in an option. For, as we saw before, the Mīmāṃsakas are very unwilling to admit option, because it involves पाक्षिक अप्रामाण्य and द्विरदृष्टकल्पना. This Section now points out a case where even at the risk of having to admit option (विकल्पप्रसक्तौ अपि),

प्रतिषेध or prohibition has to be resorted to by construing the negative particle with the suffix, because there is no other alternative (अनन्यगत्या).

'नातिरात्रे षोडशिनं गृह्णाति' represents such an example, where प्रतिषेध or निषेध has to be admitted, even though such admission leads to option. अतिरात्रः is one of the four varieties of Jyotiṣṭoma, which is a Soma sacrifice, the other three being अग्निष्टोमः, उक्थ्यः and षोडशी. षोडशिन् as a common noun means a kind of cup, used to hold the Soma juice (सोमपात्रविशेषः).

The sentence 'अतिरात्रे षोडशिनं गृह्णाति' enjoins the taking of the cup in the Atirātra sacrifice. As against this we have 'नातिरात्रे षोडशिनं गृह्णाति', which prohibits the grasping of the cup. We have seen before that when a thing enjoined by a scriptural passage is prohibited by another, option alone must be admitted as existing between the two (शास्त्रविहितस्य शास्त्रान्तरेण प्रतिषेधे विकल्प एव). So, in the present case the contingency of option (विकल्पप्रसक्तिः) between 'अतिरात्रे षोडशिनं गृह्णाति' and 'नातिरात्रे षोडशिनं गृह्णाति' arises.

We remember that when a similar contingency of option arose between 'यजतिषु येयजामहं करोति', and 'अनुयाजेषु येयजामहं न करोति', we got rid of the option by resorting to पर्युदास. We then construed न, not with करोति, which would have given us प्रतिषेध, but with अनुयाजेषु, from which we obtained the meaning अनुयाजव्यतिरिक्तेषु. Can we adopt a similar course in the present case and thus avoid option? 'No', declares Bhāskara, 'for it is impossiple to do so (असंभवात्).' How it is impossible to resort to पर्युदास in the case of 'नातिरात्रे षोडशिनं गृह्णाति' is explained in the passage, commencing with 'तथा हि'.

Adoption of पर्युदास or exclusion means the construction of the negative particle with either the धात्वर्थ or a noun in the sentence, instead of with the प्रत्ययार्थ, which would result in प्रतिषेध. In the case of 'नातिरात्रे षोडशिनं गृह्णाति' it is not possible to construe the negative particle with the धात्वर्थ. Such a construction is possible only in the case of those negative sentences that are introduced with the words 'तस्य व्रतम्'. 'नातिरात्रे षोडशिनं गृह्णाति' does not pretend to lay down any vow. So, the negative particle cannot here be construed with the धात्वर्थ.

Now, let us see what happens when we construe न with a noun in that sentence. 'नातिरात्रे षोडशिनं गृह्णाति' contains two nouns viz. षोडशिन् and अतिरात्रे. If we were to construe न with षोडशिन्, it would yield the sense षोडशिव्यतिरिक्तम् (something different from the cup). The sense of the sentence (वाक्यार्थः) would then be that one should grasp something different from a cup in the Atirātra. This sense certainly would not do (स च न संभवति). because it contradicts the direct injunction (प्रत्यक्षविधिविरोधः) regarding the grasping of the cup contained in 'अतिरात्रे षोडशिनं गृह्णाति.' The idea is that in view of the direct injunction to grasp the cup in the Atirātra we cannot possibly interpret 'नातिरात्रे षोडशिनं गृह्णाति' in such a manner as to make it lay down the grasping of something other than the cup.

Then again if we were to construe न with the sense of the word Atirātra (अतिरात्रपदार्थेन अन्वयः), the meaning of the sentence would be that one should take the cup in sacrifices other than the Atirātra. But this also contradicts the injunction which lays down the taking of the cup in the Atirātra (तद्विधिविरोधात् = अतिरात्रे षोडशिग्रहणविधिविरोधात्). Therefore, such an interpretation has also to be rejected.

Thus, there being no other course left open to us (अनन्यगत्या), we must interpret 'नातिरात्रे षोडशिनं गृह्णाति' as containing the prohibition of the taking of the cup, which has been established by another passage viz. 'अतिरात्रे षोडशिनं गृह्णाति.' It is true that under these circumstances i. e. when one passage prohibits what another has enjoined, we shall have to admit option. But such option should not be urged against us as a defect, for we fully expect it (तस्यापि अपेक्षणीयत्वात्) as an unavoidable evil under the circumstances.

अपेक्षणीयत्वात् has here been used in a somewhat peculiar sense. The usual sense of अपेक्षणीय is something which we expect as desirable. Here it means something which we expect, not as desirable, but as necessary, though undesirable. अपेक्षणीयत्वात् is, therefore, equal to अनन्यगत्या अभ्युपेयत्वात्.

It has been stated above that in the case of 'नातिरात्रे षोडशिनं गृह्णाति' it is impossible to get rid of the option by resorting to पर्युदास, as we can do in the case of 'नानुयाजेषु येयजामहं करोति'. The obvious reason for this impossibility is the difference in the nature of these two sets of sentences. 'नातिरात्रे षोडशिनं गृह्णाति' prohibits what exactly has been laid down by 'अतिरात्रे षोडशिनं गृह्णाति'. The विधि and the निषेध here refer to exactly the same thing. But 'नानुयाजेषु येयजामहं करोति' does not prohibit what exactly has been laid down by 'यजतिषु येयजामहं करोति'. For, 'यजतिषु...करोति' enjoins येयजामह in sacrifices in general and 'नानुयाजेषु...करोति' prohibits येयजामह in only the Anuyājas. So the विधि and निषेध here do not refer to exactly the same thing. As a matter of fact while the विधि is general, the निषेध is particular. If the निषेध had taken the form 'न यजतिषु येयजामहं करोति' instead of

'न अनुयाजेषु येयजामहं करोति' it would not have been possible to resort to पर्युदास in 'न यजतिषु येयजामहं करोति' and get rid of the option. Option then would have to be admitted. For, the विधि and निषेध would refer to exactly the same thing.

The up-shot of the whole discussion is that in negative sentences we either have निषेध (which is the same as प्रतिषेध and निवर्तना) or पर्युदास. Both निषेध and पर्युदास are possible in two cases each. निषेध is possible, (1) when the two बाधकs thereof viz. तस्य व्रतमित्युपक्रमः and विकल्पप्रसक्तिः are not present, as in 'न कलञ्जं भक्षयेत्'; and (2) when it is impossible to resort to पर्युदास even when there is the contingency of option as in 'नातिरात्रे षोडशिनं गृह्णाति.' पर्युदास is possible, (1) when a negative sentence is introduced by 'तस्य व्रतम्' and (2) when there is the contingency of option.

About the province of निषेध read 'अतश्च अत्र [i. e. 'नातिरात्रे षोडशिनं गृह्णाति' इत्यस्मिन् वाक्ये] पर्युदासस्य अनुपपत्तेः निषेध एव स्वीक्रियते, विकल्पोऽपि स्वीक्रियते । अनन्यगतेः । अतश्चैतत् सिद्धम् । यत्र 'तस्य व्रतम्' इत्याद्युपक्रमो विकल्पप्रसक्तिश्च नास्ति तत्र प्रतिषेधः । यथा 'न कलञ्जं भक्षयेद्' इति । यत्र वा विकल्पप्रसक्तावपि पर्युदास आश्रयितुं न शक्यते तत्र प्रतिषेधः । यथा 'नातिरात्रे षोडशिनं गृह्णाति ।' इति ।' आपदेवी

Section 71

इयान् तु विशेषः-We have just seen that प्रतिषेध or prohibition is possible in two cases viz. (1) absolute prohibition as in 'न कलञ्जं भक्षयेत्' and (2) prohibition admitted even when there is the contingency of option, as in 'नातिरात्रे षोडशिनं गृह्णाति.' But these two cases of prohibition are not exactly alike. There is a difference (विशेषः) between them. And it is this. निषेध is usually अनर्थहेतुक्रियानिवृत्तिजनक. Vide Section 62 above. This means that if we were to do a thing, which is prohibited, we would be involved in evil. The प्रतिषिध्यमान is an अनर्थहेतु. This is the usual rule, deduced from the very nature of निषेध or प्रतिषेध. Bhāskara now points out that while 'प्रतिषिध्यमानस्य अनर्थहेतुत्वम्' is true in the case of absolute prohibition, it is not true in the case of prohibition, which is admitted even when there is the contingency of option. This much is the difference (इयांस्तु विशेषः) between these two cases of prohibition.

Thus, कलञ्जभक्षण is absolutely प्रतिषिद्ध. Therefore, if one were to indulge in कलञ्जभक्षण, one would be involved in evil viz. the incurring of some kind of sin. But, षोडशिग्रहण is not absolutely prohibited. It is prohibited on account of the option that exists between 'अतिरात्रे षोडशिनं गृह्णाति' and 'नातिरात्रे षोडशिनं गृह्णाति'. In other words षोडशिग्रहण is prohibited as an alternative, which means that the ग्रहण or अग्रहण of the cup is left to our choice. This is because षोडशिग्रहण is both विहित

and निषिद्ध. If we were to take the cup, we would not be doing anything wrong. We would merely be practising the विधि about its ग्रहण. Therefore, the विकल्पात् प्रतिषिध्यमानं षोडशिग्रहणम् is not an अनर्थहेतु.

विधिनिषेधोभयस्यापि क्रत्वर्थत्वात्—This contains the reason why the प्रतिषिध्यमान षोडशिग्रहण is not an अनर्थहेतु. The reason is that both षोडशिग्रहण (विधिः) and षोडश्यग्रहण (निषेधः) are क्रत्वर्थ or in the interest of the sacrifice. What is meant is this. षोडशिग्रहण and षोडश्यग्रहण are acts, positive and negative respectively, which form part of the various physical activities that produce the outward form of the sacrifice. They have consequently nothing to do with the creation of अदृष्ट or अपूर्व, such as is produced by पुरुषार्थ things. It follows, therefore, that when a निषेध is क्रत्वर्थ, the निषिध्यमान is not an अनर्थहेतु.

The विधि and निषेध of षोडशिग्रहण are here declared to be क्रत्वर्थ. In Section 68 the विधि and प्रतिषेध of the formula 'ये यजामहे' were said to be पुरुषार्थ. What is the exact difference between these two cases of विधि and निषेध?

The answer is this: षोडशिग्रहण and षोडश्यग्रहण, being physical acts, contribute towards the outward form of the sacrifice. That is why they are regarded as क्रत्वर्थ. But the recitation and non-recitation of the formula 'ये येजामहे' involve an activity or otherwise of the tongue only. They do not produce any visible effect on the outward form of the sacrifice. That is why they are considered पुरुषार्थ.

'विधिनिषेधोभयस्यापि क्रत्वर्थत्वात्' is a clumsy expression for 'उभयोरपि विधिनिषेधयोः क्रत्वर्थत्वात्'.

यत्र तु न विकल्पः...पुरुषार्थत्वात्—In this passage Bhāskara enumerates the three conditions that make a प्रतिषिध्यमान thing an अनर्थहेतु. These three conditions are: (1) There should be no विकल्प i. e. the thing, which is prohibited, should not have been prohibited as an option i. e. it should not have been enjoined as well. (2) The establishment should be from passion and not from a scriptural passage. (3) The prohibition should be पुरुषार्थ or in the interest of man, and not क्रत्वर्थ or for the benefit of a sacrifice.

These three conditions are satisfied in the case of the निषेध of कलञ्जभक्षण. Here (1) कलञ्जभक्षण is not prohibited as an option, but is prohibited absolutely i. e. कलञ्जभक्षण is nowhere enjoined as well. (2) The प्राप्ति of कलञ्जभक्षण is from our appetite. No other authority asks us to indulge in कलञ्जभक्षण. (3) The निषेध of कलञ्जभक्षण is पुरुषार्थ, because indulgence in कलञ्जभक्षण produces no evil effect on a person in this life. It must, therefore, be supposed to give rise to some unseen evil, which we shall have to suffer after death. The avoidance of this unseen evil is the thing beneficial to man (पुरुषार्थः), which arises from the observance of the कलञ्जभक्षणनिषेध. That is why कलञ्जभक्षणनिषेध is regarded as पुरुषार्थ.

Thus all these three conditions being present in the case of the निषेध of कलञ्जभक्षण, the निषिध्यमान कलञ्जभक्षण becomes an अनर्थहेतु.

भक्षणनिषेधस्यैव—The propriety of एव here is this. In the case of षोडशिग्रहण both its विधि and निषेध were declared to be क्रत्वर्थ. But in the case of कलञ्जभक्षण only its निषेध is पुरुषार्थ, not its विधि or अनुष्ठान. That is why कलञ्जभक्षण becomes an अनर्थहेतु, but षोडशिग्रहण does not. Read 'षोडशिग्रहणविधिनत्प्रतिषेधयोरुभयोरपि क्रत्वर्थत्वात् तत्र प्रतिषिध्यमानस्य नानर्थहेतुत्वम् । अत्र तु कलञ्जभक्षणादिप्रतिषेधस्यैव पुरुषार्थत्वं न तु तदनुष्ठानस्य इति प्रतिषिध्यमानस्य कलञ्जभक्षणब्राह्मणहननादेरनर्थहेतुत्वमेव इति भावः ।' रामेश्वर

In the case of the निषेध of षोडशिग्रहण none of these three conditions is satisfied. For, षोडशिग्रहणनिषेध occurs as an option, षोडशिग्रहण is शास्त्रतः प्राप्त and the निषेध of षोडशिग्रहण is क्रत्वर्थ. Therefore, निषिध्यमान षोडशिग्रहण is not an अनर्थहेतु.

With reference to the three conditions that make a प्रतिषिध्यमान thing an अनर्थहेतु, we desire to point out that out of these three only the first is important and effective. If the first is present and the other two are not, the निषिध्यमान thing becomes an अनर्थहेतु all right. This means that in all those cases of निषेध, which do not occur as an option, the निषिध्यमान thing becomes an अनर्थहेतु, no matter whether the प्राप्ति is रागतः or शास्त्रतः, or whether the निषेध is क्रत्वर्थ or पुरुषार्थ. This will be clear from the two illustrations occurring in the next paragraph of the text.

If on the other hand a निषेध occurs as an option, the निषिध्यमान thing is not an अनर्थहेतु. It should be noted here that in such a case the प्राप्ति is always शास्त्रतः. For, option is admitted only when the विधि and the निषेध proceed from शास्त्र. Whether the निषेध is क्रत्वर्थ or पुरुषार्थ will depend upon the special circumstances of each case.

न च 'दीक्षितो न ददाति॰—It was said before that when विधि and निषेध both proceed from शास्त्र, option should be understood between them (शास्त्रविहितस्य शास्त्रान्तरेण प्रतिषेधे विकल्प एव). दान (charity, liberality or gifts) and होम (sacrifices such as Agnihotra, which a householder has to perform every day) are practices which have been enjoined by सामान्यशास्त्रs or passages of general application. As against these there is the passage 'दीक्षितो न ददाति न जुहोति,' which forbids a consecrated or initiated sacrificer, engaged in the performance of the Jyotiṣṭoma sacrifice, to indulge in ordinary charity and sacrifice. Thus, दानहोम is both शास्त्रविहित and शास्त्रनिषिद्ध. Should we, therefore, understand विकल्प or option between these शास्त्रs?

Bhāskara's answer to this question is in the negative. We have seen before that when विकल्प and निषेध go together i. e. when a negative sentence is understood to contain a निषेध even when there is the contingency of option, the प्रतिषिध्यमान thing is not an अनर्थहेतु. In the present case the प्रतिषिध्यमान दानहोम is an अनर्थहेतु (निषिध्यमानस्य अनर्थहेतुत्वात्). It follows, therefore, that option cannot exist between the विधि and निषेध of दानहोम.

निषिध्यमानस्य अनर्थहेतुत्वात्—दान and होम become अनर्थहेतु in this manner. When a sacrificer is engaged in the performance of a big sacrifice such as ज्योतिष्टोम, it is but natural that he should devote all his money and energy to the matter in hand. Therefore, if he were to indulge in his daily liberality and sacrifice, his purse and attention would be diverted from the main purpose and the principal sacrifice in hand would suffer to that extent. So the अनर्थ that would follow the practice of दान and होम on the part of a दीक्षित represents क्रतुवैगुण्य and it is only from this point of view that the प्रतिषिध्यमान दानहोम is regarded as अनर्थहेतु.

स्वतःपुरुषार्थभूतदानहोमादीनां निषेधस्य पुरुषार्थत्वाभावेऽपि—This passage gives us some characteristics of दान and होम, which figure in this discussion, and incidently supplies another reason why option cannot be admitted between the विधि and निषेध of दान-होम. In the first place दान and होम are in themselves पुरुषार्थ. This is quite natural, for liberality and sacrifice produce no visible fruit. They are supposed to create some अदृष्ट or अपूर्व, such as पुरुषार्थ things do. As दान and होम are पुरुषार्थ, their विधि is also पुरुषार्थ. But their निषेध is not पुरुषार्थ. For, as we saw before, a sacrificer is forbidden to practise ordinary दान and होम in the interest of the special sacrifice he has undertaken. Thus, the निषेध of दान-होम is क्रत्वर्थ. One manuscript of the Arthasamgraha adds 'क्रत्वर्थत्वेन' after 'पुरुषार्थत्वाभावेऽपि.' This makes the sense clearer.

Thus, the position with reference to these दान and होम is this: While their विधि is पुरुषार्थ, their निषेध is क्रत्वर्थ. Thus, as they are not of the same kind, option cannot be admitted between them. If both their विधि and निषेध had been either पुरुषार्थ or क्रत्वर्थ, option between them would have been possible. This is the second reason why option cannot exist between the विधि and the निषेध of दान-होम.

To put the matter in a nut-shell, option between the विधायक and the निषेधक शास्त्रs about दान-होम cannot be admitted, because we find (1) that the प्रतिषिध्यमान दान-होम is actually an अनर्थहेतु and (2) the two शास्त्रs are not of the same kind.

यथा ऋतौ...संपादकत्वात्—Here Bhāskara quotes another illustration to corroborate what he has said with reference to दान-होम-शास्त्रs. ऋतौ भार्यागमन is a thing, which is रागतः प्राप्त in the case of a married man. The सामान्यशास्त्रं 'ऋतौ भार्यामुपेयात्' also enjoins भार्यागमन. The विधि of भार्यागमन is पुरुषार्थ. For, the proper observance of the rules of married life is supposed to give rise to some अदृष्ट, beneficial to man after his death. 'न स्त्रियमुपेयात्' is a sentence occurring in the दर्शपूर्णमासप्रकरण. So, here is once more a case where भार्यागमन, being रागतः प्राप्त or शास्त्रतः प्राप्त, is शास्त्रनिषिद्ध. Is, therefore, option to be understood between the विधि and निषेध of भार्यागमन?

The answer to this is exactly the same as was given in the case of दान-होम. The निषेध of भार्यागमन is क्रत्वर्थ. For, if a sacrificer were to indulge in this luxury during the progress of the sacrifice, his mind would be diverted from the main purpose and imperfection in the sacrifice (क्रतुवैगुण्यम्) would be occassioned. But the विधि of भार्यागमन is पुरुषार्थ. So, the विधि of भार्यागमन and its निषेध being पुरुषार्थ and क्रत्वर्थ respectively, the two cannot be regarded as being of the same kind. Option between them is, therefore, impossible. Secondly, the निषिध्यमान भार्यागमन is known to be an अनर्थहेतु in so far as it produces the evil of क्रतुवैगुण्य. And we know that when a निषेध is coupled with an option, the निषिध्यमान is not an अनर्थहेतु. This is also why option cannot exist between the विधि and the निषेध of भार्यागमन.

The nature of a निषेध is अनर्थहेतुक्रियानिवृत्तिजनक. From this it follows as a general rule that the निषिध्यमान in an अनर्थहेतु. But it is found that all निषिध्यमान things are not really अनर्थहेतुs. This section is, therefore, devoted to the discussion as to which निषिध्यमान thing is an अनर्थहेतु and which not.

In this connection it is pointed out that there are three conditions which make a निषिध्यमान thing an अनर्थहेतु viz. विकल्पाभाव i. e. absolute prohibition, रागतः प्राप्तिः and प्रतिषेधस्य पुरुषार्थत्वम्. We have remarked above that out of these three conditions only the first matters, the other two do not. This will be clear from the following, where we arrange all the four illustrations that figure in this discussion in a tabular form.

(1) षोडशिग्रहण is not an अनर्थहेतु, because (1) there is a विकल्प, (2) its प्राप्ति is शास्त्रत: and (3) its निषेध is क्रत्वर्थ.	Here none of the three conditions, which make a प्रतिषिध्यमान thing an अनर्थहेतु, is satisfied. Therefore, the प्रतिषिध्यमानं षोडशिग्रहणम् is not an अनर्थहेतु.
(2) कलञ्जभक्षण is an अनर्थहेतु, because (1) there is no विकल्प, (2) its प्राप्ति is रागतः and (3) its निषेध is पुरुषार्थ.	Here all the three conditions are satisfied. Therefore, the प्रतिषिध्यमानं कलञ्जभक्षणम् is an अनर्थहेतु.
(3) दीक्षितस्य दानहोमादि is an अनर्थहेतु, because (1) there is no विकल्प, though (2) its प्राप्ति is शास्त्रतः and though (3) its निषेध is क्रत्वर्थ.	Here only the first condition is satisfied and the other two are not. Yet the प्रतिषिध्यमानं दानहोमादि is an अनर्थहेतु
(4) क्रतौ भार्यागमनम् is an अनर्थहेतु, because (1) there is no विकल्प and (2) its प्राप्ति is रागतः, though (3) its निषेध is क्रत्वर्थ	Here the first two conditions are satisfied. If we regard the प्राप्ति of भार्यागमन to be शास्त्रतः, then only the first condition is satisfied. Yet the प्रतिषिध्यमानं क्रतौ भार्यागमनम् is an अनर्थहेतु.

It will be noticed from the above that in cases (3) and (4) though all the three conditions are not satisfied, as they are in (2), the प्रतिषिध्यमान is an अनर्थहेतु, because the first condition, which is the one that really matters, as remarked before, is satisfied.

It should be noted that as far as Bhāskara's text is concerned, there is absolutely no doubt about the fact that according to him 'दीक्षितस्य दानहोमादि' and 'क्रतौ भार्यागमनम्,' which are निषिध्यमान, are अनर्थहेतुs. It should also be clearly understood that the अनर्थ, which proceeds from them, is क्रतुवैगुण्य or imperfection of the sacrifice. It is believed that if the sacrificer were to indulge in दानहोमादि and भार्यागमन, his purse and mind would not be solely devoted to the sacrifice, which consequently would suffer to that extent. Bhāskara's commentator Rāmeśvara also held the same view. Read his remarks: 'क्रत्वङ्गत्वोपाधिमन्तरेण केवलस्वरूपत एव पुमर्थभूतानां दानादीनां निषेधस्य पुरुषार्थत्वाभावेऽपि क्रत्वर्थत्वसंभवात् **निषिध्यमानस्य दानादेः क्रतुवैगुण्यसंपादकत्वेन अनर्थहेतुत्वम्** । तथा च तेषामनुष्ठानस्य स्वतः पुरुषार्थत्वेऽपि क्रत्वनुष्ठानकालेऽपुरुषार्थत्वात् **तत्र तेषामनुष्ठानस्य भवति अनर्थहेतुत्वम्** । क्रतौ स्त्रीगमनादेः कलञ्जभक्षणादिवद् अनर्थरूपनरकादिदुःखाहेतुत्वेऽपि क्रतुवैगुण्यसंपादकत्वेन अनर्थहेतुत्वसंभवाद् **भवति अत्रापि निषिध्यमानस्य अनर्थहेतुत्वम्** ।'

But कलञ्जभक्षण is an अनर्थहेतु in a different sense. Here अनर्थ means some unfavourable or evil अदृष्ट or अपूर्व, which would result in misery after death such as that of going to hell. Thus, though कलञ्जभक्षणम्, दीक्षितस्य दानहोमादि and क्रतौ भार्यागमनम् are all अनर्थहेतुs, the अनर्थ that proceeds from them is not of the same kind. The अनर्थ arising from कलञ्जभक्षणम् is मरणोत्तरदुःखजनकमपूर्वम्, while the अनर्थ resulting from दीक्षितस्य दानहोमादि and क्रतौ भार्यागमनम् is क्रतुवैगुण्यम्.

Now, according to some people अनर्थ in this connection must be regarded as possessing only the former sense viz. some unfavourable अपूर्व or अदृष्ट. If अनर्थ is understood in this sense, दानहोमादि and भार्यागमन on the part of a sacrificer will not be अनर्थहेतु. For, whatever imperfection दीक्षितस्य दानहोमादि and क्रतौ भार्यागमनम् may cause in the sacrifice, they do not give rise to any unfavourable अपूर्व which would redound upon the sacrificer after his death. Āpadeva holds this view. According to him cases (3) and (4) would be represented as follows:

(3) दीक्षितस्य दानहोमादि is not an अनर्थहेतु, because (2) its प्राप्ति is शास्त्रतः and (3) its निषेध is क्रत्वर्थ, though (1) there is no विकल्प.	Here though the first condition is satisfied, the other two are not. Therefore, the प्रतिषिध्यमानं दीक्षितस्य दानहोमादि is not an अनर्थहेतु.
(4) क्रतौ भार्यागमनम् is not an अनर्थहेतु, because (3) its निषेध is क्रत्वर्थ, though (1) there is no विकल्प and (2) its प्राप्ति is रागतः.	Here though the first two conditions are satisfied, the third is not. Therefore, the प्रतिषिध्यमानं क्रतौ भार्यागमनम् is not an अनर्थहेतु.

We said above, it will be remembered, that out of the three conditions that make a प्रतिषिध्यमान thing an अनर्थहेतु, only the first is important and really matters. That remark is true only when अनर्थ is understood in the sense in which Bhāskara employs it. If अनर्थ is taken in the other sense in which Āpadeva understands it, then all the three conditions become equally important, as can be seen from the representation of cases (3) and (4), according to Āpadeva, given above. From this we can see that if one or two of the conditions are not satisfied, the result viz. अनर्थहेतुत्व does not follow. Fulfilment of all the three conditions is necessary for such result.

For Āpadeva's view read :

" 'दीक्षितो न ददाति, न जुहोति' इत्यादिषु तु दानहोमादीनां शास्त्रप्राप्तावपि पुरुषार्थत्वेन प्राप्तत्वात् क्रत्वर्थत्वेन च प्रतिषेधात् तुल्यार्थत्वाभावेन विकल्पाप्रसक्तावपि **न तेषामनर्थहेतुत्वम्,** रागप्राप्त्यभावात्। रागतः प्राप्तस्यापि क्रत्वर्थत्वेन प्रतिषेधे तदनुष्ठानात् क्रतोर्वैगुण्यं, **नानर्थोत्पत्तिः,** यथा स्वस्त्र्युपगमनादिप्रतिषेधे। रागतः प्राप्तस्य पुरुषार्थत्वेन प्रतिषेधे निषिध्यमानस्य अनर्थहेतुत्वम्।' मीमांसान्यायप्रकाश

For discussion about the sentence 'दीक्षितो न ददाति न जुहोति' vide जैमिनीयन्यायमालाविस्तर on अध्याय 6, पाद 5 and अधिकरण 11 and also अध्याय 10, पाद 8 and अधिकरण 7.

Section 72

This and the following two Sections deal with Arthavāda, which is the last of the five parts into which the Veda is divided. Vide Section 10 above.

Arthavāda is defined as a sentence which aims at or conveys (पर) praise or glorification (प्राशस्त्यम् = प्रशस्तस्य भावः. प्रशस्त from प्र + शंस् to praise), or blame or censure (निन्दा). Arthavāda conveys the praise of a thing which is enjoined (विधेय) and the censure of another which is prohibited (निषेध्य). Arthavāda is thus supplementary or complimentary to (शेष) विधि and निषेध and is from that point of view of two kinds. Vide the next Section. The term अर्थवाद is thus explained: अर्थस्य प्राशस्त्यरूपस्य निन्दारूपस्य वा वादः वचनम्. It is usually translated by 'explanatory passage.'

तस्य च...पर्यवसानम्—It is an anxiom of the Mīmāṁsakas that the entire Veda must in one way or another lead up to, or be connected with, dharma, which is practically the same as yāga. The primary sense of Arthavāda is either praise or blame. Praise or blame, such as is conveyed by Arthavāda, has no direct connection with dharma. Therefore, Bhāskara tells us that Arthavāda ultimately leads to (पर्यवसानम्) dharma indirectly i. e. by indication (लक्षणा). प्रयोजनवदर्थः is the same as धर्मः or यागः. Vide Section 2 above. प्रयोजनवदर्थपर्यवसानम् is thus equal to धर्मपर्यवसानम्.

तथा हि॰—This passage explains how Arthavāda ultimately leads up to dharma by indication. 'वायुर्वै क्षेपिष्ठा देवता' and 'सोऽरोदीत् यद् अरोदीत् तद् रुद्रस्य रुद्रत्वम्' are two examples of Arthavāda. The primary sense (स्वार्थः) of the first is that vāyu is the swiftest deity. The second signifies that Agni (सः = अग्निः) cried or howled and that is why he is known as Rudra (the Crier or Howler). Now, no purpose would be served (प्रयोजनाभावः), if these two Arthavāda sentences were merely to convey their primary sense (स्वार्थप्रतिपादनम्). For, their primary sense has nothing to do with dharma. But we know that all Vedic sentences must subserve dharma. Therefore, lakṣaṇā or indication is resorted to and by means of indication the two sentences are understood to convey the praise and blame of matters which are respectively to be enjoined and prohibited (विधेयनिषेध्ययोः).

And these विधेय and निषेध्य matters, the praise and blame of which the two above Arthavādas respectively convey, are furnished by the following विधि and निषेध. 'वायव्यं श्वेतमालभेत' is an injunction which lays down the immolation or slaughter (आलभनम्) of a white animal in honour of Vāyu. Attached to this injunction is the Arthavāda 'वायुर्वै क्षेपिष्ठा देवता, वायुमेव स्वेन भागधेयेन उपधावति, स एवैनं भूतिं गमयति.' This passage contains the praise of Vāyu to the effect that he is the swiftest deity and that he confers prosperity on whomsoever pleases him with his proper oblation (स्वो भागः). Now, this praise of Vāyu, which forms the primary sense of the Arthavāda, has no direct connection with dharma or the sacrifice of a white animal, whose slaughter is laid down by the injunction 'वायव्यं श्वेतमालभेत.' Therefore, by means of indication we understand the Arthavāda passage as conveying the praise, not of Vāyu, but of the sacrifice of a white animal in his honour, which is the विधेय in the injunction 'वायव्यं श्वेतमालभेत.' Thus, the Arthavāda conveys the praise of विधेय and is consequently connected with dharma. As the Arthavāda, intimates or teaches the praise of a matter to be enjoined (विधेयार्थप्राशस्त्यबोधकतया), it has a purpose (अर्थवत्त्वम्) in the Mīmāṁsist scheme of things.

The prohibition 'बर्हिषि रजतं न देयम्' forbids the gift of silver to priests during the course of a sacrifice. The procedure is that when a dakṣiṇā or gift is to be made over to priests, it is placed or offered (देय) on the sacred sacrificial grass (बर्हिः). That is why the prohibition says that no silver is to be offered on the sacrificial grass. Now, to this prohibition belongs (शेष) the Arthavāda 'सोऽरोदीत्, यद् अरोदीत् तत् रुद्रस्य रुद्रत्वम्.' The primary sense of this Arthavāda is that Agni cried and that is why he is known as Rudra. From the story of Agni's lamentation, which is given below, we understand that silver was produced from the tears which Agni shed. Thus, the ultimate primary sense of the Arthavāda is that silver is a product of tears. But this sense has nothing to do with dharma. Therefore, by means of indication we understand from this Arthavāda the blame or censure of a matter which is prohibited viz. silver as a gift. Thus, the Arthavāda conveys the censure of a निषेध्य thing and is thus connected with निषेध. The Arthavāda consequently has a purpose in so far as it intimates the censure of a matter prohibited (निषेध्यस्य निन्दितत्वबोधकतया).

It should be noted that the Arthavāda 'सोऽरोदीत्...रुद्रत्वम्' does not convey the fact that silver is the product of Agni's tears. The proper Arthavāda to 'बर्हिषि रजतं न देयम्' is 'अश्रुजं हि रजतं यो बर्हिषि ददाति पुरा अस्य संवत्सराद् गृहे रुदन्ति.' Bhāskara is merely following Āpadeva in quoting this irrelevant Arthavāda.

For the story of Agni's lamentation read: 'सन्दर्भशुद्ध्यर्थं कथेयमत्र अनुसंधेया। पुरा कदाचित् देवासुराणां युद्धं प्रावर्तत। तत्र युद्धार्थं गच्छन्तो देवाः स्वीयमनर्घं रमणीयं च वस्तुजातमग्निसमीपेऽस्थापयन् यदि कदाचिदस्मान् असुरा जीयुः तदिदमस्माकं लोकयात्रार्थं भविष्यतीति। दृष्ट्वा च तदतिसुन्दरममूल्यं च वस्तुजातं लोभाकृष्टचित्तोऽग्निः तत् गृहीत्वा पलायत। ते च देवा असुरान् जित्वा प्रतिनिवृत्ताः यदा पलायितमग्निमवागच्छन् तदा तमान्विष्य तत् सर्वमपि धनं बलाद्गृह्णन्। **तादृशधनवियोगजं दुःखमसहमानोऽग्निररुदत्। रुदतस्तस्य नेत्राभ्यामपतदश्रु। तदेव रजतं संजातमिति।**' सारविवेचनी

स्वार्थमात्रपरत्वे... क्रियार्थत्वात्—We have seen above that the primary sense of Arthavāda is not connected with dharma or yāga. If Arthavāda were to convey only its primary sense, there would arise the contingency of its being purposeless from the Mīmāṁsaka's point of view. For, the Mimāṁsaka position is that the entire Veda (आम्नायः) is for the purpose of action i. e. yāga or sacrifice. Whatever does not subserve action or dharma is to him purposeless. Therefore, in order to make Arthavāda purposeful, we have te resort to लक्षणा and thus obtain from Arthavāda a meaning which is connected with action in the form of विधि or निषेध.

The expression 'आम्नायस्य हि क्रियार्थत्वात्' is borrowed from Jaimini's sūtra 'आम्नायस्य हि क्रियार्थत्वादानर्थक्यमतदर्थानाम्, तस्मादनित्यमुच्यते' I. ii. 1, which says that whatever is not क्रियार्थ (अतदर्थ) is purposeless.

न चेष्टापत्तिः ... नुपपत्तेः—It has been stated above that in order to remove purposelessness from Arthavāda, we have to resort to indication and obtain a meaning which will be connected with action. An objector now says that the purposelessness of Arthavāda may be regarded as a desirable contingency (इष्टापत्तिः). What does it matter if all Arthavādas are looked upon as purposeless? This is what the objector in effect asks.

The answer to this is that the injunction 'स्वाध्यायोऽध्येतव्यः' lays down that the entire Veda, in which Arthavāda is of course included is to be studied. Nobody likes to study something which is purposeless. Therefore, the same injunction suggests that the entire Veda, the study of which it lays down, has a purpose. And it can have a purpose only if it ultimately leads to matters with a purpose viz. dharma.

The position is briefly this: 'स्वाध्यायोऽध्येतव्यः' enjoins the study of the Veda. The Veda must, therefore, have a purpose, for nobody would ask us to study something which is purposeless. The Veda includes Arthavāda. Arthavāda must also, therefore, have a purpose.

If it cannot have a purpose with its primary meaning, a secondary meaning has to be culled from it in order to make it purposeful. But in no case would it be proper (अनुपपत्तिः) to regard Arthavāda as purposeless.

उपात्तत्वेन—The construction is: अध्ययनविधिना...बोधयता...सूचयता [च अर्थवादस्य] उपात्तत्वेन [तस्य] आनर्थक्यानुपपत्तेः. उपात्त accepted, covered or included. As Arthavāda is included in the अध्ययनविधि, it cannot properly be regarded as purposeless.

Section 73

We have already seen that Arthavāda conveys the praise of something which is enjoined and the censure of something which is prohibited. From this point of view Arthavāda is subsidiary or complementary or supplementary to (शेष) विधि and निषेध and is thus of two kinds. This Section deals with these two kinds of Arthavāda.

निषेध was defined before as ' पुरुषस्य निवर्तकं वाक्यम्. ' Vide Section 62 above. For विधि we may formulate a similar definition by saying that विधि is ' पुरुषस्य प्रवर्तकं वाक्यम्. ' Thus, while विधि directs a man to a thing, निषेध turns him away from another. Arthavāda helps विधि by conveying the praise of the विधेय. Similarly, Arthavāda helps निषेध by conveying the censure of the निषेध्य. Thus, Arthavāda is complementary to विधि and निषेध.

The two examples of Arthavāda, which are given in the first paragraph of this Section, have already been explained in our notes on Section 72. They need not, therefore, detain us here.

न च प्राशस्त्यादिबोधस्य...उपयोगात्—It was said above that Arthavāda helps विधि by conveying the praise of the विधेय. An objector now argues that no such help is necessary. When an injunction directs us to something, we shall undertake it even without the additional inducement of the knowledge of its praise (प्राशस्त्यबोधः). If this be so, Arthavāda will have no purpose to serve and will consequently be purposeless. This is what the objector means.

The answer to this is that though good people would readily undertake to perform whatever has been enjoined by विधि, there are others who through laziness and such other causes would be loath to go in for what has been enjoined for them. In the case of such people praise or glorification of the विधेय serves as an adequate additional inducement. Thus as the knowledge of the praise (तद्बोधस्य = प्राशस्त्यादिबोधस्य) creates activity in the lazy, it is of use in the Māmāṁsakas' scheme of things.

The same reasoning applies to निन्दापर अर्थवाद. Mere scriptural prohibition of the gift of silver in sacrifices is not enough in the case of many people to stop them from the use of silver. But an Arthavāda, which says that he, who uses silver in sacrifice, will have lamentation in his house before the year is out, proves an effective deterrent for them.

Thus, the knowledge of the praise and censure, which Arthavāda conveys, is not altogether without an object. Consequently, Arthavāda does serve a certain purpose.

We have seen so far that the import of Arthavāda is प्रशंसा and निन्दा. Some writers add परकृति: (the doings of the great) and पुराकल्प: (former happenings) and thus make Arthavāda four-fold. But परकृति and पुराकल्प are really intended to convey ultimately either praise or blame. So it is better to consider Arthavāda to be of two kinds only according as it conveys praise or blame.

For the view that Arthavāda is four-fold read: 'अर्थवादानां स्वार्थपरत्वे प्रयोजनाभावाद् अध्ययनविधिवशेन फलवदर्थज्ञानार्थत्वस्य आवश्यकत्वाद् विधेयगतप्राशस्त्यप्रतिपादनद्वारा विधिवाक्यैकवाक्यतया प्रामाण्यम् । **स च चतुर्विधः— निन्दाप्रशंसापरकृतिपुराकल्पभेदात्** । तत्र निन्दार्थवादो यथा— 'असत्त्रं वा एतद् यद् अच्छन्दोमम्' इत्यादिः, '**अश्रुजं हि रजतं यो बर्हिषि ददाति पुरा अस्य संवत्सराद् गृहे रुदन्ति**' इत्यादिश्च । प्रशंसार्थवादो यथा—'शोभनेऽस्य मुखं य एवं वेद' इत्यादिः, 'वायुर्वै क्षेपिष्ठा देवता, वायुमेव स्वेन भागधेयेन उपधावति, स एवैनं भूतिं गमयति' इत्येवमादिश्च । परेण महता पुरुषेण इदं कर्म कृतमिति प्रतिपादकोऽर्थवादः परकृतिः, यथा—'अग्निर्वा अकामयत' इत्यादिः । परप्रवक्तृकार्थप्रतिपादकः पुराकल्पः, यथा—'तमशपद् धिया धिया त्वा वध्यासुः' इत्यादिः ।

तत्र निन्दार्थवादस्य विधेयान्यनिन्दाद्वारा विधेयप्राशस्त्यपरत्वम् । 'अश्रुजम्' इत्यादि रजतनिन्दाद्वारा च विधेयभूतरजतदाननिषेधप्राशस्त्यपरत्वे विरोधाभावात् । इतरेषां त्रयाणां साक्षात् प्राशस्त्यपरत्वमेव । 'वायुर्वा' इत्यर्थवादस्य वायुः क्षिप्रगामित्वादतीव प्रशस्ता देवता, अतस्तद्दैवत्यं कर्म प्रशस्तमिति विधेयदेवतागतप्राशस्त्यप्रतिपादनद्वारा विध्येकवाक्यत्वम् । 'अग्निर्वा अकामयत' इत्यस्य अग्निदैवत्यो यागः पूर्वकालेऽग्निना कृतत्वात् प्रशस्तः, अतः आस्तिक्याद् इदानीमपि अन्यैर्यजमानैः अवश्यं कर्तव्यः इति विधेयकर्मगतप्राशस्त्यप्रतिपादनद्वारा विध्येकवाक्यत्वम् । एवमन्यत्रापि ऊह्यम् ।

क्वचित् कार्यान्तरमपि अस्ति । यथा—'अक्ताः शर्करा उपदधाति' इति विधौ 'अक्ताः' इति पदेन द्रवद्रव्यसामान्यं प्रतीयते । तच्च द्रवद्रव्यं किमिति संदेहे 'तेजो वै घृतम्' इति अर्थवादाद् घृतमिति निश्चीयते इति 'तेजो वै घृतम्' इत्यर्थवादस्य संदिग्धार्थनिर्णायकत्वेनापि प्रामाण्यम् ।'
मीमांसापरिभाषा

The following quotation would also make interesting reading: 'काम्यपशुकाण्डे विध्यर्थवादौ श्रूयेते । 'वायव्यं श्वेतमालभेत भूतिकामः' इति विधिः । 'वायुर्वै क्षेपिष्ठा देवता, वायुमेव स्वेन भागधेयेनोपधावति, स एवैनं भूतिं गमयति' इत्यर्थवादः । तत्र विधि-

वाक्यगता वायव्यादिशब्दा अर्थवादशब्दनैरपेक्ष्येणैव विशिष्टमर्थं विदधति । अर्थवादशब्दाश्च इतरनैरपेक्ष्येणैव भूतार्थमन्वाचक्षते । क्षिप्रगामी वायुः स्वोचितेन भागेन तोषितो भागप्रदाय ऐश्वर्यं प्रयच्छति इत्युक्ते रामायणभारतादाविव वृत्तान्तः कश्चित् प्रतीयते, न तु अनुष्ठेयं किंचित् । अत एकवाक्यत्वाभावाद् नास्ति अर्थवादस्य धर्मे प्रामाण्यमिति **प्राप्ते**—

ब्रूमः । मा भूत् पदैकवाक्यता । वाक्यैकवाक्यता तु विद्यते । विधिवाक्यं तावत् पुरुषं प्रेरयितुं विधेयार्थस्य प्राशस्त्यमपेक्षते । अर्थवादवाक्यं च फलवदर्थावबोधपर्यवसिताध्ययनविधिपरिगृहीतत्वेन पुरुषार्थमपेक्षते । तत्र पुरुषार्थपर्यवसितविध्यपेक्षितं प्राशस्त्यं लक्षणावृत्त्या समर्पयद् अर्थवादवाक्यं विधिवाक्येन सह एकवाक्यतामापद्यते । 'यतः क्षिप्रगामिस्वभावतया शीघ्रफलप्रदो वायुरस्य पशोर्देवता, ततः प्रशस्तामिमं वायव्यं पशुमालभेत' इति वाक्ययोरन्वयः । तस्माद् अर्थवादा धर्मे प्रमाणम् ।' जैमिनीयन्यायमालाविस्तर pp. 22–23

Section 74

In the preceding Section Arthavāda was divided into two kinds on the basis of the purpose it serves viz. the help that it gives to injunction and prohibition. This Section divides Arthavāda from another point of view viz. whether its actual content is contradicted by another means of proof, or is supported by it, or is neither contradicted nor supported. While the basis of the previous classification was the relation of Arthavāda to other things viz. विधि and निषेध, the present classification looks upon Arthavāda as independent and proceeds to divide it on the basis of the nature of its content. Thus, according to this new classification Arthavāda is of three kinds viz. (1) गुणवाद, (2) अनुवाद and (3) भूतार्थवाद. These three varieties are defined in the couplet 'विरोधे गुणवादः स्यात् etc.'

When the content of an Arthavāda is contradicted by another means of proof, it is called गुणवाद e. g. 'आदित्यो यूपः'. Here we have an identification of the sacrificial post (यूपः), to which the animal to be immolated is tied, with the sun. Now this non-difference or identity of the sun (आदित्याभेदः) with the post is contradicted by direct perception. For, we perceive that the post is not the sun. Thus, the primary meaning of the Arthavāda having been found unsuitable, indication is resorted to and the passage (अनेन = अर्थवादेन) then conveys a quality viz. brilliance such as the sun possesses. The ultimate meaning thus metaphorically obtained from the Arthavāda is that the sacrificial post is as brilliant as the sun. As this Arthavāda conveys by indication a quality, it is called गुणवाद.

Students of Alaṁkāraśāstra will recall that 'आदित्यो यूपः' is an example of गौणी लक्षणा such as is found in 'गौर्वाहीकः' or 'चन्द्रो मुखम्'.

When an Arthavāda conveys a matter which is known from some other means of proof (प्रमाणान्तरावगत), it is known as अनुवाद. This name is also significant. For, what this kind of Arthavāda does is merely to repeat what has already been known from another source. 'अग्निर्हिमस्य भेषजम्' is an example of अनुवाद. That fire is opposed to cold (अग्नौ वर्तमानं हिमेन सह विरोधित्वम्) is known from direct perception. Thus, the Arthavāda contains mere repetition of what is already known from another means of proof.

अवधारिते in the couplet should be taken equal to अवधारणे, according to 'नपुंसके भावे क्तः', which allows past passive participles to be used as abstract nouns. Thus, अवधारिते means प्रमाणान्तरेण अवधारणे. In this way we secure symmetry with विरोधे, which is also an abstract noun.

When the content of an Arthavāda is such that it can neither be contradicted nor be established by another means of proof, it is known as भूतार्थवाद. 'इन्द्रो वृत्राय वज्रमुदयच्छत्' is an example of भूतार्थवाद. Here we find that the statement that Indra raised his thunderbolt to strike at Vṛtra is such that it can neither be contradicted nor be established by any other means of proof. For, we have no means of ascertaining what happened in the fight between Indra and Vṛtra, or whether such a fight at all took place.

भूतार्थ means a thing which happened i. e. a past occurrence. A thing that has occurred is certainly real in so far as it has actually taken place. भूतार्थ thus comes to mean a real state of affairs. Compare 'आर्ये, कथयामि ते **भूतार्थम्**' शाकुन्तल i. As this Arthavāda states a past occurrence, it is properly termed भूतार्थवाद.

तद्धानात् of the couplet means विरोध-अवधारित-हानात्. In such an Arthavāda there is neither contradiction nor ascertainment. तद्धानात् is paraphrased by प्रमाणान्तरविरोध-तत्प्राप्तिरहितार्थबोधकः, where तत्प्राप्ति means प्रमाणान्तरप्राप्ति.

Section 75

The Mīmāṁsā begins with 'अथातो धर्मजिज्ञासा' and dharma is defined as 'वेदप्रतिपाद्यः प्रयोजनवदर्थः', which is the same as यागादिः. The Veda is 'विधि-मन्त्र-नामधेय-निषेध-अर्थवाद-भेदात् पञ्चविधः.' It follows, therefore, that all these five parts of the Veda must convey (प्रतिपादक) dharma such as sacrifice. The author has so far shown us how each of these five parts is धर्मप्रतिपादक. Now by way of conclusion he repeats the same thing and further tells us that some of these parts convey dharma directly and some indirectly. Thus, विधि and निषेध expound dharma directly, because they tell us what should and should not be done. मन्त्र, नामधेय and अर्थवाद convey dharma indirectly, because, though they directly do not lay down anything either positively or negatively, they are connected with either विधेय or निषेध्य. Thus, all the five parts of the Veda convey dharma either directly or indirectly.

All the five parts of the Veda are धर्मप्रतिपादक. प्रतिपादक is, however, a general term. The special function which each of these five parts performs with reference to dharma will be clear from the following :—

विधिना विहितः मन्त्रेण स्मारितः नामधेयेन परिच्छिन्नः निषेधेन निवर्तितः अर्थवादेन प्रशंसितो निन्दितो वा	} यागादिधर्मः

The purpose which each of these five parts serves with reference to dharma will be clear from the following :—

विधेः प्रयोजनवदर्थविधानेन अर्थवत्त्वम् ।

मन्त्रस्य प्रयोगसमवेतार्थस्मारकत्वेन अर्थवत्त्वम् ।

नामधेयस्य विधेयार्थपरिच्छेदकतया अर्थवत्त्वम् ।

निषेधस्य अनर्थहेतुक्रियानिवृत्तिजनकत्वेन अर्थवत्त्वम् ।

अर्थवादस्य विधेयनिषेध्ययोः प्राशस्त्यनिन्दितत्वप्रतिपादनद्वारा अर्थवत्त्वम् ।

सोऽयं धर्मः—This paragraph describes the two-fold fruit to be obtained from the practice of dharma i. e. sacrifice and others. If we practise dharma with reference to some specific fruit, it becomes the cause of winning for us that fruit. But if we perform it, not with the idea of getting any fruit for self, but with the idea of dedicating it to God, it becomes the cause of our attaining final beatitude or absolution (निःश्रेयसम्). This latter statement embodies the Bhagavadgītā doctrine of desireless action (निष्कामकर्म) by the practice of which, the Bhagavadgītā teaches us, we obtain mokṣa or final release from the cycle of birth and death. The general statement ' धर्मो यदुद्दिश्य etc ' may be thus paraphrased in specific terms : ज्योतिष्टोमादिधर्मः स्वर्गमुद्दिश्य विहितः स्वर्गोद्देशेन क्रियमाणः स्वर्गहेतुर्भवति ।

न च तदर्पणबुद्ध्या...प्रमाणत्वात्—Here an objector may ask : ' What is the authority for performing dharma with the idea of dedicating it to God ? ' The answer is the authority is the Smṛti in the form of the Bhagavadgītā itself, which says ' यत् करोषि यदश्नासि यज्जुहोसि ददासि यत् । यत् तपस्यसि कौन्तेय तत् कुरुष्व मदर्पणम् ॥ 27 शुभाशुभफलैरेवं मुच्यसे कर्मबन्धनैः । संन्यासयोगयुक्तात्मा **विमुक्तो मामुपैष्यसि** ॥ 28 ' अध्याय ix

स्मृतिचरणे०—But one may still object : The Bhagavadgītā, which is included in the Mahābhārata, is the composition of a human author (पौरुषेय) viz. Vyāsa. It falls within the class of works known as Smṛtis. Is a pauruṣeya Smṛti an authority with reference to dharma, even like apauruṣeya Śruti. ' The answer is that Jaimini has decided in what is known as the quarter dealing with Smṛtis

(स्मृतिचरणे = स्मृतिपादे,), which is the third quarter of the first chapter of his sūtras, that Smṛtis are authoritative, because they are based on Śruti (श्रुतिमूलकत्वेन). Thus, on the authority of the Bhagavadgītā there is no objection for a man,, who wants निःश्रेयस or the highest bliss, to practise dharma with the idea of dedicating it to God and thus attain salvation.

Read the following regarding the authoritativeness of Smṛtis, ''अष्टकाः कर्तव्याः' इत्यादि स्मृतिवाक्यं न धर्मे प्रमाणम्, पौरुषेयवाक्यत्वे सति मूलप्रमाणः, रहितत्वात् विप्रलम्भकवाक्यवत्। अथ मूलप्रमाणवत्त्वाय वेदार्थ एव स्मृतिभिरुच्यते इति मन्येथाः-तर्हि वेदेनैव तदर्थस्य अवगतत्वादियं स्मृतिरनर्था स्यात्। तदानीमनुवादकत्वादप्रामाण्यमिति प्राप्ते—

ब्रूमः। विमता स्मृतिर्वेदमूला, वैदिकमन्वादिप्रणीतस्मृतित्वात्, उपनयनाध्ययनादिस्मृतिवत् न च वैयर्थ्यं शङ्कनीयम्, अस्मदादीनां प्रत्यक्षेषु परोक्षेषु च नानावेदेषु विप्रकीर्णस्य अनुष्ठेयार्थस्य एकत्र संक्षिप्यमाणत्वात्। तस्मादियं स्मृतिर्धर्मे प्रमाणम्।' जैमिनीयन्यायमालाविस्तर pp. 27-28

With reference to Bhāskara's statement 'ईश्वरार्पणबुद्ध्या क्रियमाणस्तु [धर्मो] निःश्रेयसहेतुः' it must be pointed out that the doctrine of desireless action is really foreign to Mīmāṁsā. Mīmāṁsā does not believe in niṣkāma-karman. Further, according to Mīmāṁsā the highest fruit is heaven and it is obtained by the performance of certain sacrifices such as Jyotiṣṭoma. The idea that heaven is an impermanent abode and that one comes down from there on the exhaustion of one's religious merit is a later growth. It was the result of the increasing importance which came to be attached to knowledge as opposed to action. The fruit of knowledge is permanent. The fruit of action, not excluding the highest viz. heaven, must, therefore, be impermanent. Such was the kind of reasoning, which resulted in reducing heaven to the position of an exalted world, where we go to enjoy the fruit of our merit and whence we have to return on the exhaustion thereof.

Further, the idea that there is God, higher than and distinct from, the sacrificial deities such as Agni and Indra, to whom action is to be dedicated and who, being pleased by our desireless action, would grant us liberation, is also unknown to Mīmāṁsā. Altogether this statement about 'ईश्वरार्पणबुद्ध्या क्रियमाणो धर्मः'. shows clear traces of the influence of the philosophy of the Bhagavadgītā.

इति शिवम्—This represents the concluding good wishes for bliss or happiness for all—the teachers and the taught and the general readers of the book.

सुमेधसा भास्करेण—To style oneself सुमेधस् (of good intellect or intelligence) would appear to be not in good taste to modern readers. But such self-compliments are not unknown in Sanskrit literature.

श्रीमहामहोपाध्याय was probably a title held by Bhāskara.